A  University of
Hertfordshire

College Lane, Hatfield, Herts. AL10 9AB

Learning and Information Services
de Havilland Campus Learning Resources Centre, Hatfield

For renewal of Standard and One Week Loans,
please visit the web site **http://www.voyager.herts.ac.uk**

This item must be returned or the loan renewed by the due date.
The University reserves the right to recall items from loan at any time.
A fine will be charged for the late return of items.

Longman Literature in English Series

General Editors:
David Carroll, formerly University of Lancaster
Chris Walsh, Chester College of Higher Education
Michael Wheeler, University of Southampton

For a complete list of titles, see back of book

American Literature
Before 1880

Robert Lawson-Peebles

PEARSON

Longman

Harlow, England • London • New York • Boston • San Francisco • Toronto • Sydney • Singapore • Hong Kong
Tokyo • Seoul • Taipei • New Delhi • Cape Town • Madrid • Mexico City • Amsterdam • Munich • Paris • Milan

PEARSON EDUCATION LIMITED

Head Office:
Edinburgh Gate
Harlow CM20 2JE
Tel: +44 (0)1279 623623
Fax: +44 (0)1279 431059
Website: www.pearsoned.co.uk

First published in Great Britain in 2003

© Pearson Education Limited 2003

The right of Robert Lawson-Peebles to be identified as Author
of this Work has been asserted by him in accordance
with the Copyright, Designs and Patents Act 1988.

ISBN 0 582 49522 9

British Library Cataloguing in Publication Data
A CIP catalogue record for this book can be obtained from the British Library

Library of Congress Cataloging in Publication Data
A CIP catalog record for this book can be obtained from the Library of Congress

10 9 8 7 6 5 4 3 2 1

Set in 10/12pt Sabon by 35
Printed in Malaysia

The Publishers' policy is to use paper manufactured from sustainable forests.

Contents

Editors' Preface

The multi-volume Longman Literature in English Series provides students of literature with a critical introduction to the major genres in their historical and cultural context. Each volume gives a coherent account of a clearly defined area, and the series, when complete, will offer a practical and comprehensive guide to literature written in English from Anglo-Saxon times to the present. The aim of the series as a whole is to show that the most valuable and stimulating approach to the study of literature is that based upon awareness of the relations between literary forms and their historical contexts. Thus the areas covered by most of the separate volumes are defined by period and genre. Each volume offers new and informed ways of reading literary works, and provides guidance for further reading in an extensive reference section.

In recent years, the nature of English studies has been questioned in a number of increasingly radical ways. The very terms employed to define a series of this kind – period, genre, history, context, canon – have become the focus of extensive critical debate, which has necessarily influenced in varying degrees the successive volumes published since 1985. But however fierce the debate, it rages around the traditional terms and concepts.

As well as studies on all periods of English and American literature, the series includes books on criticism and literary theory and on the intellectual and cultural context. A comprehensive series of this kind must of course include other literatures written in English, and therefore a group of volumes deals with Irish and Scottish literature, and the literatures of India, Africa, the Caribbean, Australia and Canada. The forty-seven volumes of the series cover the following areas: Pre-Renaissance English Literature, English Poetry, English Drama, English Fiction, English Prose, Criticism and Literary Theory, Intellectual and Cultural Context, American Literature, Other Literatures in English.

David Carroll
Chris Walsh
Michael Wheeler

Acknowledgements

It was almost too late when I found the *History of the United States from 986 to 1905*. Its striking title was due to the excitement that one of its authors, Thomas Wentworth Higginson, felt when he, in turn, had come across *Antiquitates Americanae* (1837) and concluded that his account of American history was incomplete unless he included the Norse legends of Vinland. It was a relief to have my conviction confirmed that a book about the earlier forms of American literature would have to discuss the Vinland sagas. Indeed, my work on this book has been inspired from the outset by the belief that the Europeans imagined America before they found it – and certainly long before the Puritans landed at Plymouth Rock. I am glad that Michael Wheeler and Chris Walsh, the two series editors I have dealt with, were willing to go along with this belief, and the additional time and word-length that it inevitably involved. The dozen years that I have been working on the book have been increasingly challenged by university administration. I am especially grateful to the present Head of Exeter's School of English, Helen Taylor, for plucking me, at a crucial moment in the book's creation, from underneath piles of undergraduate application forms. I have been fortunate to be helped by the staff and book stocks of Exeter University Library, the Huntington Library in California and the British Library in London.

Usually of help, too, was my promiscuous labyrinth of files (no filing system, this one) into which, from earliest undergraduate days, went notes on books, conversations, and those anfractuous nocturnal brainwaves that I wanted to retrieve in the morning. If any part of the book has withstood the best efforts of my excellent copy-editor, Barbara Massam, it is because I have persisted beyond reason in a recovery attempt. The labyrinth allowed me to revive many conversations with teachers, friends, hosts, colleagues and students. The following, listed, as they say, in alphabetical order, may, if they are still on the planet, therefore hear echoes of their voices in the following pages: Sacvan Bercovitch, William Blazek, Malcolm Bradbury, Colin Brooks, William Boelhower, Lawrence Buell, Clive Bush, Richard Cheadle, Peter Conrad, Mark Davie, Karen Edwards, Emory Elliott, Stephen Fender, Anthony Fothergill, Wayne Franklin, G. M. Gidley, Paul Giles, Richard Gravil, Laurette Guest, Avril Henry, William Howarth, Cora Kaplan, Alberto Lena, Walton Litz, Karen Lystra, Susan Manning, Leo Marx, Bernard Mergen, Robert Middlekauff, Lee Clark Mitchell, Christopher Mulvey, David Murray, Peter New, Judith Newman, Francesca Orestano, Daniel Peck, Angelique Richardson, Martin Ridge, Paul Schlicke, Daniel Shea, Ann Swyderski, Douglas Tallack, Tony Tanner, Wil Verhoeven, Michael Wood, John Whitley and Larzer Ziff. It is not their fault if I have misinterpreted what they said. Fortunately, there have been a number of resources to hand to give the book a factual backbone;

I am thinking particularly of *The Oxford Companions* to American History and Literature, the *Annals of American Literature, 1602–1983*, and *American National Biography.*

My editors at Pearson, Heather McCallum, Casey Mein and Melanie Carter, have been willing to assist with a sympathy and patience that passeth all understanding. It is because I decided not to test their patience further that close readers of the Chronology will find that I have written little or nothing about a number of authors, amongst them Joel Barlow, Robert Montgomery Bird, Theodore and Timothy Dwight, Hannah Foster, James Kirke Paulding, Anna Seward, John Trumbull, Royall Tyler and Lydia and Jones Very.

The book is dedicated to my wife, who (with her computer) has suffered this book for a long time; and to the memory of Marcus Cunliffe, with the consciousness that he could, and did, do it better.

For Jenny Wigram
and
In Lasting Memory of Marcus Cunliffe (1922–1990)

Chapter 1

The Problem of American Literature

The case of Paul De Man

> Man in the center of space, man whom nothing protects from the sky and the earth is no doubt closer to the essential than the European, who searches for a shelter among beautiful houses polished by history and among fields marked by ancestral labor. For he is in the midst of his own struggle . . .
>
> (Paul De Man, 'The Temptation of Permanence')[1]

As Paul De Man realised, America has always presented a great challenge to its inhabitants. Likewise, it is a great challenge to write an 'American literary history'. Its three terms will not let themselves be taken for granted. Take the first term. The landmass did not receive that European name 'America' until the beginning of the sixteenth century. The nation created in 1776 out of thirteen states occupied a fraction of the territory that it would occupy in 1912, when New Mexico and Arizona became the forty-seventh and forty-eighth states. By that time the interchangeability of the terms 'United States' and 'America,' easily assumed by US nationals, had long been the despair of those Continentals living outside US borders. In the middle of the twentieth century questions of terrestrial definition became even more complex. In 1952 Puerto Rico became a self-governing commonwealth associated with the United States although, as the Puerto Ricans in Leonard Bernstein's *West Side Story* (1957) remarked, nobody seemed to know it. In 1959 Alaska became the first non-contiguous state to join the Union (it abuts Canada). Although it has the smallest population of any state, it occupies the largest space, more than twice the size of Texas although, again, Texans seem unaware of it. Also in 1959, Hawaii, a group of islands over two thousand miles west of San Francisco, complicated matters further by becoming the fiftieth state.

The question of citizenship is also complex. For Puerto Ricans it might be ambiguous. It has been even more ambiguous for Native Americans. For instance, from 1827 until 1906 the Cherokee nation had independent status, initially on its own land within the United States but for much of that period on land administered by the United States. There was little ambiguity about African-Americans. Forcibly transported to America, they had few rights in the Southern states where most lived. Abraham Lincoln signed the definitive Emancipation Proclamation in January 1863. It was a *de jure* decision, not enacted *de facto* until the conclusion of the Civil War in 1865; and then many African-Americans were denied the franchise until the Civil Rights movement of the 1960s. No nation has more consistently worried about dissidents, to the extent that 'unAmerican' is a common term. In 1798 many conservatives were concerned that the United States was being taken over by a group called the Illuminati. The problem disappeared when it became apparent that the Illuminati had been defunct for some years. Other problems were solved in a more brutal fashion. Some dissidents, like Emma Goldman, were deported; others, like Paul Robeson, were denied a passport; yet others, like John Brown or, more recently, Nicolo Sacco and Bartolomeo Vanzetti, were deprived of their lives. The citizens of the United States have not always been able to take their status on trust – which is one of the reasons why there is a greater display of patriotism there than in many countries. The titles of two well-known American histories sum up the difficulties of definition; it is (says Robert Wiebe) a 'segmented society', populated (according to Michael Kammen) by 'people of paradox'. It is fortunate that the citizens of the United Kingdom have not yet added to the problems of American literary history by agreeing to become members of the fifty-first state.

Perhaps it is appropriate that 'America' should also be the site where the two other terms, 'literary history', have also come most under question. Here again the figure of Paul De Man is exemplary. He was one of a group of philosophers and literary critics who questioned the easy assumptions frequently made about the connection between texts and their contexts. While he did not deny that language could have a truth-function, he insisted that we attend closely to the charms embedded in a text's rhetoric; for a text has an agenda which may or may not be related to the agenda it professes, or that its author thought it professed. De Man suggested that a text could create a spurious authority, and he wished to question it. This presents particularly acute problems for literary historians, who are trying to use texts to detect structures – *in* a past, which those texts may try to obscure, and *of* a past, from which literary historians are separated, more than anything, precisely by the analytical tools they are using. In other words, language has thrust us into a thicket of subjectivities, and we can only hack our way out by looking at it with the suspicion of an expert detective. As De Man put it:

> To become good literary historians, we must remember that what we usually call literary history has little or nothing to do with literature and that what we call literary interpretation – provided only it is good interpretation – is in fact literary history.[2]

De Man died in 1983. In 1987 it was discovered that he had published articles between 1939 and 1943 in the Belgian press supportive of the Nazi cause. A hubbub ensued, in which De Man and his post-war work were declared unAmerican. Certainly, De Man's early journalism is repugnant. However, the fate of his reputation reveals a number of ironies. There were numbers of Nazi sympathisers in the United States, some of them prominent. The nation only became officially anti-Nazi after 11 December 1941, when Germany declared war on the United States. The nation still contains neo-fascist groups. De Man had worked in the United States only from 1947; he may well have thought that he had left his pro-fascist past behind him in Europe. For the last few years of his life he had been one of the most respected scholars in the country. This is appropriate, for De Man's literary criticism, which his detractors had labelled immoral and sympathetic to fascism, had at its heart a cussed sense of negation, which was deeply American in spirit. One of the most influential American writers, Ralph Waldo Emerson, when challenged by English friends to produce an American idea, produced 'the dogma of no-government'. Emerson believed that 'no truer American existed' than his friend Thoreau, and Thoreau had written a famous essay on the duty of civil disobedience. Yet there has been no suggestion that Emerson and Thoreau are unAmerican. This was the final and greatest irony. De Man's 1955 essay, 'The Temptation of Permanence', written in an Emersonian mood, had therefore been prophetic. The dream of permanence is merely a temptation, a temporary shelter from an unforgivingly essential, and essentially American, sky.[3]

A literary historian therefore embarks on an American literary history with a great deal of trepidation. How does one reveal, at one and the same time, 'the historicity of the text and the textuality of history', as Sacvan Bercovitch put it in his Introduction to *The Cambridge History of American Literature*? This chapter will attempt an answer by an extended discussion of some earlier American literary histories in relation to some elements of American history. The end of the timespan covered by this book is perhaps the safest place to begin. It brings into sharp focus issues of great concern to earlier American literature. It also raises questions about the American canon, which is sometimes more problematic than its English counterpart.

James, *Hawthorne*, and the problem

In 1879 Henry James published a book about his predecessor Nathaniel Hawthorne, whom he regarded as 'the most valuable example of the American genius'. James's view of this quality of American genius was set out in the opening chapter of the essay, where he developed an environmentally-based dialectic between space and time. He used images of horizontal vacuity to indicate what he called 'the large conditions of American life', and images of vertical accretion to indicate other conditions that America, in his view, largely lacked. The shortcomings were summed up by the word 'history', which, James believed:

> as yet, has left in the United States but so thin and impalpable a deposit that we very soon touch the hard substratum of nature; and nature herself, in the western world, has the peculiarity of seeming rather crude and immature. The very air looks new and young; the light of the sun seems fresh and innocent, as if it knew as yet but few of the secrets of the world and none of the weariness of shining; the vegetation has the appearance of not having reached its majority.

Hawthorne, in contrast, was a mature bloom, 'deeply rooted in the soil'. James gave two reasons, both of them relating to history. First, Hawthorne shared his birthday with that of the United States. Born on 4 July 1804, Hawthorne, said James, was an 'unqualified and unflinching American' imbued with the patriotic spirit to be found particularly on that day when 'the great Republic enjoys her acutest fit of self-consciousness'. James was right to believe that this coincidence was significant. From very early in US history the Declaration of Independence had become a quasi-religious document. Very few nations had made such an exact or grandiloquent début, and 4 July 1776 had started the US clock just as the birth date of Christ was deemed to have begun the Christian chronicle. Later on, the show businessman George M. Cohan and the great Jazz musician Louis Armstrong would insert themselves into national history by claiming 4 July as their birthday.

The second reason gave a particular tone to Hawthorne's Americanism. Hawthorne came from the only part of America, James believed, which possessed history of any depth. The United States dated back only to 1776. Hawthorne could trace his 'pedigree' a century and a half earlier, to 'primitive New England stock'. His Puritan ancestors had moved in the 1630s from England to Salem, Massachusetts, and the family had lived there ever since. Salem, to be sure, was 'dull' and 'provincial' – qualities that James would later, in *English Hours* (1905), also use to describe Samuel Johnson's home town of Lichfield, Staffordshire. But whereas James imagined that Lichfield turned Johnson's 'great intellectual appetite . . . sick with inanition', Salem was just the place for Hawthorne, because it 'has a physiognomy in which the past plays a more important part than the present'. It was, moreover, a dark past, heavily clouded with the Puritan consciousness of sin that Hawthorne would explore in his fiction.

Hawthorne contains an early reversal of that polarity, which would occupy James for much of his career, between a virtuous but superficial New World and a corrupt but sophisticated Old World. That polarity explains why James, whose appetites were Johnsonian rather than Hawthornian, had moved to Europe in 1875, and would complete *Hawthorne* in Paris. It also suggests why Hawthorne's 'beautiful, natural, original genius' was a lonely one. James equated history with society, and just as America, New England apart, lacked history, so its air was 'unthickened and undarkened by customs and institutions'. Right at the beginning of his text, James made it clear why he thought there was a shortage of literature in America. His predecessor, he said, 'has the advantage of pointing a great moral . . . that the flower of art blooms only where the soil is deep, that it needs a complex social machinery to set a writer in motion'.

James's use of natural metaphors gives his prose a comic subsoil. That subsoil comes to the surface as broad farce when James abandons figurative language in a later passage, which has become famous:

> one might enumerate the items of high civilization, as it exists in other countries, which are absent from the texture of American life, until it should become a wonder to know what was left. No state, in the European sense of the word, and indeed barely a specific national name. No sovereign, no court, no personal loyalty, no aristocracy, no church, no clergy, no army, no diplomatic service, no country gentlemen, no palaces, no castles, nor manors, no old country-houses, nor parsonages, nor thatched cottages nor ivied ruins; no cathedrals, nor abbeys, nor little Norman

churches; no great Universities nor public schools – no Oxford, nor Eton, nor Harrow; no literature, no novels, no museums, no pictures, no political society, no sporting class – no Epsom nor Ascot![4]

The final, extended yet incomplete, sentence is a spectacular example of an anaphoric structure made up entirely of noun phrases. It constructs a rhetoric of negation defining American social reality by a series of deviations from the elements that make up James's deliberately postcard creation of England. The rhetoric of negation was used by classical writers and had been employed by a number of American writers, including Hawthorne, but never at such a scale or to such comic effect. Like much comedy, the passage operates by extreme contrast. The contrast works thematically, counterpointing plenitude with desolation. It also works tonally, combining cynicism and utopianism. Indeed, we might say that it both looks back to the disdain of Pope's *The Rape of the Lock* (1714) and forward to the epic drive for totality of Georg Lukács' *The Theory of the Novel* (1920), creating in the process a virtuosic example of mock bourgeois epic.

But American readers at the time did not find it funny. *Hawthorne* rubbed nationalist sensibilities, and provoked a storm in the Boston and New York press. Critics and reviewers objected in particular to the term 'provincial', and started to suggest that James was defecting to America's old oppressor. James was rattled by the violence of the response. There is nothing more disconcerting to a comedian than a sally taken seriously, and James showed his feelings in a letter to his friend Thomas Sergeant Perry:

> The hubbub produced by my poor little *Hawthorne* is most ridiculous; my father has sent me a great many notices, each one more abusive and more abject than the others. The vulgarity, ignorance, rabid vanity and general idiocy of them all is truly incredible. But I hold it a great piece of good fortune to have stirred up such a clatter. The whole episode projects a lurid light upon the state of American 'culture', and furnishes me with a hundred wonderful examples, where, before, I had only more or less vague impressions. Whatever might have been my own evidence for calling American taste 'provincial', my successors at least will have no excuse for not doing it.

Thereafter James's attitude to the country of his birth would be often contemptuous and usually distant. After two visits between 1881 and 1883 he did not go back to the United States until 1904, and his account of that particular visit, *The American Scene* (1907), was generally negative. Even Salem was disappointing.[5]

The contemporary history of book publishing adds a further dimension to this story. Multi-volume editions such as Heroes of the Nations and English Men of Action were popular in Britain at the time, and in 1878 Macmillan began English Men of Letters, edited by the writer and liberal politician John (later Lord) Morley (1838–1923). The venture was very successful, amounting to sixty-seven volumes by 1919, including G. K. Chesterton on Robert Browning and Anthony Trollope on Thackeray. An early attempt to get George Eliot to write on Shakespeare unfortunately came to nothing. Morley himself contributed a volume on Edmund Burke (1729–97), the Whig politician who advocated conciliation rather than military action in response to the American Revolution. The Revolution, indeed, might not have happened as far as this establishment microcosm of English writing was concerned, for one of the earliest volumes in the series was *Hawthorne*. James wrote it for Macmillan against the wishes of Morley, who objected not on grounds of nationality but rather on those of quality. He thought that an earlier book of James's had been no more than 'honest scribble work'.

It might be thought provocative to include a book on an American novelist by another, émigré, American novelist in English Men of Letters. Two years later, in 1881, the Boston publishers Houghton Mifflin responded by starting their own series, American Men of Letters, edited by Charles Dudley Warner (1829–1900), the novelist and editor best remembered now for his collaboration in *The Gilded Age* (1873) with his friend and neighbour Mark Twain. A promotional leaflet promised that when it was completed, the series 'will form an admirable survey of all that is important and of historical influence in American literature, and will be . . . a creditable representation of the literary and critical ability of America to-day'.[6] Warner himself wrote the first volume, on Washington Irving, and by 1904 the series comprised some twenty-two volumes, including books on Fenimore Cooper, Emerson, Longfellow and Thoreau, but not on Henry James. This adventure in literary nationalism had no impact on Macmillan's activities. In 1902 it began a second series of English Men of Letters, starting with Sir Leslie Stephen's *George Eliot*, and that year included a second American volume, on the Massachusetts poet John Greenleaf Whittier, this time by a Harvard-based American, Thomas Wentworth Higginson, the mentor of another Massachusetts poet, Emily Dickinson. Unabashed, when Macmillan began a third, New Series in 1926, now edited by J. C. (later Sir John) Squire (1884–1958), their first four volumes gave equal prominence to English and American writing. The two English volumes were on Meredith and Swinburne. Englishmen this time wrote the two American volumes. John Freeman wrote *Melville*, only the second appreciation of Melville ever published, and John Bailey wrote *Whitman*.

The different approaches taken by the London and Boston publishers meant some overlap. Hawthorne, Poe, Emerson and Whitman were to be found both as English Men of Letters and American Men of Letters. Those different approaches also provided some unusual opportunities for enterprising writers. In the same year, 1902, that he published his biography of Whittier for the English Men of Letters series, Higginson published *Longfellow* in the American Men of Letters series. But he was outdone by the Massachusetts critic and poet George Woodberry (1855–1930), who wrote *Edgar Allan Poe* for American Men of Letters in 1885; then challenged Henry James in 1902 by writing *Nathaniel Hawthorne*, also for American Men of Letters; and completed a hat-trick by writing *Ralph Waldo Emerson* in 1907, but for English Men of Letters.

I have given this account of James's *Hawthorne* and its context because it highlights two sets of interrelated issues that must be handled by a history of earlier American literature. One set of issues concerns the definition of terms in the titles of the two series. The century since the first appearance of English Men of Letters and American Men of Letters has thrown into question every term in those titles except the prepositions. One question concerns the final noun. John Morley and Macmillan considered a variety of titles for the series, including 'Great English Authors' and 'Masters of Literature'. The final term of the title on which they settled, 'Letters', allowed them to range well beyond imaginative literature into other fields, thus anticipating the analytical breadth of more recent critical theories like cultural materialism and new historicism. When Houghton Mifflin adopted the same phrase for their series, it allowed them to gather together a list of luminaries that gave them the additional advantage of appearing to refute James's critique of the thinness of American culture. The first list therefore included biographies of the lexicographer Noah Webster (1758–1843) and the Transcendentalist philosopher George Ripley (1802–80), the latter written by a Unitarian minister with the appropriately sonorous name of Octavius Brooks Frothingham (1822–95). Webster and Ripley will not feature significantly in this present history. The breadth suggested by the term 'Letters' will – and it should provide an answer to James's critique of the shallow American soil.

A second question concerns the noun of gender. Both publishers treated it as unproblematic, man embracing woman for this purpose, as it used to be said. English Men of Letters therefore contained volumes on Jane Austen, Fanny Burney, Maria Edgeworth, George Eliot and Elizabeth Gaskell. Margaret Fuller was the only woman to appear in American Men of Letters; and even then the book, written by the energetic Thomas Wentworth Higginson, was published under her married name of Margaret Fuller Ossoli. It can be argued that the inclusive treatment of the noun masked an inability to recognise a distinction between male and female writing, and a failure to give sufficient attention to the amount of material written by women. Feminist literary history has brought to light a range of American women's writing far greater in subject and extent than suggested by the lonely appearance of Fuller in American Men of Letters. Fuller's *Woman in the Nineteenth Century* (1845) could be said to present the first thoroughgoing American feminist programme, yet appeared long after Mary Wollstonecraft's *Vindication of the Rights of Women* (1792). Despite this, the following chapters of this book will show that women as writers and women as the subjects of writing have a more significant place in earlier American writing than in its English equivalent. Towards the end of this chapter I will try to explain why this should be so.

Third, the account of the two Men of Letters series suggests that the opening adjective for each was given a different meaning by each publisher. The adjective in the English Men of Letters series indicated language not nationality, while the adjective in American Men of Letters denoted nationality not language. Biographers like Higginson and Woodberry may have exploited the distinction, but it presented a particular problem for those trying to create a national literature for the United States. Noah Webster, fired with youthful patriotism after the revolution, attempted to create a separate American language with the aim of assisting what he called 'literary improvements'. With the exception of some orthographical changes to -or (instead of -our) and -ize (instead of -ise) suffixes, his project failed. That failure is reflected in an 1824 comment by Emerson: 'The community of language with England has doubtless deprived us of that original characteristic literary growth that has ever accompanied, I apprehend, the first bursting of a nation from the bud.'[7] It is perhaps as well that Emerson did not live to see himself included in English Men of Letters.

This brings us to the second set of issues highlighted by the two Men of Letters series. These concern the status of America within the transatlantic English-speaking community. Stephen Spender characterised the connection between the peoples on either side of the Atlantic as 'love–hate relations'. This is an unstable condition that has rarely comforted the professional student of American literature, as Henry James discovered to his cost. James's irritated response showed that he had not anticipated the offence generated by his urbane comedy, and seriously underestimated the emotional investment that many of his compatriots had in American literature. Those emotions are deep and potent because the status and contents of American literature have been the subject of debate for almost as long as its existence has been mooted. It is the subject of many questions, some of which have never been asked of English literature. Does American literature exist? If it exists, what is its relation with English literature? Is it simply a branch of English literature or does it have a separate identity? If it does, how is that identity defined? Does it have a special relation with the land after which it is named? To what extent does it reflect American politics? Has it been influenced by structures of class, race or gender that differ from those in Europe? How have non-English-speaking visitors to and inhabitants of the American continent impacted upon it? American literature has been the site of transnational, and sometimes translinguistic and transethnic, contestation. In consequence, it has never been taken for granted. It is an unsettled, often unsettling, literature. Hence the need, next, to survey American literary histories. The survey will show that different historians have asked different questions of American literature, and arrived at different answers – or decided that they cannot find any answers. Indeed, in the last few years some historians have suggested that American literature has been the object of so much debate because its major defining characteristic is instability. In a splintered postmodern western culture where there can be no answers, they feel that the characteristic of instability makes American literature the most important site to pose the most pressing literary and cultural questions.

The difficulty of American literary history

Until the revolution the little that was written about American literature tended to be confined to theory. For instance, Cotton Mather's introduction to his *Psalterium Americanum* (1718) tried to justify a plain style which would serve the practical requirements of the people. In contrast, a great deal of American literary history has been written in the two and a quarter centuries since 1776. It follows, therefore, that much literary history has been written in response to the Declaration of Independence and subsequent events in the life of the nation – hence James's comments about Hawthorne's birthday. This is not to say that it has always been narrowly nationalist. American literary history has, rather, tended to oscillate in the space defined by two opposing ideologies. Some critics have been inspired by internationalism, or by the fact that American literature has normally been in a language that they have identified as English. They have argued that American literature is part of the occidental cultural tradition or, more narrowly, a branch of English literature. Other critics have taken their cue from the politics of the United States, and have argued that its literature was special, different from other literatures. An extreme version of this is the doctrine of American exceptionalism discussed below. Yet even here the existence of English literature played a part in the definition of American literature.

The earliest post-revolutionary American literary history was written in response to adverse commentary on American culture, believed to be from British critics. A good example of such commentary appeared in *Blackwood's Edinburgh Magazine* in March 1819. This is, both in form and content, the source of James's remarks, and it makes them look generous. Ironically, although Americans read it as a typically British criticism, it too was written by an American. Joseph Green Cogswell (1786–1871) spent the years 1815–1820 in Europe. In 1817 he was a member of the first group of American students attending the University of Göttingen, and he became a friend of Goethe. While visiting Britain he anonymously contributed two articles to *Blackwood's* 'On the State of Learning in the United States of America'. Cogswell's second article boldly stated his theme in its first sentence: learning was not to be found in America. Among America's many deficiencies was a 'barrenness in creative literature'. Cogswell explained why:

> There is nothing to awaken fancy in that land of dull realities; it carries no objects that carry back the mind to the contemplation of early antiquity; no mouldering ruins to excite curiosity in the history of past ages; no memorials, commemorative of glorious deeds, to call forth patriotic enthusiasm and reverence; it has no traditions and legends and fables to afford materials for romance and poetry; no peasantry of original and various costume and character for the sketches of the pencil and the subjects of song; it has gone through no period of infancy; no pastoral state in which poetry grows out of the simplicity of language, and beautiful and picturesque descriptions of nature are produced by the constant contemplation of her.

Cogswell hoped that the problem had arisen because America was too involved in 'the pursuit of wealth'. 'The hurry of business' had prompted the neglect of 'the ideal and poetic in life'. Beneath this diagnosis, though, lay the fear of a more serious disorder, perhaps intensified by the memory of the intellectual stimulation of Göttingen and Goethe. Cogswell wondered if he would have to 'agree with Buffon and Raynal, that the human mind has suffered a deterioration in being transported across the Atlantic'.[8]

The reference to Buffon and Raynal recalls an environmentally-inspired debate, which soured transatlantic relations in the second half of the eighteenth century. The debate began with the publication of the Comte de Buffon's *Natural History* in 1749 and was renewed by l'Abbé Raynal's *Philosophical and Political History of . . . the East and West Indies* in 1770. Raynal extended to the white settlers Buffon's theories about a miasmic climate that had destroyed aboriginal potency. Settlement was too recent to allow the development of a literature and, Raynal added in later editions of the book, America's infant state had been prolonged because independence had been grasped too soon. (A version of this argument was used to oppose the independence of African states in the 1950s and 1960s.) America, according to Raynal, had not yet produced a single good poet. Because it was a timely and apparently objective analysis of the discord with America, Raynal's book was extremely popular in Britain. By 1799 fourteen editions had been published, and more copies sold than Edward Gibbon's *Decline and Fall of the Roman Empire.*

The American response to European portents of the decline and fall of their nascent empire was predictable. As we shall see in Chapter 4, the miasmatist debate provoked a rash of composition by young republicans keen to establish their nation's literary fame. The debate also explained why a relatively even-handed article, this time by a Briton who styled himself one of the 'friends and admirers' of the United States, should have received such a prompt and energetic answer. The article was published in the *Edinburgh Review* in 1820 by Sydney Smith (1771–1845), a clergyman and member of the group that founded that Whig magazine in 1802. Smith is now largely a forgotten figure, but at the beginning of the twentieth century was still regarded as sufficiently important to be included in the English Men of Letters series. His article touched off a debate that smouldered for much of the century. Indeed, its ashes still warm the ignorant. Smith's remarks came at the end of a long, highly factual review of an American statistical survey. Much of the article was more critical of Britain than America. He made a number of pointed criticisms of the burden of British taxation and 'the insanity of garrisoning little rocks and islands all over the world'. Such criticisms were, however, overlooked by Americans in the furore created by his closing remarks:

The Americans are a brave, industrious, and acute people; but they have hitherto given no indications of genius . . . They are but a recent offset indeed from England; and should make it their chief boast, for many generations to come, that they are sprung from the same race with Bacon and Shakespeare and Newton. Considering their numbers indeed, and the favourable circumstances in which they have been placed, they have yet done marvellously little to assert the honour of such a descent, or to show their English blood has been exalted or refined by their republican training and institutions . . . During the thirty or forty years of their independence, they have done absolutely nothing for the Sciences, for the Arts, for Literature, or even the statesman-like studies of Politics or Political Economy . . . In the four quarters of the globe, who reads an American book? or goes to an American play? or looks at an American picture or statue?

For many years Smith's remarks acted as a goad. In 1850 Herman Melville anticipated James's high estimation of Hawthorne by comparing him with Shakespeare. In doing so he took a view of American culture diametrically opposed to James's, predicting that 'the day will come when you shall say, Who reads a book by an Englishman that is a modern?'[9]

It might also be said that Smith prompted the start of American literary history, which begins with John Neal. In his autobiography, *Wandering Recollections of a Somewhat Busy Life* (1869), Neal claimed he quit his Baltimore law practice to spend four years in Britain specifically answering 'the insolent question . . . "*Who reads an American Book*"'. This may well be emotional hindsight by an author noted as early as 1816 for the feverish, garrulous writing which dominated his somewhat busy life. Yet the fact remains that Neal lived in Britain from 1823 to 1827. Masquerading as an Englishman under the pseudonym 'Carter Holmes', he wrote a number of articles for *Blackwood's Edinburgh Magazine*, which had been founded in 1817 as a Tory rival to Smith's *Edinburgh Review*. Six of the articles were on American writers. Neal began by telling Smith that there were many American books to be read. He also answered the miasmatist argument with another environmentalist one, suggesting that, like the natural world, the arts underwent a process of growth, maturity and decay. Neal follows the cyclical theory of history, which was frequently discussed in the eighteenth century and which would shortly feature in Thomas Cole's five paintings, *The Course of Empire* (1836), and in James Fenimore Cooper's 1848 novel, *The Crater*. The charm of the theory was that it could at the same time offer comfort to the optimist and justify the fears of the pessimist. Predisposition determined the point of entry into the cycle. Cole and Cooper were pessimists. Neal's optimism prompted him to believe that American writing, like the United States, was at present in an infant state and would yet mature. Moreover, since 'the longest-lived animals are the longest in coming to maturity', the slow growth of American writing implied a long, glorious prime. The problem, he thought, was that American writing had been either overlooked or prematurely overrated. He believed 'that there are more American writers in every branch of literature, and they are more respectable, ten times over', than the British believed; but that none of them 'would abide a temperate, firm, unsparing examination'.

Neal constructed his material to confirm his claims to objectivity, and to convey a sense of authority. The essays were presented as a dictionary, proceeding alphabetically and including material on genres (for instance, 'farces') as well as on individuals. There were entries for 126 writers in the course of the first five articles, written, Neal claimed, from memory, including in his list historians, politicians, scientists, lawyers, and editors of periodicals. Despite Neal's support of women's rights, only two of his writers were women. There were brief entries for Hannah Adams (1755–1831), whom Neal described, wrongly, as a sister of John Adams; and Mercy Otis Warren (1728–1814), whom he named Mary. In keeping with his argument about the infancy of American letters, he looked no further back than the botanist James Logan (1674–1751), whose *Experiments concerning the impregnation of the Seeds of Plants* was first published in Leyden in 1739. Most of his subjects were still alive, including two of the three whom he regarded as most 'American': James Kirke Paulding (1778–1860), and himself. Under cover of anonymity, Neal did not hesitate to discuss at length his own work. The only writer to be given more space, and on grounds of his popularity rather than his Americanism, was Washington Irving.

Neal's intention to concentrate on recent American letters was confirmed by the sixth and final essay for *Blackwood's*. Five of the six texts he discussed had been published within the preceding few months. Four were novels; Neal did not like them. Two were by writers he had previously noticed: Cooper's *Lionel Lincoln* ('a very poor book') and Paulding's *John Bull in America* ('Paulding has overshot his mark'). The third, *The Refugee*, by the Massachusetts novelist James Athearn Jones (1791–1854), was 'insupportably tedious'. The fourth novel brought another woman into Neal's list, although he was not aware of it. *A Peep at the Pilgrims* was published anonymously, and Neal, who found it 'absurd and respectable', assumed the author was male. It was written by Harriet Cheney, the daughter of Hannah Foster, whose own novel, *The Coquette* (1797), was one of the most popular books in America at the time that Neal was writing his *Blackwood's* essays. The masculine community of Neal's dictionary was cognate with his language. His final essay also reviewed the latest issue of the *North American Review*, which he rebuked for its 'bad, boyish temper'. The other text to be included in the essay had been published in Britain in 1822. It was an abridgement of a biography, by William Dunlap, of the one deceased member of his American triumvirate, Charles Brockden Brown, whom Neal regarded as 'a sound, hearty specimen of Trans-Atlantic stuff'.[10]

The next attempt at American literary history was by the Massachusetts lawyer and biographer Samuel L. Knapp (1783–1838). *Lectures on American Literature*, published in 1829, has often been noted by later critics, but rarely analysed. Yet it introduces a number of important issues that will recur in this present history. Knapp took a quite different but no less male-oriented approach from Neal. Nearly all of Knapp's subjects were dead. He believed that British prejudice had almost died, too. Indeed, he suggested that the 'evil' caused by the negative reviews had created in Britain 'a host of able vindicators of American mind and literature', to the extent that American fiction was received with much more 'éclat' in Britain than at home. This was an ironic American comment on British morality, for unlike Neal, but in common with educated conservatives on both sides of the Atlantic, Knapp regarded most fiction as corrupting. So he omitted the offending material from his book. Paulding and Neal do not appear at all. Brown is briefly mentioned only as the biographer of the Pennsylvania poet and clergyman (and Brown's brother-in-law) John Blair Linn (1777–1804), and as the subject of Dunlap's biography. Washington Irving's most 'lasting' work, in Knapp's view, is not his fiction, but rather the biography of Columbus which Irving had published just the year before.[11]

The terms in which Knapp praised Irving's *History of the Life and Voyages of Christopher Columbus* indicate his approach to American literature:

Poetry and fiction had nothing more splendid to offer, nor history to hold up, for the contemplation of man, than the life of Columbus; there was enough of vicissitude, of glory, of heart-ache, of degradation, of apotheosis, to have suited an epick bard, or an oriental enthusiast. Had the great discoverer been 'wrapt into future times', as poets have imagined him to have been, one of the most delightful visions he could have had, would have been the sight of his own great historian. Not a misery of his existence could now be spared by his biographer, for they were all wanted to finish so noble a character. Who is there now so dull as would wish to find that all the troubles of Columbus were fictitious ... Not one; his chains, his dungeon, his death, his obscure grave, are all sacred appendages to his fame; nor were his honours and his virtues to shine in that age of superstition and ignorance; three centuries, in the course of time, were required to bring forth a historian for him; for it was the decree of fate, that the events of the life of the discoverer of the new world, should be fully written by one who should arise in it.

Knapp was clearly a teleologist. This passage is structured to create a beneficent design which links 1492 and 1828 by means of an allusion to Philip Freneau's 1788 sequence, 'The Pictures of Columbus'. That design is often called *translatio imperii* and concerns the westward movement of civilisation in pursuit of the sun. Thomas Sprat's *History of the Royal Society* predicted the movement in 1667. Over a century later Edward Gibbon provided suitable corroboration of Old World decay. From the American point of view Gibbon's *Decline and Fall* could not have been written at a more significant time, for its publication began with the Declaration of Independence and it was completed with the adoption of the Federal Constitution. *Translatio imperii* was most clearly stated, however, in George Berkeley's 1726 'Verses on the Prospect of Planting Arts and Learning in America' (discussed in Chapter 3), prophesying 'the Rise of Empire and of Arts' in America to replace those that had declined in Europe. Knapp refers to the trope at a number of points in his text, and quotes Berkeley's poem in full.[12]

Knapp may also be called 'an epick bard', although one who is an enthusiast for the occident rather than the orient. *Lectures on American Literature* is epic in scale. The scale, surprisingly, is founded in the importance of language, and it provides Knapp with three advantages. First, it allowed him to create a grand yet complex model of transatlantic relations. On the one hand Knapp could present a version of the bootstrap theory, claiming that the English language was the only thing that the people of the United States had inherited from Britain; everything else they had done alone. On the other hand he could provide a unified literary and historical scheme. It suggested that 'the literature of the present day is made ... out of the ruins of the literature of former ages'; and showed that American history is an organic development of the British history which he briefly traced from before the Roman invasion. Second, the linguistic focus enabled him to follow Jefferson's *Notes on the State of Virginia* (1782) in drawing attention to Native American rhetoric. He praised the eloquence of leaders such as Logan and Tecumseh, and included a lengthy eulogy for Sequoyah, the Cherokee leader of many talents who devised an alphabet of the Cherokee language. The Cherokees had in 1828 established a bilingual newspaper, the *Cherokee Phoenix*, which Knapp praised for its 'decency and good sense'. It provided clear evidence to refute the miasmatist argument. Knapp's pleasure was reflected in enthusiastic language, which brought together a common biblical image (from Isaiah 35:1) and a reference to the mythical first king of Athens:

> The western wilderness is not only to blossom like the rose; but there, man has started up, and proved that he has not degenerated since the primitive days of Cecrops, and the romantic ages of wonderful effort and god-like renown.

The newspaper closed in 1835. Three years later, in the year of Knapp's death, the Cherokees were forcibly removed from their lands in north-west Georgia. Sequoyah is now remembered in the name of the giant redwood tree.

Third, the focus on language allowed Knapp to handle 'literature in its extended sense' so that it equated with civilisation. That sense, indeed, was extended beyond Neal's definition in order to pay attention to America's 'military and naval characters, as well as to her literary and scientifick men'. The last three 'Lectures' were devoted to a brief military history, beginning with the establishment of Jamestown in 1607 and bringing the history almost up to date with a description of West Point, founded in 1802. The *Lectures*, appropriately, ended with snapshot portraits of epic heroes, of whom the greatest was the frontiersman Daniel Boone (1734–1820). The literary legend of Boone had begun when John Filson appended the 'Boone narrative' to his *The Discovery and Settlement of Kentucke* (1784), and had been celebrated in verse in 1813 by Daniel Bryan's *The Mountain Muse*, and in 1823 when Byron included him in Canto VIII of *Don Juan*. Knapp perpetuated the legend by suggesting that Boone's character had 'a peculiarity and an elevation . . . that all the courts of Europe could not teach'. Indeed, Boone seemed to be beyond compare in testing not only the frontiers of America, but also those of longevity:

> Civilized man has no standard by which he can measure the operations of such a mind; he must go back to primitive ages to find a parallel; and then strip the travels of Theseus, and the labours of Hercules, of all the monstrous fictions – and what would the remainder be in comparison with the adventures and hardships of Boone. The whole country which these demi-gods of antiquity traversed, did not extend so far as one of Boone's hunting excursions. Bordering upon eighty years of age, Boone died in the interior of Missouri, having known but little of the decay of faculties, corporal or mental.

In his triumphalist progress from ancient myth to present-day reality, Knapp had conveniently forgotten Alexander the Great. He did not quite forget women, whom he characterised as fit mates for epic heroes. He remarked that the first white women came to America during the reign of Elizabeth I, when 'it was fashionable . . . to think women as capable of reasoning upon public affairs as men'. It was with clear relief that he noted that they had abandoned this fashion in favour of needlework and improving their handwriting, which Knapp finds easier to read than that of their menfolk. Apparently they did not write anything worth noticing in the *Lectures*, for Knapp omits women's writing completely. Woman as writer (as opposed to woman as practitioner of hand-writing) had no place in his epic scheme. This is apparent again when he looks towards the future. The imagery and Old World comparisons used for Boone occur again when Knapp adopts what has been called 'the figure of anticipation', allying America's size with the ambitions of its people:

> What are the Tibers and Scamanders, measured by the Missouri and the Amazon? Or what the loveliness of Illyssus or Avon, by the Connecticut or the Potomack? . . . Whenever a nation wills it, prodigies are born. Admiration and patronage create myriads who struggle for the mastery, and for the olympick crown. Encourage the game and the victors will come.[13]

Moses Coit Tyler (1835–1900) was Professor of English at the University of Michigan when in 1878 he published *A History of American Literature, 1607–1765*. He did not need to trouble with 'the figure of anticipation'. His pages give the impression of a country thronging with writers. Some of them had always been there, but had not been noticed by Knapp. This is particularly the case with women writers. For instance, Mary Rowlandson's captivity narrative, *The Sovereignty and Goodness of God*, was published in Cambridge, Massachusetts in 1682. It was very popular, and appeared in its sixth edition in 1828, when Knapp was writing his *Lectures*. Tyler glanced at the narrative, suggesting that the bloody conflict between the Iroquois Confederacy and the New England settlers known as King Philip's War (1675–76) has 'no more graphic or exquisite literary memorial than a little book written by a woman'. Tyler granted much more space to the work of Anne Bradstreet, also overlooked by Knapp. Her poems had been published in London in 1650 and in Boston in 1678. Tyler devoted several thousand words to them, using a more complete scholarly edition published in 1867. Indeed, some of his work relied on the material unearthed by contemporaries of Knapp who, in the wake of the Revolution, had become enthusiastic amateur historians. For instance, Tyler discussed the *Journal* of Sarah Kemble Knight, written while she was riding between Boston and New York City in 1704–5 but not published until 1825, in an edition by the Massachusetts lawyer Theodore Dwight (1764–1846).[14]

Tyler gave less attention to women's writing when in 1897, now Professor of American History at Cornell, he published the two volumes of *The Literary History of the American Revolution, 1763–1783*. He examined the work of two writers whose names had become entangled in the cobwebs of John Neal's memory: Mercy Otis Warren, and Abigail Adams (1744–1818), the wife of the second president. He did not however look at the work of other women who were writing in the later eighteenth century, and gave even less space to ethnic minorities. Neither Sequoyah nor Elias Boudinot, the editor of the *Cherokee Phoenix*, receives any mention. The only African-American writer whom Tyler noticed was Phillis Wheatley (1753?–84). He believed that her work belonged more 'to the domain of anthropology, or of hagiology, than that of poetry'. Tyler's attitude to ethnic minorities resulted from the Anglo-Saxon race theories of the period. His Preface to *The Literary History of the*

American Revolution regretted the 'needless' Revolution and hoped that the book would assist in reconciling 'these divided members of a family capable, if in substantial harmony, of leading the whole human race upward to all the higher planes of culture and happiness'. Tyler's devotion to this 'historic opportunity', as he put it, had a number of consequences. It meant an even-handed treatment of writers on both sides of the Revolution. He had praise for 'the marvelous power' of Tom Paine, but he also paid attention to those he called 'the Tories of the Revolution', who included in their number many of 'the most refined, thoughtful, and conscientious people in the colonies'. Tyler was also willing to give sympathetic space to British commentators. Sydney Smith is quoted not for his remarks on American writing but rather for his strictures on British taxation and his admiration of Franklin. The British had their tactical uses, too. Tyler sited the Declaration of Independence in the English libertarian tradition, with the result that the Declaration emerged as a document both at the heart of American literature and of international significance. There was, however, a negative side to Tyler's Anglo-Saxonism, suggested by his comments on Phillis Wheatley. In his discussion of the Declaration of Independence, he had deplored the 'appalling national temptation' to exclude 'our human brethren in bondage' from the principles 'which we ourselves had once proclaimed as the basis of every rightful government'. But principles were of no help to the brethren. Tyler referred to the horrific incarceration of an African-American in Crèvecoeur's *Letters from an American Farmer* (1782; discussed in Chapter 3), as a 'necessary barbarism'.[15]

Anglo-Saxonism was a relatively brief phase of transatlantic literary relations, if not social and political relations. Tyler's historical framework has had a longer influence. The Preface to the 1878 edition of *A History of American Literature, 1607–1765* indicates the bounds as well as the ambitions of Tyler's work. He proposed to undertake 'the history of American literature from the earliest English settlements, down to the present time'. This would have been an epic of more than Wagnerian proportions, and he had to abandon it. As it is, his tetralogy takes some 1,600 pages to cover the period from 1607 to 1783, over one thousand of them covering the last twenty years. It contained four 'epochs', the first one being both the most influential and controversial:

> our first literary epoch cannot fail to bear traces of the fact that nearly all men who made it were Englishmen who had become Americans merely by removing to America. American life, indeed, at once reacted upon their minds, and began to give its tone and hue to their words; and for every reason, what they wrote here, we rightfully claim as a part of American literature; but England has a right to claim it likewise as a part of English literature. Indeed, England and America are joint proprietors of this first tract of the great literary territory which we have undertaken to survey . . . How could it be otherwise? Is it likely that an Englishman undergoes a literary revolution by sitting down to write in America instead of in England; or that he will write either much better or much worse only for having sailed across a thousand leagues of brine?

As we shall see, it is the joint ownership of this 'literary territory' which has been the subject of debate. Yet for the great part of the century following the publication of these words, American literary histories have tended to take English settlement as their start date: either settlement in Virginia in 1607 or, more frequently, in Massachusetts in 1620. It is symptomatic that in 1962 Tyler's first two volumes should be reissued with a new Foreword written by the pioneer American Studies scholar Perry Miller (1905–63) proclaiming it a 'classic' while drawing attention to Tyler's exordium, not to the first epoch but rather to the second, which began in 1676 and ended in 1763, 'representing the earliest literary results flowing from the reactions of life in the new world upon an intellectual culture that was itself formed in the new world'.

There were good reasons why Tyler chose 1676. The conclusion of King Philip's War had ended the most serious Native American threat to the New England colonists. Bacon's Rebellion showed that colonists in Virginia were willing to stand up for rights granted to their English counterparts. The first generation born in America had come to maturity. As Tyler put it: 'That year completed the proofs that a certain uncounted throng of articulating bipeds, known as Americans – together with the words that they should articulate – were to be endured on this planet, for some ages to come.' His phrases bear a heavy teleological burden. The discussion of the Declaration of Independence had brought both his third 'epoch' and his third volume to a resonant close. The date of the Declaration provided the keystone of an elegantly symmetrical arch which ended with Tyler writing history in anticipation of the centennial of 1876. The bicentennial, which brought out its own rash of commemorations, could not provide anything so laden with significance.[16]

Nor would anyone again single-handedly attempt a project of such an extent. After Tyler, American literary histories have been brief, suggestive introductions, like *The Literature of the United States* by Marcus Cunliffe (1922–90), which announces itself in its third edition with typical modesty as 'a small book on a large topic'. Or they would be heavy, large-scale reference books, necessarily the result of teamwork. The earliest example of the latter is *A History of American Literature*, first published in 1917 as a supplement to *The Cambridge History of English Literature*. The team of thirty-six scholars involved in the first edition included two future Pulitzer Prize-winners. They were Carl Van Doren (1885–1950), the project's managing editor, whose many subsequent books included a biography of Benjamin Franklin (1938); and Vernon Parrington (1871–1929) whose trilogy *Main Currents in American Thought* (1927–30), had he lived long enough to complete it, would have challenged Tyler's work in its scale. This epic quality was the first aim announced by the editors in their Preface. Certainly, they achieved authoritative weight. Each of the two initial volumes (by 1921 it had reached four) was powered by a bibliography in excess of two hundred pages. Sydney Smith's impertinent question, which they quoted in the Preface, had been decisively squashed by scholarship. It was clear that American literature was no longer a matter of slight consequence. The editors intended to make their *History* 'a survey of the life of the American people as expressed in their writings rather than a history of *belles-lettres* alone'. The dismissive use of the French term was a key to the spirit of the *History*, which reflected the mood of a nation which had just won its first adventure in foreign warfare, the 1898 Spanish-American War, and was on the brink of entering the First World War. The editors therefore rejected what they called 'the modern aesthetic standpoint' in favour of rugged open-air qualities characterised by the man who had been their twenty-sixth President, Theodore Roosevelt (1858–1919). They produced a common defence, already seen in Cogswell's remarks in *Blackwood's* about the pursuit of wealth. Americans, they thought, had been too busy, and their energies had instead produced 'prose competently recording their practical activities and expressing their moral, religious, and political ideas'. They therefore disapproved what they called 'facile novelists and poetasters', preferring non-fiction prose – material which, they thought, would 'enlarge the spirit of American literary criticism and make it masculine'.[17]

This preference had its effect upon the canon. Anne Bradstreet, said one contributor, 'was not a poet; she was a winsome personality in an unlovely age'. She was dispatched in two pages, where Tyler had given her fourteen. In contrast, an entire chapter was devoted to the oratory of the politician and lawyer Daniel Webster (1782–1852). It was written by his successor as US senator from Massachusetts, Henry Cabot Lodge (1850–1924), a member of the elite Boston family. Lodge, who had published a biography of Webster in 1883, said bluntly that his subject 'was not a literary man at all'. Webster nevertheless had an 'uncontested place in the history of American literature' because he had unconsciously imported the lasting qualities of literature into the living force of speech. As proof, Lodge quoted several of Webster's speeches, including one given in the Senate supporting the British Empire, 'whose morning drumbeat, following the sun and keeping company with the hours, circles the earth with one continuous and unbroken strain of the martial airs of England'.[18] One wonders if the Senate cheered. Certainly, Webster's rhetoric lifted the heart of Lodge.

Not all of the contributors to *A History of American Literature* were so strongly Anglo-Saxonist, but their emphasis on literature as part of the active life meant that many writers joined Anne Bradstreet on the back seat. Carl Van Doren referred briefly to the appeal of Hannah Foster's *The Coquette* and Susannah Rowson's *Charlotte Temple* (1791) to a 'naïve underworld of fiction readers'. Yet the space accorded women writers was generous compared with that given to ethnic minorities. African-American writing was confined to one paragraph in a chapter devoted to 'Dialect Writers'. Four writers, including Frederick Douglass, were named to support the critic's contention that the life of African-American communities was better rendered by the Uncle Remus stories of the White Georgia writer Joel Chandler Harris (1848–1908).[19]

In 1948 the editors of the *Literary History of the United States* aimed 'to draw a new and truer picture', as they put it, of American literature. To do this they worked on an even more ambitious scale than that of *A History of American Literature*. It was a major academic industry, with eighty-one chapters written by some fifty-six scholars. The bibliography was in a separate volume, to which would be added a *Supplement* in 1959 and *Supplement II* in

1972. The first outlines of the picture were announced in the eloquent first paragraph of the Address to the Reader:

> The literary history of this nation began when the first settler from abroad of sensitive mind paused in his adventure long enough to feel that he was under a different sky, breathing new air, and that a New World was all before him with only his strength and Providence for guides. With him began a different emphasis upon an old theme in literature, the theme of cutting loose and faring forth, renewed under the powerful influence of a fresh continent for civilized man. It has provided, ever since those first days, an element in our native literature, whose other theme has come from a nostalgia for the rich culture of Europe, so much of which was perforce left behind.

The images employed here are revealing. References to an Old World culture, included in the glance at James's *Hawthorne* and the allusion to the closing lines of *Paradise Lost*, are seen as baggage which has to be abandoned or repacked to be carried into the new environment. American literature, the editors asserted, was both 'a *transported* European culture' and 'a *transformed* culture'. They disagreed with Tyler, placing greater emphasis on transformation. His first epoch had now become wholly American. It was the process of migration itself which created the difference. On their first page the editors referred to the Melting Pot theory, the belief that all races were transmuted into Americans by migration; and to Letter III of Crèvecoeur's *Letters from an American Farmer*, which as we shall see, had by now become the Old Testament in the Americaniser's Bible. Despite Samuel Knapp, the emphasis on American fresh-air owed little to the Boone legend. The hero of the first paragraph is a settler rather than an action-man, and Boone was only mentioned twice in the whole *History*. The environmentalism of the Turner thesis, which will be discussed towards the end of this chapter, had much more influence.[20]

The new picture of American literature had resulted from the events of thirty years and, particularly, the Second World War. It was suggested by the new title, the *Literary History of the United States*, changed from indefinite to implied definite article and from ambiguous to clear statement of nationality. The poet and critic Malcolm Cowley (1898–1989) summed up the changes in the final paragraph of his closing chapter to the *Literary History*:

> During the first half of this century, the position of American literature in foreign countries has been completely transformed. It was still regarded, before 1900, as a department of English literature, a sort of branch factory that tried to duplicate the products of the parent firm. After 1930 it came to be regarded as one of the great world literatures in its own right . . .

American critics now handled their literature with a greater sense of ease and self-confidence, which also came from the awareness that the Second World War had been largely won by American military might. But, more than this, American literature had become an ideological standard-bearer. In the Preface the editors had asserted that 'the communicable fire of Thomas Paine' was 'the antithesis of Hitler in the history of human liberty'. (In *A History of American*

Literature he had been introduced as plain Tom.) Paine's communicable fire was not extinguished with the end of the war. In March 1946, as the *Literary History of the United States* was being prepared, Winston Churchill made his 'Iron Curtain' speech at Fulton, Missouri. In their Preface, the editors regretted the isolationism which had been such a powerful motivation during the inter-war years. Tom was now involved in the Cold War as the apologist for the so-called 'Free World'.[21]

The canon underwent further adjustments as a result of the new sense of purpose. American globalism replaced Anglo-Saxonism. Loyalists received less attention than in *A History of American Literature*. Daniel Webster was now confined to three pages, and did not speak in favour of the British Empire. The American Empire would not, however, be achieved in a univocal manner. A chapter entitled 'The Mingling of Tongues', written by Henry A. Pochmann, an expert on German-American culture, proposed a variety far greater than that discussed in 1917. Pochmann discussed the literatures written in the languages of migrant groups, and quite reasonably dissented from the Melting Pot theory. He suggested instead a theory of 'cultural amalgamation' in which the 'various and lively regional cultures increase the vitality of the culture of the United States'. Native Americans, too, now had their own chapter, but not African-Americans. Frederick Douglass had disappeared, and Joel Chandler Harris was still regarded as a spokesman for the Black community. The motto on the Great Seal of the United States, *E Pluribus Unum* (out of many, one) – which had been taken, ironically enough, from the masthead of the British *Gentleman's Magazine* – had yet to be fully realised.[22]

A glance at the section headings of the *Literary History of the United States* reveals the drama of a nation growing from a temporary colonial period, covering only 110 pages of the *History*'s 1388, to democratic republic, and passing through a time of crisis (the Civil War) to continental and then international status. The headings suggested a correlation between national and personal development, for the editors believed that American literature, like the nation, was based on the ideology of individualism. The Preface listed a number of striking individuals: Jefferson, Poe, Thoreau, Melville, Lincoln, Twain, in addition to Paine. Women writers were discussed in accordance with their perceived individuality. Anne Bradstreet now had one page only, and looked pale alongside the 'imaginative power and dramatic skill' of Edward Taylor, whose poems were first published, from manuscript, in 1937. In contrast to Bradstreet, Emily Dickinson, whose poems would be published piecemeal until 1955, made her début in a literary history with an honourable mention in the Preface and a sensitively-written nine-page paean to her 'frail and heroic spirit'.[23]

The two most recent literary histories reflect the problems that have faced the United States since 1960, with disturbances at home and defeats abroad. The profession of literary criticism itself has gone through a period of great turbulence. The result is that the authoritative nature of previous literary histories has come under serious question. The answers provided by the two recent histories, though, have differed. In 1988 Emory Elliott, the General

Editor of the *Columbia Literary History of the United States*, looked back at *A History of American Literature* and the *Literary History of the United States*. He specifically linked those books with contemporary military events, and remarked that:

> there is today no unifying vision of a national identity like that shared by many scholars at the closings of the two world wars . . . the present project acknowledges diversity, complexity, and contradiction by making them structural principles, and it forgoes closure as well as consensus.

It is perhaps symptomatic of the postmodernity of the *Columbia Literary History* that it is best read from the back rather than the front. The index, occupying fifty-four pages, is longer than that of any predecessor, and to extend Elliott's simile of the text as 'a library or art gallery', acts like an enquiry desk. It is symptomatic of the loss of authority that there is no bibliography. The book proceeds in a loosely chronological fashion, but unlike its predecessors it has no clear starting date. The opening section is written by a Native American, N. Scott Momaday, and by means of a recent dictionary definition of writing as incision, proposes that prehistoric rock art in Barrier Canyon, Utah, marks 'as closely as anything can the origin of American literature'. The uncertainty of the beginning is comparable with the uncertainty of identity. Henry Pochmann, in the *Literary History of the United States*, had proposed the metaphor of the amalgam to describe the cultural variety of the United States. In 1988 a more suitable metaphor would be mosaic, denoting the change from cultural variety to multiculturalism. There are now seventy-four contributors, and sections for African-, Mexican- and Asian-American literature in addition to the groups discussed by Pochmann. Frederick Douglass makes several appearances, as does – for the first time since Tyler – Phillis Wheatley. Joel Chandler Harris still turns up, but as a reporter rather than the spokesman of Black folk culture. There are several segments devoted to women writers. Anne Bradstreet now occupies three pages. Emily Dickinson has her own section, as a 'Major Voice' alongside Mark Twain, Henry Adams and Henry James, and based on the *Complete Poems* which first appeared in 1955.[24]

Just six years separated the *Columbia Literary History of the United States* from the first volume of the new *The Cambridge History of American Literature*. Inevitably, they reveal a number of similarities. The central figures in the canon first established in 1917 are to be found in both histories, among them Jonathan Edwards, Franklin, Brockden Brown, Irving and Fenimore Cooper. Otherwise, the response to the uncertainties and polemics begun in the 1960s has differed. Where the *Columbia Literary History* abandons any pretense to authority, *The Cambridge History* overtly stakes a claim to it. In a simple, visual sense it does this by using the definite article, and providing a list of secondary texts and a chronology where the *Columbia Literary History* gave none. But there are more complex distinctions. Where the *Columbia Literary History* provides a postmodern polyphony that verges on cacophony, *The Cambridge History*, to continue the musical metaphor, is broadly symphonic in structure. The opening of the first volume.is clearly stated, with Thomas Harriot's *Brief and True Report* of 1590, and it contains four lengthy movements in the form of single-authored essays that develop its central theme.

It is in the theme itself that *The Cambridge History* indicates its status as a late twentieth-century text. That theme, paradoxically, is pluralism, with no resolution in unity. When *The Cambridge History* was in its planning stages in the mid-1980s, Bercovitch produced an ungainly but apt term, 'dissensus', to distinguish it from the consensual mode of literary history which had dominated the earlier part of this century. For instance, Emory Elliott's essay in the collection does not begin with the usual rite of passage, the voyage of the *Mayflower* in 1620, but rather with the factional crises of the 1692 witchcraft trials in Salem. The essay, the second in the collection, paints an even darker picture of the historical significance of that town than had James in *Hawthorne*. It creates a new interpretation of familiar material, much of which is in the canon of American literature. Other essays, for instance one on British-American belles-lettres of the first half of the eighteenth century, an elite Loyalist literature of clubs and salons, continue the recovery of the completely uncanonical, adding yet other voices to a plurality that cannot now be reconciled.

In one way *The Cambridge History* is inherently unAmerican, for it contradicts the motto on the Great Seal of the United States. Indeed, it questions the meaning of nationality itself. This becomes apparent when one counterpoints the two terms for the nation. The meaning of the phrase, 'the United States', is relatively clear. There were a few alternative names suggested for the nation in the early years of the Republic, such as 'Fredonia', but they quickly disappeared. In contrast, as the contributors to *The Cambridge History* show, the meaning of the term 'America' is fundamentally unstable and has changed radically over time. Myra Jehlen therefore quotes the complaint of Richard Hakluyt about the impropriety of the name 'America'. In his 1600 dedication to Robert Cecil he seemed to be suggesting 'the New World' or 'the Western Atlantis' as more appropriate alternatives. In the next chapter we shall look at some of the reasons for those alternative names. As Bercovitch points out, the nation so insecurely named can easily become 'a rhetorical battleground'.

In another way, though, *The Cambridge History* is intensely American. To quote Bercovitch again, the text 'is a federated histories of American literatures'. In its federal structure it reflects the political, social and racial organisation of the United States. It is also American and up to date in its claim to centrality. Bercovitch follows Elliott by opening his first volume with a glance back at the predecessors of 1917 and 1948. But instead of noticing the way that they reflect the cultural unity created by military events, he uses them to suggest a path along which American literary study has moved from the periphery to the core of humanistic study:

> Over the past three decades, Americanist literary criticism has expanded from a border province into a center of humanist studies . . . Virtually every recent school of criticism has found not just its followers here but many of its leading components.

And increasingly over the past three decades, American texts have provided the focus for inter- and cross-disciplinary investigation. Gender studies, ethnic studies, and popular-culture studies, among others, have penetrated to all corners of the profession, but their largest single base is American literature. The same is true with regard to controversies over multiculturalism and canon formation: the issues are transhistorical and transcultural, but the debates themselves have turned mainly on American books.[25]

Malcolm Cowley had suggested in 1948 that American literature had become 'one of the great world literatures'. Now, according to Bercovitch, it had become the central literature, at which the most important questions were directed. Sydney Smith's question seemed to have received a decisive answer. Yet for a relatively short period there was an even more decisive answer. American literature was not merely central. It was exceptional.

American exceptionalism

Goethe did not share the fears of transatlantic degeneration that seemed to worry his friend Joseph Green Cogswell. In 1827 he expressed his restlessness in a brief poem which created a negative catalogue for the purpose of reversing the Jamesian polarity: 'Amerika, du hast es besser/Als unser Continent das alte' (America, you are better off than our old continent). Many Americans, and a number of foreign observers, have believed that America was more than merely better; that it was unique, beyond compare. The belief in American exceptionalism may be traced back to 'A Modell of Christian Charity'. John Winthrop delivered the lay-sermon to his fellow-passengers on the *Arbella* as they crossed the Atlantic in 1630, bound for a new life in New England. Its Manichaean structure forged the ship's company, whether they liked it or not, into an uncomfortably exemplary community:

> we must consider that we shall be as a city upon a hill. The eyes of all people are upon us, so that if we shall deal falsely with our God in this work we have undertaken, and so cause him to withdraw his present help from us, we shall be made a story and a by-word through the world.

It was over two centuries before the word itself, 'exceptional', was applied to the United States. The French writer and politician Alexis de Tocqueville had spent eighteen months in the United States examining its penal system. The resultant two-volume *Democracy in America*, published in 1835 and 1840, moved far beyond the confines of prison to examine the implications of a franchise which was being expanded by the abolition of property qualifications and which was symbolised by its populist seventh President, Andrew Jackson (1767–1845). The cumbersome title of a chapter in the second volume – 'The example of the Americans does not prove that a democratic people can have no aptitude and no taste for science, literature, or art' – showed that de Tocqueville was specifically addressing Sydney Smith's questions. In doing so he revived Cogswell's theory of American activity, but set it in a political rather than an economic framework. De Tocqueville constructed his answer in two parts. First, he proposed a simple model of migration which was 'without a parallel in the history of the world', and which portrayed the Americans as a sophisticated European people who had moved to an undeveloped country. Second, he suggested that this 'exceptional' position had combined with a democratic polity to unite Americans in spending their initial energies on their practical needs. Once these needs had been satisfied, they would turn their attention to 'the empire of mind'.[26]

There have been many claims to American exceptionalism since de Tocqueville. The nature of the claim has sometimes changed, but its political dimensions have always acknowledged the force of de Tocqueville's enquiry into democracy, to the extent that his text joined Crèvecoeur's to complete the Americaniser's Bible by becoming its New Testament. *Democracy in America*, for instance, clearly informed the thinking of the editors of both *A History of American Literature* and the *Literary History of the United States*. It followed, as has been shown by the survey of literary histories above, that the claim to literary exceptionalism was of recent date. Much of the criticism that supports the concept of American literary exceptionality is derived from two texts, *American Renaissance*, published in April 1941 by F. O. Matthiessen (1902–50); and the essay 'Manners, Morals, and the Novel', first published in 1948 by Lionel Trilling (1905–75) and then included in his 1951 collection *The Liberal Imagination*. The two critics held somewhat different political views. Trilling's politics are encapsulated in the title of that 1951 collection. Matthiessen presented himself in a 1949 address, 'The Responsibilities of the Critic', as a Christian Socialist, which at that time was an uncomfortably complex political position to hold. Matthiessen's suicide in 1950 may have been due in part to the attentions he was receiving from the Red-hunters who were the shock-troops in the early battles of the United States' Cold War with the Soviet Union. Despite the political differences, both *American Renaissance* and *The Liberal Imagination* suggested that literature could act politically, by providing guidelines towards a better quality of life. The critics' starting-point, signalled at the beginning of each book, lay in the rejection of Vernon Parrington's trilogy *Main Currents in American Thought* which, they believed, had forced too clear a distinction between aesthetics and economics, between the life of the mind and life on the street. From that starting-point, Matthiessen and Trilling brought Matthew Arnold up to date by proposing a more dynamic and critical version of American literature, and by displaying a limited group of writers as the best expositors of the value of American democracy in a world which might be swamped by the meretricious, and which certainly had been split, initially by fascism, into two warring belief-systems.

Although contemporary events were not its subject, *American Renaissance* made references to the brutality of fascism and to the perils of 'living in the age of Hitler'. Like Alfred Kazin's *On Native Grounds: An Interpretation of Modern American Prose Literature* (1942), and like the *Literary History of the United States* (to which Matthiessen contributed), it was very much a text of its time. It was an engaged political document, which drew on a brief period in American cultural history to create a sense of value in the American present. Matthiessen focused on Emerson, Hawthorne, Melville, Thoreau and Whitman, five writers whose 'one common denominator . . . was their devotion to the possibilities of democracy'. He saw the period 1850–5 as providing 'America's way of producing a renaissance, by coming to its first maturity and affirming its rightful heritage in the whole expanse of art and culture'. In its weight and rhetoric *American Renaissance* was a response to Churchillian *gravitas*, a literary-critical version of those wartime assertions of freedom which would shortly reach their apogee in the Atlantic Charter, signed jointly by Churchill and Franklin D. Roosevelt on 14 August 1941. But in one significant way *American Renaissance* differed from the Atlantic Charter. Despite extensive discussions of British writers in *American Renaissance*, and despite Matthiessen's indebtedness to T. S. Eliot (Matthiessen had published a book on Eliot in 1935), there was a distinctly exceptionalist drive in the book, to be seen in his particular definition of 'Renaissance' as the time when a limited number of 'classic' writers joined in severing the umbilical chord which had linked the New World to the Old. This helps to explain the enormous impact of the book, for its analysis of the roots of American exceptionalism made it an appropriate text to understand the global impact of American identity – what has since been called American cultural imperialism. It also became a canonical text in the development of American Studies as a discipline. Indeed, Sacvan Bercovitch drew a link between American cultural imperialism and American Studies by calling its development in Europe an 'academic Marshall Plan'. The European Recovery Program (1947–56), named after Secretary of State and Second World War military Chief of Staff George C. Marshall (1880–1959), co-ordinated financial and material aid to those European nations which were outside the sphere of Soviet influence. Some proponents of American Studies attempted a similar intellectual co-ordination. And here, too, Matthiessen played a part by helping to set up the Salzburg Seminar in American Studies in 1947, although he was later excluded because his critical independence led him to be suspected of communist sympathies. *American Renaissance* has long outlived him and his other books. It has become so much an Americanist cultural icon that American critics still feel that they have to address Matthiessen's individual judgements and principles of selection.[27]

As befits an essayist, Lionel Trilling operated more by suggestion than by exposition. His ideas were left to be solidified and developed at greater length by others. This was particularly the case with the essay 'Manners, Morals, and the Novel'. The essay ends with a ringing assertion of the value of fiction as a vehicle for expressing freedom. It begins quite differently. It was originally an address at Kenyon College, Ohio in 1947, and it gives the impression that no alterations had been made in conveying the piece to print. This was almost certainly Trilling's intention. The subject stipulated was apparently vague, and the opening paragraphs seem like half-hearted forays into the fog in an attempt to locate a definition of 'manners':

> What I understand by manners, then, is a culture's hum and buzz of implication. I
> mean the whole evanescent context in which its explicit statements are made. It is
> that part of a culture which is made up of half-uttered or unuttered or unutterable
> expressions of value. They are hinted at by small actions, sometimes by the arts of
> dress and decoration, sometimes by tone, gesture, emphasis or rhythm, sometimes
> by the words that are used with a special frequency or a special meaning. They are
> the things that for good or bad draw the people of a culture together and that
> separate them from the people of another culture.

This passage shows that Trilling, like Matthiessen, had been deeply influenced
by Eliot. In this instance the influence is from the inclusive, anthropological
definition of culture that is apparent in Eliot's 1922 essay on the music-hall
comedienne Marie Lloyd and that, under pressure of wartime, was developed
in 'What Is A Classic?' (1944), and those essays which would later be incorporated in *Notes towards the Definition of Culture* (1948). In the last text Eliot
tried to out-James James in a definition of British culture which started where
James ended, in horse-racing, and then proceeded through an extended social
range of sporting occasions to end in 'Wensleydale cheese, boiled cabbage cut
into sections, beetroot in vinegar, nineteenth-century Gothic churches and the
music of Elgar'. Alongside *that* pungent appeal to sense-experience, American
'expressions of value' would seem all too attenuated. Attenuation, indeed, was
the distinguishing element; and the whole point of Trilling's vague opening
was that the subject itself was fogginess. In a passage which became famous,
Trilling distinguished American and English fictional representations of
reality:

> American writers of genius have not turned their minds to society. Poe and Melville
> were quite apart from it; the reality they sought was only tangential to society.
> Hawthorne was acute when he insisted that he did not write novels but romances
> – he thus expressed his awareness of the lack of social texture in his work.

Trilling then quoted James's remarks and concluded that, although 'life in
America has increasingly thickened since the nineteenth century . . . Americans
have a kind of resistance to looking closely at society'. British fiction proceeded in explicit observation of manners (although in the case of Eliot's
foodstuffs it might be an explicitness one would want to avoid). American
fiction, in contrast, proceeded by indirection.[28]
   A number of critics took up Trilling's argument. The most extensive at-
tempt to do this was *The American Novel and its Tradition* (1957), by Richard
Chase. Chase sought an American tradition that could be distinguished from
F. R. Leavis's *The Great Tradition* (1948), which he called 'Anglo-American'.
In doing so he surveyed the American novel from Charles Brockden Brown to
William Faulkner in order to identify a 'melodrama' vested in 'originality and
"Americanness"'. Unlike the 'imperial enterprise' of the English novel, 'bring-
ing order to disorder', Chase located 'Americanness' in 'the aesthetic possibil-
ities of radical forms of alienation, contradiction and disorder', which in his
view were rooted in the solitary and Manichaean qualities of New England
Puritanism. These qualities led to a distinction between the American 'Romance'

and the English 'Novel', those terms taken from Trilling. Chase's thesis was extremely influential, although (or maybe because) it involved special pleading. First, to support his thesis Chase had to erect two separate canons, American and English, each with its own identifiable qualities. This required placing an 'odd' English text like *Wuthering Heights* in the American canon! Second, it involved readings of his chosen texts which omitted the everyday 'English' minutiae of social and political implications. It is possible to see more clearly Chase's own political agenda if *The American Novel and its Tradition* is read alongside *The Democratic Vista*, published by Chase one year later and analysing what he called 'a cold-war state of mind'. Chase wished to revive a Thoreauvian dissentient 'culture of contradictions', at that time under threat by cold-war conformism and absolutely opposed to the British order symbolised by Suez, that late imperial adventure which had taken place just two years earlier.[29]

The period from 1950 to 1966 was particularly rich in monographs which aimed at establishing American literary exceptionality. It began with Henry Nash Smith's *Virgin Land* (1950), which traced the impact of the American West on American literature and society, and ended with Richard Poirier's *A World Elsewhere: The Place of Style in American Literature* (1966), which distinguished between 'works that create through language an essentially imaginative environment for the hero and works that mirror an environment already accredited by history and society'.[30] The influence of James and Trilling was clear. Those last two terms, 'history and society', tended in this period to be associated with Britain, whereas terms like 'democracy' and 'freedom' were associated with America. A selective list of the monographs would have to include: Charles Feidelson, *Symbolism and American Literature* (1953); R. W. B. Lewis, *The American Adam* (1955); Harry Levin, *The Power of Blackness* (1958); Leslie Fiedler, *Love and Death in the American Novel* (1960); Marius Bewley, *The Eccentric Design* (1963); A. N. Kaul, *The American Vision* (1964); and Leo Marx, *The Machine in the Garden* (1964). Although the aims of the monographs were not always overtly political, the period in which they appeared could be said to represent the high-point of American self-confidence, before the escalation of the Vietnam War, the increase in domestic unrest, and the arrival of European literary theory in the American academy. After 1966 the search for 'Americanness', to use Chase's term, abated, but it left in place a cluster of writers at the centre of the canon, often at the expense of those who do not clearly fit the theme of national identity, or of those who belong to marginal groups. Moreover, those canonical writers are sometimes used to support claims which cannot be substantiated from their work. This can be demonstrated by considering the cases of Emerson and Whitman.

Emerson and Whitman have long been regarded as central to the canon of United States literature. In his subtitle of his 1941 book, Matthiessen called the period of *American Renaissance* the *Age of Emerson and Whitman*. In 1979 another distinguished critic, Joel Porte, called Emerson a *Representative Man*, and explicitly related his reputation to the fortunes of the United States. Emerson and Whitman tend to be linked specifically with the concept of American exceptionalism, and studies of their work are often marked by images of fracture and novelty. Two examples illustrate this. In 1981 Larzer Ziff suggested that the writers of the American Renaissance 'not only developed new subject matter and experimented with new language within the older [English] language but also invented new forms demanded by such unprecedented material'. In 1996 a collection of essays devoted to Whitman sought 'to engage . . . and to extend into the present the bound-breaking dimensions of Whitman's life and work'. Such assertions are, of course, not without basis. The drive for originality is an important element in the work of Emerson and Whitman. One of Emerson's most famous injunctions requires Americans to have an 'original relation to the universe'. Likewise, Whitman ecstatically (if anonymously) greeted the first, 1855, edition of his own *Leaves of Grass* as the work of 'an American bard at last!' In a review of his book, Whitman presented himself as an American original, all 'gristle and beard', providing 'the first show of America' in contrast to those anaemic genteel intellectuals who 'dress by London and Paris modes'.[31]

Emerson and Whitman are certainly the embodiments of Americanism. But critics go too far when they use the work of the two writers to support the claim to exceptionalism. For instance, Oliver Wendell Holmes's biography of Emerson (published in 1884 in the American Men of Letters series) calls 'The American Scholar', Emerson's 1837 address, 'our Intellectual Declaration of Independence', thereby relating 'The American Scholar' to that document of 1776. Later critics have taken Holmes's suggestion even further, turning 'The American Scholar' into the literary version of George Washington's 'Farewell Address' (1796), which has become an icon of American isolationism. 'The American Scholar' is however neither a directly political document nor a proposal that America should isolate itself. At the beginning of the Address Emerson suggested that the American 'day of dependence, our long apprenticeship to the learning of other lands', was coming to an end. The ending of apprenticeship involves competence, self-control and professionalism, but not uniqueness. Indeed, the idea of uniqueness was antipathetic to Emerson, who was deeply read in European writing from the Greeks to the Romantics, which endowed his work with a humility, eloquently expressed in his journals:

> Literature has been before us, wherever we go . . . So is it with this young soul wandering lonely, wistful, reserved, unfriended up & down in nature. These mysteries which he ponders, which astonish & entrance him, this riddle of liberty, this dream of immortality, this drawing to love, this trembling balance of motive, and the centrality whereof these are rays, have all been explored to the recesses of consciousness, to the verge of Chaos & the Néant, by men of grander steadfastness & subtler organs of search than any now alive; so that when this tender philosopher comes from his reverie to literature, he is alarmed . . . by the terrible fidelity, with which, men long before his day, have described all & much more than all he has just seen as new Continent in the West.

Nearly two years later Emerson, pondering the relevance of his diverse reading, answered that he believed in 'Omnipresence' and noted that 'a good scholar will find Aristophanes & Hafiz & Rabelais full of American history'.[32]

Emerson's thinking fell easily into the dualisms of the Hegelian dialectic. New implies old, and originality can only be detected by contrast with imitations. As Emerson remarked in an 1859 essay, 'Quotation and Originality': 'Old and new make the warp and woof of every moment', and 'original power is usually accompanied with assimilating power'. Hegelian dialectics took their place alongside organicism. One of Emerson's favourite images was the circle. He used it in 'The American Scholar', and it provided both the structuring function and the title of an 1841 essay. In 'Circles' Emerson proceeds both dialectically, casting himself as 'an endless seeker with no Past at my back', and organically, asserting that 'the life of man is a self-evolving circle, which, from a ring imperceptibly small, rushes on all sides outwards to new and larger circles, and that without end'. Organicism, which Emerson adopted from his reading of Schlegel, Goethe and Coleridge, is to be found everywhere in his writing, and is rooted in progression and differentiation rather than rejection. It is related also to a critical method which Emerson owed to the biblical scholar Friedrich Schleiermacher, and which is today called hermeneutics. Indeed, Emerson himself provided a vivid definition of hermeneutics in his journal of June 1847:

> Every thing teaches transition, transference, metamorphosis: therein is human power, in transference, not in creation; & therein is human destiny, not in longevity but in removal. We dive & reappear in new places.
> American mind a wilderness of capabilities.

That final, incomplete, sentence encapsulates Emerson's hope, rooted in the apparent dormancy of American nature, that the New World will add to the achievements of the Old. Emerson asserted in 'Quotation and Originality' that the increment must be obtained by attention to the quotidian; or as he put it, in the well-known phrases of 'The American Scholar': 'the meal in the firkin; the milk in the pan; the ballad in the street; the news of the boat'. Emerson's optimism was restated in everyday terms in 1844 in 'The Poet':

> Our log-rolling, our stumps and their politics, our fisheries, our Negroes and Indians, our boats and our repudiations, the wrath of rogues and the pusillanimity of honest men, the northern trade, the southern planting, the western clearing, Oregan and Texas, are yet unsung. Yet America is a poem in our eyes; its ample geography dazzles the imagination, and it will not wait long for metres.

Emerson waited eleven years. His review of Whitman's *Leaves of Grass* was therefore shot through with the joy of a long-held hope finally realised. Emerson greeted the book as 'the most extraordinary piece of wit and wisdom that America has yet contributed'. The greeting, appropriately, was in terms of the relation of psychology and nature. It was the land itself which had at last created an imaginative dilation. Hitherto, Emerson thought, a 'sterile and stingy Nature' had made 'our western wits fat and mean'. But now, at the beginning of what would be 'a great career', Whitman's book seemed like 'a sunbeam'. The reference to that engine of *translatio imperii* reminds us that, to an extent, Emerson is repeating Samuel Knapp's praise of Irving's *History of the Life and Voyages of Christopher Columbus*. The difference is that Emerson saw Whitman's work as a distinctive American addition to the knowledge of the Old World rather than as an exposé of its ignorance.[33]

Whitman had intuitively grasped what Emerson had learned from his years of reading the Europeans. Not exactly noted for his humility, the poet from Brooklyn nevertheless viewed the past in the same way as the sage of Concord. Whitman's Preface to the 1855 edition of *Leaves of Grass* contains a famous phrase that is sometimes ripped out of context. The whole passage stated his wish to celebrate the American environment, and, in an appropriately all-encompassing reach, to incorporate the past into the present and into himself:

> America does not repel the past . . . The Americans of all nations at any time upon the earth have probably the fullest poetical nature. The United States themselves are essentially the greatest poem . . . The American poets are to enclose old and new for America is the race of races. Of them a bard is commensurate with a people. To him other continents arrive as contributions . . . he gives them reception for their sake and for his own sake. His spirit responds to his country's spirit . . . he incarnates its geography and natural life and rivers and lakes.

The epic that is America rests on many antecedents. Later in his life, Emerson listed in his journal some of the people to whom nineteenth-century American culture was most deeply indebted – Dante, Michelangelo, Raphael, Shakespeare, and above all Goethe, comically portrayed in a natural image: 'Goethe was the cow from which all their milk was drawn.' Goethe would nourish the next generation and thereby ensure that America was better. As Richard Poirier remarked in his account of the meaning of Emerson to the United States in the 1980s:

> the New World offers an opportunity less to disown the Old than to rediscover its true origins otherwise obscured within the encrustations of acquired culture. To be worthy of the New World, any 'new world', it is necessary to imagine what it was like when the old world was also new.[34]

The next chapter, in particular, will examine the 'true origins' of New World literature. In the final section of this chapter I will suggest the means by which American literature renewed European literature.

Songs of the earth's edge

From Columbus to Baudrillard, European commentators have believed that the factor that distinguishes America from the rest of the earth is its immensity. Claude Lévi-Strauss can stand as representative for them when he remarks:

> This impression of enormous size is peculiar to America, and can be felt everywhere . . . The feeling of unfamiliarity comes simply from the fact that the relationship between the size of human beings and the size of objects around them has been so distended as to cancel out any possibility of a common measure . . . the congenital lack of proportion between the two worlds permeates and distorts our judgments.

'American landscapes', he concluded, 'transport us into a far vaster system for which we have no equivalent.' Emerson, comparing 'that great sloven continent' with 'the trim hedge-rows and over-cultivated garden of England', clearly preferred America. There, he wrote with the longing of an American abroad:

> lies nature sleeping, over-growing, almost conscious, too much by half for man in the picture, and so giving a certain tristesse, like the rank vegetation of swamps and forests seen at night, steeped in dews and rains, which it loves; and on it man seems not able to make much impression.

On the contrary, it was America that made the impression on humankind. Crèvecoeur agreed. He had no reason to be fond of Americans, for they had driven him out of his farm in the colony of New York because of his monarchist sympathies. Yet, as we shall see in Chapter 3, he wrote in 1782 that the extensiveness of American terrain turned Europeans into Americans.[35]

The condition described by Lévi-Strauss, Emerson and Crèvecoeur could be regarded as a geopolitics. Twentieth-century geographers have tended to define geopolitics as a relationship of rivalry between major world powers.[36] Here it will be defined more broadly as the politics of spatial difference. Chapter 2 therefore begins with a discussion of the ancient Greeks, who discerned a different, maybe better, place when they looked beyond 'the Pillars of Hercules', those mountains on either side of what is now known as the Straits of Gibraltar. Geopolitics inspires Winthrop's 'city upon a hill', and is a central element of the trope of *translatio imperii* invoked by Berkeley, Knapp, and the almanac writer Nathaniel Ames discussed in Chapter 3. It informs the pessimism of the English-born Thomas Cole who, within a few years of a return visit to Europe, painted the series of canvases, *The Course of Empire*. The same landscape, overlooked by two Pillars of Hercules, forms the ground of the cycle of five paintings. The first three depict a change from wilderness to civilisation. The last two take the translation of empire to its conservative conclusion: destruction and the resurgence of wilderness, growing around the ruins of empire.[37] Such despair is nowhere to be found in the concept of 'Manifest Destiny', the phrase coined in 1845 to express the inevitable expansion of the United States westward to the Pacific. It was a concept anticipated by Charles Brockden Brown (whose work is analysed in Chapter 4), in a contribution in 1803 to the debate over the Louisiana Purchase; and its most enthusiastic expression is in the writing of William Gilpin (1813–94), the explorer who became the first governor of Colorado territory. His earlier English namesake had written somewhat anaemic picturesque travel books. The American Gilpin, in contrast, portrayed a muscular view of western 'destiny' in the *Mission of the American People* (1873). If Cole had mapped a European landform onto the New World, it was the apparently unique shape of the North American landmass that inspired Gilpin. Bounded by mountain chains and bisected by the river system of the Mississippi Valley, the physical geography of North America was shaped like a concave bowl that assisted Americans to 'subdue the continent' and in the process 'teach old nations a new civilization'.[38]

Twenty years later, the historian Frederick Jackson Turner (1861–1932) proposed a more sophisticated, and today certainly much better known, version of Gilpin's geopolitics of renewal. Turner spoke at the 1893 Conference of the American Historical Association, held in Chicago as an adjunct of the World's Columbian Exposition, itself a slightly delayed celebration of the quatercentenary of Columbus's landfall. His talk, 'The Significance of the Frontier in American History', was appropriately endowed with a strong sense of occasion. It was also elegiac, because Turner began by reflecting that, according to the US census of 1890, the frontier no longer existed. Yet its impact was vital:

> the frontier is the line of most rapid and effective Americanisation. The wilderness masters the colonist. It finds him a European in dress, industries, tools, modes of travel, and thought. It takes him from the railroad car and puts him in the birch canoe. It strips off the garments of civilization, and arrays him in the hunting shirt and the moccasin . . . In short, at the frontier the environment is at first too strong for the man. He must accept the conditions which it furnishes, or perish, and so he fits himself into the Indian clearings and follows the Indian trails. Little by little he transforms the wilderness, but the outcome is not the old Europe . . . here is a new product that is American. At first, the frontier was the Atlantic coast. It was the frontier of Europe in a very real sense. Moving westward, the frontier became more and more American.

These have become famous words largely because they have the quality of myth rather than history. As William Cronon memorably remarked, 'the frontier thesis, in effect, set American space in motion and gave it a plot'. That plot had been anticipated in many ways. Turner drew, of course, on *translatio imperii*. He was indebted to Emerson's belief (which in turn comes from Montaigne) that the aborigines have qualities which are valuable to so-called civilised humankind. Most of all, Turner was anticipated by Benjamin Rush (1745–1813), a friend of Tom Paine, a signatory to the Declaration of Independence, and the republic's first important physician. In a letter of 1786 printed in his *Essays* of 1798, Rush identified 'three different species of settlers', the first 'nearly related to an Indian in his manners', the second in which Indian manners are 'diluted', and the third, to whom 'it is proper to apply the term of *farmers*', and with whom 'we behold civilization completed'. Rush has particular praise for the third kind of settler, for he is a true republican American. 'Idleness, extravagance, and ignorance fly before him,' Rush concludes. 'Happy would it be for mankind if the kings of Europe would adopt this mode of extending their territories.'[39]

Much of Turner's thesis, then, was hardly new. Yet a few of its facets were his. First, he merged Rush's three different 'species' of settlers into a single person, 'the colonist', thereby endowing him with the regenerative rhythm of Christian mythology. Second, he reformulated the old European trope of the 'line' between civilisation and savagery in terms of geopolitics. 'Free land' – a potent phrase that Turner repeats several times – gives rise to a free people. Hence, 'the most important effect of the frontier has been the promotion of democracy here and in Europe'. Third, he stated, much more insistently than

Benjamin Rush, that the frontier Americanised. Democracy in Europe was a by-product of the frontier, consequent upon the influence of US nationalism. Finally, although Turner invoked the whole sweep of American history, and indeed looked back to the first Greek ventures into the Mediterranean, the model of transformation was a nineteenth-century one, as his depiction of 'the colonist' makes clear. If the frontier 'became more and more American' as it went westwards, it reached its Americanising apogee in 1890, at which point it disappeared from both American history and American space. The thesis is therefore dubious history. Critics have shown that it also has an inbuilt masculine bias, signalled by its language ('the wilderness *masters* the colonist. It finds *him* a European . . .'). Its 'Indian' is a stereotype. The theory of free land ignores the facts of Native American occupation. The land was free to the whites in a somewhat different sense: they stole it. The thesis has a tele-ological thrust that easily becomes triumphalism; and to many people its West no longer seems a recognisable place. Yet despite its many flaws, the thesis continues to play a role in American imagination. William Cronon noted that 'it expresses some of the deepest myths and longings many Americans still feel about their national experience'.[40]

The British geographer Sir Halford Mackinder (1861–1947) practised geo-politics on an altogether grander scale. It is possible that he knew about Turner's frontier thesis. He may have learned of it through his ally James Bryce (1838–1922), who was one of the best-informed Britons about America at the time. Bryce had written one of the most thorough political analyses, *The American Commonwealth* (1888), and he would be British ambassador to the United States from 1907 to 1913. Certainly, Mackinder's 'Heartland' theory complements the Turner thesis, and puts it in global perspective. The 'Heart-land' theory first appeared in Mackinder's 1904 essay 'The Geographical Pivot of History'. Like Turner, Mackinder invoked history on a large scale. He too believed that an epoch, in his case the Columbian epoch of exploration and expansion, had just ended. The result was a 'closed political system', which would be dominated by whomever controlled what Mackinder called the 'Heartland'. The 'Heartland' consisted of an enormous landlocked area bounded by a line extending, let's say, southwards from Archangel in north-west Russia to Isfahan in Iran, and from there north-eastwards, ending in the Cherskiy range of mountains in north-east Russia. The 'Heartland' was at the centre of an even vaster landmass, which Mackinder later named the 'World Island'. The 'World Island' is:

> a continuous land, ice-girt in the north, water-girt elsewhere, measuring 21 million square miles, or more than three times the area of North America, whose centre and north, measuring some 9 million square miles, or more than twice the area of Europe, have no available water-ways to the ocean . . .

The balance of world power, in Mackinder's view, depended on control of the 'Heartland'. In 1919 Mackinder developed his theories in *Democratic Ideals and Reality*, aimed at the politicians at Versailles. He produced a trio of maxims for them:

> *Who rules East Europe commands the Heartland:*
> *Who rules the Heartland commands the World-Island:*
> *Who rules the World-Island commands the World.*

Few people, it seemed, were interested, until Hitler's planning staff heeded Mackinder's warning, and Germany invaded Russia on 22 June 1941. Then the Allies began to pay attention. *Democratic Ideals and Reality* was reprinted in the United States in 1942 and was widely discussed. Two historians of the American West, in particular, now saw the implications of Mackinder's geopolitics for the United States. Bernard DeVoto compared Mackinder with Gilpin, while James C. Malin related him to Turner.[41]

They had been preceded by an American geographer, Charles Redway Dryer, who had been one of the few to attend to Mackinder in 1919. Dryer published a short article in 1920 which supplemented Mackinder's 'World Island' with an American 'World Ring', and ended on a troubling prophetic note:

> The American ring fence . . . is a world factor not to be overlooked. In the past America has been content to play the part of a remote satellite of the World Island, but recent events indicate other possibilities in the future . . . American lands and peoples may be sufficient to turn the scale in favor of the powers with which they are allied. If and when the Armageddon comes, even if the forces of the Old World Heartland are organized from Germany to Japan, the children of light may find themselves backed by an outer line of defense which the powers of darkness will be unable to break.[42]

The 'forces of the Old World Heartland' became the Axis Alliance in 1936. 'The American ring fence' became in 1947 the principle of containment, by which the United States sought to resist communist expansion.

It would take a bold critic to develop the literary implications of the geopolitics which had analysed the globe by 1920. Enter D. H. Lawrence. In his Foreword to the 1923 New York edition of the *Studies in Classic American Literature*, Lawrence suggested that 'two bodies of modern literature seem to me to have come to a real verge: the Russian and the American'. For Lawrence the Heartland was in Western Europe, and included Britain and Ireland. He despised the modernists who, in his view, were dominating English literature. The previous year, 1922, with the publication of *Ulysses* and *The Waste Land*, has come to be regarded as the highpoint of European modernism. Lawrence contrasted the modernists with Russians like Tolstoy, Chekhov and Dostoevsky, and Americans like Poe, Melville, Hawthorne and Whitman. Alongside such writers:

> The European moderns are all *trying* to be extreme. The great Americans I mention just were it. Which is why the world has funked them, and funks them to-day.
> The great difference between the extreme Russians and the extreme American lies in the fact that the Russians are explicit and hate eloquence and symbols, seeing in these only subterfuge, whereas the Americans refuse everything explicit and always put up a sort of double meaning. They revel in subterfuge. They prefer their truth safely swaddled in an ark of bulrushes, and deposited among the reeds until some friendly Egyptian princess comes to rescue the babe.

Well, it's high time that someone came to lift out the swaddled infant of truth that America spawned some time back. The child must be getting pretty thin, from neglect.

In the succeeding years, the child has grown fat from critical attention. Indeed, Lawrence's pugnatious, provocative book is in large measure responsible for that attention. Well before Matthiessen's *American Renaissance*, Lawrence established an American canon which included Hawthorne, Melville and Whitman. He pointed out the centrality to American culture of Franklin's *Autobiography* and Crèvecoeur's *Letters*. He noticed a writer still marginal to the canon, Edgar Allan Poe. This is not to say that Lawrence approved of the United States. There is a clear distinction between the original essays written before he visited the country, and the revisions and additions which now appear in *Studies in Classic American Literature*. His reaction appears twofold. First, the nation is an affront to Lawrence's deeply undemocratic soul. Hence his accusation in the 1923 version of his opening essay, 'The Spirit of Place', that the United States is 'a vast republic of escaped slaves' forever prating about freedom. Second, his visit reminded him in stark terms of the alienation of modern humanity; hence the addition to the earlier version of his essay on Cooper: 'white men have never probably felt so bitter anywhere, as here in America, where the very landscape, in its very beauty, seems a bit devilish and grinning, opposed to us'. Like the landscape, Lawrence remains, devilish and grinning, replacing Sydney Smith a century earlier as an irritant and inspiration, a writer often to be opposed but not to be ignored.[43]

The analytical tools of geopolitics are a great help to this study of American literature. I will suggest that the origins of American literature can be traced to a vision of the margin that became richer and more detailed as the margin was explored. When settlers moved from the 'Heartland' to the western part of the 'World Ring', their writing employed pre-existing literary resources and inflected them to take account of the major American fact, space. American literature began to express Lawrence's 'verge', in a theoretical and emotional as well as a physical sense. In its more exciting phases it has continued to do so. Succeeding chapters will treat American literature as a particularly dynamic element of a literary tradition in the English language, questioning, and only sometimes conforming to, English literature. Its sense of its marginality, in the years covered by this study, confers on it a clearer, more analytical view of the unconscious configurations of English literature. If it lacks 'institutions', to use James's term, it provides a greater space for those who have no voice, or less voice, elsewhere. It tends to take risks, to cross frontiers, to examine extremities that are often shirked by other literatures. In the phrase of Paul De Man, it reflects an attitude that is often 'closer to the essential than the European'. It is often a discomforting literature, undermining feelings of safety, questioning the reader's assurance of a place in the world, even at times repudiating the sense of self. That is why it is so important, exciting and valuable.

Notes

1. Paul De Man, 'The Temptation of Permanence', *Critical Writings, 1953–1978*, ed. Lindsay Waters (Theory and History of Literature, Vol. 66; Minneapolis: University of Minnesota Press, 1989), p. 31.

2. De Man, 'Literary History and Literary Modernity', *Blindness and Insight: Essays in the Rhetoric of Contemporary Criticism* (Theory and History of Literature, Vol. 7; 2nd edn, Minneapolis: University of Minnesota Press, 1983), p. 165.

3. Ralph Waldo Emerson, 'Stonehenge' (1856) in *English Traits, Representative Men & other Essays* (London: J. M. Dent, 1908), pp. 142–3. Emerson, 'Thoreau', and Henry David Thoreau, 'Resistance to Civil Government' (1848) in *Walden and Resistance to Civil Government*, ed. William Rossi (2nd edn, New York: W. W. Norton & Co., 1992), pp. 226–45, 323. A summary of De Man's work and its fate is given by his former editor, Lindsay Waters, in 'Paul De Man: Life and Works', in *Critical Writings, 1953–1978*, ed. Waters, pp. ix–lxxiii; and in Waters, 'Professah De Man – he dead', *American Literary History* 7 (Summer 1995), 284–303.

4. Henry James, *Hawthorne* (1879; rpt. London: Macmillan, 1967), pp. 22–3, 31, 25, 165, 89, 23, 55. James, *English Hours* (1905; rpt. London: Mercury Books, 1963), p. 47.

5. James, letter to Perry, 22 February 1880, *Henry James Letters*, ed. Leon Edel, Vol. II (Cambridge, MA: Belknap Press, 1975), p. 274. James, *The American Scene*, ed. John F. Sears (1907; rpt. Harmondsworth: Penguin, 1994), pp. 196–201.

6. Promotional leaflet in the possession of the author (Boston: Houghton Mifflin, n.d. [1884?]), n.p.

7. Noah Webster, *A Grammatical Institute of the English Language, Part I* (1783; rpt. Menston, Yorks: Scolar Press, 1968), p. 14. Emerson, Journal for January 1824, *Emerson in His Journals*, ed. Joel Porte (Cambridge, MA: Belknap Press, 1982), p. 39.

8. [Joseph Green Cogswell], 'On the State of Learning in the United States of America', *Blackwood's Edinburgh Magazine*, 4 (March 1819), 641–9. Quotations from 641, 647.

9. Sydney Smith, 'Review of Adam Seybert, *Statistical Annals of the United States of America*', *Edinburgh Review* 33 (January 1820), 74, 79. Herman Melville, 'Hawthorne and His Mosses', *Literary World* (1850), in *Hawthorne: The Critical Heritage*, ed. J. Donald Crowley (London: Routledge & Kegan Paul, 1970), p. 118.

10. [John Neal], 'American Writers', *Blackwood's Edinburgh Magazine*, 16 (September 1824), 305; 'American Writers Nos III and V', 16 (November 1824), 560 and 17 (February 1825), 203; 'Late American Books', 18 (September 1825), 316–34; 'American Writers', 16 (October 1824), 421.

11. Samuel L. Knapp, *Lectures on American Literature* (New York: Elam Bliss, 1829), pp. 187, 138, 132–3.

12. Knapp, *Lectures on American Literature*, pp. 132–3, 22, 64–5. Philip Freneau, 'The Pictures of Columbus', *Miscellaneous Works, Containing His Essays, and Additional Poems* (1788; rpt. Delmar, NY: Scholars' Facsimiles and Reprints, 1975), pp. 1–30. George Berkeley, 'Verses on the Prospect of Planting Arts and Learning in America', *Works*, ed. A. A. Luce (9 vols, London: Thomas Nelson & Sons, 1955), VII, pp. 369–73.

13. Knapp, *Lectures on American Literature*, pp. 34, 28–9, 227, 260–3, 56–7, 188–9.

14. Moses Coit Tyler, *A History of American Literature, 1607–1765* (1878; rpt. 2 vols as 1, Ithaca, NY: Cornell University Press, 1949), pp. 379–80, 239–53, 343–5.

15. Tyler, *The Literary History of the American Revolution, 1763–1783* (1897; rpt. 2 vols in 1, New York: Burt Franklin, 1970), I, pp. viii–ix, 186–7, 303, 473, 498–521; II, pp. 41, 193–8, 354, 419–23.

16. Tyler, *A History of American Literature, 1607–1765*, pp. xi, 7, 260–1. Perry Miller, 'Foreword' to *A History* (New York: Collier Books, 1962), pp. 12, 9.

17. Marcus Cunliffe, *The Literature of the United States* (1954; 3rd edn, Harmondsworth: Penguin, 1967), p. 11. *A History of American Literature*, eds. W. P. Trent, John Erskine, Stuart P. Sherman and Carl Van Doren (1917; rpt. Cambridge: Cambridge University Press, 1918), I, pp. iii–xi.

18. *A History of American Literature*, eds. Trent *et al.*, I, p. 154; II, pp. 96, 101–3.

19. *A History of American Literature*, eds. Trent *et al.*, I, p. 286; II, pp. 350–1.

20. *The Literary History of the United States*, eds. Robert E. Spiller, Willard Thorp, Thomas H. Johnson and Henry Seidel Canby (2 vols, New York: Macmillan, 1948), I, pp. xiii–xv.

21. *The Literary History of the United States*, eds. Spiller *et al.*, I, p. xvii; II, p. 1391. *A History of American Literature*, eds. Trent *et al.*, I, p. 74.

22. *The Literary History of the United States*, eds. Spiller *et al.*, II, pp. 693, 853.

23. *The Literary History of the United States*, eds. Spiller *et al.*, I, pp. xiii, xvii, 63–68; II, pp. 907–15.

24. *The Columbia Literary History of the United States*, ed. Emory Elliott (New York: Columbia University Press, 1988), pp. xi–xiii, 5.

25. Myra Jehlen, 'The Literature of Colonization', and Sacvan Bercovitch, 'Introduction', *The Cambridge History of American Literature*, ed. Bercovitch (3 vols to date, Cambridge: Cambridge University Press, 1994–), I, pp. 23, 1–5. Richard Hakluyt, *Voyages and Discoveries*, ed. Jack Beeching (Harmondsworth: Penguin, 1972), pp. 39–40.

26. Johann Wolfgang Goethe, 'Den Vereinigten Staaten', *Sämtliche Werke* (Munich: Carl Hanser Verlag, 1997), 18.1, p. 13. John Winthrop, 'A Modell of Christian Charity', in *The Puritans in America: A Narrative Anthology*, eds. Alan Heimert and Andrew Delbanco (Cambridge, MA: Harvard University Press, 1985), p. 91. Alexis de Tocqueville, *Democracy in America*, ed. Phillips Bradley (2 vols, 1835, 1840; rpt. New York: Vintage Books, 1945), II, pp. 36–8.

27. F. O. Matthiessen, *American Renaissance: Art and Expression in the Age of Emerson and Whitman* (1941; rpt. New York: Oxford University Press, 1968), pp. ix–x, 307, 368, vii. Sacvan Bercovitch, *The Rites of Assent: Transformations in the Symbolic Construction of America* (New York: Routledge, 1993), p. 375.

28. Lionel Trilling, 'Manners, Morals, and the Novel', *The Liberal Imagination* (1951; rpt. Harmondsworth: Penguin, 1970), pp. 208–9, 214–15. T. S. Eliot, *Notes towards the Definition of Culture* (London: Faber & Faber, 1948), p. 31.

29. Richard Chase, *The American Novel and its Tradition* (Garden City, NY: Doubleday, 1957), pp. 3–4, vii, 2, 11, 4.

30. Richard Poirier, *A World Elsewhere: The Place of Style in American Literature* (1966; rpt. Oxford: Oxford University Press, 1968), p. 9.

31. Larzer Ziff, *Literary Democracy: The Declaration of Cultural Independence in America* (1981; rpt. Harmondsworth: Penguin Books, 1982), p. vii. *Breaking Bounds: Whitman and American Cultural Studies*, eds. Betsy Erkkila and Jay Grossman (New York: Oxford University Press, 1996), p. 8. Ralph Waldo Emerson, 'Nature' (1837), *The Portable Emerson*, eds. Carl Bode and Malcolm Cowley (Harmondsworth: Penguin, 1981), p. 7. [Whitman], 'Walt Whitman and his Poems', *United States Review*, September 1855, in *Walt Whitman: A Critical Anthology*, ed. Francis Murphy (Harmondsworth: Penguin, 1969), pp. 29–30.

32. Oliver Wendell Holmes, *Ralph Waldo Emerson* (1884; rpt. Boston: Houghton Mifflin, 1912), p. 115. Emerson, 'The American Scholar' (1837), *The Portable Emerson*, eds. Bode and Cowley, p. 51. Emerson, Journal for June–August 1845 and March–April 1847, *Emerson in His Journals*, ed. Porte, pp. 342, 368.

33. Emerson, 'Quotation and Originality', *Letters and Social Aims* (London: Macmillan, 1891), pp. 130, 140. Emerson, 'Circles' (1841), 'The American Scholar' (1837) and 'The Poet' (1844), *The Portable Emerson*, eds. Bode and Cowley, pp. 238, 230, 69, 262. Emerson, letter 21 July 1855 to Whitman, in *Walt Whitman: A Critical Anthology*, ed. Murphy, p. 29. Emerson, Journal for June 1847, *Emerson in His Journals*, ed. Porte, p. 372.

34. Walt Whitman, 'Preface to the 1855 Edition "Leaves of Grass"', *Leaves of Grass and Selected Prose*, ed. and introd. Sculley Bradley (New York: Holt, Rinehart & Winston, 1949), pp. 453–4. Emerson, *The Journals and Miscellaneous Notebooks of Ralph Waldo Emerson* (16 vols, Cambridge, MA: Harvard University Press, 1960–82), Vol. 9, p. 382. Richard Poirier, *The Renewal of Literature: Emersonian Reflections* (London: Faber & Faber, 1987), pp. 45–6.

35. Claude Lévi-Strauss, *Tristes Tropiques*, trans. John and Doreen Weightman (1955; rpt. Harmondsworth: Penguin, 1976), pp. 95–6. Emerson, 'Stonehenge' (1856), in *English Traits, Representative Men & other Essays* (London: J. M. Dent, 1908), p. 143. J. Hector St John de Crèvecoeur, *Letters from an American Farmer* (1782; rpt. Harmondsworth: Penguin, 1981), pp. 81–2.

36. Peter J. Taylor, *Political Geography: World Economy, Nation-State and Locality* (2nd edn, London: Longman, 1989), p. 45.

37. On Thomas Cole's cycle of paintings, see Robert Hughes, *American Visions: The Epic History of Art in America* (New York: Alfred A. Knopf, 1997), pp. 147–51. Hughes provides illustrations of the second, third and fifth canvases: *The Arcadian or Pastoral State*, *Consummation*, and *Desolation*. *The Arcadian or Pastoral State* is the cover illustration of this present book.

38. William Gilpin, *Mission of the North American People, geographical, social, and political* (Philadelphia: J. B. Lippincott, 1873), p. 130. On the origin of the phrase 'Manifest Destiny', see Albert K. Weinberg, *Manifest Destiny: A Study of Nationalist Expansionism in American History* (1935; rpt. Chicago: Quadrangle Paperbacks, 1963), pp. 111–12.

39. Frederick Jackson Turner, 'The Significance of History' (1891) and 'The Significance of the Frontier in American History' (1893), in *Frederick Jackson Turner: Wisconsin's Historian of the Frontier*, ed. Martin Ridge (Madison: Wisconsin State Historical Society, 1986), pp. 27–8. William Cronon, 'Revisiting the Vanishing Frontier: The Legacy of Frederick Jackson Turner', *Western Historical Quarterly* 18, 2 (April 1987), 166. Benjamin Rush, 'An Account of the Progress of Population, Agriculture, Manners, and Government in Pennsylvania', *Essays, Literary, Moral and Philosophical* (Philadelphia: Printed by Thomas & Samuel Bradford, 1798), pp. 213–25. Rush's essay is most easily available in *The Letters of Benjamin Rush*, ed. Lyman Butterfield (2 vols, Princeton, NJ: Princeton University Press, 1951), I, pp. 400–6. The quotations are from pp. 404, 406.

40. Turner, 'The Significance of the Frontier', p. 43. Cronon, 'Revisiting the Vanishing Frontier', p. 160.

41. H. J. Mackinder, 'The Geographical Pivot of History', *The Geographical Journal* 23 (April 1904), 422–3, 431. The essay is also reprinted as an addendum to *Democratic Ideals and Reality*. Mackinder, *Democratic Ideals and Reality* (1919; rpt. New York: W. W. Norton & Co., 1962), p. 150. Bernard DeVoto, 'Geopolitics with the Dew on it', *Harper's Magazine* 188 (1944), 313–23. James C. Malin, 'Space and History', *Agricultural History* 18, 67–8.

42. Charles Redway Dryer, 'Mackinder's "World Island" and its American Satellite', *Geographical Review* 9 (January–June 1920), 205–7.

43. D. H. Lawrence, *Studies in Classic American Literature* (New York: T. Seltzer, 1923), pp. x–xi. Lawrence, *Studies in Classic American Literature* (Harmondsworth: Penguin, 1971), pp. 11, 61. Lawrence's original essays on American literature, begun in 1917, were published as Armin Arnold, ed., *The Symbolic Meaning: The Uncollected Versions of Studies in Classic American Literature* (Arundel: Centaur Press, 1962).

Chapter 2

A ProtoAmerican Literature, 800 BC to 1611

> The settler makes history; his life is an epoch, an Odyssey. He is the absolute beginning: 'This land was created by us'; he is the unceasing cause . . .
>
> (Franz Fanon, *The Wretched of the Earth*)

Beyond Atlantis

In *The Wretched of the Earth*, Franz Fanon drew attention to the Manichaean mode of thinking inherent in colonialist thought. The colonist, he suggested, conceived himself as the *maker*, creating temporal and spatial structures, which were then applied to indigenous peoples, and the lands they inhabited. The natives, too, were *made*. They were imagined by the colonist to exist outside those structures, 'interminably in an unchanging dream'.[1] It follows from Fanon's suggestion that the colonial process involves the application of preconceived, in this instance European, images. The first shapes of a literature for America emerged long before the land itself appeared to western eyes, and are to be found in the oldest surviving forms of European literature.

Those shapes derive from the expansiveness that lies at the heart of epic, and focus in particular on two methods of organising space: the imagery of the pastoral and the myth of Atlantis. Pastoral is almost certainly the earlier way of organising space. Images of the pastoral are to be found in the earliest known form of writing, in Mesopotamia around 3100 BC. For our purposes they are best illustrated by reference to the first Greek sailor's story. The Homeric poem, *The Odyssey*, was probably written in the eighth century BC. Its theme, concerning a perilous journey in an attempt to reach home, will become an important one in American literature and culture. The theme is presented in microcosm in the contrast between the fifth and seventh books of *The Odyssey*. The fifth, 'Calypso', partly concerns the anger of the god Poseidon, 'the great Earthshaker', and the storm he creates as a torment for Odysseus. The seventh, 'The Palace of Alcinous', provides a Utopian vision of the mythical island of Phaeacia, where Odysseus is shipwrecked, and which is 'like a shield laid on the misty sea'. This suggestion of a protected space is elaborated by images which represent a fond view of a periphery as seen from a mainland, a view confirmed by the long-standing identification of Phaeacia with Corfu, the island off the west coast of Greece. On the island its king, Alcinous, treats Odysseus kindly. This is in striking contrast with the treatment meted out by Alcinous' grandfather, Poseidon, and is in accord with the place, for Alcinous' house is ablaze with wealth and colour. Nearby we are presented with a pastoral vision:

> Outside the courtyard but stretching close up to the gates, and with a hedge running down on either side, lies a large orchard of four acres, where trees hang their greenery on high, the pear and the pomegranate, the apple with its glossy burden, the sweet fig and the luxuriant olive. Their fruit never fails nor runs short, winter and summer alike. It comes at all seasons of the year, and there is never a time when the West Wind's breath is not assisting, here the bud, and here the ripening fruit; so that pear after pear, apple after apple, cluster on cluster of grapes, and fig upon fig are always coming to perfection. In the same enclosure there is a fruitful vineyard, in one part of which is a warm patch of level ground, where some of the grapes are drying in the sun, while others are gathered or being trodden, and on the foremost rows hang unripe bunches that have just cast their blossom or show the first faint tinge of purple. Vegetable beds of various kinds are neatly laid out beyond the furthest row and make a smiling patch of never-failing green. The garden is served by two springs, one led in rills to all parts of the enclosure, while its fellow opposite, after providing a watering-place for the townsfolk, runs under the courtyard gate towards the great house itself. Such were the beauties with which the gods had adorned Alcinous' home.

This prose translation recreates one of the earliest extant instances of the easy relation of nature and culture that lies at the heart of the pastoral. The translator of this 1946 version, E. V. Rieu, claimed that it was accurate to the original. Forty-five years later his son, D. C. H. Rieu, publishing a revised version, suggested that the earlier one was overly poetic. This was almost certainly due to the conditions of its production. Pastoral imagery is flexible enough to undergo a number of modifications while still retaining its essence. It is a particularly potent antidote to the stresses of war, and was evoked in a number of contexts during the Second World War. In this passage the elder Rieu's translation may be regarded as a celebration of its source in terms of a release from six years of carnage. The stately tread of the sentences, an intimate closeness between narrator and reader, and the appeals to sense-experience sculpt a landscape of exuberant abundance, unshadowed by sin. The passage captures the seductions of an imagery that has pulled people westwards in search of the source of the gods', and the wind's, beneficence. It follows that the pastoral provides one of the common American images. In the words of Leo Marx, 'the pastoral ideal has been used to define the meaning of America ever since the age of discovery, and it has not yet lost its hold upon the native imagination'. As we shall see, the pastoral has informed both the earliest and many more recent visions of America. For instance, it underpinned the ideology of the Founding Fathers of 1776, it was reshaped to accommodate the technological developments of the nineteenth century, and it still invigorates the more radical elements of American politics.

The myth of Atlantis makes a brief appearance in *The Odyssey*, and contributes to the epic scale of the poem. As one of his many tasks, Odysseus is required by the enchantress Circe to travel to Hades' Kingdom of Decay to consult the soul of the blind Theban prophet Teiresias. Following her directions, he ventures out of the Mediterranean to 'the frontiers of the world', past the Gates of the Sun and through perpetual mist 'to a wild coast . . . where the tall poplars grow and the willows that so quickly shed their seeds'. This is a landscape far removed from the protected spaces of the pastoral and just beyond the bounds of Greek geographical knowledge of the eighth century BC. Four centuries later the Greek world had been greatly enlarged. That enlargement is to be found in the writings of the philosopher, Plato (c.429–347 BC), and in the exploits of the warrior, Alexander (356–323 BC). Plato looked west; Alexander east. They both played a vital part in the expansion of the Greek geographical imagination, transforming the scope of the Greek world and developing the wealth of its imagery.[2]

Atlantis is named for the first time in Plato's late dialogue, *Timaeus*, which he apparently intended as a sequel to *The Republic*. Plato presented the story of Atlantis as if it were fact. He claimed that 'the island was larger than Libya and Asia put together', and that it was located beyond the Straits of Gibraltar, forming part of a chain by which 'you might pass to the whole of the opposite continent which surrounded the true ocean'. A fragment, *Critias*, describes Atlantis in more detail. The island has a central plain sheltered from the cold north wind by 'encircling mountains, which were more numerous, huge, and beautiful than any that exist today'. It is blessed with wonderful resources. There are both hot and cold springs. Fossil fuels exist in abundance, as does 'orichalch', which normally means brass or copper but which Plato describes as of 'a higher value than any metal except gold'. The animals are many and various, and include 'the largest and most voracious of brutes', elephants. Yet the plant life is so prolific that there is plenty for all the animals. The human inhabitants also enjoy the profusion, for they can reap two harvests each year:

> Besides all this, the soil bore all aromatic substances still to be found on earth, roots, stalks, canes, gums exuded by flowers and fruits, and they throve on it. Then, as for cultivated fruits, the dry sort which is meant to be our food supply and those others we use as solid nutriment – we call the various kinds pulse – as well as the woodland kind which gives us meat and drink and oil together, the fruit of trees that ministers to our pleasure and merriment and is so hard to preserve, and that we serve as welcome dessert to a jaded man to charm away his satiety – all these were produced by that sacred island, which then lay open to the sun, in marvelous beauty and inexhaustible profusion.

In just two sentences Plato has created a riot of sense-experience. Indeed, hints of drunkenness (are some of the trees vines?) seem to be confirmed by the syntax of the second sentence, which threatens to run out of control. In an environment that combines health and pleasure the Atlantians, when sober, have created a masterpiece of design. The central plain is criss-crossed by a grid-pattern of canals that supplies trade to the capital. The capital city itself is constructed of concentric circles that alternate ring-islands, each dedicated to a specific purpose, with protective moats. At the heart of the capital is a palace 'a marvel for the size and splendor of its buildings'.

Plato has exceeded the environment of *The Odyssey*, creating a utopia by taking the pastoral to its logical conclusion, and by blending fiction with fact. For instance, the bones of pygmy elephants have been found on Crete and some of the islands of the Cyclades. Utopias, of course, are created as a comment on conditions at home. *The Republic* is a critique of Athenian democracy. If *Timaeus* and *Critias* are read together, it appears that Plato was commenting on the connection between virtue and freedom, and particularly criticising the militarism and luxury of the Persian empire that would shortly be extirpated by Alexander. As generation gave way to generation, the Atlantians lost the self-control that in his view was a vital concomitant of good fortune. Atlantians become afflicted by 'the infection of wicked coveting and pride of power'. 'Unprovoked', they 'made an expedition against the whole of Europe and Asia', invading and enslaving many of the Mediterranean states. In words which would be repeated in the Second World War, Plato recounts how Athens is 'compelled to stand alone', but defeats the invaders and proceeds to liberate the other states. *Critias* breaks off as Zeus decides to punish the Atlantians, and *Timaeus* completes the tale:

> there occurred violent earthquakes and floods, and in a single day and night of misfortune all your warlike men in a body sank into the earth, and the island of Atlantis in like manner disappeared in the depths of the sea. For which reason the sea in those parts is impassable and impenetrable, because there is a shoal of mud in the way, and this was caused by the subsidence of the island.[3]

Plato's statement that the way west was closed had little effect. The myth of a sunken volcanic island has fascinated many people including, as we shall see, the novelist James Fenimore Cooper. Indeed, following Columbus's landfall there have been many attempts to locate Atlantis. The *Historia general de las Indias* (1552) by the Spanish historian Francesco López de Gómara (1512–72), asserted that Plato's Atlantis was in fact America. So too did the political fable *The New Atlantis* by the English philosopher Francis Bacon (1561–1626), which like Plato's *Critias* was left incomplete. Bacon, though, suggested that the calamity was a latter-day flood that occurred one thousand years after the biblical universal deluge. The land emerged again when the waters receded, and later was renamed America. The land was therefore much more recently settled than the rest of the world, and consequently the inhabitants were characterised by 'rudeness and ignorance'. Bacon had produced a comic anticipation of the miasmatist debate that would generate a lot of heat in the later eighteenth century.[4]

There have been theories that Atlantis was once part of a 'land bridge' joining Northern Europe and North America, the counterpart of the land bridge joining Siberia and Alaska, at what is now the Bering Strait. One particularly piquant suggestion, which reverses Plato's chronology, was first made in 1953. Atlantis, according to this theory, was situated just north-east of the island of Heligoland. After the calamity occurred, the survivors of the Northsea people invaded Egypt, where Rameses III defeated them. But the most common theory was of a separate landmass in the Atlantic ocean between America and Africa.

The Jesuit Athanasius Kircher drew a map of it in his *Mundus Subterraneus* (1665). The theory became popular following the discovery in the nineteenth century of the Mid-Atlantic Ridge, a chain of submerged mountains. It gave rise to one of the most widely read books on the subject, *Atlantis: The Antediluvian World* (1882), by Ignatius Donnelly (1831–1901), the novelist and Minnesota politician. Donnelly suggested that Atlantis 'was the region where man first rose from a state of barbarism to civilisation', and that before it 'perished in a terrible convulsion of nature', its inhabitants colonised both the Old and New Worlds. The classical civilisations of the Mediterranean and the Pre-Columbian civilisations of America were therefore both derived from the same source.[5] Donnelly had produced a grand answer to the miasmatists. Unfortunately, the truth is likely to be more circumscribed, if still spectacular. Archaeological excavations in the 1960s and 1970s suggest that Atlantis is likely to be the Cycladic island of Santorin, north of Crete. Santorin may have been at the centre of a Minoan maritime empire that threatened both Athens and Egypt. It suffered a massive earthquake around 1500 BC, during which much of the island collapsed into the sea. Plato, who knew about Phoenician navigations in the Atlantic, may have decided to increase the potency and epic scale of his account by displacing the earthquake from Santorin to the Atlantic. If this was his decision, it was certainly effective.

The Greek expansion eastwards can be verified with much greater ease. It was the work of Alexander the Great, who succeeded his father Philip II as King of Macedon in 336 BC, when he was just twenty. In the course of his reign of twelve years and eight months Alexander destroyed Persian dominance of the eastern Mediterranean, invaded Asia Minor and penetrated the North-West Frontier. He marched as far as the River Beas, east of Amritsar in north-western India, at which point, in 326 BC, his army refused to follow him further. He reluctantly led them towards Greece, and died in Babylon. Alexander's life was marked by a thirst for kudos unprecedented and so strong that he has been called 'the first famous person'. The Greek historian Arrian (AD 90?–173?) noted that when Alexander laid a wreath on the tomb of Achilles, he called him 'a lucky man, in that he had Homer to proclaim his deeds and preserve his memory'. Yet although there was no parallel to the *Iliad* to celebrate Alexander's character and achievements, the shortcoming was made up by a group of texts, including Arrian's *The Campaigns of Alexander*, which wove the mythology of the epic hero around him. Three related elements of that mythology are important for our purposes. The first is the concept of imperial space. Alexander, said Arrian, 'had no lack of grandeur or ambition: he would never have remained idle in the enjoyment of his conquests, even had he extended his empire from Asia to Europe and from Europe to the British Isles'. Arrian conveyed a sense of that grandeur in images of amplitude. The River Indus, he wrote, exceeds the combined volumes of the Nile and Danube. It 'is a mighty stream right from its source . . . and imposes its name upon the country as it flows down to meet the sea'. It was exceeded in size only by the Ganges, which Alexander failed to reach, for the scale of his enterprise became too great for his army, and they mutinied. Arrian records

43

that Alexander told them that he wished to create a Macedonian empire to which 'there will be no boundaries but what God Himself has made for the whole world'. When they refused to satisfy his wishes, he chose a route towards Greece that led them down the Indus into the Arabian Sea 'for the mere achievement of having sailed in the Great Sea beyond India'. In the ocean he slaughtered bulls, poured a libation from a golden cup, and threw the cup and golden bowls into the ocean as a sacrifice to the god Poseidon, who had dealt so severely with Odysseus. The images of amplitude conveyed by Arrian were extended in the Apocryphal *First Book of the Maccabees*, which in its original Hebrew version may have been written four centuries after Alexander's death. It turned his desire into achievement, suggesting that he 'went through to the ends of the earth, and took spoils of many nations, insomuch that the earth was quiet before him'. Medieval romances developed the mythology further, making Alexander's spatial expansion vertical as well as horizontal. A sixth-century Greco-Egyptian story shows Alexander as the first submariner, constructing a vessel of glass and iron to go searching for monster pearls, only to be carried off by a giant fish. A ninth-century Latin poem depicts him as an early aviator, ascending in a basket of rushes powered by gryphons.[6]

Such fabulous tales are also part of the second element of the mythology of Alexander important for our purposes. The incredible becomes credible at the extreme edge of the cross-cultural interaction that inevitably arises from long-distance travel. The Greek historian Herodotus (484?–420? BC) remarked that 'the remotest parts of the world are the richest in minerals and produce the finest specimens of both animal and vegetable life'. Among nature's blessings in India were trees which produced a wool superior to that found on sheep, and ants, as big and fast as dogs, which mined the gold that existed there 'in immense quantity'. Alexander found no gold; and his chronicler, Arrian, worked hard to separate the fabulous from the probable. He dismissed stories of 'gold-mining ants and gold-guarding griffons'. But if the Indians had no gold, they did have elephants, much larger than those that had existed on Crete. Arrian regarded elephants as the most intelligent of animals, and he took care to record the Indian method of capturing them, and their various uses. The elephant made up a central, and certainly bulky, image in Indian mythology. Tamed elephants were employed in Indian armies as a kind of armoured division. They were adopted by Alexander and thereafter became a symbol of omnipotence employed, among others, by Caesar, Claudius, Pompey and Hannibal. Until the collapse of the Western Roman Empire in AD 476 the elephant, in the words of Robin Lane Fox, 'symbolized the open frontier between East and West, a frontier which Alexander had been the first man to roll back'. The elephant marked an important cultural boundary, and it is therefore appropriate that for a brief period it became one of the symbols of the cultural debate between Europe and America. The Comte de Buffon who, as we shall see, began much of the negative eighteenth-century European commentary on America, agreed with Arrian and called the elephant, after humankind, the most respectable animal on earth. The hunt for the American elephant was on. Led by Thomas Jefferson, several Americans sought evidence of elephantine life in the New World to refute European claims of degeneration. Benjamin Rush produced a version of the origin of Native Americans by suggesting that their ancestors had migrated from Asia, using elephants to cross a land bridge to America.[7]

There were other ways in which Alexander was a multiculturalist, and in consequence attracted the criticism that would later be analysed by Edward Said. Arrian echoed some of the Macedonian soldiers in Alexander's army, and accused him of 'becoming tainted with orientalism' for adopting the clothing or weapons of the so-called 'barbarian tribes' which they met, or for admitting their soldiers into his army. The Greek historian was more approving when he questioned one particularly intimate kind of cross-cultural encounter. This concerns the Amazons, the warrior-women who, as the Greek root (*maza*) of their name suggests, underwent a mastectomy so that they could shoot arrows or throw javelins more easily. According to Priam in the *Iliad*, the Amazons were 'men's equals'. They disturbed the patriarchal order of the Greek world, and so they were placed at the edge of it. Their base was believed to be south of the Black Sea, from which they travelled westwards, harassing the Greeks. But as the Greek world expanded, no trace of the Amazons was found, until Alexander's campaign took him beyond Asia Minor. After crossing the Hindu Kush, he marched towards Samarkand. There was an often-reported fable that, during the course of this journey, Thalestris approached Alexander. Attracted by his fame, the Amazon Queen wished to have a child by him, and they cohabited for thirteen days for this purpose. Arrian doubted the tale, but related a version in which Alexander was visited by a contingent of a hundred Amazons:

> They were equipped like cavalrymen, but carried axes instead of spears and light targes instead of the ordinary cavalry shield. According to some writers, their right breasts were smaller than their left, and were bared in battle. Alexander sent the women away to avoid trouble; for they might well have met with unseemly treatment from the troops, Macedonian or foreign. However, he told them to inform their Queen that he would visit her one day and get her with child.

Given the brusque masculinity of the Greeks, it might be more appropriate to replace this polite translation with the well-known modern slang dismissal. Doubtless, the intention of the tale was to change Thalestris' function from warrior to mother and thus bring her within the patriarchal structures of Macedonia. It is likely, though, that there was no encounter, and certainly there was no known issue of it. Thereafter, stories of the Amazons placed them at a safe distance. Dionysius Scytobrachian, a grammarian who lived in Alexandria during the second century BC, put them on the Isle of Hespera, at the far western edge of the world. The Greek historian Diodorus Siculus (*fl.* 60–30 BC) located Hespera 'in the western parts of Libya, on the bounds of the inhabited world', regarded as an appropriate place for women 'who followed a manner of life unlike that which prevails among us'. And it was on the bounds of the inhabited world that they were apparently rediscovered, in 1540 by the Spanish explorer Francisco de Orellana, who renamed the Marañón

River in their honour. As we shall see, America from the earliest settlement seemed an appropriate site for the alternative modes of behaviour symbolised by the Amazons.[8]

The third related element of the myth of Alexander important for our purposes is the evidence it gives of the growth of a polymorphous pan-European culture. The major, but by no means the only, source of the development of the European mythology of Alexander are a number of fables, which were written down in Alexandria, probably beginning in the third century BC. Collected as the *Alexander Romance*, they relate a number of exploits of the hero. The *Alexander Romance* was first translated into Latin around AD 338. It subsequently appeared in eighty versions in twenty-four languages, including Hebrew, Serbian, Georgian, Czech, Italian, Spanish, French, German, Russian, Irish, Scots and English. One modern English translator asserts that only the Bible exceeded the *Alexander Romance* in popularity. There are also many images of Alexander, to be found throughout the Middle East and Europe. Instances of such images are on a Byzantine ivory casket; on a relief on the north elevation of St Mark's, Venice; on a tapestry in the Palazzo Doria, Rome; on the portal of a church at Remagen; on the mosaic pavement at Otranto Cathedral; and on a misericord in Whalley Church, Lancashire. Alexander, factual and fabular, in these various languages, environments and media, was used to teach a number of moral and theological lessons.

One text, which contained all the elements of the myth already discussed, is the epic *Alexandreis*, written in Latin between 1178 and 1182 by Gautier de Châtillon (1135?–1184?). During the course of the poem's ten books, Alexander is shown being taught by Aristotle, succeeding Philip to the throne of Macedon, and then developing global ambitions. A series of victories lead Alexander eastwards, to the meeting with Thalestris and then to an India not only populated with elephants but containing such fabulous wealth that its rivers run with gold. Despite such wealth, Alexander's soldiers will go no further. In contrast, their leader regrets that the world is too small for his ambitions. This mark of *hubris* leads to the inevitable fall at Babylon. The *Alexandreis* was read throughout Europe and rendered into several languages, including Czech, Italian, Spanish, Middle Dutch and Middle High German. Shortly after 1260 Brandr Jónsson (1204?–1264), a nobleman who became Bishop of Hólar, translated it into Icelandic prose. It is *Alexanders Saga* that brings us to the point at which the European literary imagination, which had journeyed from India to Iceland, at last touched the realities of the American land.

Viking settlement

It was not until later in the eleventh century, and in two Viking sagas, that precedent literary structures began to merge with a credible awareness of America itself. Inevitably, there have been alternative claims for priority of landfall. The most clearly formulated is for St Brendan (AD 484–577), who left the west of Ireland around AD 539 and sailed for a dozen years in search of the earthly paradise in a leather boat known as a curragh. It is possible to speculate about his journey from the *Navigatio Sancti Brendani* (*Voyage of Saint Brendan*), which may not have been written until some 350 years afterwards. The text describes Brendan being driven by Atlantic winds and currents in a huge circle, the limits of which may have been as far apart as the Bahamas and Iceland. Certainly, there is plenty of evidence of the Irish reaching Iceland, and we shall see one instance of it in *Eiríks Saga*. But although Timothy Severin (in *The Brendan Voyage*, 1978) has proved that Irish shipbuilding was sufficiently advanced to make an Atlantic crossing, the *Navigatio* contains no persuasive evidence of an American landfall. It does, however, reveal one formal quality that relates it to the *Alexander Romance*. The *Navigatio* provides order to extended space by blending fact and fable for didactic purposes. It taught two kinds of lesson: geographical, for Brendan, it seemed, had travelled further than most; but mainly theological for, like *The Pilgrim's Progress* (1678), it gave a vivid account of the pitfall-ridden Christian search for the Promised Land. The *Navigatio* was popular, and presents further evidence of a pan-European culture. It survives in a large number of Latin manuscripts and was translated over time into a variety of languages, including Old Norse, Middle English, French, German and Italian. A Venetian version claims that Brendan is Venetian and sends him, like Marco Polo, eastwards.

In contrast to the Irish, the Viking claims of landfall can be believed, because archaeological evidence confirms textual evidence. The evidence begins, appropriately enough, with the generation that followed Knut the Great, the king who ruled England (from 1014), Denmark (from 1018) and Norway (from 1028) until his death in 1035. Most children know the apocryphal story of the attempt by King Canute to rule the tides as well as his three kingdoms. His nephew Sven Ulfsson (sometimes known as Sven Estridsson, for he was the son of Knut's sister Estrid) was more pragmatic. He knew the power of the sea, and he knew where it had taken the Norse. Sven ruled Denmark from 1047 to 1074. At that time, Scandinavia lay under the religious authority of the north German Archbishops of Hamburg-Bremen. They commissioned a history from one of their priests, Adam of Bremen, and after talking to Sven Ulfsson he appended a brief geography of Scandinavia. It is to be found in the *Gesta Hammaburgensis ecclesiae pontificum*, written by Adam between 1072 and 1081. It gives us the first known European sighting of America:

> He [Sven] spoke also of yet another island of the many found in that ocean. It is called Vinland because vines producing excellent wine grow wild there. That unsown crops also abound on that island we have ascertained not from fabulous reports but from the trustworthy relation of the Danes. Beyond that island, he said, no habitable land is found in that ocean, but every place beyond it is full of impenetrable ice and intense darkness.[9]

America is shown here as a borderland dividing natural profusion and a threatening desolation. The images create a typology that will recur frequently. As we shall see, the typology is central to the Puritan perception of America, but it occurs in many contexts, most recently in the work of Umberto Eco and Jean Baudrillard.

The Norse had sailed south-west from Greenland. They had settled in Greenland around 985 and remained there until about 1340 when, among other things, climatic change caused a 'Little Ice Age' and killed the settlement. From the earliest times there have been debates about exactly where the Norse sailed and what they found. A twelfth-century Icelandic *Geographical Treatise* noted that some people thought that Vínland was not an island but rather 'a continuation of Africa'. The report of vines that gave the land its name has led people to seek it far down the eastern seaboard of America. In 1885, Eben Norton Horsford, a Harvard chemistry professor and amateur archaeologist, believed that he had found evidence of Norse settlement at what is now Watertown, on the Charles River. In 1954 a Danish scholar suggested that Vínland was south of Chesapeake Bay. The most recent debate has been about the authenticity of a map of Vínland, apparently drawn in the thirteenth century, given to Yale University in 1959 and first published in 1965. Indeed, it was not until that time that modern archaeological techniques established clear proof of one Norse settlement. Excavations completed in 1968 showed that the Norse had lived on the northern tip of Newfoundland. Radiocarbon dating revealed that they were there towards the end of the tenth century.[10]

America continued to make fleeting appearances in Norse geographical and historical tracts, including the *Islendingabók (The Book of the Icelanders)*, written around 1125 by 'the father of Icelandic history', Ari Thorgilsson (1067–1148), and *Landnámabók (The Book of the Settlements)*, a somewhat later text which shows his influence. However, the fullest account of the Norse discovery and settlement of America appears in two sagas, the *Grænlendinga Saga (The Greenlanders' Saga)* and *Eirík's Saga (The Saga of Eric the Red)*. They develop the images that appeared fleetingly in Adam's history, and add others. The sagas inform us that Bjarni Herjolfsson, who had wandered off course to Greenland, sighted land 'well wooded and with low hills'. He told Leif Eriksson, the second son of Eirík the Red, who had colonized Greenland. Leif sailed west and set foot on a barren country he named Helluland ('Flat Stone Land'; probably Baffin Island), then to a land he called Markland ('Forest Land'; probably Labrador) which 'was flat and wooded, with white sandy beaches', and finally to the land that he called Vínland. Thorfinn Karlsefni, a wealthy merchant, finally settled the land. Thorfinn took with him a company of sixty-five people, including an Irish couple, who were useful as scouts, 'for they could run faster than deer'. He also took 'livestock of all kinds, for they intended to make a permanent settlement there if possible'. They began trading with the Native Americans, whom they called Skrælings (savages).[11]

Finding, naming, settling, trading: the Vínland sagas present us with two acts of assimilation. They provide the first known white description of America, the first stage of a process that would adapt the new land to the ways of the Old World. They also incorporate America into one of the oldest known literary genres, the epic. Of course, the epic is a much-discussed genre and has received many definitions. The most useful and appropriate definition for my purpose here is given by John P. McWilliams. He proposes that 'an epic must be a heroic narrative, but that heroic narrative may assume many forms'. Drawing on the work of Georg Lukács and Mikhail Bakhtin, McWilliams constructs a tradition in which nineteenth-century writers like James Fenimore Cooper and Herman Melville 'deliberately assimilated the spirit and conventions of the epic poem within the prose romance', and historians like William Hickling Prescott and Francis Parkman 'adapted the epic techniques of the historical romance into heroic history'. He shows that Walt Whitman's *Leaves of Grass* is by no means a fresh start in American literature but rather a poem that draws on a long tradition. McWilliams's specific purpose is to trace the tradition back to the eve of the new American republic.[12]

It can be traced back still further. Due to their mode of transmission, the Norse sagas portray heroism in a particularly flexible and open way. The term 'saga' originally meant an oral prose narrative. Sagas were popular, vernacular tales that did not reach a fixed form until the twelfth and thirteenth centuries, when it is likely that those who wrote them down adapted components of several different stories to achieve a narrative that would appeal to an intended audience. The Norse sagas are therefore related to the epics of the Babylonians (such as the *Epic of Gilgamesh*), the Greeks (such as *The Odyssey*), and the Anglo-Saxons (such as *Beowulf*), in the way that they are shaped from oral traditions that contain both historical and legendary elements. They present a combination of the realistic and the speculative which has been a particularly useful technique for writing about America. The novelist Philip Roth, in a well-known complaint, has put the reason for the combination in a modern setting:

> the American writer in the middle of the twentieth century has his hands full in trying to understand, describe, and then make *credible* much of American reality. It stupefies, it sickens, it infuriates, and finally it is even a kind of embarrassment to one's one [*sic* – own] meager imagination. The actuality is continually outdoing our talents, and the culture tosses up figures almost daily that are the envy of any novelist.

The complaint is hardly a new one in American writing. It occurs whenever realism has seemed a mode inadequate to its subject. Writers have therefore sometimes moved to unite the real with the legendary. In the nineteenth century the mode tended to be called Romance. In 'The Custom-House' opening to his 1850 novel *The Scarlet Letter*, Nathaniel Hawthorne characterises Romance as moonlight that invests a playroom 'with a quality of strangeness and remoteness, though still almost as vividly present as by daylight'. The critic Robert Scholes called its twentieth-century form 'fabulation', drawing the term from Caxton's 1484 translation of the eighth fable of Alfonce. Scholes discussed the work of American writers John Barth, John Hawkes, Terry Southern and Kurt Vonnegut. It has also led, on the one hand, to Norman Mailer's 'factoids', and on the other to such parodic quest-fictions as Saul Bellow's *Henderson the Rain King* (1959), which ends, appropriately, in Newfoundland.[13]

The *Grænlendinga Saga* reached written form about 1190, while *Eirík's Saga* was recorded a little later, around 1260. Of course, we do not know who the writer was and to what extent he shaped his material. Whatever shaping took place, these sagas reveal three tensions that will frequently recur in American literature. The first is between the single narrative point-of-view and the polygenesis of the material. The authoritative opening of the *Grænlendinga Saga*, for instance – 'There was a man called Thorvald . . .' (49) – soon disintegrates into a tale of so many characters, places and events that the editors of the current Penguin edition felt obliged to include a glossary of proper names. The second tension is between the pagan and the Christian. The conversion of the Icelanders at the end of the tenth century did not completely erase paganism from Icelandic literature. The conflict of the two beliefs emerges most clearly in the story of Gudrid Vifilsson, the female protagonist of the two sagas. In *Eirík's Saga* she reluctantly takes part in a pagan ceremony, summoning spirits by singing 'Warlock-songs' taught her in Iceland by her foster-mother Halldis. As a reward Thorbjorg, one of the few remaining witches in Greenland, foretells 'a great and eminent family line' for her (82–3). Both the *Grænlendinga Saga* and *Eirík's Saga* show the ghost of Gudrid's second husband forecasting a similar fate. Both tell of her third marriage, with Thorfinn Karlsefni, with whom she bears a child in Vínland. The *Grænlendinga Saga* also presents Gudrid with an apparition, a woman who carries the same name. Its closing segment relates her pilgrimage to Rome, and her final years as an anchoress. Both sagas list the many descendants of Gudrid and Karlsefni, including four bishops of the Catholic Church in Iceland.

This tension between the two beliefs makes the sagas extraordinarily difficult to interpret. They play with paganism and dabble with doubling, but end safely with a Christian hierarchy. They end, too, in history, but only after displaying a third, and related, tension, between the factual and the fabular. As I have already suggested, it is a common occurrence in American literature. Of the two sagas, the *Grænlendinga Saga* gives us more visions. To compensate, *Eirík's Saga* presents us with the first, but by no means the last, American monstrosity, the Uniped. A flat-footed attempt to explain away the Uniped as a short native in a long coat ignores the provenance of this anecdote. It is likely that the person who wrote down the saga interpolated it, in a display of learning. Fables were part of the baggage of many medieval intellectuals. Unipeds occur in Plinius Secundus (Pliny the Elder, AD 23–79), and were seen since in many places, including Ethiopia. As we shall see, the only qualification for the residence of a monstrosity was that it should be inaccessible to the audience.

Despite their impediment, Unipeds can travel, as we can see from Karlsefni's encounter with one of them. Magnus Magnusson's translation adds some black humour to the tale:

> One morning Karlsefni and his men saw something glittering on the far side of the clearing, and they shouted at it. It moved, and it proved to be a Uniped; it came bounding down towards where the ship lay. Thorvald, Eirik the Red's son, was sitting at the helm. The Uniped shot an arrow into his groin.

> Thorvald pulled out the arrow and said, 'This is a rich country we have found; there is plenty of fat around my entrails.' Soon afterwards he died of the wound. (101–2)

Thorvald's doomed laughter creates echoes that still resonate today in American literature. The Old Norse may not have stayed long in the New World, but their influence remains. There are two reasons. The first is the imagery of abundance that greeted their hungry northern eyes. It was first recorded in Adam's history and it will recur again and again in American culture. The journey from Helluland to Markland to Vínland exhibits a progression from poor to better to best. It is not the grapes alone that distinguish Vínland. The *Grænlendinga Saga* reports that the waters contained the biggest salmon the Norse had ever seen, and also that 'the country seemed to them so kind that no winter fodder would be needed for livestock: there was never any frost all winter and the grass hardly withered at all' (56). Abundance has been a frequent image of America, often in the face of stark fact. The historian David Potter suggested that abundance has informed many aspects of American culture, including its democratic politics, and its geographical (horizontal) and class (vertical) mobility. He believed, too, that American abundance created 'a wholly new institution' in modern advertising. Yet one of the oldest claims in America is that of novelty. It might indeed be said that the Norse created abundance through advertising. A famine in north-western Europe in AD 976 had afflicted Iceland worst of all and prompted migration. Eric the Red chanced on unoccupied land, a 'wilderness to the west' (50). At this point the speculator took over from the adventurer: 'he named it *Greenland*, for he said that people would be much more tempted to go there if it had an attractive name' (78). As Gwyn Jones remarked, 'the connotations of this happy title, *green*, *grass*, and *grow*, were a joyous augury to land-hungry men, and richly redolent of pastures new'. Then Leif outdid his father, producing a name for a newer land that was more intoxicating than its predecessor. It was a process that would be repeated time and again in America.[14]

Thorvald jokes about the rich country while pulling an arrow out of his belly. There is a second, darker, image pattern in the sagas, the moral counterpart of the desolation also recorded by Adam. In the sagas images of violence are intertwined with those of abundance. Indeed, it all began in violence, as William Carlos Williams points out in his 'alternative history' of America, *In the American Grain* (1925). The *Grænlendinga Saga* and *Eirík's Saga* agree that it was a blood feud rather than hunger that drove Eric the Red to seek other lands. The trade with the natives ends, almost inevitably, in violence that afflicts the whole community. At first, the Skrælings are frightened by the strangeness of Norse animals. A bull bellows at them and they flee, just as their southern kindred would later flee before the horses of Cortés. Later they get bolder and try to take Norse weapons. The murder of the first Skræling coincides with the disappearance of the double that appeared to Gudrid. The double's place is filled by Freydis, Leif's sister, an altogether tougher person who had been earlier described as 'an arrogant, overbearing woman' (52). At one point she is cut off from her party because her pregnancy has slowed her down:

> the Skrælings closed in on her. In front of her lay a dead man, Thorbrand Snorrason, with a flintstone buried in his head, and his sword beside him. She snatched up the sword and prepared to defend herself. When the Skrælings came rushing towards her she pulled one of her breasts out of her bodice and slapped it with the sword. The Skrælings were terrified at the sight of this and fled back to their boats and hastened away. (100)

Freydis's behaviour gives further evidence of the spread of Greek mythology. The Skrælings, understandably, do not wish to enter combat with an Amazon. This is the first sign of a temperament that would qualify Freydis for admission to the ranks of those tough warrior-women. It is not the last. Freydis breaks trading agreements and, coveting a larger ship, kills the owners, their crew and wives. She returns to Greenland rich and unrepentant. William Carlos Williams suggested that the violent blood of Eric the Red lived on in Freydis. The suggestion highlights the antithesis between her and the anchoress Gudrid Vifilsson. The women are the first representatives of two of the major lifestyles available to Americans: religion and crime. Many have followed in their footsteps.[15]

Knowledge of the Viking settlement in America disappeared, it seems, for eight centuries. The findings of Eben Norton Horsford and others, in the later years of the nineteenth century, caused a debate over priority of landfall, and numbers of people rushed to the defence of Columbus. One of them was Evelyn Abbot, the editor of Heroes of the Nations, one of the multi-volume editions, discussed in Chapter 1 and popular at the time. In his 1897 abridgement of Washington Irving's *Christopher Columbus* for the series, Abbot asserted that the new knowledge about the Vikings:

> does not lessen the merit of the great enterprise and achievement of Columbus. Nothing grew out of this discovery of Vinland . . . Two or three voyages were made to it . . . after which it ceased to be an object of further quest, and apparently faded from thought as if it had never been.[16]

In literary terms, however, much did grow out of the Viking discovery of Vínland. These analyses of the *Grænlendinga Saga* and *Eirík's Saga* have tried to show that, in applying precedent literary structures to the new land, the two sagas deserve to be classed as the true beginnings of American literature. The centuries between the Viking and Columbian landfalls, as we shall see, added further images that, in their turn, would be adapted in a renewed European approach to America.

The oriental impact

The American historian Daniel Boorstin once suggested that Columbus's landfall in America was a result of the Mongol Empire. This is a reasonable hypothesis. The Mongols opened the route to Cathay and thus access to the exotic silks and spices of the East. Columbus, of course, went in search not of America but rather of the short sea route to Asia. For approximately two and a half centuries until 1502, therefore, the West had no identity of its own. In whichever direction they travelled, travellers were guided by the rich tradition that Edward Said, following Arrian, has called 'Orientalism'. Images of the East were laid easily over the West. Two major sources of such images are Marco Polo's *Travels* (1295?) and *The Travels of Sir John Mandeville* (1357?; hereafter, *Mandeville*). Nowadays the two texts have been driven apart by the wedge of reality. Polo's *Travels* is believed to be fact, sometimes so devoutly that a Sinologist who dared to question its veracity caused a public uproar.[17] *Mandeville*, in contrast, was revealed by scholars in 1888 as a fraud; it is today dismissed as a pot-pourri of tall stories. Ironically, Polo's *Travels* was first known as *Il Milione* because its author was thought to have told that number of lies. Renaissance explorers, however, made no distinction between the two texts. They treated both as invaluable practical guides. They were widely circulated and translated, and were often bound together in travel collections. Columbus read *Mandeville* while preparing for his first voyage, and some time between 1492 and 1497 he annotated a copy of the Pipino edition of Polo's *Travels*. *Mandeville* accompanied Ralegh's contemporary Sir Martin Frobisher (1535?–1594) on his first attempt in 1576 to find the North-West Passage.

The material that we read in Polo's *Travels* is not clearly Polo's. First, there is some doubt whether or not Marco Polo (1254?–1324) even visited the lands that his text described. Second, the text was dictated to Rustichello of Pisa, who added some flourishes of his own, particularly a prologue in the style of the Arthurian romances that he wrote. Third, unlike the sagas, travel texts were not guided by the concept of individual authorship. The translation history of Polo's *Travels* shows that it was a compendium intended for arm-chair dreaming or practical use, like the more modern *Michelin Guide*. The original manuscript has been lost; it is not even clear in what language Rustichello took dictation. Fra Francesco Pipino wrote a Latin version, adapted to the beliefs of the Catholic Church, around 1320. It was widely circulated, but was just one of a large number of versions in several different languages. It is likely that the first printed edition was in Irish; it appeared in 1460. An Italian version, published in 1559, two years after the death of its translator, Giovanni Battista Ramusio, includes material which seems genuine but which is not to be found in Pipino. In 1503 Rodrigo Santaello made a translation into Castilian, which became the basis of the first English translation, by John Frampton, in 1579. Frampton omitted much of Ramusio's additions, and abbreviated a number of the descriptions and incidents to be found in Pipino. It will be apparent from this that any modern critic who examines Polo's *Travels* must enter a labyrinth of uncertainty. The discussion that follows looks at those elements of the text which received wide circulation and which influenced the imagery of America.

The text that we have describes an expedition by Polo's mercantile family from their Venetian base to Acre, near the present-day Haifa on the Israeli coast, and from there to the Persian Gulf, then crossing Iran to Afghanistan. So far the text makes it clear that the Polos had travelled in the steps of Alexander. Indeed, when the narrator describes Badakshan, he notes that its princes claimed descent from the marriage of Alexander to Roxane, who was believed (wrongly) to be daughter of Darius, King of the Persians.[18] Then the Polos outstripped Alexander. They travelled onwards to China and for seventeen years became part of the court of Kublai Khan (1216?–94?), the Mongol emperor. In 1292 they left China by sea, sailing to the Persian Gulf via the Straits of Malacca and the Palk Strait, returning finally to Venice in 1295, some twenty-four years after they had left. Soon after his return, Marco Polo was captured and imprisoned by the Genoese; and it was in prison that he met his amanuensis Rustichello.

The route the Polos took to China is not clear; it is not the intention of the text to examine the journey. Their itinerary is dispatched quickly in the opening pages of the text, which then shifts to description of their objectives. One of the first descriptions, of Armenia, abounds with superlatives and reveals the text's agenda:

> This is a great country. It begins at a city called ARZINGA, at which they weave the best buckrams in the world. It possesses also the best baths from natural springs that are anywhere to be found. The people of the country are Armenians, and are subject to the tartar. There are many towns and villages in the country, but the noblest of their cities is Arzinga, which is the See of an Archbishop . . .
> The country is indeed a passing great one, and in the summer it is frequented by the whole host of the Tartars of the Levant, because it furnishes them with such excellent pasture for their cattle. But in winter the cold is past all bounds, so in that season they quit this country and go to a warmer region, where they find other good pastures. At a castle called PAIPURTH, there is a very good silver mine.
> And you must know that it is in this country of Armenia that the Ark of Noah exists on top of a certain great mountain on the summit of which the snow is so constant that no one can ascend . . . (I, 47)

Facts are piled up in a manner that would later be employed, in a more temperate tone, by *Baedeker* and *Michelin*. In the Prologue Polo claims that he has seen, or has 'heard from men of credit and veracity' the 'wonderful things' that he will relate (I, 1). Those facts are subject to the three intertwined structuring functions that would later be employed in accounts of America.

The first structuring function is Christianity. The religious motives of the text, indeed, give it a false start. The Polos' first journey to the East, begun in 1260, receives scant treatment. The second, which would have begun in 1269, is held up for two years by delays over the election of Pope Gregory X and the necessary grant of Catholic credentials. The itinerary of the second journey reveals a Christianised geography which, as the reference to Noah's Ark suggests, has elements which would now be regarded as allegorical. Polo recounts two miracles. In one a cobbler's Christian faith moves a mountain and converts hordes of Saracens. In the other, a Saracen stone is used as a foundation for a pillar of a church. The Saracens recover the stone, but the pillar remains upright; and the space between its foot and the ground is still, according to Polo, to be seen. In contrast, miracles performed by the unchristian are rejected as mere sorcery. Likewise, the text dismisses unchristian faiths like the Tartar belief in metempsychosis. The peoples that the Polos meet are ranked according to their affinity with Christianity. Kublai Khan displays much interest in the religion, and is therefore accorded the greatest respect. At the other end of the scale are the people who inhabit the mountainous inland of Sumatra:

> [They] live for all the world like beasts, and eat human flesh, as well as other kinds of flesh, clean or unclean. And they worship this, that, and the other thing; for in fact the first thing they see on rising in the morning, that they do worship for the rest of the day. (II, 265)

Indiscriminacy over religion and dinner is a potent combination, and numbers of indigenous Americans and Africans would in due course be accused of both habits.

The *Travels* combines proselytism with mercantilism, which provides a second structuring function of the text. The description of Armenia above shows an appreciation of both natural resources and such human products as buckram, a stiffened cotton. In Fokien Polo finds camphor and the finest porcelain; in Malabar he finds spices, cottons, silks and precious metals. Precious stones and metals are the subject of the greatest interest, and Polo notes the many places where they are to be found. The inexhaustible source of such treasures is, of course, just out of reach. The Mongolians told Polo that Chipangu, known today as Japan, was such a cornucopia that they tried, unsuccessfully, to invade it. Polo notes that Japan has precious stones, and pearls of enormous size; but his prose becomes most excited when it considers the most prized metal. Gold 'is abundant beyond all measure', to the extent that the ruler of Chipangu

> hath a great Palace which is entirely roofed with fine gold, just as our churches are roofed with lead, insomuch that it would scarcely be possible to estimate its value. Moreover, all the pavement of the Palace, and the floors of its chambers, are entirely of gold, in plates like slabs of stone, a good two fingers thick; and the windows also are of gold, so that altogether the richness of this Palace is past all bounds and all belief. (II, 236–7)

Here Polo adds another image to the collection waiting to be applied to America, for this passage marks one source of the legend, which would in 1541 be named El Dorado ('the gilded one') by the Spanish colonist and writer Gonzalo Fernández de Oviedo y Valdes. As we shall see, though Mongolia has wealth enough, it is no El Dorado. The mercantile feature over which the text takes the greatest pains is the medium of exchange. Polo's prose takes on a breathless quality as he describes the paper currency. First circulated in 1236, it became the Mongolian predecessor of the Almighty Dollar, its effect on trade giving Kublai Khan 'more treasure than all the Kings in the World' (I, 411).

The third structuring function of the *Travels*, appropriate for the grandeur of the Mongolian empire as well as the distance the Polos travelled, is the epic. The text tests the terrain and its inhabitants against such appropriate earlier texts as *The Odyssey* and the *Alexander Romance*. Hence the description of Kublai Khan's summer palace at Chandu, built from marble and with its rooms:

> all gilt and painted with figures of men and beasts and birds, and with a variety of trees and flowers, all executed with such exquisite art that you regard them with delight and astonishment.
> Round this Palace a wall is built, inclosing a compass of 16 miles, and inside the Park there are fountains and rivers and brooks, and beautiful meadows, with all kinds of wild animals (excluding such as are of ferocious nature) . . . (I, 289)

There is one internal referent for the scene. This is a more restrained version of the earlier description of the paradisal garden of an Ismaili sheik known to the Crusaders as 'the Old Man of the Mountain'. The sheik had enclosed a valley between two mountains, turning it

> into a garden, the largest and most beautiful that ever was seen, filled with every variety of fruit. In it were erected pavilions and palaces the most elegant that can be imagined, all covered with gilding and exquisite painting. And there were runnels too, flowing freely with wine and milk and honey and water; and numbers of ladies and of the most beautiful damsels in the world, who could play on all manner of instruments, and sung most sweetly, and danced in a manner that it was charming to behold. (I, 145–6)

There is also an external referent for both of these environments: the palace and garden of Alcinous in the seventh book of *The Odyssey*. The three descriptions coalesce to provide imagery of such potency that it will recur in a number of texts. Coleridge combined the two to be found in the *Travels* when he fell asleep over two collections of travel documents by Samuel Purchas (1575?–1626) that included both Polo and *Mandeville*. The result, of course, was 'Kubla Khan' (1797–8). The imagery had its impact on Samuel Johnson's *Rasselas* (1759) and Edgar Allan Poe's 'Tamurlane' (1827), and the films *The Lost Horizon* (1937, via James Hilton's 1933 novel) and *Citizen Kane* (1941). As we shall see, it will provide one matrix for many of the early reports of America which are also to be found in Purchas's collections.

The *Travels* examines another element of the early forms of epic, the monstrous. It sorts critically through some examples to be found in *The Odyssey*, the *Alexander Romance*, and the lists of marvels often known as *Wonders of the East*. Pygmies are dismissed as nonsense; they are merely monkeys. The fable of the fire-resistant salamander is reduced to an asbestos napkin. Polo is more receptive to some other tales. In Madagascar he hears of the gryphon. It is so large and so strong, he is told, that it can lift an elephant. (Lifting Alexander, therefore, should be chick's play.) In what is nowadays Pakistan he learns of eagles which obligingly help to mine diamonds, which they leave in their droppings. An incident in Java is particularly germane, because it shows Polo struggling to reconcile observation with fable:

> There are wild elephants in the country, and numerous unicorns, which are very nearly as big. They have hair like that of a buffalo, feet like those of an elephant, and

a horn in the middle of the forehead . . . They do no mischief, however, with the horn, but with the tongue alone; for this is covered all over with long and strong prickles and when savage with any one they crush him under their knees and then rasp him with their tongue . . . They delight much to abide in mire and mud. 'Tis a passing ugly beast to look upon, and is not in the least like that which our stories tell of as being caught in the lap of a virgin; in fact, 'tis altogether different from what we fancied. (II, 265–6)

This is the moment when one fable takes its leave of the real world – as would any virgin who is kissed by a rhinoceros, or has one settle in her lap. Explorers did not seek unicorns in America, although they sought much else.

One cause of the search was *Mandeville*, which was less discriminating than Polo's *Travels*, but more popular. It was first written in French about 1357. By the end of the century it had been translated into every major European language. It was the first travel text to be printed by Richard Pynson, some five years after he had taken over Caxton's press following Caxton's death in 1491, thereby appearing in English some eighty-three years before Polo. By the end of the eighteenth century it had gone through another twenty-nine English editions and reprints. Of its contemporary English texts, only Chaucer exceeded its popularity. It is not hard to see why it was so widely read. As a compendium it outpolo'd Polo. *Mandeville* divides clearly into two sections. The first pillages such pilgrimage texts as the *Itineraria* of Odoric of Pordenone and Wilhelm von Boldensele to provide a practical guide for travellers to the Holy Land. If you come 'from the western parts of the world', you should go via Germany to the Danube, then through Greece to Constantinople, stopping long enough to see Saint Sophia, 'the best and most beautiful church in the world'. There is a guide to the Greek, Coptic, Hebrew and Saracen alphabets, an account of the Temple of Our Lord, and a detailed description of Mount Sion. The second section of *Mandeville* moves 'beyond the Holy Land' to 'diverse kingdoms, countries, and isles in the eastern part of the world, where live different kinds of men and animals, and many other marvellous things'. Those marvellous things are drawn from a variety of sources, including Herodotus, Pliny the Elder, the *Alexander Romance*, the *Wonders of the East* and Polo's *Travels*.[19]

Mandeville responds to Polo's *Travels* like a fisherman to another's tale: it improves on it. Polo talks of a circular journey which got as far east as the South China Sea. *Mandeville* talks of circumnavigation, and calculates that the world must be 31,005 miles in circumference, thereby overestimating its size by nearly 25 per cent (130). The equatorial circumference is in fact 24,902 miles. The text's account of Kublai Khan's summer palace outdoes Polo's. The place is 'more rich and noble than we had heard reported; and we should never have believed it if we had not seen it with our own eyes' (144). In consequence it is now a competitor for the description of the paradisal garden of 'the Old Man of the Mountain' (171–2). Similarly, the animal kingdom is inflated. Gryphons are 'bigger and stronger than a hundred eagles' (167). Rhinoceroses have three horns, not one, each as sharp as a sword and good for killing elephants. *Mandeville* repeats Herodotus' story of the dog-sized gold-mining ants; but they are to be found in Ceylon rather than India (183). (It is clear that Arrian is one source that has not been pillaged.) The variety of the animal world is only exceeded by the human. The Amazons which Alexander had met are relocated onto an island in the Caspian Sea (116–17). The Unipeds which the Vikings had met in America can also be seen, as Pliny the Elder had said, in Ethiopia. They are to be found, too, in the Andaman Sea, not far from Sumatra, where the archipelago provides an appropriate environment for a great array of monstrosities:

> There are many different kinds of people in these isles. In one, there is a race of great stature, like giants, foul and horrible to look at; they have one eye only, in the middle of their foreheads. They eat raw flesh and raw fish. In another part, there are ugly folk without heads, who have eyes in each shoulder; their mouths are round, like a horseshoe, in the middle of their chest. In yet another part there are headless men whose eyes and mouths are on their backs. And there are in another place folk with flat faces, without noses or eyes; but they have two small holes instead of eyes, and a flat lipless mouth. In another isle there are ugly fellows whose upper lip is so big that when they sleep in the sun they cover all their faces with it . . . (137)

The list continues, to include centaurs (save that only their feet are equine), ape-men, hermaphrodites, eight-toed people who nevertheless walk on their knees, and the pygmies dismissed by Polo. *Mandeville*'s account of the Uniped gives details that the Vikings did not have leisure to describe:

> There is still another isle where the people have only one foot, which is so broad that it will cover all the body and shade it from the sun. They will run so fast on this one foot that it is a marvel to see them. (118)

Here indeed is God's plenty. The text claims that it has been ratified by a pope, and with good reason (189). The marvels at the margins of the world are contained within an orthodox Christian cosmography. Jerusalem is portrayed at the centre of the world. The ten lost tribes of Israel still exist; they are to be found near the Caspian Sea, where they pay rent to the Amazons. The world itself is segmented by four rivers which have their source in the earthly paradise, the 'highest land on earth', the temporary home of Adam and Eve but now prohibited to humankind by the wild terrain and its wilder beasts, the speed and noise of the rivers, and by 'the flaming sword that God set up before the entrance so that no man should enter' (184–5). This last detail, but nothing else in the description of the earthly paradise, comes from the book of Genesis. *Mandeville* weaves a rich tapestry, drawing images from an enormous variety of sources, drawn from pagan as well as Christian beliefs and from earlier travel texts. It describes a globe full of detail, and teeming not just with riches, but also with incident and variety. In its Christian design *Mandeville* portrays an Old World that, as we shall see, prevented Columbus from understanding what he had stumbled on. In its readiness to describe if not to welcome a world of new and strange experiences, the text stands at the gateway to the modern. Its shapes may be detected in texts as different as Spanish and Elizabethan travel narratives, Milton's *Paradise Lost* (1667) and Poe's *The Narrative of Arthur Gordon Pym* (1838).

The Columbian complex

No doubt helped by the convenient couplet, the name Columbus and the date 1492 must be known to every English-speaking child. The Columbian landfall has been accorded special significance in western history. Yet it was just one stage in the process of Renaissance exploration, including the first circumnavigation of the earth by the Magellan expedition in 1519–22, which transformed our knowledge of the globe. In addition, the textual evidence for Columbus's voyages was, for a very long time, slight indeed. His journals were kept secret by the Spanish royal court, and were then lost. An abstract made by the Dominican historian Bartolomé de Las Casas remained unknown until 1791. It was first published by Martín Fernández de Navarrete in a Spanish collection of documents in 1825, and first appeared in an English translation, in Boston, two years later. The biography by Columbus's illegitimate son Fernando, first published in Venice in Italian in 1571, was only translated into English in 1704.[20] It was not until 1828, with Washington Irving's *The Life and Voyages of Christopher Columbus*, drawing on Navarrete's collection and published both in London and New York, that the personal fame of Columbus was finally established. By 1900 Irving's book had gone through 175 editions and abridgements, including the one for Heroes of the Nations mentioned earlier. In contrast, the only evidence circulated immediately after the first landfall was 'an account of the facts, thus abridged' to slightly less than 3000 words, dated 15 February 1493 and written by Columbus shortly before he arrived back in Spain. The response to the letter, however, was almost telegraphic. It was promptly translated into Latin, French, German and Italian, and by 1500 had spread throughout Europe.[21]

It is possible that Columbus's 'account of the facts' was widely circulated because, like Polo and *Mandeville*, it combined mercantilism and proselytism within a heroic narrative. The islands are full of fruits, spices and precious metals, as well as natives 'very inclined' to Christianity (197). Their inclination is the more welcome because, apparently, they have no concept of property. It is easy therefore for Columbus to take 'possession' of the five islands which he collectively calls 'las Indias' (191). As did the Vikings five centuries earlier, Columbus assimilates by renaming. One of the islands has the aboriginal name of Guanahani. Columbus calls it ' "San Salvador", in remembrance of the Divine Majesty, Who has marvellously bestowed all this' (191). The narrative easily takes on tones of wonderment. The natives are as beautiful and naked as they are guileless and affectionate. The islands have mountains loftier than those in Tenerife, yet covered 'with trees of a thousand kinds and tall, so that they seem to touch the sky' (192). Although he is writing about November, Columbus recalls hearing the song of a thousand birds, including the nightingale. Columbus has an eye to the future, as well, for his description of the island of Hispaniola (one of the Greater Antilles) blends the pastoral with property development:

Española is a marvel. The sierras and the mountains, the plains, the champaigns, are so lovely and so rich for planting and sowing, for breeding cattle of every kind, for building towns and villages. The harbours of the sea here are such as cannot be believed to exist unless they have been seen, and so with the rivers, many and great, and of good water, the majority of which contain gold. (194)

It has sometimes been said that American promotional literature starts here; but the Vikings had preceded Columbus, who does not in any case conceive the land as part of the Americas. The reference to the nightingale, which is not native to America, indicates that images from elsewhere have been projected onto the land. Columbus's letter reveals the influence of Polo, *Mandeville* and their predecessors. He shapes his islands to his understanding of Polo's East. He fortifies a town on Hispaniola so that it is particularly well fitted for trade with 'the Grand Khan' (198). As with Polo, too, the greatest treasures are just over the horizon. The natives obligingly tell him of an island populated by people with no hair but with 'incalculable gold' (200). In these circumstances it is *Mandeville* that provides the appropriate imagery. Columbus finds none of that text's 'human monstrosities', but they cannot be far away (200). He hears of the island of 'Carib', occupied by cannibals; of 'Matitino', populated only by warrior women; and of 'Avan' (Havana), where 'people are born with tails' (198). The demonisation of Cuba by the United States thus has a venerable history.

Two voyages later Columbus was still trying to accommodate his discoveries to earlier models. The narrative of his Third Voyage tells of a westward passage in which 'the ships mounted gently nearer to the sky'. This observational error prompted Columbus to revise Ptolemy. Ptolemy had not seen the southern hemisphere, and reasonably conjectured that the earth was round. On the basis of his experience, Columbus was able to correct this. The earth had 'the shape of a pear', because as 'Holy Scripture' (and also *Mandeville*) dictated, the earthly paradise was located in the East, on higher ground.[22] Columbus went to his death believing that he had found the earthly paradise. In other words, Columbus shaped his findings to fit the old Christian cosmography. This state of affairs could not last long. It has been argued that 'America' is quite properly named after Amerigo Vespucci. For in his letter of March 1503 to Lorenzo Pietro de Medici, Vespucci reported that he had found 'a new world'. The ancients, he said, had lied:

> My last voyage has proved it, for I have found a continent in that southern part; more populous and more full of animals than our Europe, or Asia, or Africa, and even more temperate and pleasant than any other region known to us.

It is likely that Vespucci, too, told some lies. His first two voyages may not have taken place, and he reported meeting giants, and natives so healthy 'that they live for 150 years, and are rarely sick'. But the central fact, of the existence of a continent unknown to the ancients, rang true. The letter to de Medici, under the title *Mundus Novus*, was promptly printed in Rome and shortly thereafter in many European cities. It was as 'America' that this New World first appeared on a map in 1507, and the name stuck despite the misgivings of its cartographer, Martin Waldseemüller.[23]

Yet it is the first Columbian landfall which is treated as the benchmark, starting the debate over the value and meaning of the New World. Columbus, one might say, became a *cause célèbre* long before he became a celebrity. The French priest and intellectual l'Abbé Raynal remarked in 1770 that 'no event has been so interesting to mankind in general, and to the inhabitants of Europe in particular, as the discovery of the new world, and the passage to India by the Cape of Good Hope'.[24] The New World was now competing with the East for the attention of Europeans. It both took on some of the imaginative structures that had been applied to the East, and added some of its own. The result, as scholars have begun to show in recent years, is a network of cross-cultural relations of even greater complexity than had existed before. What follows is necessarily a simplification of a multivalent circumatlantic discourse that we have still fully to understand.

A good place to start is Mark Twain's ironic commentary on the first landfall, to be found in 'Pudd'nhead Wilson's Calendar': '*October 12. – The Discovery.* – It was wonderful to find America, but it would have been more wonderful to miss it.'[25] The sentence points to the universal acceptance of the significance of the landfall, but suggests that there has been a division of opinion over its consequences. Europeans, who for more than four centuries constituted the majority of those who migrated to America, did not unequivocally approve of the discovery. When Raynal offered a prize for the best essay answering the question 'Has the discovery of America been beneficial or harmful to the human race', the competitors were divided. Perhaps Raynal was, too, for he made no award. The 'dispute of the New World', as the scholar Antonello Gerbi called it, has continued to divide American as well as European writers. As we shall see, Twain was by no means alone.

Despite Twain, the first and larger body of opinion is celebratory. No one summed up this view more confidently than Francisco López de Gómara, who in 1552 proclaimed the return to Spain of Cortés (and his own employment as the conquistador's secretary) by asserting that 'the greatest event since the creation of the world, second only to the incarnation and death of he who created it, is the discovery of the Indies'. The reasons for celebration have changed over time, but may be summed up in terms of four themes. The first, implicit in de Gómara's assertion, was religious. Even a Puritan could join with a Catholic in contemplating the possibility that the whole world would now be illuminated by the gospel. In *Magnalia Christi Americana*, probably begun in 1693, the Massachusetts minister and historian Cotton Mather (1663–1728) belatedly marked the bicentennial by noting the result of Columbus's 'wonderful *Impulse*'. Indeed, as we shall see, it was not only Puritans who would examine the implications of Columbus's belief that he had found the earthly paradise, affirming that America was a land reserved for the godly.[26]

The second theme was philosophical, using the New World as a vehicle for speculation upon human nature. One of the first writers to develop this theme was the Frenchman Michel de Montaigne (1533–92), in his essay 'Of the Caniballes'. By the time, 1580, that Montaigne had published his essay,

Columbus's informants had been proved right. Not only did cannibals exist in America, they had become part of its symbology. But the account of them in Montaigne's essay, given here in John Florio's 1603 translation, is the very reverse of horror. The cannibals:

> hath no kinde of traffike [trade], no knowledge of Letters, no intelligence of numbers, no name of magistrate, nor of politike superioritie; no use of service, of riches or of povertie; no contracts, no successions, no partitions, no occupation but idle; no respect of kindred, but common, no apparrell but natural, no manuring of lands, no use of wine, corne or mettle. The very words that import lying, falshood, treason, dissimulations, covetousnes, envie, detraction, and pardon, were never heard of amongst them . . .
>
> Furthermore, they live in a country of so exceeding pleasant and temperate situation, that as my testimonies have told me, it is verie rare to see a sicke body amongst them; and they have further assured me they never saw any man there, either shaking with the palsy, toothless, with eies dropping, or crooked and stooping through age.[27]

This passage is to a large extent a fine, if wily, example of the rhetoric of negation discussed in Chapter 1. The first sentence presents an apparently neutral list of the qualities of a sophisticated European economy which the cannibals lack. The second sentence marks an abrupt change in the character of the list, showing that they also lack the corruption on which such an economy rests. Together, the two sentences show that Montaigne has an excellent 'knowledge of Letters', and is uncomfortably a member and beneficiary of the economy he deplores. The superiority of the state of nature is confirmed by the closing portrait of a version of Vespucci's medical utopia. The state of nature, Montaigne suggests, is without original sin. The theme would be taken up by Rousseau in *Du Contrat Social* (1762), and would become an important element of the New World/Old World dialectic central to transatlantic relations and explored most fully by Henry James.

The third theme was scientific. From José de Acosta's *Historia natural y moral de las Indias* of 1590 to Alexander von Humboldt's *Kosmos* of 1845, the landfall was associated with the new experimental methodology. Acosta, for instance, drew attention to Columbus's navigation, noting 'that the Ancients had no knowledge of the secrets of the Loadstone'. The German astronomer Johan Kepler (1571–1630) compared Columbus with Galileo, and favoured Columbus's empiricism over Ptolemy's theoretical speculation – but omitted the navigator's erroneous conclusion discussed above. The fourth theme was mercantile. The Spanish exploration, from the very beginning, was in search, in the words of Cortés, of 'gold, pearls, precious stones and spices, and many wonderful and unknown things'. The image of America as a continent rich in resources was reformulated in capitalist terms by the Scots economist Adam Smith (1723–90), who repeated Raynal, but with the conviction of Gómara, when in *The Wealth of Nations* he asserted that the discovery of America was one of 'the two greatest and most important events recorded in the history of mankind'. The New World and the easy passage to the East

Indies opened 'a new and inexhaustible market to all the commodities of Europe', giving rise 'to new divisions of labour and improvements of art'. In view of the status of the United States as the world's most powerful capitalist nation, the publication date of *The Wealth of Nations*, 1776, has taken on a significance that Smith might have regretted but would almost certainly have regarded as appropriate. In 1893, two centuries after Mather remembered Columbus's landfall in Christian terms, the Chicago Columbian Exposition celebrated it in terms of technology and the capitalist market. The exposition cost $30 million to stage and was larger than the centennial expositions of Philadelphia in 1876 and Paris in 1889 combined. A large statue of Columbus acted as the centrepiece of the exposition, looking out on the buildings containing all the products of American ingenuity. Some contemporary journalists described the exposition as the fulfilment of Columbus's dream, while Frederick Jackson Turner used the occasion to present his frontier theory. The quatercentennial was the highpoint of Columbus's reputation as an all-American symbol.[28]

The quincentennial was far less celebratory. One of the best known of the books issued to mark the event was Kirkpatrick Sale's *The Conquest of Paradise*, which – as its title perhaps suggests – is a catalogue of the adversities which resulted from the Columbian landfall.[29] Sale could be regarded as a member of Twain's second group, those who thought it would have been better to have missed America. Smaller in number but more vociferous than the celebrants, they tend to explore two themes. The first is that the discovery of America was a disaster for those who were discovered and for such third parties as the Africans who were enslaved. The settlement established by Columbus in 1492 on Hispaniola began a process of exploitative imperialism which would be repeated, with variations, across the continent, leading directly to present-day concerns about the destruction of the Amazonian rain forest. Before the arrival of the Spanish, Hispaniola had been occupied by a tribe of food-gathering natives called the Tainos. The men were forced into labour and the women into concubinage. Those who resisted were maimed or killed. The crops were consumed by cattle imported by the settlers. Illnesses such as measles and smallpox completed the attrition begun by social dislocation. Within a few years the tribe was extinct.

In 1912 a Spanish journalist, Julián Juderías, coined the phrase 'the Black Legend' to describe the contempt in which Spain was held for the attitudes and acts which led to such genocide. We shall shortly see some English examples of that contempt. This is not to say, of course, that the English, or any other colonising nation for that matter, were exempt from the practices which the Spanish initiated in the New World. Indeed, it was Spanish priests who first criticised those practices. In 1539 the Dominican jurist Francisco de Vitoria (1485?–1546?) lectured at the University of Salamanca on 'these barbarians in the New World, commonly called Indians'. In a closely reasoned argument, Vitoria asserted that Spain had numbers of rights in the New World – including rights of exploitation, government, trade, and conversion to Christianity. Yet it was also clear to him that the natives were neither juvenile nor mad; and

certainly were not 'continual enemies of the Christian religion'. It would therefore, he concluded, 'be harsh to deny to them, who have never done us any
wrong, the rights we concede to Saracens and Jews'. The question, then, was
not to how to justify absolute dominion, but rather how to regulate relations
between contending parties, relations which were better exercised peacefully,
because 'amity between men is part of natural law'. In pursuit of this Vitoria
set down a number of principles which would become central to modern
international law.[30] It was another Dominican, Bartolomé de Las Casas, who
listed the atrocities which had troubled Vitoria. Las Casas went to Hispaniola
in 1502 as a settler and underwent a conversion experience, to become the
first Christian priest ordained in the New World. He wrote a number of
works, including the abstract of the log of Columbus's First Voyage. In 1552
he published in Seville his most notorious book, the *Brevissima relación de
la destruyción de las Indias*. It was translated into Latin, Dutch, English and
French. It was from accounts of Spanish cruelty to the natives like this that
Montaigne drew his inspiration for 'Of the Caniballes'. As an alternative Las
Casas proposed the conversion of the natives to Christianity by the peaceful
means of trade. He also suggested to the Spanish royal court that it should use
Africans instead of submitting the natives of the Caribbean to heavy labour. It
is one of the deepest ironies that Las Casas can be regarded both as the source
of the 'Black Legend' and as the initiator of the Black slave trade.

The second theme is that the discovery of America was a disaster for those
who discovered it. This theme is hinted at in Bacon's *The New Atlantis*, but
came into full flower with the publication in 1749 of the first volume of the
Histoire naturelle by the Comte de Buffon. A New World, said Buffon, is an
undeveloped world and therefore threatening:

> Here the earth never saw her surface adorned with those rich crops, which demon-
> strate her fecundity and constitute the opulence of polished nations. In this aban-
> doned condition, everything languishes, corrupts, and proves abortive.

Buffon, however, looked forward to the time when American farming would
transform the continent into 'the most fertile, the most wholesome, and the
richest in the whole world'.[31] His work initiated a debate about the wisdom
of having discovered America. Raynal was a relatively restrained contributor
to the debate. The least restrained contribution was by a Dutch monk. Cornelius de Pauw's *Recherches philosophiques sur les Américains*, published in
1768–9, is a brilliant orchestration of adverse images inherited from such
texts as *Mandeville* and supplemented by over two and a half centuries of
anti-American prejudices. It provided the fullest vision to date of America as
hell:

> At the time of the discovery of America, its climate was unfavorable to most quad-
> ruped animals, which in fact are one-sixth smaller in the New World than their
> counterparts in the old continent. In particular, the climate was injurious to the
> natives who, to an astonishing degree, were stupified, enervated, and vitiated in all
> parts of their organism.

The land itself, either bristling with mountain peaks or covered with forests and marshlands, presented the aspect of an immense and sterile desert. The first adventurers to settle there underwent the horrors of famine or the great sufferings of thirst. The Spaniards, from time to time, were forced to eat Americans [natives] and even other Spaniards for lack of nourishment . . . The first French colonists sent into this hapless world also ended by eating each other . . .

The surface of the earth, full of putrefaction, was flooded with lizards, snakes, serpents, reptiles, and insects that were monstrous by their size and the power of their poison extracted from the juice of this earth, so barren, so vitiated, so abandoned . . .

De Pauw believed that America had been swamped by a second flood centuries after Noah's. Twice damned, the continent was so malignant that it infected with syphilis everyone who breathed its tainted air. It had been believed for some time that syphilis had been America's gift to the world. De Pauw blamed a monk of another order, a Benedictine with the appropriate name of Boil. Boil had sailed with Columbus, but hated him so much that he infected Europe. As a result Columbus was excommunicated, imprisoned, and 'repented for having discovered a new world'. Many have since agreed with Twain that it would have been better had Columbus missed America. Sigmund Freud, for instance, only half in jest, asserted that America was 'a bad experiment conducted by Providence'. The events since Freud made that remark in 1926 have prompted many to agree with him.[32]

To the Virginian voyage

Bloody Mary was only partly to blame. There were a number of reasons why the English showed only occasional interest in America before the later years of the sixteenth century. The papal division of America between Spain and Portugal had been confirmed by the Treaty of Tordesillas of 1494. In the sixty-odd years before the accession of Elizabeth I, the English monarch most willing to ignore the interdict was Henry VII (1457–1509). Yet when on 24 June 1497 John Cabot made the first definite European landfall on the American mainland since the Vikings, his sponsor was more occupied with domestic peripheries. Henry VII had simultaneously to wage war with James IV of Scotland, and crush a rebellion in Cornwall. Further voyages, by Cabot and others, produced little to excite his interest: no gold, no pearls, just a few wild cats, some parrots, and a couple of Micmac Indians, who changed their furs for English dress, and were paraded by Henry in Westminster. Sebastian Cabot, John's son, made an attempt in 1508 to find the North-West Passage to Cathay. A Venetian account of 1536 noted, with a mixture of sarcasm and relief, that its failure brought to an end the first period of English New World exploration:

Sebastian Cabot, the son of a Venetian . . . had two ships from Henry, King of England, father of the present Henry, who has become a Lutheran and worse, and with 300 men navigated so far that he found the sea frozen . . . Whence it was

65

necessary for Cabot to turn back without effecting what he intended, but with a resolve to return to that project at a time when the sea should not be frozen. He found the King dead, and his son cared little for such an enterprise.

Sebastian Cabot gave up and spent the next forty years in the service of Spain. His project would lead to the exploitation of the cod banks of Newfoundland. But Henry VIII (1491–1547) had other fish to fry: a succession of six wives, and three doubting advisors, the Thomases Wolsey, Cromwell and More. Henry's son, Edward VI (1537–53), did not live long enough to translate his Protestantism into an overseas policy. Mary I (1516–58) gained her sanguinary soubriquet from her oppression of Protestants. Her devotion to Catholicism was confirmed by her marriage in 1554 to Philip II of Spain. The neglect of the New World by her father and half-brother was now replaced by an enthusiastic enforcement of the Catholic prohibition of any English interest in it.[33]

It follows that before 1558 there was barely any English writing about America. A 1511 translation of a German broadside talks of an America containing 'many wonders of beestes and fowles' previously unknown; cannibals who prefer their relatives smoked; and a lifestyle, for those who are not eaten, that is so healthy that Vespucci's estimate of longevity has had to be doubled to 300 years.[34] It is clear that the discovery had been incorporated into a textual system which owed more to *Mandeville* than to the realities of Spanish settlement. It is therefore perhaps appropriate that the first known literary use of America by an Englishman, and the first example of the New World/Old World dialectic, is as a vehicle for political philosophy. It is an indicator of its status as a contribution to an intellectual debate that Sir Thomas More's *Utopia* was first published in Latin, in Louvain in 1516.

The complex construction of the text ensures that *Utopia* has an argument that is far from ponderous. The first edition was prefaced by a group of letters, two of them from More to his friend Peter Giles (1486–1533), a citizen of Antwerp, editor (suitably) of *Aesop's Fables*, and a character in the text. The letters seem to confirm the veracity of the main text, which consists of two books, each with its own narrator. The first, narrated by 'More' (the reason why inverted commas are used will become apparent in a moment), is largely a dialogue between the narrator and Raphael Hythloday. The second is an account by Hythloday of the island of Utopia, similar in size to England. Hythloday is a learned traveller, who 'accompanied Vespucci on the last three of his four voyages, accounts of which are now common reading everywhere'. This last statement is correct. *The First Four Voyages of Amerigo Vespucci* was initially published in Lisbon in 1504, quickly appeared in several editions, and was widely read. 'More' and Giles eagerly ask him questions, not 'about monsters, which are the routine of travelers' tales', but about 'governments solidly established and sensibly ruled'. The suggestion that this is going to be a straightforward political treatise has, however, already been undermined by linguistic and geographical information. One of the prefatory letters contains a Mandevillean touch, a Utopian alphabet. We are also told that when Vespucci returns to Europe from the furthest point in his last voyage, north of Rio de Janeiro, Hythloday remains behind and travels further westward from there, 'by strange good fortune', to Ceylon, and thence back to his home in Portugal. In other words, Hythloday circled the globe before Magellan's party; and somewhere on the journey he visited Utopia, once connected by an isthmus to a continent (America?) but now isolated by a channel dug by its founder, Utopus. Just over two centuries later, in *Gulliver's Travels* (1726), Swift would use a similar landform and location for Brobdingnag, also the purpose of developing a commentary on European behaviour and institutions. The comparison with *Gulliver's Travels*, however, shows that More's viewpoint is far less splenetic, and also far from clear. In the first place, it is difficult to establish a clear authorial viewpoint. 'More' the narrator cannot be taken as the voice of More the author, for there is evidence that 'More' puts forward views that would be anathema to More. Second, the debate in Book 1 acts to question the detailed conclusions of Book 2. Third, *Utopia* differs from Phaeacia, in *The Odyssey*, and Plato's Atlantis by occasionally using the tactic, later used by Swift, of coarse comic inversion. Hence the inversion of the myth of El Dorado. Although the Utopians 'have accumulated a vast treasure . . . they hold gold and silver up to scorn in every possible way':

> their chamber pots and stools – all their humblest vessels, for use in the common halls and private homes – are made of gold and silver. The chains and heavy fetters of slaves are also made of these metals. Finally, criminals who are to bear through life the mark of some disgraceful act are forced to wear golden rings on their ears, golden bands on their fingers, golden chains around their necks, and even golden crowns on their heads.[35]

Was More suspicious of *The First Four Voyages of Amerigo Vespucci*? We do not know. It is clear, though, that the weight and detail of the description of Utopia, apparently authenticated by that text, is at odds with the shifty narrative structure. It could be argued that More, along with Vespucci, is one of the first transatlantic tricksters. He will not be the last.

Utopia did not appear in English until 1551, sixteen years after More had been beheaded by Henry VIII for refusing to reject papal authority. He found that he could not play tricks with his religious belief. It was his brother-in-law who first depicted America in the vernacular, and in its own right. John Rastell's play, *The Four Elements*, was written sometime after 1517. Rastell was a builder, lawyer, printer and writer. He also tried to open the trade routes from England to America. In 1517 Rastell diverted Henry VIII sufficiently from his other interests to obtain permission to trade in foreign parts. His print shop had given him access to all the latest information on America, but due to some skullduggery by his partners the expedition got no further than Cork. The play records his anger at the failure of a venture which seemed so promising. Yet the failure does not diminish a sense of imperial space, found in the mythology of Alexander, made possible once more by Vespucci's *Mundus Novus*, and proved by the Cabot voyages:

This See is called the great Occyan,
So great it is that never man
Coude tell it sith the worlde began,
  Tyll nowe, within this twenty yere,
Westwarde be founde new landes
That we never harde tell of before this
By wrytynge nor other meanys,
  Yet many nowe have ben there.

And that contrey is so large of rome,
Much lenger than all christendome,
  Without fable or gyle;
For dyvers maryners have it tryed
And sayled streyght by the coste syde
  Above fyve thousand myle.

This is no El Dorado. Rastell gives a realistic merchant's view of the land's resources: no iron, but copper, and an enormous amount of wood. The fish are so plentiful that seamen can fill a hundred boatloads per year. But it is the French rather than the English that have the trade. Rastell's brief account of America is set as a nationalist lament:

O, what a thynge had be than,
Yf that they be englyshe men
  Myght have ben the furst of all
That there shulde have take possessyon
And made furst buyldynge and habytacion,
  A memory perpetuall!

And also what an honorable thynge,
Bothe to the realme and to the kynge,
To have had his domynyon extendynge
  There into so farre a grounde,
Whiche the noble kynge of late memory,
The moste wyse prynce the seventh Herry,
  Causyd furst for to be founde.[36]

If it was Elizabeth I (1533–1603) who began to answer Rastell's demand for an extending dominion, she did so largely as an adjunct of her opposition to Spain and the Catholic Church. She began her reign in 1558 by reversing Mary's prohibition of English involvement in the New World. Her religious policies led in 1570 to her excommunication by the Pope; and the last eighteen years of her reign were marked by open war with Spain. Elizabethan texts which deal with the New World consequently tend to handle four interlinked themes. The first, simplest and most self-serving was an attempt to dislodge Spanish claims to ownership by disputing priority of landfall. In 1578 the scientist John Dee (1527–1608) compiled a list of those explorers who would substantiate a British claim to America. Dee mentioned Cabot's mainland landfall and Martin Frobisher's north-western explorations, but also St Brendan, and the Welsh Prince Madoc who, it was believed, escaped Welsh civil war by sailing west in AD 1170. The story of Madoc was elaborated in David Powel's *Historie of Cambria* (1584). On Madoc's return to Wales, he spoke of the contrast between 'the pleasant and fruitfull countreys that he had seene' and the 'barren and wilde grounde' over which the Welsh were fighting. He persuaded sufficient people to fill ten ships to return to America with him. Nothing further was heard of him, but tales of finding Welsh Indians persisted at least until 1805. The most industrious exponent of English America was Richard Hakluyt (1552?–1616). In 1582 he began his *Divers Voyages touching the Discovery of America* by repeating the letters patent given by Henry VII to John Cabot. In 1589 Hakluyt continued his project with his enormous collection of exploration narratives, totalling three quarters of a million words and with an appropriately epic title: *The principall Navigations, Voiages and Discoveries of the English nation, made by Sea or over Land, in the most remote and farthest distant Quarters of the earth at any time within the compasse of these 1500 yeeres*. The 'Epistle Dedicatory in the first edition' indicates that the collection is the literary equivalent of the Armada the year before, scattering 'the obloquy of our nation' with its enormous battery of documents, some of them taken from *Mandeville*. Further editions followed in 1598 and 1600, the latter extending material on 'the fourth part of the world, more commonly than properly called America; but by the chiefest authors The New World'. Then as now, naming as well as dating was subject to nationalist sensitivities. After Hakluyt's death his collection was continued by Samuel Purchas. *Purchas his Pilgrimes* was widely read, and had an impact on Cotton Mather a century before Coleridge, if to less spectacular effect. In *Magnalia Christi Americana*, Mather claimed that America had been settled by 'Britains . . . *Three or Four Hundred Years before* the Spaniards *coming thither*'.[37]

The second Elizabethan theme is Hispanophobia. The earliest views of American natives are therefore as the victims of Spanish atrocities. The most useful source was Las Casas' *Brevissima relación*, first translated into English in 1583. It portrays the natives living in a state of primal innocence and, paradoxically, in social organisations not unlike those of Europe. Then the Spanish arrive:

> The Spaniards with their Horses, their Speares and Lances, began to commit murders, and strange cruelties: they entred into Townes, Borowes, and Villages, sparing neither children nor old men, neither women with childe, neither them that lay In, but that they ripped their bellies, and cut them in peeces, as if they had beene opening of Lambes shut up in their fold . . . They took the little soules by the heeles, ramping them from the mothers dugges, and crushed their heads against the clifts. Others they cast into the Rivers laughing and mocking . . .

There are other atrocity stories. One describes a child being dismembered and fed to dogs. Another anticipates the Nazi technology of mass murder: gibbets large enough to hang thirteen people, who were then put to the torch while they were still alive. The genocide was such that Las Casas estimated that some three million natives had been killed in Hispaniola alone.[38]

Such atrocity stories became a regular part of the imagery of America. There were a number of reasons for this. Tensions between Britain and Spain recurred until the mid-eighteenth century, ensuring that Las Casas was often available, in fresh translations and embellishments. Extended extracts appeared in Purchas's *Pilgrimes* between 1613 and 1626, while translations of the complete text appeared in 1689 and 1745. One translation was published in 1656 by John Phillips (1631–1706), the nephew and secretary of John Milton. Entitled *The Tears of the Indians*, it was dedicated to Oliver Cromwell. Its illustrations confirm how widespread the 'Black Legend' had become. They were drawn from a 1596 volume in the series, often simply called *America*, published in Frankfurt by the Flemish engraver Theodor de Bry (1528–98). One illustration shows a Spaniard tending the fire under a mass gibbet, while his compatriot swings a child by the ankles, ready to smash his head against a wall. A second suggests cannibalism; dismembered parts hang from hooks, as if in a butcher's shopfront. The text concludes that some twenty million natives have been slaughtered. It calls on the English 'to revenge the Blood of that innocent People'. Such atrocity stories are highly effective as propaganda, and are easily transferable. For instance, reports of the Massacre of Fort William Henry (1757), during the French and Indian War, transformed the Spanish into French, and the natives into dogs:

> The French immediately after the Capitulation, most perfidiously, let their Indian Blood-Hounds loose upon our People . . . The Throats of most, if not all the Women, were cut, their Bellies ripped open, their Bowels torn out and thrown upon the Faces of their dead or dying Bodies . . . the Children were taken by the Heels, and their Brains beat out against the Trees or Stones, and not one of them saved.

The English, of course, were not exempt from bad behaviour. If they used Las Casas to deplore genocide, they also took up his suggestion about the virtues of an alternative labour source. In 1562 Sir John Hawkins showed that it was possible to turn a handsome profit by shipping African slaves to Hispaniola. It quickly became an industry. The city of Bristol, once noted for the Cabot explorations, was one of a number of ports which made much money from slaving until the trade was outlawed in 1807.[39]

The Elizabethans tended to believe, as some English do now, that English bad behaviour was somehow different from that of others. Images of Spanish and French atrocities quoted above are marked with hints of the diabolic. In contrast, the English thought themselves to be the elect. 'God is English', claimed John Aylmer, Bishop of London, when in 1558 he shielded the new Queen from the 'late blowne Blaste' of John Knox against women in power. From this belief comes the third Elizabethan New World theme: a concatenation of images promoting English expansion as part of a Protestant mission. If one became rich and famous in the process, it was simply further evidence of God's grace. Promotional texts were often impelled by a utopian drive, to be seen, for instance, in the translations of John Frampton, a Bristol merchant expelled from Seville by the Inquisition. He spent the latter part of his life encouraging English expansion by 'Englishing' Spanish texts. Among them were a Castilian edition of Polo's *Travels* (1579), *The Arte of Navigation* (1581), and *Joyfull Newes out of the New Founde Worlde* (1577), which detailed the wonderful crops that could be harvested in America, including tobacco, which was thought to have 'merveilous Medicinable vertues'. More's *Utopia* had become part of the explorer's geographical furniture. It inspired Sir Humphrey Gilbert (1539?–83) to make plans, in his *Discourse of a Discovery for a New Passage to Cataia* (1576), for an English settlement in America as well as for exploration of the North-West Passage to China. Both would serve the cause against Spain. Settlement would promote a trade war, would help the problem of poverty in England, and line some pockets. When two years later Gilbert set out on his first expedition to America, the poet Thomas Churchyard (1520?–1604?), whose verse had the smell of his surname, celebrated his departure and summed up this theme: 'For Countreys wealth, for private gayne/or glory seeke we all.' The expedition got no further than the Cape Verde Islands. A second one in 1583 was somewhat more successful. It reached Newfoundland, which Gilbert annexed for the English crown; but he could persuade nobody to settle there, and he was drowned when his ship went down in a storm on the return voyage. This setback only increased the sense of mission. In his account of Gilbert's last voyage, Edward Haie argued that Cabot's discovery was part of God's grand plan, for:

> the countreys lying North of Florida, God hath reserved the same to be reduced unto Christian civility by the English nation . . . the English nation onely hath right . . . to prosecute effectually the full possession of those so ample and pleasant countries apperteining unto the crowne of England: the same (as is to be conjectured by infallible arguments of the worlds end approching) . . . by the revolution and course of Gods word and religion, which from the beginning hath moved from the East, towards, & at last unto the West, where it is like to end.[40]

Running as an undercurrent beneath the belief in the Protestant mission, and perhaps reinforcing its apocalyptic sense, was the fourth theme, the exotic. For instance, Edward Topsell's *Historie of Foure-Footed Beastes* (1607) included animals such as dogs and horses together with creatures that were neither European nor domestic. The book ignored Polo and instead used the authority of the Bible to assert that the unicorn existed. It drew on travellers' tales from Libya to depict the Lamia, which had 'a Womans face, and very beautifull', with four legs and a tail; from India, for her male counterpart, the Mantichora, with a body resembling a lion but with the head of a well-groomed Elizabethan male, a triple row of teeth and a spiked tail; and from Patagonia, for the Su, which did not seem to resemble anything, but was 'a very deformed shape, and monstrous presence, a great ravener and an untameable wild beast'. Many other writers gave close attention to the 'savage', often placed at the nexus of the human and the bestial, and thus frequently associated with cannibalism. For instance, Shakespeare jokes twice, at the expense of Falstaff's voraciousness and at the (knowing?) simplicity of the Host of the Garter Inn when, in *The Merry Wives of Windsor* (1602), the Host expects that Falstaff will 'speak like an Anthropophaginian'. Illustrations to texts and maps muster around the savage some enormous creatures, such as armadillos acting as horses and alligators as big as whales. Size had perhaps become more important, because there were now fewer monsters than had appeared in the East of *Mandeville*. For instance, while Hakluyt reprinted an account of Unipeds seen in Armenia, none was reported in the New World, despite the Viking encounter. Enough of the exotic remained, though, to make America exciting, even fearsome. In 1597 an English translator of foreign travel texts anticipated that headless men would be discovered in America. As we shall see, Ralegh believed that he was right. Like Topsell's *Historie*, such beliefs would survive the realities of settlement, influencing De Pauw, and even Diderot's *Encyclopédie* (1751), which talks of an America populated by pygmies and giants, winged serpents and savages whose knees bend backwards.[41]

The four themes are to be found in three texts which can be used to sum up Elizabethan America. The first, indeed the first book written by an Englishman about America, is Thomas Harriot's *A briefe and true report of the new found land of Virginia*. Harriot (1560–1621) was a scientist who lived in Virginia for two years from 1586. The first edition of his book was promptly published on his return to England in 1588. A second edition, published in 1590, became the first volume in de Bry's *America*. It appeared in Latin, French and German as well as English, and included, as an appendix, drawings by John White engraved by de Bry. The title of the text claims scientific objectivity, and to an extent this is true; but it also locates itself in the textual system inherited from the East. It is structured as a list like the *Wonders of the East*, although there is little that is monstrous about it. Like Polo's *Travels*, *A briefe and true report* combines proselytism with mercantilism. It begins with an account of 'marchantable commodities'. Harriot describes a Virginia that is rich in such resources as wood, grapes, copper, pearls, deer and 'Civet cattes'. The silk worms are 'as bigge as our ordinary walnuttes', and properly managed 'there will rise as great profite in time to the Virginians, as there of doth now to the Persians, Turkes, Italians and Spaniards'.[42]

Similarly managed, the natives will become good servants and Protestants. Harriot spends some time analysing the native religion, seeking similar doctrines, such as the immortality of the soul, which would make it 'the easier and sooner reformed' (25). This is done without the atrocities that marked accounts of Spanish settlement. The natives can be violent, but two circumstances assist the English. One is providential. Any native village which resists them is struck down with disease. Harriot, blending science with the supernatural, calls it 'this marvellous accident' (29). The other has no trace of the supernatural, but Harriot presents it as a list of European wonders:

Most thinges they sawe with us, as Methematicall instruments, sea compasses, the vertue of the loadstone in drawing yron, a perspective glasse whereby was shewed manie strange sightes, burning glasses, wildfire woorkes, gunnes, bookes, writing and reading, spring clocks that seeme to goe of themselves, and manie other thinges that wee had, were so straunge unto them, and so farre exceeded their capacities to comprehend the reason and meanes how they should be made and done, that they thought they were rather the works of gods then of men . . . (27)

Together, Providence and technology will persuade the natives into a relationship which Harriot describes in terms drawn from the marriage ceremony in the *Book of Common Prayer* (1549): 'there is good hope that they may be brought through discreet dealing and governement to the imbracing of the trueth, and consequently to honour, obey, feare and love us' (29). There is no suggestion of sexual relations here; that will emerge in later texts. Hints that the interior is even better provide the hope that the union of white master and red servant, together with abundant crops, a salubrious climate and medicinal plants such as the sassafras – here Harriot cites Frampton's *Joyfull Newes* – could produce a utopia.

The illustrations confirm Harriot's analysis. De Bry's engravings embellished John White's drawings of various native activities (including what may be the first ever barbecue) and set them in a placid context, presenting a stark contrast to the images of Spanish atrocity which de Bry would include in the volume he published six years later. Two overhead views of native villages summarise the activities. One, of 'Pomeiooc', resembles a miniature version of Kublai Khan's summer palace (67). The other, of 'Secota', looks in its ordered plenitude like the kitchen garden of Alcinous (69). The English successors to Odysseus and Marco Polo have not travelled in vain. De Bry's use of the pastoral is enhanced by other illustrations which suggest that America presents a fresh start for Europeans. Supposedly from originals by White but perhaps from a French contemporary, de Bry provides five engravings of Picts 'which in the olde tyme dyd habite one part of the great Bretainne' (75). They have been added to provide comparisons of the savage state. The Picts, however, are more bloodthirsty. All, men and women alike, are armed, and the Pict in the first illustration is particularly welcoming: he displays two severed heads. Perhaps the second chance will be the better chance. This seems also to be suggested by the very first engraving. The foreground is occupied by a svelte Adam and Eve, at the moment when Eve plucks the apple. But there is no despair at the Fall, for the background is occupied by a pastoral scene: cows graze and a man hoes while a woman cradles her child. By placing the moment of biblical transition in a setting of everyday tranquillity, the scene looks forward to the closure of *Paradise Lost*.

Tranquillity is not a condition to be found in the second text to sum up Elizabethan America, *The Discoverie of the Large, Rich and Bewtiful Empyre of Guiana* (1596), by Sir Walter Ralegh. Like Thomas Harriot, Ralegh's intent was to promote colonisation. Ralegh's title, however, suggests a method that was more spectacular, and more in keeping with his gift for self-presentation. It certainly found a ready audience. Four different editions of the text appeared in 1596. De Bry included it in the eighth part of his *America*, and Hakluyt included it in the 1600 edition of his *Principall Navigations*. By that time it had been translated into Latin, German and Dutch. Its popularity was perhaps due to its epic form, which draws on and takes its place alongside such earlier examples as the *Alexander Romance*, Polo's *Travels*, and *Mandeville*. The epic seemed appropriate for an undertaking of this magnitude. When George Chapman wrote his poem 'De Guiana, Carmen Epicum' as the preface to

Lawrence Keymis's *A Relation of the Second Voyage to Guiana*, published in the same year as Ralegh's text, the poem easily took on the title and grand shapes of epic.

The Discoverie of Guiana is presented as a chivalric quest. It has a cast of villains, the cruel Spaniards led by Anthonio de Berrio, whom Ralegh captures. The heroes are identified by linking freedom with that common image of Elizabeth I, virginity. Hence Ralegh's speech to Trinidadian chiefs (casiqui):

> I made them understand that I was the servant of a Queene, who was the great Casique of the north, and a virgin, and had more Casiqui under her than there were trees in their Iland: that she was an enemy to the Castellani [Castilians] in respect of their tyrannie and oppression, and that she delivered all such nations about her, as were by them oppressed, and having freed all the coast of the northern world from their servitude had sent me to free them also . . . I shewed them her majesty's picture which they so admired and honored, as it had been easy to have brought them Idolatrous thereof.

The image of chastity is then extended from the Queen to all women in order to distinguish English and Spanish modes of colonisation. The Spanish, he wrote, daily took the wives and daughters from the natives:

> and used them for the satisfying of their owne lusts. But I protest before the majestie of the living God, that I neither know nor beleeve, that any of our companie one or other, by violence of otherwise, ever knew any of their women, and yet we saw many hundreds, and had many in our power, and of those very yoong, and excellently favored, which came among us without deceit, starke naked.

Where Harriot used technology and a freak contagion to win over the natives, Ralegh uses abstinence, symbolised by an icon. Guiana itself is then gendered. Annette Kolodny has identified a tradition of terrestrial rape in American letters.[43] In contrast, Guiana is here depicted as undefiled in order to make it the rightful inheritance of the Elizabethans. It 'is a Countrey that hath yet her Maydenhead, never sackt, turned, nor wrought' (196). It is a country also noted for its spaciousness, its salubrity, and particularly its wealth. One of its cities, Manoa, contains so much precious metal that Ralegh accepts the Spaniards' name of El Dorado for it – but he doesn't visit it (140–1).

Once again, the monsters are at the margins. Like Polo, Ralegh attempts to distinguish truth from fable. He hears so often about headless men that he believes the story:

> they are called *Ewaipanoma*: they are reported to have their eyes in their shoulders, and their mouths in the middle of their breasts . . . Such a nation was written of by *Maundevile*, whose reportes were held for fables many yeares, and yet since the East *Indies* were discovered, wee finde his relations true of such thinges as heeretofore were held incredible. (178)

He also believes that, although they do not amputate their right breasts, the Amazons also exist (146). The distinction between their behaviour and that of Elizabeth I allows him to close his text with a flourish:

where the south border of *Guiana* reacheth to the Dominion and Empire of the *Amazones*,
those women shall heereby heare the name of a
virgin, which is not onely able to defend her
owne territories and her neighbors, but
also invade and conquere so
great Empyres and so
farre removed.

(199)

Strictly, the date of *The Tempest*, 1611, means that it is not an Elizabethan text. Nor does Shakespeare make it clear that his island is off the coast of America, although he had read William Strachey's 1610 account of being shipwrecked on Bermuda. Yet it is precisely the lack of specificity that ensures that *The Tempest* belongs here, as the third text to sum up Elizabethan attitudes to the New World. First, it criticises a group of earlier texts, from More's *Utopia* to Florio's translation of Montaigne's 'Of the Caniballes', that pre-date the first successful English settlement of 1607. Second, in looking back, it also looks forward. In an influential book, Leo Marx suggested that 'the topography of *The Tempest* anticipates the moral geography of the American imagination'. In reflecting on the past, *The Tempest* sketches imaginative attitudes that will be developed in the future. It does this through a dramatic structure which projects the audience into a special, sealed environment. The storm in the first scene and the relaxed, easy pleading of Prospero's Epilogue act as a framework which allows the audience, for a while, to suspend judgement while important questions are examined about the relation of nature and culture. *The Tempest* is both axial and axiological. Its questions fall into three groups; they interrogate naive utopianism, the savage, and sophisticated utopianism.

As soon as the court party lands on Prospero's island, Gonzalo and Adrian employ images of renewal and pastoral beauty to celebrate their fortunate fall. Their naivety is exposed by the cutting interjections of their sardonically realist companions, Antonio and Sebastian. Within a couple of minutes, Gonzalo is planning what he shall do with the land, in a negative catalogue that is drawn from 'Of the Caniballes'. His intentions for the island, in particular, are exposed as cant, for he proposes to exercise absolute power to get rid of absolute power. As Antonio remarks with great economy, 'the latter end of his commonwealth forgets the beginning'. Antonio also snipes at Gonzalo's intention to rid his commonwealth of work. If everyone is idle they will become 'whores and knaves'.[44] Knaves themselves, Antonio and Sebastian reveal the corruption at the heart of the Elizabethan attacks on the Spanish empire, and their own imperial ambitions.

A central aim of Shakespeare's critique is the philosophy informing Montaigne's essay, that source of Gonzalo's negative catalogue. Caliban, his name of course an anagram of those tribes praised by Montaigne, is a monstrous representative of original sin. Miranda, who should know, tells him he is 'capable of all ill' (I. ii. 354). No evidence is presented to the contrary. Caliban is easily perverted by Stephano and Trinculo. Although at the close of the play he claims he will 'be wise hereafter/And seek for grace', there is no suggestion that his promises will be fulfilled (V. i. 295–6). Caliban is a commentary on those curious rearrangements of human and animal form which, it seems, now live at the margins of Spanish America. Gonzalo is prepared to believe that there are 'men/Whose heads stood in their breasts' (III. iii. 48–9). To Trinculo, Caliban smells like a strange and ancient fish, and later he calls him 'half a fish and half a monster' (III. ii. 28). But Caliban is quite a different piscine kettle; for he is a frightening, deformed version of the nexus between the human and the animal. Prospero is wrong when he says that nurture cannot stick to him. He has been able to acquire a language which sometimes sounds eerily like the music of the football terraces – ''Ban, 'Ban, Ca-Caliban' – but which can also respond eloquently to the 'sweet airs' of the island (II. ii. 184–5; III. ii. 134). What does not stick to Caliban is morality. He is the Wild Man of European myth, the character striding across the maps of the New World, the untameable ignoble savage who lives outside and threatens so-called civilised society, the kind of creature that Montaigne would not want to meet.

Gonzalo suggests that 'nature should produce/Without sweat and endeavour' (II. i. 162–3). Prospero believes that others should sweat and endeavour to produce for him. He wishes to inhabit a sophisticated utopia. His expulsion from Milan forces him to turn his secret studies into a technology. Unlike Gonzalo, who dreams of renouncing power, Prospero exercises it through his implements, Caliban and Ariel. As Leo Marx has shown, a clear comparison between the utopias of Gonzalo and Prospero emerges during the speech of Ceres, goddess of agriculture. Both utopias envision a natural landscape to present ideals of abundance and happiness. But Ceres, together with the other spirits, has been summoned by Prospero 'to enact' his present fancies (IV. i. 121). She is a tool like Caliban and Ariel. Their characteristic season is not summer, the perpetual season of Gonzalo's dream, but spring, the time of planting, and autumn, the time of reaping. Yet there are limits to Prospero's sophisticated utopia. Prospero loses control, of himself and thus of the masque, which falls apart. His anger is momentary, but leads to the most solemnly perspicuous moment in the play:

> Our revels now are ended. These our actors,
> As I foretold you, were all spirits, and
> Are melted into air, into thin air;
> And, like the baseless fabric of this vision,
> The cloud-capped towers, the gorgeous palaces,
> The solemn temples, the great globe itself,
> Yea, all which it inherit, shall dissolve,
> And, like this insubstantial pageant faded,
> Leave not a rack behind. We are such stuff
> As dreams are made on; and our little life
> Is rounded with a sleep. (IV. i. 148–58)

The speech conjures images which go back to the palace of Alcinous in *The Odyssey*, but looks forward to the close of the play and the return to Milan, leaving the island to its natives. Even a sophisticated utopia is a dream; and

American writers and politicians from Jefferson to Paul De Man would allude this speech and worry about the thin impalpability (to use James's terms) of the construct.

More directly, the speech sums up the Elizabethan experience of America. The dream is encapsulated in Michael Drayton's 'To the Virginian Voyage' (1606), written in support of 'industrious Hackluit' to 'inflame' heroes to settle in America. Virginia, in defiance of *Mandeville* and Columbus, is called 'Earth's onely Paradise', replete with such resources as gold, pearls:

> And the fruitfull'st Soyle,
>   Without your Toyle,
> Three Harvests more,
> All greater then your Wish.

Gonzalo's dream has here run riot, to the extent that in its triple fecundity Virginia matches the Elysian Fields of the Greeks.[45] In contrast, the reality was desolate. By the time Ralegh set off for Guiana in 1595 none of the English attempts at settlement had succeeded. The 1583 expedition, led by his step-brother Sir Humphrey Gilbert and including his own ship *The Bark Ralegh*, came to nothing. The first, 1585, settlement on Roanoke Island, led by his cousin Sir Richard Grenville and including Harriot, had to be evacuated. A second settlement was led by John White in 1587. White had soon to go back to England for supplies, and his return was delayed, among other things, by the Armada. When he was finally able to get back to the colony in 1590, the colonists had disappeared, including his daughter and granddaughter, the first child born in English America. No trace of them was ever found. Nor is there any trace of these failures in Ralegh's *The Discoverie of Guiana*, in 'To the Virginian Voyage', or later in the various publications of John Smith. It was a process of erasure which would sometimes be found in later American literature as it developed, despite Prospero's warning, the theme of the second chance.

Notes

1. Franz Fanon, *The Wretched of the Earth*, trans. Constance Farrington (1965; rpt. Harmondsworth: Penguin, 1967), pp. 39–40.

2. *The Odyssey*, trans. E. V. Rieu (Harmondsworth: Penguin, 1946), Books V, VII, X and XI, pp. 99, 95, 115, 168–71. *The Odyssey*, trans. D. C. H. Rieu (Harmondsworth: Penguin, 1991), p. viii. Leo Marx, *The Machine in the Garden* (New York: Oxford University Press, 1964), p. 3.

3. Plato, *Timaeus* 24e–25d (trans. Benjamin Jowett), and *Critias* 114e–118b, 121a–c (trans. A. E. Taylor), in *The Collected Dialogues of Plato*, eds. Edith Hamilton and Huntington Cairns (Princeton, NJ: Princeton University Press, 1961), pp. 1159–60, 1219–21, 1224. *Plato: The Atlantis Story*, introd. Christopher Gill (Bristol: Bristol Classical Press, 1980).

4. Francis Bacon, *The New Atlantis and The Great Instauration*, ed. Jerry Weinberger (revised edn., Arlington Heights, IL: Harlan Davidson, 1989), p. 54.

5. Ignatius Donnelly, *Atlantis: The Antediluvian World* (1882; revised by Egerton Sykes, London: Sidgwick & Jackson, 1950), pp. 1–2.

6. Leo Braudy, *The Frenzy of Renown: Fame & Its History* (New York: Random House, 1997), p. 32. Arrian, *The Campaigns of Alexander*, trans. Aubrey de Selincourt, introd. J. R. Hamilton (1958; rpt. Harmondsworth: Penguin, 1971), pp. 67, 349, 259, 264, 293, 328. *1 Maccabees 3*, *The Bible: Authorized King James Version*, eds. Robert Carroll and Stephen Prickett (Oxford: Oxford University Press, 1997), Apocrypha, p. 180.

7. Herodotus, *The Histories*, trans. Aubrey de Selincourt (Harmondsworth: Penguin, 1954), Book III, pp. 218–19. Arrian, *The Campaigns of Alexander*, p. 260. Arrian, *Indica* 13–14, trans. P. A. Brunt (Cambridge, MA: Harvard University Press, 1983), pp. 343–9. Robin Lane Fox, *Alexander the Great* (London: Allen Lane, 1973), p. 338. Georges Louis Le Clerc, Comte de Buffon, *Natural History, General and Particular*, trans. William Smellie (2nd edn., 9 vols, Edinburgh: William Creech, 1780–5), VI, p. 1. Benjamin Rush, draft letter 25 September 1812 to David Hosack, *The Letters of Benjamin Rush*, ed. Lyman H. Butterfield (2 vols, Princeton, NJ: Princeton University Press, 1951), II, p. 1163.

8. Arrian, *The Campaigns of Alexander*, pp. 213, 356–7, 369. Homer, *The Iliad* 3.189, trans. Richmond Lattimore (1951; rpt. Chicago: University of Chicago Press, 1961), p. 105. Diodorus of Sicily, *The Library of History* 53.1–4, trans. C. H. Oldfather (12 vols, Cambridge, MA: Harvard University Press, 1953), II, pp. 249, 251.

9. Adam of Bremen, *History of the Archbishops of Hamburg-Bremen*, trans. Francis J. Tschan (New York: Columbia University Press, 1959), p. 219.

10. *Geographical Treatise*, quoted by R. M. Perkins, 'Norse Implications', in Helen Wallis *et al.*, 'The Strange Case of the Vinland Map: A Symposium', *Geographical Journal* 140, 2 (July 1974), 203. Eben Norton Horsford, *The Discovery of the Ancient City of Norumbega. A Communication to the President and Council of the American Geographical Society, at their Special Session in Watertown November 21, 1889* (Boston: Houghton Mifflin, 1889), pp. 5, 38.

11. *The Vinland Sagas: The Norse Discovery of America*, trans. and eds. Magnus Magnusson and Hermann Pálsson (Harmondsworth: Penguin, 1965), pp. 53, 55, 65, 95. Future references will be given in parentheses after the quotation.

12. John P. McWilliams, Jr., *The American Epic: Transforming a Genre, 1770–1860* (Cambridge: Cambridge University Press, 1989), pp. 4, 2.

13. Philip Roth, 'Writing American Fiction', *Reading Myself and Others* (New York: Farrar, Straus and Giroux, 1976), p. 120. Roth's emphasis. Nathaniel Hawthorne, *The Scarlet Letter and Selected Tales*, ed. Thomas E. Connolly (Harmondsworth: Penguin, 1970), p. 66.

14. David M. Potter, *People of Plenty: Economic Abundance and the American Character* (Chicago: University of Chicago Press, 1954), p. 167. Gwyn Jones, *The Norse Atlantic Saga* (London: Oxford University Press, 1964), pp. 47, 85–6.

15. William Carlos Williams, *In the American Grain* (1925; rpt. Harmondsworth: Penguin, 1971), pp. 21, 24.

16. Evelyn Abbot, 'Note' in Washington Irving, *Columbus: His Life and Voyages* (New York: G. P. Putnam's Sons, 1897), p. v.

17. Daniel J. Boorstin, *The Discoverers* (1983; rpt. Harmondsworth: Penguin, 1986), pp. 125–7. Edward W. Said, *Orientalism* (1978; rpt. New York: Vintage Books, 1979), pp. 1–4. Frances Wood, 'Marco Polo – a man or merely a manuscript?' *Financial Times*, 13 July 1996, p. III.

18. *The Book of Ser Marco Polo the Venetian, Concerning the Kingdoms and Marvels of the East*, trans. and ed. Henry Yule (2nd edn, 2 vols, London: John Murray, 1875), I, p. 165. Future references to this edition will be given in parentheses after the quotation. The old Yule edition is used here because it combines great scholarship with a translation that does not attempt to erase, as do some later editions, the fables that are important to this discussion.

19. *The Travels of Sir John Mandeville*, trans. and introd. C. W. R. D. Moseley (Harmondsworth: Penguin, 1983), pp. 45–6, 111. Future references to this edition will be given in parentheses after the quotation.

20. Cristoforo Colombo, *Personal Narrative of the First Voyage of Columbus to America. From a manuscript recently discovered in Spain*, trans. Samuel Kettell (Boston: T. B. Wait & Son, 1827). Awnsham Churchill and John Churchill, *A Collection of Voyages and Travels, some now first printed from original manuscripts. Others translated out of foreign languages, and now first publish'd in English* (London: A. & J. Churchill, 1704).

21. *The Journal of Christopher Columbus*, trans. Cecil Jane (London: Anthony Blond, 1968), pp. xv–xvi, xxi–xxii, 201. Future references to this edition will be given in parentheses after the quotation.

22. *The Four Voyages of Christopher Columbus*, ed. and trans. J. M. Cohen (Harmondsworth: Penguin, 1969), pp. 218–22.

23. Amerigo Vespucci, *The Letters of Amerigo Vespucci*, trans. Clements R. Markham (1894; rpt. New York: Burt Franklin, 1970), pp. 42, 47, xvii–xviii.

24. Guillaume, l'Abbé Raynal, *A Philosophical and Political History of the Settlement and Trade of the Europeans in the East and West Indies* (1770), trans. J. Justamond (4 vols, London: T. Cadell, 1776), I, p. 1.

25. Mark Twain, *Pudd'nhead Wilson* (1894; rpt. Harmondsworth: Penguin, 1969), p. 224.

26. Francisco López de Gómera, Dedication to Charles V, *Historia general de las Indias* (n.p.: n.p., 1552), fo. iiv (my translation). Cotton Mather, *Magnalia Christi Americana* (1702; rpt. Cambridge, MA: The Belknap Press of Harvard University Press, 1977), p. 119.

27. Michel de Montaigne, 'Of the Caniballes,' *Essays*, trans. John Florio (3 vols, 1603; rpt. London: David Nutt, 1892), I, pp. 222–3.

28. Father Joseph de Acosta, *The Natural and Moral History of the Indies*, trans. Edward Grimeston (1604; rpt. 2 vols, New York: Burt Franklin, 1970), I, p. 49. Johann Keppler, *Dissertatio cum Nuncio Siderio nuper ad mortales misso a Galilaeo Galilaei* (Prague: 1610). Hernán Cortés, *Letters from Mexico*, ed. A. R. Pagden (London: Oxford University Press, 1972), p. 267. Adam Smith, *The Wealth of Nations* (1776; rpt. 2 vols, Oxford: Clarendon Press, 1976), II, p. 626; I, p. 448.

29. Kirkpatrick Sale, *The Conquest of Paradise: Christopher Columbus and the Columbian Legacy* (1990; rpt. New York: Plume, 1991), p. 353.

30. Francisco de Vitoria, 'On the American Indians' (1539), *Political Writings*, trans. and eds. Anthony Pagden and Jeremy Lawrance (Cambridge: Cambridge University Press, 1991), pp. 233, 251, 279.

31. Buffon, *Natural History*, V, pp. 136–9.

32. Cornelius de Pauw, *Recherches philosophiques sur les Américains* (3 vols, Berlin: n.p., 1771), I, pp. 4–7, 19, 35. Max Eastman, 'Differing With Sigmund Freud,' rpt. in *Broken Image: Foreign Critiques of America*, ed. Gerald E. Stearn (New York: Random House, 1972), p. 222.

33. James A. Williamson, *The Cabot Voyages and Bristol Discovery Under Henry VII* (Cambridge: Cambridge University Press for the Hakluyt Society, 1962), pp. 52, 63, 85. *The Great Chronicle of London* (1501/2), and Marcantonio Contarini, 1536 report, in Williamson, *The Cabot Voyages*, pp. 220, 146.

34. Broadside of 1511, quoted in *The English Literatures of America, 1500–1800*, eds. Myra Jehlen and Michael Warner (New York: Routledge, 1997), p. 43.

35. Thomas More, *Utopia*, trans. and ed. Robert M. Adams (2nd edn, New York: W. W. Norton & Co., 1992), pp. 5, 7, 46–7.

36. John Rastell, *Four Elements*, in *Three Rastell Plays*, ed. Richard Axton (Cambridge: D. S. Brewer, 1979), pp. 49–51.

37. John Dee, 'Statements on the date of the discovery of North America', in Williamson, *The Cabot Voyages*, pp. 201–2. David Powel, *Historie of Cambria* (1584), rpt. in Richard Hakluyt, *The Principal Navigations* (12 vols, Glasgow: James MacLehose, 1903–5), VII, p. 134. Richard Hakluyt, *Voyages and Discoveries*, ed. Jack Beeching (Harmondsworth: Penguin, 1972), pp. 32, 39. Mather, *Magnalia Christi Americana*, p. 118.

38. Bartolom de Las Casas, *The Spanish Colonie, or Briefe chronicle of the actes and gestes of the Spaniardes in the West Indies . . .*, rpt. in *Hakluytus Posthumous, or Purchas his Pilgrimes* (20 vols, Glasgow: James MacLehose, 1905–7), XVIII, pp. 88–91.

39. John Phillips, 'Dedication' to Las Casas, *The Tears of the Indians*, trans. Phillips (London: Nathaniel Brook, 1656), n.p. *The Pennsylvania Gazette* No. 1496 (25 August 1757), p. 2; also printed in the *New-York Mercury* and *The London Magazine* in 1757.

40. John Aylmer, *An Harborowe for Faithfull and Trewe Subjects* (1558; rpt. New York: Da Capo, 1972), n.p. John Frampton, *Joyfull Newes out of the New Founde Worlde*, introd. Stephen Gaselee (2 vols, London: Constable & Co., 1925), I, p. 75. Sir Humphrey Gilbert, *Discourse of a Discovery for a New Passage to Cataia* (1576), rpt. in Hakluyt, *The Principal Navigations*, VII, pp. 186–7. Thomas Churchyard, *The Discourse of The Queenes Maiesties entertainement in Suffolke and Norffolke* (London: Henry Bynneman, [1578]), n.p. Edward Haie, rpt. in Hakluyt, *The Principal Navigations*, VIII, pp. 36–8.

41. [Edward Topsell], *The Historie of Foure-Footed Beastes* (1607; rpt. New York: Da Capo Press, 1973), pp. 712, 441–2, 452–5, 660. William Shakespeare, *The Merry Wives of Windsor* (Harmondsworth: Penguin, 1973), IV. v. 8, p. 134. Hakluyt, *The Principal Navigations*, I, p. 154. R. R. Cawley, *Unpathed Waters: Studies in the Influence of Voyages on Elizabethan Literature* (1940; rpt. London: Frank Cass & Co., 1967), p. 104. See also illustrations in Beatriz Pastor Bodmer, *The Armature of Conquest: Spanish Accounts of the Discovery of America, 1492–1589*, trans. Lydia Longstreth Hunt (Stanford, CA: Stanford University Press, 1992), n.p.

42. Thomas Harriot, *A briefe and true report of the new found land of Virginia* (1590; rpt. New York: Dover, 1972), pp. 7–8, 10. Future references to this edition will be given in parentheses after the quotation.

43. Sir Walter Ralegh, *The Discoverie of the Large, Rich and Bewtiful Empyre of Guiana*, ed. and introd. Neil L. Whitehead (Manchester: Manchester University Press, 1997), pp. 134, 165. Future references to this edition will be given in parentheses after the quotation. Annette Kolodny, *The Lay of the Land: Metaphor as Experience and History in American Life and Letters* (Chapel Hill, NC: University of North Carolina Press, 1975).

44. Leo Marx, *The Machine in the Garden: Technology and the Pastoral Ideal in America* (London: Oxford University Press, 1964), p. 72. Shakespeare, *The Tempest* (Harmondsworth: Penguin, 1968), II, i. 160–1, 170–1. Future references to this edition will be given in parentheses after the quotation.

45. Michael Drayton, 'To the Virginian Voyage', in *Works*, ed. J. William Hebel (5 vols, Oxford: Shakespeare Head Press, 1932), II, pp. 363–4.

Chapter 3

From Settlement to Revolution, 1607–1783

America, a nation of immigrants, has created great literature out of the phenomenon of cultural transplantation, out of examining the ways in which people cope with a new world . . .

(Salman Rushdie, 'Imaginary Homelands')[1]

Virginia and the naming of New England

In 1603 Elizabeth I died and James VI of Scotland took the additional title of James I of England. The consequences were far-reaching. He removed his court from Edinburgh to London, and fifteen years later he removed the head of Sir Walter Ralegh, who died still promising to find gold. No two acts more clearly signalled the decline of the cockalorum style of colonisation, to be replaced by negotiation and more prosaic forms of trade. James (1566–1625) was portrayed as the creature of Spain, particularly by the followers of Ralegh. Yet it could be argued that accommodation with Spain was part of a larger imperial enterprise, which embraced both external and internal colonisation. James ended the Anglo-Scots border wars, and the Irish and Spanish wars. His wish to extend the union of crowns into full political union would not be realised until 1707. In contrast, the pace and success of external colonisation increased markedly, with British settlements in Virginia (at Jamestown, founded in 1607), Bermuda, Newfoundland and New Plymouth. External colonisation continued apace after the accession of Charles I in 1625, with settlements in Barbados, Nevis, Massachusetts, Maryland, Montserrat, Antigua, Connecticut and Rhode Island. Jamaica was captured in 1655 in Cromwell's war against Spain (1655–8). In 1663 Charles II granted a patent to land between Virginia and Florida, named Carolina in his honour. The colonial ambitions of Charles's younger brother, the Duke of York (and on Charles's death in 1685 James II), led to an attack against New Netherland in 1664, and the capture of Delaware, and Surinam, on the mainland south-east of the West Indies. Surinam was exchanged in 1667 for New Amsterdam, which was renamed New York. With the foundation of South Carolina in 1670 the British North American coastline, stretching from northern Florida to southern Maine, had taken on the shape it would retain until the French and Indian War. Colonialism was, however, by no means a uniform activity. Styles of settlement varied greatly, and those variations gave rise to different forms of literary expression.

One of the earliest writers to examine Virginia was William Strachey (1572–1621). Strachey's account of his shipwreck on Bermuda on his way to Virginia in 1609 had influenced *The Tempest*. He reached his goal in 1610, becoming the first secretary of the Virginia Company, remaining there for a year. He completed *The Historie of Travell into Virginia Britania* in London in 1612. The first task of the text was to establish British title. His 'Praemonition to the Reader' carefully distinguished British title to Virginia from that of Spain to Florida. He both claims priority, citing Madoc, and 'our Industry and expences', as opposed to papal donation. The text's two books reverse the normal sequence. The second begins with an account of Atlantis, and then summarises English exploration in 'this straung and new half world'. The first two chapters of Book One establish a pattern that will later be developed in Jefferson's *Notes on the State of Virginia*, detailing the boundaries and topography of the colony. The closing chapter of the book describes its flora and fauna, including 'Lyons'. (By Jefferson's time they would be identified as pumas.) Comparison with *Notes on the State of Virginia* reveals Strachey's central interest, and the reason for its antichronistic structure. Unlike Jefferson, who devotes only one chapter to 'the Aborigines', Strachey gives them seven of the book's ten chapters. Strachey creates an ethnology that reveals both a strenuous attempt to understand the inhabitants of this strange new world, and a strong adherence to hierarchy:

> Although the Country people be very barbarous, yet have they amongst them such governement, as that their Magistrates for good Comaunding, and their people for due subiection and obeying excell many places that would be accompted Civile . . .[2]

The government, by the London Company, of colonial Virginia in its early years was not always so well managed. The colonists suffered periods of hardship and native attack, and they were also often at odds with leaders both in Virginia and London. The result was writing which approaches, and then crosses, what D. H. Lawrence called a 'real verge'. One text that approaches the verge is *Ovid's Metamorphosis Englished*, by George Sandys (1578–1644). His father, Edwin Sandys, had been Archbishop of York, and one of those involved in the translation project that resulted in the Bishops' Bible (1572), the Anglican response to the Calvinist Geneva Bible. It seems that George Sandys inherited his father's gift for translation, for the greater part of his writing was devoted to 'Englishing' classical and religious texts. He was an experienced traveller and in 1615 had published an elegant, formally controlled account of his travels in the Middle East. *A Relation of a Journey begun in An. Dom: 1610* included some verses translated from Ovid's *Metamorphoses*, and in 1621 Sandys published his version of its first five books. In that year he moved to Virginia as an official of the London Company in Jamestown. Shortly afterwards, Michael Drayton wrote him a poetic letter:

> And (worthy GEORGE) by industry and use,
> Let's see what lines *Virginia* will produce;
> Goe on with OVID, as you have begunne,
> With the first five Bookes; let your numbers run

> Glib as the former, so shall it live long,
> And doe much honour to the *English* tongue:
> Intice the Muses thither to repaire,
> Intreat them gently, trayne them to that aire . . .

Drayton, who in 1606 had constructed a Virginian Utopia out of thin air, now asked Sandys to give him details of the 'soyle' and savages.[3]

Sandys no doubt had many stories to tell Drayton; but it was when he revised his *Ovid's Metamorphosis Englished* that he supplied written evidence of the impact of Virginia's 'aire'. Ovid had written his text before he was banished, in AD 8, from the heart of the Roman imperium. Sandys began his translation before he left the heart of the growing British imperium, and completed his work on the last ten books in Virginia. It was the first translation of a classical text made in America. It was first published in 1626, the year after Sandys had returned to London from Virginia, and then revised in 1632. This revision does not reveal a triumphal arrival of the imperium in Virginia, but rather the impact of the periphery on the centre, resulting in writing somewhat less 'glib' than before. The language of Sandys's dedication to Charles I suggested that he had Drayton's poem more in mind when he remarked that the book was:

> Sprung from the Stocke of the Ancient Romanes; but bred in the New-World, of the rudeness whereof it cannot but participate; especially having Warres and Tumults to bring it to light instead of the Muses.[4]

Sandys had survived a massacre of the settlers in 1622 and, as we shall see, some other terrible events. The experience had scarred his view of Virginia. Indeed, in the fifteenth book of the poem Sandys suggested that some of the things he had 'seene in *America*' had turned his world upside down:

> Where once was solid land, Seas have I seene;
> And solid land, where once deepe Seas have beene.
> Shels, far from Seas, like quarries in the ground;
> And anchors have on mountaine tops beene found. (674)

The things that Sandys had seen lent credence to his reading about Spanish America, which in turn explained one of *Mandeville*'s tales. When they first saw Cortés's cavalry, the Mexicans did not distinguish horse and rider and thus believed that they were centaurs (565). By 1646 the Mexicans' mistake had become one of the 'Vulgar Errors' in Sir Thomas Browne's *Pseudodoxia Epidemica*. Yet if one fable was dispatched, another was maintained. Sandys's reading about Florida confirmed what he had heard during his travels in Egypt. Hermaphrodites are often to be found in Florida, where they 'are so hated by the rest of the Indians, that they use them as beasts to carry their burthens; to suck their wounds, and to attend on the diseased' (208–9). But aborigines too were monstrous. Sandys asserted that their culture was characterised by 'injustice and cruelty, as ever accompanied by Atheisme and a contempt for the Deity'. They should therefore be 'numbred among beasts'. He noted ironically that at least they were superior to Polyphemus, the son of

Poseidon in *The Odyssey*. Each day Polyphemus had devoured two of Odysseus' shipmates, his guests. The aborigines only ate their enemies. But there was no irony in the description of those occasions, 'seene by some of our Country-men', when the heads of a dozen defeated warriors had been boiled in a pot, for 'the heads of men they account among their delicates, which are only to be eaten by the great ones' (649–50). The type of beast nearest to the native, Sandys thought, was the frog: 'the Heiroglyphick of impudence and clamor'. The comparison was not intended to be comic. Sandys noted that a plague of frogs had troubled the Egyptians, driven the Abderites out of their country and 'depopulated a Citty in *France*'. There was also something macabre about the frog. Sandys remarked that a frog still hopped after it had suffered that favourite sport, disembowelling (295). America and its inhabitants were pro-foundly unsettling.

Safely back in London, Sandys could reflect on the impact that Virginia had made on his beliefs. The realities of Virginia were sometimes even more dis-turbing. Writers from Polo to Shakespeare had portrayed the savage man as the nexus of the human and the bestial. In Virginia the English settlers them-selves crossed the line into bestiality when they too began to practise cannibal-ism. In 1624, while Sandys was still in Virginia, an anonymous author penned 'The Tragicall Relation of the Virginia Assembly'. The 'Relation' admits to cannibalism, and in doing so draws more on Thomas Kyd's *The Spanish Tragedy* (1596) than on the grandeur of Sophocles or Shakespeare. In seeking the appropriate way in which to convey the horrors of starvation, the text also creates a mixture of vivid vernacular and black humour which would become a common American style and be turned to high art by Mark Twain:

> In those 12 yeers of Sir Tho: Smith his government, we averr that the Colony for the most parte remayned in great want and misery . . . soe lamentable was our scarsitie that we were constrayned to eate Doggs, Catts, ratts, Snakes, Toadstooles, horse hides and what nott, one man out of the mysery that he endured, killinge his wife powdered her upp [salted her] to eate her, for which he was burned. Many besides fedd on the Corps[es] of dead men, and one who had gotten insatiable, out of custome to that foode could not be restrayned, untill such tyme as he was executed for it, and in deede soe miserable was our estate, that the happyest day that ever some of them hoped to see, was when the Indyans had killed a mare, they wishinge while she was a boylinge that Sir Tho: Smith were uppon her backe in the kettle.[5]

Such humour, and such admissions, is not to be found in the work of the best-known, or most notorious, writer of early Virginian settlement, John Smith. Smith was with the first shipload of settlers to arrive in Virginia. His time there was marked by controversy, and he stayed only two years, leaving in October 1609. Yet he would spend much of the rest of his life writing about North America, and generally promoting settlement there. His first publica-tion was a brief pamphlet entitled *A True Relation of Such Occurences and Accidents of Noate as Hath Hapned in Virginia Since the First Planting of That Collony*. Published in 1608, it is the earliest printed first-hand account of the colony, and its title indicates an emphasis on heroic narrative, for by stages Smith turned Strachey's ethnology into an adventure story. While Strachey describes the Algonquin leader Powhatan as 'a goodly old-man . . . well beaten with many cold and stormy wynters', Smith concentrates on his aristocratic demeanour, 'with such a grave and Maiesticall countenance, as drave me into admiration to see such state in a naked Salvage'.[6] *A Map of Virginia* (1612) develops his theme, injecting the pastoral with suggestions of something more:

> Here are mountains, hills, plains, valleys, rivers and brooks all running most pleasantly into a fair bay, compassed, but for the mouth, with fruitful and delightsome land. These waters wash from the rocks such glistering tinctures that the ground in some places seemeth as gilded; where both the rocks and the earth are so splendent to behold that better judgments than ours might have been persuaded they contain more than probabilities.

In part *A Map of Virginia* is a promotional text, anticipating the language of the real-estate agent in the way that it integrates hints of El Dorado with instant deniability. In part, too, it continues Smith's heroic agenda, with extended accounts of conversations with Powhatan (now a 'subtil Salvage') and another native leader, Opechancanough, that are models of elegant classical rhetoric (II, 133).

In 1614 and 1615 Smith made two voyages to the coast between Penobscot and Cape Cod, the first to explore and trade, the second with a group of settlers. They were intercepted en route by a French pirate and taken to France. Smith escaped, and probably spent the rest of his life in England, writing about his life and America. The two were closely intertwined in a heroic narrative. In *A Description of New England* (1616) Smith compares his efforts with those of Samson, Hercules and Alexander, and denigrates 'those who would live at home idly', extolling instead a life of work:

> Who can desire more content, that hath small meanes; or but only his merit to advance his fortune, then to tread, and plant that ground hee hath purchased by the hazard of his life? If he have but the taste of virtue and magnanimitie, what to such a minde can bee more pleasant, then planting and building a foundation for his Posteritie, gotte from the rude earth, by Gods blessing and his owne industrie, without prejudice to any? (I, 180, 208)

A Description of New England is the first text to name that land, and to announce the theme of small means but great spirits that is the heart of the American Dream. Perhaps the experience of being captured by pirates had cured Smith of easy money. Certainly, the narrative derides 'spoil, piracie, and such villany' as the occupation of 'the Portugall, Spanyard, Dutch, French or Turke'; and gold is now dismissed as 'the Masters device to get a voyage'. Even whales are a waste of time: 'we saw many, and spent much time in chasing them'. Instead the heroic has now become the quotidian, and will be rewarded in a rich land that abounds with furs, and the sea with fish (I, 217, 186).

Smith's experience of Virginia and New England was brought together in his most extensive work, *The Generall Historie of Virginia, New-England,*

and the Summer Isles (nowadays known as Bermuda). Published in 1624, the *Generall Historie* was his most widely read and frequently anthologised publication. No doubt this was in part because of its usefulness. In the spirit of the compendia, Smith plundered much detail from Strachey's manuscript *Historie of Travell*. The text's popularity was mainly due to its heroic narrative, now dealing with Smith's adventures in the third person and including, for the first time in print, a story that became the first legend of Anglo-American settlement. In this narrative Smith has been captured by Powhatan:

> At his entrance before the King, all the people gave a great shout. The Queen of *Appomattuck* was appointed to bring him water to wash his hands, and another brought him a bunch of feathers, instead of a Towell to dry them: having feasted after their best barbarous manner they could, a long consultation was held, but the conclusion was, two great stones were brought before *Powhatan*: then as many as could layd hands on him, dragged him to them, and thereon laid his head, and being ready with their clubs, to beat out his braines, *Pocahontas* the Kings dearest daughter, when no entreaty could prevaile, got his head in her arms, and laid her owne upon his to save him from death: whereat the King was contented he should live . . . (II, 400)

It has been suggested that this story is a fabrication, or that Smith had misinterpreted an Algonquin rite of passage. Certainly, Pocahontas existed. She became converted to Christianity and married, not John Smith but John Rolfe, moving with him to England, where she was received by James I. She died in 1617 before she could return to Virginia, and is buried in the Thames port with the apt name of Gravesend. After the revolution, the story was revived as a foundation myth for the United States, and its elements have been recreated in various media, including John Davis's novel *The First Settlers of Virginia* (1805), Victor Nehlig's painting *Pocahontas and John Smith* (1870), Hart Crane's poem *The Bridge* (1930), and *Pocahontas*, the Disney feature-length cartoon (1995).

Perhaps inspired by the success of the *Generall Historie* and the Pocahontas story, Smith now wrote his most ambitious book, briefer than the *Generall Historie* but with a geographical reach only exceeded by its heroic narrative. *The True Travels, Adventures, and Observations of Captaine John Smith in Europe, Asia, Affrica, and America* (1630) repeats the adjective that opened the title of his first publication, but more than ever tests the reader's credulity. Smith tells how, in 1596, he first fought with other British volunteers in the Dutch War of Independence against Spain; then sailed as a pirate to the Mediterranean and captured a Venetian ship. He joined the Austrian army and serially killed three Turkish officers in single combat before being captured in a battle. He was enslaved by the Turks but rescued by the beautiful Lady Tragabigzanda, who sent him to Russia. He escaped from Russia and returned after an absence of nine years to England and the Virginia Company. It is a tale reaching towards Mandevillean proportions, and the wonder is that some of it has been found to be indeed true. Smith called on some of the episodes in his earlier life and works – the capture by pirates, the rescue by a woman – to assist in shaping his text as a blend of the picaresque with the chivalric romance.

To that extent it might be said that Smith was an Elizabethan after his time. Yet a comparison with Ralegh highlights the novelty of Smith's work. A passage written by Smith soon after Ralegh's death and added to the close of the first edition of *New Englands Trials* (1620) promises 'no Mines of golde' but suggests instead the model of the Dutch, who obtained their wealth by fishing:

> Therefore (honourable and worthy Countrymen) let not the meannesse of the word *Fish* distaste you, for it will afford as good gold as the mines of *Guiana*, or *Tumbatu*, with lesse hazard and charge, and more certaintie and facilitie. (I, 272)

The work ethic has been substituted for El Dorado, or 'Tumbatu' (Timbuktu) for that matter. Ralegh's outlandish attempts to emulate the Spanish have been replaced by Smith's emphasis on careful Dutch styles of trade. Smith domesticates the epic by inserting calculation and perseverance. The result is that the failure of Roanoke is replaced by the success of Jamestown, rightly named after the careful king.

A second comparison must be made, however, to place Smith with greater precision. When the Pilgrim Fathers set out from Holland in 1620, Smith offered to lead them to Virginia. According to him they declined on the grounds of cost, took his books instead, and ended up in New Plymouth. Smith noted their landfall and survival in the second, 1622, edition of *New Englands Trials*. After a further group of Puritans, led by John Winthrop, had settled in Massachusetts Bay in 1630, he preached obedience. In his last pamphlet, *Advertisements for the unexperienced Planters of New-England, Or Anywhere* (1631), Smith attacked the earlier settlers at New Plymouth for refusing his offer of leadership. As a result, 'accident, ignorance and wilfulnesse' had almost led to the demise of their settlement. He portrayed the Pilgrim Fathers as factious schismatics and, dedicating his pamphlet to the Archbishops of Canterbury and York, he recommended to Winthrop 'the prime authority of the Church of England'. In a prefatory poem, 'The Sea Marke', he depicted himself as a battered hulk which now acts as a warning to seafarers; and he hoped that Winthrop and his followers would also pay heed (II, 926, 946, 959). It is likely that Smith's advice would have annoyed Winthrop. Although more moderate than the Pilgrim Fathers, Winthrop and his followers were forced out of England precisely by the Anglican establishment, led by William Laud (Bishop of London from 1628 and Archbishop of Canterbury from 1633), which was restoring elements of pre-Reformation liturgical practice. There is no record of Winthrop's feelings about Smith. An illustrious Bostonian successor will therefore have to speak for him. Henry Brooks Adams (1838–1918) traced his American family back to Thomas Brooks, who emigrated in 1630 with Winthrop, and Henry Adams, who migrated in 1638 to Massachusetts. In 1861 he began his career as a historian by closely examining Smith's writing, and the Pocahontas story in particular. The resulting article, which aimed, Adams said, at 'nothing less than the entire erasure of one of the most attractive portions of American history', appeared in the *North American Review* in January 1867. It began a debate about Smith's reliability that has not yet ceased. The date that Adams started research on Smith is significant; it is also the year of the outbreak of the American Civil War. There is more than a hint of sectional rivalry in the way that Adams describes the beginning of his task as throwing stones at a figure who is 'picturesque but un-puritanic'.[7] Too careful a planter to be an Elizabethan swashbuckler, Smith was also too much an Anglican cavalier to suit the Yankees, or their Puritan forbears. It would be a gross exaggeration to say that had Smith led the New England settlers, the Civil War would not have happened. Yet Smith applied the shapes of chivalric romance to a colony that would embrace them fervently. In the absence of Smith, New England and its writing took a quite different course.

The varieties of writing in New England

In the wake of migration comes controversy. Certainly, that was the case with the first great European migration to North America, by the English Puritans. Many nationalists have treated Plymouth Rock as the foundation stone of the United States, and scholars from Perry Miller to Andrew Delbanco have proposed that the Puritans and their legacy have defined important aspects of American identity. Others have regretted that identity, and blamed the Puritans. For instance, William Carlos Williams suggests in his 'alternative history' of America, *In the American Grain*, that:

> The result of that brave setting out of the pilgrims has been an atavism that thwarts and destroys . . . It has become 'the most lawless country in the civilized world,' a panorama of murders, perversions, a terrific ungoverned strength, excusable only because of the horrid beauty of its great machines . . . What prevented the normal growth? Was it England, the northern strain, the soil they landed on? It was, of course, the whole weight of the wild continent that made their condition of mind advantageous, forcing it to reproduce its own likeness, and no more.

Williams wrote that in 1925. In the succeeding three-quarters of a century or more the 'violence and despair' of the United States has increased manifold.[8] Yet American Puritanism was not the monolith that many assumed it to have been. Puritanism is a portmanteau term describing a large number of people, on both sides of the Atlantic, many of whom would not have accepted the label. They were often unified only in dissent from the communion of the Church of England, believing that it had not gone far enough in detaching itself from the Roman Catholic Church. American Puritans, like their English counterparts, had a variety of political as well as religious aims. Shades of difference detectable between New Plymouth and Massachusetts Bay would develop into a spectrum as the numbers of migrants and settlements increased. Furthermore, the migrants were extremely willing to express their views in writing, and a great deal of that writing found its way into print. What follows is an attempt to provide a shape to the writing of New England by relating a limited number of texts to the first eighty years in its history.

It is likely that those who sailed from Plymouth in the *Mayflower* in September 1620 were impelled by a variety of aims. The intention of their leaders was to remove them from a European Protestantism they believed to have become corrupt. But the venture also had an economic element. They were financed by a group of London merchants, and they received a grant of land through the offices of Sir Edwin Sandys, successor as treasurer of the London Company to Sir Thomas Smith, and elder brother of George Sandys who had translated Ovid in Virginia. In 1623 there was a further proposal for settlement in New England, not as a godly sanctuary but rather to provide a commercial market, and a potential home both for the unemployed and for the impoverished gentry. The writings of Puritan leaders like William Bradford and John Winthrop should therefore be read with the understanding that their agenda was not necessarily the same as those who financed them, or even, to their despair, those whom they led.

The first signs seemed propitious enough. In 1622, just two years after the first settlement in New England, *A Relation or Journall of the beginning and proceedings of the English Plantation setled at Plimoth . . .* was published in London. The text has become known as *Mourt's Relation*, a suitably sombre title for a Puritan settlement, following its listing under that name in Thomas Prince's 1736 *A Chronological History of New England*. It reports two events that are often regarded as foundation stones of the United States. One is political. In the Mayflower Compact, the forty-one male adults who arrived at Cape Cod in November 1620 agreed 'to combine ourselves together into a civil politic' and to 'frame such just and equal laws, ordinances, acts, constitutions . . . as shall be thought most meet and convenient for the general good of the colony'. The other is social; the first Thanksgiving. To celebrate their first harvest in 1621, the settlers invited Massasoit and some ninety of his tribe for three days of feasting and entertainment. The natives provided deer and the settlers 'fowl'. There was as yet no prescription that the 'fowl' should be turkey.[9]

The change in the text's title is perhaps an indicator of its incorporation into the myth of the United States. The reality was somewhat different. Its full title indicates that it is a promotional text, and refers to the success, after difficulties, of *certaine English Adventurers both Merchants and others*. The 'others', identified in the text as loyal to the Church of England, were in fact members of the Leyden congregation, which had separated from the Church. They made up the majority of the *Mayflower*'s complement, and they obliged all the males to adopt the Mayflower Compact because they feared 'some appearance of faction' among those they called 'strangers'. The Thanksgiving ceremony, the subject of countless drawings by American schoolchildren, took place thanks to a peace treaty agreed between the settlers and Massasoit which was kept until he died in 1661. As we shall see, relations with the Wampanoags under Massasoit's son Metacomet were far less jovial, setting the trend for the future. When in 1863 Abraham Lincoln adopted Thanksgiving as a national ceremony, it was in a nation riven by the Civil War and after two centuries during which the whites had decimated the natives and driven the remnants of the tribes westwards. *Mourt's Relation* is therefore a monument to the power of rhetoric.

Another event of 1622 was the death of the first leader of the Plymouth settlement, John Carver. In his place William Bradford was elected governor, and re-elected another twenty-nine times until 1656. The qualities of leadership that so impressed his community include, once again, a rhetorical power that is to be seen in *Of Plymouth Plantation*. Bradford wrote the journal in two segments. The first is a continuous narrative, written about 1630, which traces the departure of the group from England to Holland, and thence to Cape Cod, closing with the building of 'the first house for commone use', appropriately on Christmas Day, 1620.[10] The second 'Booke', probably written between 1644 and 1650, continued the account by means of annual instalments until 1646. Bradford announced at the outset that his text is concerned to reveal events in 'a plain stile, with singuler regard unto the simple trueth in all things' (25). Maybe so; but Bradford also writes with an awareness of the mission in which he is playing a leading part. The result is a text that wishes to convey a sense of great drama. The account of their arrival at New Plymouth is therefore structured to convey with unflinching clarity a mixture of relief and foreboding:

> Being thus arived in a good harbor and brought safe to land, they fell upon their knees & blessed the God of heaven, who had brought them over the vast & furious ocean, and delivered them from all the periles & miseries thereof, againe to set their feete on the firm and stable earth, their proper elemente . . . But hear I cannot but stay and make a pause, and stand half amased at this poore peoples presente condition; and so I thinke will the reader too, when he well considers the same. Being thus passed the vast ocean, and a sea of troubles before in their preparation . . . they had now no freinds to welcome them, nor inns to entertaine or refresh their weatherbeaten bodies, no houses or much less townes to repaire too, to seeke for succoure. It is recorded in scripture as a mercie to the apostle & his shipwraked company, that the barbarians shewed them no smale kindnes in refreshing them, but these savage barbarians, when they mette with them (as after will appeare) were readier to fill their sids full of arrows then otherwise. And for the season it was winter . . . Besids, what could they see but a hideous and desolate wilderness, full of wild beasts & willd men . . . for which way soever they turnd their eys (save upward to the heavens) they could have litle solace or content in respect of any outward objects. For summer being done, all things stand upon them with a weatherbeaten face; and the whole countrie, full of woods & thickets, represented a wild and savage heiw. If they looked behind them, ther was the mighty ocean which they had passed, and was now as a maine barre & goulfe to seperate them from all the civill parts of the world . . . What could now sustaine them but the spirite of God & his grace? May not & ought not the children of these fathers, rightly say: *Our faithers were Englishmen which came over this great ocean, and were ready to perish in this wilderness; but they cried unto the Lord, and he heard their voice and looked on their adversity* . . . (59–61)

This passage has been quoted at some length not just because it records a famous moment in American history, but also because it reveals some traits that would influence later American writing. First, the passage employs great art to convey the 'plain stile' that Bradford proclaimed. If he spoke as he wrote, it is little wonder that Bradford was re-elected governor year after year. He uses images drawn from everyday life, one of them – the sea of troubles

– shared with the most famous soliloquy in the language (*Hamlet* III. i. 56). The passage alludes on several occasions to the central Protestant text, the English Bible. It compares their own experience of 'barbarians' with that of St Paul (Acts 27–8), and moves into the vernacular for an imagined reported speech which includes a quotation from Psalm 107:6.

The comparison with St Paul indicates Bradford's sense of his mission. Remember Paul in prison: 'I have fought a good fight . . . Henceforth is laid up for me a crown of righteousness' (II Timothy 4:7–8). Bradford too regards himself as one of the elect, and this gives his text, and this passage, its teleological structure. And, as with St Paul, struggle is central to the mission. The result is an intolerance that strikes many modern readers as inhumane. Bradford feels obliged to recall that during the transatlantic crossing there was 'a spetiall worke of Gods providence'. A profane and healthy young sailor who mocked the seasick, threatening to throw them overboard, himself died of a disease 'and so was him selfe the first that was throwne overboard'. It was 'the just hand of God upon him' (57). During the course of his life Bradford felt that the just hand of God should fall on a number of people, particularly those younger than he.

'All things stand upon them with a weatherbeaten face.' A new territory exacerbated Bradford's claustral sense. Feeling isolated, Bradford populated the woods with his fears, and employed an imagery of the aborigines quite different from that to be found in Harriot's ethnology or Smith's adventuring. 'Wild' was his description both for the environment and the beings that occupied it. The related term 'wilderness' had a special significance that Bradford shared with many others. It derived from the Old English 'wildêornes', which identified areas occupied by wild beasts. It was an environment that commented, too, on the humans who lived there. In *Sir Gawain and the Green Knight*, written in the later fourteenth century, 'the wilderness of Wirral' (near Liverpool) is portrayed as an area where 'few lived . . . who loved either God or man wholeheartedly'. The Puritans increased the diabolic character of the wilderness. It was beyond the light of civilisation, beyond the Christian order of St Augustine's City of God, a place occupied by the devil. The English Puritan John Corbet, for instance, writing in 1645 of the siege of Gloucester, talked of the Royalist forces – 'those miserable Welshmen' – as denizens of the 'dark corners of the earth'. In 1662 the Congregational minister and poet Michael Wigglesworth multiplied that sense of threat when he expanded the corner to a continent that had never before seen the light of English Puritanism:

> Beyond the great Atlantick flood
>   There is a region vast,
> A country where no English foot
>   In former ages past:
> A waste and howling wilderness,
>   Where none inhabited
> But hellish fiends and brutish men
>   That Devils worshiped.

> This region was in darkness plac't
> Far off from heavens light,
> Amidst the shaddows of grim death
> And of Eternal night . . .

Bradford too blurs the distinction between the human and the animal. In his 'hideous and desolate wilderness' beasts and men are linked by the adjective 'wild'. The English Puritans found themselves on a brink in America which threatened their nationality, their civility, their religion, even their humanity.[11]

The Massachusetts Bay settlement was somewhat different from the one in New Plymouth. John Winthrop, who led the group that migrated there in 1630, claimed that they did not want to separate from the Church of England, but wished rather to revitalise it in the wilderness. In consequence Winthrop's sermon, 'A Modell of Christian Charity', quoted in Chapter 1 as the source of American exceptionalism, also contains Utopian elements when it emphasises the communitarian side of Dissent:

> Wee must be willing to abridge our selves of our superfluities, for the supply of others necessities . . . wee must delight in each other . . . rejoyce together, mourne together, labour, and suffer together . . . soe shall wee keepe the unitie of the spirit in the bond of peace . . . wee shall finde that the God of Israell is among us, when tenn of us shall be able to resist a thousand of our enemies, when hee shall make us a prayse and glory, that men shall say of succeeding plantacions: the lord make it like that of New England.

In constructing what he called 'a more near bond of marriage' among themselves, and between the community and God, Winthrop seemed to approach the protocommunism of the Digger Gerrard Winstanley (1609–1660?). Indeed, Winthrop reproved his deputy-governor, Thomas Dudley, for building a house that was too grand. But he would later use the image of marriage in another respect, to reconcile liberty with authority. A woman was free to choose her husband, but once married to him was subject to his rule. Winthrop's communitarianism, therefore, only went so far. It was not unusual. His limited concept of liberty would also be found in Milton's *Paradise Lost*. His Calvinist sense of the division between the elect and the damned was similar to that of Bradford. Unlike Harriot in Virginia, Winthrop talked of disease among the aborigines as no 'marvellous accident', but rather as evidence of God's intention that the land should be cleared for his community. Unfortunately, his community rarely seemed to deserve God's favour. Winthrop's *Journal*, begun on the *Arbella* in 1630 and continued spasmodically until he died in 1649, shows a vision darkened by the dissent and backsliding of others.[12]

Both Winthrop's communal utopianism, and the plain style proposed but not entirely followed by William Bradford, is evident in the first text of any substance printed in America, *The Bay Psalm Book*, translated by Richard Mather, John Eliot and Thomas Weld, and published in 1640. For about a century it was used over much of New England and had spread as far south as Philadelphia. The last, twenty-seventh, edition appeared in 1762, by which time it was being supplanted by the psalms and hymns of the English Dissenter

Isaac Watts. Watts's publications were enormously popular, but after the revolution his references to the British monarchy made his *Psalms of David* (1719) unsuitable. Joel Barlow and Timothy Dwight produced republican versions. For worship has, of course, its political dimension. *The Bay Psalm Book* could perhaps be regarded as an adjunct of the democratisation of religion which began in England with the translations of the Bible by William Tyndale in 1525 and Miles Coverdale in 1535. It is also part of another change introduced by the Reformation, from choral to communal singing, replacing hierarchical with a more participatory mode of churchgoing. *The Bay Psalm Book* is the fifteenth English metrical translation intended for musical worship, continuing a process begun in 1549. Yet participation remained within the bounds of the clearly limited concept of liberty found in Winthrop's 'A Modell of Christian Charity' and Milton's *Paradise Lost*. The dedication of the 1611 Bible, known in Britain as the Authorised Version and in America as the King James Bible, worried that 'men should have been in doubt which way they were to walk'. Likewise, John Cotton's Preface to *The Bay Psalm Book* asserted that 'in singing ordinary psalmes the whole Church is to joyne together in heart and voyce to prayse the Lord'.[13]

Such considerations influenced most translations of the Psalms. The particular character of *The Bay Psalm Book* can be seen by comparing its version of the most well-known psalm, XXIII, with the translation made four years earlier, in 1636, by George Sandys, now back in London:

> *Sandys*
> The Lord my shepherd, me His sheep
> Will from consuming famine keep.
> He fosters me in fragrant meads,
> By softly-sliding waters leads.
>
> My soul refresh'd with pleasant juice,
> And lest they should his name traduce,
> Then when I wander in the maze
> Of tempting sin, informs my ways.[14]
>
> *The Bay Psalm Book*
> The Lord to mee a shepheard is,
> want therefore shall not I.
> Hee in the folds of tender-grasse,
> doth cause mee downe to lie;
> To waters calme me gently leads
> Restore my soule doth hee:
> He doth in paths of righteousnes:
> for his names sake leade mee. (Ev–E2r)

Both translations are intended to be set to music and therefore use one of the commonest English verse forms, iambic tetrameter. The similarities end there. Sandys's title, a *Paraphrase upon the Psalmes*, made no claim to fidelity. In contrast, John Cotton's Preface to *The Bay Psalm Book*, said that it was the translators' 'faithfull indeavour, to keepe close to the originall text' (n.p.).

Sandys creates a conventional (indeed, now a comic) sense of the poetic in his tendency to use repetitive sounds and multisyllabic terms. He was even sometimes forced to seek some strained synonyms by the need to close his couplet (for instance, juice/traduce). *The Bay Psalm Book* could be called antipoetic in the stern march of its monosyllables and thumping rhymes. The translators' use of the ABAB rhyme scheme and their willingness to use half-rhyme (or to abandon rhyme altogether) gave them the extra space to negotiate a more accurate translation. The community envisaged by *The Bay Psalm Book* is larger and less educated than that sought by Sandys, but has a more individual relation with God – hence the rhyme hee/mee.

With its simple language, *The Bay Psalm Book* is the sacred equivalent of Winstanley's 'Digger's Song': 'You noble Diggers all, stand up now, stand up now.' The sense of community it creates is not, however, directed by Winstanley's egalitarianism but rather by an overriding need for proximity to God's word. As Cotton said in the Preface:

> If therefore the verses are not alwayes so smooth and elegant as some may desire or expect; let them consider that Gods Altar needs not our pollishings: Ex.20. for wee have respected rather a plaine translation, then to smooth our verses with the sweetnes of any paraphrase, and soe have attended Conscience rather then Elegance, fidelity rather then poetry . . . (n.p)

Verified by Exodus 20:25 ('And if thou wilt make me an altar of stone, thou shalt not build it of hewn stone'), *The Bay Psalm Book* has a rigorous austerity that attempts to be the verse equivalent of plain glass, giving a clear view of Heaven. It did not appeal to all. The Episcopalian James Fenimore Cooper, in *The Last of the Mohicans* (1826), called it a 'miserable travesty of the Song of David'. Yet in its attempt to skin the language to reveal the bones of truth in a world of lies it could be said to anticipate the early work of Ernest Hemingway.[15]

The dream of a community unified in heart and voice had already begun to fade. By 1637 the leaders of New England felt beleaguered: by the Pequot War, by Thomas Morton and Roger Williams, and by the Antinomian Crisis precipitated by Anne Hutchinson. The Pequot War, the first serious conflict between the settlers and the natives, shows how the fear of the wilderness and its denizens could easily shift into genocide. In retribution for Pequot attacks against frontier traders and settlers, John Underhill, a Massachusetts soldier, was commissioned to kill all the men and enslave all the women and children of the tribe. In May 1637 a Pequot fort on the Mystic River was surrounded by a combined force of Massachusetts and Connecticut militia. Some five hundred of its inhabitants, women and children as well as men, were slaughtered. The survivors were scattered. William Bradford gave a summary of the war in *Of Plymouth Plantation*, and detailed accounts of it were published in London in 1638, one of them by Underhill. Bradford repeated the moral of the profane sailor tipped overboard; the victory was 'a sweete sacrifice', and further evidence of God's providence (184). Underhill's *Newes from America* (1638) imagined that now that the necessary victory against Satan's servants, the aborigines, had been accomplished, the land would be transformed into a Protestant utopia.

In his life as well as his one book, *New English Canaan*, Thomas Morton (1590?–1647) projected a different Utopia, built upon work but substituting Dionysus for the angry God of the Puritans. They interpreted Morton's presence as a serious threat, and dealt with him accordingly. He was jailed by them several times, deported to England twice, expelled once to Maine, had his goods confiscated and his house torched. The charges laid against him were largely to do with illegal trade with the aborigines and disputes with the leadership of the Bay Colony. Yet Bradford portrays the difficulties with Morton as something altogether more concupiscent. Inoculating his story by beginning it as if it were a chapter from the King James Version, Bradford warmed his chill fingers over the misdeeds of Morton, for once confirming H. L. Mencken's 1925 definition of Puritanism as 'the haunting fear that someone, somewhere, may be happy':

> And Morton became lord of misrule, and maintained (as it were) a schoole of Athisme ... quaffing and drinking both wine & strong waters in great exsess ... They allso set up a May-pole, drinking and dancing aboute it many days togeather, inviting the Indean women, for their consorts, dancing and frisking togither, (like so many fair- ies, or furies rather,) and worse practices ... Morton likewise (to shew his poetrie) composed sundry rimes & verses, some tending to lasciviousnes, and others to the detraction & scandall of some persons, which he affixed to this idle or idoll May- polle. They chainged also the name of their place, and in stead of calling it Mounte Wollaston, they call it Merie-mounte, as if this joylity would have lasted ever. (141)

It did not. Morton was deported, the maypole cut down, and the place renamed Mount Dagon, after a god worshiped by the Philistines whose idol was demolished, leaving only the stump (I Samuel 5:4). Mount Dagon can now be found under the secular and prosaic name of Quincy, Massachusetts.

It is likely that the verses tacked by Morton to the maypole are among those that survive in the *New English Canaan*. It first appeared in Amsterdam in 1637. In part the text is an account of the unparalleled beauty and resources of New England, and, in the words of the title of its first 'Booke', the 'tractable nature and love towards the English' of the aborigines. In part it is an Angli- can attack on the 'cruell Schismaticks', who are often caricatured. One of those who sat in judgement over him, Dr Samuel Fuller becomes 'Dr. Noddy', while Plymouth Colony's military leader, Miles Standish, is 'Captain Shrimp'. Some of the poems elaborate on the love between the two races. 'The Songe' is a celebration of booze and sex, while 'The Authors Prologue' is a wedding poem, somewhat more bawdy than Spenser's 'Epithalamion' (1594), provid- ing an extended play on literal and tropic meanings of the term 'husbandry' by taking Ralegh's imagery of Guiana one stage further:

> Like a faire virgin, longing to be sped,
> And meete her lover in a Nuptiall bed,
> Deck'd in rich ornaments t'advaunce her state
> And excellence, being most fortunate,

> When most enjoy'd, so would our Canaan be
> If well imploy'd by art and industry
> Whose offspring, now shewes that her fruitfull wombe
> Not being enjoy'd, is like a glorious tombe,
> Admired things producing which there dye,
> And ly fast bound in darck obscurity . . .

William Carlos Williams, who admired Morton's *New English Canaan* for its 'lightness', made the same distinction between his practices and those of nearby Bay Colony. 'Their religious zeal', he said, prompted them 'not toward germination but the confinements of a tomb'. Other writers too have appreciated the sprightly life that Morton and his book brought to a sometimes plain New England, including Whittier, Longfellow, Stephen Vincent Benét and, of course, Nathaniel Hawthorne. But for the New England leaders Morton was an Elizabethan roisterer after his time, the thorn that always seemed to spring back to pierce the soul.[16]

Roger Williams was a different kind of thorn in the side of the New England leaders, and a different mediator between them and the wilderness. Educated at Cambridge, he took orders in the Church of England, then migrated in 1631 to Boston, but refused a post there because the church had not rejected Anglicanism. In 1633 he became a minister in Salem, but was banished from there in 1635, largely for two reasons. He claimed that Charles I had no title to native land, which the settlers had therefore to purchase from the natives. He also asserted that civil magistrates had no power to punish people for their religious opinions. He went beyond the boundaries of the Bay Colony, to the land of the Narragansetts, buying some land from them and founding what became known as the Providence Plantations, and later Rhode Island. He became a Baptist in 1639, but soon rejected that sect and for the remainder of his life called himself a 'seeker'. The term could be taken to describe his entire life, for it indicates the tenacity with which he clung to his beliefs. Others thought him unstable. Bradford called him 'a man godly & zealous, having many precious parts, but very unsettled in judgmente' (166). Williams in turn believed that it was others, rather than he, who were unsettled, and for the worst reasons: 'ready to be converted and turned forward and backward, as the *Weather-cock*, according as the powerfull *wind* of a prevailing *Sword* and *Authority*, shall blow from the various *points* and *quarters* of it'. This time a comparison with Gerrard Winstanley produces a greater equivalence. Both men rejected established authority and replaced it with a radical individualism. Winstanley thought that 'he that speaks from the original light within, can truly say, I know what I say and I know whom I worship'. Williams's similar belief in the sanctity of the individual conscience was embedded in the Patent for Providence Plantations that he obtained from the Roundhead Parliament, and repeated in 1663 in the Charter for Rhode Island granted by Charles II.[17] Both men could when necessary use simple language to communicate directly to ordinary people, Winstanley in his songs and Williams, as we shall see, in his poetry. Both men held unflinchingly to the belief in the 'original light within'. Yet Williams enjoyed much greater success than Winstanley.

The Digger colony at Cobham, Surrey, lasted less than one year, and nothing definite is known of Winstanley after 1660. Williams obtained a patent from the Long Parliament in 1644 which was confirmed by Charles II in 1663. Rhode Island offered a haven to Jews and Quakers refused sanctuary elsewhere, and its charter remained generally in force until the revolution. There are two explanations of Williams's greater success. One is personal. Williams, like Winstanley, held uncompromising beliefs and had a combative style, best seen in the two texts addressing John Cotton's orthodoxy, *The Bloudy Tenent of Persecution* (1643) and *The Bloudy Tenent yet More Bloudy* (1651). Yet, as Bradford's comment indicates, he was also an interesting and engaging man who made a number of important friends, including Winthrop, Cromwell and Milton. The other explanation is environmental. The conditions of a periphery, and the liberality of the Narragansetts, provided Williams with a space denied to Winstanley by the gentry and freeholders of Cobham, who burnt his houses and trampled his crops.

The impact made by the periphery on Williams is shown most clearly in his *A Key into the Language of America*, written, he said, on the voyage back to England to obtain the charter for Providence Plantation, and published in London in 1643. To an extent the text can be regarded as a cultural anthropology. As an attempt to mediate between two civilisations, it can be placed alongside Harriot's *A briefe and true report*, Daniel Gookin's histories of the aborigines, and John Eliot's work with the Algonkian language – including his translation of the Bible in 1661 and 1663 (the first complete Bible published in the colonies), and his *Indian Primer* (1669). Williams's title, however, hints that his work will be more complex than a primer. It is an ironic response to *The Gate of Tongues Unlocked and Opened*, the primer in foreign languages written by the Czech educationalist Comenius. *The Gate of Tongues* was translated into English in 1633, with a subtitle that made it a favourite with hard-pressed scholars: *A short way of teaching and thorowly learning, within a yeere and a half at the furthest, the Latin, English, French, and any other tongue.* By 1643 it had reached its sixth edition.[18] In contrast, Williams's title suggests that his text will be rich in implication rather than laden with explication; and this is confirmed by the opening address 'To the Reader': 'A little *Key* may open a *Box*, where lies a *bunch* of *Keyes*.' The text is organised into a series of chapters, each devoted to a specific subject ('Of Salutation', 'Of Fowle', 'Of Marriage' and so on), and each containing Algonkian vocabularies interspersed with comments and concluding with a poem. In design it is quite different too from that other explicatory genre, the sermon. *A Key* is not a simple text. Critics have given varying interpretations, and their readings tend to be conjectural. The titular metaphor, adapted from Comenius, will help to highlight the problem, but not solve it. At face value, Williams presents us with a phrase book of 'the Narrogansett *Dialect*'. This is the key that gets us into the box. Williams then goes on to claim more: that his text '*will be of great use in all parts of the Countrey*' – that it will, as his title says, open the rest of America to us. But what we are given is 'a *bunch* of *Keyes*' with unclear directions to take us to the locks.

To provide a problem but no clear solution changes the relationship between the stated audience, Williams's '*Deare and Wellbeloved* Friends and Countreymen, *in old and new* England', and the objects of attention, the aborigines of America. The alphabets of *Mandeville* asserted an order in accord with its Christian design. Harriot's *A briefe and true report* is even clearer. The 'bookes, writing and reading', of the whites create a superiority which is blessed by Providence (27). In contrast, *A Key* leaves us blundering in an alien undergrowth, which the aborigines are much better at deciphering. The consequence is a rearrangement of the antinomy savage/civilised and a redefinition of the concept of wilderness. This discomforting result can be seen in one of Williams's more limpid poems:

> *Adulteries, Murthers, Robberies, Thefts,*
>   *Wild* Indians *punish these!*
> *And hold the Scales of Instice* [*sic* – justice] *so,*
>   *That no man farthing leese.*
>
> *When Indians hear the horrid filths,*
>   *Of* Irish, English *Men,*
> *The horrid Oaths and Murthers late,*
>   *Thus say these* Indians *then.*
>
> *We weare no Cloaths, have many Gods,*
>   *And yet our sinnes are lesse*:
> *You are Barbarians, Pagans wild,*
>   *Your Land's the Wildernesse.*

There are wildernesses the world over, wherever human beings create '*horrid filths*'. As Roger Williams put it in 1652, during his second visit to England: 'We have *Indians* at home, *Indians* in Cornewall, *Indians* in Wales, *Indians* in Ireland.' It was a message that most of his contemporaries did not wish to hear.[19]

The ethnohistorian James Axtell has suggested that the presence of an alternative, aboriginal culture increased the New England suspicion of subversion within, and hence severity in correcting it.[20] It is also likely that the Dissenters had learned fear even before discrimination forced them to flee England. I suggested in the previous chapter that a dread of external perversion, together with an awareness of its possible impact on internal order, was embedded in Greek imperialism. The New England leaders were nothing if not classically learned. In 1635 the Boston Latin School was founded. It still exists. Initially, it prepared its students for Harvard, founded the following year at a site on the Charles River opposite Boston and in 1639 named Cambridge in honour of the university in England attended by many of the first generation of leaders. When Anne Hutchinson was asked to appear before the Boston General Court, her examiners included Governor Winthrop, John Eliot (one of the translators of *The Bay Psalm Book*) and Thomas Shepard, all educated at Cambridge University; and Thomas Dudley, a founder of Harvard.

The records of the trial show that Anne Hutchinson was not overawed by this array of intellect. Indeed, if Edward Johnson's mimicry of vernacular in his *History of New-England* (1653) is to be believed, her appeal was precisely to 'ignorant and unlettered Men and Women':

> Come along with me, says one of them, i'le bring you to a Woman that Preaches better Gospell then any of your black-coates that have been at the Ninneversity, a Woman of another kinde of spirit, who hath had many Revelations of things to come, and for my part, saith hee, I had rather hear such a one that speakes from the meere motion of the spirit, without any study at all, then any of your learned Scollers.

Anne Hutchinson (1591–1643) and her husband William had in 1634 followed John Cotton from Boston, Lincolnshire to Boston, Massachusetts. She continued her midwifery practice in her new home, and began preaching before lay meetings. Her message, derived from Genesis 17, urged a covenant of grace rather than one of works; in other words, that faith alone was necessary for salvation, rather than deeds. Boston quickly split into two camps, and Hutchinson was accused of Antinomianism, the belief that those saved by grace are no longer subject to moral law. During her trial Hutchinson ran rings round her accusers until she told Thomas Dudley that she had had 'an immediate revelation'; that she had heard the voice of God. Dudley's gasped repetition – 'How! an immediate revelation' – indicates the shock created by her statement. Undismayed, she elaborated on the nature of her inspiration, even threatening the court that 'if you go on in this course . . . you will bring a curse upon you and your posterity'. Her fate was sealed. She was convicted of heresy and banished with her family and followers to Rhode Island.[21]

The Antinomian Crisis is not unlike the later Salem witchcraft trials. Treating the trials as a type of the McCarthy hearings of 1953–4, Arthur Miller, in his Preface to *The Crucible* (1953), called them 'one of the strangest and most awful chapters in human history'. Awful certainly, but not strange. The events in Boston in 1637 and Salem in 1692 were ostensibly about heresy, but can also be understood as conflicts of class, learning and gender. Both events were exacerbated by being grounded in a peripheral culture. Milton in Old England and Winthrop in the New believed in the same model of gender relations, focused on the institution of marriage and summed up by the words love, mutuality and hierarchy. In two circumstances the subordination of women was weakened. One was during the unstable conditions of the English Civil War; the other was on a periphery. In England groups such as the Family of Love and the Ranters practised their so-called 'heresies' overtly; and Samuel Torshell, an English minister, theorised that the state of grace was blind to gender. 'The *Soul*', he wrote, 'knows no difference of *Sexe*, as neither doe the *Angels*.' Anne Hutchinson put Torshell's theory into practice. Her spectacular success was no doubt partly due to her striking abilities. It was also partly due to an environment which had been settled only for six years and which was as yet, to use James's phrase, 'undarkened by customs and institutions'. Winthrop's response was more severe in Boston than it would have been in London. Because of the crisis, 'All things are turned upside down among us,' he later said. The dispute had spread from the church 'into Civill and Publike affaires', had created marital disharmony, and had even diminished an expedition against the Pequots. Fearful of the environment, Winthrop also took advantage of it. He expelled Hutchinson to a more distant and dangerous periphery. In 1643 he noted that she and her family had been killed by natives, conveying no sense of sorrow but adding merely that they 'had cast off ordinances and churches'.[22]

Winthrop also demonised her. The title of the pamphlet he published in London the year after Hutchinson's death indicated that he had classed her with other heretics who were becoming more prominent in England. But in *A Short Story of the Rise, Reign, and Ruin of the Antinomians, Familists and Libertines* he went further. He accused 'this *American Jesabel*', as he called her, of combining her work as a preacher with that of a midwife to produce monstrosities. On the day that Hutchinson had been cast out from the church one of her followers, Mary Dyer, had been delivered prematurely of a still-born child. Winthrop exhumed the body and wrote an account of what he found in his *Journal*. His description, slightly altered, was printed in *A Short Story* as tangible proof of the evil influence of Anne Hutchinson:

> it had no head but a face, which stood so low upon the breast, as the eares (which were like an Apes) grew upon the shoulders.
>
> The eyes stood farre out, so did the mouth, the nose was hooking upward, the brest and back was full of sharp prickles, like a Thornback, the navell and all the belly with the distinction of the sex, were, where the lower part of the back and hips should have been, and those back parts were on the side the face stood.
>
> The arms and hands, with the thighs and legges, were as other childrens, but in stead of toes, it had upon each foot three claws, with talons like a young fowle. Upon the back above the belly it had two great holes, like mouthes, and in each of them stuck out a piece of flesh.
>
> It had no forehead, but in the place thereof, above the eyes, foure hornes, whereof two were above an inch long, hard, and sharpe, the other two were somewhat shorter.

Modern medicine would be much more circumspect in its description; perhaps it was simply a twisted foetus. Winthrop produced something altogether more sophisticated. Using his learning, he has drawn on a reservoir of images from many sources, including *Mandeville*'s description of some of the inhabitants of the Andaman Sea and the symbology of deformity reflected in *Richard III*. In a land as yet little explored, such Old World images are readily marshalled to explain a stillbirth, and take on a fresh and frightening life. It appears that the Court had acted just in time. A few more weeks, and Mary Dyer might have given birth to a devil. Perhaps we need to go to a later frontier, in the *Alien* trilogy of movies, to find anything as horrific. Yet Thomas Weld, the Massachusetts agent who wrote the Preface to *A Short Story*, tried to outdo it. He summarised Winthrop's account of the stillborn child, and then produced this description of Anne Hutchinson:

> *Mistris* Hutchinson *being big with child . . . she brought forth not one, (as Mistris Dier did) but (which was more strange to amazement) 30. monstrous births or thereabouts, at once; some of them bigger, some lesser, some of one shape, some of another; few of any perfect shape, none at all of them (as farre as ever I could learne) of humane shape.*

Weld embroiders an account of Anne Hutchinson's 'monstrous birth' that appears in Winthrop's *Journal*. Using the detailed clinical description in the *Journal*, a scholar has suggested that Hutchinson suffered from a hydatidiform mole, an abnormal growth in the placenta. But the interpretive power of the Puritan imagination far exceeded that of present-day medicine. Anne Hutchinson was therefore a warning to women settlers. If they wished to benefit from the protean conditions of a peripheral culture, they would have to be more circumspect.[23]

The evidence of Anne Bradstreet's poetry shows that she had learned the lesson of Anne Hutchinson's fate. Bradstreet was the daughter of Thomas Dudley, who built too fine a house for John Winthrop's taste, and who sat in judgement on Hutchinson. She migrated to the Bay Colony in the *Arbella* with her parents and her husband Simon Bradstreet, a graduate of Emmanuel College, Cambridge, who became one of the Colony's leading figures, and in 1679 its governor. In the only book published in her lifetime, *The Tenth Muse Lately sprung up in America* (1650), Bradstreet arrived at three interwoven solutions to the problem highlighted by the fate of Hutchinson. The first solution invoked antecedents, the second the question of poetic form, and the third, using her connections, family. Bradstreet wrote just three formal elegies, a triptych of which the central panel was Queen Elizabeth I. In suggesting that women 'are heires together with men of the grace of life', Samuel Torshell had proposed Elizabeth as an example of a woman who was '*able to rule the whole world*'. Bradstreet's elegy makes a similar point:

> No Phoenix pen, nor Spencer's poetry,
> No Speed's nor Camden's learned history,
> Eliza's works wars, praise, can e'er compact;
> The world's the theatre where she did act ...
> Who was so good, so just, so learn'd, so wise,
> From all the kings on earth she won the prize ...
> She hath wiped off th'aspersion of her sex,
> That women wisdom lack to play the rex ...[24]

William Camden's *Annals* (1615, 1625) of Elizabeth's reign, and John Speed's county maps, *The Theatre of the Empire of Great Britain* (1611), are both too circumscribed to account for Elizabeth. So too are Spenser's poetry and Bradstreet's own 'phoenix' pen. Appropriately, the other two panels of her triptych are painted in less brilliant colours. She praises the 'Learning, valour, wisdom' of Sidney, who posthumously (he died at the Battle of Zutphen in 1586) became the model of the Elizabethan soldier-poet (189). Her third elegy is for Guillaume Du Bartas (1544–90), whose epic poem expounding the Creation exceeded twenty thousand lines but failed to complete its second week. Joshua Sylvester began publishing an English translation in 1592. It was a great success; by 1641 *The Divine Weeks and Works* had gone through nine editions. With its length, scope and grandeur, *The Divine Weeks and Works* satisfied the need for a Protestant epic, until *Paradise Lost* replaced it in 1667. Bradstreet's elegy to 'Great, dear, sweet Bartas' creates an anti-epic, including the ultimate bathetic effect, some eighty-six years before Pope wrote his essay 'Of the Art of Sinking in Poetry':

> My dazzled sight of late reviewed thy lines,
> Where art, and more than art, in nature shines ...
> Which rays darting upon some richer ground,
> Had caused flowers and fruits soon to abound;
> But barren I my daisy here do bring,
> A homely flower in this my latter spring ... (192)

Positioning herself behind such antecedents as Elizabeth, Sidney and Du Bartas, Bradstreet could afford to display the humility that is to be found everywhere in her poetry, but at its most extreme here. Humility was vital. Nathaniel Ward, the Massachusetts clergyman best known for *The Simple Cobler of Aggawam* (1647), his grumbling attack on religious tolerance, highlighted Bradstreet's delicate situation when, in his introductory poem to *The Tenth Muse*, he called her 'a right Du Bartas girl', but warned men that they had best 'look to't, lest women wear the spurs' (4). He need not have worried. Bradstreet, unlike Hutchinson, succeeded precisely because she publicly disavowed spurs. 'The Prologue', for instance, might have Hutchinson in mind, and stakes a limited claim only after constructing a strictly gendered space:

> Men have precedency and still excel,
> It is but vain unjustly to wage war,
> Men can do best, and women know it well.
> Preeminence in all and each is yours;
> Yet grant some small acknowledgement of ours. (16)

These lines, often quoted, seem strange and quite unacceptable today. Hardly feminist, they nevertheless are part of a negotiation creating an interstice which will be opened further by later women writers.

The second solution to the Hutchinson problem involved poetic form. The opening of the 'Prologue' shows that Bradstreet, who was very well read, drew her techniques from a variety of classical writers:

> To sing of wars, of captains, and of kings,
> Of cities founded, commonwealths begun,
> For my mean pen are too superior things ... (15)

The first line alludes to Virgil's *Aeneid* ('This is a tale of arms and of a man'), while the second brings together an allusion to Livy's *History of Rome* with a reference to Bradstreet's own situation as a member of a first family of the Bay Colony. The third line undermines the first two by using a rhetoric of incapacity which harks back to such Latin writers as Horace. The result aimed to reassure Bradstreet's audience, predominantly male, by fusing a group of familiar allusions and generic formulas with the deference expected of the gender. It follows that her most successful, and most anthologised, poems are those which apply her sense of poetic form to her present-day life. Her overt attempt at traditional epic, the 'Quaternion', four poems of four books each on 'The Humours', 'The Ages of Man', 'The Seasons' and 'The Four

Monarchies', is stilted and bathetic in comparison with Du Bartas and Ralegh. Her major achievement, and the third solution to the Hutchinson problem, is rather to be found in the poems devoted to the Bradstreets, which embody the Puritan sense of pilgrimage in the life of a family. This solution is sketched in *The Tenth Muse*, but fully developed in the poems that Bradstreet added for a second edition, but not printed until 1678, six years after her death. The sequence of poems on her husband's absence in England contains one of the great hymns to domestic love:

> If ever two were one, then surely we.
> If ever man were lov'd by wife, then thee;
> If ever wife was happy in a man,
> Compare with me ye women if you can . . . (225)

A third group of poems, written in a small notebook, were not published until 1867. They are dedicated to her children:

> This book by any yet unread.
> I leave for you when I am dead,
> That being gone, here you may find
> What was in your living mother's mind. (240)

Her mind was much upon her family, and many of her poems provide a vivid record of domestic life in Puritan Massachusetts. Some are precisely dated, as if they are entries in the family Bible. They include poems on the deaths of her parents, the various illnesses that occurred, the burning of a house, and particularly those on the deaths of three young grandchildren. Unlike Bradstreet's 'Dialogues and Lamentations', these are far from ritual exercises in religious trial and devotion. They convey a strong sense of the struggle to reconcile present loss with deeply-held belief:

> No sooner come, but gone, and fall'n asleep,
> Acquaintance short, yet parting caused us weep;
> Three flowers, two scarcely blown, the last i'th' bud,
> Cropt by th'Almighty's hand; yet is He good . . . (237)

As in 'To my Dear and loving Husband', the use of everyday language, with its frequent monosyllables and everyday images, communicates the texture of the commonplace. Taken together, the family poems democratise the form of the epic, inflecting a traditional form to take account of the facts of life in a colony. It was an achievement anticipated in that title, *The Tenth Muse Lately sprung up in America*, uniting gender with genre, and centre with periphery.

Like Janus, the double-faced Roman god of doorways, Bradstreet's poetry looked two ways: back towards the Old World and forward into the New. This ambivalence is to be found in much Puritan writing, and indeed is demanded by the rationale of their migration. In 1648 Richard Mather drafted the 'Cambridge Platform', a statement granting quasi-establishment powers to their church, and not abolished in Massachusetts until 1833. When the 'Cambridge Platform' was published in 1649 as *A Platform of Church-Discipline*, its Preface firmly declared that 'we . . . are by nature English men'. Similarly,

John Cotton asserted that they had undertaken this 'hazardous and voluntary banishment into this remote wilderness' to set up a purer but not different church. Scholars have suggested that the history of the more public Puritan poetry written in America can be constructed in terms of the fortunes of their English counterparts. Bradstreet's 'Dialogue between Old England and the New', is subtitled 'concerning their present Troubles'. Dated 1642, it begins in concern about 'these sad alarms', and ends after the admonition: 'Bring forth the beast that ruled the world with's beck,/And tear his flesh, and set your feet on's neck . . .' (187). The publication of *The Tenth Muse* (including this 'Dialogue') in 1650 may mark the apogee of Anglo-American Puritanism. In January 1649 Charles I had been executed, and the New Model Army under Cromwell had achieved great success in Ireland and Scotland. In 1653 Cromwell became Lord Protector, and his forces defeated the Dutch and Spanish. But the various Puritan interests held together by Cromwell crumbled after his death in 1658, leading to the Restoration of 1660. Michael Wigglesworth's long ballad *The Day of Doom*, published in 1662 and very widely read in New England, is a more immediate response to the Restoration than its English counterpart, *Paradise Lost*, published five years later. Its 224 stanzas are constructed as a sermon, with marginal references to the Bible and occasional moments of direct address, when with magnificent ire the preacher separates the saints from the sinners. Since stanza 8 the latter have been in no doubt as to their fate, and they suffer until stanza 201, when God finally appears and pronounces judgement:

> *Ye sinful wights, and cursed sprights, that work Iniquity,*
> *Depart together from me for ever to endless Misery;*
> *Your portion take in yonder Lake, where Fire and Brimstone flameth:*
> *Suffer the smart, which your desert as it's due wages claimeth.*

And off they go, leaving the few 'perfect Saints' to reign eternally in Heaven with God.[25]

Very soon the Saints felt assailed from both sides. Increasingly isolated from England after the Restoration, they quickly found further troubles to the West. The death of Massasoit in 1661 began a period of deteriorating relations with some native tribes, which came to a climax with King Philip's War, its title taken from the settlers' name for Massasoit's son Metacomet. The War began with a dispute over land rights. The Wampanoags took the same view about native ownership as Roger Williams: that the land was theirs, and in the absence of purchase had merely been lent to the settlers. Their attempt to recover their property led to serious violence, with the Wampanoags, now possessing firearms and assisted by some other tribes (including the Narragansetts), attacking villages and destroying crops and livestock. Their campaign collapsed when Metacomet was killed in 1676, but the spoliation was so severe that New Englanders did not resettle that part of the frontier until 1720. The War was spatially constricting but stylistically fertile, producing a new genre, the captivity narrative. In February 1676 a group of Narragansetts attacked Lancaster, Massachusetts and took some hostages, including Mary Rowlandson (1636–1711), who was held for nearly twelve weeks before she was ransomed. Six years later she published an account of her experience: *The Sovereignty & Goodness of God, Together with the Faithfulness of His Promises Displayed; Being a Narrative of the Captivity and Restauration of Mrs. Mary Rowlandson.*

Variously titled, the narrative has reappeared in a large number of editions and anthologies. It owes its success to the ways in which it unites four earlier forms. Critics have shown that three of them are deeply embedded in the Puritan experience. One is the sermon, with its didacticism, and care with Biblical precedent. An example is Winthrop's 'A Modell of Christian Charity'. Another is the jeremiad, the lament over backsliding of which Michael Wigglesworth is one of the most wrathful practitioners. The third is spiritual autobiography. It can be traced back to the *Confessions* of St Augustine (AD 354–430), the Bishop of Hippo (in North Africa), whose account of his sins and conversion to Christianity in AD 386 became a model for the self-scrutiny and successful outcome which was a central element of Protestant theocracy. The Puritans on both sides of the Atlantic kept a balance sheet of their relationship with God. (The metaphor of accountancy is deliberate, for that modern profession in its careful precision could be regarded as an heir to Puritanism.) In England John Bunyan's *Grace Abounding to the Chief of Sinners*, written while he was in prison, was published in 1666, while *The Autobiography of Thomas Shepard*, who died in 1649, was probably the first American autobiography, treating the transatlantic crossing as the conversion experience. The fourth source, adding much-needed spice to the other three, was the atrocity story. This was a reconfiguration of the 'Black Legend' discussed in Chapter 2, with the aborigines now taking the role previously played by the Spanish. The narrative thus begins:

> On the tenth of February 1675 [1676] came the Indians with great numbers upon Lancaster. Their first coming was about sunrising. Hearing the noise of some guns, we looked out; several houses were burning and the smoke ascending to heaven. There were five persons taken in one house; the father and mother and a sucking child they knocked on the head; the other two they took and carried away alive . . . Another there was who running along was shot and wounded and fell down; he begged of them his life, promising them money (as they told me), but they would not hearken to him but knocked him in [the] head, stripped him naked, and split open his bowels.

The aborigines are immediately established as representatives of evil, the inhabitants of 'the vast and desolate wilderness' into which she is forced to travel. They present the protagonist with a series of trials that she must undergo before, in 'a remarkable change of providence', she is released. References to the medieval trope of the wheel of fortune indicate a dialectic of good and evil, which is embedded in the structure of the work. The text is organised as a series of 'removes' rather than chapters. This has two counterpointed functions. It provides an inland version Shepard's transatlantic conversion experience, analogous to the wandering of the Israelites in Egypt; and it plots the aborigines' 'usual manner to remove when they had done any mischief, lest they should be found out'. Native duplicity is contrasted with the narrative style, which in its horrific detail makes claims to tell the truth, and which provides a series of confessions, underpinned by biblical reference. Native mobility, sometimes depicted in animal terms, is also contrasted with the quiescence of the closure: 'I have learned to look beyond present and smaller troubles and to be quieted under them, as Moses said, Exod. 14:13, "Stand still and see the salvation of the Lord".'[26]

The captivity narrative was a much-read public form until the later nineteenth century; it was renewed in the slave narrative; and its plot reappeared in such Western movies as John Ford's *The Searchers* (1956). In contrast, the poetry of Edward Taylor was not published until 1937. It was essentially as private communion that nearly all of his work passed down within his family, until it was given to Yale University Library in 1883, where it lay forgotten for many years. The bulk of the poetry is made up of two sets of 'Preparatory Meditations', 217 introspective poems written before administering the Eucharist, for Taylor was pastor of the frontier town of Westfield, Massachusetts, from 1679 until his death. Taylor's models were the *Spiritual Exercises* (1548) of St Ignatius Loyola, the founder of the Jesuits, and the English metaphysical poets whom he had read at school in Leicestershire. Yet his work has travelled far from Catholic devotions, and from the obliqueness of Donne's most clever conceits. Neither is it, despite the number of poems, repetitious. It resembles, rather, a series of draft statements towards a spiritual autobiography, each one inspired by the Bible. Hence Meditation 46 in the First Series, which takes its cue from Revelations 3:5 – 'He that overcometh, the same shall be clothed in white raiment':

> I'm but a jumble of gross Elements
> A Snaile Horn where an Evill Spirit tents.
>
> A Dirt ball dresst in milk white Lawn, and deckt
>   In Tissue tagd with gold, or Ermins flush,
> That mocks the starrs, and sets them in a fret
>   To se themselves out shone thus. Oh they blush.
>   Wonders stand gastard here. But yet my Lord,
>   This is but faint to what thou dost afford.[27]

The address to God and the simplicity of the language resembles George Herbert's *The Temple* (1633). Many of the terms used here would be familiar to his ordinary parishioners in 1692, when the poem was written, even perhaps 'gastard', a dialect term used from Derby to Essex that still remains with us in the form 'aghast'. The coarseness of the metaphors for the self is far greater than in Herbert. Taylor emphasises that coarseness, running variations on 'A Dirt ball' throughout the poem. Taylor is sometimes portrayed as a mystic, but there is little that is otherworldly in his poetry, which is unpretentious, frank, even comic – a quality not often associated with the Puritans. A comparison of one of his miscellaneous poems, 'A Fig for thee Oh! Death', with Donne's tenth Divine Meditation, 'Death be not proud', reveals that

Taylor's syntax, and therefore his argument, is much more simple, direct and pugnacious. His most famous poem, 'Huswifery', while a fully worked conceit, shares none of the attention-seeking smartness of Donne's compass conceit. Like the variations on 'A Dirt ball', the conceit is lucid and unstrained, and, once again, the self is modestly portrayed. It is God who is the housewife, and Taylor merely the wheel on which He spins. It could be argued that modesty is the leading characteristic of Taylor's work, and it is this that allies it with the poetry of Anne Bradstreet, whose *Tenth Muse* was on his shelves.

Modesty is not a feature of the work of Cotton Mather, either in attitude or quantity. A theocrat to the core, he believed that he had inherited not only the leadership of Massachusetts and its church, but also the obligation to record its achievements. As he wrote in 1690: '*I were a very* Degenerate *person, if I should not be touched with an* Ambition, *to be a Servant of the* CHURCHES IN *this now famous Countrey, which my two Grand-fathers* COTTON *and* MATHER *had so considerable a stroke in the first planting of.*' He served with a ferocity that was powered by a combustible mixture of energy, pride and guilt – guilt, because pride was sinful. A 1940 bibliography of his works listed 468 printed items, including history, biography, poetry, science, medicine, philosophy and theology. One of his longer works, *Magnalia Christi Americana* (in English, *The Great Works of Christ in America*), is discussed here because it was intended as the greatest summation of events in New England since first settlement. It also revealed a New England in the process of change. The text is something of a compendium. It was begun around 1693, included seventeen of his earlier publications, was completed in 1698 and published in London in 1702. Mather tried to provide his text, covering some eight hundred pages, with a unifying theme in its opening paragraph:

> I write the *Wonders* of the CHRISTIAN RELIGION, flying from the Depravations of *Europe*, to the *American Strand*: And, assisted by the Holy Author of that *Religion*, I do, with all Conscience of *Truth*, required therein by Him, who is the *Truth* it self, Report the *Wonderful Displays* of his Infinite Power, Wisdom, Goodness, and Faithfulness, wherewith His Divine Providence hath *Irradiated* an *Indian Wilderness*.

As an opening flourish this is marginally less grandiose than the exordium to Book One of *Paradise Lost*. Mather reports rather than justifies the ways of God, and limits those ways to just one corner of the universe. Perhaps because of this restriction, but more likely because prose is the chosen medium, he feels no need to invoke the Muses. Nevertheless, the epic intent is clear. Mather's style is far from plain. He exceeds Milton in writing that is lofty, complex, learned and allusive, yet garnished with the occasional, rather ponderous, word-play. The text sees Columbus's landfall as an analogue of Genesis 1:1, creating a New World for the expression of 'Two Benefits, *Literature* and *Religion*, which dawned upon the miserable World, one just *before*, t'other just *after*, the first famed *Navigation* hither'. The conjunction of the three events is providential. The invention of print and the arrival of the Reformation result in the English Bible; America is where its precepts will be practised. This is just the first 'wonder'. The rest are worked out in seven books, covering the settlement of New England; the lives of its governors; 'the Lives of Sixty Famous Divines'; the foundation of Harvard; the constitutions of the churches; 'A Faithful Record of many Illustrious, Wonderful Providences'; and *'The Wars of the Lord'*.[28]

The structure of the text therefore extends the Puritan moral geography stated in the opening paragraph and already seen in the work of Bradford and Wigglesworth. Like Montaigne in the essay discussed in Chapter 2, 'Of the Caniballes', Mather regards the Old World as corrupt, but its 'depravations' are religious rather than temporal. The state of nature is now the abode of the devil rather than a sign of purity. Mather, like Rowlandson, demonises the aborigines. His biography of John Eliot in Book III emphasises the difficulty of the task that the missionary has undertaken and, in one of his adventures in word-play, Mather remarks that the anagram of Eliot is 'TOILE'. The aborigine 'way of living', he says, 'is infinitely barbarous'. He pities Eliot for the pains that he has taken to learn Algonkian, and gives lengthy transliterations of individual words to show that the language is 'tedious' and inefficient.[29] It is here, though, that a somewhat different note can be detected, and one which signals that the Anglo-American world was growing more complex as he was writing.

The first generation of settlers had been dying off and, as a way of combating declining church membership, the Massachusetts synod introduced the 'Half-way Covenant' in 1662, offering baptism to children of those who had not had a conversion-experience. In the Connecticut Valley some ministers went further, treating the Eucharist as a symbol of conversion, and therefore opening church membership to all those who desired it. Settlement in Massachusetts was increasing, and Boston had become a major port, with all the conveniences which make up a port: fine houses for the wealthy merchants, and taverns and brothels for the sailors. The 'Glorious Revolution' of 1688 and the flight of James II had, in the eyes of many New Englanders, averted a 'Popish plot' – phrases echoed the following year in a local uprising when the authoritarian governor, Sir Edmund Andros, was deposed and returned to England. But in 1691 William and Mary replaced the original Massachusetts Charter of 1629 with one which enfranchised all Christians except Catholics. The *'American Strand'* had become very different from the one imagined by Bradford's pilgrims when they fell to their knees in 1620.

Mather's attitude to the aborigines in *Magnalia Christi Americana* reveals the complexities of a text that tries to unite the traditional with the modern. On the one hand, the moral geography of the text reveals that Mather is as traditional a Puritan as Bradford or Winthrop; on the other, his description of the native language shows that he despises the aborigines because, he believes, they are in a state of nature. Without going so far as to separate the sacred and profane (in this respect there is no comparison to be made with Jefferson), Mather is distinctly more modern in civil matters than he is in religious. In *Magnalia Christi Americana* this becomes clear in the biography of Sir William Phips, the first Royal Governor of Massachusetts appointed under the new Charter. Mather wrote a lengthy eulogy of Phips which was first published in

1697, two years after he died. Phips was born in 1651 in humble circumstances 'at a despicable Plantation' in Maine (278). As captain of a frigate in the British navy, he discovered a sunken Spanish treasure-ship off Haiti. He sailed to Britain with the treasure and, according to Mather, behaved with such 'Honesty, Fidelity and Ability' that William III knighted him, the first American to receive that honour. Mather concluded that Phips should be called '*The Knight of Honesty*':

> for it was *Honesty* with *Industry* that raised him; and he became a Mighty River, without the running in of Muddy Water to make him so. Reader, now make a Pause, and behold *One Raised by God!* (284)

Although Mather later describes Phips's (convenient) conversion experience, he has here negotiated an accommodation between traditional Puritan beliefs and the modern trading state by describing new characteristics, which qualify a person for admission to the elect. A less positive assessment would reveal Phips as a throwback to the Elizabethan adventurer, but Mather portrays him as a thoroughly modern man, lauding his business acumen. Mather may have eulogised Phips because he supported Increase Mather, Cotton's father, in his struggle against Andros. It is more likely that he praised him because he wanted to see in Phips the future of Puritanism. Incorporated into *Magnalia Christi Americana*, the biography of Phips creates a trajectory from Bradford and Winthrop by emphasising work. It is possible to see the shadow of Mather himself in his account of Phips. This is partly because Mather too was a thoroughly modern man in such secular matters as science and medicine, for instance in his advocacy of inoculation and in his election to the Royal Society in 1714. It is also because of the value they both apparently placed in sheer hard work. In 1722, at the age of fifty-nine, Mather had this advice for those who contemplated the ministry: 'Be up and be doing. *Activity, Activity*, in the *Service* of GOD.' The ministry provided many '*Opportunities to do Good*', a theme Mather emphasised at length in *Bonifacius*, better known as *Essays to Do Good* (1710), a text which was influenced by Daniel Defoe's 'Essay on Projects' and which in turn influenced Benjamin Franklin.[30] Mather portrays Phips as an artisan-capitalist; a man who, like Robinson Crusoe, makes things, and makes them happen. Yet at the moment when Phips finds the treasure, Mather transforms him from subject to object in reporting celebration as gratitude: '*Thanks be to God! We are made*' (284). As we shall see in the final section of this chapter, the self-made man will emerge as an important American myth. Mather contributed to that myth, except that for him God had a greater hand in the making.

The rising empire

In 1726, George Berkeley, the Anglican bishop and idealist philosopher, wrote his only serious poem, 'On the Prospect of Planting Arts and Learning in America':

> In happy Climes the Seat of Innocence,
>   Where Nature guides and Virtue rules,
> Where Men shall not impose for Truth and Sense,
>   The Pedantry of Courts and Schools:
>
> There shall be sung another golden Age,
>   The Rise of Empire and of Arts,
> The good and great inspiring epic Rage,
>   The wisest Heads and noblest Hearts . . .
>
> Westward the Course of Empire takes its Way;
>   The first four Acts already past,
> A fifth shall close the Drama with the Day:
>   Time's noblest Offspring is the last.[31]

The immediate intention of the poem was to promote the foundation of a college in Bermuda. Berkeley set off for Rhode Island in 1728 to work on his plans for the college. While in Rhode Island he founded a Literary and Philosophical Society, and wrote *Alciphron*, a set of Socratic dialogues refuting deism. The Bermudan project came to nothing, and late in 1731 Berkeley returned to Britain, where he published *Alciphron*.

The importance of Berkeley's contribution to American culture is out of proportion with its brevity. Unlike the project, the poem made a great impact. It extends to America one of the oldest tropes in European civilisation, *translatio imperii*, discussed briefly in Chapter 1 and concerning the westward movement of civilisation. This was an idea that became increasingly popular in what is sometimes known as the First British Empire. Berkeley's poem was published in 1752, the year before his death and long after the project collapsed. It is likely that it was read by Nathaniel Ames (1708–64), a Massachusetts doctor who compiled one of the most popular almanacs in the colonies. The almanac for 1758 energetically extends *translatio imperii*, and redraws on a continental scale the Puritan line between darkness and light:

the Progress of Humane Literature (like the Sun) is from the East to the West; thus it has travelled thro' *Asia* and *Europe*, and now is arrived at the Eastern Shore of *America*. As the Coelestial Light of the Gospel was directed here by the Finger of GOD, it will doubtless, finally drive the long! long! Night of Heathenish Darkness from *America*: – So Arts and Sciences will change the Face of Nature in their Tour from Hence over the Appalachian Mountains to the Western Ocean; and as they march thro' the vast Desert, the Residence of wild Beasts will be broken up, and their obscene Howl cease for ever.[32]

Ames uses the term 'Desert' in its older sense of vacant land, for he asserts that the land west of the Appalachian mountains is so fertile that it has become 'the Garden of the World'. He also anticipates that 'inestimable Treasures of Gold and Silver' will be found to the West. This prediction also came true. Gold was eventually found in 1848 in the Sacramento Valley, not too far from Berkeley, the Northern California city named in honour of the philosopher who had written the phrase 'Westward the Course of Empire takes its Way'.

Until the American Revolution, the 'Progress of Humane Literature' extended down the coastline from Boston in the north to Surinam in the south, made only occasional forays westwards, and did not always display the triumphalism of *translatio imperii*. Two texts by the prolific writer Aphra Behn display colonial administrations in a poor light. One is read today, in part, because of its treatment of slavery. The novel *Oroonoko*, published in 1688, is subtitled *A True History* and is apparently based on an incident in 1664 in Surinam while it was still under British administration. Behn claimed to have witnessed the incident, but her account also reveals extensive reading. The depiction of Surinam recalls Harriot's *A briefe and true report of the new found land of Virginia* and Ralegh's *The Discoverie of Guiana*. It is a riot of sense-experience conveyed in the present tense:

> 'tis there eternal Spring . . . groves of oranges, lemons, citrons, figs, nutmegs, and noble aromatics, continually bearing their fragrancies. The trees appearing all like nosegays adorned with flowers of different kind; some are all white, some purple, some scarlet, some blue, some yellow; bearing, at the same time, ripe fruit and blooming young, or producing every day new.[33]

The text organises the inhabitants of Surinam into four racial groups. The aborigines are appropriate to this Berkeleian 'Seat of Innocence'. They are depicted 'like our first Parents before the Fall', revealing 'that simple Nature is the most harmless, inoffensive and virtuous mistress' (76–7). The snakes in Eden are no longer the Spanish, but the British themselves. The belief that the colonies were being populated by those cast out of British society is reflected in Behn's comment on the Council of Surinam, which:

> consisted of such notorious villains as Newgate never transported . . . and had no sort of Principles to make them worthy the name of men. But, at the very council table, would contradict and fight with one another, and swear so bloodily that 'twas terrible to hear, and see them. (133–4)

The British have found that the aborigines are not amenable to slavery, and so have imported a third racial group, Africans from the Gold Coast. They give their slaves new, often classical, names, and work them viciously.

So far, Behn has given a reasonably accurate account of the slave trade. Enslavement of Africans was embodied in colonial law at this time, for instance in Virginia in 1661 and Maryland in 1663, creating an institution that would become central to the Southern economy. By 1665 Surinam had some three thousand slaves, and when Behn died in 1689 there were around two hundred thousand slaves in the British colonies. It is, however, difficult to argue that *Oroonoko* is an abolitionist text, despite its later popular reputation. This is because of the presence of a fourth racial group, which is represented by the eponymous hero, an African prince sold into slavery by his grandfather. Behn isolates Oroonoko, denying him African characteristics in favour of those that are classical: 'his Nose was rising and *Roman*, instead of *African* and flat'. He is portrayed as an honourable classical hero not unlike Cato in Addison's 1713 play of that name, but with the additional advantages of a modern

European education. His adventures show that Behn has read the *Alexander Romance*, and his description recalls some of the figures in Plutarch's *Lives*, which had just been published in a new translation by John Dryden, and on which both Behn and Addison would draw. Given Behn's attitude to the white planters, the outcome is inevitably tragic. The catalyst is a slave rebellion led by Oroonoko, which of course fails. The text concludes with Oroonoko dismembered and killed by the British in a manner which recalls both classical and Elizabethan brutality. Yet Oroonoko is not a precursor of later African-American heroes, for instance Nat Turner (1800–31), who saw himself as a religious leader destined to lead his people to freedom. When Oroonoko is captured, he admits that his followers deserve their status: 'he was ashamed of what he had done, in endeavouring to make those free, who were by nature slaves, poor wretched rogues, fit to be used as Christians' tools' (130). Behn's argument, then, makes rank superior to race. A number of references in the text confirms her passionate adherence to the Stuarts, and hatred of the inter-regnum. Her text, dedicated to Lord Maitland, a Catholic who in 1688 followed James II into exile, maps a British religious and political dispute onto the South American mainland.

Behn's exotic plot was popular, so the next year she wrote it again, this time as a play. *The Widow Ranter* was not produced until after her death, with Dryden providing the Prologue. In the play Behn moved northwards, dealing with Bacon's Rebellion, but retaining some of the same components: aborigines, a hero who leads a doomed rebellion, and a corrupt colonial administration. Nathaniel Bacon (1647–76) was a Virginia planter who led an uprising against the oppressive policies of Sir William Berkeley, the colonial governor. The uprising collapsed when Bacon died of malaria. The rebellion is sometimes seen as a democratic uprising and thus a precursor of the Revolution. This is not Behn's view. Although she may have had first-hand information about the rebellion, she rewrote it to accord with her elitist attitudes. Berkeley, who was restored to office by Charles II in 1660, is therefore omitted from *The Widow Ranter*. Bacon is presented as a tragic Tory hero, a virtuous nobleman who dies by his own hand. The names of many of the characters – Boozer, Bragg, Dunce – indicate her view of an upstart colonial administration occupied by corrupt provincial bumpkins who have no business in government. The penultimate speech in the play uses the vernacular to display a disdain of ordinary provincial people often to be found in Restoration drama:

> TIMOROUS: Gadzoors, I never thrived since I was a statesman, left planting, and fell to promising and lying; I'll to my old trade again, bask under the shade of my own tobacco, and drink my punch in peace. (324)

Ebenezer Cook, a writer about whom very little is known, may be the author of two poems treating Nathaniel Bacon and tobacco. The poems seem to have been aimed at Aphra Behn, for they provide images which deflate her portrayal of colonial heroism. 'The History of Colonel Nathaniel Bacon's Rebellion', in Cook's collection *The Maryland Muse* (1731), shows that Bacon is no more a hero than anyone else in the ill-fated uprising. The work for which he is better known, *The Sot-Weed Factor* (1708), if only because it inspired John Barth's 1960 novel of the same title, asserts that America is inhabited only by morons and rascals. Cook had lived in both London and Maryland, and claimed to be an expert. Indeed, the poem is so knowing that its satire is more difficult to situate than Benjamin Franklin's. The narrator of the poem is himself a merchant, who describes a long and rough journey across the Atlantic to Maryland in a leaky ship 'Freighted with Fools' as well as his merchandise. On arrival he finds it difficult to distinguish the planters and the agents (factors) from their slaves, so tanned are they. Although the merchant does not say if it is the sun or the tobacco that has blackened the whites, he makes it clear that they have the mark of Cain.

The Sot-Weed Factor is an early contribution to the imagery of America as Hell that would be developed as the century progressed. Frampton's *Joyfull Newes out of the New Founde Worlde* (1577) had said that tobacco had 'merveilous Medicinable vertues'. Now the smoke issuing from the mouths of the inhabitants is merely a harbinger of the evil that is realised during the rest of the poem. After a night shared with frogs, mosquitoes and rattlesnakes, the merchant sets out with guide named Oronooko. A footnote blandly explains that he was named for the type of tobacco he planted; yet the slight rearrangement of the name of Behn's Surinam hero hints at ignoble behaviour, which is confirmed when the guide deserts the merchant. The noble sexuality exemplified by Behn's hero is transformed into something altogether more seedy. Cook draws on Harriot's *A briefe and true report* for material quite unlike Behn's pastoral. A naked aborigine appears and the protagonist compares him, like Harriot's engraver Theodor de Bry, with the Picts, but this time to turn him into a slimily odorous eighteenth-century version of rough trade:

> His manly Shoulders such as please,
> Widows and Wives, were bath'd in Grease
> Of Cub and Bear, whose supple Oil,
> Prepar'd his Limbs 'gainst Heat or Toil.
> Thus naked Pict in Battel faught,
> Or undisguis'd his Mistress sought;
> And knowing well his Ware was good,
> Refus'd to screen it with a Hood . . .

After adventures which strip the merchant of his goods as well as his clothes, he flees to England, throwing this curse behind him:

> May Canniballs transported o'er the Sea
> Prey on these Slaves, as they have done on me;
> May never Merchant's, trading Sails explore
> This Cruel, this Inhospitable Shoar;
> But left abandon'd by the World to starve,
> May they sustain the Fate they well deserve:
> May they turn Savage, or as Indians Wild,
> From Trade, Converse, and Happiness exil'd;
> Recreant to Heaven, may they adore the Sun,
> And into Pagan Superstitions run

> For Vengence ripe . . .
> May Wrath Divine then lay those Regions wast
> Where no Man's Faithful, nor a Woman Chast.[34]

The journal of Sarah Kemble Knight (1666–1727) adopts a somewhat less scabrous attitude of metropolitan hauteur towards colonial rustics. The standard is now set by Boston and New York. Madam Knight, as she was known, was reputed to have taught Benjamin Franklin. A courageous woman, sharp of eye and of tongue, she made an unaccompanied business trip between those two cities in the winter of 1704–5, and recorded her impressions:

> Being at a merchants house, in comes a tall country fellow, with his alfogeos full of Tobacco; for they seldom Loose their Cudd, but keep Chewing and Spitting as long as they'r eyes are open, – he advanced to the middle of the Room, makes an Awkward Nodd, and spitting a Large deal of Aromatick Tincture, he gave a scrape with his shovel like shoo, leaving a small shovel full of dirt on the floor . . . Stood staring rown'd him, like a Catt let out of a Basckett. At last, like the creature Balaam Rode on, he opened his mouth and said: have You any Ribinen for Hatbands to see I pray? . . . the Ribin is bro't and opened. Bumpkin Simpers, cryes *its confounded Gay I vow*; and beckning to the door, in comes Joan Tawdry, dropping about 50 curtsees . . . hee shows her the Ribin. *Law, You*, sais shee, *its right Gent* . . .

This vignette achieves its vividness by counterpointing the linguistic virtuosity of Knight against the homely language of the country folk. Bumpkin Simpers and Joan Tawdry, together with their vernacular, might have come out of Restoration drama. They are unlikely to have encountered the terms 'Aromatick Tincture' (tobacco), and particularly 'alfogeos', which is a corruption of the Spanish 'alforjas', meaning cheeks (much later it would come to mean saddlebags). Knight believed that, for lack of education, country people made themselves ridiculous. Yet this disdain of the ordinary people was moderated by a vision of a future America better than Boston or New York, transforming the countryside and comforting her on a dark, threatening night:

> Now Returned my distressed apprehensions of where I was: the dolesome woods, my Company next to none, Going I knew not whither, and encompassed with Terrifying darkness . . . [then] the Tall and thick Trees at a distance, especially when the moon glar'd light through the branches, fill'd my Imagination with the pleasent delusion of a Sumpteous citty, fill'd with famous Buildings and churches, with their spiring steeples, Balconies, Galleries and I know not what: Granduers which I had heard of, and which the stories of foreign countries had given me the Idea of.

Such imagery, sometimes called 'the figure of anticipation', became a common rhetorical tactic after the revolution, used among others by Samuel Knapp (as we saw in Chapter 1); and by Timothy Dwight, who first published Knight's journal in 1825, when it also seemed to provide the United States with a usable if sometimes disreputable past.[35]

Madam Knight's journey from Boston to New York, covering some two hundred miles of 'wilderness', provides another kind of anticipation, of intercolonial travel and, in some respects, of growing convergence. David Hackett Fischer has charted four distinct waves of migration from Britain to

America. In addition to the migration of Puritans to Massachusetts and the Royalists to the South, Quakers moved to the Delaware Valley following William Penn's selection of Philadelphia in 1682 as a capital, while others left 'North Britain' in the wake of the Jacobite Rebellions, settling in frontier areas from Maine to South Carolina. In certain circumstances the differences highlighted by Fischer seemed to be swept aside. One such circumstance was the first Great Awakening. It is likely to have begun in 1719 in New Jersey, when Theodore Frelinghuysen, a German immigrant preacher, led revival meetings in the Raritan Valley. Within a few years, the awakening had become transatlantic in impact, spreading throughout the colonies and changing the nature of worship in Britain. Two instances will suffice. Jonathan Edwards's *A Faithful Narrative of the Surprising Work of God* (1737), describing a revival in Northampton, Massachusetts, influenced both John Wesley, and hence the founding of the Methodist Church in Britain, and George Whitefield, the English evangelist on the first of his several tours of America, in Savannah, Georgia. In 1742, the account of a group conversion in Cambuslang, near Glasgow in Scotland, was promptly reprinted in Boston and Philadelphia. By 1770 the awakening had splintered, leaving a number of colleges, each devoted to different shades of Protestantism: Princeton (founded 1746), Columbia (initially King's College, 1754), Brown (1764), Rutgers (1766) and Dartmouth (1769).[36]

The work of Jonathan Edwards, like that of Anne Bradstreet, is Janus-faced, but temporally rather than spatially. His preaching, an important factor in the awakening, looks back to Wigglesworth in its hellfire. Perhaps because of that, 'Sinners in the Hands of an Angry God' is his best-known work. It conveys vividly the urgency of his message:

> The God that holds you over the pit of hell, much as one holds a spider, or some loathsome insect over a fire, abhors you, and is dreadfully provoked: his wrath towards you burns like fire; he looks upon you as worthy of nothing else, but to be cast into the fire; he is of purer eyes than to bear to have you in his sight; you are ten thousand times more abominable in his eyes, than the most hateful venomous serpent is in ours. You have offended him infinitely more than ever a stubborn rebel did his prince; and yet it is nothing but his hand that holds you from falling into the fire every moment. It is to be ascribed to nothing else, that you did not go to hell the last night; that you was suffered to awake again in this world, after you closed your eyes to sleep.[37]

The listeners repented in flocks. Yet here is Edwards again, writing about that offending insect in an early essay, 'Of insects':

> Of all Insects no one is more wonderfull than the Spider especially with Respect to their sagacity and admirable way of working . . . we have Observed that they never fly except in fair Weather and we may now observe that it is never fair weather neither in this Country nor any other except when the Wind blows from the Midland Parts and so towards the Sea, so here in newengland I have Observed that they never fly except when the wind is westerly and I never saw them fly but when they were hastening Directly towards the sea . . . (8–9)

Of course, it is the difference between the metaphorical and the natural. But it is more than that. The essay looks forward to Thoreau in its concern for accurate observation, emphasised by that repeated verb, and its need to make a meticulous record – the essay includes a diagram on web making. Yet Edwards's 'Personal Narrative' indicates that he differs from Thoreau in his emphasis on Design:

> God's excellency, his wisdom, his purity and love, seemed to appear in every thing; in the sun, moon, and stars; in the clouds, and blue sky; in the grass, flowers, trees; in the water, and all nature . . . (60–1)

The New World seemed the purest expression of God's excellency. In *Some Thoughts Concerning the Revival of Religion in New England* (1742), Edwards noted that the Old World was steeped in the blood of Christ and the Christian martyrs. Edwards resembled Wigglesworth and the first generations of Puritans in his criticisms of the Old World, but he also rejected their fear of the New. In the New World humankind had been given, miraculously, the chance to start afresh, and the conversion of the aborigines was crucial evidence of the working of God's will. Edwards gave the funeral oration for David Brainerd (1718–47), a missionary to the natives who, had he lived, would have become Edwards's son-in-law; and in 1749 Edwards published Brainerd's *Journal*. The *Journal*, kept by Brainerd on the orders of the Scottish Society for Propagating Christian Knowledge, showed Edwards that his success in converting the natives was an example of 'the wonderful works of God's grace' (179). The act of writing itself was for Edwards less an account of self-scrutiny than an expression of the immanence of God and a record of the wonders of His will.

The awakening was religious evidence of the incorporation of America into a transatlantic world. Cosmopolitanism of a more secular kind is to be found in the writings of William Byrd of Westover, the name of his Virginia residence sometimes added to distinguish him from the English composer. In at least three ways, Byrd was a conspicuous consumer. He loved English culture, and stuffed Westover with furniture, paintings and books. His library, containing some four thousand volumes, was twice the size of Cotton Mather's and was believed to be the largest at the time in the English colonies. He loved the South, which at times seemed as if it might become paradise:

> All the Land we Travell'd over this day, that is to say from the river Irvin to Sable Creek, is exceedingly rich, both on the Virginia Side of the Line, and that of Carolina. Besides whole Forests of Canes, that adorn the Banks of the River and Creeks thereabouts, the fertility of the Soil throws out such a Quantity of Winter Grass, that Horses and Cattle might keep themselves in Heart all the cold Season without the help of any Fodder . . . I question not but there are 30,000 Acres . . . as fertile as the Lands were said to be about Babylon, which yielded, if Herodotus tells us right, an Increase of no less that 2 or 300 for one. But this hath the Advantage of being a higher and consequently a much healthier, Situation than that. So that a Colony of 1000 families might, with the help of Moderate Industry, pass their time very happily there.[38]

116

So he bought it. Byrd, who helped to scotch Berkeley's Bermudan plan, here reveals his own imperial agenda, one that is somewhat less idealistic than Berkeley's. The land is viewed statistically, as a commodity, in terms of its prospects for agricultural production. Byrd draws on his classical learning to point up the advantages of his land. He also draws on John Locke, whose *Second Treatise of Government* (1690) compared England and America to expound a labour theory of value:

> An acre of land that bears here [in England] twenty bushels of wheat, and another in America which, with the same husbandry, would do the like, are without doubt of the same natural, intrinsic value. But yet the benefit mankind receives from the one, in a year, is worth £5, and from the other possibly not worth a penny, if all the profit an Indian received from it were to be valued and sold here; at least I may truly say, not 1/1000. 'Tis labour then which puts the greatest part of value upon land, without which it would scarcely be worth anything . . .

Locke brought the comparison to a close with a remark that became famous: 'in the beginning all the world was America', and therefore title created by labour can be extended by trade 'to disproportionate and unequal possession of the earth'.[39] It became one of the major arguments for the dispossession of the aborigines.

Byrd's thirst for disproportionate and unequal possession was such that, at his death, he owned nearly 180,000 acres, tended by large numbers of slaves and servants. The particular example, quoted above, of this form of consumption is taken from the *History of the Dividing Line betwixt Virginia and North Carolina*, his account of a surveying trip westwards in 1728 to settle a boundary dispute. A Virginian to the core, Byrd used the labour theory of value to distinguish his colony from the neighbouring one of North Carolina. (Ironically enough, it was Locke who drew up a Constitution for the proprietors of North Carolina; it was never incorporated into law.) A central theme of the *History of the Dividing Line* is the laziness of the Carolinians, 'Drones' whose behaviour, together with the hot climate, crosses the divide to infect some of the southern Virginians. This theme also appears in Byrd's *Secret History of the Dividing Line*, which comments on the other history, giving nicknames to the surveying party and detailing some of their unofficial exploits:

> My Landlord had unluckily sold our Men some Brandy, which produced much disorder, making some too Cholerick, and others too loving. So that a Damsel who came to assist in the Kitchen wou'd certainly have been ravish't, if her timely consent had not prevented the Violence. Nor did my Landlady think herself safe in the hands of such furious Lovers, and therefore fortify'd her Bed chamber and defended it with a Chamber-Pot charg'd to the Brim with Female Ammunition. (66, 147–9)

The glee with which this Falstaffian anecdote is related indicates the third form of Byrd's voraciousness. His sexual prowess during his lengthy visits to London is proudly noted in diaries, which recall Samuel Pepys's voyeurism in their use of shorthand to record and yet keep to oneself a lively social life. Byrd's activities in London are somewhat different from those on the Virginia frontier where, now calling himself 'Steddy', he seems more concerned to record the frequent indiscretions of others. Neither of the two accounts of the expedition were published until long after Byrd's death in 1744. Their publication histories indicate their differing significance to the culture of the United States. The *History of the Dividing Line* was published in 1841 by the Southern separatist William Ruffin, and was used to demonstrate the longevity of a Southern plantation system hierarchically organised with cultured Anglophile landlords and a large labour force, often made up of slaves. The *Secret History* remained unpublished until 1929. Its crude, sexist, sometimes black comedy looks forward to the south-western humour which would influence Twain, and which Twain's flamboyant status would in turn valorise. If the *History* is now valued for descriptions of a rural South which can be placed alongside Jefferson's *Notes on the State of Virginia* (1782) and William Bartram's *Travels Through North and South Carolina, Georgia, East and West Florida* (1791), the *Secret History* is an early example of a tradition which is altogether rougher.

Religious and secular cosmopolitanism were combined in the figure of William Smith. A product of the Scottish educational system, Smith migrated to New York in 1751, where he began publishing fabular homilies and proposals for the education of the aborigines. He made his reputation, however, with a pamphlet advocating, for the settlers, a liberal education of the kind that at the time was transforming the Scottish universities and English Dissenting academies. *A General Idea of the College of Mirania* (1753) sketches a Utopia where the education system unites the growing range of migrant nationalities into a hierarchical yet organically related society that is loyal to the British Crown. A preface combines the imagery of Berkeley's poem, which had been published the year before, with a 'figure of anticipation' resembling Madam Knight's:

> Oh! Science! onward thus thy realm extend
> O'er realms yet unexplor'd till time shall end . . .
> Not trackless deserts shall thy progress stay,
> Rocks, mountains, floods, before thee shall give way . . .
> Where wolves now howl shall polish'd villas rise,
> And towery cities grow into the skies!
> 'Earth's farthest ends our glory shall behold,
> And the new world launch forth to meet the old.'[40]

The closing imperial quotation, slightly altered from Pope's 'Windsor Forest' (1713), brings to an end a remarkable anticipation of the shape of the modern United States, with vertical cities surrounded by horizontal suburbs. It is hardly surprising that Smith's pamphlet attracted the attention of Benjamin Franklin, who offered Smith the post of first provost of the College of Philadelphia.

Once established in Philadelphia, Smith put in place the cultural model recommended by his English patron, Thomas Herring (1693–1757), the Archbishop of Canterbury. Smith's curriculum abandoned classical scholarship in favour of modern languages, public speaking and the arts. His students were encouraged to act, and he revised popular English plays to make them relevant. In 1757 Smith staged a version of James Thomson's *Alfred: A Masque* (1740) in direct response to the initial British defeat of the French and Indian War (1755–63). The British general Edward Braddock was mortally wounded at the Battle of the Monongahela in July 1755, and the retreat of the remnants of his force was headed by the colonel of the provincial soldiers, George Washington. In the succeeding months, much of Pennsylvania was threatened by Indian attack. Smith staged *Alfred*, he said, because 'the situation of *England* under the *Danish* invasion, is an exact representation of our present state under the outrages of a savage enemy'. Alfred was an appropriate model, and not just because of the defeat of the Danes. He began the process of the unification of the English, introduced educational and literary reforms and, according to Thomson's play, was 'Modest of Carriage, and of Speech most Gracious'. Smith's adaptation was a great success. A detailed account of the production, with lengthy quotations, was printed in four issues of *The Pennsylvania Gazette*, and extracts appeared in the London *Gentleman's Magazine*. It also had an impact on both British and United States symbology that is both imperceptible and, apparently, ineradicable. In Britain the play survives only in Thomas Arne's song, 'Rule, Britannia'. In the United States the play survives in the imagery of George Washington. Smith was both directly and indirectly responsible for the imagery of the modest leader that is indelibly associated with Washington. He created the imagery not only in the adaptation of *Alfred*, but also in a sermon in 1778 when he compared Washington with Cincinnatus, retelling Livy's story of the Roman called from the plough to help a besieged Roman army, leading the army to victory, and then resigning his office to return to his small farm. Five years later Washington resigned as commander-in-chief of the Continental forces, thus hypostatising the imagery woven by Smith. Smith, it might be said, also furthered such imagery indirectly through Mason Weems's *The Life of Washington*, which first appeared in 1800. Smith was related to Weems, and may have encouraged his career as a parson, bookseller and writer. It is in *The Life* that the famous stories of Washington are first told – such as the tale of the cherry tree. It is there, too, that he appears both as a modest man and as 'the father of his country'. The two images were interdependent; both were essential to the belief that Washington was at once a leader and a representative of his people.[41]

The 1760s marked the high point of Smith's career. A trusted colonial servant, he was commissioned in 1762 to report on the state of the Anglican Church in the colonies. Three years later he published, in Philadelphia, an account of the expedition, led by the Swiss soldier Henry Bouquet, which brought an end to the native uprising known as Pontiac's Rebellion. In the account Smith described new methods of Indian fighting and proposed new schemes for frontier settlement. The book was an immediate success; it was reprinted in London in 1766 by the Geographer Royal, came out in three more editions between 1768 and 1770, and appeared in French translations in 1769 and 1778. Then Smith's career fell apart as discord grew between Britain and America. He attempted to steer a middle course, denouncing British attempts to tax the colonies but suggesting that independence would be disastrous for America. He was imprisoned briefly in 1776, and in 1779 the charter of his College of Philadelphia was revoked. Although he was eventually reappointed as provost, remaining until the College became the University of Pennsylvania in 1791, he never regained the influence he had wielded in mid-century. Yet Smith left a legacy of educational and cultural achievement. In 1757 he had founded *The American Magazine* and in 1769 the American Philosophical Society. He fostered many careers in addition to that of Weems. They included David Rittenhouse, the distinguished astronomer; Francis Hopkinson, the poet and composer of the first book of music published in America; Thomas Godfrey, another poet whose blank-verse play *The Prince of Parthia* became in 1767 the first professionally performed drama in America; and Benjamin West, the painter, who made portraits of Smith and his wife but is better-known for such grand historical canvases as *The Death of General Wolfe* (1770) and *Penn's Treaty with the Indians* (1771). The parallel careers of Hopkinson (1737–91), who was a signatory to the Declaration of Independence, the designer of the Stars and Stripes, and judge of admiralty for Pennsylvania, and West (1738–1820), who became a founder of the Royal Academy and in 1792 succeeded Joshua Reynolds as its president, suggest that Smith's vision of the Anglo-American cultural empire, prophesied by Berkeley in 1726, might have come to pass. It perished on the rocks of the physical empire created by the Treaty of Paris in 1763.

The fall of the British American Empire

In March 1781 Edward Gibbon appended a chapter of 'General Observations' to the second instalment of *The History of the Decline and Fall of the Roman Empire*. The chapter's speculations had a contemporary relevance. The tide of war in America had turned against the British; their forces had been defeated in the Carolinas, at King's Mountain in August 1780 and at Cowpens in January 1781. A further defeat at Yorktown, Virginia on 19 October 1781 would end British resistance to American independence. Gibbon, both in Parliament and at the Board of Trade, was only too familiar with the conduct of American affairs. It is not clear that he intended to draw a parallel between the fate of the Roman and British empires; yet some of the remarks in his 'General Observations' were easily applied to the British American Empire:

> the decline of Rome was the natural and inevitable effect of immoderate greatness. Prosperity ripened the principle of decay; the causes of destruction multiplied with the extent of conquest; and as soon as time or accident had removed the artificial supports, the stupendous fabric yielded to the pressure of its own weight. The story of its ruin is simple and obvious . . .[42]

The British Empire was extended and reduced in the space of the twenty years between two peace treaties, both signed in Paris. The Treaty of Paris of 1763 concluded the French and Indian War, with French Canada and the Spanish Floridas being ceded to Britain. The effect was to exclude France from the continent, and to increase British territory there more than twofold. The increased burden of administration prompted the British government to impose taxes which were resented in colonies with no voice in the British Parliament. That resentment was exacerbated by the metropolitan disdain of the colonials which we have seen occasionally reflected in the texts discussed in the previous section. The counterpoint of expansion and declension that informs Gibbon's sonorous prose provides a simple framework for what was, at the time, a complex set of problems. They were not solved until the Treaty of 1783, again at Paris, with the British recognising the independence of the United States, with the Mississippi River as its western boundary. Britain retained just Canada, Honduras and the West Indies. The result is a redefinition of American literature, for after 1783 it would no longer include texts written in or about what might be called the British-American rump. Yet, as we shall see, questions of definition would still be problematic. In the concluding section of this chapter, the rise and fall of the British American Empire will be seen in the work of two writers, Benjamin Franklin and J. Hector St John de Crèvecoeur.

Franklin's lifetime was marked by great change. He was born in Boston in 1706, the year before the union of Scottish and English parliaments. *Magnalia Christi Americana* had been published four years earlier. Madam Knight had made the difficult journey to New York two years earlier. The sons and daughters of the Pilgrim Fathers could still be seen in Boston streets. Cotton Mather's father Increase published *A Discourse Concerning Earthquakes* in 1706; he would live for another seventeen years. When Franklin died in 1790 Burke published his *Reflections on the Revolution in France*, and Blake published *The Marriage of Heaven and Hell*. Philadelphia had become the nation's capital, and would remain so until 1800. In 1791 the Bill of Rights was ratified and the first bank of the United States incorporated. In 1792 the cornerstone of the White House was laid, the New York stock exchange opened, and Kentucky admitted as the fifteenth state of the Union. The America into which Franklin was born had a fragmented colonial structure. When he died it was a republic with an embryonic modern economy. He played a large part in the transformation.

There were, of course, continuities with the past. Critics have pointed to the similarities between Franklin and Cotton Mather, particularly with the emphasis on works to be found in Mather's biography of Sir William Phips in *Magnalia Christi Americana*, and in the *Essays to Do Good*. Yet until late in life, Franklin preferred to distance himself from Mather and the Puritan tradition. He did this in three ways. The first was satire. The 16-year-old Franklin anonymously submitted a series of fourteen essays to his brother's newspaper, *The New-England Courant*, supposedly from one Silence Dogood, the widow of a Puritan clergyman. The essays poked fun at such New England institutions as the funeral elegy, and Harvard College. The second method in which Franklin distanced himself from Mather was physical. In 1723, the year after he wrote the 'Dogood Papers', he left Boston to start a new life in

Philadelphia. The third method was to claim intellectual kinship with his family rather than with the theocracy. At the beginning of his *Autobiography*, Franklin quoted (and lightly rewrote) a poem written by his maternal grandfather Peter Folger (1617–90), heralding it as a turning point:

> It was in favor of Liberty of Conscience, & in behalf of the Baptists, Quakers, & other Sectaries, that had been under Persecution; ascribing the Indian Wars & other Distresses, that had befallen the Country to that Persecution, as so many judgments of God . . .

Franklin called the poem 'homespun'.[43] This is rather kind, for 'Looking-Glass for the Times' (1676) is no more than doggerel. In it Folger pleaded for religious liberty, and suggested that the Indian Wars were not a trial of Protestant faith but rather retribution for the bigotry of Massachusetts:

> If we do love our brethren,
>   and do to them, I say,
> As we would they should do to us
>   we should be quiet straightway.
>
> But if that we a smiting go,
>   of fellow-servants so,
> No marvel if our wars increase
>   and things so heavy go.[44]

This was a neat reversal of the usual Puritan explanation of 'distresses'. It also signalled that there were views about the future of America quite different from the Puritan.

In one way, however, Franklin differed from his grandfather. Franklin noted, in his *Autobiography*, that Folger wished to 'be known as the Author' of his poem. In the original poem Folger gave a good reason why he felt so strongly about the inclusion of his name in the verse:

> But I shall cease and set my name
>   to what I here insert,
> Because to be a libeller,
>   I hate it with my heart.
>
> From *Sherbon* town, where now I dwell,
>   my name I do put here,
> Without offence your real friend,
>   It is PETER FOLGER.[45]

In the extract that Franklin included in his *Autobiography*, he renamed his grandfather 'Folgier' to complete the rhyme. In contrast, he polished his own name out of existence, partly no doubt because of his fears of libel. Beginning with the 'Dogood Papers', Franklin frequently used pseudonyms (one scholar counted more than forty of them), or withheld his name from his publications. The result is an extraordinarily shifty authorial persona. The 'Dogood Papers' were not attributed to him until 1864, and the Franklin canon may never be finally established.

The authorial evasiveness of the *Autobiography* is an aspect that distinguishes it markedly from its Puritan forbears. Franklin left it in four incomplete segments. The first segment, written in England in 1771 and covering the years to 1730, appeared in Paris in French translation in 1791, shortly after his death, and in German translation in Berlin the following year. The first English edition, a retranslation from the French, was published in London in 1793. The second segment was written in France in 1784 and is less a narrative than a set of precepts. The third segment, written in Philadelphia in 1788–9, takes up the narrative again and covers the years 1731–57. A final segment was added just before Franklin died in 1790. The first three segments were edited by his grandson and published in London and Philadelphia in 1818, but a full edition did not appear until 1868. The Benjamin Franklin that figures so prominently in American culture is, then, something of a posthumous imposition upon a complex, changing man reacting to complex, changing times. Herman Melville, writing in 1855 on the basis of the 1818 edition, identified the problem of locating the essential Franklin:

> Having carefully weighed the world, Franklin could act any part in it. By nature turned to knowledge, his mind was often grave, but never serious. At times he had seriousness – extreme seriousness – for others, but never for himself. Tranquillity was to him instead of it. This philosophical levity of tranquillity, so to speak, is shown in his easy variety of pursuits. Printer, postmaster, almanac maker, essayist, chemist, orator, tinker, statesman, humorist, philosopher, parlor man, political economist, professor of housewifery, ambassador, projector, maxim-monger, herb-doctor, wit:
> – Jack of all trades, master of each and mastered by none – the type and genius of his land. Franklin was everything but a poet.[46]

For Melville, a poet was a Romantic who wrestled over deep feelings, like the brow-clutching theological student in his long poem *Clarel* (1876). In contrast, he sees Franklin as a multifaceted set of brilliant surfaces.

Each segment of the *Autobiography* has a somewhat different intent. The first, written at the home of an English friend, Jonathan Shipley, the Bishop of St Asaph, is addressed to his illegitimate son William, then the Royal Governor of New Jersey. It is appropriately informal, even rambling. It covers the years when Franklin moved from Boston to Philadelphia, worked for the British-born printer Samuel Keimer and then, misled by promises made by the governor of Pennsylvania, William Keith, sailed to Britain to buy equipment to set up his own business. After working in London for two printing houses, he returned to Philadelphia, worked again for Keimer, opened a small print shop, and got married. Described in this way, the first segment hardly seems the stuff of legend; yet the bare facts are transfigured by several factors, apparent throughout most of this narration, but notably at the moment when the narrator first enters Philadelphia and goes to a bakery

> and ask'd for Biscuit, intending such as we had in Boston, but they it seems were not made in Philadelphia, then I ask'd for a three-penny Loaf, and was told they had none such: so not considering or knowing the Difference of Money & the greater Cheapness nor the Names of his Bread, I bad him give me three penny worth of any

123

sort. He gave me accordingly three great Puffy Rolls. I was surpris'd at the Quantity, but took it, and having no room in my Pockets, walk'd off, with a Roll under each Arm, & eating the other. Thus I went up Market Street as far as fourth Street, passing by the Door of Mr Read, my future Wife's Father, when she standing at the Door saw me, & thought I made as I certainly did a most awkward ridiculous Appearance. (27–8)

This incident, trivial in itself, becomes luminous through the fusion of three genres. The picaresque and the *Bildungsroman* leavens and transforms the solemn retrospection required of autobiography. The young man coming to town is a common moment of the picaresque. The immediate comic predecessor of Franklin's 1771 description is the entry of the eponymous hero into London in Book Thirteen of *Tom Jones* (1749). Fielding accompanies Jones's arrival with references to the *Odyssey* and the *Aeneid*; reducing Cerberus, the many-headed canine guardian at the gates of Hell (in Book VI of the *Aeneid*) to a porter in his lodge. The episode in Philadelphia extends Fielding's comic reduction of epic, with Franklin as Aeneas carrying the sop past Cerberus, in the shape of his future wife.

After passing Debby Read's lodge, the narrator accounts for many '*errata*' before he marries her (which may in itself be an *erratum*, but one that, the reference to Cerberus apart, is excluded from the *Autobiography*). The learning process is of course the central motif of the *Bildungsroman*. When the poet Gottfried Bürger, the translator of the German edition of 1792, entitled his text *Benjamin Franklin's Jugendjahre*, he accurately located it in the tradition that would reach its peak in Goethe's *Wilhelm Meister's Lehrjahre* (1795–6). Unlike many *Bildungsromane*, however, Franklin's learning process is not structured around a spiritual crisis. Spirituality has to a large extent been excluded. Having given away two of the puffy rolls, the narrator follows a crowd into a Quaker Meeting House, and promptly falls asleep. This is one of the first signs that God is reduced to the status of a benevolent bystander in the progress of this particular pilgrim, who moves through an Anglo-American environment of great materiality, similar to that of Defoe's *Moll Flanders* (1722). The narrative is saturated with the economic. The narrator's discovery of the price of bread in Philadelphia is the first step in a process of learning the mechanics of industry and frugality that would be detailed in 'Father Abraham's Speech'. Full of the homespun versifying that Franklin learned from his grandfather, the speech was included in the twenty-sixth and last edition of *Poor Richard's Almanack* (1758) and then republished under the title (not Franklin's own) of 'The Way to Wealth'.

At the very beginning of the 1771 segment, the narrator signalled his motivation:

Having emerg'd from the Poverty & Obscurity in which I was born & bred, to a State of Affluence and some degree of Reputation in the World . . . the conducing Means I made use of, which, with the Blessing of God, so well succeeded, my Posterity may like to know, as they may find some of them suitable to their own situations, & therefore fit to be imitated. (3)

124

This has, of course, become known as the American Dream. Franklin may be called the first modern dreamer in the way that he restates Cotton Mather's emphasis on activity. Mather's account of Sir William Phips, with its climactic phrase, '*Thanks be to God! We are made*', showed God rewarding those who toiled in His service. Franklin, in contrast, emphasised the transitive form of the verb. He made many things, including a clock, a duplicating machine, the lightning rod, the Franklin stove (which prevents smoke blowing back into a room), and the glass harmonica, for which Mozart wrote a sonata. His work on electrostatics is recorded in his *Experiments and Observations on Electricity* (1751–4). As a result of these and other works, when he returned to England in 1757 as agent for the Pennsylvania Assembly he had become the most famous inhabitant of the colonies, and was recognised for his achievements by the award of an honorary doctorate at Oxford. It was as the foremost American that he worked in Britain for much of the time until 1775, attempting, like William Smith (who in other respects had become a political enemy), to obtain colonial rights within an imperial framework. The theme of rags-to-riches was written in England before Franklin accepted that the colonies should secede from the British Empire. It should therefore be placed alongside the work of Defoe as an important element of Anglo-American imperialism rather than be regarded as a foundation-stone of the American Dream. Teleology has here smothered historical accuracy.

The second segment of the *Autobiography* was written at Passy, while Franklin was the United States' minister to France. It is no longer addressed to his son, because William had remained loyal to the British Crown. The text reflects Franklin's different status. It is prefaced by two letters of recommendation, the second of which urges publication because the work will 'present a table of the internal circumstances of your country, which will very much tend to invite to it settlers of virtuous and manly minds' (79). Those circumstances are largely internal to Franklin; after describing the creation of the Philadelphia Public Library, the segment is mainly devoted to the inculcation of qualities that are then tabulated in 'the Art of Virtue' – and parodied by Scott Fitzgerald towards the close of *The Great Gatsby* (1925). The third and fourth segments, written in the United States, return to narrative form, yet interpret the period 1731–57 in the light of the revolution. The narrator describes Franklin's 1754 Albany Plan, that the colonies unite for their defence, as if it were the 1787 Constitution in embryo. The many failures of the British are symbolised by the account of the death of General Braddock after the Battle of the Monongahela. William Smith had used the event to rally the colonists by staging Thomson's *Alfred*. Franklin, some thirty years later, uses it for quite different purposes:

> This General was I think a brave Man, and might probably have made a Figure as a good Officer in some European War. But he had too much self-confidence, too high an Opinion of the Validity of Regular Troops, and too mean a One of both Americans and Indians . . . This whole Transaction gave us Americans the first Suspicion that our exalted Ideas of the Prowess of British Regulars had not been well founded . . . [Braddock] being grievously wounded . . . was totally silent, all the first

Day, and at Night only said, Who'd have thought it? . . . was silent again the following Days, only saying at last, We shall better know how to deal with them another
time; and dy'd a few Minutes after. (157–60)

Of course, they do not know better next time. In a text devoted to learning,
the British are shown failing to learn how to deal with the Americans, and the
result is the death of the British American Empire.

D. H. Lawrence hated Franklin with all the passion of which he was
capable:

The Perfectibility of Man! Ah heaven, what a dreary theme! . . . Oh, but I have a
strange and fugitive self shut out and howling like a wolf or a coyote under the ideal
windows. See his red eyes in the dark? . . .
   The perfectibility of man, dear God! When every man as long as he remains alive
is in himself a multitude of conflicting men. Which of these do you choose to perfect,
at the expense of every other?
   Old Daddy Franklin will tell you. He'll rig him up for you, the pattern American.
Oh, Franklin was the first downright American. He knew what he was about, the
sharp little man. He set up the first dummy American.[47]

Together with many other critics, Lawrence has treated the *Autobiography* as
the unity that the title suggests but the text does not deserve. He has been sold
a dummy. In his anger he fails to see the fractured nature of the text, and reads
its first segment in the light of the later ones. He misses the sly humour of the
first, Anglo-American segment, and therefore overlooks the red-eyed Franklin.

It is precisely Franklin's wolfishness which unites his imperial and republican lives, and establishes an American genre. For if there is anything one can
trust about Franklin, it is that he is not to be trusted. There is so much guile
lurking in his work that it is extraordinarily difficult wholly to take him at his
word, from the 'Dogood Papers' to the letter on his religious beliefs, written
five weeks before he died. In such texts as the infamous 'Advice to a Friend on
Choosing a Mistress' (1745), he uses the destabilising comic techniques of
irony and satire with such consummate urbanity that it brings out the moral
shock-troops, who find themselves facing an empty field with the sound of
laughter coming from the trees. Franklin's comic style is the literary equivalent
of the guerrilla tactics which defeated Braddock and which were adopted so
successfully by the Continental Army for much of the Revolution. The most
trustworthy of his works is perhaps the hoax – otherwise the point of the
deception would be lost. This is the case with 'Rules by Which a Great Empire
May Be Reduced to a Small One' and 'An Edict by the King of Prussia', the
two essays written in 1773 to show the British administration the effect of
their policies. It is also the case with the article signed 'A Traveller' and
written in 1765 as a contribution to the miasmatist debate. American sheep,
he had been told, were so affected by the adverse climate that their wool
would not make a single pair of socks. That is a lie, he said, 'The very Tails of
the American Sheep are so laden with Wool, that each has a Car or Waggon
on four little Wheels to support and keep it from trailing on the Ground.' The
miasmatist tales are as ludicrous as

the Account, said to be from Quebec, in the Papers of last Week, that the Inhabitants of Canada are making preparations for a Cod and Whale Fishery this Summer in the Upper Lakes. Ignorant People may object that the Upper Lakes are fresh, and that Cod and Whale are Salt-water Fish: But let them know, Sir, that Cod, like other Fish, when attacked by their Enemies, fly into any Water where they think they can be safest; that Whales, when they have a mind to eat Cod, pursue them wherever they fly; and that the grand Leap of the Whale in that Chace up the Fall of Niagara is esteemed by all who have seen it, as one of the finest Spectacles in Nature!

The world, he concluded, had grown too credulous. Unfortunately, nobody told the Swedish scientist Per (or Pehr) Kalm (1715–79), who fell victim to a number of tall tales, including one from the Philadelphia botanist John Bartram (1699–1777). Kalm solemnly reported that American bears killed cows by biting a hole in their hide and blowing into the hole 'till the animal swells excessively and dies'. Kalm did not say if he actually had seen any ballooning cows. To adopt Lawrence's terms, Franklin was not the first, but he definitely was a downright American in his deflating use of humour. The American critic Constance Rourke called humour 'a fashioning instrument in America . . . its mode has often been swift and coarse and ruthless, beyond art and beyond established civilization'. Franklin, who was not above dressing in buckskins for the ladies of Paris, was perhaps the most artful practitioner in a form whose mongrel pedigree goes from Mike Fink to Mark Twain.[48]

A different kind of authorial uncertainty informs the *Letters from an American Farmer*, the best-known work of Crèvecoeur. He was born in France into the ancient Norman family of de Crèvecoeur, and was christened Michel-Guillaume-Jean. He served in the French army during the French and Indian War, was injured and resigned his commission in 1759. He moved to British America, changed his name to J. Hector St John, and in 1769 began farming in Orange County, New York. It was under this Anglicised name, and assuming the narrative mask of a farmer from Carlisle, Pennsylvania, that he published the *Letters*, in London in 1782. It was immediately successful. A second edition appeared there the next year, followed by editions in Dublin and Belfast. It was then translated into French, German and Dutch. Coming at the close of hostilities between the United States and Britain, the book was for Europeans their major primer on the United States for more than a decade. In contrast, the first American edition, which appeared in 1793, was a failure, and for a century the book went out of print on both sides of the Atlantic. It was not reprinted until 1904, now under the name of J. Hector St John Crèvecoeur. The ennobling preposition has since been returned to the author's name, and the text has become the first of the two major French commentaries on the United States. (The second, by another nobleman, Alexis de Tocqueville, will be discussed in Chapter 5.)

Comparisons with two other epistolary texts will highlight the particular structure of the *Letters*, and the ways in which it expresses the complexities of the rise and fall of the British American Empire. Samuel Richardson's *Pamela; or, Virtue Rewarded* (1740) began the popularity of the epistolary novel. It contains many voices, each expressing the privacy of the individual experience.

Crèvecoeur's *Letters* has few voices. Andrew the Hebridean is introduced in Letter III as an example of the transformation which will be examined shortly. The Russian Iw-n Al-z occupies Letter XI, reporting a visit to the farm of John Bartram, the botanist who had tricked Per Kalm but who is now on his best behaviour, keen to demonstrate the realisation of the ancient pastoral dream by means of modern agriculture. These voices are contained within St John's narrative and serve to amplify points made by him. In place of the shards of Richardsonian subjectivity, then, is a greater sense of open-air community. The letters are instead structured spatially, organised to examine aspects of the four distinct regions that Crèvecoeur treats: the agricultural middle provinces, the fisheries of the north-east, the frontier West and the slaveholding South.

The realism of the *Letters* becomes apparent when it is compared with a second epistolary text. John Dickinson's *Letters from a Farmer in Pennsylvania* began to appear in 1767 in *The Pennsylvania Chronicle* as a set of twelve essays addressed, anonymously, to '*My Dear Countrymen*'. They were bound together as a pamphlet in 1768, and became the most widely known of the many published colonial complaints against British taxation. The farmer concludes in Letter XII:

> Let these truths be indelibly impressed on our minds – that we cannot be happy, without being free – that we cannot be free, without being secure in our property – that we cannot be secure in our property, if, without our consent, others may, as by right, take it away – that taxes imposed on us by parliament, do thus take it away.[49]

The persona of a plain-speaking smallholder, farming on the banks of the Delaware, was merely rhetorical, and fooled nobody. The carefully-constructed step-by-step argument here was clearly the product of a legal mind, and the authorship of the letters was quickly known. John Dickinson (1732–1808) was a London-trained Philadelphia lawyer. The components of his argument were incorporated by Jefferson into the Declaration of Independence, which ironically Dickinson refused to sign because, like William Smith, he believed that colonial rights were best exercised within the empire. In contrast, we are driven to believe that St John really is a farmer, because his agrarianism combines literal and tropic meanings. They reflect the seven years when Crèvecoeur farmed in colonial New York, and was raising a family with the daughter of a prosperous Anglo-American family. Indeed, some passages such as the account of beekeeping are conveyed in such loving detail that their parabolic intent only emerges when the text is considered as a whole.

It is only in recent years that this has been done. Perhaps because of the superficial similarity to Dickinson's text – twelve letters written by a Pennsylvania farmer – and perhaps because of the opening address to l'Abbé Raynal, the *Letters* has often been given a literal reading as a defence of America against European strictures. This is largely owing to two partial accounts which have been confirmed by two of the major American literary histories of this century. The first account sees the book as a hymn of praise to American agrarianism. This account, which may well have appealed to Thomas Jefferson (who knew and admired Crèvecoeur), has its modern incarnation in the 1904 edition, when W. P. Trent, who would later become one of the editors of the 1917 *A History of American Literature*, praised the author as 'a pioneer poet-naturalist'.[50] Pioneering and agrarianism are most clearly seen in Letter III, which answers its titular question – 'What Is an American?' – by turning American space into a psychological imperative which is neatly congruent with the theme of rags-to-riches in the first segment of Franklin's *Autobiography*:

> An European, when he first arrives, seems limited in his intentions, as well as in his view; but he very suddenly alters his scale; two hundred miles formerly appeared a very great distance, it is now but a trifle; he no sooner breathes our air than he forms schemes and embarks in designs he never would have thought of in his own country. There the plenitude of society confines many useful ideas and often extinguishes the most laudable schemes, which here ripen into maturity. Thus Europeans become Americans.[51]

The second partial account of the *Letters* also draws on Letter III, which discusses 'this new man':

> He is neither an European nor the descendant of an European, hence that strange mixture of blood, which you will find in no other country. I could point out to a family whose grandfather was an Englishman, whose wife was Dutch, whose son married a French woman, and whose present four sons have now four wives of different nations. *He* is an American, who, leaving behind him all his ancient prejudices and manners, receives new ones from the new mode of life he has embraced, the new government he obeys, and the new rank he holds. He becomes an American by being received in the broad lap of our great *Alma Mater*. Here individuals of all nations are melted into a new race of men, whose labours and posterity will one day cause great changes in the world. (69–70)

This passage has become famous because of its invocation of renewal, and because it seems to give a revolutionary pedigree to the ideology informing the second great wave of migration, which developed in the 1880s and which is celebrated in *The Melting-Pot*, the 1909 play by Israel Zangwill. For this reason, Crèvecoeur is canonised as 'one of our most sympathetic immigrants' on the first page of the 'Address to the Reader' in the 1948 *Literary History of the United States*, which was discussed in Chapter 1.[52] There are ironies here which escaped the editors of the *Literary History*. The individuals discussed in Chapter III are not from 'all nations', but rather from western Europe. They were able to achieve a greater measure of assimilation than those from the second wave, who tended to be from southern and eastern Europe, and against whom there was a nativist backlash which led to a Quota Act in 1924. Migration to the United States is today still conducted under a quota system.

By looking at Letter III in isolation it appears that 'the new government' the American obeys is the one created by the Declaration of Independence. This is not the case; the politics of the text is ardently colonial. Crèvecoeur suggests that the American spirit derives from 'the original genius and strong desire of the people ratified and confirmed by the crown. This is the great chain that links us all . . .' (69). In other words, he was seeking a colonial system similar to that of William Smith, John Dickinson and Benjamin Franklin before 1773. It is the image of George III which unifies the various colonies. These are examined from an agrarian point of view. Both fishermen and frontiersmen are seen at odds with the genial hierarchy that is part of St John's colonial model. There is, too, a horrific reversal of agrarianism, a detailed account of Southern 'Strange Fruit', a slave hanging in a cage from a tree and being consumed by nature. Moral lessons conveyed by the metaphoric subsoil of the text surface in Letter XII, 'Distresses of a Frontier Man'. The 'great chain' has been broken; the revolution is regarded with terror, as a fratricidal civil war. In imagery that recalls the Puritan fear of the wilderness, St John shows that the once-benign environment is now stalked by wild beasts, human and animal. The imagery now also reflects Crèvecoeur's life after 1776. On the outbreak of the Revolutionary War he was threatened by patriots and, moving alone to New York City in 1778, was briefly imprisoned by the British. Following a nervous breakdown, he was allowed to take ship to Britain, where he arranged the publication of his text.

The 'Distresses' were also horribly prophetic. Crèvecoeur returned in 1783 to the United States as French consul, to discover that his wife was dead, his house destroyed and his children vanished. His experience was not unusual. The property of those loyal to the Crown was normally confiscated and, despite the provisions of the Treaty of Paris, in most cases not restored. Loyalists continued to be persecuted. Some were lynched. Those who could do so left the country. Around eighty thousand migrated to Canada. A nation founded on the sanctity of property blinked at its destruction; and one whose title proclaimed its unity remained divided. Yet such problems were erased by many American histories, and two texts which in part were devoted to an analysis of the rise of the British American Empire were misinterpreted so that they seemed to explain only the distinctive character of the United States. Even D. H. Lawrence unwittingly connived in this, suggesting that while Franklin was the '*practical* prototype of the American', Crèvecoeur was 'the emotional'.[53] He was wrong on both counts. Just as the shapes of American literature developed from European prototypes, so the Americanism of Franklin and Crèvecoeur was rooted in an Anglo-American empire that the new United States found it convenient to forget.

Notes

1. Salman Rushdie, *Imaginary Homelands: Essays and Criticism, 1981–1991* (London: Granta Books, 1991), p. 20.

2. William Strachey, *The Historie of Travell into Virginia Britania*, eds. Louis B. Wright and Virginia Freund (London: Hakluyt Society, 1953), pp. 9, 139, 77.

3. Michael Drayton, 'To Master George Sandys', in *Works*, ed. J. William Hebel (5 vols, Oxford: Shakespeare Head Press, 1932), III, pp. 206–8.

4. George Sandys, *Ovid's Metamorphosis Englished, Mythologiz'd And Represented in Figures*, eds. Karl K. Hulley and Stanley T. Vandersall (Lincoln, NE: University of Nebraska Press, 1970), p. 3.

5. 'The Tragicall Relation of the Virginia Assembly' (1624), in *Narratives of Early Virginia 1606–1625*, ed. Lyon Gardiner Tyler (New York: Scribner, 1907), pp. 422–3.

6. Strachey, *The Historie of Travell into Virginia Britania*, p. 57. John Smith, *A True Relation of Such Occurences and Accidents of Noate as Hath Hapned in Virginia Since the First Planting of That Collony*, in *Travels and Works*, ed. Edward Arber (2 vols, Edinburgh: John Grant, 1910), I, p. 19. Future references to *Travels and Works* will be given in parentheses after the quotation.

7. Henry Adams, 'Captaine John Smith', in Charles F. Adams and Henry Adams, *Chapters of Erie, and Other Essays* (Boston: James R. Osgood, 1871), p. 193. Adams, *The Education of Henry Adams* (1918; rpt. Harmondsworth: Penguin, 1995), p. 214.

8. William Carlos Williams, *In the American Grain* (1925; rpt. Harmondsworth: Penguin, 1971), pp. 82–3.

9. *Mourt's Relation*, ed. Dwight B. Heath (Bedford, MA: Applewood Books, 1963), pp. 18, 82.

10. William Bradford, *Of Plymouth Plantation*, ed. Harvey Wish (New York: Capricorn Books, 1962), p. 68. Future references to this text will be given in parentheses after the quotation.

11. *Sir Gawain and the Green Knight*, ed. W. R. J. Barron (Manchester: Manchester University Press, 1974), ll.701–2, p. 65. John Corbet, *An Historicall Relation of the Military Government of Gloucester* (London: Robert Bostock, 1645), pp. 16, 10. Michael Wigglesworth, 'God's Controversy with New-England', *The Poems of Michael Wigglesworth*, ed. Ronald A. Bosco (Lanham, MD: University Press of America, 1989), p. 90.

12. John Winthrop, 'A Model of Christian Charity', in *The Puritans in America: A Narrative Anthology*, eds. Alan Heimert and Andrew Delbanco (Cambridge, MA: Harvard University Press, 1985), pp. 90–1. Winthrop, 'Speech to the General Court, 3 July 1645', in *The Puritans*, eds. Perry Miller and Thomas H. Johnson (revised edn, 2 vols, New York: Harper & Row, 1963), I, p. 205. Winthrop, *Reasons to be Considered for the Intended Plantation in New England* (1629), in *The Puritans in America: A Narrative Anthology*, eds. Heimert and Delbanco, p. 71.

13. 'Preface', *The Bay Psalm Book* (1640; rpt. Chicago: University of Chicago Press, 1956), n.p. Future references to this text will be given in parentheses after the quotation.

14. Sandys, *Poetical Works*, ed. Richard Hooper (2 vols, London: John Russell, 1872), I, pp. 118–19.

15. Gerrard Winstanley, *The Law of Freedom and Other Writings*, ed. Christopher Hill (Harmondsworth: Penguin, 1973), p. 393. James Fenimore Cooper, *The Last of the Mohicans* (Albany, NY: State University of New York Press, 1983), p. 84.

16. Thomas Morton, *New English Canaan* (1637; rpt. New York: Da Capo, 1969), pp. 188, 134–5, 10. Williams, *In the American Grain*, pp. 91, 80.

17. Roger Williams, *The Hireling Ministry None of Christs* (1652), in *The Complete Writings of Roger Williams*, ed. Perry Miller (7 vols, New York: Russell & Russell, 1963), VII, p. 168. Winstanley, *The New Law of Righteousness*, in *The Works of Gerrard Winstanley*, ed. G. H. Sabine (Ithaca, NY: Cornell University Press, 1941), p. 224.

18. [Comenius], *The Gate of Tongues Unlocked and Opened . . . That is, A short way of teaching and thorowly learning, within a yeere and a half at the furthest, the Latin, English, French, and any other tongue . . .* (2nd edn, London: Michael Sparkes, 1643), t.p.

19. Williams, *A Key into the Language of America* (1643; rpt. Menston: Scolar Press, 1971), pp. A2r–v, [A8r], 137. Williams, *The Hireling Ministry None of Christs*, in *The Complete Writings of Roger Williams*, ed. Miller, VII, p. 168.

20. James Axtell, 'Colonial America Without the Indians', in *After Columbus: Essays in the Ethnohistory of Colonial North America* (New York: Oxford University Press, 1988), pp. 236–7.

21. Edward Johnson, *The Wonder-Working Providence of Scion's Saviour in New-England*, ed. J. Franklin Jameson (1910; rpt. New York: Barnes & Noble, 1967), p. 127. 'The Examination of Mrs. Anne Hutchinson at the Court at Newtown', in David D. Hall, *The Antinomian Controversy 1636–1638: A Documentary History* (2nd edn, Durham, NC: Duke University Press, 1990), pp. 337–8.

22. Arthur Miller, *The Crucible* (1953; rpt. Harmondsworth: Penguin, 1968), p. [11]. Samuel Torshell, *The Womans Glorie* (2nd edn, London: n.p., 1650), p. 11. Textual emphases. Henry James, *Hawthorne* (1879; rpt. London: Macmillan, 1967), p. 89. Winthrop, entry for September 1643, *The Journal of John Winthrop 1630–1649*, eds. Richard S. Dunn and Laetitia Yeandle (Cambridge, MA: Belknap Press, 1996), p. 239.

23. Winthrop, *The Journal of John Winthrop 1630–1649*, eds. Dunn and Yeandle, pp. 141–2, 146–7. [Winthrop], *A Short Story of the Rise, Reign, and Ruin of the Antinomians, Familists and Libertines* (1644), and [Weld], 'Preface', *A Short Story*, both reprinted in Hall, *The Antinomian Controversy*, pp. 310, 280–1, 214.

24. Torshell, *The Womans Glorie*, pp. 13, 87–8. Textual emphases. Anne Bradstreet, 'In Honour of that High and Mighty Princess Queen Elizabeth of happy memory', in *The Works of Anne Bradstreet*, ed. Jeannine Hensley (Cambridge, MA: Harvard University Press, 1967), pp. 195–6. Future references to this text will be given in parentheses after the quotation.

25. Edward Winslow, introd., *A Platform of Church-Discipline* (London: Peter Coles, 1653), p. 1. John Cotton, *The Way of Congregational Churches Cleared* (1648), in *John Cotton on the Congregational Churches of New England*, ed. Larzer Ziff (Cambridge, MA: The Belknap Press of Harvard University Press, 1968), pp. 304–5. Wigglesworth, *The Day of Doom*, in *The Puritans*, eds. Miller and Johnson, II, pp. 602, 606.

26. Mary Rowlandson, *The Sovereignty & Goodness of God*, in *Puritans Among the Indians: Accounts of Captivity and Redemption 1676–1724*, eds. Alden T. Vaughan and Edward W. Clark (Cambridge, MA: Harvard University Press, 1981), pp. 33, 37, 70, 64, 75. Until 1752, the Julian calendar was used in the British empire.

27. *The Poems of Edward Taylor*, ed. Donald E. Stanford (New Haven, CT: Yale University Press, 1960), p. 74.

28. Cotton Mather, *A Companion for Communicants* (Boston: 1690), quoted in Robert Middlekauff, *The Mathers: Three Generations of Puritan Intellectuals, 1596–1728* (New York: Oxford University Press, 1971), p. 197. Mather, *Magnalia Christi Americana* (1702; rpt., Cambridge, MA: The Belknap Press of Harvard University Press, 1977), pp. 89, 118, t.p. Future references to this text will be given in parentheses after the quotation.

29. Mather, *Magnalia Christi Americana* (3rd edn, 1853; rpt. Edinburgh: Banner of Truth Trust, 1979), pp. 559–62.

30. Mather, *The Minister* (Boston: n.p., 1722), pp. 14, 34.

31. George Berkeley, 'On the Prospect of Planting Arts and Learning in America', in *The White Men's Burdens: An Anthology of British Poetry of the Empire*, eds. Chris Brooks and Peter Faulkner (Exeter: Exeter University Press, 1996), pp. 70–1.

32. Nathaniel Ames, *An Astronomical Diary: or, An Almanack for the Year of our Lord Christ 1758* (Boston: Printed for J. Draper, n.d.), [pp. 15–16].

33. Aphra Behn, *Oroonoko* in *Oroonoko, The Rover, and Other Works*, ed. Janet Todd (Harmondsworth: Penguin, 1992), pp. 115–16. Future references to this edition will be given in parentheses after the quotation.

34. John Frampton, *Joyfull Newes out of the New Founde Worlde*, introd. Stephen Gaselee (2 vols, London: Constable & Co., 1925) I, p. 75. Ebenezer Cook, *The Sot-Weed*

Factor, in *The English Literatures of America, 1500–1800*, eds. Myra Jehlen and Michael Warner (New York: Routledge, 1997), pp. 1014, 1021, 1026, 1031.

35. Sarah Kemble Knight, *Journal*, in *The English Literatures of America, 1500–1800*, eds. Jehlen and Warner, pp. 426, 419.

36. David Hackett Fischer, *Albion's Seed: Four British Folkways in America* (New York: Oxford University Press, 1989). Jonathan Edwards, *A Faithful Narrative of the Surprising Work of God* (London: John Oswald, 1737). *A Short Narrative of the Extraordinary Work at Cambuslang* (Boston: S. Kneeland and T. Green, 1742).

37. Edwards, 'Sinners in the Hands of an Angry God', in *Jonathan Edwards: Representative Selections*, eds. Clarence H. Faust and Thomas H. Johnson (New York: Hill & Wang, 1962), p. 164. Future references to this text will be given in parentheses after the quotation.

38. William Byrd, *Histories of the Dividing Line betwixt Virginia and North Carolina*, ed. William K. Boyd (New York: Dover, 1967), pp. 268–70. Future references to this text will be given in parentheses after the quotation.

39. John Locke, *The Second Treatise of Government*, in *Political Writings*, ed. David Wootton (Harmondsworth: Penguin, 1993), pp. 282, 285–6.

40. William Smith, *A General Idea of the College of Mirania*, rpt. in *Works* (2 vols, Philadelphia: Hugh Maxwell & William Fry, 1803), I, pp. 180–1.

41. Mason L. Weems, *The Life of Washington*, ed. Marcus Cunliffe (Cambridge, MA: The Belknap Press of Harvard University Press, 1962), pp. 172–5.

42. Edward Gibbon, *The History of the Decline and Fall of the Roman Empire*, ed. J. B. Bury (7 vols, London: Methuen, 1909), IV, pp. 173–4.

43. Benjamin Franklin, *The Autobiography and Other Writings*, ed. Kenneth Silverman (Harmondsworth: Penguin, 1986), p. 8. Further references to this text are usually given in parentheses after the quotation.

44. Peter Folger, 'Looking-Glass for the Times' in A. Evert and George L. Duyckinck, *Cyclopaedia of American Literature* (2 vols, 1854; rpt. Detroit: Gale Research Co., 1965), I, p. 61.

45. Franklin, *The Autobiography and Other Writings*, ed. Silverman, p. 8. Folger, 'Looking-Glass for the Times' in *Cyclopaedia of American Literature*, I, p. 61.

46. Herman Melville, 'Dr. Franklin and Latin Quarter', *Israel Potter* (New York: Sagamore Press, 1957), p. 66.

47. D. H. Lawrence, *Studies in Classic American Literature* (1924; rpt. Harmondsworth: Penguin, 1971), p. 15.

48. Franklin, *The Papers of Benjamin Franklin*, ed. Leonard W. Labaree (New Haven, CT: Yale University Press, 1968), XII, pp. 134–5. Per Kalm, *Travels into North America*, trans. John R. Forster (3 vols, Warrington: William Eyres, 1770), I, pp. 116–17. Constance Rourke, *American Humor: A Study of the National Character* (1931; rpt. New York: Harcourt Brace Jovanovich, 1959), p. 297.

49. John Dickinson, *Letters from a Farmer in Pennsylvania* (Boston: Mein & Fleeming, 1768), pp. 5, 137.

50. W. P. Trent, 'Prefatory Note' to J. Hector St John Crèvecoeur, *Letters from an American Farmer* (1782; rpt. New York: Fox, Duffield, 1904), p. viii.

51. J. Hector St John de Crèvecoeur, *Letters from an American Farmer* (1782; rpt. Harmondsworth: Penguin, 1981), pp. 81–2. Further references to this text will be given in parentheses after the quotation.

52. *The Literary History of the United States*, eds. Robert E. Spiller, Willard Thorp, Thomas H. Johnson and Henry Seidel Canby (2 vols, New York: Macmillan, 1948), I, p. xiii.

53. Lawrence, *Studies in Classic American Literature*, p. 29.

Chapter 4

The New Republic, 1776–1826

It is not indeed the fine Arts, which our Country requires. The Usefull, the mechanic Arts are those which We have occasion for in a young Country, as yet simple and not far advanced in Luxury . . . I must study Politicks and War that my sons may have liberty to study Mathematicks and Philosophy. My sons ought to study Mathematicks and Philosophy, Geography, natural History, Naval Architecture, navigation, Commerce and Agriculture, in order to give their Children a right to study Painting, Poetry, Musick, Architecture, Statuary, Tapestry and Porcelaine.

(John Adams)[1]

The age of Paine

In May 1780, John Adams could not imagine a role for the arts in the new Republic. There was a very good reason. The outcome of the Revolution was still uncertain. In that month Continental troops surrendered to superior British forces at Charleston, South Carolina. It would have taken great prescience to think that the tide would turn and that, seventeen months later, the British would finally surrender at Yorktown. Yet the tenor of Adams's letter is predictive and, as we have seen in Chapter 1, it was a view repeated by Joseph Green Cogswell in 1819, and by Alexis de Tocqueville in 1840. All three men thought that there was little space for works of the imagination in the new nation. The problem, though, was one of perception rather than reality. Certainly, as this chapter will show, some writers believed that the circumstances of the time cramped their abilities. But it would be quite untrue to say that no arts existed in the early Republic. Adams's prediction was wrong in two ways. First, his model of cultural change lasted too long. One might say that its three stages occurred not in three generations but could instead be represented by the first three presidents. George Washington (1732–99) might be called the warrior-president. John Adams (1735–1826), who succeeded Washington in 1797, could be called a philosopher-president. Thomas Jefferson (1743–1826), who succeeded Adams in 1801, was the president as man of letters. Second, the written works of the new Republic certainly appeared, but in forms that were unfamiliar to Adams, and which he loathed. Adams himself recognised the fact in 1805 when, in a magnificent burst of furious rhetoric, he gave the age its name:

I am willing you should call this the Age of Frivolity as you do: and would not object if you had named it the Age of Folly, Vice, Frenzy, Fury, Brutality, Daemons, Buonaparte, Tom Paine, or the Age of the burning Brand from the bottomless Pitt:

134

or any thing but the Age of Reason. I know not whether any Man in the World has had more influence on its inhabitants or affairs for the last thirty years than Tom Paine ... For such a mongrel between Pigg and Puppy, begotten by a wild Boar on a Bitch Wolf, never before in any Age of the World was suffered by the Poltroonery of mankind, to run through such a Career of Mischief. Call it then the Age of Paine.[2]

Thomas Paine was as much a symbol as a writer. There is even a felicity in his upbringing: how appropriate it is that the son and apprentice of a corsetmaker should become one of the most fervent advocates of freedom. Indeed, much of his later life involved a rejection of the past. He shrugged off the first thirty-seven years of his life when, with the help of Benjamin Franklin, he moved to Philadelphia in 1774. The process of renewal began again in 1787 when he moved back to Europe in support of the revolutionary cause. In 1792 he was made an honorary French citizen by the Assembly, only to have it revoked during the Reign of Terror a year later. He returned again to the United States in 1802, but never exercised the influence that he had possessed in earlier years. He died in poverty in 1809, maligned by many, as well as Adams, who feared his radical freethinking.

'It was the cause of America that made me an author', he wrote on 19 April 1783, the eighth anniversary of the Battle of Lexington and Concord, and eight days after Congress had proclaimed a cessation of hostilities against Britain. That claim was not literally true, for in Britain he had published a pamphlet on behalf of excise officers. It led to his dismissal from the service. But because Paine was at his best in times of turmoil, the claim could be said to have a certain metaphorical force. It was written in the penultimate issue of *The American Crisis*, a series of sixteen essays that Paine began at a low-point in the fortunes of the Continental Army. The opening phrases of the first essay of the series have the weight of the moral maxims that they have since become:

These are times that try men's souls. The summer soldier and the sunshine patriot will, in this crisis, shrink from the service of their country; but he that stands it now, deserves the love and thanks of man and woman. Tyranny, like hell, is not easily conquered; yet we have this consolation with us, that the harder the conflict, the more glorious the triumph. What we obtain too cheap, we esteem too lightly: it is dearness only that gives every thing its value.

The metaphors of economics perhaps show the influence of Franklin. Otherwise, the style – the artfully simple use of monosyllables, the frequent resort to alliteration – is identifiably Paine's own. As an inspirational document it ranks with the address of Henry V to his soldiers before the walls of Harfleur. The essential difference is that while Shakespeare wrote the address almost two centuries after the siege of Harfleur, Paine's pamphlet was before the event. It was written on a drumhead while he was a soldier with Washington's forces, during their retreat across New Jersey. It was intended to catch the ear of the widest audience. By Washington's command it was read out to the soldiers before they crossed the freezing Delaware River to attack the Hessians at

Trenton, on Christmas Eve 1776. The attack was a success, and is often regarded as a turning point in the Revolutionary War. It might be said therefore that Paine's authorship was instrumental in making the United States. There is the closest relationship between his demotic style and the American democracy.[3]

That style also invigorates *Common Sense*, the pamphlet he published when he lived in Philadelphia in January 1776:

> ...we have every opportunity and every encouragement before us, to form the noblest, purest constitution on the face of the earth. We have it in our power to begin the world over again. A situation, similar to the present, hath not happened since the days of Noah until now. The birth-day of a new world is at hand...[4]

The claim to American novelty, for all the potency of its recourse to the Bible, is hardly new. Neither is the sense of American space, which Paine inflated from geography into geopolitics. Yet the pamphlet is so urgently argued that it did more than any other document to prepare the way for the Declaration of the Fourth of July. The pamphlet's complaints against George III and his government were reinforced by an assertion of American amplitude, and a little geopolitical chicanery. In common with many other English people (to the natural resentment of the Scots and Welsh), Paine equated England with Britain for much of the pamphlet. But when he compared the size of the combatant countries, Scotland and Wales vanished and even poor England shrivelled:

> In this extensive quarter of the globe, we forget the narrow limits of three hundred and sixty miles (the extent of England) and carry our friendship on a larger scale... (85)

Paine also anticipated Crèvecoeur by turning American space into a psychological imperative. Americans, he said, had 'continental minds'. Their politics and vision should expand accordingly. They should not get 'into holes and corners', cramping themselves into a reconciliation with Britain; tyranny, he thought, could only be sustained in a small country (118). His imagery was extremely persuasive. One of the earliest responses to *Common Sense* called it 'a wonderful production ... completely calculated for the meridian of America'.[5]

Paine raked over the past as a counterpoint to American novelty. In particular, he used the device of a dialogue with a dead person, begun by the Greek satirist Lucian (*c*. AD 115–200) and modernised by François Fénelon (1651–1715), Matthew Prior (1664–1721) and George Lyttelton (1709–73). The most recent figure disinterred by Paine was General Richard Montgomery (1738–75), who died leading an abortive attack by the Continental Army against Quebec. In the dialogue, Paine has Montgomery place himself in a tradition, from Hampden to Wolfe, of those who had sacrificed themselves 'upon the altar of liberty'. A year earlier, in 'A Dialogue Between General Wolfe and General Gage', Paine had resuscitated James Wolfe himself, who died leading the British attack on Quebec in 1759. Wolfe tells Gage, an old army friend and now commander-in-chief of British forces in America, that he has come 'to deprive your fellow subjects of their liberty', which is 'a business unworthy a British soldier, and a freeman'. Paine's use of military heroes to speak for the revolutionary cause was too much for William Smith. In a 1776 pamphlet Smith turned the tables on Paine, suggesting that Montgomery was instead a hero in the tradition of Alfred and Ralegh, claiming liberty within the British Empire.

Imperialism was anathema to Paine. Another figure, which he brought back from the dead, was Robert Clive (1725–74). The 'Reflections on the Life and Death of Lord Clive', published in March 1775, suggest that the suicide of the conqueror of India was the inevitable outcome of such imperial ambitions. One month earlier Paine had imagined a worse fate for the most famous imperialist of all. In the 'New Anecdotes of Alexander the Great', Paine transformed the River Schuylkill into the Styx. He crosses it to discover the destiny of the Greek. He sees a grand chariot, and finds that Alexander is not one of the splendid occupants, but rather one of the horses. The hero suffers other humiliations. When threatened with punishment, the Greek warrior becomes a ball of dung, and rolls away. As Paine leaves, a bug alights on his dress. He is about to crush it, when it screams: '*Spare Alexander the* GREAT.' Paine picks up the bug:

> he exhibited a most contemptible figure of the downfall of tyrant greatness. Affected with a mixture of concern and compassion (*which he was always a stranger to*) I suffered him to nibble on a pimple that was newly risen on my hand, in order to refresh him; after which, I placed him on a tree to hide him, but a Tom Tit coming by, chopped him up with as little mercy as he put whole kingdoms to the sword.[6]

Paine attacked the institutions of the Old World with an imagination that anticipates Kafka and a vitriol that stings like Twain at his most acid. It is hardly surprising, then, that many agreed with Adams in regarding him as the archetype of the sanguinary revolutionary. *The Rights of Man* (1791–2) and *The Age of Reason* (1794–5) enhanced Paine's notoriety. The first book was his response to Edmund Burke's *Reflections on the Revolution in France* (1790). It was published while he lived in London, and prompted his flight to Paris and his conviction *in absentia* for treason. He wrote the second while in prison in France, ironically for being an English enemy of the Montagnards. Although *The Age of Reason* is a deist comment on sectarianism, it was reviled as an attack on the sanctity of the Bible. Paine was the symbol of the demotic literary revolutionary, united with others who had little in common with him. In an 1804 review Francis Jeffrey, one of the founders of the *Edinburgh Review* with Sydney Smith (whose comment on American culture was discussed in Chapter 1), used a heavily ironic tone to link:

> the laudable exertions of Mr. Thomas Paine to bring disaffection and infidelity within the comprehension of the ordinary people . . . [with] the charitable endeavours of Messrs Wirdsworth [*sic*] & Co., to accommodate them with an appropriate vein of poetry. Both these were superfluities which they might have done very tolerably without.[7]

It is difficult now to bracket Thomas Jefferson with Paine as a dangerous incendiary. Yet for much of his life he was regarded as such, particularly during the long and acrimonious debate that accompanied his election as third president in 1801. Jefferson's relief at the close of this unpleasant period is clear from a letter written to the scientist Joseph Priestley:

> We can no longer say there is nothing new under the sun. For this whole chapter in the history of man is new. The great extent of our republic is new. Its sparse habitation is new. The mighty wave of public opinion which has rolled over it is new. But the most pleasing novelty is, its so quickly subsiding over such an extent of surface to its true level again.[8]

The images that Jefferson uses here shows that he shares with Paine the sensation of the novelty and amplitude of American space, to the extent that he rejects the famous assertion in Ecclesiastes 1:9 that 'there is no new *thing* under the sun'. He regarded American space as such a distinguishing feature that within three years he doubled it by the purchase of Louisiana from France. Yet those images also suggest a political difference with Paine. Stormy disorder gives way to sunny order, expressed spatially by means of the written word. Ordering devices are to be found throughout the many hundreds of letters that Jefferson wrote, and particularly in the two texts for which he is now most remembered, the Declaration of Independence, and the *Notes on the State of Virginia* (1782).

The Declaration of Independence shares Paine's anger against tyranny in its long list of indictments against George III. The list has now been forgotten; its sarcasm has subsided, smoothed by the ordering tactics of the famous opening sentences:

> When in the Course of Human Events it becomes necessary for one people to dissolve the political bands which have connected them with another, and to assume among the Powers of the earth, the separate and equal station to which the Laws of Nature and Nature's God entitle them, a decent respect for the opinions of mankind requires that they should declare the causes which impel them to the separation.
>
> We hold these truths to be self-evident, that all men are created equal, that they are endowed by their Creator with certain inalienable Rights, that among these are Life, Liberty and the Pursuit of Happiness; that to secure these rights, Governments are instituted among Men, deriving their just powers from the consent of the governed; that whenever any Form of Government becomes destructive to these ends, it is the Right of the People to alter or abolish it, and to institute a new Government, laying its foundation on such principles, and organizing its powers in such form, as to them shall seem most likely to effect their Safety and Happiness. (235)

Scholars have often noted Jefferson's indebtedness, in writing these sonorous phrases, to Locke's *Second Treatise of Government* and to the rationality of the Scottish Enlightenment. In its turn, the Declaration has become a founding document not only for the United States, but also generally for liberal political thought. Some critics have remarked that the definition of equality is silent about the slaves who were making up an increasingly large proportion of the population of the South. Jefferson, it will be remembered, was a relatively benign slaveholder. References to 'safety and happiness' also obliterate the harm and misery caused to large numbers, Crèvecoeur and William Smith among them, who held a different view about the way America should be ordered. 'Decent respect' for others was sometimes missing from the Republic. The most famous triadic phrase of the Declaration – those self-evident truths – provides a model for republican behaviour that, as we shall see, was not always followed.

If the Declaration of Independence creates an overall design for the new nation, the *Notes on the State of Virginia* provides an exemplary ordering structure for one of its components. Initially intended by Jefferson to be a private response to a list of questions from François Barbé de Marbois, secretary to the French minister to the United States, the *Notes* reshuffles the 'Queries' to follow a pattern established by William Strachey's *The Historie of Travell into Virginia Britania* (1612) and recommended by the 'General Heads for a Natural History of a Country' recommended by Robert Boyle (1627–91), the founder of the scientific Royal Society. The Queries therefore start with scientific measurement (the boundaries), move through a description of the country (Queries II–XII) to a discussion of the Constitutions, laws and institutions (Queries XIII–XXII), and conclude with a list of 'Histories, Memorials, and State-Papers' (Query XXIII). Within the ordered structure Jefferson tries to answer the criticism of such miasmatists as Buffon, and analyses the tourist attractions of the Natural Bridge and the passage of the Potomac through the Blue Ridge Mountains in terms of the Burkean aesthetics of the Beautiful and Sublime. He proposes the emancipation of the slaves (it would not be effected for another seventy-three years), yet in discussing them follows the conventional hierarchy of racism. At the apex of his system is the independent farmer:

> Those who labour in the earth are the chosen people of God, if ever he had a chosen people, whose breasts he has made his peculiar deposit for substantial and genuine virtue. It is the focus in which he keeps alive that sacred fire, which otherwise might escape from the face of the earth. Corruption of morals in the mass of cultivators is a phænomenon of which no age or nation has furnished an example.

Jefferson's attachment to the agrarian ideal resembles Crèvecoeur's; and is such that he proposes that 'our workshops remain in Europe'. He suggests that such trades as are necessary to support husbandry should be encouraged in the United States. Indeed, like Franklin, Jefferson tinkered with innovations, such as the mould-board plough. But as long as the twin evils of industrialisation and urbanisation are kept away from the republic, it will be free of the 'canker which soon eats to the heart of its laws and constitution', and will be preserved 'in vigour' (217). We shall see if this prediction came true.

Writing in a vacuum

'Rip Van Winkle', Washington Irving's best-known short story, was first published in 1819. It presents in exaggerated form the difficulties confronting many US writers in the first fifty years of the existence of the United States. Those difficulties were not foreseen by Jefferson, but had been predicted by Adams, and summarised by Henry James when he remarked that 'it takes an accumulation of history and custom' to nurture imaginative writing. American history is marked not by accumulation, but rather by discontinuity. Irving's tale alludes to three periods in his country's history, each one sealed off from the other. Rip moves between all three; he becomes, like Kurt Vonnegut's Billy Pilgrim, 'unstuck in time'. Fortunately for Rip the end result is fun, for the second time-shift, from 1776 to 1796, shuffles his termagant wife off this mortal coil. The first takes Rip back to the time of the settlement of New Netherland in 1624, following the Dutch title established by the voyage of Hendrick Hudson in 1609, up the river that now bears his name. This time-shift carries Rip across one of the fissures in American history, for New Netherland changed its owner and name (to New York and New Jersey) after the British attack in 1664. The second is marked by a clear historical reference:

> Instead of the great tree that used to shelter the quiet little Dutch inn of yore, there was now reared a tall naked pole, with something on the top that looked like a red nightcap, and from it was fluttering a flag, on which was a singular assemblage of stars and stripes – all this was strange and incomprehensible. He recognised on the sign, however, the ruby face of King George, under which he had smoked so many a peaceful pipe; but even this was singularly metamorphosed. The red coat was changed for one of blue and buff, a sword held in the hand instead of a sceptre, the head was decorated with a cocked hat, and underneath was painted in large characters, GENERAL WASHINGTON.

Rip has stumbled into the election of 1796, contested between the Federalists, who supported Britain in its War against France, and Jefferson's Democratic-Republicans, sympathetic to the French Revolution. The Phrygian cap atop the flagpole and the rhetoric of the politician outside the door of Jonathan Doolittle's inn indicates that Rip's Hudson Valley village is Francophile. This is confirmed by the bystanders' angry reaction to Rip's hasty remark that he is 'a loyal subject of the king'. It is a dangerous if brief interlude. For Rip is not really loyal to anything, save perhaps his drink, and a dog, now dead. He is not even loyal to himself; in his readiness 'to attend to anybody's business but his own' he is the reverse of Benjamin Franklin, a lengthier version of whose *Autobiography* had appeared the year before, in 1818.[9]

Perhaps the only thing that Rip shares with Franklin is the ability to sleep through an American institution. In Franklin's case it is the Quaker Meeting. In Rip's it is much more. He sleeps through the Revolution, the subsequent period of confederacy, the Constitutional Convention, the election of George Washington as first President in 1789 and re-election for a second term in 1792. He is not around to read the Declaration of Independence (1776), the Articles of Confederation (1781), the Constitution (1787) and the Bill of Rights (1789). He misses, in other words, the documents which created the United States and which have subsequently taken on such quasi-religious significance that they apparently make the United States different from every other nation. Rip has a serious identity problem.

The fracturing of time also strips meaning from space. The disorientation experienced by Rip is explained in 'The Author's Account of Himself', which Irving added to the collection of pieces he published in London as *The Sketch Book of Geoffrey Crayon, Gent.* Irving discusses 'the charms of storied and poetical association' (2), which drew him in 1815 to Europe, where he would remain for seventeen years. In using the term 'association' Irving is drawing on a well-established causal theory relating all mental activity to sensations and feelings. Associationism was first fully explored in David Hartley's *Observations on Man* (1749), and then developed by Edmund Burke in his 1757 *Enquiry into the Origin of Our Ideas of the Sublime and Beautiful.* By 1815 picturesque tourism had long been popular, with such areas as the Alps and the Lake District tramped over by those bent on gratifying their wish for a sensational joyride. The problem for Irving was that while America was full of possibilities 'for the sublime and beautiful of natural scenery' (2), its lack of associations made the continent resemble a blank slate. Locke's remark, 'in the beginning all the world was America', had for Irving a psychological rather than a mercantile meaning.

Rip's twenty-year snooze in the Catskill Mountains was a counterpart of Irving's inability, at this stage, to deduce value from the environment. It is no help that this scenery would shortly inspire the Hudson River school of landscape painters. History, indeed, seemed to be dismantling what little significance there was. When Rip returned to his village in 1796, the venerable tree had been replaced by a liberty pole, and the old Dutch inn by the 'Union Hotel', which is falling apart. The painter has taken the easy option with its sign, repainting the dress of the figure rather than the whole sign. George III has thus been 'singularly metamorphosed' to a president whose identity has to be confirmed by the addition of his name (37). This last is a particularly ironic touch by Irving, born in 1783 and named for the great leader. An environment drained of significance is accompanied by degeneration of the inhabitants. Rip is a feeble offspring 'of the Van Winkles who figured so gallantly in the chivalrous days of Peter Stuyvesant' (27). It seems that Irving was forced to agree with Joseph Green Cogswell, who also left the United States in 1815 and whose articles for *Blackwood's*, discussed in Chapter 1, worried that the miasmatist theories put forward by Buffon and Raynal were correct.

Such worries infected the form of Irving's text. The anaemic gentility suggested by the title is confirmed in a casual collection of short stories, essays and travel pieces. The articles about Britain, particularly the quintet of sketches about Christmas, full of a rubicund plum-pudding jollity which anticipates Dickens, seemed the most substantial and were so successful that they led to a sequel, *Bracebridge Hall*, two years later. The American pieces appeared in contrast to be attenuated; and the two most famous, 'Rip Van Winkle' and 'The Legend of Sleepy Hollow', were in any case adaptations from Old World sources. 'Rip Van Winkle' is taken from an old German tale, 'Peter Klaus'. The story of Ichabod Crane and the Headless Horseman of Sleepy Hollow

– who may or may not be Brom Bones – owes something to *Sir Gawain and the Green Knight* and 'Der wilde Jäger', a poem by Gottfried Bürger, the translator of *Benjamin Franklin's Jugendjahre*. It is little wonder that the authorial uncertainty, which informs the *Letters from an American Farmer*, is also apparent here. It is not clear if 'The Author's Account of Himself' is by Crayon, or Diedrich Knickerbocker, or Irving. Its tone is hesitant and self-deprecating. The sketches are of 'nooks, and corners, and by-places' rather than the buildings and landscapes which gave the Old World its solid centrality (3). The whole text seems to confirm James's remark 'that the flower of art blooms only where the soil is deep'.[10] Yet, to continue that metaphor, Irving helped to deepen the soil when he adapted his sources to create two tall New York tales. He furthered the process of mythological sedimentation by adding to a comic American crew that already included Franklin's Niagara-jumping whales and Bartram's ballooning cows.

The problems of authenticity, noticeable in *The Sketch Book of Geoffrey Crayon, Gent.*, also marked the careers of Hugh Henry Brackenridge and Philip Freneau. Those careers began in 1771 with 'The Rising Glory of America', a poem written jointly in celebration of *translatio imperii* within the setting of British America. It draws on Berkeley's poem, 'On the Prospect of Planting Arts and Learning in America', and adds echoes of Milton, the King James Bible and Drayton's 'To the Virginian Voyage' to create the Anglo-American Dream, a prelapsarian vision where:

> . . . tim'rous deer with rabid tygers stray
> O'er mead or lofty hill or grassy plain.
> Another Jordan's stream shall glide along
> And Siloah's brook in circling eddies flow,
> Groves shall adorn their verdant banks, on which
> The happy people free from second death
> Shall find secure repose; no fierce disease,
> No fevers, slow consumption, direful plague
> Death's ancient ministers, again renew
> Perpetual war with man: Fair fruits shall bloom,
> Fair to the eye, sweet to the taste . . . Music's charms
> Shall swell the lofty soul and harmony
> Triumphant reign; thro' ev'ry grove shall sound
> The cymbal and the lyre, joys too divine
> For fallen man to know. Such days the world
> And such, America, thou first shall have
> When ages yet to come have run their round . . .

This utopianism survived the collapse of the Anglo-American Empire. When in 1779 Brackenridge began publishing the *United States Magazine*, his Preface to its first issue indicated both his anger at British disdain and his happiness that it was apparently being answered by the growing public interest in literature:

> For what is man without taste and the acquirements of genius? An Ouran-Outan with the human shape and the soul of a beast.

It was the language of our enemies at the commencement of the debate between America and what is called the mother country, that in righteous judgement for our wickedness, it would be well to leave us to that independency which we seemed to affect, and to suffer us to sink down to so many Ouran-Outans of the wood, lost to the light of science which, from the other side of the Atlantic, had just begun to break upon us. They have been made to see, and even to confess the vanity of this kind of auguration.

The image-pattern here repeats the one to be found in Nathaniel Ames's 1758 almanac, discussed in Chapter 3. The dark woods, the home of beasts, are contrasted with the light of science and culture. Brackenridge's emotions are all the more raw because as a child he had lived through the unstable conditions of the Pennsylvania frontier following Braddock's defeat in 1755. An uneasy awareness of the beast lurking in man would inform his writing for much of his life.[11]

The *United States Magazine* was published throughout 1779, with contributions from Freneau as well as Brackenridge. Then, that December, it closed. Brackenridge blamed the war, the inflation of republican currency, and also those with no interest in literature, 'the people who inhabit the region of stupidity, and cannot bear to have the tranquillity of their repose disturbed by the villainous jargon of a book'. He hoped that the magazine would be merely suspended until better times.[12] It never reopened. In 1780 Brackenridge was admitted to the Philadelphia bar. The following year he moved back to the Pennsylvania frontier, only to discover that Pittsburgh was the capital of the region of stupidity, noted for the disorder of those he characterised as orangutans. Even farmers were prone to unrest. According to such revolutionary ideologues as Thomas Jefferson and Benjamin Rush, they were the upholders of republican virtue. Yet, having learnt to react against a taxation system imposed by Britain, they now rejected the system set up by their own government. The first years of the Republic were marked by a series of frontier rebellions, the best known of which were Shays's Rebellion of 1786–7, the Whiskey Rebellion of 1794, and Fries's Rebellion of 1798. These uprisings seemed to suggest that the United States was importing the bloodshed and demagoguery that, as we shall see, came to be associated with the French Revolution.

Brackenridge's frontier experience is reflected in *Modern Chivalry*, his longest fiction and the work for which he is now remembered. Published serially between 1792 and 1815 and totalling more than eight hundred pages, it was for many years regarded as a sprawling, even incoherent, picaresque novel. Recently, however, a number of critics have revealed its tightly controlled satirical form with a sophisticated, experimental narrative stance. *Modern Chivalry* draws upon Old World antecedents yet reveals an awareness of writing in the cultural vacuities of a new republic and a newly settled territory. It can be regarded as the first novel to discuss the new United States, and anticipates the work of Brockden Brown and Fenimore Cooper. It presents the adventures of Captain Farrago, who is depicted as the epitome of the rural gentry. With his intellectual power, classical learning, rhetorical gifts and natural modesty, Farrago is modelled on the ideal of the republican leader. Yet, as the opening of the novel indicates, he is not without the potential for delusion:

> the idea had come in to his head, to saddle an old horse that he had, and ride about the world a little, with his man Teague at his heels, to see how things were going on here and there, and to observe human nature. For it is a mistake to suppose, that a man cannot learn man by reading him in a corner, as well as on the widest space of transaction. At any rate, it may yield amusement.

The echo of *Don Quixote* is clearly apparent. On setting out, Farrago discovers that the Republic is dismissive of his qualities. It is money rather than learning that leads to status. As a result, rogues are to be found everywhere, particularly in the nation's capital, Philadelphia, which is awash with 'fat swabs, that guzzle wine, and smoke segars'.[13]

Farrago is dogged by his servant, Teague Oregan, who might be called the first in a long line of fictional American confidence tricksters. He represents the bribery and vote-seeking that had apparently been growing in the years before the Revolution but are now unchecked in the new democracy. In such a political environment the confidence trickster is the perfect operator, for he is able to present himself in whatever role the electorate wishes. Oregan can therefore outpoint Farrago at every turn. He presents himself as a clergyman, a Greek scholar, a philosopher, a senator and Indian treaty-maker. He is enormously popular with businessmen, voters and women alike. They all want to know 'Major' Oregan, for Teague makes himself superior to his master although, as Farrago snorts, 'he is about as much a Major as my horse' (229).

Brackenridge's experience during the Whiskey Rebellion is reflected in an episode which is both the most comic and most ominous in the novel. Oregan gets himself appointed as an excise officer. When he tries to collect the taxes a mob treat him to tar and feathers, giving him 'the appearance of the wild fowl of the forest' (305). His pretentiousness has come home to roost, completing the erosion of the human and animal anticipated in Farrago's equine comment. The comic fate of Oregan extends over two chapters, and is the richer because it is interrupted by a discussion of Thomas Paine's *Rights of Man*. The servant is left to roam, and climbs a tree to escape the attention of wolves, then attracts a pair of hunters, who debate his species:

> At first they took him for a bear; but seeing the feathers, it was decided that he must be of the fowl kind. Nevertheless his face and form, which appeared to be human, made him a monster in creation, or at least a new species of animal, never before known in these woods. (317)

The hunters take him in a cage to Philadelphia, where he receives the attentions of the American Philosophical Society:

> If this animal is to be referred to the quadruped, or beast kind, it would most naturally be classed with the Ouran Outang, or Wild Man of Africa: If with the bird kind, we shall be totally at a loss to assign the genus. For although it has a head and face not unlike the ouzel, or the grey owl, yet in the body it has no resemblance. Nevertheless, we should certainly give it a place amongst fowls, were it not that it

has . . . an epiglottis, from the articulation of its sounds, by which it has come to imitate our speech, with a pronunciation not unlike that kind of brogue, which we remark in some of our west country Irish. (319–20)

It seems that the British disdain, attacked by Brackenridge in the Preface to the *United States Magazine*, has a basis after all. Humans in America have regressed. The members of the American Philosophical Society are also right, for the creature speaks with an Irish accent. Oregan, as his name suggests, is a redheaded Irish immigrant: ill dressed, when he is dressed, and often called a bogtrotter, when his identity is certain.

The aborigines too were the subjects of Brackenridge's racism. In 1783 he edited two captivity narratives, adding 'observations' which used the Lockeian labour theory of value to deny aborigines any rights to land, and referring to them as 'the animals, vulgarly called Indians'.[14] In *Modern Chivalry*, he used them to make more explicit the connection he saw between demagoguery and bestiality. On his travels Farrago meets a man who proposes to pay Oregan to become an Indian chief. He needs to conclude a treaty, and 'as some unknown gibberish is necessary, to pass for an Indian language, we generally make use of Welch, or Low Dutch, or Irish' (55). Towards the close of the novel, Brackenridge extends his argument, blending racism with comedy. If you treat with Indians, why not give the vote to animals?:

> The late disorderly elections in the districts, was owing to this very proposition to give beasts votes; whereas in the opinion of most persons, if any were sober, on that day, there were beasts enough on the ground . . . who can reconcile it to themselves, to cheat and to wrangle in support of the frauds they have committed. (659)

In a disordered world the separate spheres of whites, aborigines and beasts apparently become indistinguishable. The only way to achieve any kind of order, thought Brackenridge, who in 1799 had become a justice of the Pennsylvania Supreme Court, was to cling to the legal system ratified ten years earlier:

> But for the constitution and the laws, what would you differ from the racoons and opossums of the woods? It is this which makes *all the difference that we find between man and beast*. (755)

Thirty-six years after Brackenridge had rebuked the British for suggesting that independence would lead to regression of the Americans, he treated the central legal document of his country as the only guarantee against that outcome. He could never escape the uneasy feeling that the orang-utans were waiting at the margins to dispute the distinction between man and beast, and to rip the Constitution to shreds. The experience of those years had only served to deepen his unease.

In 1789 Freneau, now without Brackenridge's help, produced in 'The Vanity of Existence', a landscape that outstrips *Modern Chivalry* in its disillusion:

> In youth, gay scenes attract our eyes,
> And not suspecting their decay
> Life's flowery fields before us rise,
> Regardless of its winter day.

> But vain pursuits and joys as vain,
> Convince us life is but a dream.
> Death is to wake, to rise again
> To that true life you best esteem.
>
> So nightly on some shallow tide,
> Oft have I seen a splendid show;
> Reflected stars on either side,
> And glittering moons were seen below.
>
> But when the tide had ebbed away,
> The scene fantastic with it fled,
> A bank of mud around me lay,
> And sea-weed on the river's bed. (II, 91)

Freneau, sometimes known as 'the poet of the American Revolution', wrote with a simplicity and power far removed from the derivative utopian maunderings of 'The Rising Glory of America'. This happened because he had seen too many deeds of death to believe any longer in prelapsarian possibility. For instance, 'George the Third's Soliloquy', written in 1779, looks at the Revolution not from the point of view of a patriot, but rather from that of the unfortunate monarch. As a result, the war is presented as Crèvecoeur saw it, as an internecine struggle, with George III sending gangs of jailbirds and cutthroats to put down what he calls a slave rebellion.

Freneau himself saw the dark side of the revolution one year later when he was a passenger in a ship captured by the British navy. He was confined in a prison-ship with the appropriate name of *Scorpion*. With some three hundred others he was fed beef crawling with maggots, and was almost stifled by the heat and stench. Offenders were beaten senseless by Hessian guards. Many died of disease. Freneau himself caught a fever, and was released, transformed after only six weeks of imprisonment into a grey cadaver of a man. The experience prompted one of his most angry poems, 'The British Prison Ship'. Its negative view of British imperialism contains a grim prevision of the tyrannies of the mid-twentieth century:

> Death has no charms – his realms dejected lie
> In the dull climate of a clouded sky;
> Death has no charms, except in British eyes,
> See, arm'd for death, the infernal miscreants rise;
> See how they pant to stain the world with gore,
> And millions murder'd, still would murder more;
> This selfish race, from all the world disjoin'd,
> Perpetual discord spread throughout mankind,
> Aim to extend their empire o'er the ball,
> Subject, destroy, absorb, and conquer all . . . (II, 38)

The conclusion of the Revolution brought only partial remission of such holocaust imagery. It is likely that Freneau's happiest time was the period from 1791 to 1793 when he edited *The National Gazette* for Thomas Jefferson, who defended his appointment on the grounds that a democracy would give more employment to 'men of genius' than one where government was 'transmitted through the loins of knaves & fools'.[15] Jefferson was wrong. Freneau rarely had adequate employment; and this is reflected in his work, which alternates between public poems celebrating republicanism, and more private ones reflecting anger or despair. The former can be represented by 'The Pictures of Columbus', the poem written as an accolade to Washington when the victorious general was feted in Philadelphia early in 1782:

> Illustrious hero, may you live to see
> These new Republics powerful, great, and free;
> Peace, heaven born peace, o'er spacious regions spread,
> While discord, sinking, veils her ghastly head. (II, 109)

Quite often, the 'spacious regions' of Freneau's imagination were dreary and overcast. Or they are rent with storms, as in 'The House of Night' (1779), which looks forward to the terrestrial instability of some of Poe's work. Some examples will suggest that the Revolutionary War was for Freneau not just an isolated event, but was the exemplar of a world damned by violence, tyranny and folly. In 1776 he had visited the Isle of Santa Cruz, now St Croix in the US Virgin Islands, but then belonging to Denmark. His long poem, 'The Beauties of Santa Cruz', initially depict the island as 'an earthly paradise', a relief from 'northern glooms'. Then a slave appears, 'with years, and pain, and ceaseless toil opprest'. This reminder of the economy of the West Indies is a signal for a hurricane that seems to indicate the approach of the Apocalypse. The return 'to milder stars, and skies of clearer blue' provides a closure to the poem that is unconvincing (I, pp. 249–68).

A short story written in 1788, ironically entitled 'Light, Summer Reading' deals with madness. A woman has been rejected in love and her mind has become 'disordered'. The doctor tending her suggests that 'we are all more or less affected with idiotism at times'. An optimist, he believes that the human imagination can transform 'every thing that happens in real life to the more agreeable landscapes of an inchanted and fictitious country'. The woman dies.[16] The doctor is based on Benjamin Rush, the leading American physician. Rush was notorious for bleeding and purging, his panacea against the epidemics of yellow fever that afflicted many towns and cities on the eastern seaboard from 1793 to 1805. He became for Freneau the exemplar of an overrated, overpaid, disputatious and often incompetent profession. Freneau wrote a number of poems on medicine, which seemed to have become (and perhaps still is) the republican equivalent of the colonial ministry. One, 'On the Free Use of the Lancet', reflects on the epidemics and concludes by looking favourably on what we now call homeopathy:

> Old Shelah, with her herbs and teas,
> And scarce a shilling for her fees . . .
> Did more to dispossess the fever,
> Did more from dying beds deliver
> Than all the hippocratian host
> Could by the lancet's virtue boast;
> To which, I trow, full many a ghost
> Will have a grudge forever. (III, 160)

Freneau bore a grudge, too. To use William Carlos Williams's phrase, poetry is a tough racket, and tougher still where the free market has replaced the system of patronage common in the Old World. This was a bitter pill for the poet of the Revolution to swallow. In 'The City Poet', Freneau looked back at the success of Alexander Pope, and noted despairingly: 'A poet where there is no king,/Is but a disregarded thing/An atom on the wheel.' In 'To a New-England Poet', another late poem, he noted enviously that the success Irving had achieved in Britain had in turn increased his status in its old adversary, the United States. Those writers who remained faithful to 'such a *tasteless land*' were repaid with starvation. He published the last collection of his work in 1815. The two addresses to the poet were published in a small journal. His last known poem, dated 1827 and simply called 'Winter', did not appear in print until 1945:

> The Sun hangs low! – So much the worse, we say,
> For those whose pleasure is a Summer's day;
> Few are the joys which stormy Nature yields
> From blasting winds and deserted fields;
> Their only pleasure in that season found
> When orchards bloom and flowers bedeck the ground.
>
> But, are no Joys to these cold months assign'd?
> Has winter nothing to delight the Mind?
> No friendly Sun that beams a distant ray,
> No Social Moons that light us on our way? –
> Yes, there are Joys that may all storms defy,
> The chill of Nature, and a frozen Sky.
>
> Happy with wine we may indulge an hour;
> The noblest beverage of the mildest power.
> Happy, with Love, to solace every care,
> Happy with sense and wit an hour to share;
> These to the mind a thousand pleasures bring
> And give to winter's frosts the smiles of spring,
> Above all praise pre-eminence they claim
> Nor leave a sting behind – remorse and shame.[17]

By 1827 Freneau had become an impoverished alcoholic. Here 'the noblest beverage', introduced by the shift into affirmation, provides merely a temporary refuge for one who now regards the United States as a country stripped of its agreeable landscapes. The chill of this poem was eerily predictive. Five years later, in 1832, Freneau died in a blizzard.

Experiment and failure: Charles Brockden Brown

In the address 'To the Public' in *Edgar Huntly* (1799), Charles Brockden Brown set out his proposal for 'a series of adventures, growing out of the condition of our country' which would therefore appeal to Americans:

Puerile superstition and exploded manners; Gothic castles and chimeras, are the materials usually employed for this end. The incidents of Indian hostility, and the perils of the western wilderness, are far more suitable; and, for a native of America to overlook these, would admit of no apology. These, therefore, are the ingredients of this tale . . .

Although these remarks prefaced his fourth completed novel, it is an indicator of the intention informing all of his writing up to that time. Brown's objective as the first professional novelist in the United States was to distinguish his work from such pre-existing British forms as the Gothic and sentimental. His aim was to go further than British fiction dared go, and to do it by matching American reality. In a 1793 letter to a friend he attacked the work of the English sentimental novelist: 'Richardsons fictions have, I doubt not, been, a thousand times parallelled or exceeded by realities.' For two years he wrote with the fervour of excess, dashing off those four novels as well as other works, including *Alcuin: A Dialogue* (1798), on women's rights.[18]

A remark in the 'Memoirs of Stephen Calvert', a tale begun in 1798 but never completed, presents the core of his thought about psychology:

The constitution of man is compounded and modified with endless variety. The wisest and soberest of human beings is, in some respects, a madman; that is, he acts against his better reason, and his feet stand still, or go south, when every motive is busy in impelling him north.

The passage opens with a reference to a founding document of the United States, but ends in complexity using, paradoxically, the simple metaphor of two cardinal points of the compass. The term 'reasonable', which plays such an important part in the Constitution, and the concept of 'self-evident' truths, which begins the Declaration of Independence, have no place in Brown's fictions. There is no simple explanation for the psychology of the characters in the four novels published between 1798 and 1800. Likewise, beneath their sometimes apparently haphazard plotting there is a fear that there may be no connection between the mind and the physical universe. Both are ultimately indecipherable. If his attack on reason made Brown question the basis on which the United States was founded, his attack on associationism made him question the basis of much European literature, from Richardsonian sentimentalism onwards. Irving's belief that the New World was a Lockeian blank slate implied that, in due course, it would be impressed with meaning. In contrast, Brown's galloping fictions dragged him at times towards the belief that the concept of meaning was finally meaningless. He hints at this conclusion in a 1794 poem, 'Devotion':

. . . long has been the march
And weary through the thorny tracts that lead
To nothing in the metaphysic wilderness.

Brown anticipated later attacks on Romanticism to be found, for instance, in Aldous Huxley's charge that Wordsworth's feeling for nature depends on strictly limited environmental conditions.[19]

Brown's attack on associationism begins on the first page of *Wieland* (1798), his first completed novel. The narrator, Clara Wieland, complains:

> I address no supplication to the Deity . . . The storm that tore up our happiness, and changed into dreariness and desert the blooming scene of our existence, is lulled into grim repose; but not until the victim was transfixed and mangled; till every obstacle was dissipated by its rage; till every remnant of good was wrested from our grasp and exterminated.[20]

Her complaint, with its echoes of the Book of Job is, like much else in this novel, based on misconception. Towards the end of the novel it seems that a 'double-tongued deceiver' is to blame (244). *Wieland* is a sarcastically inventive variation on the plot of seduction that had occupied so many English fictions in the eighteenth century. The seducer, Carwin, must surely be the first character in fiction (or out of it, for that matter) to pursue his evil intentions using ventriloquism. He admits to Clara that he had filled her mind 'with faith in shadows and confidence in dreams' (211). The irony is that while Clara is led astray by the false sense-impressions caused by ventriloquism, she ignores the genuine warnings of her brother's murderous intentions because they come to her in a dream.

Wieland also includes an attack on European aesthetics. Clara remarks that an ancestor was 'the founder of the German Theatre', and that she is related to the contemporary poet, Christoph Martin Wieland (1733–1813), now best known for *Oberon* (1780) and his translations of Shakespeare into German. Her father expresses his aesthetic taste, cramped by years of 'mercantile servitude', in building a gazebo, 'edged by twelve Tuscan columns', and overlooking both the Schuylkill River and 'a rising scene of cornfields and orchards' (7, 11). This perfect pastoral scene, resembling Jefferson's Monticello, is the site of an inexplicable visitation. Clara's father is subject to a spontaneous combustion, some fifty-five years before Dickens similarly dispatched Krook, in *Bleak House*. The icon of the American farmer is no safer. Wieland's son intends to be an inventive gentleman farmer, not unlike Jefferson. A moment of 'irradiation' (167) does not combust him but converts him to a religious fanatic who kills his wife and children. This *American Tale*, as the novel's subtitle has it, suggests that the new republic is a very dangerous place.

Brown's second published novel, *Ormond* (1799), again uses a female narrator, Constantia Dudley, partly to develop the discussion of women's rights also to be found in *Alcuin*, and partly to extend his attack on associationism. The attack is now focused on the theories of physiognomy. Constantia 'delighted to investigate the human countenance, and treasured up numberless conclusions as to the coincidence between mental and external qualities'.[21] As a result, she is as helpless as Clara Wieland, but this time when confronted by the masks assumed by confidence tricksters. Like Clara, she comes from an artistic family. Her father's training in Europe as a painter disables him, first figuratively, because he does not have the practical skills to detect fraud, and then literally, because after the loss of his fortune and the death of his wife he goes blind.

Into the lives of Constantia and her stricken father comes Ormond, a protean scoundrel who is connected 'with schemers and reasoners, who aimed at
the new-modelling of the world' (252). Brown was one of a number of Americans concerned that the United States was being taken over by the Illuminati.
Although the Illuminati were harmless European utopians who had organised
in 1776 and disbanded in 1787, they were treated as a group of international
conspirators in *Proofs of a Conspiracy against all the Religions and Governments of Europe*, published by an Edinburgh professor, John Robison, in
1796. Within a year the book had been reprinted in New York and Philadelphia,
and it gave rise to the first, but by no means the last, conspiracy scare in the
United States. Ormond is the third Brown Illuminatus; Ludloe and Carwin, in
the *Memoirs of Carwin* (the unfinished sequel to *Wieland*) had been members
of that sect. In pursuit of his schemes Ormond goes into 'the heart of desert
America' (252), and it is from here that he returns to Constantia's New Jersey
mansion. It is:

> illuminated by a spacious window, through which a landscape of uncommon ampli-
> tude and beauty was presented to the view . . . her eyes rested for a moment on the
> variegated hues, which were poured out upon the western sky, and upon the scene of
> intermingled waters, copses and fields. The view comprized a part of the road which
> led to this dwelling. It was partially and distantly seen, and the passage of horses or
> men, was betokened chiefly by the dust which was raised by their footsteps.
>   A token of this kind now caught her attention. It fixed her eye, chiefly by the
> picturesque effect produced by interposing its obscurity between her and the splen-
> dours which the sun had left. Presently, she gained a faint view of a man and horse.
> (268–9)

It is Ormond. Having arranged the death of her father, and now he has come
to rape Constantia. This set-piece anticipates the verbal canvases constructed
by Hawthorne and James. In particular, the emergence of a figure from the
canvas, and hence the development of the plot, looks forward to the 'Strether
by the River' sequence in Book Eleventh of James's *The Ambassadors* (1903).
Brown here draws on Burke's remark in his 1757 *Enquiry* that 'to make any
thing very terrible, obscurity seems in general to be necessary'.[22] By careful
placement of key terms he links Illuminism with the Picturesque, and the
result 'fixes' Constantia's eyes. She does not, however, share her father's fate.
She kills Ormond with a penknife.

So far, Brown had used the American environment as a critique of European thought. In his third novel, *Arthur Mervyn*, he attended directly to Philadelphia, and (as its subtitle indicates) the plague year of 1793. In terms of
structure, it is Brown's most complex novel. Its two parts, published in 1799
and 1800, present a set of conflicting statements, which force the reader to
question the reliability of the narrators. An unreliable narrative structure is at
one with a tale that is a complex development of Fielding's *Tom Jones* (1749).
It reveals a widespread duplicity and demoralisation that is exacerbated by
the extreme conditions of the plague. The opening of the novel finds the
eponymous hero in a setting that reflects the agrarian ideal of the Republic:
a small farm in Chester County, near Philadelphia. The ideal is immediately

destroyed. Arthur's father remarries 'a wild girl from the pine forests of New Jersey' and Arthur is alienated from his patrimony. He decides to seek 'asylum' in Philadelphia. This allusion to the ideology of migration leads again to disappointment. Arthur's entry into the city is an ironic inversion of Franklin's famous arrival. He is tricked out of his money; then into a yard where his vision is restricted by darkness and looming buildings; then into a house; then into a bedroom. Suddenly realising he is alone in alien and compromising territory, Arthur hides in a cupboard, where he is in 'utter darkness' and 'without the privilege of upright deportment'.[23] The pastoral vistas with which the novel opened have been reduced almost to the smallest possible space for humankind. Only a coffin is smaller, and plenty of those will appear in the novel. There is no greater contrast with the ideology of migration, and nothing better illustrates the disjunction of appearance and reality. Crouching in the cupboard, Arthur can only conjecture about the outside world. He is screened from reality just as a mask screens the intentions of a confidence trickster. In the second part of the novel, Arthur affirms that people must draw conclusions from what is 'exposed to their view'; not to do so would prove them 'brutish' (341). Within its opening four chapters he has graphically and comically disproved his later remark.

Less funny events await Arthur. He catches yellow fever and is taken to hospital. Brown draws on his own experience (for close friends died of the disease) as well as on contemporary documents to create a horrifically vivid account of a Philadelphia hospital:

> The atmosphere was loaded with mortal stenches. A vapour, suffocating and malignant, scarcely allowed me to breathe. No suitable receptacle was provided for the evacuations produced by medicine or disease. My nearest neighbour was struggling with death, and my bed . . . was moist with the detestable matter which had flowed from his stomach.
>
> You will scarcely believe that, in this scene of horrors, the sounds of laughter should be overheard. While the upper rooms of this building, are filled with the sick and dying, the lower apartments are the scene of carrousals and mirth. The wretches who are hired, at enormous wages, to tend the sick and convey away the dead, neglect their duties and consume the cordials, which are provided for the patients, in debauchery and riot.
>
> A female visage, bloated with malignity and drunkenness, occasionally looked in. Dying eyes were cast upon her, invoking the boon, perhaps, of a drop of cold water, or her assistance to change a posture which compelled him to behold the ghastly writhing or deathful *smile* of his neighbour. (173; italics in original)

Inevitably, the living are sometimes treated as dead, an error that Edgar Allan Poe would turn into a motif. The passage here shifts from natural to moral infirmity, for the plague is both a cause and a metaphor of spiritual corruption. Its shifts too from past to present tense, and invokes all the sense-impressions to increase its impact. The passage's detail concentrates, in a manner which prefigures Dickens, on parts of the body, focussing on the link between physical and moral illness. The mirth of the attendants seems unnatural alongside the rictus of death that the narrative emphasises. In turn, the events inside the hospital are a metaphor for those outside. The plagues destroys 'all sentiments of nature'. Husbands desert wives, parents forsake children, the city dwellers flee into the country and, in a demonstration of the comment in the 'Memoirs of Stephen Calvert', some are hurried madly by 'their misguided steps' into the very danger they are seeking to escape (129). The City of Brotherly Love is no asylum.

In the second part of the novel the simple opposition of city and country disappears. When Arthur fell ill he looked forward to becoming a ploughman because it was 'friendly to health, liberty and pleasure' (11). These remarks, so close to the famous triad of the Declaration of Independence, suggest again that Jefferson is being parodied. The parody is confirmed when Arthur says that, like Wieland Junior, he wants to exercise a 'spirit of improvement' on a small farm (291). Both expectations lead to the disappointment we have now come to expect. Arthur returns to a Quaker farm in which he had found asylum, to find the place 'vacant, negligent, forlorn' (272). The plague has spread to the country and killed the farmer, whereon 'his servants fled from the house and the neighbours refused to approach it' (276). Moral frailty can be found in a pastoral setting, too. Once again, Arthur changes his mind. He now becomes interested in 'manners, professions and social institutions' (293). He rejects a farmer's daughter and returns to Philadelphia, where he marries a wealthy Jewish widow, ironically named Fielding.

Brown's closest engagement with American terrain is to be found in *Edgar Huntly*. The novel has been related to the Indian captivity narrative, to such European aesthetic forms as the Gothic, and to contemporary thinking, by Benjamin Rush among others, on the nature of the unconscious. It is perhaps best remembered for anticipating Edgar Allan Poe's more extensive exercises in detection and the use of the double. In this instance, the double leads the eponymous hero into a wilderness that is both realistic and 'metaphysic'. The novel is constructed as a series of letters from Edgar to Mary Waldegrave, concerning his investigations into the activities of an Irish servant, Clithero Edny, who sleepwalks near the site of the murder of Mary's brother. Edgar resolves to track him. In the pursuit he goes beyond his 'customary paths' (93) until he passes through a cave onto a narrow ledge overlooking a gulf. It leads to a sublime waterfall:

> A sort of sanctity and awe environed it, owing to the consciousness of absolute and utter loneliness. It was probable that human feet had never before gained this recess, that human eyes had never been fixed upon these gushing waters . . . Since the birth of this continent, I was probably the first who had deviated thus remotely . . . (99)

This sensation, which replicates the wonder of the first discoverers of the 'New World', is shown three sentences later to be specious. A face pops out among the 'phantastic shapes, and endless irregularities' (99) of the scene. It is Clithero, whose scanty, ragged clothing and long, matted hair suggests that he has confirmed the fears of Hugh Henry Brackenridge, regressing from the despised Irish to the detested Indian. Edgar calls out to him – *'Man! Clithero!'* (100) – and he vanishes. Obsessed with finding Clithero, Edgar sets out again in search of him, but meets a cougar instead. He resolves in future to arm himself.

An incidental remark relates Edgar's search to the American Dream:

> Our countrymen are prone to enterprize, and are scattered over every sea and every land in pursuit of that wealth which will not screen them from disease and infirmity, which is missed much oftener than found, and which, when gained, by no means compensates them for the hardships and vicissitudes endured in the pursuit. (147)

One of the vicissitudes occurs in the sixteenth chapter of the novel. It is marked by a collapse in consciousness and of narrative flow, quite at odds with the steady daily progress that, since Franklin's *Autobiography*, has become an essential element of the Dream. At the beginning of the chapter Edgar is in total darkness. So too is the reader, for there is a complete break in the narrative. The reader's disorientation thus matches Edgar's, and the pace of the narrative is reduced so that every movement of Edgar's fearful imagination is charted. The syntactical structure of the chapter provides another anticipation of the later works of Henry James, this time in the slow shifts of consciousness plotted by the slowly moving prose, with moments of revelation achieved at the close of the sentences.

The reader finally discovers that Edgar has shadowed Clithero in another way: he has been sleepwalking in the wilderness, has fallen into a pit and knocked himself unconscious. Edgar emerges 'from oblivion by degrees so slow and so faint, that their succession cannot be marked'. His thoughts are 'wildering and mazy', and initially he cannot seem to move (152). He thinks he may have become blind because he is 'wrapt in the murkiest and most impenetrable gloom' (153). He cannot get his bearings, and imagines that he is in a dungeon, or has been buried alive. It is a living death that both recalls the hospital scene in *Arthur Mervyn* and anticipates Poe. Eventually the darkness diminishes and Edgar sees two obscure flames. They are the eyes of a panther. Fortunately Edgar's tomahawk is to hand, and he kills the animal. This unusual stroke of good luck would later be criticised as improbable by Fenimore Cooper in his 'Preface' to *The Spy*. But probability has no role to play in a scene designed to show the degradation to which humans can sink. Edgar makes a 'banquet' of the 'warm blood and reeking fibres' of the animal (161). This is the moment of realisation of such hints earlier in the text as a change in the environment from paths to mazes, and the confusion of habitual distinctions between civility, savagery and bestiality. Clithero had previously acted as a leader. Now Edgar has outstripped him, and the motif of doubling disappears to show the supposedly superior man grovelling on the ground with the agony brought on by the meal. At this point Edgar embodies the antipode of republican ideology.

Chapter 16 of *Edgar Huntly*, then, both summarises revolutionary fears and anticipates, in subject and form, more modern American literature. It does not mark the end of Edgar's demoralisation. He escapes from the pit and rescues a white girl from a band of Indians. But there is no triumphalism in the presentation of this adventure. Brown goes beyond even the more lurid elements of the captivity narrative to show a punitive killing in grisly detail, for his protagonist is an inefficient killer. Finally Edgar, 'prompted by some freak of fancy', sticks the native's musket upright in the ground (194). This is yet another anticipation, this time of the symbology of death in later wars. Twenty-three years after it had been founded in fratricide, the United States in 1799 is still being sprinkled with blood. It will become a deluge.

In another context near the close of the novel, Edgar outlines both his own experiences and those of the other narrators in the novels published between 1798 and 1800:

> Few, perhaps, among mankind have undergone vicissitudes of peril and wonder equal to mine. The miracles of poetry, the transitions of enchantment, are beggarly and mean compared with those which I had experienced: Passage into new forms, overleaping the bars of time and space, reversal of the laws of inanimate and intelligent existence had been mine to perform and to witness. (229)

Driven perhaps for commercial reasons – only *Edgar Huntly* went into a second edition in his lifetime – Brown tried no more such experiments. His last two novels, *Clara Howard* and *Jane Talbot*, both published in 1801, are concerned with the moral adjustments necessary to convert a young man into a bridegroom. Brown himself got married, and in 1803 he specifically rejected his former 'exertions'. This did not involve a complete rejection of fiction. Brown's writing between 1803 and his death in 1810 included nine or ten fragments, comprising some 100,000 words, of history of a family from Roman times to the present. Some time was also spent writing essays for the magazines he edited, and preparing a *System of Geography*, which was lost. No more was American terrain a means for outstripping English fiction. Indeed, in an article published in 1806 he remarked that the picturesque had the virtue of recreating 'exquisite scenes'. He also wrote a number of pamphlets, some of them supporting what would become known as Manifest Destiny, in which the whole continent would be 'occupied by one language; one people; one mode of government; one system of salutary laws'. The westward occupation of America was no longer seen as a problematic or bloody exercise.[24]

Transatlantic domesticity

Brown's change in 1801 towards that form characterised as 'domestic fiction' may have been an attempt to capitalise on its popularity. Despite an official posture of rejection of British precedents, domestic fiction adapted them to American circumstances. The domestic ideology of the United States can clearly be seen in Mason Weems's *The Life of Washington* (1800), mentioned in Chapter 3. 'The father of his country' is portrayed as a modest, loving, religious man, in contrast to such contemporary revolutionary leaders as Charles Lee, Alexander Hamilton and Aaron Burr, who were fatally flawed by 'pursuing the phantom honour'.[25] The images of Washington were part of the changes in familial ideology, placing him at the centre of a national family which at first sight rejected hierarchy and patriarchy in favour of egalitarianism and affection. The replacement of George III with another figurehead, not entirely coincidentally called George, involved changes greater than the simple painting out of a red coat in 'Rip Van Winkle'. Yet, as we shall see, the model of British family was not entirely obliterated.

The new familial structure of the United States can be seen to a limited extent in the text sometimes claimed as the first American novel, *The Power of Sympathy* (1789), by William Hill Brown. It proposes education for girls as an antidote to seduction. The structure is more fully displayed in David Humphreys' *A Poem, on the Happiness of America* (1786), a 'Rising Glory' poem like that of Brackenridge and Freneau. It uses Washington's return to his home at Mount Vernon, at the close of the War, as a vehicle to praise the domestic felicity at the heart of the new nation. Three comparisons animate the poem. The first contrasts the 'freedom' and 'laws' of the United States with earlier empires, which were 'the work of guilt,/On conquest, blood, or usurpation built'. Second, 'hallowed wedlock', is contrasted with the 'eastern manners', which delivered up 'beauteous slaves' to 'loath'd masters':

> Here uncontroul'd, and foll'wing nature's voice,
> The happy lovers make th' unchanging choice,
> While mutual passions in their bosoms glow,
> While soft confessions in their kisses flow,
> While their right hands in plighted faith are given,
> Their vows accordant reach approving Heaven.

The result of national and marital bliss is reflected in a pastoral landscape of 'a thousand groves' and 'laughing fields', highlighted by a third contrast, this time with London:

> The eye no view of waining cities meets,
> Of mould'ring domes, of narrow, fetid streets;
> Of grey-hair'd wretches who ne'er own'd a shed,
> And beggars dying for want of bread.

The negation in that first line is another example of the tendency to define American social reality as a series of departures from the perceived social systems of the Old World. It takes its place with Montaigne's essay 'Of the Caniballes' and Henry James's 'no Epsom, nor Ascot' passage in *Hawthorne* as an example of the rhetoric of negation discussed in Chapter 1. It was a recipe for inertia. The documents that created American exceptionalism were, as we have seen, the Declaration of Independence and the Constitution. Humphreys's poem implies that they were sufficient to protect the institution at the heart of the United States. It attributes the daily operation of marital relations to the concept of separate spheres. American women should value 'home-felt bliss' rather than attempting to 'wrest his bold prerogatives from man'. The result could be foretold. The United States for many years followed English precedents respecting marital relations. Abigail Adams's often-quoted letter to her husband requested laws to persuade American males 'to give up the harsh title of Master for the more tender and endearing one of Friend', and threatened to 'foment a Rebelion' if 'perticulier care and attention is not paid to the Laidies'. The letter met with no response.[26]

The transatlantic publication record of the British conduct books suggests that American women accepted Humphreys's recipe with even greater willingness than did the British. The conduct books were the major purveyors of morals in the eighteenth century. They had initially been intended for young men; but in the latter decades of the century were increasingly aimed at young women. One of the most widely read was *A Father's Legacy to his Daughters*, by Dr John Gregory, Professor of Medicine at Edinburgh University. It was first published in Britain in 1774, appropriately the year after he died. It was first reprinted in the United States in 1775, in three editions, in Philadelphia, New York and Annapolis. Even more popular than in Britain, *A Father's Legacy* was last published in New York in 1844, by which time some thirty-three editions had appeared, in twelve towns and cities from Albany, New York to Wilmington, Delaware. In the same period only twenty-one British editions had been published.

Perhaps Edward Moore's *Fables for the Female Sex* provides the most notable instance of the popularity of the conduct books in the United States. It was first published in Britain in 1744, but did not appear in an American edition until 1787, forty-three years later, and four years after the conclusion of the Revolutionary War. *Fables for the Female Sex* has a transatlantic publication record similar to *A Father's Legacy*. Between 1787 and 1815 twelve American editions had appeared, in comparison with seven British editions over a similar period. It was normally renamed *Fables for the Ladies* in the United States, presumably to avoid the offending three-letter word. The text contains sixteen fables, of which the third, 'The Nightingale and the Glow-Worm', confines virgins to the home:

> The prudent nymph, whose cheeks disclose
> The lily, and the blushing rose,
> From publick view her charms will screen,
> And rarely in the crowd be seen;
> This simple truth will keep her wise,
> 'The fairest fruit attracts the flies.'[27]

This suggests an image of American manhood rather less pleasant than the one symbolised by modest George Washington. It shows the pressure to which the familial ideology could be subject.

The reasons why this should have happened arise from relations between Britain, the United States and France. Citizens of the United States initially welcomed the French Revolution as an extension to Europe of the American republican experiment. As 'Rip Van Winkle' indicates, opinions soon became divided. It was Burke's *Reflections on the Revolution in France*, describing among other things a systematic plan by the French intelligentsia to destroy Christianity, which sounded the first warning note. Burke's book became an omen, apparently confirmed by the activities of Citizen Genêt, the first

Minister from the French Republic to the United States, who undermined the nation's neutrality in 1793 by trying to recruit a private army to attack British and Spanish colonies. The affair is hinted at in Brown's *Ormond*. Franco-American relations were also affected by the execution of Louis XVI, the Reign of Terror, and the XYZ Affair of 1797–8, when French officials demanded bribes from the American ambassadors. The term 'Jacobin', originally indicating a founder of the French Revolution, came to be applied to any troublemaker or moral subversive.

Fears of subversion of the American familial ideology are to be found in reactions to Mary Wollstonecraft. As in Britain, her *A Vindication of the Rights of Woman* (1792) was favourably received. But when in 1798 William Godwin published his *Memoirs of the Author of a Vindication of the Rights of Woman*, revealing her unrestrained emotions and suicide, she became associated with, as William Cobbett put it, 'the sentiments and the manners of the impious Amazons of republican France'.[28] Such fears probably also account for the initial popularity of the first best-selling novel in the United States. Like the conduct books, Susannah Rowson's *Charlotte Temple* was more popular in the United States than in Britain. *Charlotte: Tale of Truth*, as it was first known, appeared in Britain in 1791, with limited success. It was first imported by Mathew Carey in Philadelphia in 1792. He then published it in 1794, and changed its title in 1797 to the one by which it has since been known. In 1812 Carey believed that more than fifty thousand copies had been sold, although even this is likely to be an underestimate, for there were many pirated editions. There were also abridgements, alterations and serialisations, one of which asserted that Charlotte was 'The Fastest Girl in New York'. It has been estimated that more than two hundred editions had been published by the beginning of the twentieth century, by which time its popularity had significantly declined.

The author confirmed the novel's first title in the text: 'I am writing a tale of truth: I mean to write it to the heart'.[29] Its truth-telling included fidelity to some aspects of the life of its author. The story of Susannah Haswell's family is at points similar to that of Crèvecoeur's, and is not untypical of the Anglo-American world of the time. She was born in Portsmouth, England in 1762. Her father was in the British navy; her mother died shortly after giving birth. Her father became an exciseman, remarried and purchased property in Nantaskett, Massachusetts. An extremely hazardous Atlantic crossing when she was five was followed by happy years in the colony. These were brought to an abrupt end by the Revolution. Her father's property was confiscated, and after moving several times they returned penniless to England in 1778 in an exchange of prisoners. She gained the patronage of Georgiana Cavendish, Duchess of Devonshire, to whom she dedicated her first novel, *Victoria*, published in 1786. That same year she married William Rowson, a somewhat shiftless man whose greatest ability seemed to be playing the trumpet. After his hardware business failed they moved to Philadelphia, arriving in 1793 in the midst of the yellow fever epidemic. Her career as a novelist was supple-mented by acting, playwriting and songwriting. She moved to Boston and in 1797 gave up the stage in favour of a Young Ladies' Academy. She died in 1824. It follows that the fortunes of a woman in a changeable and uncertain world is central to *Charlotte Temple*.

Writing to the heart is an even more vital feature of the text. In terms of the depth of emotion that it evoked from its American audience, *Charlotte Temple* is comparable with *Uncle Tom's Cabin* (1852) and *Death of a Salesman* (1949). One scholar reviewed inscriptions in early editions to show the extent to which readers identified with the tale. The following poem, written in an 1812 edition by its reader, gives a charmingly garbled summary of the plot that nevertheless goes to its heart and indicates its allure:

> She was fair and sweet as the Lilly Inosentas [*sic*]
> The young lamb folly misled
> her love betrayed her misery
> Cros'd the awful final ocean
> in the twentieth year of her age – So ended the unfortunate Charlotte.[30]

A comparison with one of the most widely read conduct novels in England, Fanny Burney's *Evelina* (1778), will suggest why *Charlotte Temple* was so popular with American audiences. Both novels, to use Burney's subtitle, are concerned with *The History of a Young Lady's Entrance into the World*. The results of that entrance, and hence the narrative style, differ markedly. *Evelina* teaches by means of a comedy that is sometimes slapstick. *Charlotte Temple* is aimed at extracting tears, not laughter. Its seriousness reaches towards tragedy, and is conveyed in a painstakingly didactic narrative. For instance, Chapter XXXIII is entitled 'Which People Void of Feeling Need Not Read' (124) – a rare privilege, but one which nobody would dare to exercise.

The novel is riddled with instructions that provide rules for avoiding an evil that is physically present. A second comparison with *Evelina* will make this clear. Burney's novel is cast so that its heroine is thrust into the company of people who are inconsiderate and foolish. Its epistolary form allows the reader to chart the relation between Evelina's declining innocence and her developing critical distance from her companions. The casting of *Charlotte Temple* places its heroine amongst a greater range of characters, in terms of class and moral stature. There are, to be sure, a few types to be found in both novels. Montraville could be *Evelina*'s Willoughby with an added dash of thoughtlessness and impetuosity. La Rue is a younger, more harmful version of *Evelina*'s painted Madame Duval; both could be taken for, in Cobbett's words, those 'impious Amazons of republican France'. But there is no character in *Evelina* like Belcour, who is evil personified. One has to move outside the conduct format to another genre, to *Ormond*, to find a character of this malevolence. *Charlotte Temple*, though, lacks the complexity of Brown's novels. Its third-person narrative, in keeping with its didacticism, makes the reader clearly aware of both Belcour's evil and Charlotte's helplessness. Unlike Evelina, Charlotte remains an innocent. It is only the reader who learns, with a horrified fascination, of Charlotte's impotence in the face of Satan. Belcour is easily able to overwhelm the 'Natural Sense of Propriety Inherent in the Female Bosom', as the title of Chapter VII has it (27). Charlotte's path runs steadily downwards, from the opening encounter as she exits from church (appropriately, for the last time in the novel), to elopement, seduction, abandonment, destitution, childbirth and death.

The moral landscape of *Charlotte Temple* is polarised. It is not the usual Atlantic polarity, examined most comprehensively by Henry James, between a virtuous but embryonic New World and a corrupt but sophisticated Old World. The representative Great Good Place is Charlotte's childhood home, somewhere in southern England, where 'Plenty, and her handmaid, Prudence, presided at their board, Hospitality stood at their gate, Peace smiled on each face, Content reigned in each heart, and Love and Health strewed roses on their pillows' (21–2). The Great Bad Place is everywhere else. Britain and the United States differ only in the extent of their degeneracy. In a flashback, the narrative describes a Britain whose aristocracy is plagued by snobbery, profligacy and penury, rooted in primogeniture and loveless marriages:

> Mr. Temple was the youngest son of a nobleman whose fortune was by no means adequate to the antiquity, grandeur, and I may add, pride of the family. He saw his elder brother made completely wretched by marrying a disagreeable woman, whose fortune helped to prop the sinking dignity of the house; and he beheld his sisters legally prostituted to old, decrepit men, whose titles gave them consequence in the eyes of the world, and whose affluence rendered them splendidly miserable. (6)

So far, the text has created a vision of Britain that is part of the ideology of the new republic, shared, for instance, with David Humphreys. Yet in *Charlotte Temple* the United States is far from being the 'new world' sloughing off the sins of the old, as Paine had promised in *Common Sense*. It is a worse kind of Hell, a savage periphery portrayed, ironically enough, in exactly the terms celebrated by Paine: space and economics. The setting of most of the chapters is wartime New York. The officers and their wives come and go, following military demands; two places mentioned are Rhode Island and St Eustatia, the Leeward Island fought over by the British, Dutch and French in 1781. Their transience has the effect of stripping from Charlotte the moral supports which would have been available in the Great Good Place. Left alone, Charlotte is at the mercy of the economic imperative. In *Reflections on the Revolution in France*, Burke asserted that the 'age of chivalry' had been replaced by '[t]hat of sophisters, economists, and calculators'. As a result, 'a woman is but an animal; and an animal not of the highest order'.[31] Rowson's calculating animal is the farmer's wife, who comes for her rent. She rejects Charlotte's request for charity in a vividly rendered vernacular:

> charity indeed: why, Mistress, charity begins at home, and I have seven children at home, *honest, lawful* children, and it is my duty to keep them; and do you think I will give away my property to a nasty, impudent hussey, to maintain her and her bastard; an I was saying to my husband the other day what will this world come to; honest women are nothing now-a-days, while the harlotings are set up for fine ladies, and look upon us no more nor the dirt they walk upon: but let me tell you, my fine spoken Ma'am, I must have my money; so seeing as how you can't pay it, why you must troop, and leave all your fine gimcracks and fal der ralls behind you. I don't ask for no more nor my right, and nobody shall dare for to go for to hinder me of it. (113)

Rowson constructs in just two sentences a torrent of words, many of them redundant, to reveal the inhumanity created by the new social and economic order. Charity may now begin at home, but home for Charlotte is thousands of miles away and now unreachable, across 'the awful final ocean'. She is 'doomed to linger out a wretched existence in a strange land, and sink broken-hearted into an untimely grave' (77). Charlotte wanders off, into the intense cold that is New York in winter – a figure who, according to David Humphreys, was to be found in the Old World, not the New. Like another death, that of Willy Loman in Miller's *Death of a Salesman*, Charlotte's demise rubbed raw the emotions of American audiences because it exposed the deficiencies in the American Dream. For this reason the novel retained its power for over a century. A memoir of 1903 noted that a myth, that Charlotte was buried in New York's Trinity Churchyard, had greater magnetism than the myth of the Republic, symbolised by the statuary of its leaders:

> In that churchyard are graves of heroes, philosophers, and martyrs, whose names are familiar to the youngest scholar, and whose memory is dear to the wisest and best. Their graves, tho marked by imposing monuments, win but a glance of curiosity, while the turf over Charlotte Temple is kept fresh by falling tears.[32]

Transatlantic difficulties: the early work of James Fenimore Cooper

Despite the antecedence of, among others, works by Susannah Rowson, Charles Brockden Brown and Washington Irving, James Fenimore Cooper has often been treated as the first 'real' American novelist. This estimate comes from a critical tradition, still important today, which goes back to the historian Francis Parkman (1823–93). In an elegiac review of the 'Author's Revised Edition' of Cooper's *Works* (for Cooper had died in 1851), Parkman claimed that 'of all American writers, Cooper is the most original, the most thoroughly national'. His work was 'a faithful mirror of that rude . . . nature, which to European eyes appears so strange and new'.[33] The tradition deriving from Parkman depends on particularly narrow interpretations of his 'Leatherstocking' novels, named after the frontiersman who appears in all of them, and who wears galligaskins made from the deer he kills. The rude nature of Natty Bumppo is, however, just one aspect of those five novels; and Cooper wrote twenty-nine other novels, five travel narratives, four political texts, three histories, one biography and one comic drama.

An output of this magnitude indicates a strong sense of profession. It was animated by an even stronger sense of family. Lawrence was right when he notated 'the essential keyboard of Cooper's soul' as 'MY WIFE . . . MY WORK/ THE DEAR CHILDREN'. The story goes that his first novel, *Precaution* (1820), was written in response to a challenge from his wife. It was just as likely driven by the need to restore a lost fortune. Cooper's father, a lawyer and Federalist politician, had become rich by speculating in land, including

Cooperstown, founded by Otsego Lake in New York State. By 1820, when Cooper began writing, the estate was encumbered with large debts. And so, like Sir Walter Scott six years later, he wrote to restore his financial honour. No doubt he also did so because of the De Lanceys. His wife's family were Huguenot migrants. By the Revolution they had built a transatlantic familial network of great distinction. In 1848 Cooper sketched a genealogy of them, noting that they were even related to the Duke of Wellington. Cooper was proud of the family he had married into; and his pride impacted on themes and characters in his fiction, developing into a sustained social and political critique of the United States. That critique is animated by two intertwined themes: the centrality of the family and the sanctity of property. In using both themes Cooper regarded himself as a true revolutionary and, as he wrote later, 'as good a democrat as there is in America'. We have seen the importance of family to revolutionary ideology. The sanctity of 'property' too was an important element of the Revolution, central to John Dickinson's dispute with the British government and only at a late stage replaced by 'happiness' in the Declaration of Independence. To shape these themes Cooper drew both on Scott and Jane Austen. From Scott he took the technique of the multiple point-of-view, which he used for one of the first accounts in fiction of the Battle of Waterloo. A long time ago it was established that another source for *Precaution* was *Persuasion* (1818). Austen's novel must have seemed particularly apposite to Cooper, for its tale of romance between a young naval officer with no ship and no money and an aristocratic girl of nineteen was very close to his own early life. The influence of Austen, too, is to be found in Cooper's second publication, *Tales for Fifteen*, two cautionary stories for young girls probably written early in 1821 and published under the pseudonym of Jane Morgan.[34]

Discussions of Cooper's work often begin with his third publication, *The Spy* (1821), concerning espionage and guerrilla warfare in the revolution. The site of battle is quite unlike Waterloo; it is the so-called 'neutral ground' of Westchester County, New York. The term is ironic, for Westchester County is where familial and national divisions are worked out, and the result is the devastation of property. Here again Cooper used family history. His wife's uncle, James De Lancey (1746–1804), had led a unit of Loyalist irregulars known as the 'Cow-Boys'. They are presented more leniently than the Skinners, the aptly named patriot irregulars. The Skinners destroy the home of 'the spy', Harvey Birch, and then burn down the Locusts, the family home of the Whartons. Its blackened walls become 'dreary memorials of the content and security that had so lately reigned within'. One of the Skinners proclaims that ' "the law of the neutral ground is the law of the strongest" ' as he begins to wreck the Birch home, and the implications for the future of the United States are bleak indeed.[35]

It could be argued that the bleakness of *The Spy* is an inevitable result of the portrayal of a conflict regarded more as a 'civil war' (as Cooper put it in his 1831 Preface to the novel) than a war of liberation. The other novels published by 1826 reveal a picture that is only intermittently happier. *The Pioneers* (1823) contains an examination of the relation of the Old and New

Worlds. Its theme is summarised by its epigraph, taken from an 1818 poem by James Kirke Paulding, *The Backwoodsman*:

> Extremes of habits, manners, time and space,
> Brought close together, here stood face to face,
> And gave at once a contrast to the view,
> That other lands and ages never knew.[36]

The first paragraph confirms that the novel is mistitled. Cooper is not concerned about 'the pioneers who first broke ground', but rather yeomen who will be buried on their farms, and their children, who will inherit them. The morality of inheritance is indebted to Burke's *Reflections on the Revolution in France*, which asserted that property owners were 'temporary possessors' rather than 'entire masters'. They did not have the right to 'commit waste on the inheritance, by destroying at their pleasure the whole original fabric of their society; hazarding to leave to those who come after them a ruin instead of an habitation'. Yet again, Cooper draws upon his family history. Judge Marmaduke Temple, the leading landowner of Otsego County, is clearly based on Cooper's father, while the Loyalist Effingham family resembles the De Lanceys. This is not, however, a *roman-à-clef*. Cooper develops Paulding's 'extremes' by contrasting the female figures with the environment, and never more so than when Elizabeth Temple and her friend Louisa come face to face with a panther:

> Elizabeth now lay wholly at the mercy of the beast . . . Her hands were clasped in the attitude of prayer, but her eyes were still drawn to her terrible enemy; her cheeks were blanched to the whiteness of marble, and her lips were slightly separated with horror. (308–9)

That closing noun indicates that, while the women are facing the panther, we are facing a Gothic efflorescence of sentiment. Cooper surrounds the *pietà* with a series of sacred and profane images, encompassing devotion, purity, eroticism and morbidity. It is, in the root sense of the term, a frontier moment, in which culture, in the form of a European aesthetic, confronts nature, in the form of the beast. The scene is set for the intervention of Natty Bumppo.

Natty's role in the novel is instrumental rather than central to the plot. Much of the novel is concerned with contrasts that are both less extreme and less easily resolved than the panther scene. It problematises the plot conventions of Austenian comedy by placing them in the dynamic, changing environment of 1793. Plot developments are therefore less about social interaction than about achieving a stable habitat. A Burkean debate about trusteeship is central to the novel. Almost all of Chapter 3 is devoted to allowing 'Elizabeth to dwell on a scene which was rapidly altering under the hands of man' (40). Those alterations are viewed critically: the descriptions are either comic or ironic, and the chapter is opened by an epigraph that presents the alterations as a rape. Elizabeth Temple's view of Templeton echoes two famous turning points in Austen's fiction: Elizabeth Bennet's first view of Pemberley and Emma Woodhouse's view of Donwell Abbey. The view of Templeton, with its felled trees and gimcrack buildings, becomes in consequence a devastating comment on the failures of settlement. Judge Temple is aware that settlement should only be conducted with restraint. His cousin Richard Jones, the architect of his ramshackle house, is one of the people of plenty. With no thought for the future, he cuts trees, catches bass with a seine and shoots pigeon with a cannon, bringing down so many that 'none pretended to collect the game, which lay scattered over the fields in such profusion, as to cover the ground with the fluttering victims' (246).

The attitude of Richard Jones is contrasted with that of Natty Bumppo, who deplores the 'wasty ways' of the settlers. Despite the frontiersman's function as an ecological commentator, Cooper was unable to fully integrate him into the plot. In part the problem is thematic: despite the title, the novel is not about the backwoods that are Natty's real home. In part the problem arises from instability in the characterisation of Natty. He enters the novel as a Shakespearian fool, a grouchy buckskin buffoon with a drip on the end of his nose. He leaves it as a superb marksman, a deeply serious figure who no longer makes wise jokes about society (as befits a Shakespearian fool), but is rather at odds with it. The failure of integration was detrimental to the design of *The Pioneers*, and its attempt to provide a balanced discussion between the virtues of natural and civil law. The failure results in a double ending to the novel. The second depicts the departure westwards of Natty, after refusing the offer of some of 'the new-fashioned money that they've been making at Albany, out of paper!' (455). The first is more appropriate to the main plot. The Temple and Effingham families have been united by a marriage, which is celebrated by one of the earliest of Cooper's descriptions of American nature:

> ... they gained the open fields, and her eye roamed over the placid lake, covered with wild fowl, already journeying from the great northern waters, to seek a warmer sun, but lingering to play in the limpid sheet of the Otsego, and to the sides of the mountain, which were gay with the thousand dies of autumn, as if to grace their bridal ... (448)

The quiet beauty of this scene is superbly rendered. Elizabeth's point-of-view is again adopted, this time to convey a sense of benediction uniting the environment with the nuptial rite. The sense of unity, together with a gentle rocking rhythm created by alternating short and long clauses, indicates that Cooper is drawing on Edmund Spenser's 'Prothalamian'. As with the debt to Austen, Cooper adapts the epithalamic tradition to the wilderness. Instead of the 'Sweete Themmes' we have Lake Otsego, and instead of flowers and 'meades adorn'd with daintie gemmes', he gives us wild fowl and mountains. That Cooper did not end his song at this point is an indication of his awareness of the flaws in the culture of the United States, and its implications for American nature.

After writing his first sea fiction, *The Pilot* (1824), and another about the Revolution, *Lionel Lincoln* (1825), Cooper brought back Natty Bumppo in *The Last of the Mohicans* (1826), and this time was able to integrate his frontier skills fully into the plot structure. The novel deals with domesticity in a military setting, and draws on the Captivity Narrative. It is set during the

French and Indian War, and the centre of the text, both metaphorically and literally (for it occupies Chapter 17 of the novel's thirty-three, and brings the first volume to a close), is based on a notorious incident during the War. Fort William Henry had been besieged by a mixed force under General Montcalm of French (including Crèvecoeur), Canadians and a number of native tribes, among them Hurons. The commander of the Fort, a Colonel Monro, obtained a safe passage for the garrison in exchange for surrender. The natives, however, did not abide by the agreement, and killed and captured a number of Britons and colonials. Estimates of the number massacred varied widely, from a dozen to over fifteen hundred; but the number did not signify in the resulting furore in the British colonies. The French were vilified for allowing the atrocities, detailed accounts of which circulated, first in the colonial press and then in histories of the War.

Cooper drew on a variety of sources, including personal knowledge of the area, for his description of the massacre. He again used a multiple point-of-view, including this close-up when a Huron snatched a child from its mother and 'holding it by the feet'

> . . . dashed the head of the infant against a rock, and cast its quivering remains to her very feet. For an instant, the mother stood, like a statue of despair, looking wildly down at the unseemly object, which had so lately nestled in her bosom and smiled in her face; and then she raised her eyes to heaven, as if calling on God to curse the perpetrator of the foul deed. She was spared the sin of such a prayer; for . . . excited by the sight of blood, the Huron mercifully drove his tomahawk into her own brain. The mother sunk under the blow, and fell, grasping at her child, in death, with the same engrossing love, that had caused her to cherish it when living.[37]

This is another 'frontier moment'. Its components and its Christian references are similar to those of the meeting between Elizabeth Temple and the panther in *The Pioneers*. In constructing it Cooper drew verbatim on the accounts of the massacre. These in turn were versions of the 'Black Legend' discussed in Chapter 2, with the natives taking the role previously reserved for the Spanish. The detail that Cooper omitted, but his sources did not, was the disembowelling.

We have here another example of the reshaping of a pre-existing literary resource in order to give voice to a recent event. That event lies at the heart of Cooper's text and acts as a synecdoche of the plot, which concerns the reunion and break-up of the Munro family (Cooper changes the surname slightly). In the preceding Chapter 16, Cooper provides a fleeting vision of domestic contentment. The centre of the group is occupied by Alice Munro, a young girl earlier described as of 'dazzling complexion, fair golden hair, and bright blue eyes' – in short, a virgin who might have modelled for *Fables for the Ladies*. Alice sits on her father's knee. Cora, her raven-haired elder sister, whose 'rich blood' bespeaks a different mother and greater experience, looks on 'with that species of maternal fondness, which characterised her love for Alice' (18, 156). This intimate interior has its counterpart in Chapter 15, when Cooper paints another moment of rest by describing an American sunset:

> The mountains looked green, and fresh, and lovely; tempered with the milder light, or softened in shadow, as thin vapours floated between them and the sun. The numerous islands rested on the bosom of the Horican, some low and sunken, as if imbedded in the waters, and others appearing to hover above the element, in little hillocks of green velvet; among which the fishermen of the beleaguering army peacefully rowed their skiffs, or floated at rest on the glassy mirror, in quiet pursuit of their employment.
>
> The scene was at once animated and still. All that pertained to nature was sweet, or simply grand; while those parts which depended on the temper and movements of man, were lively and playful. (148–9)

In its softness and transience, this is the pastoral counterpart of the domestic scene between Munro and his two daughters. Cooper uses images of that most Christian of activities ('I will make you fishers of men': Matthew 4:19) and an antinomy – 'animated and still' – to suggest a beneficent collaboration between humankind and 'mother' nature. Elsewhere, he shows that nature also has a life independent of humankind. For instance, earlier in the novel, when Natty's party make their way towards Fort William Henry, they stop 'in the midst of a breathing stillness' that is Glens Falls (48). By making a metaphorical connection between the human and terrestrial bodies, Cooper shows an understanding of nature closer to our modern ecological concerns than to the demonised environment of the Puritans or the voids imagined by many of his contemporaries.

The episode at the Fort provides a temporary point of rest between the twin plots of flight and pursuit, and mark the point of transition from the world of the white races and their Eurocentric beliefs in 'history' to the native world of myth, magic and bewitchment. The comparison between the two worlds is not favourable to the whites. The opening paragraph of the novel proposes that the French and Indian War has been caused by offstage figures whose machinations create a land riven by conflict and deception and lead to a bloodletting far more widespread than that caused by Napoleon and Wellington in *Precaution*:

> there was no recess of the woods so dark, nor any secret place so lovely, that it might claim exemption from those who had pledged their blood to satiate their vengeance, or to uphold the cold and selfish policy of the distant monarchs of Europe. (13)

Natty is the most adept and prolific killer in an environment soaked in blood. Cooper makes him responsible for the massacre at 'Bloody Pond', another incident during the war. Natty claims that he led the scouts who surprised a band of resting French and Canadians and, contravening the European laws of war, filled the pond with the dead and wounded so that it was 'coloured with blood, as natural water never yet flowed from the bowels of the 'arth'. He boasts that there isn't a square mile in the neighbourhood that he hasn't stained with the blood of enemy or beast (136–7).

Natty's native opponent, Magua, is his moral superior because the murders he commits are in accord with the native laws of war. Magua is surrounded with demonic imagery, most clearly when he is likened to 'the Prince of Darkness'

(284). The reference to *Paradise Lost* is apposite because, like Milton's Satan, Magua is a magnificent figure, a superb warrior, a subtle speechmaker, and an effective and resourceful leader. Yet his demonic behaviour has been caused by an insult. The story emerges when Magua is disputing the truce at William Henry with Montcalm. Munro had humiliated him in a beating so severe that his back still bears the scars. The comparison with *Paradise Lost* reflects badly on Munro: he is not God but merely another racist British officer. We are reminded of the significance of the humiliation by a series of six epigraphs drawn from *The Merchant of Venice*, one of them on the title page of the novel. Magua is treated as Shylock and in seeking redress for a racial insult is turned into Satan. The consequences are more devastating for the innocent Mohicans than for the Munro family. Colonel Munro is left to mourn the murder of Cora, while Chingachgook has, with the death of his son Uncas, to face the extinction of his tribe. Cooper embeds the motif of *ubi sunt*, the formula for lamenting a vanished past, into the title and structure of the novel, bringing it to an end with the threnody of the old chief Tamenund. Motivated by greed and insensitive to native civilisation, the whites draw down the inevitable retribution of death and destruction. The hope of America and its land was wasted even before the creation of the United States.

In 1856 the French novelist George Sand accurately identified the pain which gives *The Last of the Mohicans* its power when she remarked that in this novel Cooper 'let loose from his breast this conscience-stricken cry; "In order to be what we are, we had to kill a great people and devastate a mighty land"'.[38] Although there is nothing in his correspondence to suggest that his analysis of genocide had driven him from his country, Cooper left the United States four months after the publication of the novel by which he is still largely remembered. He did not return for seven years.

Notes

1. John Adams, letter [May 1780] to Abigail Adams, *The Book of Abigail and John: Selected Letters of the Adams Family 1762–1784*, eds. L. H. Butterfield, Marc Friedlaender and Mary-Jo Kline (Cambridge, MA: Harvard University Press, 1975), p. 260.

2. John Adams, Letter 29 October 1805, *Statesman and Friend: Correspondence of John Adams with Benjamin Waterhouse*, ed. Worthington Chauncy Ford (Boston: Little, Brown, 1927), p. 31.

3. Thomas Paine, 'The American Crisis,' XIII and I, in *The Life and Major Writings of Thomas Paine*, ed. Philip S. Foner (1945; rpt. New York: The Citadel Press, 1961), pp. 235, 50.

4. Paine, *Common Sense*, ed. Isaac Kramnick (Harmondsworth: Penguin, 1976), p. 120. Further references to this text will be given in parentheses after the quotation.

5. *Constitutional Gazette*, 24 February 1776, quoted in Moses Coit Tyler, *The Literary History of the American Revolution* (1897; rpt. 2 vols in 1, New York, Burt Franklin, 1970) I, pp. 472–3.

6. Paine, 'A Dialogue Between General Wolfe and General Gage in a Wood near Boston', 'New Anecdotes of Alexander the Great', 'Reflections on the Life and Death of Lord

Clive' (1775) and 'A Dialogue' (1776), in *The Writings of Thomas Paine*, ed. Moncure Daniel Conway (1894; rpt. London: Routledge/Thoemmes Press, 1996), pp. 10–13, 26–35, 161–7. William Smith, *An Oration in Memory of General Montgomery* (2nd edn, London: J. Almon, 1776).

7. Francis Jeffrey, review of Maria Edgeworth, *Popular Tales*, in *The Edinburgh Review*, 4 (1804), 329–30.

8. Thomas Jefferson, letter to Joseph Priestley 21 March 1801, in *The Portable Thomas Jefferson*, ed. Merrill D. Peterson (Harmondsworth: Penguin, 1977), p. 484. Future references to this text will be given in parentheses after the quotation.

9. Henry James, *Hawthorne* (1879; rpt. London: Macmillan, 1967), p. 55. Kurt Vonnegut, *Slaughterhouse 5* (1969; rpt. London: Triad Panther, 1979), p. 23. Washington Irving, 'Rip Van Winkle', *The Sketch Book of Geoffrey Crayon, Gent.* (1820; rpt. London: Dent, 1963), pp. 37–9, 29. Further references to this text will be given in parentheses after the quotation.

10. James, *Hawthorne*, p. 23.

11. Philip Freneau, *The Poems of Philip Freneau*, ed. Fred Lewis Pattee (3 vols, 1902; rpt. New York: Russell & Russell, 1963), I, pp. 81–2. Further references to this edition will be given in parentheses after the quotation. Hugh Henry Brackenridge, 'Preface', *United States Magazine*, I (January 1779), 3.

12. *United States Magazine*, I (December 1779), 483.

13. Brackenridge, *Modern Chivalry*, ed. Claude M. Newlin (New York: Hafner Publishing Co., 1968), pp. 6, 105. Further references to this text will be given in parentheses after the quotation.

14. [Brackenridge, ed.], *Narratives of a Late Expedition against the Indians* (1783; rpt. New York: Garland Publishing, 1978), p. 32.

15. Jefferson, letter to George Washington 9 September 1792, in *Writings* (New York: Library of America, 1984), p. 999.

16. Freneau, 'Light, Summer Reading', *The Miscellaneous Works* (1788; rpt. Delmar, NY: Scholars' Facsimiles and Reprints, 1975), pp. 251–69.

17. Freneau, *The Last Poems of Philip Freneau*, ed. Lewis Leary (1945; rpt. Westport, CT: Greenwood Press, 1970), pp. 31–2, 112–13, 123.

18. Charles Brockden Brown, *Edgar Huntly; Or, Memoirs of a Sleep-Walker* (1799; rpt. Harmondsworth: Penguin, 1988), pp. [3–4]. Further references to this edition will be given in parentheses after the quotation. Letter 16 August 1793, MSS Bowdoin College, Maine.

19. Brown, 'Memoirs of Stephen Calvert', in *Alcuin, A Dialogue; Memoirs of Stephen Calvert* (Kent, OH: Kent State University Press, 1984), pp. 179–80. Brown, 'Devotion', MSS Bowdoin College, Maine. Aldous Huxley, 'Wordsworth in the Tropics', *Collected Essays* (London: Chatto & Windus, 1960).

20. Brown, *Wieland; or, The Transformation. An American Tale* (Kent, OH: Kent State University Press, 1977), pp. 5–6. Further references to this edition will be given in parentheses after the quotation.

21. Brown, *Ormond; or, The Secret Witness* (Kent, OH: Kent State University Press, 1982), p. 77. Further references to this edition will be given in parentheses after the quotation.

22. Edmund Burke, *Enquiry into the Origin of Our Ideas of the Sublime and Beautiful*, ed. David Womersley (1757; rpt. London: Penguin, 1998), p. 102.

23. Brown, *Arthur Mervyn; or, Memoirs of the Year 1793, First and Second Parts* (Kent, OH: Kent State University Press, 1980), pp. 18, 21, 25–7, 42, 38. Further references to this edition will be given in parentheses after the quotation.

24. Brown, 'The Editors' Address to the Public', *The Literary Magazine, and American Register*, I, No. 1 (1 October 1803), 4. Brown, *An Address to the Congress of the United States on the Utility and Justice of Restrictions upon Foreign Commerce* (Philadelphia: C. & A. Conrad, 1809), pp. 89–90. Brown, 'On the Picturesque', *The Literary Magazine*, VI, No. 34 (July 1806).

25. Mason L. Weems, *The Life of Washington*, ed. Marcus Cunliffe (Cambridge, MA: The Belknap Press of Harvard University Press, 1962), pp. 172–5.

26. David Humphreys, *A Poem, on the Happiness of America: Addressed to the Citizens of the United States* ([London]: n.p., [1786]), pp. 11–12, 20, 22, 26–7. Abigail Adams, letter 31 March 1776 to John Adams, *The Book of Abigail and John*, eds. Butterfield, Friedlaender and Kline, p. 121.

27. Edward Moore, *Fables for the Ladies* (Philadelphia: Thomas Dobson, 1787), p. 16.

28. Cobbett, Preface to Richard Polwhele, *The Unsex'd Females* (New York: William Cobbett, 1800), pp. v–vi.

29. Susanna Rowson, *Charlotte Temple*, ed. Ann Douglas (Harmondsworth: Penguin, 1991), p. 108. References to this text will in future be given in parentheses after the quotation.

30. MS poem, unknown author, quoted in Cathy N. Davidson, *Revolution and the Word: The Rise of the Novel in America* (New York: Oxford University Press, 1986), p. 75.

31. Burke, *Reflections on the Revolution in France* (1790; rpt., Harmondsworth: Penguin, 1968), pp. 170–1.

32. 'H.S.B.', letter 12 September 1903 in the *New York Evening Post* quoted in Cathy N. Davidson, 'Introduction' to *Charlotte Temple* (New York: Oxford University Press, 1986), p. xiv.

33. Francis Parkman, 'The Works of James Fenimore Cooper', *North American Review*, 74 (January 1852), 147.

34. D. H. Lawrence, *Studies in Classic American Literature* (1924; rpt. Harmondsworth: Penguin, 1971), p. 53. Cooper, *The American Democrat* (1838; rpt. Harmondsworth: Penguin, 1969), p. 70.

35. Cooper, *The Spy*, ed. J. E. Morpurgo (London: Oxford University Press, 1968), pp. 261, 264, 176.

36. Cooper, *The Pioneers*, ed. James Franklin Beard (Albany: State University of New York Press, 1980), pp. 15–16, title page. References to this text will in future be given in parentheses after the quotation. Burke, *Reflections on the Revolution in France*, p. 192.

37. Cooper, *The Last of the Mohicans*, eds. James A. Sappenfield and E. N. Feltskog (Albany, NY: State University of New York Press, 1983), p. 175. References to this text will in future be given in parentheses after the quotation.

38. George Sand, 'Fenimore Cooper', in *Fenimore Cooper: The Critical Heritage*, eds. George Dekker and John P. McWilliams (London: Routledge & Kegan Paul, 1973), p. 267.

Chapter 5

Growth and Identity, 1812–1865

It is quite obvious, that, so far as taste and forms alone are concerned, the Literature of England and that of America must be fashioned after the same models. The Authors previously to the revolution are common Property, and it is quite idle to say that the American has not just as good a right to claim Milton, and Shakspeare . . . as an Englishman. The Americans having continued to cultivate, and to cultivate extensively, an acquaintance with the writers of the mother Country since the separation, it is evident they must have kept pace with the trifling changes of the day. The only peculiarity that can, or ought to be, expected in their Literature, is that which is connected with the promulgation of their distinctive political opinions.

(James Fenimore Cooper, *Notions of the Americans*)[1]

Transatlantic trifles

After the end of the revolution, European commentary on America shifted in emphasis from concern about its miasmic environment to debate about the politics and society of the new nation. The leading commentators were the British and French. British aggressiveness was reawakened by the War of 1812. The United States declared war on Britain in June 1812 for two reasons: interference with neutral shipping during the conflict with France, and incursions from Canada into the west. The war lasted two and a half years. It is now chiefly remembered for two engagements, the British capture of Washington DC, where they burnt the Capitol and the White House; and the Battle of New Orleans, where the US Army, led by General Andrew Jackson, won its only major victory of the war, two weeks after a peace treaty had been signed in Ghent. More than many wars, the War of 1812 is rich in black ironies. It settled neither of the complaints against Britain, and led instead to an extended war of words.

The War of 1812 encouraged a self-justificatory and bellicose Americanism, epitomised by the song whose status was confirmed in 1931 when it was made the US National Anthem. A Washington lawyer, Francis Scott Key (1779–1843), wrote the poem after seeing Fort McHenry in Baltimore withstand a British bombardment:

> O say, can you see, by the dawn's early light,
>> What so proudly we hailed at the twilight's last gleaming –
> Whose broad stripes and bright stars, through the clouds of the fight,
>> O'er the ramparts we watched were so gallantly streaming . . .

> Praise the power that hath made and preserved us a nation.
>   Then conquer we must, when our cause it is just,
> And this be our motto, – 'In God is our trust':
>   And the star-spangled banner in triumph shall wave
> O'er the land of the free, and the home of the brave.[2]

Phrases from 'The Star-Spangled Banner' are deeply embedded in the culture of the United States. They have found their way onto US coins and stamps, and even inspired such jokes as the shopkeeper's sign: 'In God we trust/All others cash.'

For many British the poem was no joke, and not simply because it was set to an English drinking-song. (A number of songs celebrating the Republic, including 'America', are set to British tunes.) More important, it was indicative of a bragging chauvinism that is still part of the British imagery of US citizens. It was such imagery that had caused Sydney Smith to abandon his positive remarks about the United States in his 1820 review, discussed in Chapter 1, ending by asking if anyone knew any of the cultural products of 'this self-adulating race'. The British war of words was conducted in quarterly journals like Sydney Smith's *Edinburgh Review*, and in books written by such travellers as Henry Fearon (*Sketches of America*, 1818), Basil Hall (*Travels in North America*, 1830), Thomas Hamilton (*Men and Manners in America*, 1833) and Harriet Martineau (*Society in America*, 1837). The most notorious representative of such carping British texts remains *Domestic Manners of the Americans* (1832) by Frances Trollope, who insisted at length that they had none. She recalled her three and a half years in the United States 'with a general feeling of irksomeness and fatigue of spirits'. It was the 'want of refinement' that she found most irksome. Whilst in Washington, for instance, she went to a theatre patronised by the nation's leaders. Their behaviour, she believed, was having unfortunate physiognomic consequences:

> The spitting was incessant . . . I am inclined to think this most vile and universal habit of chewing tobacco is the cause of a remarkable peculiarity in the male physiognomy of Americans; their lips are almost uniformly thin and compressed . . . the act of expressing the juices of this loathsome herb enforces exactly that position of the lips . . .

American expectorations were one reason for Charles Dickens's disappointment at what he found during his first visit to the United States. That disappointment is recorded in *American Notes* (1842), and in the American chapters of his transatlantic novel, *Martin Chuzzlewit* (1843–4). They are populated by an array of uncouth, noisy, irascible braggarts, whose 'smart' sharp practices create, among other things, a hellhole ironically named Eden, the slimy, miasmic speculators' paradise based on Dickens's memory of Cairo, Illinois.[3]

In contrast, French texts written about America were less excremental, more speculative. They followed the tradition begun by Montaigne's 'Of the Caniballes' and continued by such *philosophes* as Buffon and Raynal. Alexis de Tocqueville wrote the text that has since become the most famous. After obtaining letters of recommendation from Cooper, de Tocqueville visited the

United States from May 1831 to February 1832, ten years before Dickens and with one aim in common: to see American prisons. The result was *Democracy in America*, published in two volumes in 1835 and 1840. They differ in focus and tone. The first volume produces a cosily organic view of American democracy by locating its origins in the New England town meeting, from which the events of 1776 are an evolution rather than a revolution. Its tone is generally optimistic, and it ends with a vision of the future in which 'the destinies of half the globe' will be dominated by the Russians and the 'Anglo-Americans', a term which de Tocqueville uses frequently. In the second volume, de Tocqueville looks at the cultural consequences of democracy, and his view is less sanguine. The darker hints in the first volume, contained in such phrases as 'the tyranny of the majority', develop into a vision of an insipid utilitarian society where the pressures to conform create a nervous individualism which has no room for eccentricity or excellence. This time the conclusion is equivocal, uncertain if 'the principle of equality', which de Tocqueville regards as inevitable, will lead 'to servitude or freedom, to knowledge or barbarism, to prosperity or wretchedness'.[4] De Tocqueville had reason to be uncertain. The years from 1812 to 1865 were not simply marked by an uneasy political and cultural relationship with Europe. The United States underwent phenomenal population growth and consequent changes in political and social structure, expanded westwards, and was marked by a division between Northern and Southern states that would only be resolved in a bloody civil war.

Fenimore Cooper and the follies of democracy

Later in his life, James Fenimore Cooper was noted for his willingness to go to law in defence of his distinctive opinions. His writing was a vehicle for his forthright convictions, and it provides a clear index of many of the debates in the United States during the second period of its existence. He died in 1851, ten years before the Civil War broke out. Yet even here it could be said that his depiction of violence, based on his awareness that the Revolution was itself a civil war, anticipated the greatest conflict in the history of the United States. From 1826 to 1833, Cooper travelled widely in Europe and met many politicians, artists and writers with an interest in the United States, including de Tocqueville, Scott, Coleridge, Godwin and Sydney Smith. As a result, the international elements of his work developed and his critique of the politics and culture of his homeland became more outspoken. No writer kept pace with 'the trifling changes of the day' in Europe more than he. Indeed, it is likely that Cooper used that adjective ironically, for he had the clearest sense of the emblematic importance of the apparently inconsequential.

Although Cooper had already used the habit of spitting tobacco as the dénouement of one of the *Tales for Fifteen*, he began his European sojourn by defending his country against the viciousness of the British attacks. In *Notions of the Americans* (1828), Cooper praised republican institutions, yet had to agree with critics about the lack of cultural variety in his homeland. He tried initially to turn this into a virtue, by thinking like de Tocqueville in Anglo-American terms and refusing to make a nationalist separation of American from English literature. He soon was forced to admit that it was difficult for American literature to become distinctive. There were two reasons. American publishers paid no overseas copyright fees, and could market foreign work more cheaply than the domestic. Cooper believed that this problem was temporary; it would remain a source of much anger until an international copyright law was adopted in 1891. The work of British writers was widely distributed in the United States, often in pirated editions. Dickens made such an issue of piracy during his first visit to the United States in 1842 that it soured his relations with many of its citizens. Yet British literature was fashionable as well as cheap, which prompted such literary visitors as Dickens. This was the second obstacle for an American literature. In Cooper's view American culture could not provide the materials to allow its literature to compete with the British, and he used the rhetoric of negation to express his sense of its inadequacy:

> There are no annals for the Historian; no follies (beyond the most vulgar and common place) for the satirist; no manners, for the dramatist; no obscure fictions for the writers of romance; no gross and hardy offences against decorum for the moralist; nor any of the rich artificial auxiliaries of Poetry . . .[5]

The rhetoric had first been used by Montaigne and later by David Humphreys to compare America favourably with Europe. In *Notions of the Americans*, Cooper used it to depict American vacuity, thereby anticipating the extended burlesque version by Henry James in *Hawthorne*.

The novels Cooper had written before he left the United States were hardly a sustained hymn of praise to his homeland. His vision of the United States darkened further in the decade following the publication of *Notions of the Americans*. The problem, in part, was Europe. The seven years that he had lived there provided him with a wealth of material, including five travel volumes collectively titled *Gleanings in Europe* (1836–8). They allowed him to develop the textual examination of European politics, society and landscape that previously he had mainly encountered through the works of others. The result was a more complex view of the United States than that found in *Notions of the Americans*, more nuanced as well as more negative. The United States did not seem to have France's political instability, but its culture was inferior. With his eye for a synecdoche, he fixed on Europe's visiting card and showed at length how it acted as a social enabler and emollient. 'These things will quite likely strike you as of little moment', he noted, yet 'ordinary life is altogether coloured by things that, in themselves, may appear trifling', using that adjective again in a comment with which Frances Trollope would have heartily agreed.

In *Gleanings in Europe* Cooper depicted the society of the United States as colourless, characterised by 'an overwhelming mediocrity', an opinion anticipated in *Notions of the Americans* and now shared with de Tocqueville's *Democracy in America*. Within the next few years Cooper also became uncertain about the answer to de Tocqueville's question about 'the principle of equality'. His attempt to negotiate a path between the political and social systems of Europe and the United States began with a trio of novels examining the evil consequences of such Old World systems as Venetian republicanism (*The Bravo*, 1831); the German nobility (*The Heidenmauer*, 1832); and the Swiss hereditary aristocracy (*The Headsman*, 1833). The political lessons learnt from Europe were then applied to the United States. *The Monikins* (1835) is an allegorical satire which extends Brackenridge's *Modern Chivalry* by comparing the politics of Leaphigh (Britain), dominated by a rigid class system, with Leapthrough (France), which is unstable and unprincipled, and with Leaplow (the United States), dominated by commercialism and a popular opinion manipulated by demagogues and the press. The outcome of his investigations in these four novels could be represented by the words of Mordaunt Littlepage as he opens his narrative in Cooper's 1845 novel, *The Chainbearer*:

> the great error of democracy [is that it] fancies truth is to be proved by counting noses; while aristocracy commits the antagonist blunder of believing that excellence is inherited from male to male, and that too in the order of primogeniture! It is not easy to say where one is to look for truth in this life.

Cooper's inability to isolate a monolithic 'truth' increased the dialectic between society and nature apparent in his earlier fiction, and intensified his despair about his country. The shape of his later work can be seen most clearly by organising a selection of his novels into three groups: those that criticised society, property and civil law; those that praised nature and natural law; and those that pondered on the future of the United States.[6]

The themes animating, indeed frequently dominating, his social fictions are summed up in *The American Democrat* (1838):

> Social station, in the main, is a consequence of property. So long as there is civilization there must be the rights of property, and so long as there are the rights of property, their obvious consequences must follow ... As property is the base of all civilization, its existence and security are indispensible to social improvement.

This is a particularly powerful concept of property, and it lay at the heart of his model political system. That system was transatlantic. It combined elements of the social and political structures of Britain and the United States to create a complex organism which was hierarchical yet open, honouring rank yet not opposed to change, formed in the image of a family in which each member, including the servants, had a role to play and was respected for it. The model is exhibited in *The Redskins* (1846), when Hugh Littlepage describes his inheritance:

> The whole of the land in sight – the rich bottoms, then waving with grass – the side-hills, the woods, the distant mountains – the orchards, dwellings, barns, and all the other accessories of rural life that appertained to the soil, were mine, and had thus become without a single act of injustice to any human being, so far as I knew and believed.

174

The owner's sense of quiet possession is strongly expressed. So too is a sense of order which was a feature of British society. In *Gleanings in Europe: England* (1837) Cooper praised Britain for 'the perfect order in which every thing is kept, and the perfect method with which every thing is done'. He also believed that Britain's rigid class system was politically and spatially exclusive. It had the most severe consequences for those most excluded, female servants. Their condition he thought 'less enviable than that of Asiatic slaves'; it turned a metropolitan centre like London into a 'huge theatre of misery and vice'. Cooper believed that servants played a vital role in a unified familial society. In the United States, property was therefore not equated with exclusion. Hugh Littlepage's description of his land integrates wilderness with farmland to convey a sense of spatial openness that accords with the assertion of justice.[7]

This was Cooper's ideal. It became increasingly outdated, for changes in population were impacting both on patterns of voting and on concepts of property. The population of the United States increased from almost four million in 1790 to over twenty-three million in 1850, much of the increase swelling such ports as New York, Boston and Philadelphia. The balance of population of the Northern states in particular was shifting from rural to urban. The suffrage was still restricted to males (votes for women were only introduced by the Eighteenth Amendment to the Constitution in 1920), but it was extended far beyond the limited class of freeholders. The election of Andrew Jackson as president in 1828 was the clearest marker of the change from elite to democratic government. Like George Washington, Jackson was a war hero. The similarity between the two men ended there. Jackson was born on the South Carolina frontier in poor circumstances, and owed his election to the ordinary people with whom he identified. The change in government was accompanied by changes to the concept of property. Theories of property rights shifted from the agrarian ideal of a limited republic towards the economic and social efficiency of a modernising utilitarian world. The conservative correlation of property and liberty came increasingly under attack.

Cooper fought a bitter rearguard battle against such changes through his social novels. For these he abandoned the allegorical format of *The Monikins*, inspired instead by two property conflicts in which he had special interests. The first was the Three Mile Point controversy. It concerned a tract of land of particularly scenic value on the shore of Lake Otsego, inherited from the Judge by the Cooper family and by concession used by local villagers as a public amenity. When Cooper returned to Otsego in 1834, he felt that the land had been misused, and issued a trespass warning. The villagers responded by holding a meeting and voting that the land was public property. This was a minor instance of de Tocqueville's 'tyranny of the majority', but Cooper's synecdochal method of thinking prompted him to believe that the future of the United States hung upon its outcome. His antidote was a pair of novels, *Homeward Bound* and *Home As Found*, both published in 1838.

The two novels bring up to date the story of the Effingham family, last seen in *The Pioneers* and now even more clearly based on Cooper's autobiography. As their titles suggest, the first novel brings the family home after an extended stay in Europe; the second takes them to their estate in Templeton and into conflict with some of its citizens. Once again, the family is constructed around a beautiful young woman. Eve Effingham possesses elegance and simplicity in thought and appearance. Proud of her country yet aware of its faults, she embodies Cooper's belief that the leisured elite provides the refinement and discrimination essential to the progress of a civilised nation. In another Burkean debate about trusteeship she is supported by her relatives and a group of yeomen who are granted the narrator's approval in proportion to their contact with, and edification by, the Effingham family. Opposed to them are a group of shiftless people, 'adventurers in quest of advancement', devoted only to the expediency of the present moment. They are led by two figures given names which hark back to the earlier allegorical method: Aristabulous Bragg, an unctuous and cunning lawyer, and Steadfast Dodge, a Yankee newspaperman whose nature is interwoven with 'the publicity principle'. Eventually the shiftless fail in the face of the ceremony that unites property and family, a marriage. *Home As Found* ends with Eve and her new husband contemplating a future 'under auspices so favorable as to seem almost providential'.[8]

Auspices are much less favourable in the Littlepage Trilogy (1845–6), which is a defence of property-ownership in the face of the Anti-Rent War, a conflict that broke out in New York State in 1839 between landlords and agricultural tenants. The conflict itself is now a footnote in New York history, but once again Cooper believed that it would shake the foundations of the Republic. The trilogy tests the equation of property and civilisation asserted in *The American Democrat*, and sets it in a broad perspective. Cooper extends the historical canvas created by his novels of 1821–6 by providing precise historical markers in Ticonderoga (a French fort captured by the British in 1759), the Revolution, and the Anti-Rent War. Each novel, moreover, is carefully linked to its neighbour by a web of cross-reference, by Cooper's footnotes, and by two dynasties, the Littlepages and the Newcomes. The Littlepages represent genteel America, and are shown growing from a colonial naivety, to cultural independence realised through foreign travel. The more sophisticated members of the family leaven their patriotism with a healthy critique of their country. Around them, once again in the form of an extended family, is gathered a collection of friends, yeomen and retainers, most of whom are endowed with good sense if not the grace and linguistic refinement of the gentry. The gentility of the family and its succession is planted in landed property. The property is defended by an elderly Littlepage in Burkean terms as 'historically connected' with the family name and 'associated with all the higher feelings of humanity', yet the class structure that it underpins is relatively open, because the only qualification for entry is merit.[9] The setting, family and trilogy is presided over by two representatives of oppressed groups, the Black, Jaap and the Native American, Susquesus, who perform great services for the family but, unlike the servants depicted in *Gleanings in Europe: England*, are not servile. Indeed, they take on the quality of household gods as the trilogy progresses.

Antithetically opposed to the Littlepages is the aptly named Newcome family, who descend from an émigré Yankee. Cooper merely outlines their history, since they function only as antitypes of the Littlepages. De Tocqueville had seen the New England town meeting as the fount of American democracy. Cooper is far less positive. He describes the Newcomes in *The Chainbearer* as 'the yeomen of New England . . . imbued with all the distinctive notions of their very peculiar state of society' – trying, as it were, to vote themselves farms. Their attitude to property is based on utility rather than sentiment. Their founder, Jason Newcome, is a rising entrepreneur who sees the cash nexus as the basis of property-ownership, and external objects as the mark of rank. The method of the Newcomes is, like Brackenridge's Teague Oregan, subversive. The trilogy is therefore conceived as a series of struggles that shift from open warfare with an external enemy to guerrilla action by an internal enemy. In *Satanstoe*, the French-employed natives attack the Littlepage property. In the second novel, *The Chainbearer*, the attack is taken up by a white who lives on the margins of civilisation, the squatter Aaron Thousandacres, whose attitudes recall the Skinners in *The Spy*, and whose vernacular utterances capture the essence of the Anti-Rent arguments:

> There's two rights to all the land on 'arth, and the whull world over. One of these rights is what I call a king's right, or that which depends on writin's, and laws, and sich like contrivances; and the other depends on possession. It stands to reason, that fact is better than any writin' about it can be.[10]

Possession, in other words, is ten-tenths of the law. The violent 'neutral ground' of the revolution in *The Spy* is now also seen as a feature of both pre- and post-revolutionary America. The political change simply means a declension in civility, and in the final novel, *The Redskins*, a depleted Littlepage group are shown conducting a last-ditch stand against a community which is largely subverted by Newcome doctrine, and which attacks the property disguised as 'Injins'. *The Redskins* closes with Hugh Littlepage contemplating emigration to Europe.

That Cooper himself did not return to the Old World may be an indication of his deep attachment to New York State, sustaining a residual utopianism to be found in the novels which deal with nature and natural law. Two of them resuscitated Natty Bumppo, ironically at the suggestion of Cooper's British publisher. Of the two, *The Pathfinder* (1840) is closer to *The Last of the Mohicans*, creating a similar conflict between good and evil, white and native characters, and repeating the historical setting, the French and Indian War. There are two significant changes. The first is in the presentation of the environment. In *The Last of the Mohicans* Cooper had emphasised the life of the natural setting in contrast to the deadly deeds of those who fought in it. The woods were ubiquitous, but not sublime. Indeed, in *Gleanings in Europe: Italy* Cooper had remarked that American scenery had 'very little of the grand, or the magnificent'. Yet the lessons he had learned in describing Italian scenery were applied to Upper New York, with a consequent increment in its status. The setting now takes on the role of a chorus, commenting on human activity.

The Pathfinder thus opens with an extended celebration of American trees, bracketed by a brief rehearsal of Burkean aesthetics:

> The sublimity connected with vastness, is familiar to every eye . . . the eye ranged over an ocean of leaves, glorious and rich in the varied but lively verdure of a generous vegetation, and shaded by the luxuriant tints that belong to the forty second degree of latitude. The elm, with its graceful and weeping top, the rich varieties of maple, most of the noble oaks of the American forest, with the broad leafed linden, known in the parlance of the country as the bass-wood, mingled their uppermost branches, forming one broad and seemingly interminable carpet of foliage, that stretched away towards the setting sun, until it bounded the horizon, by blending with the clouds, as the waves and sky meet at the base of the vault of Heaven. Here and there . . . the tall, straight trunk of the pine, pierced the vast field, rising high above it, like some grand monument reared by art on the plain of leaves.
>
> It was the vastness of the view, the nearly unbroken surface of verdure, that contained the principle of grandeur. The beauty was to be traced in the delicate tints, relieved by gradations of light and shadow, while the solemn repose, induced a feeling allied to awe.

There is no concern here about the lack of 'associations' that had so disturbed Washington Irving. Cooper had a different view of American history, and from the very beginning of his career he regarded writers of fiction as its primary custodians. He soon gained the assistance of the visual arts. Starting with *The Pioneers*, Cooper's work, as an 1823 journal put it, 'excited a sensation among the artists, altogether unprecedented in the history of our domestic literature'. Thomas Cole's painting, *Cora Kneeling at the Feet of Tamenund*, made soon after the publication of *The Last of the Mohicans*, is probably the best known of a large number of illustrations of incidents in Cooper's novels. Although Cole, an English-born painter, himself bemoaned the lack of a 'storied past' in America, the activity of laying paint on canvas itself began to create the needed 'associations'.[11]

The second significant change since *The Last of the Mohicans* concerns the characters, who are now more clearly judged in relation to their respect for natural law. The principal beneficiary is Natty. Changes in his stature begun in *The Pioneers* come to fruition in both *The Pathfinder* and *The Deerslayer*. He is the eponymous hero, an extraordinary figure more than ever endowed with superhuman qualities. He first appears in *The Pathfinder* as a man 'of middle age' yet 'in the flower of his strength and activity'. When the action of the novel is complete, his figure is seen leaning on its rifle, 'motionless, as if it were a statue set up in that solitary place, to commemorate the scenes of which it had so lately been the site and the witness'. The iconic process continues in *The Deerslayer*. The setting is Lake Glimmerglass, the fictional name for Cooper's beloved Lake Otsego, in an earlier Anglo-French conflict, King George's War (1744–8). Natty is in his early twenties, with similar physical qualities but now with a face expressing 'guileless truth, sustained by an earnestness of purpose, and a sincerity of feeling'. Natty is the embodiment of innocence; he is also a killer. Natty, more than ever before, is isolated, his occasional social and sexual drives being sublimated in a firmer grasp of his rifle. His natural environment is the virgin forest, for both bear 'the impress . . . of the divine hand of their creator'. The moral unity of nature and Natty (now called Hawkeye) is confirmed when, in a coda to the novel, the return of the hero to an 'unchanged' Lake Glimmerglass prompts the narrator to close with a lament the 'world of transgressions and selfishness'.[12]

With its terrible beauty, *The Deerslayer* would have been the perfect capstone for Cooper's career. It united protagonist and environment with an intensity that answered his earlier worries about American vacuity. In it, Cooper wrote the final version of a character who would become a central element of the iconography of the United States. The significance of Natty Bumppo can be summarised by relating him to earlier contributions to American culture. He is an epic hero in the mould of Alexander the Great, and has the killer instincts of Eric the Red. He is a version of Daniel Boone (1734–1820), the frontiersman who broke through the Cumberland Gap in 1775 to discover Kentucky, and whose exploits were turned into legend in John Filson's *The Discovery, Settlement, and Present State of Kentucke* (1784). He is also a representative of the minuteman, the armed citizen who, like the volunteer farmers at Lexington and Concord (1775), is ready for combat at a minute's notice. D. H. Lawrence rightly compared him with a sanitised Odysseus, for all the 'Leatherstocking' novels contain elements of the quest motif. Lawrence grasped the significance of Natty even more clearly when he called him 'a saint with a gun . . . who lives by death, by killing'.[13] Killing becomes an expression of moral purity, and Natty the incarnation of the Second Amendment to the Constitution, which in the cause of national freedom confirms 'the right of the people to keep and bear arms'. His figure recurs again and again in the national culture, for instance in characters created by Herman Melville and Dashiell Hammett, in the screen personae (often indistinguishable from the offscreen personae) of John Wayne and Clint Eastwood, and in the imagery cultivated by the twenty-sixth and fortieth Presidents of the United States, Teddy Roosevelt and Ronald Reagan.

William Carlos Williams lamented that the migration to the New World had resulted in 'souls . . . bent into grotesque designs of violence and despair'. Although Cooper may not have anticipated the deadly consequences of the canonisation of Natty, he certainly had deep forebodings about the future of the United States. These are to be found in most concentrated form in two novels that mark almost the span of his later career, *The Prairie* (1827) and *The Crater* (1847). *The Prairie*, completed shortly after Cooper arrived in Europe, is a sequel to *The Pioneers*. It begins by moving westwards, in the footsteps of Natty Bumppo who is now in his mid-eighties. It ends with his death. It is therefore a valedictory novel, extending the linked images of waste and death to be found in *The Pioneers*. The opening paragraphs of *The Prairie*, emphasising the 'bleak and solitary' environment, is an appropriate setting for the Bush family, who are slovenly, unruly squatters:

> The meagre herbage of the Prairie promised nothing, in favor of a hard and unyielding soil, over which the wheels of the vehicles rattled as lightly as if they travelled on

a beaten road; neither wagons nor beasts making any deeper impression, than to mark that bruised and withered grass, which the cattle plucked, from time to time, and as often rejected, as food too sour, for even hunger to render palatable.

The atmosphere here, rendered principally by the adjectives, is one of transience and contention. This is not a site for achieving a lasting balance between nature and culture. Instead, for a large part of the novel, Cooper sweeps the arena clean so that the implications of possession may be examined.[14]

The Bushes are 'seeking for the Eldorado of the West', and to increase their chances of wealth, they have kidnapped a young woman (11). Cooper provides a modern setting for a variety of *topoi*: the myth of abundance, the genre of the captivity narrative, and the typology of a borderland dividing profusion and desolation, first seen in *Gesta Hammaburgensis ecclesiae pontificum* of Adam of Bremen. The novel begins in the spring of 1804, and with reference to the Louisiana Purchase. Jefferson completed the purchase from France on 20 December 1803; it had doubled the territory of the United States. It was a controversial act. Some, like Charles Brockden Brown, supported it. Others believed that so much new territory would entice lawless people and might even threaten the integrity of the United States. Cooper, who parodied Jefferson scornfully in the figure of the comic intellectual, Obed Bat, was an opponent. One of the sources of *The Prairie* was an *Account* (1810) written by an army officer, Zebulon Pike, of the expeditions he had led into Minnesota and Colorado. Pike reported seeing much 'barren soil', and he hoped that it would limit the expansion of the United States. The uncultivated areas would be left to the Native Americans.[15]

Natty repeats Pike's 'barrier' theory early in *The Prairie* (24). Yet, by 1827, Cooper knew that Pike's optimistic prediction was not being realised. An expanded Union merely expands the greed of its settlers. As Mahtoree, the chief of the Teton Sioux, remarks, 'the land is too small'. The 'red-man' will be driven out by whites who 'are always hungry' (335). The one thoroughly evil man in the novel, Abiram White, expresses a rapacious and viciously manipulative view of nature that infects the other members of the Bush family: ' "The 'arth was made for our comfort; and for that matter, so ar' its creatur's" ', (22). White's brother-in-law, the patriarchal Ishmael Bush, chafes against all laws, human, divine and natural. He presents the antitype of the newly-wed Elizabeth in *The Pioneers*, looking at Lake Otsego. Indeed, *The Prairie* inverts the epithalamian. There is no sweet Otsego and no woods to echo the merry music, but a barren land whose coarse vegetation creates the illusion of the 'sameness and chilling dreariness' of an ocean, 'heaving heavily' after a tempest (13). There is no 'bridal', but rather an abducted bride, Inez Middleton. *The Prairie* is a tale of transgressions, and the most perverse act is committed by Abiram White when he shoots his nephew Asa in the back. This pushes Ishmael too far. He invokes the Old Testament law of an eye for an eye and a tooth for a tooth (Exodus 21:22); and this eventual resort to law signals a reversal of the journey pattern. The Bush family turn their back on the setting sun and return to 'the settled country' (355). They are 'blended' into 'the settlements', where some of their descendants are 'reclaimed from their law-less and semi-barbarous lives' (364). The final vector of the novel is thus eastwards, and its closure celebrates an integrated community within a limited republic.

Twenty years later there was no room even for such limited optimism. In *The Crater* Cooper returned to the method he had used in *The Monikins*, and wrote an allegory of the history of the United States. The novel brings together two creation myths: that of Atlantis, which first appeared in Plato's *Timaeus*, and that of the constructor, like Sir William Phips and Benjamin Franklin. The constructor in this instance is Mark Woolston. He is shipwrecked on a Pacific reef and forced, as his helper Bob Betts puts it, 'to Robinson Crusoe it'.[16] Woolston Crusoes it with success. A volcanic island appears from the sea and is settled by Woolston and a group of like-minded colonists. Soon 'the whole party in Eden was comfortably established' (230). An extended family is cre-ated in an environment described in terms similar to Plato's island of Phaeacia. Mark becomes governor, and rules as a benign autocrat until the colonists, flushed with success in beating off some pirates, get 'an exaggerated view' of themselves (472). They start to call themselves 'the people' and prate about their 'rights', encouraged by some 'intruders', new immigrants who include among their number a lawyer, a printer and four ministers of religion, each one from a different sect. The pastoral utopia quickly collapses from internal divisions. Mark and his immediate family leave, and his volcanic paradise disappears beneath the ocean as suddenly as it emerged. Sinners in the hands of an angry novelist, 'the colony of the crater perished to a man' in a dreadful earthquake, leaving the narrator to warn that those who boast of 'their vaunted climates and productions, have temporary possession of but small portions of a globe ... which will one day be suddenly struck out of its orbit, as it was originally put there by the hand that made it' (504). The outbreak of the Civil War would have given Cooper ample proof that his warnings of an apocalypse had not been heeded.

Yankee attitudes

'I was just going to say, when I was interrupted...' This is the opening sentence of *The Autocrat at the Breakfast Table* (1858), the first of three collections of conversation pieces by Oliver Wendell Holmes (1809–94). It is a good indicator of the loquacity of many New Englanders, in the pulpit, on the platform, and in print. Time has not been kind to Holmes, nor to many other writers of the heyday of New England, which lasted from around 1830 to the 1870s. Their names, often tripartite to proclaim their pedigree – Charles Eliot Norton, James Russell Lowell, William Ellery Channing – peep out from the faded spines of fusty second-hand editions. There are a number of reasons why the popularity of the New England writers suffered a decline. The Brah-mins, the term for the priestly caste of the Hindus humorously applied to the upper-crust New Englanders, were increasingly seen as an anachronism in the post-bellum industrial era. Holmes himself anticipated the decline of his patrician circle when, in the opening chapter of his 1861 novel, *Elsie Venner*, he contrasted the robust 'common country-boy' who will 'become distinguished in practical life' from the pale scholar who descends from this 'harmless, inoffensive, untitled aristocracy'. Untitled though they might be, they were famous for their snobbery, which is recorded in this mordant little poem, addressed by Samuel C. Bushnell (1852–1930) to the intellectual capital of New England:

> I come from the city of Boston,
> The home of the bean and the cod,
> Where Cabots speak only to Lowells,
> And Lowells speak only to God.[17]

Speaking only to God was a mark of Puritanism. The Brahmins were further damaged by their Puritan heritage, for it became associated with a cramped, desiccated, pernicious religiosity, even a murderous hypocrisy. The 1925 attacks on the Puritans by H. L. Mencken and William Carlos Williams (discussed in Chapter 3) brought to a climax a half-century of Puritan-baiting. Nor was the New England tradition of oratory, derived from the Puritan ideal of an educated ministry, exempt from suspicion. As we have seen in Chapter 1, Henry Cabot Lodge had to indulge in special pleading to include the supreme orator, Daniel Webster, in the 1917 *A History of American Literature*. Given the prejudices of a New Yorker, it was perhaps inevitable that Fenimore Cooper would be one of the first to distrust Yankee oratory, seeing it as a vehicle for political chicanery. Using a term he would repeat in *The Chainbearer*, Cooper suggested that Webster was 'not a great man – merely a man of great peculiarities'. After the Civil War, the dislike of oratory spread to the west. Mark Twain, whose hatred of the pretentiousness of eloquence was passed on to Ernest Hemingway, used the character of Huck Finn to call it 'soul butter and hogwash'.[18]

Samuel Clemens's 1877 encounter with the Bostonians, whom he thought all too proper, is an indicator of the waning influence of New England. He was invited to speak at the *Atlantic Monthly* dinner for John Greenleaf Whittier's seventieth birthday. His speech imagines a meeting with a California miner. Clemens, 'callow and conceited', uses his pen name. The miner responds by complaining that Twain is the fourth 'littery man that's been here in twenty-four hours'. Three of the senior figures at the dinner had preceded him: Emerson (described as 'a seedy little bit of a chap'), Holmes ('fat as a balloon') and Longfellow ('built like a prizefighter' with a hairbrush coiffure). The miner was unhappy. They had drunk his liquor and played cards, quarrelled and quoted – or misquoted – their better-known lines at each other. As they left in the morning 'Longfellow' declaimed his most famous flawed metaphor:

> Lives of great men all remind us
> We can make our lives sublime;
> And departing, leave behind us
> Footprints in the sands of time.

With these words he stole the miner's only pair of boots. The sketch ends with Twain consoling the miner with the thought that, like the King and the Duke in *The Adventures of Huckleberry Finn* eight years later, these men were impostors.[19]

Even while he was speaking Clemens believed that he was making a hideous mistake. He thought that his extended slapstick joke had given so much offence that he later wrote an abject letter of apology to the figures he had caricatured. The evidence, on the contrary, suggests that they had either enjoyed, or slumbered through, his performance. The incident, and the discomfort which Clemens felt for the rest of his life, indicates a clash of values between cynical south-western humour and genteel north-eastern respectability which, ironically, moved in his favour and branded the Yankees as old-fashioned.[20] Yet the record shows that in earlier years the Yankees wrote work that, while not quite scaling the heights of Twainian scurrility, was often far from staid. The New England hegemony was at its greatest before the Civil War, when its nonconformist values became political commitment in the abolitionist crusade and turned its preachers into (often embattled) heroes.

The preacher whose heroic status has survived longest is Ralph Waldo Emerson. As we saw in Chapter 1, Oliver Wendell Holmes and a number of later writers described Emerson's 1837 Harvard address, 'The American Scholar', as the literary equivalent of the Declaration of Independence. Certainly, it is a call for cultural freedom. Drawing on the last line of 'The Star-Spangled Banner', Emerson required the American scholar to be 'free and brave'. While 'there is a portion of reading quite indispensable to a wise man', the scholar should become an outdoor 'Man Thinking' rather than a 'book-worm'. Books, nature and action all had their place in the development of Man Thinking, and the ultimate aim was independence. 'The American Scholar' thus concludes in masculinist and martial terms:

> We will walk on our own feet; we will work with our own hands; we will speak with our own minds. The study of letters shall no longer be a name for pity, for doubt, for sensual indulgence. The dread of man and the love of man shall be a wall of defence and a wreath of joy around all. A nation of men will for the first time exist, because each believes himself inspired by the Divine Soul which also inspires all men.[21]

Emerson's call for freedom could be linked with patriotism. His 'Concord Hymn', written the same year, therefore commemorates the bridge where 'once the embattled farmers stood/And fired the shot heard round the world' (664). But it was much more an assertion of the spirit of intransigent individualism. That spirit led him to resign his pastorate of the Second Boston Church in 1832, and prompted him in July 1838 to deliver what has become known as the Divinity School Address. He gave it at his Alma Mater, Harvard. As a result he was reviled as an infidel, and for almost thirty years was not invited back. The Address is a sustained attack on established religion, at one point by a vivid imagery of a winter Sunday contrasting the 'real' snowstorm outside the church with the 'merely spectral' preacher inside it (83). Here, as elsewhere, Emerson's dialectical method recalls Blake, particularly with the counterpoint in the *Songs of Innocence and of Experience* between the childhood joy in nature and such confining institutions as schools and 'black'ning' churches. The book which made Emerson well known, *Nature* (1836), therefore begins by contrasting the 'retrospective' age which 'builds the sepulchres of the fathers' with 'nature, whose floods of life stream around and through us' (7). Likewise, that summer Sunday evening in the Harvard Divinity School, the Senior Class were treated by this descendant of an old Puritan family not to an argument constructed around the familiar jeremiad, but rather to one rejecting 'the traditional and limited' (80) method of preaching in favour of a joyous sense of the flood of life, conveyed in a headlong rush of short phrases:

> In this refulgent summer, it has been a luxury to draw the breath of life. The grass grows, the buds burst, the meadow is spotted with fire and gold in the tint of flowers. The air is full of birds, and sweet with the breath of the pine, the balm-of-Gilead, and the new hay. Night brings no gloom to the heart with its welcome shade. Through the transparent darkness the stars pour their almost spiritual rays. Man under them seems a young child, and his huge globe a toy. The cool night bathes the world as with a river, and prepares his eyes again for the crimson dawn. The mystery of nature was never displayed more happily. (72)

Emerson's injunction to the young ministers-to-be, 'obey thyself' (79), was an important element of his thinking. It was heresy to their tutors, but such individualism has since become a central strand in the ideology of the United States, and one reason why Emerson has in recent years been both lionised and defamed.

The 'Divinity School Address' is also typical of Emerson's work in showing that he does not preach mere egotism. God irradiates the natural world as well as the self. To an extent, this belief was drawn from Europe. Emerson had learnt from the Romantics to see a connection between the natural and human worlds more dynamic and regenerative than the relatively simple pleasure/pain matrix of Burkean psychology that had been practised by Jefferson. He had also learnt from Kant, and Kant's German acolytes Schelling and Richter, who had also had a strong influence on such British Romantics as Coleridge. Emerson noted in his 1842 lecture, 'The Transcendentalist', that the idealistic philosophy took its name from Kant's rejection, in *The Critique of Pure Reason* (1781), of Lockeian empiricism. Transcendental knowledge, said Kant, is not concerned with objects that we sense, but with the way that we sense them. So far there seemed little difference between Transcendentalism and Romanticism. Yet in the United States Transcendentalism became infused with a spirit that is more utopian and hedonistic, giving the philosophy a distinctively American colour. So while Wordsworth, in his 1805 Preface to *Lyrical Ballads*, famously characterised 'all good poetry' as 'the spontaneous overflow of powerful feelings', Emerson described a state more akin to exhilaration. In his 1842 essay he asserts that the Transcendentalist believes 'in miracle . . . in inspiration, and in ecstasy' (96).

The causes of the difference were temporal, spiritual and spatial. By the time Emerson wrote *Nature* in 1836, Romanticism in Europe had sputtered out. Its early stirrings had coincided with the French Revolution. Indeed, Kant's German followers had interpreted such events as the storming of the Bastille as Kantian philosophy in action. Within a few years the belief in collective action which had characterised the opening stages of the French Revolution had metamorphosed into a heroic yet 'pernicious' individualism. Thus, in his essay on Napoleon in *Representative Men* (1850), Emerson began by suggesting that the general had become an emperor because he acted as a focus for 'the power and affections of vast numbers'; yet he had failed and had left a 'demoralized' Europe precisely because he lacked 'moral principle'. As we shall see in a moment, Napoleon was merely 'the man of the World' (325, 344–5). It was the poet, rather, who was the more representative man because he united moral with heroic individualism. In 'The Poet', an 1844 essay, Emerson restated Wordsworth's Preface to *Lyrical Ballads* with greater enthusiasm. 'The poet is the sayer, the namer, and represents beauty,' he asserted, 'he is a sovereign, and stands on the centre' (244). Emerson had learnt most from the Swedish mystic Emanuel Swedenborg (1688–1772), who taught that it was possible to intuit direct knowledge of the Divine. The poet was therefore the singer both of God and the world. He penetrated 'into that region where the air is music', providing transcripts which became 'the songs of the nations' (244). America was the best place to apply Swedenborg's teaching because its woods and fields presented to Emerson, as he put it in *Nature*, a vision of 'the plantations of God' where 'we return to reason and faith' (10–11).

Emerson believed that his fellow Americans had rarely met the challenge presented by nature. In his journal for 18 May 1843 he expressed the problem which he spent much of his life addressing:

> Our American lives are somewhat poor & pallid, Franklins & Washingtons, no fiery grain ... But why go to Europe? Best swallow this pill of America which Fate brings & sing a land unsung. Here stars, here birds, here trees, here hills abound and vast tendencies concur of a new Order ... The young men complain that here in America is no past, no tradition, only shopkeeping, no ghost, no god in the landscape, no stimulus.[22]

The raw material was there, waiting to be voiced; yet it seemed that all Emerson's juniors could do was to rehearse the negative catalogue to be found in Cooper's *Notions of the Americans*. The difficulty was how to get beyond the bare generic nouns (birds, trees, hills) and sing the land in a manner worthy of it. As he put it in 'The Poet', his countrymen needed to 'hear those primal warblings and attempt to write them down' (244). If this sounds comic it is because semiotics, pioneered among others by the Swiss linguist Ferdinand de Saussure (1857–1913), has erected a wall between the Transcendentalists and us. Semiotics is based on the belief that language is an arbitrary construct, while Emerson held a view, now almost entirely disregarded, of language as autochthon. He thought, too, that an American language would not emerge as a result of the tinkering of the lexicographer Noah Webster, but because a poet would appear who would give voice to the words that were waiting, there in the abundant land.

Emerson's first attempts at giving voice to the primal warblings are to be found in the journals – there are over two hundred of them – which he kept for much of his mature life. The opening entry, for 25 January 1820 (when he was a Junior at Harvard), is headed 'The Wide World' rather than the more usual 'Common Place Book'. The entry for the second day indicates, with a note of conscious comedy which would often recur, how the voicing would be achieved: 'I do hereby nominate & appoint "Imagination" the generallissimo & chief marshal of all the luckless raggamuffin Ideas which may be collected & imprisoned hereafter in these pages.' Far from being luckless and imprisoned, his ideas leap from the pages of the journals. They reveal a life the reverse of 'poor & pallid'; rather a ragamuffin drunk with both word and world:

> The world is a Dancer; it is a Rosary; it is a Torrent; it is a Boat; a Mist; a Spider's Snare; it is what you will; and the metaphor will hold, & it will give the imagination keen pleasure . . . There is no thing small or mean to the soul . . . Must I call the heaven & the earth a maypole & country fair with booths or an anthill or an old coat in order to give you the shock of pleasure which the imagination loves and the sense of spiritual greatness? Call it a blossom, a rod, a wreath of parsley, a tamarisk-crown, a cock, a sparrow, the ear instantly hears & the spirit leaps to the trope . . .[23]

The journals became the lectures, and the lectures became the books. For instance, a visit to Britain in 1847–8 and meetings with Wordsworth, Dickens and Carlyle gave rise to a lecture series in 1849 and then *English Traits* in 1856. The process of recension made his prose slightly less tipsy, but never less exuberant. It is relaxed, informal, epigrammatic; still carrying, a century and a half later, a sense of his platform style. By the time he stopped keeping a journal, in 1875 at the age of 72, his energetic expression had become second nature. He grew old, but – fortunately like Mark Twain – he never grew up. James Russell Lowell, coming out of an 1867 lecture, wrote to a friend about seeing stars and hearing trumpets. William James, in an address at the centenary of Emerson's birth, talked of the essays as if they were the writer still speaking.

The effect of Emerson's journals on his poetry is less happy. In his search, as he put it in 'The Poet', for 'a thought so passionate and alive that like the spirit of a plant or an animal it has an architecture of its own', he believed that 'it is not metres, but a metre-making argument that makes a poem' (245). The inattention to form means that, at its worst, the poetry submits to a thumping metre and clanging rhyme that recalls Emerson's didactic Bostonian predecessors, the translators of *The Bay Psalm Book*. At its best, for instance in the 'Ode' inscribed to William Henry Channing (1810–84), a Christian socialist friend of Emerson, the poetry directs the emotions by using its lines to convey the irregular breathing of the angry speaker:

> But who is he that prates
> Of the culture of mankind.
> Of better arts and life?
> Go, blindworm, go,
> Behold the famous States
> Harrying Mexico
> With rifle and with knife! (647)

The poem was inspired by the outbreak of the Mexican War. The war was caused partly as a result of the US annexation of Texas in 1845, and partly by the wish of Southern planters, who controlled Congress, to extend their slave-holding territory further south-west. At its conclusion Mexico ceded territory to the United States which would become part of the states of California, Colorado and New Mexico. In January 1848, one month before the Treaty of Guadalupe Hidalgo ended the war, gold was discovered in the Sacramento Valley, and within the next year the Gold Rush began. Emerson's 'Ode', it seemed, was prophetic. It drew a comparison with the Russian acquisition of Poland to suggest that patriotism was being used cynically, as a mask for imperialism and at the service of material gain:

'Tis the day of the chattel,
Web to weave, and corn to grind;
Things are in the saddle,
And ride mankind. (648)

At this point Emerson begins to sound uncannily like a precursor of Lenin. Indeed, in 1848 Emerson saw the conditions of Manchester that inspired Marx and Engels's *Communist Manifesto*. That essay on Napoleon, published two years later, therefore begins in hope by invoking Swedenborg and ends in despair, suggesting that the Frenchman's leadership became 'pernicious' because 'our civilization is essentially one of property, of fences, of exclusive-ness' (345). The use of the plural determiner, 'our', is deliberate; for the United States, if anything, is more curst by materialism than France. The sole inter-ruption to the negative catalogue in that journal entry for May 1843 is 'shopkeeping', a noun extended into a gerund, a maggot at the core of America. Much of Emerson's work is marked by an intense hatred of materialism. His cure, however, did not lie in collective action, but rather in moral individual-ism – or, as he put it in a journal entry for 1847, 'to a right aristocracy . . . to the men who are incomparably superior to the populace in ways agreeable to the populace'. Emerson counted Daniel Webster among the aristocracy. Then, on 7 March 1850, Webster spoke in the Senate in favour of what has since become known as the Compromise of 1850. The Compromise was a series of resolutions designed to prevent growing divisions between the Northern and Southern states. It involved a notorious Fugitive Slave Law. Emerson thought that this was the vilest apostasy by Webster, because slavery turned people into property. 'The word *liberty* in the mouth of Mr Webster sounds like the word *love* in the mouth of a courtezan,' he wrote furiously in his journal, 'the fame of Webster ends in this nasty law.'[24]

Yet there was still hope. As long as the United States remained a democracy it would create 'a right aristocracy'. The species could even be found in Britain, the natural home of the wrong aristocracy. A talk Emerson gave about Carlyle in 1881, the year of Carlyle's death and a year before Emerson's own, said that while 'holding an honored place in the best society, he has stood for the people' (626). But the United States was the natural environment of the people; and the 1787 Constitution, beginning 'We the people', the best guarantor of the future. Emerson was in no doubt in what direction the future lay. In an 1844 lecture, 'The Young American', he saw the rapid development of the railroad not as an expression of capitalism but as a means of communication to the West, which he regarded as a 'sanative and Americanizing influence':

> We, in the Atlantic states, by position, have been commercial, and have . . . imbibed easily an European culture. Luckily for us, now that steam has narrowed the Atlantic to a strait, the nervous, rocky West is intruding a new and continental element into the national mind, and we shall yet have an American genius.[25]

To an extent this is one of several anticipations of the phrase, 'go west, young man', for which the newspaper editor, Horace Greeley, is famous. It was, however, western influence rather than the West itself which would produce the American genius. One of Emerson's later essays, 'Fate' (1860), was organised around a distinction similar to that made by Oliver Wendell Holmes in *Elsie Venner*. More clearly than Holmes, Emerson rejected the 'clean shirt and white neckcloth of a student in divinity' – in other words his forbears and his own earlier life – in favour of those who could survive in a 'rough and surly' world (349–50). One genius that did come from the West was Abraham Lincoln. Emerson praised Lincoln's 'simplicity' and, at the Concord memorial service for the dead President, called him 'the true representative of this continent'. There were, however, two other representatives closer to hand, Henry Thoreau and Walt Whitman.

When Emerson published his eulogy on Thoreau, he used yet another negative catalogue:

> He was bred to no profession; he never married; he lived alone; he never went to church; he never voted; he refused to pay a tax to the state; he ate no flesh; he drank no wine; he never knew the use of tobacco; and, though a naturalist, he used neither trap nor gun . . . He had no temptations to fight against; no appetites, no passions, no taste for elegant trifles.[26]

For these reasons 'no truer American existed'. Emerson's negations are a little overdone. Thoreau did teach for three periods, and he did work occasionally for the family pencil factory, improving the design of the Thoreau pencils until they were the best in the United States. Otherwise, this is a fairly accurate if rather emaciated account of Thoreau's life, and another instance of Emerson's shrewdness. Thoreau was an abstainer before his time, and his work is far better known now than it ever was in his life. His first book, *A Week on the Concord and Merrimack Rivers*, was printed in one thousand copies in 1849. In 1853 his publisher asked him to take back the 706 unsold copies, after which Thoreau noted, 'I have now a library of nearly nine hundred volumes, over seven hundred of which I wrote myself.' Thoreau is now one of the best-known American political and literary figures. This happened because he turned the negative catalogue, so often an American grumble, into an affirmation. Shortly after he spent a day in jail for refusing to pay his poll tax, Thoreau published 'Resistance to Civil Government'. As 'Civil Disobedience' (the title it was posthumously given in 1866) it has become a classic statement of moral self-reliance and passive resistance: 'The only obligation which I have a right to assume, is to do at any time what I think right.'[27] It influenced Gandhi and Martin Luther King; and valorises anyone who brandishes a placard or sits down in front of a tank.

A later American critic and naturalist, Joseph Wood Krutch, wrote that Thoreau began 'by swallowing Emerson whole'. Perhaps 'chewed over' would be a more appropriate metaphor. Before he ever knew Emerson, Thoreau had had a visitation (no less word is appropriate) with Orestes Brownson (1803–76). He later told Brownson that staying with him was 'the morning of a new *Lebenstag* . . . as a dream that is dreamt, but which returns from time to time in all its original freshness'.[28] Brownson gave Thoreau the 'fiery grain' which Emerson prescribed but could not provide. Brownson was an autodidact, an ardent and intellectually restless polemicist who began his mature life as a Presbyterian before becoming, in turn, a Universalist, a Marxist before Marx, a Unitarian, then embracing Catholicism in 1844, the year before the century's most notorious conversion to Catholicism, that of John Henry (later Cardinal) Newman. When Thoreau boarded with him in 1836, Brownson was a Transcendentalist. In that year he published *New Views of Christianity, Society and the Church*, which argued that life is a continuous struggle between spiritual and material values. Struggle was the key word for Brownson. Even after he became the leading Catholic in New England, Brownson struggled, much to the dismay of the Holy See. He had an opinion on almost everything, and over time almost every opinion on anything. When furious about his opinions, he chewed tobacco and thumped tables. But the chewing and thumping was nothing compared to the writing. Brownson began the *Boston Quarterly Review* in 1838; it has been estimated that he wrote 150,000 words in each of its first two years. He was ejected from the *Boston Quarterly Review*, and then from the *Democratic Review* and, unabashed, set up his own Catholic vehicle, *Brownson's Quarterly Review*, which he edited, and to a large extent wrote, for twenty-two years.

Between them, Brownson and Emerson provided the lexicon to make Thoreau the quintessential Yankee cuss – which was why he could joke about the fate of *A Week on the Concord and Merrimack Rivers*. At first sight, *A Week* is a long-winded tale of a short trip that Thoreau made with his brother in a boat, which had cost them 'a week's labor', to the White Mountains of New Hampshire. In typical cussed fashion, Thoreau keeps interrupting the narrative with quotations, poems and homespun philosophy:

> The routine which is in the sunshine and the finest days, as that which has conquered and prevailed, commends itself to us by its very antiquity and apparent solidity and necessity. Our weakness needs it, and our strength uses it. We cannot draw on our boots without bracing ourselves against it. If there were but one erect and solid standing tree in the woods, all creatures would go and rub against it and make sure of their footing.

It is only in the last half-century that the book has been appreciated as a carefully crafted whole. The obviously cyclical construction of the text – with chapters for each day from Saturday to Friday – is related to other cycles. Morning to night, up river and down, climbing and descending the mountains, the passage of the seasons: all are versions of a 'routine' which binds humankind to the natural world, and to the past. The introductory section therefore begins a series of references to pre-European American history by reminding us that the Concord River had been called the Musketaquid. The 'Saturday' chapter opens with a quotation from the English poet Francis Quarles (1592–1644), an apologist for Charles I, the king beheaded in 1649. It then depicts the brothers passing 'the still visible abutments' of the North Bridge, a reminder of the Battle of Lexington and Concord which began the Revolution; and quotes Emerson's 'Concord Hymn, Sung at the Completion of the Battle Monument, July 4, 1837'. Although the Republic may have 'conquered' the Concord River – the assonance seems obvious when the verb is ripped out of context – reminders and memorials of earlier republics and earlier ages encrust both text and environment. As Emerson remarked in 1859, 'old and new make the warp and woof of every moment'.[29]

Thoreau built a hut on Emerson's land at Walden Pond. It cost $28.125 – the precise figure mattered to Thoreau. He moved in on 4 July 1845, and nine years later published *Walden*, the only other book that appeared in his lifetime and, with 'Civil Disobedience', the text for which he is best remembered. He claimed that the date of moving was an 'accident'. It is hard to believe that Thoreau ever did anything by accident. It was, rather, his own declaration of independence, as willed an event as the text itself. He lived in the hut for two years, two months and two days; but *Walden* is constructed around the cycle of a year, ending in the spring, the Transcendentalist season of potentiality:

> the sun shines bright and warm this first spring morning, recreating the world, and you . . . bless the new day, feel the spring influence with the innocence of infancy . . .

Here again is the rhetoric of novelty of Thomas Jefferson and Tom Paine, with more than a dash of pantheism drawn from Emerson and the 'original freshness' learnt from Brownson. This time, instead of appearing diffused by the journey-pattern, the text achieves great concentration by focusing on the lowest common denominator: one person, living in a limited space for a limited time.[30]

Walden is affirmation as natural therapy. Thoreau's purpose was to relieve 'the mass of men', who 'lead lives of quiet desperation'. The text is constructed to scrub away the dead scales which hamper sensitivity, and instead 'to live deep and suck out all the marrow of life'. It does this by reconnecting the cycle of nature with the one apparently lost by humankind. Thus physical movement in autumn is replaced by a contraction in winter as a necessary preparation for the rejuvenation of spring. This means that, whilst the text abides by Jefferson's agrarian ideal, it is not opposed to change and development. In contrast to the way that Dickens portrays a destructive railway in *Dombey and Son* (1846–8), Thoreau does not disapprove of technology. All depends on the way that it is used:

Our inventions are wont to be pretty toys, which distract our attention from serious things. They are but improved means to an unimproved end, an end which it was already too easy to arrive at; as railroads lead to Boston or New York. We are in great haste to construct a magnetic telegraph from Maine to Texas; but Maine and Texas, it may be, have nothing important to communicate.

In the right circumstances, technology is a boon. The trains that pass Walden Pond give others access to 'this vision of serenity and purity'. Similarly, Thoreau's rejection of materialism is presented as book-keeping. The first chapter, 'Economy', therefore repeats the concern of Franklin's *Autobiography* to render 'some account' of frugality, to show 'that a man may use as simple a diet as the animals, and yet retain health and strength'. Thoreau, like the animals, did not pay rent for the land. It helped maintain his economy and did not destroy his argument. He was concerned with restoring animal vitality to a generation he regarded as jaded. Several generations passed before he attracted many listeners.[31]

Thoreau's other books are posthumous creations, the earliest edited from journals and published essays by his sister, Sophia, and his friends Emerson and Ellery Channing. *Excursions* (1863), *The Maine Woods* (1864), *Cape Cod* (1865) and *A Yankee in Canada* (1866) resume the form of the anecdotal saunter. The journals themselves were published in four extracts in the 1880s, and in almost complete form in 1906. They were kept, after one or two false starts, on a daily basis from 22 October 1837 to 3 November 1861. By this time it was clear to him that he did not have long to live – and his journals were about the conduct of life, to borrow the title of one of Emerson's books. Thoreau's conduct of life might be called applied self-examination. While Emerson floated on air, Thoreau was down on his knees, doing detailed work on leaves and seeds. His concern for recording the environment owes something to *Rural Hours* (1850), by Susan Fenimore Cooper, the novelist's daughter, and would be continued by the naturalists John Muir (1838–1914) and John Burroughs (1837–1921). His awareness that humans are animals with technological abilities is echoed, in different ways, by the ecologist Rachel Carson, in *Silent Spring* (1962), and by *Walden Two* (1948), the utopian novel by the behavioural psychologist B. F. Skinner.

The fate of Longfellow's work was the reverse of Thoreau's. On the first day that it appeared in 1858, *The Courtship of Miles Standish* was an international publishing event, selling over fifteen thousand copies in Boston and London. At his death he was one of the most popular authors in the English-speaking world, the only American with a place in Poet's Corner in Westminster Abbey. Now, it seems, few adults will admit to reading him. When the poet and novelist Howard Nemerov (1920–91) edited a small selection of Longfellow's poems in 1959, he lamented the bard's disappearance, even from the half-time recitals at football games. Twenty-nine years later, when Lawrence Buell edited another selection, he explained the problem that still existed: 'Longfellow has fared badly within a critical framework that is scholarly (the fondness for intricacy), modernist (the equation of alienated pessimism with the authentic), and American-centered.' This is a particularly unhappy fate for an author more concerned than most to contribute to American literature. Longfellow's third prose work, *Kavanagh* (1849), a depiction of village life in New England, contains a debate about literary nationalism. Hathaway, a visiting writer, demands 'a national literature commensurate with our mountains and rivers', written by those who are 'untutored, wild, original, free'. Churchill, a local schoolteacher who is the vehicle for Longfellow's view, employs the melting-pot theory to suggest a literature drawn from English origins but made universal because 'the blood of all nations is mingling with our own'.[32]

Longfellow's contemporaries praised or criticised him precisely because his work was informed by the melting-pot theory. His most famous long poem, *The Song of Hiawatha* (1855), uses material about native tribes Longfellow had read in the work of the Moravian missionary John Heckewelder (1743–1823) – also a source for Cooper – and the ethnologist Henry Schoolcraft (1793–1864), and seen in engravings by George Catlin (1796–1872). In the notes that accompanied the first publication of the poem, Longfellow called it an 'Indian Edda', after the thirteenth-century collections of Old Norse poems. Traces of *The Odyssey* and *Beowulf* are also to be found in *The Song of Hiawatha*. The poem is most closely based on the *Kalevala* ('Land of Heroes'), the Finnish epic which reached printed form in 1822, and which was first arranged into alliterative eight-syllabled trochees in 1835. Longfellow read the *Kalevala* in Finnish; it did not appear in the United States in an English translation until 1888. Longfellow's scholarly attempt to reveal the place of Native Americans in a universal mythology was criticised at the time as plagiarism. The criticism did nothing to diminish its immense popularity. An extract from 'Hiawatha's Childhood' may help to explain why:

> By the shores of Gitche Gumee,
> By the shining Big-Sea-Water,
> Stood the wigwam of Nokomis,
> Daughter of the Moon, Nokomis,
> Dark behind it rose the forest,
> Rose the black and gloomy pine-trees,
> Rose the firs with cones upon them;
> Bright before it beat the water,
> Beat the clear and sunny water,
> Beat the shining Big-Sea-Water.
>   There the wrinkled, old Nokomis
> Nursed the little Hiawatha,
> Rocked him in his linden cradle,
> Bedded soft in moss and rushes,
> Safely bound with reindeer sinews;
> Stilled his fretful wail by saying,
> 'Hush! the Naked Bear will hear thee!'

This is a version of the story of Moses in the bulrushes (Exodus 2:2), with Nokomis doubling as the daughter of both Levi and Pharaoh, and the Naked Bear as an ursine Pharaoh, muttering offstage threats. The scene is no longer the Nile, but the southern shore of Lake Superior, dressed as a darker version of the Lake Glimmerglass that appears in Cooper's *The Deerslayer*. *The Song of Hiawatha* combines the shapes of a Mosaic epic trajectory with the *ubi sunt* motif from *The Last of the Mohicans* (discussed in Chapter 4), as Hiawatha paddles off at the close of the poem 'to the land of the Hereafter!' In this way Longfellow gave international significance to an increasingly outmoded American way of life. It was a form of pleasingly plangent sentimentalism shared not only with Schoolcraft and Catlin but also, for instance, with the Boston historian Francis Parkman (1823–93). In the account of his 1846 expedition, *The Oregon Trail* (1849), Parkman dismissed those 'picturesque tourists, painters, poets and novelists' who had never travelled 'beyond the extreme frontier'. Yet he too, confronted by the sight of a 'savage multitude' of Oglalah Sioux descending 'grand and imposing' mountains, admitted that 'only the pen of Scott could have done it justice in description'. This did not prevent him making his own attempt. He depicted 'that perilous wilderness, eight hundred miles removed beyond the faintest vestige of civilization' in images of the Colosseum and St Peter's, in Rome, and of 'the peak of Mount Etna towering above its inky mantle of clouds'. Parkman gave a similar treatment to another vanishing culture, that of the French in North America. When he wrote the introduction to his multi-volume *France and England in North America* (1865–92), he noted that 'the French dominion is a memory of the past; and when we evoke its departed shades, they rise upon us from their graves in strange, romantic guise'.[33] A range of writers in mid-century created a usable American past by clothing it with myths and images that belonged to the Old World. At the time they were rewarded with great popularity. In the later twentieth century texts such as *The Song of Hiawatha* were accused of sentimental savagism. Yet, while Longfellow's poem is no longer recited at sporting events, vestiges of its former glory remain in its continued appeal to the more imaginative child.

Ironically, Longfellow's greatest innovation, trochaic tetrameter, proved to be usable in a less flattering way. A friend, the writer Bayard Taylor (1825–78), warned Longfellow that the metre would attract parodies. There have been many of them. Taylor himself used it affectionately to evoke a pungent local atmosphere in the courtship comedy of Hiram Hover, a trapper, and Huldah Hyde, who gathers herbs for a living but is looking for something better:

> 'Why', he murmured, loth to leave her,
> 'Gather yarbs for chills and fever,
>   When a lovyer bold and true,
>   Only waits to gather you?'
> 'Go', she answered, 'I'm not hasty,
> I prefer a man more tasty;
>   Leastways, one to please me well
>   Should not have a beasty smell'.

Then Huldah buys a fur coat and realises, in an age long before diamonds were a girl's best friend and fur was politically incorrect, that fashion for women means money in the bank for the trapper, and happiness ever after for them both.[34]

Some of Longfellow's other work recreates colonial history. *Evangeline* (1847) concerns, like *The Last of the Mohicans*, an episode in the French and Indian War, but this time a British atrocity, the forced transportation of some six thousand French-Canadians from Nova Scotia to Louisiana and elsewhere. There are a number of sources here, including Goethe and Milton. Yet from them Longfellow creates a lament that surpasses *Hiawatha*, the long hexameter line accommodating a tone of sorrow that can barely restrain anger:

> Far asunder, on separate coasts, the Acadians landed;
> Scattered were they, like flakes of snow, when the wind from the northeast,
> Strikes aslant through the fogs that darken the Banks of Newfoundland.
> Friendless, homeless, hopeless, they wandered from city to city,
> From the cold lakes of the North to sultry Southern savannas . . .
> Friends they sought and homes; and many, despairing, heart-broken,
> Asked of the earth but a grave, and no longer a friend nor a fireside.
> Written their history stands on tablets of stone in the churchyards.[35]

This particular attempt to write American history, rarely recorded save 'on tablets of stone', is reminiscent of the Jewish diaspora and would speak more clearly to present-day concerns than Longfellow's other colonial memories, such as *The Courtship of Miles Standish*, 'Paul Revere's Ride' (1861), or *The New England Tragedies* (1868). It may be going too far to suggest that Longfellow would have retained his audience had he followed the advice of Hathaway, in *Kavanagh*, and sought originality rather than universality. Yet the predictions of Holmes and Emerson came true. After Longfellow's death, Clemens's miner and Bayard Taylor's 'beasty' trapper became the representative American voices. The earnest anglicised voice of Longfellow, like those of the other Brahmins, was overwhelmed by the forces of the vernacular, sunk beneath the cynicism of the *Hiawatha* parodies. Longfellow's work would survive in popular phrases. 'The Village Blacksmith' would become the music-hall song 'Under the spreading chestnut tree' (in turn parodied by Orwell in *Nineteen Eighty-Four*, 1949). 'The Bridge' would be transformed into the scurrilous 'She stood on the bridge at midnight'. 'Paul Revere's Ride' would endure in an early Count Basie recording, 'Listen, My Children, and You Shall Hear'. It was an apt, if not always happy, outcome.

Explorations of identity: Hawthorne

In 1837 Nathaniel Hawthorne sent a copy of *Twice-Told Tales* to Longfellow, who had been in the same class at Bowdoin College, Maine, and who was by then an established writer. Hawthorne had wanted for some sixteen years to be a writer, but had met with limited success. His first, anonymous, publication was *Fanshawe* (1828). The novel, which he never acknowledged, concerned a reclusive scholar forced, by love, to become briefly a man of action.

By 1837 he had also published a children's reader and a number of sketches and short stories, some of which were reprinted in the appropriately titled *Twice-Told Tales*. Longfellow's review of the book made Hawthorne's name. It praised the tales for the way that they illuminated a New England present which otherwise seemed 'dull, common-place, and prosaic'. As a result they were 'national in their character'. In this instance the Brahmin confusion of New England with the nation prompted Longfellow to write a review that was notably prophetic, particularly as Hawthorne's starting-point was an authorial uncertainty similar to Irving's. In a letter to Longfellow, Hawthorne said that he had been 'carried apart from society'. He was therefore in precisely the same position as his first protagonist, the similarly-named Fanshawe. From this unpromising corner, Hawthorne reached out much further than Irving to develop a commentary on the United States, to the extent that Henry James marvelled that he had been able to extract so much from its apparently immature 'vegetation'.[36]

Hawthorne made a virtue of his exile. It was a frequent motif in his work, related to his insistence on calling his fictions 'Romances' rather than novels, 'having a great deal more to do', as he said in his Preface to *The House of the Seven Gables* (1851), 'with the clouds overhead, than with any portion of the actual soil of the County of Essex'. The English novelist Anthony Trollope followed Longfellow's prognosis, and treated Hawthorne's fictions as a symptom of a general condition, suggesting that American literature was 'speculative', devoted to 'dreams'. In contrast, the bully British thrived – in a phrase that Trollope borrowed from Hawthorne – on their 'beef and ale'. Trollope's analysis was taken up in turn by a group of American critics, such as Richard Chase, keen in the mid-twentieth century on establishing literary exceptionalism. Yet it is unlikely that Trollope's remarks would have cut much ice with his mother, the indignant Frances. She knew the earthy side of the Americans, and probably would have seen through Hawthorne's diffidence. The reclusive narrator is no more than a convenient persona for commenting on contemporary American society.[37]

Two examples. One of Hawthorne's earliest surviving sketches, 'Mrs. Hutchinson' (1830), retells the story of the Antinomian Crisis as a portent of the proliferation of women's writing in Hawthorne's time. The narrator of the tale presents Anne Hutchinson as an exemplar of the woman who goes too far. While her judges are hardly presented with sympathy, Anne reveals 'unknown to herself . . . a flash of carnal pride' which is her undoing. Likewise, there are nowadays 'public women' who pursue their 'ambition' through the press. The case of Hutchinson warns those 'ink-stained Amazons' that 'woman, when she feels the impulse of genius like a command of Heaven within her, should be aware that she is relinquishing a part of the loveliness of her sex'. Hawthorne invokes the common belief in the separation of spheres, unacceptable to us today, which would resurface in his infamous 1855 comment about the 'damned mob of scribbling women'. A later tale, more frequently anthologised, rewrites John Bunyan's *The Pilgrim's Progress* (1678) in terms of contemporary technology. In 'The Celestial Rail-Road'

(1843) Hawthorne, unlike Thoreau, sees no virtue in technological development. It merely speeds the path to hell. ' "The whole concern is a bubble," ' remarks Mr Stick-to-the-right. Another pilgrim, Mr Foot-it-to-Heaven, adds that ' "every man who buys a ticket must lay his account with losing the purchase-money – which is the value of his own soul" '.[38] Hawthorne, it seems, was deeply discomforted by railroads. In his memoir of his stay in England, *Our Old Home* (1863), he remarked that the countryside was never intended to be viewed in the linear manner that the railroad demanded. Likewise, a railroad journey in the 1851 novel, *The House of the Seven Gables*, is presented as a fortunately temporary dislocation of perspective.

The House of the Seven Gables can be read as a more general attack on American society. Hawthorne wrote two sentences in his notebook in 1849, when he was developing the plot of his novel: 'To inherit a great fortune. To inherit a great misfortune.'[39] They present in miniature much of his thought about the relationships between family, property and nationality. The noun 'fortune' (meaning both destiny and wealth) and its opposite, 'misfortune' (meaning adversity, but never meaning the absence of wealth), together present a semantic play on the concept of transmission between generations. The positive noun modifies the verb, 'to inherit', to convey an idea of the transmission of property, involving legal mechanisms to secure that transmission. The negative noun modifies the same verb in a different way, now suggesting the transmission of physical characteristics, and involving genetic mechanisms, which until recently were unlike legal mechanisms in that they contained no element of choice, but rather carried ideas of fate and fatality.

The political structure of the United States exacerbated the difference between the two kinds of inheritance. As the narrator of *The House of the Seven Gables* remarked about Hepzibah Pyncheon, at the point when she is transformed by poverty from 'patrician lady' to 'plebeian woman':

> In this republican country, amid the fluctuating waves of our social life, somebody is always at the drowning-point. The tragedy is enacted with as continual a repetition as that of a popular drama on a holiday; and, nevertheless, is felt as deeply, perhaps, as when an hereditary noble sinks below his order. More deeply; since, with us, rank is the grosser substance of wealth and a splendid establishment, and has no spiritual existence after the death of these, but dies hopelessly along with them. (38)

This suggests that property becomes a separate institution when social structure is based on genetic transmission. Loss of status does not necessarily follow loss of a fine house in an aristocracy. In a democracy it often does. We have seen the operation of economics in the writing of Franklin and Paine; and have observed its dreadful effect on the eponymous Charlotte Temple. The impact on Hepzibah is less deadly but still demeaning. Hepzibah is identified with any other huckster the minute that the urchin Ned Higgins hands over his cent for a gingerbread. The copper coin leaves an indelibly 'sordid stain' (51).

In *The House of the Seven Gables* Hawthorne underlines the identity of property and humanity by drawing on Poe's 1839 tale 'The Fall of the House

of Usher'. The narrator, approaching the house in Pyncheon-street, remarks on its 'human countenance' (1). The house implies the person who owns it. When he tells the legend of Alice Pyncheon, the daguerrotypist Holgrave remarks that the spirit of the founder, Colonel Pyncheon, seems to pervade the place. When Gervayse Pyncheon agrees to transfer the property to Matthew Maule, the portrait of the Colonel seems to start out of its frame. A resemblance between the Colonel and the house's present owner, Judge Jaffrey, is intuited by his niece Phoebe and displayed in a comparison between the Colonel's portrait and the Judge's daguerrotype. This modern technology updates the old Puritan belief in types. The Colonel is a type of the Judge, who in turn is a type of the economic individual, whose:

> field of action lies among the external phenomena of life. They possess vast ability in grasping, and arranging, and appropriating to themselves, the big, heavy, solid un-realities, such as gold, landed estate, offices of trust and emolument, and public honors. With these materials, and with deeds of goodly aspect, done in the public eye, an individual of this class builds up, as it were, a tall and stately edifice, which, in the view of other people and ultimately in his own view, is no other than the man's character, or the man himself. Behold, therefore, a palace!

The shift from direct speech into metaphor, signalled by the phrase 'as it were', replicates the process by which an individual, intending to stamp a property with his own mark, is stamped by it. The exclamation mark at the close of the passage triumphantly proclaims the end of the process: the palace is the man and the metaphor has again become direct speech. The account of the palace that follows is an exercise in double meaning. In describing the edifice, the narrator is also describing the Judge. Most visitors are impressed by the edifice, but occasionally someone arrives 'before whose sadly gifted eye the whole structure melts into thin air', revealing 'the secret abomination' beneath. Holgrave is one such gifted person, who remarks: ' "To plant a family! The idea is at the bottom of most of the wrong and mischief which men do" ' (229–30, 185).

Despite all the mischief, *The House of the Seven Gables* ends happily, with the marriage of Holgrave and Phoebe and the house released of its curse. Hawthorne joined numbers of critics in believing that it was his best lengthy work so far. Modern critics have usually disagreed. They have seen his first novel, *The Scarlet Letter* (1850), as his most accomplished. With an allegorical architecture already sketched in 'The Celestial Rail-Road', *The Scarlet Letter* lent itself most clearly to mid-twentieth-century concerns. Similarly, of almost one hundred short stories, it is those portraying the Puritan past which have tended to be the most frequently reprinted. Several of them anticipate the sombre colouring of *The Scarlet Letter*. 'Young Goodman Brown' (1835) deals with a witches' sabbath outside Salem, while 'Alice Doane's Appeal' (also 1835) harks back to the notorious witchcraft trials in that town, and portrays Cotton Mather 'as the representative of all the hateful features of his time'. 'The Minister's Black Veil' (1836) and 'The Gray Champion' (1835) discuss incidents of 'darkness, and adversity, and peril'; while 'The May-Pole of Merry Mount' (1836) and 'Endicott and the Red Cross' (1838) look at moments in the harsh administration of John Endecott, who preceded John Winthrop to Massachusetts Bay. Such stories gave grist to the anti-Puritan mill of H. L. Mencken and William Carlos Williams, and prompted Lionel Trilling to compare Hawthorne with Kafka, although he noted that there was a 'decisive difference between them, that for Hawthorne the world is always and ineluctably *there* in a very stubborn and uncompromising way'.[40] Later critics have not been so discriminating. By erasing Hawthorne's contemporary world, they have been able to play several different kinds of enjoyable interpretative games with his works.

Hawthorne was, albeit reluctantly, a man of his world. Writing fiction did not provide adequate support, and on three occasions he accepted political appointments. The first was as measurer of salt and coal in the Boston Custom House; the second as surveyor of Salem Custom House, a job which lasted until he was ousted by political opponents in 1849. It was this second experience that informed the 'Custom House' Preface to *The Scarlet Letter*. In their search for interpretative potency, some critics pass quickly over 'The Custom House', or omit it entirely. But, despite Hawthorne's dissembling remarks in the Preface to the second edition – for 'The Custom House' had upset some fellow Salemites – it is integral to the meaning of the novel. In a work structured by symbols, many are shared between the two parts: light, mirrors, birds, vegetation. 'The Custom House' acts as a link between the past and the present, and as, in a comment by the narrator which is often separated from its context:

> a neutral territory, somewhere between the real world and fairy-land, where the Actual and the Imaginary may meet, and each imbue itself with the nature of the other.[41]

The meeting-point occurs when the scarlet letter found in the upper room seems to burn the hand of Mr Surveyor Pue. Similarly, the narrator points to a rose bush believed to have 'sprung up under the footsteps of the sainted Ann Hutchinson, as she entered the prison door'. In a direct address, he presents one of its roses to the reader:

> It may serve, let us hope, to symbolize some sweet moral blossom, that may be found along the track, or relieve the darkening close of a tale of human frailty and sorrow. (76)

This sounds whimsical. It could be an indicator of narrative uncertainty, or a confirmation of the irony already apparent in the reference to Anne Hutchinson as 'sainted'. The whimsy is developed by the portrayal of a 'sweet moral blossom' in each part. In 'The Custom House' it is, oddly enough, a 'man of business' bred 'from boyhood in the Custom-House' and of such perfect 'integrity' that he was 'thoroughly adapted to the situation which he held' (55). In *The Scarlet Letter* it is, of course, Pearl, the love-child who is at home in the woods and fields surrounding Salem. Otherwise, these are tales not of whimsy but of human frailty, like the weeds that convey physical and moral decay in the Salem of 1850 and two centuries earlier.

Decay, both within and across generations, is one of the central themes of the text. The retired sea-captains that form the majority of the staff of the Custom House are likened to the living dead. So too is Chillingworth, who in the pursuit of revenge for Hester's adultery, both infects Dimmesdale and becomes more deformed himself. When Dimmesdale dies, Chillingworth, as befits a Poesque double, loses his 'vital and intellectual force' (272). He soon follows Dimmesdale to the grave. The sins which afflict the community as a whole impact on later generations. The narrator remarks that, unlike 'those wives and maidens of English birth and breeding', who owed their robust figures and stout morals to its 'beef and ale', those of colonial origins revealed 'a fainter bloom, a more delicate and briefer beauty, and a slighter physical frame' (78). Hawthorne had read the theories of Buffon and Raynal about American degeneration and, it seems, agreed with them. There is a hint at the close that Pearl might have escaped to a healthier environment overseas.

Hester Prynne is a complex creation. She is often described as one of the most courageous figures in American literature. Certainly, she becomes one of the first semioticians; she succeeds in assigning fresh signifieds to the signifier 'A'. But her courage may only increase the extent of her failure. Her prophecy of 'a new truth' establishing 'the whole relation between man and woman on a surer ground of mutual happiness' is given not in direct speech, but by the narrator just one sentence before he records her death (275). This is the last of several hints that she is a type of Anne Hutchinson, which suggests another instance, in Hawthorne's view, of a woman who goes too far. Typology is rooted in recurrence rather than development, and hence is pessimistic. There was little enough optimism to be found in the history of Hawthorne's Puritan ancestors. The first American Hathorne, Major William, had been a pitiless judge. His son John had followed in his father's footsteps, gaining a kind of fame as one of the magistrates in the Salem trials of the 1690s. His mother's forbears, the sisters Anstice and Margaret Manning, had suffered from Salem justice. Convicted in 1681 of incest with their brother, they were whipped and made to stand on high stools during prayer day in the Salem meeting house. A Massachusetts law passed in the 1690s would have condemned them to wear a capital 'I' on their clothes. Shortly before their descendant published *Fanshawe*, he added a 'w' to his surname. If Hawthorne's orthographical change was an attempt to distance himself from Salem, it was even less successful than Hester's semiotic one. He remained under its thrall whenever he wrote about the New England past.

The Blithedale Romance (1852) deals with the New England present. Once again, although Hawthorne dissembles, the text has autobiographical elements. It is based on Brook Farm, a co-operative community nine miles from Boston which existed from 1841 to 1847. Under George Ripley, the Transcendental Club established the community to apply its theories of utopian socialism. Those interested included some of the leading New England intellectuals of the time: Theodore Parker, Orestes Brownson, Elizabeth Peabody, Margaret Fuller, Bronson Alcott and Emerson. Unlike these, Hawthorne actually lived on the Farm for some six months in 1841. The life of the community was simple, the intention co-operative. As Emerson put it in a journal entry: 'At Brook Farm one man ploughed all day, & one looked out of the window all day & drew his picture, and both received the same wages.' In 1843 it came under the influence of Albert Brisbane (1809–90), a follower of the theories of Charles Fourier, and the group began calling itself a 'phalanx'. The change in title did not assure longevity; the group dissolved in October 1847, shortly after a fire destroyed the nearly-completed meeting-place, the 'phalanstery'. Emerson gave the epitaph for Brook Farm in an essay, published post-humously in 1883. Brook Farm, he wrote, was 'a perpetual picnic, a French Revolution in small, an Age of Reason in a patty-pan'.[42]

Emerson's dismissal is savoury; Hawthorne's is scathing. The narrator, Miles Coverdale, is a version of Hawthorne himself, and his tale is less concerned with a utopian community than with a love triangle between the former black-smith Hollingsworth and Zenobia and Priscilla, who are modelled on the Munro daughters in *The Last of the Mohicans*. Zenobia and Priscilla, too, are half-sisters. Zenobia, says Coverdale, is 'truly a magnificent woman', so pulchritudinous that he feels obliged to close his eyes, 'as if it were not quite the privilege of modesty to gaze at her'. In contrast, Coverdale describes Priscilla as insipid, prepubescent, as yet incapable of 'taking a very decided place among creatures of flesh and blood'. She seems out of place in Coverdale's early vision of the community, presented as an exaggerated version of pastoral:

> Emerging into the genial sunshine, I half fancied that the labors of the brotherhood had already realized some of Fourier's predictions. Their enlightened culture of the soil, and the virtues with which they sanctified their life, had begun to produce an effect upon the material world and its climate. In my new enthusiasm, man looked strong and stately! – and woman, oh, how beautiful! – and the earth, a green garden, blossoming with many-colored delights![43]

The vision proves yet again to have a baseless fabric, to the extent that Coverdale becomes 'dizzy'. He repeats the capitalist image of Mr Stick-to-the-right, seeing Blithedale as an 'insubstantial bubble' (140). Yet Coverdale is no simple pilgrim, and the choice of his name is deeply ironic. Miles Coverdale (1488–1568) made the first translation of the complete Bible into English in 1535 and became a Puritan leader in the reign of Elizabeth. Hawthorne's Coverdale is hardly a type of his distinguished namesake, and his language is drawn more from Chaucer's 'The Miller's Tale' than the Bible. Coverdale spends much time observing the 'backside of the universe' (148). His narra-tion is scatological and sexual, replete with voyeuristic images, notoriously so in the reference to Priscilla's silk purses. One does not need to resort to Freud to find an image-pattern that is onanistic, even paedophile. Zenobia, by far the bolder of the two women, accuses him of 'groping for emotions in the dark corners of the heart' (214). So she has to go. Soon afterwards she drowns herself; and Coverdale finds one of her shoes, washes off the mud, and hangs on to it as a keepsake.

There is a good reason why Coverdale preferred Zenobia dead. The original Zenobia was queen of the Syrian town of Palmyra, captured in AD 273 by the

Emperor Aurelian, who restored unity to the Roman republic. It is likely that Hawthorne also chose the name for its homonymy to the Greek *xenos*, meaning strange or different. Coverdale coyly says that Zenobia is 'not her real name' (13). Many people at the time were quite clear that she was based on Margaret Fuller, who had drowned two years earlier in a shipwreck close to Fire Island, New York. She had been returning from Italy with Count Ossoli, whom she may have married and who had supported Mazzini, a founder of a later and much more short-lived Roman republic. In 1852 Emerson contributed to the *Memoirs of Margaret Fuller Ossoli* (edited by William Henry Channing), and noted in his journal that she had a 'rich & brilliant genius' but that Hawthorne had given her 'a dismal mask'. It is not hard to see why: Hawthorne regarded Fuller as a modern Anne Hutchinson, an 'ink-stained Amazon'. In her best-selling publication, *Woman in the Nineteenth Century* (1845), Fuller had attacked Hamlet's comment on Gertrude, 'frailty, thy name is woman' (I. ii. 146), making it an epigraph to her book and trawling the past to reveal numbers of women, real and fictional, who were far from frail. Like Mary Wollstonecraft before her, she preached equality for women:

> if you ask me what offices they may fill; I reply – any. I do not care what case you put; let them be sea-captains, if you will. I do not doubt there are women well-fitted for such an office . . .[44]

Like Wollstonecraft, too, Fuller had had to endure the criticism that her views had turned her into an 'unsex'd female'. Hawthorne, whose father had been a sea-captain, held a somewhat more complex view. Zenobia is the reverse of unsexed. An 'unconstrained' woman who is 'not exactly maidenlike', she is even too much for brawny Hollingsworth, who marries the frail Priscilla instead (47).

Coverdale remains a bachelor, and near the close of his narration mentions time spent 'rather agreeably' in Europe (246). In the year after publishing *The Blithedale Romance*, Hawthorne followed Coverdale abroad, taking up his third political appointment, as US consul in Liverpool. His four years in England were agreeable, but the only work that resulted was the affectionate memoir *Our Old Home* (1863). A two-year stay in Italy led to his last completed novel, *The Marble Faun* (1860). Its first chapter introduces the four major characters, who are cast in pairs, like those in *The Blithedale Romance*. There are two Americans. Kenyon is a sculptor, while Hilda is a copyist with 'clear and delicate' perceptions which help the accuracy of her imitations. She is a 'slender, brown-haired, New England girl' who is 'not overflowing with animal spirits'. Miriam, in contrast, is another unconstrained woman, this time of uncertain origins. Not one to take things at second hand, she is a painter: 'a beautiful and attractive woman', whose 'nature had a great deal of colour and, in accordance with it, so likewise did her pictures'. That Hawthorne was still brooding about Margaret Fuller, years after her death, is confirmed by his notebook for 1858, which records a meeting with a non-fictional American sculptor, Joseph Mozier, who had known Fuller and Ossoli in Rome. Ossoli 'was the handsomest man whom Mr. Mozier ever saw, but . . . half an idiot, and without any pretensions to be a gentleman'. Fuller 'was a great humbug' who had 'quite lost all power of literary production'. Hawthorne added that he liked her more now; she had collapsed 'like the weakest of her sisters' precisely because she had tried to transform herself into 'a work of art'. 'Providence' had been kind in ending her life before her 'awful joke' had been exposed.[45]

Hawthorne's notes caused a scandal when they were published in his son's biography in 1884. They served a more creative purpose in *The Marble Faun*, fleshed out into Miriam and the fourth character, Donatello. He is an Italian nobleman who bears a striking resemblance to the marble Faun of Praxiteles at the Roman Capitol. The likeness is 'the key-note' of the narrative, for Donatello is handsome and sensual, but 'anything but intellectually brilliant', and 'endowed with no principle of virtue' (19, 10). The two shortcomings, exaggerated by being constructed as rebuttals, are premonitory. Donatello is a Don Giovanni who tries to be 'the wildest dancer of them all' but, lacking Giovanni's intellectual and (im)moral stamina, can only dance to Miriam's tune (39). Inspired by love for her, Donatello commits a crime which, thrusting him from nature into guilt, from art into time, unites him with Miriam:

> She turned to him – the guilty, blood-stained, lonely woman – she turned to her fellow-criminal, the youth, so lately innocent, whom she had drawn into her doom. She pressed him close, close to her bosom, with a clinging embrace that brought their two hearts together, till the horrour and agony of each was combined into one emotion, and that, a kind of rapture. (139)

This is a complex moment. Its portrayal of the dissolution of identity seemingly relates it to the *Liebestod* of *Tristan und Isolde*, being written by Richard Wagner at about the same time. It may also contribute to the formal uncertainty which, as some critics have noted, characterises this novel more than the others that Hawthorne had completed. The sanctity of the individual is, after all, a central component of the bourgeois ideology of fiction. Yet Miriam is hardly a Wagnerian redemptive female. 'Carnal pride', to use the words of Hawthorne's early essay on Anne Hutchinson, has here been taken to Gothic excess. Later on, indeed, Miriam admits to a 'betrayal of woman's cause' by her 'lack of feminine modesty' (229). When Miriam and Donatello embrace they represent a resolution of the alternatives represented by another sculpture in the Capitol: 'a symbol (as apt at this moment as it was two thousand years ago) of the Human Soul, with its choice of Innocence or Evil close at hand, in the pretty figure of a child, clasping a dove to her bosom, but assaulted by a snake' (7).

At first sight this seems to be another Hawthornian attempt at conspicuous symbology. *The Marble Faun* is, however, far more than an Old World setting of 'The May-Pole of Merry Mount', with grim Puritans contending with frisking fauns and nymphs. The novel is more successful at escaping the gloom of Salem than it is from the dominating absence of Margaret Fuller. If *The Scarlet Letter* is overly weighted by a symbolic system which depends on the mediating presence of 'The Custom House', *The Marble Faun* benefits from a setting which, as that parenthesis suggests, is timeless yet transitory, bringing the symbology vividly to life. *The Marble Faun* is set in present-day Rome, a decade after Mazzini's republican uprising had been crushed and the Pope restored, with 'the Eternal City' once again at the heart of a religious empire. Hawthorne's description of the Pincian Hill therefore intersects a loving, long-breathed account of its gardens with references to 'the red-trowsered French soldiers' who now keep order, and their military band which 'flings out rich music over the poor old city, floating her with strains as loud as those of her own echoless triumphs' (79–80). Those triumphs are recorded in the visual remains of the earlier pagan empire, still existing alongside the religious. There is, for instance, an equestrian statue of Marcus Aurelius, emperor of Rome a century before Aurelian, portrayed with moonlight clothing 'the figure as it were with an imperial robe of light', making it 'the most majestic representation of the kingly character that ever the world has seen' (132). Counterpointed against these descriptions of the classical and religious empire are frequent references to the decay of the city and the disease of its populace.

The complexity of this analysis of Rome is signalled by that opening symbol 'of the Human Soul', which does not present the normal opposition of good/evil or innocence/experience, but the more oblique one of innocence/evil. Innocence, then, takes on a quality more dynamic, more susceptible to change than in relation to its conventional antonym, or that could be allowed by Manichaeism. The implications of this are worked out in the figure of Hilda, who has witnessed Donatello's crime and seeks to relieve her 'troubled heart'. The narrative is close to Hilda as she enters St Peter's, the 'World's Cathedral', and observes the other penitents as they escape the miasma of Rome:

> In the hottest fever-fit of life, they can always find, ready for their need, a cool, quiet, beautiful place of worship. They may enter its sacred precincts, at any hour, leaving the fret and trouble of the world behind them, and purifying themselves with a touch of holy-water at the threshold. In the calm interiour, fragrant of rich and soothing incense, they may hold converse with some Saint, their awful, kindly friend. And, most precious privilege of all, whatever perplexity, sorrow, guilt, may weigh upon their souls, they can fling down the dark burthen at the foot of the Cross, and go forth – to sin no more, nor be any longer disquieted – but to live again in the freshness and elasticity of innocence! (274, 282–3)

All this should be anathema to a God-fearing Puritan. But clearly it is not to Hilda, who confesses to a priest and reaches an understanding of, if not a conversion to, the richness of the Catholic faith and the serenity assured by the confessional. Neither is it to Hawthorne. The longest description of timebound Rome, 'like a long-decaying corpse', with 'narrow, crooked, intricate streets . . . where a chill wind forces its deadly breath into our lungs', is contained within Hawthorne's longest sentence, over 370 words. Constructed from repeated subordinate clauses and Jamesian in its nuancing sensitivity, the sentence shows that love and hate are not antonyms, but are intimately wound into each other (259–60). The physical exile from Salem had prompted Hawthorne to distance himself emotionally from his Puritan inheritance, and to create one of the most extended yet delicate dialogues between the Old and

New Worlds. It was a dialogue which would become one of the central themes of Henry James, who in 1879 published the first full-length critique of Hawthorne in that transatlantic series, English Men of Letters.

Explorations of identity: the fiction of Melville

In 1850 Herman Melville wrote an effusive review, 'Hawthorne and His Mosses', in which he praised 'this great power of blackness' in Hawthorne, proclaiming him a truly national author yet comparing him with Shakespeare for 'those occasional flashings-forth of the intuitive Truth in him; those short, quick probings at the very axis of reality'. The two men became friends about the same time, and in 1851 Melville dedicated *Moby-Dick* to Hawthorne. For Melville, this was an unfortunate turning point. Whereas Hawthorne's reputation continued to grow, Melville's began a long decline. In 1879 Henry James's *Hawthorne* became the first volume devoted to an American in the English Men of Letters series. It took another forty-seven years before Melville was included in a later series, in a volume written by an Englishman, John Freeman, as part of the revival of interest in his work in the 1920s. 'Hawthorne and His Mosses' hints at the reason for the striking contrast in the popularity of the two writers. England 'is in many things alien to us', he wrote. 'China has more bonds of real love for us than she.' To put it bluntly, if Hawthorne looked back, Melville looked outwards. Hawthorne's 'probings at the very axis of reality' were grounded in a strong sense of the nation's Anglo-American past. Melville sought the axis of reality, rather, in space. As the poet Charles Olson (1910–70) put it, opening his account of Melville:

> I take SPACE to be the central fact to man born in America, from Folsom Cave to now. I spell it large because it comes large here. Large, and without mercy.

In his increasingly complicated examination of that 'central fact', Melville had little mercy on his readers, and they repaid him in kind.[46]

The publications in the five years before *Moby-Dick* were popular, in some respects sensational. In February 1846 the London publisher John Murray brought out in his Home and Colonial Library Melville's *Narrative of a Four Months' Residence among the Natives of a Valley of the Marquesas Islands*. A month later the narrative appeared in New York as *Typee*, the title by which the book is now known. The subtitle of both editions, *A Peep at Polynesian Life*, hints at voyeurism, while the text claims to discuss matters omitted by the earlier South Sea narratives that it mentions. Indeed, *Typee* was so unlike them that some critics suspected that it was mere fiction, while others were horrified by the sexuality displayed even in the early expurgated editions. The lengthy description of 'the beauteous nymph Fayaway', at once 'the very perfection of female grace' and 'a child of nature' turned her into a sex symbol of a potency to be found in the paintings of Paul Gauguin, and not seen in Europe until the appearance of Josephine Baker in Paris in 1925, at just the time that Melville's work was being read once again. The narrative in *Typee* is simple and vivid: it relates the adventures of two sailors who jumped ship, the disappearance of one (who reappears again in a brief sequel), and the eventual return to 'civilization' of the other. The structure is more complex: the text is constructed as a fortunate fall out of time into sex, separated from the seagoing narrative by moments of unconsciousness, and confirmed by the name 'Tommo', which is given to the narrator only while he is in this timeless existence. Even the landscape is sexualised in this waking dream. Sometimes it is quite crude, as in the mention of a 'Buggerry Island' – which can no longer be found on the map. More often the presentation is sophisticated, as in the description of the bay of Nukahiva, the rhythm of the prose and use of key words presenting a paradisal environment in terms of coition:

> From the verge of the water the land rises uniformly on all sides, with green and sloping acclivities, until from gently rolling hill-sides and moderate elevations it insensibly swells into lofty and majestic heights, whose blue outlines, ranged all around, close in the view. The beautiful aspect of the shore is heightened by deep and romantic glens, which come down to it at almost equal distances, all apparently radiating from a common centre, and the upper extremities of which are lost to the eye beneath the shadow of the mountains. Down each of these little valleys flows a clear stream, here and there assuming the form of a slender cascade, then stealing invisibly along until it bursts upon the sight again in larger and more noisy water-falls, and at last demurely wanders along to the sea.[47]

Melville is not merely employing the cunning displacements of Victorian pornography. The depiction of sex as nature, and natural, is a critique of shipboard licentiousness, presented as 'unholy passions'; and of the intrusiveness of 'European civilizers', comically depicted as the striptease of a missionary's wife (50, 39). Industrial societies also fare poorly; in 'civilization' sexual activity is no recreation but driven by need, accompanied by penalties, and marked by discontinuity from all other acts (165). The critique of industrialisation here anticipates Marcuse and unexpectedly aligns Melville with the Southern apologists for chattel slavery, with whom he probably did not agree. It is part of a thoroughgoing analysis in which the 'civilized world' fares badly. In an extended passage, Tommo asserts that 'for every advantage she imparts', civilisation 'holds a hundred evils in reserve'. Using yet another negative catalogue, this one derived from Swift's splendidly splenetic list in *Gulliver's Travels*, he combines the biblical comment that 'money is the root of all evil' (I Timothy 6:10) with an analysis resembling Montaigne's 'Of the Caniballes', to conclude that:

> In this secluded abode of happiness there were no cross old women, no cruel step-dames, no withered spinsters, no love-sick maidens, no sour old bachelors, no in-attentive husbands, no melancholy young men, no blubbering youngsters, and no squalling brats. All was mirth, fun, and high good humour. Blue devils, hypochondria, and doleful dumps, went and hid themselves among the nooks and crannies of the rocks. (182)

And yet, unlike Poe in *The Narrative of Arthur Gordon Pym* (1838), Melville returns the narrator rather than the narrative to 'civilization'. Also unlike

Montaigne, he treated cannibalism objectively, as the evil lurking behind the innocent facade of the Typees. Melville was reluctantly committed to the 'civilization' of the United States, and *Typee* was intended as an antidote to its 'doleful dumps'. His readership, however, required a further holiday, and he obliged with a sequel, *Omoo* (1847). It was quickly followed by a further four sea-novels: *Mardi* (1849), *Redburn* (1849), *White-Jacket* (1850) and *Moby-Dick* (1851).

The record to 1851 seems to support Albert Camus's remark that 'Melville never wrote anything but the same book, which he began again and again'.[48] This is true at first sight. As with many, Melville's early experiences coloured his life. He was proud of his family, and was related through his father to Scottish nobility and through his mother to the Dutch patroons. Good connections, but no money. The family fortune had been wiped out, and Melville therefore began work at the age of twelve, doing a variety of jobs until he signed on as a seaman. He worked on a number of ships. First it was the merchantman *St Lawrence* in 1839, bound from New York for Liverpool. Then, in 1841, it was the whaler *Acushnet*. Finally, in 1843, it was the frigate USS *United States*. The variety of seagoing inspired much of his writing, for it gave him the best possible exercise in comparative sociology. It took him to many different places, and introduced him to the greatest possible variety of humankind. He met the natives of Liverpool and the Marquesas. He took orders from merchant and naval officers. He worked with fellow sailors ranging from 'the scum of the sea' – to adapt a remark of the Duke of Wellington – to other well-born out-of-pocket or adventurous young men like Charles Dana, who in 1840 would publish his own experiences in *Two Years Before the Mast*.

Camus's comment, however, is only true at first sight. Most travel narratives end up at a different place. *Mardi* is an allegory that mixes *Gulliver's Travels* with a number of other texts, including *The Travels of Sir John Mandeville*, thereby replacing Swift's unifying disgust with a rich multiplicity of viewpoints. It ends, therefore, with no conclusion but with the narrator, Taji, pursued by 'three fixed specters . . . over an endless sea'. *Redburn*, in contrast, is a version of Melville's voyage on the *St Lawrence*. Told by Wellingborough Redburn, the son of a middle-class family oppressed by 'sad disappointments', it gives a realistic account of the noxious existence both aboard ship and in Liverpool, interrupted by the occasional general comment:

> There is something in the contemplation of the mode in which America has been settled, that, in a noble breast, should forever extinguish the prejudices of national dislikes.
>
> Settled by the people of all nations, all nations may claim her for their own . . . our blood is as the flood of the Amazon, made up of a thousand noble currents all pouring into one. We are not a nation, so much as a world . . .

Redburn therefore joins Longfellow's *Kavanagh*, published in the same year, in calling on the melting-pot theory as a source of Americanism.[49]

White-Jacket contains a more direct comment on the United States. Like Dana's *Two Years Before the Mast*, it includes horrific accounts of the authoritarian system aboard American ships, maintained by a practice of flogging (145). Dana, Melville and others protested that flogging transformed free men into slaves. Congress reasserted the distinction between Blacks and whites by prohibiting flogging in the same month, September 1850, that it passed the Fugitive Slave Act. Melville shows, though, that flogging is symptomatic of a greater evil on board. The narrator suggests that the reasons for maintaining a force of marines aboard naval vessels is not only to man the guns, but to act as watchdogs to the sailors:

> what standing armies are to nations, what turnkeys are to jails, these marines are to the seamen in all large men-of-war. Their muskets are their keys ... the mutual contempt, and even hatred, subsisting between these two bodies of men – both clinging to one keel, both lodged in one household – is held by most Navy officers as the height of the perfection of Navy discipline ... Thus they reason: secure of this antagonism between the marine and the sailor, we can always rely upon it, that if the sailor mutinies, it needs no great incitement for the marine to thrust his bayonet through his heart; if the marine revolts, the pike of the sailor is impatient to charge. Checks and balances, blood against blood, *that* is the cry and the argument.[50]

This is an indictment of another savage naval practice. It is also a fear, expressed metaphorically, about a nation, the 'household', divided by racial animosity. The passage begins with the phrase designed to provoke American anger: 'standing army'. One of the complaints against George III in the Declaration of Independence was that he had 'kept among us, in times of peace, Standing Armies without the Consent of our legislature'; while the Second and Third Amendments to the Constitution, which went into effect in 1791, were designed so that the United States relied in peacetime on a militia, rather than a regular army, with its potential threat to liberty. The indictment ends with an ironic use of the argument for 'checks and balances', which inspired the Constitutional separation of executive, legislative and judicial branches of the US government. The argument for 'checks and balances' here uses that political philosophy to oppose the melting-pot theory, the mingled 'blood' of the seagoing 'household'. The founding documents of the United States are therefore ignored or perverted in order to prevent liberty.

White-Jacket, together with its predecessors, could be said to have used the sea-story as a vehicle for reflecting on the cultural space of the United States. They might perhaps be called dry runs for *Moby-Dick*, for in this novel there is the greatest leverage between plot and reflection. The plot is simple. As Ruth says in *Wonderful Town*, Leonard Bernstein's 1952 musical: 'I was re-reading *Moby Dick* the other day ... it's about this whale.' Indeed it is. Melville's epic, like Poe's *The Narrative of Arthur Gordon Pym*, is based on Jeremiah Reynolds's 1839 account of 'Mocha Dick'. Reynolds described 'Mocha Dick' as 'a freak of nature'. He added that 'this renowned monster, who had come off victorious in a hundred fights with his pursuers, was an old bull whale, of prodigious size and strength'. Melville turned a freak into a force of nature, and developed Reynolds's brief tale into a plot which takes the central narrator, the youthful Ishmael, to the Massachusetts port of New Bedford, where he meets a Polynesian prince, Queequeg. They join a whaler crewed by many different races, and sail into the South Seas, where the obsessive hatred of Captain Ahab leads them into a search for the great whale. This narrative threads its way through a text of such size that George Ripley, in an astute review in Greeley's New York *Tribune*, called it 'a "Whaliad", or the Epic of that veritable old leviathan'.[51]

The two nouns of Ripley's explanatory subtitle give us an entry to *Moby-Dick*. The novel contains many of the features and conventions of epic, to be found in texts like the *Epic of Gilgamesh* and *The Odyssey* and first mapped onto America in the Norse sagas. An element of epic is, of course, the participation of the supernatural, which in this instance is the whale. Ripley included in his review a description of the leviathan paraphrased from the Book of Job (41:7, 26–9). Most biblical exegetes believed that the leviathan (the Hebrew name for a water monster) was a whale and, together with that other invincible monster, the behemoth, was a symbol of the immense, inscrutable power of God. Ripley, who in 1841 had resigned his Unitarian ministry to pursue his Transcendentalist beliefs in reform, created a more complex symbol by calling Moby Dick 'the whale-demon' (609). This is nothing compared with the symbology produced by Ishmael in the chapter where he speculates on the meaning of 'The Whiteness of the Whale'. Ishmael begins by signalling the importance of his speculation, for if we do not understand him 'all these chapters might be naught' (159). There follows an account of the meaning of whiteness to different cultures, and the chapter ends with three short and two extended sentences, necessarily abbreviated here, as Ishmael tries to explain the monomania with which Ahab has infected the crew:

> Is it that by its indefiniteness it shadows forth the heartless voids and immensities of the universe, and thus stabs us from behind with the thought of annihilation, when beholding the white depths of the milky way? Or is it, that as in essence whiteness is not so much a color as the visible absence of color, and at the same time the concrete of all colors; is it for these reasons that there is such a dumb blankness, full of meaning, in a wide landscape of snows – a colorless, all-color of atheism from which we shrink? And when we consider that other theory of the natural philosophers, that all other earthly hues . . . are but subtile deceits, not actually inherent in substances, but only laid on from without; so that all deified Nature absolutely paints like the harlot, whose allurements cover nothing but the charnel-house within; and when we proceed further, and consider that the mystical cosmetic which produces every one of her hues, the great principle of light, for ever remains white or colorless in itself, and if operating without medium upon matter, would touch all objects, even tulips and roses, with its own blank tinge – pondering all this, the palsied universe lies before us like a leper; and . . . so the wretched infidel gazes himself blind at the monumental white shroud that wraps all the prospect around him. And of these things the Albino whale was the symbol. Wonder ye then at the fiery hunt? (165)

What are we to make of this? It is as if Taji has turned, and is pursuing the 'specters'; or as if Ishmael has picked up *The Narrative of Arthur Gordon Pym*, treated its closure as incomplete and, pushing past the 'shrouded human figure' that blocks the way to the final chasm, has begun an exploration of the blankness of the inexpressible.[52]

We can disperse some of the fog around Ishmael's speculation if we refer to Melville's reading, and to geometry. Remember that, while he was working on *Moby-Dick*, Melville praised both Hawthorne and Shakespeare for 'those short, quick probings at the very axis of reality'. He was also reading Thomas Carlyle's *Sartor Resartus*, which first appeared in a complete edition in Boston in 1836. While it would be going too far to call Ishmael a seagoing son of Diogenes Teufelsdrökh, his narration here has taken on the fustian qualities of the Professor's speech. In particular, Ishmael has swallowed Teufelsdrökh's lesson that 'the Universe . . . bears visible record of invisible things; but is, in the transcendental sense, symbolical as well as real'.[53] Carlyle is another writer probing at the axis of reality. He can do no more than probe because, geometrically, an axis is a straight line, and hence one-dimensional and invisible. It can be calculated only by reference to the system that rotates symmetrically about it. It nevertheless exists, and both Ishmael and Teufelsdrökh conceive it as lying at the nexus between physics and metaphysics, anchoring the nature of belief to that of the universe. This is why so much of the text is given over, as Ishmael puts it, to a 'systematized exhibition of the whale' (115).

Ahab shares Ishmael's belief that the visible is the record of invisible things. Unlike Ishmael, Ahab tries to grasp the invisible. Ishmael uses verbs of meditation, Ahab verbs of violent action. Starbuck, his God-fearing first mate, accuses Ahab of blasphemy for wishing ' "vengeance on a dumb brute" '. In front of the assembled crew, Ahab responds:

> 'All visible objects, man, are but as pasteboard masks . . . If man will strike, strike through the mask! How can the prisoner reach outside except by thrusting through the wall? To me, the white whale is that wall, shoved near to me . . . He tasks me; he heaps me; I see in him outrageous strength, with an inscrutable malice sinewing it. That inscrutable thing is chiefly what I hate; and be the white whale agent, or be the white whale principal, I will wreak that hate upon him. Talk not to me of blasphemy, man; I'd strike the sun if it insulted me.' (140)

Ahab orders the three mates to cross lances and, grasping 'the three level, radiating lances at their crossed centre', touches the 'axis'. This sacramental act seems to release another natural force: 'by some nameless, interior volition, he would fain have shocked into them the same fiery emotion accumulated within the Leyden jar of his own magnetic life'. The 'shock' of Ahab's 'electric thing' suggests a second nexus, between physics and metaphysics. In the century since the first capacitor was invented in the Dutch town of Leiden, experiments conducted by scientists on both continents, including Benjamin Franklin, pointed to the conclusion that electricity could be the origin of life itself. Mary Shelley's novel, *Frankenstein* (1818), invoked the myth of Prometheus to link modern science with sacrilege. Melville, who had read *Frankenstein* while preparing *Moby-Dick*, made Ahab an overreacher like Shelley's scientist, and depicts the quarterdeck committal as a Black Mass (141–2).

Moby-Dick, like *Frankenstein*, is deeply indebted to *Paradise Lost*. Ahab has many of the qualities of Milton's Satan. Captain Peleg calls him a 'grand, ungodly, god-like man' (78). The link between Satan and Ahab is underlined when they both set sail. Milton's narrator deploys the imagery of sailing to describe Satan's plan to visit the earth: 'Into this wilde Abyss the warie Fiend/ Stood on the brink of Hell and lookd a while,/Pondering his Voyage' (II, 917–19). When he first sees Ahab, Ishmael imagines his leader as Satan, staring ahead of the ship with 'an infinity of firmest fortitude, a determinate, unsurrenderable wilfulness, in the fixed and fearless, forward dedication of that glance' (109). Like Satan, Ahab uses guile to exercise absolute control over Pandemonium, his floating palace, the *Pequod*. Yet Ahab is not sportive. He merely threatens the sun. In contrast, Satan plays with homonymy (sun, Son) to associate the pagan myth of Icarus to his own sin of 'Pride and worse Ambition' (IV, 37–40). It is Father Mapple who points the lesson of Ahab's voyage, before it takes place. His text is the best-known tale of a whale: 'Now the lord had prepared a great fish to swallow up Jonah' (Jonah 1:17). Mapple calls the Book of Jonah ' "one of the smallest strands in the mighty cable of the Scriptures" ' but his lengthy hellfire exegesis, decked out with lessons in seamanship, turns it into one of the Bible's most solemn admonitions: ' "if we obey God, we must disobey ourselves" ' (46–53). The voyage of the *Pequod* is an illustration of Mapple's sermon, an elaboration on the consequences of the sin of *hubris*.

Ahab and Mapple are solemn creatures. But *Moby-Dick*, like *Paradise Lost*, has its moments of fun. For, as George Ripley spotted when he called *Moby-Dick* a 'Whaliad', the novel is a burlesque as well as an epic. It begins with a parodic retelling of St John's retelling of Genesis: 'In the beginning was the Word, and the Word was with God, and the Word was God' (St John 1:1). The Word is an 'Etymology' provided by 'a Late Consumptive Usher to a Grammar School'. He is succeeded by a 'mere painstaking burrower and grub-worm of a poor devil of a Sub-Sub' Librarian, who supplies several pages of 'Extracts', beginning with Genesis 1:21, 'And God created great whales', and including the text of Mapple's sermon (7–8). Only when this recital is exhausted is the narrator allowed to step onstage with his famous injunction, 'Call me Ishmael' (18). He has named himself after a 'wild man', the son of the Jewish patriarch Abraham by his Egyptian handmaid Hagar (Genesis 16:12) and destined, according to tradition, to become the ancestor of the Arabs. He sees himself, with some reason, as an outsider, yet with a guardian angel, like the biblical Ishmael (Genesis 21:17–18). His narration from the outset warms the chilling northeasterly winds of Calvinism with a cheering breeziness.

The repeated fricatives in Ishmael's first description of Ahab suggest that his frightened view of the fearsome captain is mediated by humour. Ishmael has, moreover, just described the 'pivot-hole' bored in the planking; Ahab maintains his upright, 'singular posture' by sticking his whale-stump into it (109). Writing with hindsight, Ishmael knows that the tectonics of the Christian practice of carpentry will save none but himself. He can therefore afford a droll view of Calvinism. He dismisses Mapple's sermon in favour of another night in bed with the Polynesian prince. In Chapter 83, 'Jonah Historically Regarded', Ishmael dwells upon Mapple's text and destroys it with common sense, anticipating those modern Bible critics who suggest that the Book can only be intelligible as a parody. In contrast, the 'cosy, loving' night with Queequeg is treated with warmth rather than ridicule. Ishmael's 'melting' feelings both recall the sexual paradise of *Typee*, and anticipate Chapter 94. 'A Squeeze of the Hand' describes the intimacy of squeezing sperm-oil with Ishmael's shipmates, and ends with a comical vision of 'long rows of angels in paradise, each with his hands in a jar of spermaceti' (56–7, 287–8, 322–3). This, too, has its source in *Paradise Lost*. When Adam asks Raphael if the 'heav'nly Spirits' express love by 'virtual or immediat touch', the archangel, blushing, responds that when angels embrace they 'obstacle find none of membrane, joint, or limb' (VIII, 615–29). Melting feelings occur both in Heaven and the Spouter-Inn.

So the text proceeds on its broad highway, tacking between encyclopaedia and action story, between epic and burlesque. It is a function both of its diversity and loose construction that it can respond to many differing approaches. It has been read from many points of view, including those of myth-criticism, psychoanalysis, cultural materialism, deconstruction and postcolonialism.[54] It has often been treated as an analysis of the wider significance of the United States which, after the Civil War, increasingly regarded itself as the beacon of freedom. In 1923 D. H. Lawrence added lines about a 'terrible fatality' to his essay on *Moby-Dick*, asserting that America equalled 'the doom of our white day'. F. O. Matthiessen had a cooler and perhaps more complex view. He wrote in 1941 that 'Melville's hopes for American democracy, his dread of its lack of humane warmth, his apprehension of the actual privations and defeats of the common man, and his depth of compassion for courageous struggle unite in giving fervor to the declaration of his purpose in writing *Moby-Dick*.' One could steer a path between those two views by suggesting that the novel links a contemplation of the cultural space of the United States with an enquiry into the origins of sin within the physics of the universe. It follows that what begins as ceticide ends as a holocaust.[55]

There have been a number of reinterpretations of *Moby-Dick* in the century of total war. In particular, Melville's theme of a compulsive, claustrophobic all-male environment, where a boat is both hunter and hunted, recurs in many of the novels and films about submarine warfare that have been made since the 1930s. One instance is Mark Rascovich's novel, *The Bedford Incident* (1963), which maps Melville's novel very precisely onto a Cold War incident in the Denmark Strait, to the extent of nicknaming the American captain Ahab, and the Soviet submarine *Moby Dick*. James B. Harris's film, made two years later, is much more effective because it drops the nicknames and develops Melville's themes in the light of *Dr Strangelove* (Stanley Kubrick, 1963), to show how the crew of the USS *Bedford* is driven into a nuclear exchange with the submarine. Cyril James, a Trinidadian Marxist cricket commentator, explains most clearly the modern significance of *Moby-Dick*, by suggesting that it predicts modern political conditions where a 'society of free individualism would give birth to totalitarianism and be unable to defend itself against it'. *Moby-Dick*, one might say, slept until it was awakened by Hitler's kiss.[56]

Melville's love affair with his American readership ended with the appearance of the first negative reviews of *Moby-Dick*. Thereafter, the relationship would be antagonistic. *Pierre* (1852) was greeted as 'a mystic romance, in which are conjured up unreal nightmare-conceptions, a confused phantasmagoria of distorted fancies and conceits, ghostly abstractions and fitful shadows'. In retrospect, it is not surprising that the novel received such a response. It begins in a mock pastoral, when Pierre, 'issuing from the embowered and high-gabled old home of his fathers', is greeted by a high-summer 'verdant trance', through which 'nothing came but the brindled kine, dreamily wandering to their pastures, followed, not driven, by ruddy-cheeked, white-footed boys'. There follows an account 'full of blood, violence, wrong, and iniquity of every kind'. These words are from an incomplete pamphlet of one 'Plotinus Plinlimmon', that is inserted into the text with the instruction that 'each person can now skip, or read and rail for himself'.[57] The novel, it is now clear, appeared in the wrong century. It looks back to the jokey, self-conscious narratives of Lawrence Sterne, and forward to the comic-apocalyptic mode of Nathanael West. *Israel Potter* (1855) fared little better. Melville drew on the supposed *Life and Adventures of I. R. Potter, who was a soldier in the American Revolution* (1824) and from it fashioned a picaresque narrative in which the protagonist takes part in the Battle of Bunker Hill, is captured by the British and shipped to England, consorts with revolutionary sympathisers, meets Franklin in Paris, befriends John Paul Jones and takes part in his most famous battle, and eventually returns poverty-stricken to the United States, to 'record his fortunes' only to have them 'faded out of print'. It received a mixed response – an English reviewer called it 'not a bad shilling's worth for any railway reader' – but it soon followed the fate of its model.[58]

In 1856 Melville collected some short stories he had published in magazines within the previous three years, and added a title-sketch. *The Piazza Tales* were briefly reviewed and coolly received. It included some tales now frequently anthologised. Melville's view is now more pessimistic. The sea-story, 'Benito Cereno', gives an account of race relations much more deceptive and troubling than the paradisal *Typee*. 'The Encantadas, or Enchanted Isles' reveal little enchantment. They are a set of ten sketches about 'a group rather of extinct volcanoes than of isles; looking much as the world at large might, after a penal conflagration'. They are more depressing than Cooper's angry *The Crater*, for the isles are a microcosm of the cemetery that is the earth. Even more depressing is 'Bartleby', which is deeply cynical about the value of composition. For Bartleby is a copyist. His work involves him in the mere act of writing, without any external referents. Despite this, he seems initially to 'gorge himself' on documents, but then, without explanation, he begins to refuse his duties. He does so by adopting the rhetorical structure, 'I would prefer not to.' That structure begins to run his life, then leads him inexorably into the final negation of death.[59]

The Confidence-Man, published in London and New York on April Fool's Day 1857, is an extended play on the two meanings of the title. On the first of April, a man boards the steamboat *Fidèle*, another scale model of the *United*

States, bound down the Mississippi from St Louis to New Orleans. He writes on a slate a version of the comments of St Paul on charity, from his First Epistle to the Corinthians: 'Charity thinketh no evil . . . suffereth long, and is kind . . . endureth all things . . . believeth all things . . . never faileth.' The other passengers think he is mad. They prefer a phrase from another sacred text, 'The Star-Spangled Banner', but invert it to 'NO TRUST', the sign seen on shop doors ashore, and also gracing the barber's shop aboard. They have no confidence in the teachings of St Paul, who begins his account of charity like this:

> Though I speak with the tongues of men and of angels, and have not charity, I am become as sounding brass, or a tinkling cymbal. (I Corinthians 13:1)

Charity, then, distinguishes language from noise. But the man is a deaf-mute, and the distinction means nothing to him. The theme of the text is summarised by a handbill found in the saloon, where the gamblers congregate: 'ODE ON THE INTIMATIONS OF DISTRUST IN MAN, UNWILLINGLY INFERRED FROM REPEATED REPULSES, IN DISINTERESTED ENDEAVOURS TO PROCURE HIS CONFIDENCE.' What follows is a series of masques, in which confidence is undermined by a wide range of confidence-men. The trickster is one of the earliest figures in the literature of the United States, begun by Teague Oregan in Brackenridge's *Modern Chivalry*, and still is an important figure in American culture. With this novel, Melville came closest to Edgar Allan Poe's interest in metamorphosis. The response to *The Confidence-Man*, like that to Poe's work, was mixed. One London reviewer thanked Melville for attacking 'the money-getting spirit which appears to pervade every class of man in the States, almost like a monomania'. Another, noting that the text ended with the suggestion that 'something further may follow of this Masquerade', responded 'the less the merrier'. Whether Melville's last sentence was a confidence-trick or not, we shall never know. He published no further prose in his lifetime.[60]

Melville did, however, leave one tale unpublished. In an authorial intrusion in *Moby-Dick*, he noted that 'small erections may be finished by their first architects; grand ones, true ones, ever leave the copestone to posterity' (125). The architectural imagery was repeated in Melville's *opus posthumous*, completed shortly before his death in 1891 but not published until 1924. A factual narrative will always, he wrote, 'be less finished than an architectural finial'.[61] The timing of the tale is certainly precise enough; it is the summer of 1797, shortly after the British naval mutinies of Spithead and the Nore. There is also, as there had been for all Melville's sea stories, a personal dimension. A cousin, Guert Gansevoort, had served in 1842 as an investigating officer when three members of the US warship *Somers* were hanged for mutiny. The *Somers* affair was controversial; among other things, the case against the men was slim. James Fenimore Cooper, in a review attached to the published *Proceedings* of the affair, believed that the events on the ship had been illegal and had therefore dishonoured the United States. He reflected on the affair in his 1844 novel, *Afloat and Ashore*, as did Melville in *White-Jacket*. Melville's second response, in *Billy Budd*, was altogether more ambiguous, to the extent that critics have debated the meaning of the text ever since. It is not so much that Melville equivocated about his cousin's role in the *Somers* affair. The narrator in *Billy Budd* suggests that the captain of HMS *Bellipotent*, just like the USS *Somers*, felt that military 'urgency' overrode other considerations (391). The ambiguity of the text arises more from the conflict of laws and their appropriate styles. It is the subtle blend of allegory and realism that makes *Billy Budd* the copestone of Melville's nautical works.

The three characters who are the protagonists of the tale are realistically described, yet their roles are heavily freighted with biblical allegory, principally from Genesis and the four Gospels. John Claggart is the basilisk of the *Bellipotent*. His pallid face, surrounded by 'silken jet curls', separates him from his 'bronzed' shipmates as much as his office (342). He is master-at-arms, responsible for discipline aboard ship; sailors dislike him more than they do the marines. The eponymous Billy, too, is of uncertain origins. The likeness ends there, for Billy is a handsome and innocent foundling, faithful to his duty, and a natural leader. Edward Vere is both the captain and an aristocrat, and therefore an appointed leader on two grounds. Yet he is also an exceptional captain, intrepid and resolute, an intellectual who wears lightly if firmly the absolute power conferred upon him by the laws of war. He is a bachelor 'old enough to have been Billy's father' (392). When Billy kills Claggart he releases the sailors from an evil tyranny, but invokes the judgement of his shipboard father. The foremast from which the Foretopman is hung remains in the memory of the sailors: 'to them a chip of it was as a piece of the Cross' (408). It is a more true memorial to Billy than the official record, 'News from the Mediterranean', which acts as one of the three codas to the tale. It is not clear whether 'News from the Mediterranean' was intended as an ironic comment on the *Proceedings* of the *Somers* affair, or on the numerous but more informal newspaper reports. It may never be clear; but opacity is essential to a resurrection, such as happened to the text of *Billy Budd*.

The nation in flux: Edgar Allan Poe

Edgar Allan Poe has always had an uncertain reputation. James Russell Lowell, writing 'A Fable for Critics' the year before Poe's death, set the tone for subsequent criticism with his vicious little couplet:

> There comes Poe, with his raven, like Barnaby Rudge,
> Three-fifths of him genius and two-fifths sheer fudge.[62]

Unfortunately for Poe, American writers and critics have tended to fasten on the fudge. Henry James, for instance, declared that 'an enthusiasm for Poe is the mark of a decidedly primitive stage of reflection'. T. S. Eliot followed him by saying that Poe had 'the intellect of a highly gifted young person before puberty'. Allen Tate was one of several twentieth-century Southern writers indebted to Poe, and believed that his great-grandfather was acquainted with the writer. Yet even he imagined his forbear standing 'smiling and bowing at the madman Poe'.

In contrast, the three-fifths which apparently constituted Poe's genius has consistently been lionised by the French, to the extent that Malcolm Cowley once suggested a name change to 'Aidgarpo'. Baudelaire, the first translator, said in a letter that 'Edgar Poe, who isn't much in America, must become a great man in France – at least that is what I want.' Baudelaire's wish has been realised, for Poe has been praised, among others, by the writers Gautier, Rimbaud, Maupassant, Verne, Maeterlinck and the Goncourt brothers. The epigrammatic style of his 'Marginalia' – brief *jeux d'esprit* appended to those magazines with which he was involved – persists in the work of the sociologist Jean Baudrillard. His tales have been subject to close semiotic and psychoanalytic analysis by such as Marie Buonaparte, Roland Barthes, Jacques Lacan and Jacques Derrida. He inspired a painting by Gauguin and music by Debussy. Where the French have led others have followed. Lawrence wrote an approving essay in *Studies in Classic American Literature*, calling him 'almost more a scientist than an artist' – an insight that may help to account for the rapturous response of the French. Poe has also been appreciated in Austria, Germany, Italy, Portugal, Russia (where he influenced the work of Dostoevsky) and Spain. The impact of his work is even to be found, it is said, in Serbian and Croatian literature.[63]

The divergence between Poe's reputation inside and outside America has caused deracination. Poe is admired for his complex symbolism, his literary theories, his psychological insights, his pioneering detective stories, and his skill with science fiction. Appropriately, he has come to be seen as a forerunner of twentieth-century science by suggesting that science is not just 'dull realities', as he put it in his 1827 'Sonnet – To Science', but is vitally influenced by human perception. The problem is that these aspects of Poe are generic. They emphasise his cosmopolitan qualities. Until recently he has usually not been identified as an American writer. The 1926 interpretation by Joseph Wood Krutch, influenced by Freud, represented a common view:

> The works of Poe have no place in the American literary tradition . . . it is very near the absolute truth to say that for him the American scene was non-existent.

Poe seems to be a deeply unsettling writer, brilliant but elusive, even unAmerican. Indeed, he seems so shifty that the editor of a 1915 Spanish collection of his poems claimed that he had died by spontaneous combustion.[64]

There is little doubt that Poe's work and life helped cause such extravagant assessments of him. He argued with many of the well-known literary figures of his age, and was noted for his damning judgements. He disliked Wordsworth, and what he called 'the cant of the lakists'. Carlyle bored him to death. Elizabeth Barrett Browning, he thought, was imitative and affected, although that did not stop him imitating her in 'The Raven'. His judgements of Americans were worse. The work of one American contemporary, Rufus Dawes, was, he wrote, 'downright nonsense'. The poems of Joseph Rodman Drake were 'puerilities', while those of Fitz-Greene Halleck were 'essentially inferior, upon the whole, to those of his friend Drake'. A novel by Morris Mattson was 'utter folly, bombast, and insanity'. A poem by Cornelius Mathews was, quite simply, 'trash'.[65] Had he known about it, Henri Murger might have added spice to *Scènes de la Vie de Bohème* by using Poe's life. That life included a spectacular if brief military career; experiments with drugs; marriage to a cousin half his age; and death by the time he was forty, of alcoholism. The story goes that, in a stupor, he was captured by a political gang and made to cast his vote several times, a subterfuge unapproved by the framers of the democratic process but not unusual at the time.

This is a record of which a sophomore with literary ambitions might be proud. It is not one normally regarded as the basis of solid achievement. But William Carlos Williams thought otherwise:

> Americans have never recognized themselves. How can they? It is impossible until someone invent the ORIGINAL terms. As long as we are content to be called by somebody else's terms, we are incapable of being anything but our own dupes.
>
> Thus Poe must suffer by his own originality. Invent that which is new . . . and there's none to know what you have done. It is new because there's no name. This is the cause of Poe's lack of recognition . . . Here Poe emerges – in no sense the bizarre, isolate writer, the curious literary figure. On the contrary, in him American literature is anchored, in him alone, on solid ground.[66]

I will follow Williams in trying to locate a solid ground for Edgar Allan Poe. The solid ground is paradoxically instable.

The starting point is dispossession. Poe wrote in 1836:

> You are aware of the great barrier in the path of an American writer. He is read, if at all, in preference to the combined and established wit of the world. I say established; for it is with literature as with law or empire – an established name is an estate in tenure, or a throne in possession. Besides, one might suppose that books, like their authors, improve by travel – their having crossed the sea is, with us, so great a distinction. Our antiquaries abandon time for distance; our very fops glance from the binding to the bottom of the title-page, where the mystic letters which spell London, Paris, or Genoa, are precisely so many letters of recommendation.

Poe first published these remarks as the Preface to his 1831 *Poems: Second Edition*, and reprinted them with minor alterations as the 'Letter to B—' in the July 1836 issue of the *Southern Literary Messenger* where he, as its editor, recommended them for their 'vigor and originality'. Vigorous they may be; but it is likely that only the judicial and imperial similes are original. As early as 1788, in a poem called 'Literary Importation', Philip Freneau expressed his indignation; while, as we have seen, Cooper and Emerson added their voices to what would, in the years before the Civil War, become a chorus of American complaint. It is William Ellery Channing who most clearly anticipates Poe's remarks, when he wrote in 1830 that American literature seemed to be 'only an echo of what is thought and written under the aristocracies beyond the ocean'. James Russell Lowell made the point all too clearly by comparing Poe to the novel published by Dickens in 1841, *Barnaby Rudge*.[67]

Poe thought that the British had no more right than anyone else to claim precedence. In *Eureka*, a complex but now outmoded philosophy of science published in 1848, he asserted that 'the plots of God are perfect', and that 'the Universe is a plot of God'. It followed that imperfection was inherent in the human condition. Poe seemed all the better equipped to detect such imperfections, because he perceived himself to be – and frequently acted as – an outsider. Indeed, he saw himself as marginal to two literary establishments, the British and the Bostonian. Such an extreme form of exclusion turned Poe into a permanent 'liminar'. This term, coined by the anthropologist Victor Turner, denoted those who underwent a temporary rite of passage, during which they were separated from the norms of everyday life. Turner illustrates liminality by means of the play which, in Leo Marx's words, 'anticipates the moral geography of the American imagination':

> Symbolic structures, elaborately contrived, are exhibited to liminars at most sacred episodes in the marginal rites, and are then, despite the time and labor taken to construct them, destroyed. Shakespeare's 'cloud-capped palaces,' as his master of liminality, Prospero, declared, 'leave not a rack behind.' The fabrications of liminality, being free from the pragmatics of the common sense world, are 'baseless fabrics of this vision' – like *The Tempest* itself.[68]

Even Thomas Jefferson, who could claim to be the architect of the Republic, was profoundly worried by the transience suggested by Prospero's speech. For Poe, transience was characteristic of all architecture.

The poet Richard Wilbur has suggested that an 'architectural allegory' is at the root of all Poe's imaginative work. That architectural allegory can operate in both the smallest and grandest scales, as a metaphor for a synapse or as the organising principle of the physical universe. Poe turned the architecture, as it were, upside down, revealing the instability concealed within an imperial order such as 'the established wit of the world'. A good example of Poe's inverted architecture is 'The Raven'. The poem originated from a review of *Barnaby Rudge* written by Poe in 1841, in which he drew attention to the:

> raven, whose croakings are to be frequently, appropriately, and prophetically heard in the coarse [*sic*] of the narrative, and whose whole character will perform, in regard to that of the idiot [Barnaby], much the same part as does, in music, the accompaniment in respect to the air. Each is distinct. Each differs remarkably from the other. Yet between them is a strong analogical resemblance, and although each may exist apart, they form together a whole which would be imperfect, wanting either.

'The Raven' was not published until 1845. It was an immediate success and has continued to be so, to the extent that it has become Poe's trademark, as Lowell's 'A Fable for Critics' and countless book covers have shown. Its fame is partly due to its theme, about grief for a lost lover so intolerable that it drives the protagonist into frenzy and death; and partly due to the melancholic and morbid connections its audiences have made, not without reason, with its author. Poe certainly prized his most famous work, but on technical rather than thematic or personal grounds. In 'The Philosophy of Composition' (1846) he discussed it at length in terms of the mathematics of effect. When he responded to 'A Fable for Critics' in an 1849 review, he attacked Lowell not for the insult to 'The Raven' or his intelligence, but rather for a failure 'with the anapaestic rhythm; it is exceedingly awkward in the hands of one who knows nothing about it'. Poe scored points against Dickens on similar, technical grounds. He turned the somewhat desultory relationship between a bird and a madman in *Barnaby Rudge* into a virtuoso 108-line colloquy. In addition, he adopted the musical metaphor from his review, but reversed the relationship. It is the raven that mutters the 'air', the anapaestic melody 'Nevermore', while the narrator embroiders increasingly frenzied variations around it, until the melody becomes a closing comment on the narrator's fate. The result was a victory for Poe. While *Barnaby Rudge* is hardly 'a quaint and curious volume of forgotten lore', it is Poe's nameless raven that is remembered rather than Dickens's bird, the far more voluble Grip.[69]

Poe revealed symbolic architecture as a baseless fabric by means of five kinds of metamorphosis. The first is between the solid and the liquid, for instance in the 1838 tale, 'Ligeia', where the tapestries are decorated by arabesque characters which seem 'changeable in aspect', creating a 'phantasmagoric effect . . . vastly heightened by the artificial introduction of a strong continual current of wind behind the draperies – giving a hideous and uneasy animation to the whole'. A similar kind of hideous animation is to be found in the 1843 story 'The Pit and the Pendulum', where the narrator is entombed in a room which gets smaller and smaller. The second metamorphosis is from silence into language. Poe's approach to language renders the science of semiotics questionable; it allies him, unusually, with Emerson, who once dismissed Poe as 'that jingle man'. For, like Emerson, Poe suggests that language is in the land, waiting to speak. The protagonist of Poe's only novel, *The Narrative of Arthur Gordon Pym*, spends several pages of his narrative discussing and drawing the shapes of the chasms of Tsalal, during a voyage to the South Pole. The chasms resemble hieroglyphics. Poe would reconstruct this episode from *Pym* in the 1843 story 'The Gold Bug', both in its terrain and its concerns over the origin of language.[70] This concern is, in turn, related to a third type of metamorphosis, between the human and the animal. Humankind was supposedly elevated above animal kind by the ability to speak and by discriminating over its food. In 'The Murders in the Rue Morgue' (1841) the police are baffled by murders committed by someone speaking an unidentifiable language. Poe's detective, C. Auguste Dupin, discovers that the language is indeed unidentifiable, for the murderer is an orang-utan. The animal becomes human in *The Narrative of Arthur Gordon Pym*: one of the characters, a misshapen half-breed called Dirk Peters, is said to resemble an orang-utan. In the same tale humans become animal: Pym and his companions are driven by hunger to cannibalism.

A fourth metamorphosis is from one human being into another. This raises doubts about the sanctity of the individual, and hence one of the important ideologies of the United States, liberal individualism. Poe asks awkward questions about the definition of an individual. Do alcohol or drugs permanently change states of consciousness and thus one of the defining elements of individuality? Poe's use of the mathematics of effect seems, on the other hand, to suggest that instability is the norm; to read a Poe story is to be taken on a switchback of shifting emotions, moving swiftly from hilarity into horror. Or is one's skin an adequate means of differentiation? Poe had particular praise for an 1836 novel by Robert Montgomery Bird (1803–54). *Sheppard Lee* was 'an original in *American* Belles Lettres'. It deals with multiple metempsychosis: young Lee's spirit enters into a 'dead man's nostrils', six times in succession. Metempsychosis fascinated Poe – as it would Hitchcock in *Vertigo*. Yet he was more restrained than Bird. In 'Ligeia' he portrayed just one transformation. The will to live of the eponymous corpse with 'the raven-black, the glossy, the luxuriant and naturally-curling tresses' is so great that it occupies the body of the fair-haired Rowena, the narrator's second wife, in the process giving her a new hair-do. Poe was willing to undertake greater experiments with the double. In *The Narrative of Arthur Gordon Pym* there are no less than three doubles: Pym and Augustus Barnard, the man who smuggles him aboard the whaler, Pym and the simian Dirk Peters, and Pym and his dog, his 'inseparable companion', for which he has 'an affection far more ardent than common'. In 'William Wilson' (1840), the protagonist is pursued by a youth who resembles him and who bears the same name. Eventually the protagonist is driven to murder his namesake. As the namesake expires, the protagonist hears this sentence, but does not know if he or the namesake utters it: '*In me didst thou exist – and, in my death, see by this image, which is thine own, how utterly thou hast murdered thyself.*'[71]

Both 'Ligeia' and the 1839 tale 'The Fall of the House of Usher' are examples of twinning, and of the fifth metamorphosis identified by Poe: between life and death. Most people regard this as a one-way trip. Not Poe. Ligeia moves from death into (another's) life. Or perhaps the journey can be halted. An 1845 tale, 'The Facts in the Case of M. Valdemar' describes an attempt to delay death by mesmerism. In contrast, conventional medicine seemed in too much of a hurry. One of Poe's themes derives from the contemporary fear of premature burial. In 'The Premature Burial' (1844) the narrator gives a number of examples, including his own, the result of a misdiagnosed catalepsy. Poe was also interested in describing death, an endeavour that would fascinate a number of later writers, including William Faulkner. Poe combined a horrific dream in *The Narrative of Arthur Gordon Pym* with the progressive 'vaguenesses' of Roderick Usher's paintings to create a mobile landscape of death in the 1844 poem 'Dream-Land':

> Mountains toppling evermore
> Into seas without a shore;
> Seas that restlessly aspire,
> Surging, unto skies of fire;
> Lakes that endlessly outspread
> Their lone waters – lone and dead, –

Sometimes parts of the body live on, as in 'The Tell-Tale Heart' (1843). The narrator, subject to nervous disease, kills an innocent old man. He dismembers the body and buries the pieces under the floor. Police officers come to invest-igate. They discover nothing, but the old man's heart keeps beating. Poe sets the prose in a trochaic rhythm which replicates the heartbeat, 'louder! louder! louder! *louder!*' – until the narrator confesses to the murder.[72]

Given Poe's beliefs in transience, it is hardly surprising that his literary nationalism, in some respects like Longfellow's, is unusual and has often been overlooked. It rejects the temporal and spatial co-ordinates by which we con-ventionally gauge our attachment. Poe dismissed as superficial those who, like George Jones in *Ancient America* (1845), sought in America a history to match that of the Old World. He was even more amused by the bathos which inevitably followed from the frequent attempts to extol such icons of American amplitude as the Niagara Falls. He thought that for a writer to confine himself to American themes 'is rather a political than a literary idea'. American literat-ure is instead created by drawing on 'the Republic of Letters', the phrase used by Jefferson and the revolutionary intellectuals.[73] As one of the nation's most active editors and reviewers, Poe was ideally placed to transform his daily drudgery into a world of glistening, dangerous and original imagination. Poe had, for instance, a detailed knowledge of the reports of westward explora-tion. He turned to advantage Nicholas Biddle's 1814 edition of the journals of the Lewis and Clark Expedition, the first to cross the North American continent. For instance, he mapped the West onto Pym's South Seas, creating a strange new frontier where the earth and sea seem interchangeable. He also rewrote the account of the Expedition as 'The Journal of Julius Rodman' (1840), emphasising some of its strange encounters, and claiming priority of discovery for Rodman.

Poe was particularly fascinated by whirlpools and volcanoes, because they seemed to support the old theory that the earth was hollow. In 1818 John Cleves Symmes, a US Army officer, proposed that the earth was not only hollow but 'habitable within', and that entry may be achieved through the North and South Poles. Two years later Symmes added much detail in a Utopian fiction called *Symzonia*. It was hardly surprising that Symmes's theory was contro-versial. Detractors sneered at what they called 'Symmes's hole' or, with a little more elegance and geographical precision, 'holes in the poles'. Yet there was sufficient support for the theory to prompt the US Congress to fund an expedi-tion. Poe was spellbound by the theory, precisely because it answered his worry, expressed in a review, that there was no new land left to discover. He wrote about the theory in magazine articles, and referred to it in three tales. The 1833 'MS Found in a Bottle' ends when the narrator's vessel plunges into a whirlpool at the South Pole. In the 1835 'Unparalleled Adventure of one Hans Pfaall', the narrator goes to the North Pole in a balloon, en route for the moon. As he crosses the Pole, Pfaall sees that it is concave, with a sharply defined centre. The most extended treatment of Symmes's theory is *The Nar-rative of Arthur Gordon Pym*, which is also based on a proposal to explore the South Seas, by Jeremiah Reynolds, another Symzonian acolyte who also wrote the account of 'Mocha Dick'. The narrative ends as Pym's canoe 'rushed into the embraces of the cataract' somewhere near the South Pole.

Poe's form of literary nationalism made him question the Monroe Doctrine. James Monroe, the fifth president, noted in his 1823 Annual Message to Congress that Europe had long been 'agitated' by wars, and pledged the United States to a policy of non-intervention. He also asserted, in words which have since become a keystone of the foreign policy of the United States, that 'the American continents, by the free and independent condition which they have assumed and maintain, are henceforth not to be considered as subjects for future colonization by any European powers'. This, together with Washington's 'Farewell Address', is one of the central assertions that the United States is a sacred, isolated space. In Poe's view isolationism was useless, and he demonstrated its futility when, in 'The Masque of the Red Death' (1842), he mapped some aspects of *The Tempest* onto contemporary America. In particular, Poe changes the Masque scene into an orgy, multiplies the number of Prospero's followers, and distends Prospero's 'gorgeous palace':

> This was an extensive and magnificent structure, the creation of the prince's own eccentric yet august taste. A strong and lofty wall girdled it in. This wall had gates of iron. The courtiers, having entered, brought furnaces and massy hammers and welded the bolts. They resolved to leave means neither of ingress or egress to the sudden impulses of despair or of frenzy from within. The abbey was amply provisioned. With such precautions the courtiers might bid defiance to contagion. The external world could take care of itself.

Poe's punning mind has transfigured Prospero's fabric into an interior decorator's delight, but this vision proves to be just as baseless. The external world is already inside. Poe's Prince Prospero and his company discover that the Red Death, whose manifestation is 'the redness and horror of blood', has come, in that vivid phrase, 'like a thief in the night'. He finds, as did his Shakespearean forebear, that the sacred space is nothing but an 'insubstantial pageant', and that 'Darkness and Decay and the Red Death held illimitable dominion over all'. 'The Masque of the Red Death' has had many imitators, but none more vivid than Stephen King's *The Shining* (1977). Prospero has now become Jack Torrance, the 'amply provisioned' abbey is the Overlook Hotel, and the Masque is now a masked ball, held on 29 August 1945 to celebrate victory against Japan. But the high noon of *Pax Americana* disappears at midnight in a welter of blood, 'like an obscene rain shower', that finally unhinges Torrance.[74]

Poe was often at odds with the imperial power of Boston. He once wrote that he liked Boston, for he was born there. Yet any claim the city might have had to originality was swamped by the noise of the frogs, his pet name for the Transcendentalists, 'the word-compounders and quibble concoctors of Frogpondium'. Above all, Poe hated Longfellow, whom he regarded as Top Frog. Despite their similar views on literary nationalism, Poe attacked Longfellow again and again, in several journals and over several years. He suggested that Longfellow had, 'through his social and literary position as a man of property and a professor at Harvard, a whole legion of active quacks at his control'. Quacking frogs? Poe's anger had, for once, made him fail to see the humour of his mixed metaphors. Nevertheless, whether it was frogs or ducks that occupied Boston, they had a small 'estate in tenure'. Poe therefore was particularly enraged about Longfellow's *The Waif* (1845), an anthology maintaining the tenure and constructed to confirm Longfellow as the leading poet. Around him, in Poe's view, hopped a sycophantic cabal of 'muddle-pates' and 'the merest nobodies'. Their work was fatally marred by vagueness. They wandered into 'the Cloud-Land of Metaphysics' and lost all precision.[75] And Poe, the frog–duck collision apart, was nothing if not precise. Pages of his reviews were devoted to making detailed metrical analyses, exposing flawed metaphors, undertaking the kind of work for which the New Critics would become famous.

Poe believed that the Bostonians were establishing a hegemony at the expense of his own region. Over eighty years before the Southern Agrarians issued their manifesto in *I'll Take My Stand* (1930), Poe asserted that it was 'high time that the literary South took its own interests into its own charge'. Those interests haunt his writing. Poe's sense of himself as a Virginia gentleman may have caused the verbal whipping he handed out to his literary opponents. Certainly, his distaste for the growing democracy in the United States appears in a description of 'the tyranny of the majority', phrased more vividly than anything de Tocqueville attempted, as 'the most odious and unsupportable despotism than ever was heard upon the face of the Earth'. Poe celebrated 1848, the year of European revolutions, by writing the satire, 'Mellonta Tauta' (Greek for 'these things are in the future'). In another balloon ride, this time in the year 2848, the narrator suggests that 'democracy is a very admirable form of government – for dogs'.[76]

If the Southern gentleman revered anything above himself, it was the Southern lady. The pedestals, on which Poe placed his ladies, include 'Annabel Lee', and 'To Helen', whose beauty equals that of her Trojan predecessor, pulling the wanderer back 'To his own native shore', which is compared, in those famous lines, 'To the glory that was Greece,/And the grandeur that was Rome'. The glory that apparently was the South rested on the institution of slavery. In the *Southern Literary Messenger* and in a number of personal contacts Poe supported the arguments in favour of slavery. In his magazines he promoted the vision of the South – that fatal combination of chivalry and violence – to be found in the novels of such colleagues as Robert Montgomery Bird, William Gilmore Simms, Augustus Longstreet and Beverley Tucker. In 1850 Tucker, a law professor at Jefferson's College of William and Mary, would speak out in favour of Secession. 'The Fall of the House of Usher' can be read as a fateful prevision of Secession. Of all his tales of doom, this one contains the fullest metaphor of the South, and looks forward most clearly to the work of William Faulkner. 'The Haunted Palace', the poem within the tale, celebrates a vision of the aristocratic South, yet fears the 'hideous throng' who rush out to 'a discordant melody'. The House of Usher, the narrator recalls, represents 'both the family and the family mansion'. The twinning of Roderick and Madeline contains, if one wishes to be Freudian, a hint at incest; there had never been an 'enduring branch' of the family. It is a sign of the doom also to be found in the other two tales of doubling that frame 'The Fall of the House of Usher':

The Narrative of Arthur Gordon Pym and 'William Wilson'. The premature burial of Madeline could be read as a failed attempt to perpetuate Southern womanhood 'in the maturity of youth', as the narrator paradoxically puts it. The collapse of the fissured house might be a premonition of the collapse of the baseless fabric that was the so-called United States. If this interpretation places a great deal of weight on the fragile yet highly embellished architecture of the tale, one must remember that Poe, like Cooper, always did think synecdochically. 'The Little Longfellow War', as he once put it, was therefore a synecdoche of something altogether more serious.[77] The rift between South and North grew wider and wider until, ten years and six months after Poe died, it became open warfare.

Disunion and civil war

In the first, 1835, volume of *Democracy in America*, Alexis de Tocqueville recalled a journey down the Ohio River. At the point where the Ohio joins the Mississippi, near Cairo at the southmost point of Illinois, he imagined that the traveller:

> may be said to sail between liberty and servitude; and a transient inspection of surrounding objects will convince him which of the two is more favorable to humanity.
>
> Upon the left bank of the stream the population is sparse; from time to time one descries a troop of slaves loitering in the half-desert fields; the primeval forest re-appears at every turn; society seems to be asleep, man to be idle, and nature alone offers a scene of activity and life.
>
> From the right bank, on the contrary, a confused hum is heard, which proclaims afar the presence of industry; the fields are covered with abundant harvests; the elegance of the dwellings announces the taste and activity of the laborers; and man appears to be in the enjoyment of that wealth and contentment which is the reward of labor.

In the second volume, five years later, the memory had been sharpened into a prediction that 'if ever America undergoes great revolutions, it will be brought about by the presence of the black race on the soil of the United States; that is to say, they will owe their origin, not to the equality, but to the inequality of condition'.[78] His prediction of 'revolution' came true on 12 April 1861, when the Civil War began. De Tocqueville's analyses of the causes were reasonably accurate, too. At the heart of Southern Secession was a complex set of cultural differences, with attitudes to slavery at its cutting edge.

The South regarded itself as a memorial to Jefferson's agrarian ideal. John Taylor of Caroline (1753–1824), a leading Southern political philosopher, held agriculture in the highest esteem: 'by combining a thorough knowledge of the real affairs of life, with ... the strongest invitations to the practice of morality, it becomes the best architect of a complete man'. Unlike Edgar Allan Poe, many Southern writers and apologists accepted the architectural meta-phor, creating a myth of the ante-bellum South that can still be found. One of the most relentless mythmakers was William Gilmore Simms (1806–70) who, with a large number of historical novels beginning with *Guy Rivers* (1834), did for South Carolina what Faulkner a century later would do for northern Mississippi, but with a fraction of Faulkner's ability. Poe thought that Simms was 'immeasurably the best writer of fiction in America', except for Brockden Brown, Hawthorne and Cooper, although that did not stop him pillorying Simms's style. Simms, indeed, was frequently compared with Cooper, which was reasonable, since both were indebted to Scott. But where Cooper usually created characters, Simms produced Southern stereotypes: gentlemen, belles and cheerfully complaisant slaves with burlesque dialects. Repair the fissure in the House of Usher, cure its residents of their unfortunate habits, and you have a shadow of Simms's sanative South – which is why Poe recruited Simms for the defence against the Northern hegemony. Twain must have had Simms in mind when he diagnosed the 'Sir Walter disease' and accused Scott of being 'in great measure responsible for the war'. There was, as usual, more than a grain of truth in Twain's gross exaggeration. Simms was one of those responsible for creating the enchantment which helped the South fall in love with itself and divorce the North. He paid a heavy price: his mansion, 'Woodlands', was burnt twice during the War, and his great reputation crashed. There has been little sign of recovery.[79]

The case of John Pendleton Kennedy (1795–1870) is different. Kennedy created in his novels *Swallow Barn* (1832) and *Horse-Shoe Robinson* (1835) a cast of Simmsean stereotypes, set in a pastoral idyll:

> The soil of this district is remarkable for its blood-red hue. The side of every bank glowed in the sun with this bright vermillion tint . . . The contrast of this with the luxuriant grass and the yellow stubble, with the grey and mossy rock, and with the deep green shade of the surrounding forest, perpetually solicited the notice of the lover of landscape . . .[80]

With its subordinate clauses laid on like paint, this picture clearly reflects a love affair. It is a love affair remembered. Kennedy's South is in decline. Although his pedigree was impeccable – he was related through his mother not only to John Taylor but also to Edmund Pendleton, a leading Virginian revolutionary lawyer – he was sufficiently of the present to know that they were of the past; and he supported the Union during the war.

Of all the political apologists for the South, none was more comprehensive than George Fitzhugh (1806–81). In *Sociology for the South* (1854) – the first American text to refer to that social science in its title – the Virginia lawyer pursued two theses. The first was that white superiority was grounded in nature and proved by Scripture. The South was in fact doing its African-American population a favour. The plantation system, he thought, acted as a welfare state, with Blacks as the contented recipients of white beneficence, and the whites receiving in return Black loyalty and labour. But in the North it was clear to Fitzhugh that 'free laborers have less liberty than slaves, are worse paid and provided for, and have no valuable rights'. This was Fitzhugh's second thesis, contained in his subtitle, *the Failure of Free Society*. Much of his evidence was, like Karl Marx's, drawn from Britain, with its 'wage slavery'. Worse still, it was clear to Fitzhugh that Jefferson's hope, that 'workshops' would remain in Europe, had not been realised. Every day the modern industrialising North provided him with more evidence that the concept of freedom was a chimera. Capitalists were no more than overdressed cannibals, and the myth of freedom merely resulted in a babel of squabbling, reminiscent of the French Revolution. As Fitzhugh put it, in a series of exasperated questions, in *Cannibals All!* (1857):

> Why have you Bloomer's and Women's Right's men, and strong minded women, and Mormons, and anti-renters, and 'vote yourself a farm' men, Millerites, and Spiritual Rappers, and Shakers, and Widow Wakemanites, and Agrarians, and Grahamites, and a thousand other superstitious and infidel Isms at the North? Why is there faith in nothing, and speculation about everything? Why is this unsettled, half-demented state of the human mind co-extensive in time and space with free society?

Fitzhugh was right about the number of 'Isms' in the North, but wrong about their instability. They formed a coalition, united only in the cause of freedom for African-Americans, yet forging a myth of the Union which helped bring victory to the North.[81]

If a myth could be said to be started by anyone, this one was begun by William Lloyd Garrison (1805–79). One of his early biographers, John Jay Chapman, believed that Garrison 'vitalized and permanently changed this nation as much as one man ever did'. Garrison's editorial to the first issue of his journal, *The Liberator* (1831), declared his determination 'to lift up the standard of emancipation in the eyes of the nation, *within sight of Bunker Hill and in the birth place of liberty*'. By referring to the place which, however mistakenly (the battle was fought on another hill), became a rallying-cry for the revolution, Garrison anchored his cause in one of the founding myths of the nation. The reference to Bunker Hill was also a sign of Garrison's militancy, usually a vital ingredient for a myth. Garrison was certainly the most militant of the abolitionist leaders. Although many of his opinions changed over time, he was constant to his two central articles of faith, equal rights for women and freedom for African-Americans. Garrison quarrelled with many supporters and, it seemed, would go out of his way to invite trouble. It was inevitable that when a slave revolt began in August 1831, led by Nat Turner (1800–31), many Southerners accused Garrison of responsibility for the 'insurrection'. The only link between the two men, however, was an urgent sense of religious mission. Turner's captors allowed him to be interviewed by a lawyer; and in *The Confessions of Nat Turner*, published shortly after he was hanged, Turner is reported as having seen a number of visions, and having watched the heavens for a sign 'when I should arise and prepare myself, and slay my enemies with their own weapons'.[82]

One of the most effective weapons for the North in the ante-bellum period was the slave narrative. A number were published, including *Narratives of the Sufferings of Lewis and Milton Clarke* (1846), *The Narrative of the Life and Adventures of Henry Bibb* (1849) and *Twelve Years a Slave: The Narrative of*

Solomon Northup (1853). The best known is the *Narrative of the Life of Frederick Douglass, An American Slave*, first published in 1845 with a Preface by Garrison enjoining the reader to agree that there should be ' "NO COMPROMISE WITH SLAVERY! NO UNION WITH SLAVEHOLDERS!" ' Douglass's *Narrative* presents a persuasive case against slavery, but is also more complex, giving the first clear instance of what was called 'double-consciousness' by the Black activist W. E. B. Du Bois (1868–1963): 'two souls, two thoughts, two unreconciled strivings; two warring ideals in one dark body'.[83] The white 'ideal' is to be found in the ways that Douglass fashions pre-existing models to create a suitable anti-slavery text for the North. Take the opening of the narrative:

> I was born in Tuckahoe, near Hillsborough, and about twelve miles from Easton, in Talbot County, Maryland. I have no accurate knowledge of my age, never having seen any authentic record containing it. By far the larger part of the slaves know as little of their ages as horses know of theirs, and it is the wish of most masters within my knowledge to keep their slaves thus ignorant.

In its precise detail, Douglass's *Narrative* is here indebted to *Robinson Crusoe* (1719). Douglass imitates the first paragraph of Defoe's novel for two reasons. The first, ironically, is to distinguish the *Narrative* from some earlier texts by asserting authenticity. As we have seen, it was a white lawyer who took Nat Turner's confession. In 1838 there was a scandal about the narrative of one James Williams which, it was alleged, was only a novel. Charles Ball's *Slavery in the United States* (1836) was ghostwritten by a white, while *American Slavery As It Is: Testimony of a Thousand Witnesses* (1839) – one of the sources of *Uncle Tom's Cabin* – was compiled from newspaper reports by a Massachusetts reformer, Theodore Weld (1803–95).

Douglass's second reason for imitating *Robinson Crusoe* is to show how slavery perverts the cherished American institution of the family. In a few lines, Defoe provides much detail about the background of his protagonist. In contrast, Douglass reveals that slaves do not know their ages or, as we discover within the next page, their parentage. After the reference to his white father, Douglass left to others the task of exploring the sexual complexities of the Black–white relation in the South. William Wells Brown (1814?–84) wrote what is probably the first novel by an African-American. It was a version of the rumour, which had been circulating since 1802, about the relationship between Thomas Jefferson and one of his slaves, Sally Hemings. Brown's novel was published in London in 1853 as *Clotel; or, The President's Daughter*. When he revised the novel for publication in Boston in 1864, Brown omitted Jefferson's name and made the title less salacious: *Clotelle: a tale of the Southern States*. The relationship has more recently been given fresh treatments by Barbara Chase-Riboud's novel *Sally Hemings* (1979) and by the film *Jefferson in Paris* (1995). They are all less distressing than *Incidents in the Life of a Slave Girl* (1861), published under the pseudonym of Linda Brent but written by Harriet Jacobs (1813?–97) with the assistance of the Massachusetts novelist and abolitionist Lydia Maria Child (1802–80). Jacobs reveals the 'living death' of sexual slavery, made more horrific by appearing through a mist of circumlocution.

Douglass's *Narrative* draws more extensively on two forms about abduction and release, the American captivity narrative such as Mary Rowlandson's *The Sovereignty & Goodness of God*, and one of the earliest works by an African published in English, *The Interesting Narrative of the Life of Olaudah Equiano* (1789). While both these texts profess a deep-seated religious belief, Douglass's *Narrative* is more secular. His work is closest to the economic structure of Franklin's *Autobiography*, with its account of a rise from obscurity by means of self-education, its emphasis on freedom achieved through hard work, and its use of the secular turning point. It is a battle with his master, Edward Covey, rather than the light on the road to Damascus which 'rekindled the few expiring embers of freedom'. The close of the *Narrative* is marked by religious imagery – Douglass's 'soul was set all on fire', and he takes up his 'cross' – but the object of devotion is the abolitionist cause rather than God.

The Black 'ideal', to use Du Bois's term, is to be found in the hints of an alternative African-American tradition, which surfaces in the account of slaves singing:

> they would make the dense old woods, for miles around, reverberate with their wild songs, revealing at once the highest joy and the deepest sadness. They would compose and sing as they went along, consulting neither time nor tune. The thought that came up, came out – if not in the word, in the sound; – and as frequently in the one as in the other . . .
> 'I am going away to the Great House Farm!
> O, yea! O, yea! O!'

Emphasising sound as much as meaning, uniting joy and sadness, drawing attention to improvisation and, in that last line, to syncopation, Douglass highlights the qualities of Black music which would, in the next half-century, become Jazz and, in the hands of a genius like Louis Armstrong, change the nature of western popular and classical music. Perhaps it was Douglass's feeling for the phrasing of Black music which made him the most inspirational abolitionist speaker, in Britain and Ireland as well as the North. Certainly, the way Douglass promoted Black identity established him as a hero for the twentieth-century Civil Rights movement.[84]

In the last fifteen years of the ante-bellum Douglass displaced Phillis Wheatley as the African-American figurehead of the abolitionist movement. Wheatley's *Poems on Various Subjects* (1773) had been heralded, by Garrison and others, as the pre-eminent African-American work, a decisive answer to those Southerners who dismissed any possibility of African-American achievement. But, both as a person and a poet, Wheatley became less useful to abolitionism than Douglass. Like Jupiter Hammon (1720?–1800?), she was considered a freak. Wheatley was educated by her owner, becoming a precocious student whose poems were admired precisely because they were produced by a young Black woman. She visited Britain and, in a period when freakishness was fashionable, experienced (like the young Mozart) the intense interest of London society, only to return to Boston, poverty and neglect. Her poetry, moreover, was too apologetic and outdated for abolitionist militancy:

> 'Twas mercy bought me from my Pagan land,
> Taught my benighted soul to understand
> That there's a God, that there's a Saviour too:
> Once I redemption neither sought nor knew.
> Some view our sable race with scornful eye,
> 'Their colour is a diabolic die.'
> Remember, *Christians, Negros*, black as *Cain*,
> May be refin'd, and join th' angelic train.[85]

The most influential text, during the ante-bellum and since, did not need to put its African-American characters through a conversion experience. Harriet Beecher Stowe's *Uncle Tom's Cabin* (1852) is a heavily embroidered version of the slave narrative. Although Stowe was a prolific writer, this novel was by far her most popular, and with good reason. It shares some of the characteristics of Susannah Rowson's *Charlotte Temple*, if only to outmatch them. *Uncle Tom's Cabin* contains the occasional direct address by the author to the reader professing truth to reality as well as emotions. It is structured as a moral geography, this time running from North to South, with an Ohio Quaker settlement presented as a colourful pastoral and Simon Legree's plantation portrayed, following Psalm 74:20, as one of the dark places of the earth. *Uncle Tom's Cabin* also outstrips *Charlotte Temple* in its portrayal of evil. Legree is one of the more evil creations in literature, and he pays, with nightmares of a maternal spectre that pursue him into death. The several plots are intertwined but the two most extensive ones run in opposite directions: with Eliza and George northwards to Canada and freedom, and with Uncle Tom southwards to New Orleans and death. There are a number of dramatic setpieces – the flight of Eliza across the wintry Ohio River, bloodstains marking her passage across the packed ice; and the deaths of Eva and Tom.

Some critics dismissed Tom as a passive child. With the development of Black Rights in the twentieth century the term 'Uncle Tom' became an insult, and Richard Wright's *Uncle Tom's Children* (1938) announced a new Black generation who would not accept the grinning, shuffling stereotype that Tom had become. The original Tom was not a stereotype, and to dismiss him as a child misses the point. Tom is an older version of Eva because children, in accordance with Mark 19:14, are vital to Stowe's moral scheme. Tom quotes Luke 10:21, 'that thou hast hid these things from the wise and prudent, and hast revealed them unto babes'. In this respect, Stowe is a Transcendentalist like Bronson Alcott, believing that the innocent are the most perspicacious. To this extent, Tom is a Christ figure; as Christ was always a child, so is he. At one point Mary Bird, a minor character, says that she knows nothing about politics but can read the Bible. The text is less feigning; it applies the New Testament to contemporary politics with great dexterity. At its heart lies the sanctity of the family, unmodified by skin pigmentation. The result was a novel which had a great impact on its readership, selling more than a million copies in its first year. When Stowe visited the White House in 1862, President Lincoln is supposed to have said, with a typically dry overstatement that contains a germ of truth: 'So you're the little woman who wrote the book that made this great war!'[86]

The lyrics for the Union during 'this great war' were written in 1861 by Julia Ward Howe (1819–1910), a poet, biographer of Margaret Fuller and later a leader of the women's suffrage movement. The provenance of the music is complex. Its beginnings have been traced at least back to an 1858 Methodist hymn, but it became better known as 'John Brown's Body', first to memorialise a Union army sergeant, and then the abolitionist hanged for treason after his abortive raid in 1859 on Harper's Ferry, Virginia. Brown's raid polarised the South and the North, and Brown's death made him a martyr for freedom. Julia Ward Howe's poem caught the tone of Brown's fanaticism, deftly uniting it with an imagery of evangelical fervour drawn largely from the Old Testament. The song has become an informal national anthem, the most bellicose thread in the fibre of American culture. It steps forward in full colour whenever the United States goes to war, for example, in Woodrow Wilson's 1917 Declaration of War, accepting 'the gage of battle' against Germany. Its shadow also reappears at times of crisis, providing, for instance, the title for John Steinbeck's best-known novel, about the Dust Bowl in the 1930s:

> Mine eyes have seen the glory of the coming of the Lord:
> He is trampling out the vintage where the grapes of wrath are stored;
> He hath loosed the fatal lightning of His terrible swift sword:
>   His truth is marching on . . .
>
> I have read a fiery gospel writ in burnished rows of steel:
> 'As ye deal with my contemners, so with you my grace shall deal;
> Let the Hero, born of woman, crush the serpent with his heel,
>   Since God is marching on' . . .
>
> In the beauty of the lilies Christ was born across the sea,
> With a glory in his bosom that transfigures you and me:
> As he died to make men holy, let us die to make men free,
>   While God is marching on.[87]

It has been estimated that 802,000 soldiers, Union and Confederate, died as a result of the four years that God marched on. The Second World War has been the only conflict in which there were more American casualties, and it was not, of course, fought on American soil. That the Civil War was so bloody was not just a function of the clash between the two systems of belief entitled by de Tocqueville 'liberty' and 'servitude'. It could be characterised, as well, as the consequence of two unevenly-matched armies fighting different kinds of war. The South thought of it as a war for cavaliers. The Confederate Army was led for much of the war, appropriately, by a Virginia gentleman, Robert E. Lee. For the North it was more a war of supply and attrition. The most famous general and eventually the commander-in-chief of the Union army was, again appropriately, a modest Ohio farm-boy who in 1869 would become eighteenth President, Ulysses S. Grant. Because the North fought the more modern war, it eventually won.

Some of the war's bloodiest battles were recorded by a new technology, photography. The best-known name associated with the three and a half thousand photographs of the Civil War is Mathew Brady, although he is likely to have taken very few of them. One of the most often reprinted is by Timothy O'Sullivan. 'A Harvest of Death, Gettysburg, July, 1863', is the inevitable and bitter fruit of Julia Ward Howe's earlier vintage. The dead lie scattered across a hillside, most of them in a horrific parody of the military 'at ease': heads back, chests out, legs apart, never to snap back to attention.[88] During the course of the three-day Battle of Gettysburg, there were some forty-three thousand casualties, over one-quarter of the combatants. One soldier's story must represent the terror that Gettysburg meant for all. Harriet Beecher Stowe's son Frederick had interrupted the study of medicine to become an officer in the Union army. He received a head wound at Gettysburg which left him 'shattered in mind and body'. After the war he gave up medicine and tried, with the support of his parents, a variety of enterprises. They all failed. He moved to San Francisco, where he was met by friends. He left them, promising to return shortly. Some forty years later his brother noted that 'from that hour to this there has been nothing to throw the least light upon his fate'.[89]

There were two speakers on 19 November 1863, the day that the site of the battle was dedicated as a national cemetery. The first was Edward Everett, a Massachusetts politician, former President of Harvard, and an orator in the mould of his friend Daniel Webster. Everett's oration lasted two hours, his speech peppered with hellfire images similar to Howe's 'Battle Hymn of the Republic'. The second speaker was Abraham Lincoln. His speech lasted three minutes. This version contains just 272 words:

> Four scores and seven years ago our fathers brought forth on this continent, a new nation, conceived in Liberty, and dedicated to the proposition that all men are created equal.
>
> Now we are engaged in a great civil war, testing whether that nation, or any nation so conceived and so dedicated, can long endure. We are met on a great battle-field of that war. We have come to dedicate a portion of that field, as a final resting place for those who here gave their lives that that nation might live. It is altogether fitting and proper that we should do this.
>
> But, in a larger sense, we can not dedicate – we can not consecrate – we can not hallow – this ground. The brave men, living and dead, who struggled here, have consecrated it, far above our poor power to add or detract. The world will little note, nor long remember what we say here, but it can never forget what they did here. It is for us the living, rather, to be dedicated here to the unfinished work which they who fought here have thus far so nobly advanced. It is rather for us to be here dedicated to the great task remaining before us – that from these honored dead we take increased devotion to that cause for which they gave the last full measure of devotion – that we here highly resolve that these dead shall not have died in vain – that this nation, under God, shall have a new birth of freedom – and that government of the people, by the people, for the people, shall not perish from the earth.[90]

Too brief to make much impact during the ceremony, the speech is now known as the 'Gettysburg Address', and has become one of the sacred documents of the United States, in stature equal to the Declaration of Independence. Lincoln was wrong; the speech has been long remembered. Some of the reasons for its potency are obvious: the quotation from the Declaration, the triple use of the phrase 'the people', the invocation of novelty that was already a component of the national rhetoric. Some are less so. Lincoln's use of biblical allusion – unlike Howe and Everett – is very sparing. The speech begins with a reference to Luke 2:7 ('she brought forth her first-born son') and ends with one to John 11:50 ('that one man should die for the people, and that the whole nation perish not'). Between those two allusions the language resembles that of another Midwesterner, Mark Twain, in its simple, largely monosyllabic, appeal. Indeed, Garry Wills suggested that the Address marks a revolution in literary style. The references to the Gospels, though, compare the nation with Christ and structure the speech as a dialectic, not between North and South, but between life and death. The speech therefore, even while the Civil War is proceeding, begins to minister to its trauma by hoping for the resurrection of the United States, sanctified by the blood of *all* combatants, reconciled in death. On 14 April 1865, five days after Lee's surrender at Appomattox, Lincoln was shot while watching a play in Washington, the first President to be assassinated and the last martyr to the cause of Union.

Notes

1. James Fenimore Cooper, *Notions of the Americans* (1828; rpt. Albany, NY: State University of New York Press, 1991), p. 342.

2. Francis Scott Key, 'The Star-Spangled Banner', in *American Issues, Volume One: The Social Record*, eds. Willard Thorp, Merle Curti and Carlos Baker (Chicago: J. B. Lippincott Co., 1944), p. 101.

3. Sydney Smith, 'Review of Adam Seybert, *Statistical Annals of the United States of America*', *Edinburgh Review*, 33 (January 1820), 79. Frances Trollope, *Domestic Manners of the Americans* (1832; rpt. Oxford: Oxford University Press, 1984), pp. 363, 39, 197–8.

4. Alexis de Tocqueville, *Democracy in America*, ed. Phillips Bradley (2 vols, New York: Vintage Books, 1945), I, pp. 452, 269; II, p. 352.

5. Cooper, *Notions of the Americans*, p. 348.

6. Cooper, *Gleanings in Europe: Italy* (1838; rpt. Albany, NY: State University of New York Press, 1981), p. 51. Cooper, *Gleanings in Europe: The Rhine* (1836; rpt. Albany, NY: State University of New York Press, 1986), p. 175. Cooper, *Gleanings in Europe: France* (1837; rpt. Albany, NY: State University of New York Press, 1983), p. 145. Cooper, *Gleanings in Europe: England* (1837; rpt. Albany, NY: State University of New York Press, 1986), p. 210. Cooper, *The Chainbearer* (Boston: Dana Estes & Co., n.d.), p. 21.

7. Cooper, *The American Democrat* (1838; rpt. Harmondsworth: Penguin, 1969), pp. 135, 186. Cooper, *The Redskins* (Boston: Dana Estes & Co., n.d.), p. 139. Cooper, *Gleanings in Europe: England*, pp. 19, 177, 276–8.

8. Cooper, *Home as Found* (1838; rpt. New York: Capricorn Books, 1961), pp. 165, 432, 447.

9. Cooper, *The Redskins*, p. 34.

10. Cooper, *The Chainbearer*, pp. 21, 387.

11. Cooper, *Gleanings in Europe: Italy*, p. 95. Cooper, *The Pathfinder* (1840; rpt. Albany, NY: State University of New York Press, 1981), pp. 7–9. *The Port Folio*, 15 (June 1823), 520. Thomas Cole, 'Essay on American Scenery', *The American Monthly Magazine*, 7 (1836), p. 11.

12. Cooper, *The Pathfinder*, pp. 17–18, 35, 461, 468. Cooper, *The Deerslayer* (Oxford: Oxford University Press, 1993), pp. 21, 278, 546, 548.

13. D. H. Lawrence, *Studies in Classic American Literature* (1924; rpt. Harmondsworth: Penguin, 1971), pp. 55, 69.

14. William Carlos Williams, *In the American Grain* (1925; rpt. Harmondsworth: Penguin, 1971), p. 82. Cooper, *The Prairie* (1827; rpt. Harmondsworth: Penguin, 1987), p. 11. Further references to this text will be given in parentheses after the quotation.

15. Zebulon M. Pike, *An Account of the Expeditions to the Sources of the Mississippi, and through the Western Parts of Louisiana . . .* (Philadelphia: C. & A. Conrad & Co., 1810), Appendix to Part II, p. 8.

16. Cooper, *The Crater* (Boston: Dana Estes & Co., n.d.), p. 61. Further references to this text will be given in parentheses after the quotation.

17. Oliver Wendell Holmes, *The Autocrat at the Breakfast Table* (1858; rpt. London: Dent, 1906), p. 5. Holmes, *Elsie Venner* (1861; rpt. Boston: Houghton Mifflin, 1897), p. 4. Samuel C. Bushnell, 'Boston', *The Oxford Book of American Light Verse*, ed. William Harmon (New York: Oxford University Press, 1979), p. 204.

18. Cooper, Letter 31 January 1841 in *The Letters and Journals of James Fenimore Cooper*, ed. James Franklin Beard (6 vols, Cambridge, MA: Harvard University Press, 1964), IV, p. 114. Mark Twain, *The Adventures of Huckleberry Finn* (1884; rpt. Harmondsworth: Penguin, 1966), p. 228.

19. Twain, 'Whittier Birthday Speech', *Tales, Speeches, Essays, and Sketches*, ed. Tom Quirk (Harmondsworth: Penguin, 1994), pp. 134–9.

20. The context and significance of the 'Whittier Birthday Speech' incident is discussed in Henry Nash Smith, *Mark Twain: The Development of a Writer* (1962; rpt. New York: Atheneum, 1974), pp. 94–112.

21. Ralph Waldo Emerson, 'The American Scholar' (1837), *The Portable Emerson*, eds. Carl Bode and Malcolm Cowley (Harmondsworth: Penguin, 1981), pp. 58–71. Further references to this text will be given in parentheses after the quotation.

22. Emerson, Journal for 18 May 1843, *Emerson in His Journals*, ed. Joel Porte (Cambridge, MA: Belknap Press, 1982), p. 307.

23. Emerson, Journals for 25–26 January 1820, July–August 1841, *Emerson in His Journals*, ed. Porte, pp. 3, 256.

24. Emerson, Journal entries for June 1847 and April–May 1851, *Emerson in His Journals*, ed. Porte, pp. 372, 421–2.

25. Emerson, 'The Young American' (1844), *Essays & Lectures* (New York: The Library of America, 1983), pp. 216–17.

26. Emerson, 'Thoreau', *The Portable Emerson*, eds. Bode and Cowley, pp. 578, 575.

27. Henry David Thoreau, 'Resistance to Civil Government', *Walden and Resistance to Civil Government*, ed. William Rossi (2nd edn, New York: W. W. Norton & Co., 1992), p. 227.

28. Joseph Wood Krutch, *Henry David Thoreau* (1948; rpt. New York: William Morrow, 1974), p. 168. *The Correspondence of Henry David Thoreau*, eds. Walter Harding and Carl Bode (New York: New York University Press, 1958) p. 19.

29. Thoreau, *A Week on the Concord and Merrimack Rivers*, ed. Carl F. Hovde (Princeton, NJ: Princeton University Press, 1980), pp. 5, 15, 17, 217. Emerson, 'Quotation and Originality', *Letters and Social Aims* (London: Macmillan, 1891), p. 130.

30. Thoreau, *Walden and Resistance to Civil Government*, pp. 33, 57, 210.

31. Thoreau, *Walden and Resistance to Civil Government*, pp. 5, 61, 35, 130, 41.

32. Howard Nemerov, 'Introduction' to *The Laurel Poetry Series: Longfellow* (New York: Dell, 1959), p. 9. Lawrence Buell, 'Introduction', to *Longfellow, Selected Poems* (Harmondsworth: Penguin, 1988), p. viii. Henry Wadsworth Longfellow, *Kavanagh*, in *Works* (18 vols, New York City: AMS Press, 1966), VIII, pp. 365–9.

33. Longfellow, *The Song of Hiawatha*, ed. Daniel Aaron (London: Everyman, 1993), pp. 20–1, 160. Francis Parkman, *The Oregon Trail* (1849; rpt. Harmondsworth: Penguin, 1982), pp. 68, 344, 338–9. Parkman, *France and England in North America* (2 vols, New York: The Library of America, 1983), II, p. 15.

34. Bayard Taylor, 'The Ballad of Hiram Hover', *The Oxford Book of American Light Verse*, ed. Harmon, pp. 100–1.

35. Longfellow, 'Evangeline', *Selected Poems*, pp. 38–9.

36. [Longfellow], review of *Twice-Told Tales*, *North American Review* (1837), and Nathaniel Hawthorne, letter 11 June 1837 to Longfellow, rpt. in *Hawthorne: The Critical Heritage*, ed. J. Donald Crowley (London: Routledge & Kegan Paul, 1970), pp. 57–8, 55. Henry James, *Hawthorne* (1879; rpt. London: Macmillan, 1967), p. 165.

37. Hawthorne, *The House of the Seven Gables* (1851; rpt. Oxford: Oxford University Press, 1991), p. 3. Further references to this text will be given in parentheses after the quotation. Anthony Trollope, 'The Genius of Nathaniel Hawthorne', *North American Review* (1879), in *Hawthorne: The Critical Heritage*, ed. Crowley, p. 515.

38. Hawthorne, 'Mrs. Hutchinson' and 'The Celestial Rail-Road', in *Selected Tales and Sketches*, ed. Michael J. Colacurcio (Harmondsworth: Penguin, 1987), pp. 14–15, 19, 331.

39. Hawthorne, entry for 23 October 1849, *The American Notebooks* (Columbus, OH: Ohio State University Press, 1972), p. 293.

40. Hawthorne, 'Alice Doane's Appeal' and 'The Gray Champion', in *Selected Tales and Sketches*, ed. Colacurcio, pp. 122, 132. Lionel Trilling, *Beyond Culture* (1965; rpt. Harmondsworth: Penguin, 1967), p. 175.

41. Hawthorne, *The Scarlet Letter*, ed. Thomas Connolly (Harmondsworth: Penguin, 1970), p. 66. Further references to this text will be given in parentheses after the quotation.

42. Emerson, Journal entries for May–June 1847, *Emerson in His Journals*, ed. Porte, p. 371. Emerson, 'Historic Notes of Life and Letters in New England', *The Portable Emerson*, eds. Bode and Cowley, p. 617.

43. Hawthorne, *The Blithedale Romance* (1852; rpt. Oxford: Oxford University Press, 1991), pp. 61–2. Further references to this text will be given in parentheses after the quotation.

44. Emerson, Journal entry for March 1868, *Emerson in His Journals*, ed. Porte, p. 540. Margaret Fuller, *Woman in the Nineteenth Century*, in *The Portable Margaret Fuller*, ed. Mary Kelley (New York: Penguin, 1994), pp. 328–9.

45. Hawthorne, *The Marble Faun* (London: Everyman, 1995), pp. 8, 51, 19–20. Further references to this text will be given in parentheses after the quotation. Hawthorne, *The French and Italian Notebooks*, ed. Thomas Woodson (Columbus, OH: Ohio State University Press, 1980), pp. 155–6.

46. Herman Melville, 'Hawthorne and His Mosses', *Literary World* (1850), in *Hawthorne: The Critical Heritage*, ed. Crowley, pp. 116, 121, 119. Charles Olson, *Call Me Ishmael* (1947; rpt. London: Jonathan Cape, 1967), p. 15.

47. Melville, *Typee* (1846; rpt. Harmondsworth: Penguin, 1972), pp. 133–4, 58–9. Further references to this text will be given in parentheses.

48. Albert Camus, 'Herman Melville', *Lyrical and Critical*, trans. Philip Thody (London: Hamish Hamilton, 1967), p. 206.

49. Melville, *Mardi* (Evanston and Chicago: Northwestern University Press and The Newberry Library, 1970), p. 654. Melville, *Redburn* (1849; rpt. Harmondsworth: Penguin, 1976), pp. 43, 238–9.

50. Melville, *White-Jacket; or, The World in a Man-of-War* (1850; rpt. London: Oxford University Press, 1966), p. 392. Melville's emphasis.

51. J. N. Reynolds, 'Mocha Dick', and George Ripley, 1851 review, in Melville, *Moby-Dick*, eds. Hershel Parker and Harrison Hayford (New York: W. W. Norton, 2002), p. 551. Further references to this text will be given in parentheses.

52. Edgar Allan Poe, *The Narrative of Arthur Gordon Pym* (1838; rpt. Harmondsworth: Penguin, 1975), p. 239.

53. Thomas Carlyle, *Sartor Resartus* (1836; rpt. London: Dent, 1967), pp. 167–8.

54. A useful introduction to the various approaches to the text is *Herman Melville, Moby-Dick*, ed. Nick Selby (Cambridge: Icon Books, 1998).

55. Lawrence, *Studies in Classic American Literature*, pp. 168–9. F. O. Matthiessen, *American Renaissance: Art and Expression in the Age of Emerson and Whitman* (1941; rpt. New York: Oxford University Press, 1968), p. 444.

56. Cyril L. R. James, *Mariners, Renegades, and Castaways: The Story of Herman Melville and the World We Live In* (1953; rpt. Detroit: Bewick/Ed, 1978), p. 60.

57. Review in the *Literary World* (August 1852), rpt. in *Melville: The Critical Heritage*, ed. Watson G. Branch (London: Routledge & Kegan Paul, 1974), p. 302. Melville, *Pierre; Or, the Ambiguities* (1852; rpt. New York: Signet, 1964), pp. 23, 249, 243.

58. Melville, *Israel Potter* (New York: Sagamore Press, 1957), p. 241. Review in the *Athenaeum* (June 1855), rpt. in *Melville: The Critical Heritage*, ed. Branch, p. 344.

59. Melville, *Billy Budd, Sailor and Other Stories*, ed. Harold Beaver (Harmondsworth: Penguin, 1967), pp. 131, 194, 67–8.

60. Melville, *The Confidence-Man* (Oxford: Oxford University Press, 1989), pp. 2–4, 67, 336. Review in the *Illustrated Times* (April 1857), and the *Saturday Review* (May 1857), rpt. in *Melville: The Critical Heritage*, ed. Branch, pp. 381, 383.

61. Melville, *Billy Budd, Sailor and Other Stories*, ed. Beaver, p. 405. Further references to this text will be given parenthetically.

62. James Russell Lowell, 'A Fable for Critics', *The Poetical Works of James Russell Lowell* (London: Ward, Lock, Bowden & Co., n.d.), p. 363.

63. James, Eliot, Tate, Baudelaire, in *Poe: A Collection of Critical Essays*, ed. Robert Regan (Englewood Cliffs, NJ: Prentice-Hall, 1967), pp. 39, 64, 66, 164. Jay B. Hubbell, 'Edgar Allan Poe', *Eight American Authors*, ed. James Woodress (New York: W. W. Norton, 1971), pp. 22–4, 31. Lawrence, *Studies in Classic American Literature*, p. 70.

64. Poe, 'Sonnet – To Science', *Selected Writings*, ed. David Galloway (Harmondsworth: Penguin, 1967), p. 27. Krutch, *Edgar Allan Poe: A Study in Genius* (1926; rpt. New York: Russell & Russell, 1965), pp. 192, 197.

65. Poe, *Essays and Reviews* (New York: Library of America, 1984), pp. 501, 522, 530, 838, 824.

66. Williams, *In the American Grain*, pp. 227–8.

67. Poe, 'Letter to B–' (1836) *Essays and Reviews*, pp. 5–6. Channing, 'Remarks on National Literature', *Works* (London: 'Christian Life' Publishing, 1884), p. 138.

68. Poe, *Eureka*, in *The Science Fiction of Edgar Allan Poe*, ed. Harold Beaver (Harmondsworth: Penguin, 1976), p. 292. Leo Marx, *The Machine in the Garden: Technology and the Pastoral Ideal in America* (London: Oxford University Press, 1964), p. 72. Victor Turner and Edith Turner, *Image and Pilgrimage in Christian Culture: Anthropological Perspectives* (Oxford: Basil Blackwell, 1978), pp. 249–50. Victor Turner, *On the Edge of the Bush: Anthropology as Experience*, ed. Edith Turner (Tucson, AZ: University of Arizona Press, 1985), p. 161.

69. Richard Wilbur, 'The House of Poe', *Poe: A Collection of Critical Essays*, ed. Regan, p. 118. Poe, *Essays and Reviews*, p. 222. Poe, 'The Raven', *Selected Writings*, ed. Galloway, pp. 77–80.

70. Poe, 'Ligeia', *Selected Writings*, ed. Galloway, pp. 119–20. Poe, *The Narrative of Arthur Gordon Pym*, pp. 224–6.

71. Poe, *Essays and Reviews*, p. 392. Poe, 'Ligeia' and 'William Wilson', *Selected Writings*, ed. Galloway, pp. 111, 178. Poe, *The Narrative of Arthur Gordon Pym*, p. 67.

72. Poe, *Tales and Poems* (4 vols, London: John C. Nimmo, 1884), IV, p. 146. Poe, 'The Fall of the House of Usher' and 'The Tell-Tale Heart', *Selected Writings*, ed. Galloway, pp. 145, 281–2. Emphasis in text. Poe, 'Dream-Land', *Complete Poems and Selected Essays*, ed. Richard Gray (London: Dent, 1993), p. 69.

73. Poe, *Essays and Reviews*, pp. 1076, 1035.

74. Poe, *The Narrative of Arthur Gordon Pym*, p. 239. James Monroe (5th President of US), Annual Message to Congress, December 1823, in Richard D. Heffner, *A Documentary History of the United States* (New York: New American Library, 1965), pp. 89–91. Poe, 'The Masque of the Red Death' (1842), *Selected Writings*, ed. Galloway, pp. 254, 260. Stephen King, *The Shining* (London: New English Library, 1977), pp. 148, 332, 98.

75. Poe, *Essays and Reviews*, pp. 1169, 670–777, 1120.

76. Poe, 'Marginalia', *Southern Literary Messenger*, April 1849, in *Essays and Reviews*, p. 1440. Poe, 'Mellonta Tauta', *The Science Fiction of Edgar Allan Poe*, ed. Beaver, p. 319.

77. Poe, 'To Helen' and 'The Fall of the House of Usher', *Selected Writings*, ed. Galloway, pp. 68, 140, 147–8, 151. Poe, *Essays and Reviews*, p. 725.

78. De Tocqueville, *Democracy in America*, ed. Bradley, I, pp. 376–7; II, p. 270.

79. John Taylor, *Arator: Being a Series of Agricultural Essays, Practical and Political* (Baltimore: John M. Carter, 1817), p. 180. Poe, *Essays and Reviews*, p. 1342. Twain, *Life on the Mississippi* (1883; rpt. New York: New American Library, 1961), pp. 265–6.

80. John Pendleton Kennedy, *Horse-Shoe Robinson* (1835; rpt. New York: Hafner, 1962), p. 19.

81. George Fitzhugh, *Sociology for the South, or the Failure of Free Society* in *Ante Bellum*, ed. Harvey Wish (New York: Capricorn, 1960), pp. 32, 54, 59, 65, 82, 95. Fitzhugh, *Cannibals All! or, Slaves Without Masters* (1857), ed. C. Vann Woodward (Cambridge, MA: Harvard University Press, 1960), p. 103.

82. John Jay Chapman, *William Lloyd Garrison* (New York: Moffat, Yard, 1913), p. 8. William Lloyd Garrison, 'To the Public', *The Liberator*, 1 January 1831, in *William Lloyd Garrison and the Fight Against Slavery*, ed. William E. Cain (Boston: Bedford Books, 1995), p. 71. Emphasis in text. *The Confessions of Nat Turner, the Leader of the Late Insurrection in Southampton, Va., as Fully and Voluntarily Made to Thomas R. Gray* (1831) in *The Confessions of Nat Turner and related documents*, ed. Kenneth S. Greenberg (Boston: Bedford Books, 1996), p. 48.

83. W. E. B. Du Bois, *The Souls of Black Folk* (1903; rpt. New York: Vintage, 1986), pp. 8–9.

84. *Narrative of the Life of Frederick Douglass, An American Slave* (1845; rpt. Harmondsworth: Penguin, 1982), pp. 42, 47, 57, 113, 151. Harriet A. Jacobs, *Incidents in the Life of a Slave Girl, Written by Herself*, ed. Jean Fagan Yellin (Cambridge, MA: Harvard University Press, 1987), p. 53.

85. Wheatley, 'On Being Brought from Africa to America' (1768), *The Collected Works of Phillis Wheatley*, ed. John C. Shields (New York: Oxford University Press, 1988), p. 18. Emphases in text.

86. Charles Edward Stowe and Lyman Beecher Stowe, *Harriet Beecher Stowe: The Story of Her Life* (Boston: Houghton Mifflin, 1911), p. 203.

87. Julia Ward Howe, 'The Battle Hymn of the Republic', *The New Oxford Book of American Verse*, ed. Richard Ellmann (New York: Oxford University Press, 1976), p. 181. Woodrow Wilson, 'Message to Congress, 2 April 1917', in *American Issues, Volume One: The Social Record*, eds. Thorp, Curti and Baker, pp. 933–5.

88. The photograph is reprinted in Alan Trachtenberg, *Reading American Photographs* (New York: Hill and Wang, 1989), p. 102, plate 27; and in Timothy Sweet, *Traces of War: Poetry, Photography, and the Crisis of the Union* (Baltimore: The Johns Hopkins University Press, 1990), p. 126 fig. 11.

89. Stowe and Stowe, *Harriet Beecher Stowe: The Story of Her Life*, pp. 205, 217–18, 277–9.

90. Abraham Lincoln, 'Address delivered at the Dedication of the National Cemetery, 19 November 1863', in Garry Wills, *Lincoln at Gettysburg: The Words that Remade America* (New York, Simon & Schuster, 1992), p. 263. Wills counted six variants of the Address. The one I have quoted is the last authorised by Lincoln. Wills also reprints the text of Edward Everett's preceding speech. See Wills, pp. 148, 191–203, 213–47, 269 fn 33.

Chapter 6

Prospects for the Great Republic, 1865–1880

One may say that the Civil War marks an era in the history of the American mind. It introduced into the national consciousness a certain sense of proportion and relation, of the world being a more complicated place than it had hitherto seemed, the future more treacherous, success more difficult . . . the good American, in days to come, will be a more critical person than his complacent and confident grandfather. He has eaten of the tree of knowledge.

(Henry James, *Hawthorne*)[1]

Battle-pieces: the aftermath of war

In 1933 Gertrude Stein claimed that the United States was now 'the oldest country in the world'. Because of 'the civil war and the commercial conceptions that followed it America created the twentieth century' more than three decades before other countries entered it.[2] Stein's sequence of causes was inaccurate. 'Commercial conceptions' preceded the Civil War and, indeed, had helped widen the schism between North and South. By the middle of the century the United States had become internationally renowned for its innovative gadgetry. Cyrus McCormick's mechanical reaper and Samuel Colt's 'six-shooter' were great attractions at the Great Exhibition, opened by Queen Victoria at the Crystal Palace in 1851. Yet Stein's conclusion was accurate enough. As Henry James suggested in *Hawthorne*, the Civil War was both a national disaster and a rite of passage. Although Mark Twain among others would give renewed emphasis to the depiction of youth, even youth would now be shadowed and darkened in a land that could no longer pretend innocence. American literature in the brief post-bellum period covered by this chapter therefore prefigures work written in what would become known as 'the century of total war'. I will discuss the authors active in the period 1865–80 more briefly than their predecessors, but will also outline some themes that would be developed further by American literature after 1880.

Wars are difficult to write about, and civil wars are more difficult still. Looking back at the war in *Specimen Days and Collect* (1882), Walt Whitman preferred to remember the 'countless minor scenes', including 'the typic one': the 'Bravest Soldier' who, missed by the burial squads, 'crumbles in mother earth, unburied and unknown'. Who, thought Whitman:

can write the story? Of many a score – aye, thousands, north and south, of unwrit heroes, unknown heroisms, incredible, impromptu, first-class desperations – who tells? No history ever – no poem sings, no music sounds those bravest men of all . . . Future years will never know the seething hell . . . and it is best they should not – the real war will never get in the books.[3]

In a famous analysis of the South published in 1941, the Southern journalist Wilbur Cash noted that the Civil War had not yet produced a really great novel. The Civil War did not get the large-scale memorial that Tolstoy gave to Napoleon's invasion of Russia, nor the attempts by American writers – among them James Jones, Norman Mailer, Kurt Vonnegut and Joseph Heller – to capture the madness and bravery of the Second World War. One reason was that relatively few professional writers actually experienced combat in the Civil War, partly because of the system of paying for a substitute to do the fighting.

Ambrose Bierce (1842–1914?), one of those who did fight, wrote a few short stories years after the war. Collected in *Tales of Soldiers and Civilians* (1891), they use techniques learnt from Poe to create fleeting psychological states and surprise endings. As befits a civil war, the tales record such events as a Union soldier killing his Confederate father ('A Horseman in the Sky') or an artillery officer shelling his own home and killing his wife and child ('The Affair at Coulter's Notch'). They also reflect a malevolence learnt in the war and exaggerated by the corruption that marked the succeeding, so-called Gilded Age. Like Frederick Beecher Stowe, Bierce was deeply unsettled by the war, and he sought a similar fate. In 1913 he went to Mexico to find 'the good, kind darkness', and was never seen again. Stephen Crane (1871–1900), although born well after the war, was similarly marked by it. Drawing on *War and Peace* (1865–72) and a popular history called *Battles and Leaders of the Civil War* (1888), he wrote the short novel often regarded as the most vivid memorial to the war. *The Red Badge of Courage* (1895) deals with the baptism by fire of a recruit to the Union army. It was so successful that it pushed Crane into war. He spent much of the remaining five years of his life as a war reporter, his experience giving him an outlook similar to Bierce, as the title poem of his collection *War is Kind* (1899) reveals:

> Do not weep, maiden, for war is kind.
> Because your lover threw wild hands toward the sky
> And the affrighted steed ran on alone,
> Do not weep.
> War is kind . . .
> Swift blazing flag of the regiment
> Eagle with crest of red and gold,
> These men were born to drill and die.
> Point for them the virtue of slaughter,
> Make plain to them the excellence of killing
> And a field where a thousand corpses lie.[4]

Bierce and Crane reflected a common experience of the War, often characterised as the first modern war, in terms of a chaos difficult to comprehend. It was an attitude which would be developed after the First World War by

Ernest Hemingway, for instance in those sardonic phrases lampooning the 'Gettysburg Address' in the 'Caporetto' segment of *A Farewell to Arms.*

Oliver Wendell Holmes Jr (1841–1935), a Union officer, son of the conversationalist and later to become one of the most distinguished American lawyers, wrote a diary that often records events in a tumbling sequence of fragments. This suggests a second reason for the paucity of Civil War fiction. The ordered, linear structure of the pre-modernist novel was ill-equipped to handle chaos. Poetry was a more capable genre, and much poetry was written in the years during and immediately after the Civil War, some by Herman Melville. Melville had turned exclusively to poetry in 1858. He did not find a publisher until 1866, when Harpers agreed to bring out *Battle-Pieces and Aspects of the War*, which he began writing shortly before its end. The text begins with a memory of the execution of John Brown, and continues with an unsentimental record of incidents in the war, such as the Battle of Gettysburg:

> Before our lines it seemed a beach
> Which wild September gales have strown
> With havoc on wreck, and dashed therewith
>   Pale crews unknown –
> Men, arms, and steeds. The evening sun
> Died on the face of each lifeless one,
> And died along the winding marge of fight
>   And searching-parties lone.

A seagoing imagination still held sway, even at inland Gettysburg. A distanced account created disenchantment, and again Melville received some poor reviews. One critic feared that the poetry reflected more Melville's 'inner consciousness' than the war, while another said that 'the poetic nature and the technical faculty of poetry writing are not identical'. Despite this discouragement, Melville continued to battle with poetry. *Clarel*, published in 1876 at the expense of a relative, is an epic, 18,000-line meditation that had its origin in Melville's visit to Palestine. Almost inevitably, the critics rejected the book. Melville responded by ridiculing the idea of an audience. His last two volumes of poetry, *John Marr and Other Sailors* (1888) and *Timoleon* (1891), were published privately, at his own expense, in editions of twenty-five copies each.[5]

The public sphere was, as usual, more receptive to those who wrote and published more conventionally. Two well-established writers published poems about the Civil War as part of their ongoing commitment to the genre. The work of one, Longfellow, was considered in Chapter 5. His 'Killed at the Ford' (1866) concerns an unsuspecting night-time patrol that meets a sniper:

> Sudden and swift a whistling ball
> Came out of a wood, and the voice was still;
> Something I heard in the darkness fall,
> And for a moment my blood grew chill;
> I spake in a whisper, as he who speaks
> In a room where some one is lying dead;
> But he made no answer to what I said.

The work of another, John Greenleaf Whittier, will be sketched shortly. His 'Barbara Frietchie' (1863) records a confrontation between a Confederate general, 'Stonewall' Jackson, and an elderly woman who raises the Union flag during the Confederate occupation of Frederick, Maryland:

> 'Shoot, if you must, this old grey head,
> But spare your country's flag,' she said.

'Stonewall' Jackson, so named because he stood 'like a stone wall' in the face of fire at the first Battle of Bull Run, was mortally wounded at the Battle of Chancellorsville by a bullet from one of his own snipers. Melville devoted two poems to him; he was a 'stoic' who 'stoutly stood for Wrong'. Whittier, in simpler poetry, gave him a more vivid memorial in 'Barbara Frietchie':

> The nobler nature within him stirred
> To life at that woman's deed and word:
>
> 'Who touches a hair of yon grey head
> Dies like a dog! March on!' he said . . .
>
> Barbara Frietchie's work is o'er,
> And the Rebel rides on his raids no more.
>
> Honour to her! and let a tear
> Fall, for her sake, on Stonewall's bier.[6]

The most memorable poetry, for both sides of the Civil War, was not the aggressively patriotic verse like Julia Ward Howe's 'Battle Hymn of the Republic'. It was, rather, that poetry which adopted the healing remedy of Lincoln's 'Gettysburg Address'. The remedy could perhaps only be properly administered by those who were both involved and observers. For the Union side, the work of Walt Whitman will be discussed shortly. For the Confederacy, the work of a South Carolinian poet, Henry Timrod (1828–67), is perhaps the best. Timrod had to leave the Confederate army because of tuberculosis, and he spent much of the war as a reporter. A life marked by sadness and poverty kept even his patriotic poetry in check, and conveyed a restraint and nobility to such memorial verses as 'The Unknown Dead':

> Of them, their patriot zeal and pride,
> The lofty faith that with them died,
> No grateful page shall farther tell
> Than that so many bravely fell;
> And we can only dimly guess
> What worlds of all this world's distress,
> What utter woe, despair, and dearth,
> Their fate has brought to many a hearth.[7]

With a sympathy, as well as a half rhyme, that looks forward to Wilfred Owen, Timrod's work showed great promise for the reunited republic. But, also like Owen, he died too soon.

The local and the universal

In 1939 William Carlos Williams proclaimed that 'the local is the universal'. In the fifteen years from 1865 to 1880, a number of writers sketched what has been called 'local colour', showing that the United States was made up of several quite distinctive areas. They developed interests that had often started before the war and would continue beyond the turn of the century. A good example is John Greenleaf Whittier. Whittier's first inspiration was Robert Burns, and some of his earliest poems, signed 'Donald', were in Scots vernacular. Then Whittier found his own voice, transforming Burns to celebrate Massachusetts. 'Skipper Ireson's Ride' (1828, revised 1857) is a Yankee version of 'Tam O'Shanter'. Tam's witches give way to 'the women of Marblehead', who speak out forthrightly in their own dialect. Ireson is no 'blethering, blustering, drunken blellum', but rather a captain with a 'horrd horrt' who commits the cardinal sin of the sea, by failing to go to the aid of a sinking ship. So the women tar and feather him, and ride him in a cart, stopping only when he repents his hard-hearted act. The close of the poem reflects Whittier's Quaker belief in the primacy of the individual conscience. That belief drew him away from his native Haverhill in 1829, taking him first into politics, and then into abolitionism. For more than twenty years, Whittier worked tirelessly in the cause of abolition, to the extent that Frederick Douglass called him 'the slave's poet'.[8] In 'Ichabod' (1850), one of the best-known abolitionist poems, Whittier joined Emerson in attacking Daniel Webster for his Compromise Speech, but replaced Emerson's anger with sorrow for Webster's 'dim,/Dishonored brow' (326). An examined conscience would be punishment enough.

The end of the Civil War also ended Whittier's political role, and he spent the rest of his career portraying New England in verse. *Snow-Bound* (1866) is another transformation of Burns, this time of 'The Cotter's Saturday Night'. It is an extended reminiscence about the pleasures of Whittier's family hearth during the bitter north-eastern winter. He was modest about *Snow-Bound*, as he was about all his poetry, but it has roots as deep in Massachusetts as *The Scarlet Letter*. It uses iambic tetrameter to retell old tales and to celebrate, although not to illustrate, the vernacular:

> Our mother, while she turned her wheel
> Or run the new-knit stocking-heel,
> Told how the Indian hordes came down
> At midnight on Cocheco town,
> And how her own great-uncle bore
> His cruel scalp-mark to fourscore.
> Recalling, in her fitting phrase,
>   So rich and picturesque and free
>   (The common unrhymed poetry
> Of simple life and country ways),
> The story of her early days . . . (67)

William Carlos Williams would later devote his career to capturing 'the common unrhymed poetry' of his own New Jersey locality. Whittier's 'Yankee homespun', as it has been called, would also be written by Robert Frost (1874–1963), who was born in San Francisco but would live much of his life, as the title of his 1914 collection put it, *North of Boston*.

Even further north of Boston, Sarah Orne Jewett (1849–1909) wrote sketches of the coastal villages of Maine, which she portrayed as remote from the modernising urban centres:

> Deephaven seemed more like one of those lazy little English seaside towns than any other. It was not in the least American. There was no excitement about anything; there were no manufactories; nobody seemed in the least hurry. The only foreigners were a few standard sailors. I do not know when a house or a new building of any kind had been built; the men were farmers, or went outward in boats, or inward in fish wagons, or sometimes mackerel and halibut fishing in schooners for the city markets.

Deephaven (1877) collected a series of pieces written in the previous six years. Four novels and a large number of articles and sketches followed it. Jewett's best-known collection is *The Country of the Pointed Firs* (1896), detailing a visit to Dunnet Landing. The place's distance from the 'noisy world' allows Jewett to unite the mundane with the sublime in a way that recalls the closing lines of *Paradise Lost*. Her protagonist, the widowed herbalist Mrs Todd, therefore appears to the narrator both like the mythical Antigone of Sophoclean tragedy and 'a renewal of some historic soul, with her sorrows and the remoteness of a daily life busied with rustic simplicities and the scents of primeval herbs'.[9] Jewett's style of regional realism would be applied by her friend Willa Cather (1873–1947) to states as remote from Maine as Nebraska and New Mexico.

A more strident form of regional realism is to be found in *A Fool's Errand* (1879), by Albion W. Tourgée (1838–1905). Tourgée served in the Union army, and after the war moved from Ohio to North Carolina, where he became, first a political journalist, and then a judge. The South had been devastated by the war, was divided over the recovery programme known as Reconstruction, and corrupted by some Northern migrants, who were called 'carpetbaggers'. Then both freedmen and reformers were threatened by violent white supremacists, a band of Confederate veterans known as the Ku Klux Klan. (A new Klan emerged in 1915; it still exists.) The Klan may have prompted Tourgée to leave the South in 1879, around the time that his semi-autobiographical *A Fool's Errand* appeared. Its protagonist is an erstwhile Union colonel called Comfort Servosse who moves to 'Verdenton', a lightly fictionalised version of Greensboro, North Carolina. Servosse tries to assist equality and justice by selling lands to the freedmen and drawing up plans for the political future of the South. But Servosse realises that his work has been blocked by 'that *pseudo* South that has the power'. He presents the hope for the future in an echo of Lincoln's 'Gettysburg Address':

> The Nation expected the liberated slave to be an ally of freedom. It was altogether right and proper that it should desire and expect this. But it made the fatal mistake of expecting the freedman to do successful battle on his part of the line, without training or knowledge. This mistake must be remedied.[10]

With the failure of his work, Tourgée pinned his hopes on a more modest plea for Black education. The plea would be answered by the creation of the Tuskegee Institute in 1881 and would be reasserted twenty years later in *Up from Slavery*, the autobiography of its founder, Booker T. Washington.

Thomas Nelson Page, Joel Chandler Harris and Thomas Dixon portrayed Tourgée's '*pseudo* South'. The tales of the Virginian Page (1853–1922) might be said to be fictional apologia for the slavery theories of George Fitzhugh. *In Ole Virginia* (1887) collects stories that depict the Old South in terms of a benevolent personal relationship between master and slave, based on a mutual perception of the unbridgeable gulf between them. The Uncle Remus stories of the Georgian Harris still reveal that gulf, yet within a greater domestic closeness between Black and white. First collected in *Uncle Remus: His Songs and His Sayings* (1880), the tales were so popular that Harris eventually wrote 180 of them in ten collections, ending with *Uncle Remus and the Little Boy* in 1910. The stories, which are probably based on a wide range of oral folk tales, portray a post-bellum stability that is a wishful version of the ante-bellum plantation. The agenda of Page and Harris may be found in the most popular portrayal of the Southern plantation: Margaret Mitchell's *Gone With the Wind* (1936).

Thomas Nelson Page's later novel, *Red Rock* (1898), presents a more sombre view of the post-bellum South. It sees Reconstruction as Northern oppression and portrays a mulatto, ironically called Moses, in bestial terms. The North Carolinian Thomas Dixon (1864–1946) takes Page's racist agenda further. *The Clansman* (1905), the second and best-known volume of Dixon's Reconstruction trilogy, rewrites history by including Abraham Lincoln, and having him say, just before his assassination, that he 'can conceive of no greater calamity than the assimilation of the Negro into our social and political life as our equal', and adding that 'a mulatto citizenship would be too dear a price to pay even for emancipation'.[11] With Lincoln apparently making a link between racial equality and sexuality, Dixon sets the scene for two Souths. The ante-bellum South is seen as the Garden of Eden before the Fall. After emancipation brutish Black rapists, supported by carpetbaggers, stalk the South. The Ku Klux Klan is a racist version of the Seventh Cavalry, arriving just in time to save it. The novel was popular, and was adapted by W. G. Griffith into the first large-scale narrative film, *The Birth of a Nation* (1915).

The Scots dramatist J. M. Barrie thought that to sit in a steam laundry and read the best-known work of George Washington Cable was 'the quickest way of reaching the strange city of New Orleans'. Cable (1844–1925) certainly gives a pungent rendering of the Deep South, together with a sophisticated approach to its social and racial complexities. The short story, 'Belles Demoiselles Plantation' (1874), is a good indicator of Cable's awareness of the instability of its society. The plantation, on the banks of the Mississippi, is depicted as a pastoral paradise, yet with an uneasy undertone:

> The house stood unusually near the river, facing eastward, and standing foursquare, with an immense veranda about its sides, and a flight of steps in front spreading

broadly downward, as we open arms to a child. From the veranda nine miles of river were seen; and in their compass, near at hand, the shady garden full of rare and beautiful flowers; farther away broad fields of cane and rice, and the distant quarters of slaves, and on the horizon everywhere a dark belt of cypress forest.

The plantation is owned by 'Colonel De Charleu', a 'bitter-proud' widower with seven 'goddesses' of daughters and an 'extremely distant relative' called 'Injin Charlie', the sole relic of 'injudicious alliances, and deaths in the gutters of old New Orleans'. One day the plantation slides into the Mississippi, taking the seven goddesses with it, and leaves the dying Colonel to be nursed by Injin Charlie. The tale is all the more potent because the disappearance of 'Belles Demoiselles Plantation' is no mere fictional fiat, like Cooper's *The Crater*. Mark Twain, beginning his *Life on the Mississippi* (1883), noted that 'the Mississippi is well worth reading about':

> Considering the Missouri its main branch, it is the longest river in the world – four thousand three hundred miles . . . It discharges three times as much water as the St. Lawrence, twenty-five times as much as the Rhine, and three hundred and thirty-eight times as much as the Thames . . . The area of its drainage basin is as great as the combined areas of England, Wales, Scotland, Ireland, France, Spain, Portugal, Germany, Austria, Italy and Turkey; and almost all this wide region is fertile . . .

And, because of the power of the river, a dangerous place to live. Cable had therefore united metaphor and reality in the climax of his tale.[12]

The instability that arises from complex social, sexual and racial relations are dealt with more fully in Cable's *The Grandissimes* (1880). Running like a thread through the novel is a dispute between two aristocratic Louisiana families, the Grandissimes and the De Grapions, which occasionally erupts into violence. The plot focuses on two half-brothers, one white and one mulatto. To emphasise their brotherhood they both have the same name, Honoré Grandissime. Yet they receive very different treatment from the community. While the white Honoré is respected and admired, the mulatto Honoré is shunned, and leads a shadowy existence, despite being the wealthier of the two. A cousin of the white Honoré, Raoul Innerarity, sums up the communal view in his Louisiana dialect:

> 'I t'ink, me, dat hanny w'ite man is a gen'leman; but I don't care if a man are good like a h-angel, if 'e har not pu'e w'ite, 'ow can 'e be a gen'leman?' (137)

Joseph Frowenfeld, the young Northerner who comes to New Orleans, sees the problem clearly: 'here is a structure of society defective, dangerous, erected on views of human relations which the world is abandoning as false' (165). He is told to moderate his opinions, but is proved right. When the two Honorés unite their business interests, the town is horrified and two deaths ensue, one of an innocent bystander. The one person who has a secure sense of self-worth is an African prince sold into slavery. In telling the story of Bras-Coupé, which Cable initially wrote as a separate short story in 1873, he draws on the figure of Oroonoko, the eponymous hero of Aphra Behn's novel; but he gives his prince a happier ending. Bras-Coupé dies in ecstasy, believing that he is returning to his lands in Africa. Frowenfeld, talking to the mulatto Honoré, points Cable's moral:

> 'you – your class – the free quadroons – are the saddest slaves of all. Your men, for a little property, and your women, for a little amorous attention, let themselves be shorn even of the virtue of discontent, and for a paltry bait of sham freedom have consented to endure a tyrannous contumely which flattens them into the dirt like grass under a slab.' (215–16)

Cable's conclusion was unacceptable to his compatriots, and in 1885 he moved to a more congenial environment in Massachusetts. His work would be taken up, in yet more complex form, by William Faulkner (1897–1962).

Faulkner also drew on the tradition of dialect humour, which was to be found in all regions of the United States. Augustus Longstreet spoke for Georgia, Seba Smith for Maine, Frances Whitcher for New York, Finley Peter Dunne for the Chicago Irish. Many adopted pseudonyms. Johnson J. Hooper of Alabama became 'Simon Suggs', while Henry Clay Lewis became 'Madison Tensas, the Louisiana Swamp Doctor', noted for his deadly prescriptions. Others went a stage further, turning the pseudonym itself into a parodic vehicle. Thus Robert H. Newell of New York became 'Orpheus C. Kerr', certainly less successful than Hawthorne in finding jobs; David Ross Locke became 'Petroleum Vesuvius Nasby, late pastor uv the Church uv the New Dispensation' in Ohio; while George Washington Harris was more quietly suggestive with 'Sut Lovingood', although his character, the 'nat'ral born durn'd fool' from East Tennessee, was himself loud-mouthed enough. The humourists were known on the busy, lucrative post-bellum lecture circuit by their pseudonyms, creating personae which would be refined and developed by Twain. Their task, when they went into print, was to transliterate their dialect vividly but readably. Henry Wheeler Shaw (1818–85) was, before Twain, one of the most successful, giving a vivid impression of a Massachusetts front porch philosopher. Hence 'Josh Billings' on the 'pashunt mule':

> The mule is haf hoss and haf jackass, and then kums tu a full stop, natur diskovering her mistake. Tha weigh more, accordin tu their heft, than enny other kreetur, except a crowbar. Tha kant hear enny quicker, nor further than the hoss, yet their ears are big enuff fur snow shoes . . . Tha are a modern invenshun; i don't think the Bible deludes to them at tall . . . Tha never hav no disease that a good club won't heal . . . I herd tell ov one who fell oph from the tow path, on the Eri kanawl, and sunk . . . but he kept rite on towing the boat tu the nex stashun, breathin' thru his ears, which stuck out of the water about 2 feet 6 inches; i didn't see this did, but an auctioneer told me ov it, and i never knew an auctioneer tu lie unless it was absolutely convenient.[13]

The unusual orthography might have pleased Noah Webster, who spent a considerable time trying to create an identifiably American language. The rest – the deformed syntax, poor logic, bad jokes, double negatives, in one case a triple negative – would have been offensive to him. That was the point. The humourists turned their dialects into a joyfully violent perversion of the 'littery', as Clemens put it in his Whittier Birthday Speech. Their grip on the naive, violent, everyday realities of American life is repeated in the writing of Sherwood Anderson and Ernest Hemingway, while their dry, disrespectful humour acts as a subversive undercurrent in the work of Hemingway's social and stylistic antithesis, Henry James.

The achievement of Samuel Clemens was to transform the humourists' tendency to aphorism into continuous narrative, the baroque anacoluthia of their transliterated humour into a simple vernacular style, and their pseudonymity into a persona of such elemental force that the author almost disappeared. It is sometimes difficult to detect the early life of Clemens beneath the smokescreen of bravado, but we do know that he was a competent Mississippi riverboat pilot; that he briefly dashed around the Missouri countryside pretending to be Confederate cavalry; that he prospected without success for gold, wrote for several newspapers, hung around with Artemus Ward and fellow California journalist 'Dan De Quille', and learnt some of his trade from Bret Harte (1836–1902), whose *Condensed Novels and Other Papers* (1867) were toxic satires of such popular novelists as Cooper, Dickens and Irving. We also know that he tried on several pseudonyms for size, including 'W. Epaminondas Adrastus Blab', before being transmogrified into 'Mark Twain', a choice that is at once believable and redolent of Clemens's fondest memory, of piloting a Mississippi riverboat.

More than with the other humourists, a complex dynamic existed between Samuel Clemens and his pseudonym. Mark Twain was a mixed blessing. Like a double that is just out of control, Twain prompted Clemens to make his most outrageous flights of fancy. Then Clemens had to meet the costs, as the aftermath to the Whittier Birthday Speech showed. Duality is a central element of Clemens's thought, and is apparent early in *The Adventures of Tom Sawyer* (1876), with the first entry of one of the major characters in fiction, swinging, by the tail, a cat with rigor mortis:

> Huckleberry was cordially hated and dreaded by all the mothers of the town because he was idle, and lawless, and vulgar, and bad – and because all their children admired him so, and delighted in his forbidden society, and wished they dared to be like him. Tom was like the rest of the respectable boys in that he envied Huckleberry his gaudy outcast condition, and was under strict orders not to play with him. So he played with him every time he got a chance . . . Huckleberry came and went of his own free will. He slept on door-steps in fine weather, and in empty hogsheads in wet; he did not have to go to school or church, or call any being master, or obey anybody; he could go fishing when and where he chose, and stay as long as it suited him; nobody forbade him to fight; he could sit up as late as he pleased . . . he never had to wash, nor put on clean clothes; he could swear wonderfully. In a word, everything that goes to make life precious, that boy had.

Signalled by the oxymoron 'cordially hated', this is an exercise in wish-fulfilment, with Tom Sawyer acting as a surrogate for Clemens, and Huck Finn as the imaginative vehicle for Twain. Clemens, however, was here too confined by the conventions of the middle class to be swept along by the wondrous childhood of Huck. At the close of the tale Huck is 'snaked' into the middle class by the Widow Douglas, which means clean clothes and a wash.[14] There are similarly unsatisfactory results when Tom takes charge again in *Tom Sawyer Abroad* (1894) and *Tom Sawyer, Detective* (1896). In contrast, when Twain is given too much imaginative rope, as in *The Tragedy of Pudd'nhead Wilson* (1894), the result is an interesting but disordered mess. On just one occasion the tension between Twain and Clemens was sufficiently equal to produce a masterpiece, *The Adventures of Huckleberry Finn* (1885), which of course reverses the ending of *The Adventures of Tom Sawyer*.

Twain also made Clemens brave enough to puncture the over-inflated. Clemens's attacks began with his first success, 'Jim Smiley and His Jumping Frog' (1865). The Jumping Frog was named 'Dan'l Webster', and the tale could be interpreted as a metaphor of the grounding of that most famous American orator. The attacks continued in the account of Clemens's western travels, *Roughing It* (1872). The handwriting of Horace Greeley, the most famous newspaper editor of his day, is so illegible that Greeley's signature is repeatedly read as 'HEVACE EVEELOJ . . . a harmless affectation of Hebrew'. The consequence is that Greeley's advice on the properties of turnips is understood too late to prevent the death of a young man besotted with the plant, the death in turn leading to the madness of the storyteller. Clemens's attacks on humbug reached their comic pinnacle in *The Adventures of Huckleberry Finn*, which contains a version of the central soliloquy of the English canon:

> To be or not to be; that is the bare bodkin
> That makes calamity of so long life;
> For who would fardels bear, till Birnam Wood do come to Dunsinane,
> But that the fear of something after death
> Murders the innocent sleep,
> Great nature's second course,
> And makes us rather sling the arrows of outrageous fortune
> Than fly to others that we know not of.

The soliloquy, which continues for another seventeen sublime lines, almost succeeds in making sense. It brings into near-collision five lines from two different scenes of *Hamlet*, five lines from four different scenes of *Macbeth*, and one line from *Richard III*. It ends by sending Ophelia to a nunnery.[15] Unfortunately, even Shakespeare of this calibre isn't strong enough meat for the tobacco-chewing population of Brocksville, Arkansas. The King and the Duke are forced to drop the Bard in favour of the more licentious Royal Nonsuch show, and they continue a downward path which ends when they are run out of town like Skipper Ireson, dressed in feathers and tar.

The appearance of Twain in Clemens's life could be seen as a comic modernisation of the Antinomian crisis, with Twain an overreacher like Anne Hutchinson. So Clemens paid. The first sign of serious strain, as opposed to the middle-class embarrassment of the Whittier Birthday Speech, is to be found in *A Connecticut Yankee in King Arthur's Court* (1889). The target for comic deflation this time was the Age of Chivalry. It had been suggested by Clemens's attack on Sir Walter Scott, in *Life on the Mississippi*, for stopping 'progress' by recreating the 'sham chivalries of a brainless and worthless long-vanished society'.[16] When Hank Morgan, the Yankee, an engineer at a Colt firearms factory, gets knocked back to AD 513, the scene is set for another sally at the deadly vacuities of sentimental language. But 'progress' ends in a holocaust, with twenty-five thousand knights slain by thirteen Gatling guns. This horrific preview of the First World War also anticipated Clemens's late misanthropic work, such as *The Man That Corrupted Hadleyburg* (1900) and *What Is Man?* (1906). Humbug, it seemed, was such a fundamental part of human nature that violence rather than humour was the only antidote. But the 'gaudy outcast' epitomised by Huck Finn would survive. As a concession to modern sensibilities Americans may have disposed of dead cats, but the large number of road movies show that the impulse to light out for the territory is still deeply embedded in their psyche.

E Pluribus Unum

The victory of the North in the Civil War had satisfied Lincoln's wish to preserve the Union, and confirmed the motto on its Great Seal, *E Pluribus Unum*. The railroads, beginning with the creation of the first transcontinental link in 1869, continued the task by spreading a network of lines across the nation. Andrew Carnegie (1835–1919), who had begun his career as a railroad man and rose to become the best-known industrialist of the time, aptly characterised the country's dominant values with a railroad image: 'The Republic thunders past with the rush of an express.' The writer who celebrated those values with the greatest enthusiasm was Horatio Alger (1832–99) who, beginning with *Fame and Fortune* in 1868, wrote some 130 novels preaching the American Dream. The essence of Alger's work can be distilled by comparing *Mark, the Match Boy*, published the next year, with the fairy tale that is probably its source, Hans Christian Andersen's 'The Little Match-Girl' (in translation, 1851). Afraid of going home without having sold any matches, the girl freezes with a smile on her face, the matches having illuminated memories of the grandmother with whom she is reunited in death. The protagonist of *Mark, the Match Boy* begins with the same fear, but thanks to a benevolent journalist is able to pay for a warm night in the cabin of a ferryboat. This is the first of a series of steps, which lead to the reunion of Mark and his grandfather in Milwaukee. In other words, blessed are those who seek their reward on earth; Alger's plots, combining aggressive opportunism with bourgeois conformity, will provide opportunities for them. The novels sold more than twenty million copies but, ironically, they did little to reward Alger. Alger's publishers prospered; he died in poverty.[17]

Hawthorne in *The House of the Seven Gables* had questioned Alger's message, even before he had formulated it. That message would receive its decisive answer in Nathanael West's 1934 parody *A Cool Million*. There were many, too, who disagreed with Carnegie's triumphalism. They included Henry George who, in his best-selling *Progress and Poverty* (1879), suggested why it was possible for those two nouns in his title to co-exist. In 1873 Twain co-operated with Charles Dudley Warner to publish the novel that would give the period its name. *The Gilded Age* satirised the values of the time savagely. Its main speculator, Colonel Beriah Sellers – his name a stroke of parodic genius – has one expensive 'vision' after another. The most costly, for it ends in the bankruptcy of Sellers and others, is a projected railroad from St Louis to Corruptionville, named 'after Congress itself'.[18] The railroad will travel via Slouchburg, Doodleville, Brimstone, Babylon, Bloody Run, Hail Columbia, Hark-from-the-Tomb and Hallelujah. It was the Midwest counterpart to Hawthorne's 'Celestial Rail-Road'.

If there was one writer more equipped than the others to celebrate the nation as a whole, it was Walt Whitman. He staked out the ground he would cultivate all his life in the well-known words beginning the second paragraph of his Preface to the first, 1855, edition of *Leaves of Grass*. 'The Americans of all nations at any time upon the earth have probably the fullest poetical nature,' he wrote, 'the United States themselves are essentially the greatest poem.' Other nations appear 'tame and orderly' compared with 'their ampler largeness and stir'.[19] Apart from the braggadocio, vital and far from empty, the other noticeable aspect here is the unusual locution. Whitman left school when he was eleven years old, and turned a potential hindrance into a virtue, freeing his writing from the straitjacket of the grammarian. For much of his life he moved from job to job: printer, teacher, journalist, newspaper editor, government clerk, builder. He made a virtue of that, too, for it gave him authority to speak for the people. His first long work, which sold more copies in his lifetime than anything else he wrote, was a temperance tract, *Franklin Evans; or the Inebriate* (1842). This may seem odd, in view of the way he projects himself in the first poem of the 1855 *Leaves of Grass*, later called 'Song of Myself':

> Walt Whitman, an American, one of the roughs, a kosmos,
> Disorderly fleshy and sensual . . . eating drinking and breeding,
> No sentimentalist . . . no stander above men and women and apart from
>   them . . . no more modest than immodest.
>
> Unscrew the locks from the doors!
> Unscrew the doors themselves from their jambs! (50)

This seems a sure prescription for the temperance writer to find himself in a Saturday-night police cell. It is confirmed by the engraving facing the first, anonymous, title page: of a slouching, louche, open-necked lout, flashing his flannel underwear. Perhaps the temperance-tract was hack work. Yet the first poem begins with a refusal to become intoxicated; and Whitman may have learnt the technique of drunken writing from that Concord sobersides, Emerson, whom he had heard lecture on 'The Poet' in 1842.

Whitman also learnt from William Cullen Bryant (1794–1878), the editor of the New York *Evening Post* and a very popular poet at the time. Emerson wrote in his journal that Bryant was 'American . . . Dared name a jay & a gentian, crows', adding that his poetry was 'sincere'. This seems half-hearted praise. On the one hand, in poems like 'To the Fringed Gentian' and 'To a

Water-Fowl', Bryant was prepared to address apostrophes to the common flora and fauna of the American countryside. On the other hand, his poetry was conventional, drawn above all from Wordsworth, one of whose most famous poems was about daffodils. Yet Bryant did try to isolate the specific qualities of his environment. Emerson added in his journal that he felt that Bryant had actually visited the places he wrote about. Whitman, in a late tribute, called him the 'bard of the river and the wood, ever conveying a taste of open air'. In 'The Prairies' Bryant wrote, for instance, that these 'gardens of the Desert' had no name in 'the speech of England' – the noun was originally French. He saw that 'this great solitude is quick with life', and imagined a time when it would be filled by 'the laugh of children' as well as the hum of insects. The poem of Bryant that is best remembered, probably because it is addressed to the painter Thomas Cole on his return to Europe in 1829, shows precisely what would have appealed to Whitman:

> Thine eyes shall see the light of distant skies;
>   Yet, COLE! thy heart shall bear to Europe's strand
> A living image of our own bright land,
>   Such as upon thy glorious canvas lies;
> Lone lakes – savannas where the bison roves –
>   Rocks rich with summer garlands – solemn streams –
> Skies, where the desert eagle wheels and screams –
>   Spring bloom and autumn blaze of boundless groves.
> Fair scenes shall greet thee where thou goest – fair,
>   But different – everywhere the trace of men,
>   Paths, homes, graves, ruins, from the lowest glen
> To where life shrinks from the fierce Alpine air.
>   Gaze on them, till the tears shall dim they sight,
>   But keep that earlier, wilder image bright.

It can be argued that Cole did not listen to Bryant's advice; he returned to the United States with a taste for Italian landscape. Whitman, in contrast, paid close attention. He discarded Bryant's traditional forms – here it is, of course, a sonnet – but kept that wilder image bright by using Bryant's lists and ambient terminology. Indeed, in his drive for wildness Whitman went beyond Bryant, and used vernacular. He was, after all, like Sut Lovingood and Josh Billings, one of the 'roughs'.

Apart from Emerson and Bryant, Whitman's other influences included the King James Bible, Milton – both for the rolling lines and the everyday imagery – and Italian opera. The opening of that first 1855 poem has the multi-tempo dramatic form of the nineteenth-century aria, even more than when it was rewritten as 'Song of Myself', despite the later reference to singing. One can almost hear the tenor voice:

> I celebrate myself,
>   And what I assume you shall assume,
> For every atom belonging to me as good belongs to you.
>
> I loafe and invite my soul,
>   I lean and loafe at my ease . . . observing a spear of summer grass.

The ellipsis marks are breathing directions like the line endings, rather than signs of an omission. Whitman, indeed, omitted as little as possible. One reviewer talked of Whitman's 'heroic nudity'. Others were less broad-minded, muttering darkly about the poet's lack of shame. The wittiest response came from an almost exact contemporary, the critic Edwin P. Whipple, who, as reported by Emerson, said that *Leaves of Grass* contained 'every leaf but the fig leaf'. It was sensuality, not intoxication, which earned Whitman his reputation. He was fired from the Indian Affairs Department in 1865 for writing a 'dirty book', and *Leaves of Grass* hit the headlines in 1882 for being the first book to be 'banned in Boston'.[20]

Whitman's sexuality, as opposed to his sensuality, has been a much-discussed topic. There may be hints of homosexuality in the 'Calamus Poems', added to the third, 1860, edition of *Leaves of Grass*. These are balanced by assertions that may be bisexual. For instance, in 'Whoever You Are Holding Me Now In Hand' – a question that is never answered – Whitman talks of 'the comrade's long-dwelling kiss or the new husband's kiss' (271). Maybe, like some of the First World War poetry that he influenced, it was homoeroticism that was the guiding emotion. Certainly, from that very first poem in the 1855 edition he was frank about sex:

> I mind how we lay in June, such a transparent summer morning;
> You settled your head athwart my hips and gently turned over upon me,
> And parted the shirt from my bosom-bone, and plunged your tongue to my
>   barestript heart,
> And reached till you felt my beard, and reached till you held my feet. (30)

Which seems to suggest a well-developed technique, no matter the gender of the addressee. Ultimately, gender was not the point. Sex; 'the largeness of nature or the nation'; the enormous lists, beginning with the first 1855 poem and far more ambitious than anything Emerson attempted; the extent of the social reach, from the 'greasy or pimpled' to the President – all were gathered into the poetry to make it the embodiment of *E Pluribus Unum* (6, 90). As Whitman said in one of his most famous lines, 'I am large . . . I contain multitudes' (87).

This did not mean that he lacked discrimination. In 'To the States', a poem added to the 1860 edition of *Leaves of Grass*, he attacked the 'scum floating atop of the waters/Who are they as bats and night-dogs askant in the capitol?' (415). This 'filthy Presidentiad' was the collective name for the presidencies of Millard Fillmore, Franklin Pierce and James Buchanan, lasting collectively from 1850 to 1861. Fillmore had presided over the Compromise of 1850, which had offended Emerson so much. Pierce, according to Teddy Roosevelt, was 'a small politician, of low capacity and mean surroundings . . . ever ready to do any work the slavery leaders set him'. Buchanan favoured the admission of Kansas to the Union as a slave state, turning it, after the Kansas-Nebraska Act (1854), into a bloody battleground between abolitionists and pro-slavery supporters. While he was not as agitated as the abolitionists, Whitman's key doctrine of freedom was at odds with slavery. He therefore treated those who had engineered the elections of these presidents to a magnificent prose flyting in 'The Eighteenth Presidency!':

WHO ARE THEY PERSONALLY?

Office-holders, office-seekers, robbers, pimps, exclusives, malignants, conspirators, murderers, fancy-men, post-masters, custom-house clerks, contractors, kept-editors, spaniels well-trained to carry and fetch, jobbers, infidels, disunionists, terrorists, mail-riflers, slave-catchers, pushers of slavery . . . blind men, deaf men, pimpled men, scarred inside with the vile disorder, gaudy outside with gold chains made from the people's money and harlot's money twisted together; crawling, serpentine men, the lousy combings and born freedom sellers of the earth. (1313–14)

In a land of political favouritism no distinction is made between those who legally obtain posts for political favours, like Hawthorne, who wrote the campaign biography for Pierce; those who can trap escaped slaves under the Fugitive Slave Act of 1850, repealed by Lincoln's administration in 1864; and those who act outside the law, such as murderers and thieves. Indeed, Whitman's anger here has turned him briefly against those, like prostitutes and men with skin afflictions, whom he normally treated as equal partners in his grand democracy.

Whitman saw Lincoln as an honest antidote to the political jobbery that had tarnished the government. Lincoln was, he thought, an 'idiomatic western genius', or – better yet – 'a hoosier Michael Angelo', bringing together the name of the Renaissance polymath with the term applied to the inhabitants of Indiana. This was one reason why, after Lincoln's assassination, Whitman joined other poets, one of them Bryant, in writing poems in honour of the President. But he outdid the others by writing four poems for Lincoln, one of them 206 lines long, because the President's martyrdom to the Union was at the heart of Whitman's ideology.[21] Whitman had little involvement in the Civil War until he was sent by his family to find his younger brother, a Union officer wounded in December 1862 at the Battle of Fredericksburg. Whitman found him at the battle site, then accompanied a squad of wounded soldiers back to Washington. For the remainder of the war he remained in the Union capital as a volunteer nurse. He also visited the sites of the battles of Chancellorsville and Vicksburg (May and July 1863) as soon as they were over. These experiences are recorded in *Drum-Taps* (1865), the finest group of poems inspired by the war.

The sequence follows the progress of the war. It begins with parades in Manhattan, but quickly abandons partisanship with 'From Paumanok Starting I Fly like a Bird', involving an imaginary journey over all parts of the country. It then examines some battlefront scenes where 'guidon flags flutter gayly in the wind', and at night soldiers sit 'by the bivouac's fitful flame' (435–6). The first sombre note appears with 'Come Up from the Fields Father'. The poem begins like a Victorian ballad, but darkens as the family reads a letter in broken sentences, 'not our son's writing'. One of Whitman's tasks in Washington hospitals was to write just such letters for the wounded and dying. In this case the poem uses omniscient narrative to inform the reader that, as the family read the letter, 'the only son is dead' (436–8). 'Come Up from the Fields Father' is a preparation for 'The Wound-Dresser', which uses Whitman's intimate sense of sympathy to convey first-person immediacy to the hospital scene:

> I dress the perforated shoulder, the foot with the bullet-wound,
> Cleanse the one with a gnawing and putrid gangrene, so sickening,
>   so offensive,
> While the attendant stands beside me holding the tray and pail. (445)

The sequence ends with the poet returning to the imaginary journey over the reunited republic. Later in 1865 Whitman published *Sequel to Drum-Taps*, including the four poems which make up the 'Memories of President Lincoln'. The most popular at the time was 'O Captain! My Captain!', perhaps for its ballad-like quality. The most memorable now is the extended elegy, 'When Lilacs Last in the Dooryard Bloom'd'. It is a processional for 'the sweetest, wisest soul of all my days and lands', and contains the themes of 'Come Up from the Fields Father' and 'The Wound-Dresser', but finally refuses to mourn, for death is but an 'outlet song of life' (459–67). The poem, in other words, performs the same function as Lincoln's 'Gettysburg Address', spoken two years earlier.

Whitman never again wrote as well. 'Passage to India', added to the fifth, 1871, edition, and 'Prayer of Columbus', added to the sixth, 1876, edition of *Leaves of Grass*, mark a return to Whitman's optimistic poetry. The first poem celebrates the Suez Canal, the transcontinental railroad and 'seas inlaid with eloquent gentle wires' (the transatlantic cable) as new technologies uniting the whole world (531–40). The second is a prayer which begins with Columbus 'a batter'd wreck'd old man', possibly a self-portrait, and ends with 'anthems in new tongues I hear saluting me' (540–2). Whitman had turned himself, for good or ill, into a representative American, and the United States will become the representative nation. *Democratic Vistas*, published in 1871, uses Puritan theology to assert that America is the 'type of progress, and of essential faith in man' (977). The 'fruition of democracy' still 'resides altogether in the future', but there will come 'a new age and a new man' (957), based on the ideology rooted in Whitman's poetry from the first edition of *Leaves of Grass* onwards:

> the main thing being the average, the bodily, the concrete, the democratic, the popular, on which all the superstructures of the future are to permanently rest. (994)

It was a return to the geopolitics of Thomas Paine, one of the 'good and faithful men' whose fame, as Whitman said in an 1877 address, should be burnished 'newer, truer and brighter, continually' (799). Whitman regarded himself, with some reason, as one of those men, but his aspirations had now inflated to the whole world, undimmed by present fears of American materialism and corruption. The world, certainly its western part, responded with enthusiasm. Whitman has had many followers. He influenced the British composers who emerged in the early twentieth century, Delius, Holst and Vaughan

Williams; and the Beat writers of mid-century. His most enthusiastic acolyte is perhaps Allen Ginsberg, who has devoted a number of poems to his 'dear father, graybeard, lonely old courage-teacher'.[22]

A complex fate

The end of the Civil War gave the United States a renewed sense of mission. Even with its outcome still far from certain, Abraham Lincoln had closed his 1862 Annual Message to Congress with words heavy with portent:

> Fellow-citizens, *we* cannot escape history ... In *giving* freedom to the *slave*, we *assure* freedom to the *free* – honorable alike in what we give, and what we preserve. We shall nobly save, or meanly lose, the last best, hope of earth.

As expressed by Lincoln, the Civil War both inserted the United States into history and set it a task that it would not be able to complete. The victory of the North had given the United States an ideological freight far more burdensome than the one given to Europe by the First World War. No citizen would now try to follow George Fitzhugh in questioning the fundamental value of freedom. At the close of 1865 William Lloyd Garrison ceased publishing his journal, *The Liberator*, contending that it had finally achieved its purpose. Henceforth the United States would designate itself the beacon of freedom to the world, symbolised by the Statue of Liberty, the centennial gift from France eventually erected in New York harbour in 1886, with the Emma Lazarus sonnet carved on its base:

> 'Give me your tired, your poor,
> Your huddled masses yearning to breathe free ...'[23]

The international status of the United States is reflected in the work of two quite different writers, Emily Dickinson and Henry James.

When she died in 1886, Dickinson's death certificate recorded her occupation as 'At Home'. The statement is both accurate and diminishing. Dickinson spent the first ten and last thirty years of her life in 'The Homestead', the house built by her grandfather in the small Massachusetts college town of Amherst. She had withdrawn from Amherst life to the extent that, when Mabel Loomis Todd arrived in the town in 1881, Dickinson had achieved local celebrity for her reclusiveness:

> I must tell you about the *character* of Amherst. It is a lady whom the people call the *Myth* ... She has not been outside of her own house in fifteen years, except once to see a new church, when she crept out at night, & viewed it by moonlight ... She dresses wholly in white, & her mind is said to be perfectly wonderful. She writes finely, but no one *ever* sees her. Her sister ... invited me to come & sing to her mother sometime ... People tell me that the *myth* will hear every note – she will be near, but unseen.

Todd's letter to her parents names and perpetuates the myth of Emily Dickinson, and marks the first step in her own involvement with the poet and her family.

Todd sang at the Dickinson house, and Dickinson hid and listened. The only time that Todd saw Dickinson she was in her coffin. Dickinson doubtless heard Todd on other occasions, too, because Todd soon began an enthusiastic and long-lasting affair with Dickinson's brother Austin, a darkly Byronic figure living in the mansion next door. Todd's records show that she and Austin often consummated their relationship in the dining room of 'The Homestead' while Dickinson was upstairs, or even in the garden. After Dickinson's death, Todd published three volumes of her poetry (1890, 1891, 1896) and one volume of her letters (1894).[24] They were the first widespread indication that Dickinson indeed wrote finely. Although some of Dickinson's work circulated privately, only ten poems were published in her lifetime, between 1852 and 1878, principally in the local newspaper edited by Austin's friend Samuel Bowles, the *Springfield Daily Republican*, and in the *Brooklyn Drum Beat*, an 1864 fund-raising publication. Dickinson's younger sister Lavinia discovered the vast majority of her work shortly after her death. The variorum edition of 1998 numbers 1,789 poems, although there were doubtless many more that did not survive.

The posthumous publication of Dickinson's work has caused many problems of editing and interpretation. Todd, together with her co-editor for the first two editions, the indefatigable Thomas Wentworth Higginson, regularised the poems and grouped some of them together as love poems. Thomas H. Johnson, who in 1955 produced the first accurate edition of her poems, and Ralph W. Franklin, the editor of the 1998 edition, attempted a chronological order, thereby making the poems available to autobiographical interpretation. The two earliest extant poems, 'Awake ye muses nine' and 'Sic transit gloria mundi', are valentines, beginning the lengthy sequence with a hothouse intensity seemingly confirmed by the lyric brevity of almost all of the poems. There has been considerable speculation about the 'Master' who is the addressee of several poems and three passionate draft letters. There have been some recent suggestions that the 'Master' may be female. Everything appears to confirm Todd's initial impression of Dickinson as a permanent teenager or a woman-on-the-edge. For these reasons, among others, Dickinson was a popular model for the twentieth-century female poet.

The poems, and the way that Dickinson herself ordered them, reveal a somewhat different picture. From 1858 until about 1865, Dickinson rewrote her poems and stitched them together, sometimes with variants, into forty booklets known as fascicles. The first fascicle did not include the two valentines.[25] Yet even they are nuanced. 'Sic transit gloria mundi' is a mordant title for a valentine, while 'Awake ye muses nine' contains the following line: 'The worm doth woo the mortal, death claims a living bride' (Franklin 1). Later revisions were kept in unbound groups. Dickinson's intentions in grouping her poems are unclear and have been subject to scholarly debate. Numbers of poems were sent to friends, then revised for the fascicles, and sometimes revised again later. The revisions can lead to radically different readings. For instance, 'I showed her Hights she never saw', probably written in the summer of 1862, was sent in the following form to Susan Dickinson, wife of the unfaithful Austin:

> I showed her Hights she never saw –
> 'Would'st Climb,' I said?
> She said – 'Not so' –
> 'With *me* –' I said – With *me*?
> I showed her Secrets – Morning's Nest –
> The Rope the Nights were put across –
> And *now* – 'Would'st have me for a Guest'?
> She could not find her Yes –
> And then, I brake my life – And Lo,
> A Light, for her, did solemn glow,
> The larger, as her face withdrew –
> And *could* she, further, 'No'?

The poem was rewritten in Fascicle 16:

> He showed me Hights I never saw –
> 'Would'st Climb' – He said?
> I said, 'Not so' –
> 'With me' – He said – 'With me'?
>
> He showed me secrets – Morning's Nest –
> The Rope the Nights were put across –
> 'And now, Would'st have me for a Guest'?
> I could not find my 'Yes' –
>
> And then – He brake His Life – And Lo,
> A light for me, did solemn glow –
> The steadier, as my face withdrew –
> And could I further 'No'? (Franklin 346)

The differences in punctuation, emphases, stanzaic arrangement, and one adjective, may be significant. The most obvious difference, though, is in the subject of the poem. The first version might lend itself to a lesbian reading, the second to a heterosexual – unless the persona in the poem is male. Or, to strip the words of potential metaphoric meanings, perhaps both versions are about bird nesting.

With all their ambiguities and difficulties, Dickinson's poems can be organised into three groups: local, national and international. The local are those which reveal a New England voice. That voice is earnestly yet often comically individualistic, intimate with the King James Bible, grappling with the reality of death, anxious to record the soul's account with God, disdainful of any intermediary – hence the dismissal of the clergy in 'Bees are Black' as 'Buccaneers of Buzz' (Franklin 1426). 'I died for Beauty', for instance, acts as a comic scourge for the Romantic indulgence of Keats's 'Ode on a Grecian Urn':

> I died for Beauty – but was scarce
> Adjusted in the Tomb
> When One who died for Truth, was lain
> In an adjoining Room –

He questioned softly 'Why I failed'?
'For Beauty', I replied –
'And I – for Truth – Themself are One
We Bretheren, are', He said –

And so, as Kinsmen, me a Night
We talked between the Rooms –
Until the Moss had reached our lips –
And covered up – Our names – (Franklin 448)

Time cancels all antinomies. Dickinson's inventive and multi-purpose use of the dash, so much a feature of her poems in modern editions, here indicates the passage of time, and a conversation where the speakers believe they now have all the time in the world, until the final comic delay and then release into silence. The dashes may also act as breathing directions. It was once suggested that Dickinson's poems may be sung to one of two melodies: either – as here – to that of 'The Yellow Rose of Texas', or to that of 'John Brown's Body'. There is an element of truth in this burlesque reduction. If Whitman's rhythms are based on Italian arias, Dickinson's are rooted in the more regular communal phrases of the hymnal.

Dickinson's national poems reflect on the Civil War, the years in which she wrote the majority of her work. Her recruitment to the Union side resulted to an extent from her growing relationship with Thomas Wentworth Higginson (1823–1911). When Henry James reviewed Higginson's autobiography, *Cheerful Yesterdays* (1898), he noted that it is 'the abbreviated record of a very full life, in which action and art have been unusually mingled', and added that 'Colonel Higginson has the interesting quality of having reflected almost everything that was in the New England air, of vibrating with it all around'.[26] Higginson was the quintessential Brahmin reformer. He supported women's and workers' rights. He hated slavery, assisted fugitive slaves, led an armed group to Kansas after the passage of the Kansas-Nebraska Act, and aided John Brown. Dickinson, too, was one of his 'vibrations', and for her he became military hero as man-of-letters. His 'Letter to a Young Contributor' in the *Atlantic Monthly* (1862), encouraging women to publish, prompted Dickinson to write to him and enclose four poems. By the time he received her letter he had joined the Union army, and would shortly be chosen to lead the First South Carolina Volunteers, the first regiment comprised of slaves freed by Union forces. He was wounded in action, leading his freedmen, and would record his experience in *Army Life in a Black Regiment* (1870). The relationship between Dickinson and her 'preceptor', as she called him, lasted until her death and was largely conducted by letter. They only met twice, Higginson apparently being relieved that their relationship was mediated by the postal system.

Others, including several from Amherst College who were wounded or killed in the Civil War, joined Higginson in heralding a tendency toward romance in Dickinson's poetry. Twain would have rejected it as 'sham chivalry', but it endowed her lyrics with the spaciousness of epic. The Civil War is to be found in the references to artillery as well as cavalry in her poetry; in the sound of the Dead March in 'I felt a Funeral, in my Brain' (Franklin 340); but most of all in 'Lay this laurel on the one'. It was written in 1877, apparently inspired by Higginson's 'Decoration' (1874). Higginson's poem begins with the military ritual of the unknown soldier:

> Mid the flower-wreath'd tombs I stand,
> Bearing lilies in my hand.
> Comrades! in what soldier-grave
> Sleeps the bravest of the brave?

The question is answered after a further five stanzas in a closure that is both chivalric and chivalrous, declaring Higginson's feminism:

> Turning from my comrades' eyes,
> Kneeling where a woman lies,
> I strew lilies on the grave
> Of the bravest of the brave.

Dickinson responded to 'Decoration' with a poem that, Higginson admitted, 'is the condensed essence of that & so far finer':

> Lay this Laurel on the one
> Triumphed – and remained unknown –
> Laurel fell your futile tree –
> Such a Victor cannot be –
>
> Lay this Laurel on the one –
> Too intrinsic for Renown
> Laurel – vail your deathless tree –
> Him thou chastenest – That is he –[27]

Her poem remains as one of the finest memorials to the Civil War, together with the Saint-Gaudens bas-relief on Boston Common, dedicated to Robert Gould Shaw and his (Black) 54th Massachusetts Regiment, and the poem that it in turn inspired, Robert Lowell's 'For the Union Dead' (1960).

The poems that place Dickinson in the international English literary tradition have been often identified, and can be handled briefly. They include the poems that locate Dickinson as a feminist, either paying homage to Elizabeth Barrett Browning, Charlotte Brontë and George Eliot, or subverting male identity and its public forum. 'I'm Nobody!' therefore seems to begin precisely from the forum of male dialect humour, but turns into a devastating attack on the inflated creature, which Twain would later use to puncture a man more public than he:

> I'm Nobody! Who are you?
> Are you – Nobody – too?
> Then there's a pair of us!
> Don't tell! they'd banish us – you know!
>
> How dreary – to be – Somebody!
> How public – like a Frog –
> To tell your name – the livelong June –
> To an admiring Bog! (Franklin 260)

When Dickinson's poems were first published in 1890 some reviewers re-cognised that they signalled something new. Indeed they do; they anticipate the concise precision of imagism, the fragments that are modernism, the defamiliarising agenda of formalism, and the dream world of psychoanalysis. All of these anticipations can be seen in her most famous piece:

> After great pain, a formal feeling comes –
> The Nerves sit ceremonious, like Tombs –
> The stiff Heart questions 'was it He, that bore,'
> And 'Yesterday, or Centuries before'?
>
> The Feet, mechanical, go round –
> Of Ground, or Air, or Ought –
> A Wooden way
> Regardless grown,
> A Quartz contentment, like a stone –
>
> This is the Hour of Lead –
> Remembered, if outlived,
> As Freezing persons, recollect the Snow –
> First – Chill – then Stupor – then the letting go – (Franklin 372)

In terms both of construction and sensory observation, this poem is perfectly realised. The last line summarises the stages of the three stanzas, with the dashes acting both as sutures binding the broken groups and as markers on the road to the final release. Dickinson may have spent much of her time 'At Home', but it was she who most clearly proved William Carlos Williams's dictum that the local is the universal.

Henry James spent much of his life away from 'home'. Yet like Dickinson, his early work expresses the new international status of the United States, ironically in its discussion of a freedom for which some of their contemporaries were not yet ready, the freedom of the imagination. Henry James was the grandson of one of the wealthiest men in the United States, and the son of an inquisitive religious philosopher with a taste for transatlantic travel. This endowment had a great impact on James that would be worked out in his fiction. The trend was set by a visit to Europe very soon after he was born. The visits continued as he grew older, and in 1875 he moved permanently to Europe, first to France and then to England. Many of James's American contemporaries thought of Europe as a den of iniquity. They reacted negat-ively to lascivious dances, such as the can-can, and even ballet; and were particularly horrified by the dress of the dancers. That lightweight cloth, gauze, became subject to some heavy Puritan interpretations. Samuel Clemens exposed this humbug in the aptly-named *The Innocents Abroad* (1869), the result of his first visit to Europe in 1867. He reported seeing the can-can at the Jardin Mabille in Paris. 'I placed my hands before my face for very shame,' he wrote, 'but I looked through my fingers.' Europe was such a feast for James's imagination that he did not even go through the pretence of shielding his face. In part it was European society that inspired him. The younger American novelist Harold Frederic said that James's enthusiasm for social events was

259

such that 'he has licked dust from the floor of every third rate hostess in London'. In part it was the environment. Even a visit to Blunderstone, near Great Yarmouth in Suffolk, sent his hypersensitive consciousness into associationist overdrive, making him sniff like a dog, he wrote, for 'an impression in every bush'. In contrast, James's book on Hawthorne suggested, with a comic extension that contained a kernel of truth, that the United States provided a surfeit only of absences, enough to induce imaginative if not canine suicide. As the Baroness Eugenia Münster remarks in James's 1878 novel, *The Europeans*, the country around Boston 'seemed to be all foreground'.[28]

Discussing social matters by implication, James's 1876–7 novel, *The American*, might be regarded as the antithesis of *The Europeans*. It provides an illustration of the cognitive gymnastics that Europe offered to the sensitive American. Christopher Newman, the wealthy but naive veteran of the Civil War whose name carries an obvious weight of American symbology, wishes to marry the sister of a 'penniless patrician', the Marquis Urbain de Bellegarde. He becomes aware of the difficulties confronting him simply by watching the Marquis put on a pair of gloves:

> Newman for a few moments watched him sliding his white hands into the white kid, and as he did so his feeling took a singular turn. M. de Bellegarde's good wishes seemed to descend out of the white expanse of his sublime serenity with the soft scattered movement of a shower of snow-flakes. Yet Newman was not irritated; he did not feel that he was being patronised; he was conscious of no especial impulse to introduce a discord into so noble a harmony. Only he felt himself suddenly in personal contact with the forces with which . . . he would have to contend, and he became sensible of their intensity.[29]

Temporally, this passage spans a few moments only. Its cognitive dimension is enormous, signalling the struggle that will occupy the rest of the novel, and bringing into focus the conflict of New with Old World social and cultural structures. The second sentence, with its imagery and smooth structure, unpunctuated and assisted by sibilants, conveys the self-assurance of the French aristocrat. The following two sentences convey the perceptual agility of the American, rhythmically irregular and clinched by the appropriate final noun, 'intensity'. The Civil War veteran is now much less naive.

It follows that Rome would provide the most rich education to American senses, and James, like Hawthorne before him, responded to the 'Eternal City' with particular intensity. He would treat the city, and Italy in general, as the setting for a significant proportion of his novels and short stories. The discussion here will be confined to two texts published before 1880, *Roderick Hudson* (1875) and *Daisy Miller* (1879). From his earliest publications, James wrote both fiction and criticism. Occasionally, he would combine those functions. *Roderick Hudson* is a rewrite of *The Marble Faun*; just as *The Portrait of a Lady* (1880–1) would be a rewrite of George Eliot's *Middlemarch* (1871–2). The plot and character structure of *Roderick Hudson* is close to Hawthorne's novel. At an early point, shortly after Roderick Hudson, an amateur sculptor, and Rowland Mallett, his wealthy patron, have reached Rome, the narrator reflects on the artistic influence of the city very much as Hawthorne had done: 'Rome is the natural home of those spirits . . . with a deep relish for the artificial element in life and the infinite superpositions of history'.[30] This is in sharp contrast to the family back in New England. 'Rome is an evil word in my mother's vocabulary,' says Roderick, 'Northampton is in the centre of Christendom and Rome far away in outlying dusk, into which it can do no proper moral man any good to penetrate' (77). The novel, however, goes beyond the presentation of Rome as a moral guide-book. The relationship between the characters and Rome reverses Hawthornian symbolism. In *The Marble Faun* the characters were subject to a governing design. In *Roderick Hudson* they are judged in terms of their appreciation of Rome. Mary Garland, the girl from 'West Nazareth', New England, feels that 'the great amenities of the world . . . were shaping her with a divinely intelligent touch' (270). Roderick, in contrast, is an egotist upon whom Rome finally has no impact. As the other girl, Christina Light, comically observes, as an artist Roderick has 'gone up like a rocket', but she fears he will 'come down like the stick' (216).

It is the observer, Rowland Mallett, who comes to understand Rome most fully. In the Preface that James wrote for the 1908 New York edition, he recalled that Mallett's consciousness was 'the centre of interest' in the novel (45). During his second winter in Rome he feels 'his roots striking and spreading in the Roman soil'. It is 'a perfect response to his prevision that to live in Rome was an education to the senses and the imagination' (159–60). Later, as Mallett conducts Mary Garland around the Vatican, the home, in the New England view, of the Antichrist, he:

> found himself expounding aesthetics . . . the sun was already scorching in the great square between the colonnades, where the twin fountains flashed almost fiercely, the marble coolness of the long image-bordered vistas made them a delightful refuge . . . Here and there was an open window, where they lingered and leaned, looking out into the warm dead air, over the towers of the city, at the soft-hued historic hills, at the stately shabby gardens of the palace, or at some sunny empty grass-grown court lost in the heart of the labyrinthine pile. (270–1)

Rowland's deep, if not quite unshadowed, sense of tranquillity is expressed in the easy rhythm of the clauses, at one with his sense of the beauty of the scene. Shortly afterwards he tells Mary that he is quite unAmerican: 'I have no practical occupation, and yet I have kept up a certain spirit.' Living is an art in itself, and Mary responds that Rowland has 'lived a great deal for *us*' (274–5).

Daisy Miller depicts another side of Rome, and shows that the American innocent cannot survive in its 'warm dead air'. The tale has symbolic implications for the concept of the United States as a nation in the years after the Civil War. By extinguishing the life of its eponymous heroine, embodying many of the ideals of the American Dream, *Daisy Miller* comments on the need for the United States to reconsider its national identity. In his introduction to the New York edition, James had called Daisy 'pure poetry'. Indeed, Daisy as an art-object may be regarded as the textual equivalent of the Statue of Liberty. As Randolph says, introducing his sister to Winterbourne and the reader, 'She's an American girl.' 'Innocent by definition' according to Leslie Fiedler, she moves through the text, disturbing gender and power relations in a way that is subversively attractive.[31] Unlike the other expatriate Americans, who have enthusiastically embraced European ideals of propriety, Daisy abides by American ideals of individualism, and refuses to conform. As a result she becomes 'regarded by her compatriots as abnormal' (106). James constructs the narrative by looking at Daisy through the guiding consciousness of Winterbourne, whose name, suggesting icy rigidity, is confirmed by his education at Geneva, 'the little metropolis of Calvinism' (48). Fixed according to the belief that played a large part in the founding of one republic, it is entirely apt that her death should be caused by her presence at the heart of another republic from which the United States took so many of its ideals. As 'a lover of the picturesque' but with none of the sensitivity of Rowland Mallet, Winterbourne feels that he must stop by the Colosseum at night:

> The place had never seemed to him more impressive. One half of the gigantic circus was in deep shade while the other was sleeping in the luminous dusk. As he stood there he began to murmur Byron's famous lines, out of *Manfred*; but before he had finished his quotation he remembered that if nocturnal meditations in the Colosseum are recommended by the poets, they are deprecated by the doctors. The historic atmosphere was there, certainly; but the historic atmosphere, scientifically considered, was no better than a villainous miasma. Winterbourne walked to the middle of the arena, to take a more general glance, intending thereafter to make a hasty retreat. The great cross in the centre was covered with shadow; it was only as he drew near it that he made it out distinctly. Then he saw that two persons were stationed upon the low steps which formed its base. (110)

It is, of course, Daisy and her *cicerone*, Giovanelli, at this particular station of the cross. This scene, located at the ancient site of sacrifice and martyrdom, intersects a dying aesthetic with a medical theory, summarised in the term 'miasma', coined by Horace Walpole in Italy. With figures emerging from a canvas, it both looks back to Brown's *Wieland* and forward to the 'Strether by the River' sequence in *The Ambassadors*. It epitomises the dangerous attractions of the Old World for the New, and reverses the polarity that, with the myth of Atlantis, first drew adventurers from their fastness in the Mediterranean. The scene at the Colosseum is a masterpiece of narration that is both reflective and refractive. It shows that, of all American writers, James was the best equipped to meet the new adventure. As he noted, in a letter to Charles Eliot Norton in 1872, shortly before travelling to Europe:

> It's a complex fate, being an American, and one of the responsibilities it entails is fighting against a superstitious valuation of Europe. – It will be rather a sell, getting over there and finding the problems of the universe rather multiplied than diminished.[32]

The complex origins, challenges and destiny of American literature could wish for no better testimonial.

Notes

1. Henry James, *Hawthorne* (1879; rpt. London: Macmillan, 1967), p. 135.

2. Gertrude Stein, *The Autobiography of Alice B. Toklas* (1933; rpt. New York: Vintage, 1961), p. 78.

3. Walt Whitman, *Specimen Days and Collect*, in *Complete Poetry and Collected Prose* (New York: The Library of America, 1982), pp. 724, 778.

4. Stephen Crane, 'War Is Kind', in *The Portable Stephen Crane*, ed. Joseph Katz (New York: Penguin, 1977), p. 542.

5. *Touched with Fire. Civil War letters and diary of Oliver Wendell Holmes, Jr.*, ed. Mark deWolfe Howe (Cambridge, MA: Harvard University Press, 1946). Herman Melville, *Poems* (London: Constable, 1924), p. 62. Reviews in the *Atlantic Monthly* (February 1867) and *New York World* (October 1866), rpt. in *Melville: The Critical Heritage*, ed. Watson G. Branch (London: Routledge & Kegan Paul, 1974), pp. 396, 393. For a sympathetic approach to Melville's poetry, see Lawrence Buell, 'Melville the Poet', *The Cambridge Companion to Herman Melville* (Cambridge: Cambridge University Press, 1998), pp. 135–56.

6. Henry Wadsworth Longfellow, 'Killed at the Ford', *Works* (London: Routledge, 1886), V, p. 138. Melville, 'Stonewall Jackson', *Poems*, pp. 59–61. John Greenleaf Whittier, 'Barbara Frietchie', *The Poetical Works of John Greenleaf Whittier* (London: Frederick Warne, n.d.), p. 251.

7. Henry Timrod, 'The Unknown Dead', *The Collected Poems of Henry Timrod*, eds. Edd Winfield Parks and Aileen Wells Parks (Athens, GA: University of Georgia Press, 1965), p. 127.

8. William Carlos Williams, 'Introduction to Charles Sheeler, 1939', in *Selected Essays* (1954; rpt. New York: New Directions, 1969), p. 231. Whittier, *The Poetical Works*, pp. 210–12. Further references to this text will be given in parentheses after the quotation. Robert Burns, *Poems and Selected Letters*, ed. Anthony Hepburn (London: Collins, 1959), pp. 348–53. *Narrative of the Life of Frederick Douglass, An American Slave* (1845; rpt. Harmondsworth: Penguin, 1982), p. 92.

9. Sarah Orne Jewett, *Deephaven and Other Stories*, ed. Richard Cary (New Haven, CT: College and University Press, 1966), p. 84. Jewett, *The Country of the Pointed Firs*, in *Four Stories by American Women*, ed. Cynthia Griffin Wolff (Harmondsworth: Penguin, 1990), p. 95.

10. Albion W. Tourgée, *A Fool's Errand*, ed. John Hope Franklin (Cambridge, MA: Harvard University Press, 1961), pp. 388–9. Emphasis in text.

11. Thomas Dixon, *The Clansman* (1905; rpt. London: William Heinemann, 1915), p. 34.

12. J. M. Barrie, 'Note' to George Washington Cable, *The Grandissimes* (London: Hodder and Stoughton, 1898), p. xi. Further references to this text will be given in parentheses after the quotation. Cable, 'Belles Demoiselles Plantation', in *Creoles and Cajuns: Stories of Old Louisiana*, ed. Arlin Turner (Gloucester, MA: Peter Smith, 1965), pp. 63–4. Mark Twain, *Life on the Mississippi* (1883; rpt. New York: New American Library, 1961), p. 1.

13. Henry Wheeler Shaw, *The Complete Works of Josh Billings* (New York: G. W. Dillingham Co., 1867), pp. 163–4.

14. Twain, *The Adventures of Tom Sawyer* (1876; rpt. Harmondsworth: Puffin, 1950), pp. 45–6, 221.

15. Twain, *Roughing It* (1872; rpt. Harmondsworth: Penguin, 1981), pp. 501–9. Twain, *The Adventures of Huckleberry Finn* (1884; rpt. Harmondsworth: Penguin, 1966), p. 198.

16. Twain, *Life on the Mississippi*, pp. 265–6.

17. Andrew Carnegie, *Triumphant Democracy* (New York: Scribner's, 1886), p. 1. Hans Christian Andersen, 'The Little Match-Girl', *Danish Fairy Legends and Tales* (London: Henry G. Bohn, 1861), pp. 324–6. Horatio Alger, *Ragged Dick and Mark, the Match Boy* (New York: Collier Books, 1962).

18. Mark Twain and Charles Dudley Warner, *The Gilded Age: A Tale of Today* (1873; rpt. New York: Signet, 1969), p. 198.

19. Whitman, *Complete Poetry and Collected Prose*, p. 5. Further references to this text will be given in parentheses after the quotation.

20. Ralph Waldo Emerson, Journal entries for 19 October 1864 and 26 April 1856, *Emerson in His Journals*, ed. Joel Porte (Cambridge, MA: Belknap Press, 1982), pp. 525, 467. Whitman, 'My Tribute to Four Poets', *Specimen Days, Complete Poetry and Collected Prose*, p. 902. William Cullen Bryant, 'The Prairies' and 'To Cole, the Painter, Departing for Europe', *The Life and Works of William Cullen Bryant*, ed. Parke Godwin (6 vols, New York: D. Appleton & Co., 1883–5) III, pp. 228–32, 219.

21. Whitman, quoted in Daniel Aaron, *The Unwritten War* (New York: Oxford University Press, 1973), p. 70.

22. Allen Ginsberg, 'A Supermarket in California', *Collected Poems 1947–1980* (1985; rpt. London: Penguin, 1987), p. 136.

23. Abraham Lincoln, 'Annual Message to Congress, 1 December 1862', in *The Portable Abraham Lincoln*, ed. Andrew Delbanco (1992; rpt. New York: Penguin, 1993), pp. 269–70. Emphases in text. Emma Lazarus, 'The New Colossus' (1883), *The Faber Book of America*, eds. Christopher Ricks and William L. Vance (London: Faber & Faber, 1992), p. 43.

24. Mabel Todd, letter 6 November 1881, in Jay Leyda, *The Years and Hours of Emily Dickinson* (1960; rpt. 2 vols, New York: Archon Books, 1970), II, p. 357. Emphases in text. Polly Longsworth, *Austin and Mabel: the Amherst affair and love letters of Austin Dickinson and Mabel Loomis Todd* (New York: Farrar, Straus & Giroux, 1984).

25. *The Poems of Emily Dickinson: Variorum Edition*, ed. R. W. Franklin (3 vols, Cambridge, MA: Harvard University Press, 1998), I, p. 10; III, pp. 1542–4. Further references to this edition are given in parentheses after the quotation, giving the editor's surname and poem number.

26. James, *The American Essays*, ed. Leon Edel (New York: Vintage Books, 1956), p. 239.

27. Thomas Wentworth Higginson, *The Afternoon Landscape: poems and translations* (London: Longmans & Co., 1889), pp. 24–5. Millicent Todd Bingham, *Ancestors' Brocades: The Literary Discovery of Emily Dickinson* (1945; rpt. New York: Dover Publications, 1967), pp. 129–30. Franklin 1428.

28. Twain, *The Innocents Abroad* (1869; rpt. London: Collins, n.d.), p. 90. Harold Frederic, quoted in Scott Donaldson, Introduction to Frederic, *The Damnation of Theron Ware* (1896; rpt. Harmondsworth: Penguin, 1986), pp. xv–xvi. James, *English Hours* (1905; rpt. London: Mercury Books, 1963), p. 196. James, *The Europeans* (1878; rpt. Oxford: Oxford University Press, 1985), p. 28.

29. James, *The American* (1876–7; rpt. New York: New American Library, 1963), pp. 91, 122.

30. James, *Roderick Hudson* (1875; rpt. Harmondsworth: Penguin, 1969), p. 108. Further references to this text will be given in parentheses after the quotation.

31. James, *Daisy Miller* (Harmondsworth: Penguin, 1986), pp. 43, 50. Further references to this text will be given in parentheses after the quotation. Leslie A. Fiedler, *Love and Death in the American Novel* (New York: Criterion Books, 1960), pp. 299–300.

32. James, letter to Charles Eliot Norton, 4 February 1872, *Letters*, ed. Leon Edel (London: Macmillan, 1974), I, p. 274.

Chronology

1516	More *Utopia*		
1517?	Rastell *The Four Elements*		
1519			Cortez lands in Mexico Magellan reaches Rio de Janeiro
1524			Verrazano explores east coast
1526			African slaves imported by Spain
1530			Cabeza de Vaca explores New Mexico
1535			Cortez names California
1540			Coronado explores north of Mexico
1541			De Soto explores Mississippi River
1547			Edward VI (1547–53)
1552		Lopez de Gomara *Historia de las Indias*	
		Las Casas *Brevissima relación de la destruyción de las Indias*	
1553		Eden *A Treatyse of the New India*	Mary I (1553–8), 'Bloody Mary'
1555		Eden *Decades of the New World*	
1558			Elizabeth I (1558–1603)
1577		Frampton *Joyfull Newes out of the New Founde Worlde*	
1580	Montaigne 'Of the Caniballes'		
1582		Hakluyt *Divers Voyages*	
1584			First, unsuccessful, English settlement at Roanoake
1588		Hariot *Virginia*	Defeat of Spanish Armada
1589		Hakluyt *Principal Navigations*	
1590		Acosta *Natural and Moral History of the Indies*	
1596		De Bry *America* Ralegh *Guiana* Keymis *Second Voyage to Guiana*	

1598		Hakluyt *Principall Navigations* I–III (1598–1600)	
1602			Bartholomew Gosnold explores Massachusetts Bay, names Cape Cod
1603			James I (1603–25)
1604			French settlement in Nova Scotia
1605			Samuel Champlain explores Isles of Shoals
1606			Virginia Companies of Plymouth and London founded
1607			Jamestown founded
1608		Smith *A True Relation*	John Smith explores Maryland coast
1609			Henry Hudson names Hudson River
1610			Hudson explores Delaware Bay Santa Fe founded
1611	Shakespeare *The Tempest* (not printed until 1623)	The Bible, King James version	
1612		Smith, *Map of Virginia* Strachey, *Historie of Travaile into Virginia Britania*	
1613		Purchas, *Purchas his Pilgrimage*	
1614			Smith explores north-east coast, names New England
1616		Smith, *Description of New England*	
1619			African slaves imported to Jamestown
1620		Smith, *New Englands Trials*	*Mayflower* lands at Plymouth Rock
1622		*Mourt's Relation*	William Bradford Governor of Plymouth Colony
1623	Shakespeare *First Folio*		First permanent English settlement in area of Maine First permanent Dutch settlement at Fort Orange, New York
1624		Smith *General Historie*	

1625		Purchas *Purchas his Pilgrimes*	Charles I (1625–49)
1626	Bacon *The New Atlantis* Sandys *Ovid's Metamorphosis English'd*		Dutch colony founded on Hudson River Peter Minuit buys Manhattan from natives
1630		Smith *The True Travels*	John Winthrop arrives in Massachusetts Bay Colony
1631		Smith *Advertisements for the unexperienced Planters of New-England*	
1632			Charles I grants Maryland to Lord Baltimore
1633			Archbishop Laud purges Puritans from Anglican Church
1634			First English settlement in Connecticut
1636			Roger Williams banished from Massachusetts, founds Providence Antinomian Crisis Harvard founded
1637		Morton *New English Canaan*	Pequot War
1638			First printing press in America
1640		*Bay Psalm Book*	
1643			Swedish settlement in Pennsylvania
1644		Williams *The Bloudy Tenent*	
1647		Ward *The Simple Cobler of Aggawam*	
1648			'Cambridge Platform'
1649		Winthrop *History of New England* (published 1825–6)	Execution of Charles I Interregnum (1649–60)
1650	Bradstreet *Tenth Muse*	Bradford completes *History of Plimoth Plantation*, published 1856	
1652		Williams *The Bloudy Tenent Yet More Bloudy*	Maine becomes part of Massachusetts
1653			Oliver Cromwell becomes Protector
1655			Swedish settlement ceded to Dutch

1656		Phillips *The Tears of the Indians*	
1660			Restoration of Charles II (1660–85)
1662	Wigglesworth *Day of Doom*		
1663		Eliot translation of the Bible into Algonkian	Charles II grants charter to Rhode Island and Providence Plantations
1664			Dutch colonies captured by British
1667	Milton *Paradise Lost*		Anglo-Dutch War ends
1669		Eliot *The Indian Primer*	La Salle begins exploration of Ohio and Great Lakes
1672		Penn *Quakerism*	
1676	Folger *A Looking-Glass for the Times*		Bacon's Rebellion
1678	Bradstreet *Severall Poems* Bunyan *Pilgrim's Progress*		
1679			New Hampshire established as province separate from Massachusetts English Habeas Corpus Act
1681			Charles II grants land to William Penn
1682		Rowlandson *Narrative of the Captivity*	
1683			Penn buys land from natives
1685			James II (1685–8)
1688	Behn *Oroonoko*		Glorious Revolution William and Mary (1688–1702)
1690		Locke *Second Treatise of Government*	
1692			Salem witchcraft trials
1693		Cotton Mather *The Wonders of the Invisible World*	College of William & Mary founded
1701			Antoine Cadillac founds Detroit Yale founded

1702		Cotton Mather *Magnalia Christi Americana*	New Jersey becomes royal province Queen Anne (1702–14) Queen Anne's War begins
1704		Knight *Journal*, published 1825	
1706		Increase Mather *A Discourse Concerning Earthquakes*	Benjamin Franklin born
1707			Union of English and Scottish Parliaments
1708	Cook *Sot-Weed Factor*	Oldmixon *The British Empire in America*	
1710		Cotton Mather *Bonifacius: An Essay to Do Good*	
1713			Treaty of Utrecht ends Queen Anne's War
1714			George I (1714–27)
1715			First Jacobite Rebellion
1718		Cotton Mather *Psalterium Americanum*	de Bienville founds New Orleans
1720			South Sea Bubble
1721		Increase and Cotton Mather both write about inoculations	First smallpox inoculations, in Boston
1722		Franklin 'Dogood Papers'	
1726	Berkeley 'On the Prospect of Planting Arts and Learning in America'		
1727		Prince *Earthquakes are the Works of God*	George II (1727–60)
1728		Byrd *History of the Dividing Line* (published 1841)	Vitus Bering discovers Straits
1729		Sewall *Diary* (published 1878–82)	North and South Carolina become separate royal colonies
1732		Byrd *A Progress to the Mines*, published 1841	Charter for Georgia colony granted George Washington born

1733		Franklin *Poor Richard's Almanack*, first issue Byrd *Journey to the Land of Eden*, published 1841	
1737		Edwards *A Faithful Narrative of the Surprising Work of God*	
1738			George Whitefield's first visit to America
1741		Edwards *Sinners in the Hands of an Angry God*	Bering explores Alaska Franklin stove
1743		Franklin *A Proposal for Promoting Useful Knowledge*	Thomas Jefferson born Pierre de la Verendrye explores upper Missouri and Black Hills
1745		Franklin 'Advice to a Young Man on Choosing a Mistress'	Second Jacobite Rebellion
1746		Brainerd *Mirabilia Dei Inter Indicos*	College of New Jersey (later Princeton) founded
1749	Fielding *Tom Jones*	Edwards *Life of David Brainerd* Buffon *Histoire naturelle*	George II charters first Ohio Co. Franklin invents lightning rod
1750			Thomas Walker crosses Cumberland Gap
1753		Smith *A General Idea of the College of Mirania*	Spain cedes Florida to Britain
1754			Continental Congress meets at Albany
1755			French & Indian War begins General Braddock defeated and killed Acadians deported from Nova Scotia
1758		Franklin *Father Abraham's Speech*	
1760			George III (1760–1820)
1762			France cedes Louisiana to Spain
1763			French & Indian War ends
1765		Blackstone *Commentaries on the Laws of England*	Stamp Act

1766	Rogers *Ponteach*	Stamp Act repealed
1767		Dickinson *Farmer's Letters*	Townshend Acts (import duties) Mason-Dixon line separates Maryland and Pennsylvania
1768		de Pauw *Recherches philosophiques sur les Américains* (2 vols, 1768–9)	
1770	Brackenridge and Freneau *Father Bombo's Pilgrimage to Mecca*	Kalm *Travels* Raynal *Philosophical and Political History of the East and West Indies*	Boston 'massacre'
1772	Brackenridge and Freneau *The Rising Glory of America*		Somerset Case
1773	Wheatley *Poems*	Cook *Account of a Voyage Around the World*	Boston Tea Party
1774		Jefferson *A Summary View of the Rights of British America*	Coercive Acts Continental Congress meets
1775			Daniel Boone establishes Boonesboro War of Independence begins at Lexington and Concord Battle of Bunker Hill
1776	Brackenridge *The Battle of Bunkers-Hill*	Paine *Common Sense* William Smith *Plain Truth* Paine *The American Crisis* Adam Smith *The Wealth of Nations*	Declaration of Independence
1777			Articles of Confederation Valley Forge
1778	Burney *Evelina*		James Cook lands at Kauai
1781	Freneau 'The British Prison-Ship'		British surrender at Yorktown
1782		Crèvecoeur *Letters*	
1783			Britain recognises US independence at Treaty of Paris, and exchanges Florida with Spain for Bahamas
1786	Freneau *Poems*		Shays's Rebellion

1787	Tyler *The Contrast* Barlow *Vision of Columbus*		Constitutional Convention Northwest Ordinance Constitution ratified by Delaware, Pennsylvania and New Jersey
1788	Freneau *Miscellaneous Works*		Constitution ratified by Georgia, Connecticut, Massachusetts, Maryland, South Carolina, New Hampshire, Virginia and New York
1789	W. Brown *Power of Sympathy*	Morse *American Geography* Ramsay *History of the American Revolution* *The Interesting Narrative of the Life of Olaudah Equiano*	Constitution ratified by North Carolina and Rhode Island 1st President: George Washington (1789–97) Alien and Sedition Laws Storming of the Bastille Baptist minister makes first bourbon whiskey
1790	Warren *Poems*	Burke *Reflections on the Revolution in France*	Philadelphia becomes US capital Benjamin Franklin dies
1791	Rowson *Charlotte*	Bartram *Travels* Franklin *Mémoires de la vie privée* Paine *The Rights of Man*	Vermont becomes 14th State Bill of Rights (first 10 Amendments to Constitution) becomes law
1792	Brackenridge *Modern Chivalry* (completed 1815)	*Benjamin Franklin's Jugendjahre* Wollstonecraft *Vindication of the Rights of Woman*	Kentucky becomes 15th State Whitney cotton gin invented George Vancouver explores Puget Sound
1793			Yellow fever epidemic in Philadelphia Franco-British War begins
1794	Dwight *Greenfield Hill*	Paine *The Age of Reason*	Whiskey Rebellion
1796		Washington *Farewell Address*	Tennessee becomes 16th State John Adams elected 2nd President (1797–1801)
1798	Brown *Alcuin* Brown *Wieland*		Illuminati scare
1799	Brown *Ormond* Brown *Arthur Mervyn*, Part 1 Brown *Edgar Huntly*		George Washington dies
1800	Brown *Arthur Mervyn*, Part 2	Weems *Life of Washington*	Spain cedes Louisiana to France US capital moves to Washington Thomas Jefferson elected 3rd President (1801–9) Library of Congress established

1801	Brown *Clara Howard* Brown *Jane Talbot*	Crèvecoeur *Voyage*	
1802	Irving *Letters of Jonathan Oldstyle, Gent.*		US Military Academy founded at West Point, NY
1803			Louisiana Purchase Ohio becomes 17th State
1804			Napoleon crowns himself emperor Lewis and Clark Expedition begins
1806		Webster *Compendious Dictionary*	Lewis and Clark Expedition returns Zebulon Pike explores 'Pike's Peak'
1807	Irving *Salmagundi*		Fulton launches steamboat
1808			James Madison elected 4th President (1809–17) Import of slaves banned
1809	Irving *History of New York* Campbell *Gertrude of Wyoming*		Abraham Lincoln born
1810		Cooper *A Guide to the Wilderness*	US annexes West Florida
1811			Astor's Pacific Fur Co. builds Astoria
1812	Paulding *Diverting History of John Bull and Brother Jonathan*		Louisiana becomes 18th State US declares war on Britain
1814	Francis Scott Key 'Star-Spangled Banner'	Allen *History of Lewis and Clark Expedition*	Washington DC burned by British War of 1812 ends
1815	Freneau *A Collection of Poems*	Dunlap *Life of Charles Brockden Brown*	Battle of New Orleans Battle of Waterloo
1816			James Monroe elected 5th President (1817–25) Indiana becomes 19th State
1817	Bryant 'Thanatopsis' Neal *Keep Cool*		Mississippi become 20th State
1818	Bryant, 'To a Waterfowl' Paulding *The Backwoodsman*		US–Canada boundary fixed at 49th Parallel Illinois becomes 21st State

1819	Irving *Sketch Book*		East Florida bought from Spain Alabama becomes 22nd State
1820	Cooper *Precaution*		Maine becomes 23rd State George IV (1820–30)
1821	Cooper *The Spy* Bryant *Poems*		Missouri Compromise Missouri becomes 24th State Texas becomes part of Mexico
1822	Irving *Bracebridge Hall*		
1823	Cooper *The Pioneers*	McGuffey, first *McGuffey Reader*	Monroe Doctrine
1824	Cooper *The Pilot* Irving *Tales of a Traveller*	Neal *American Writers*	John Quincy Adams elected 6th President (1825–9)
1825	Cooper *Lionel Lincoln*		Erie Canal opened
1826	Cooper *The Last of the Mohicans*	Kent *Commentaries on American Law*	John Adams and Thomas Jefferson die Cooper leaves for Europe
1827	Cooper *The Prairie* Poe *Tamerlane*	Audubon *Birds of America*	
1828	Cooper *The Red Rover*	Irving *The Life and Voyages of Christopher Columbus* Cooper *Notions of the Americans* Webster *American Dictionary* *Cherokee Phoenix* first published	Andrew Jackson elected 7th President (1829–37)
1829	Cooper *The Wept of Wish-Ton-Wish* Hale *Sketches of American Character*	Irving *Conquest of Granada* Knapp *Lectures on American Literature*	
1830	Cooper *The Water-Witch*	Smith *Book of Mormon*	William IV (1830–7)
1831	Poe *Poems* Whittier *Legends of New England* Cooper *The Bravo*		Nat Turner's Rebellion
1832	Cooper *The Heidenmauer* Bryant *Poems*	Irving *The Alhambra* Trollope *Domestic Manners of the Americans*	

1833	Longfellow *Outre-Mer* Cooper *The* *Headsman*		American Anti-Slavery Society formed
1834	Bryant *Poems*	Crockett *Life* Bancroft *History of* *the United States* (10 vols, 1834–74)	McCormick reaper patented
1835	Cooper *The* *Monikins* Irving *Crayon* *Miscellany* Kennedy *Horse-* *Shoe Robinson*	De Tocqueville *Democracy in* *America*, Vol. 1 *Cherokee Phoenix* closes	Samuel Colt patents revolver
1836	Bird *Sheppard* *Lee* Cole's five paintings *The* *Course of Empire*	Irving *Astoria* Emerson *Nature*	Martin Van Buren elected 8th President (1837–41) Arkansas becomes 25th State Battles of Alamo and San Jacinto Republic of Texas formed
1837	Hawthorne *Twice-Told Tales*	Emerson 'The American Scholar'	Michigan becomes 26th State Queen Victoria (1837–1901)
1838	Poe *Narrative* *of Arthur* *Gordon Pym* Cooper *Homeward* *Bound*; *Home* *As Found*	Emerson 'The Divinity School Address' Simms *Slavery* *in America* Cooper *Chronicles of* *Cooperstown*; *The* *American Democrat*	Underground Railroad formed Samuel Morse invents telegraphic code
1839	Longfellow *Hyperion*; *Voices* *of the Night* Very, *Essays and* *Poems*	Reynolds 'Mocha Dick' Cooper *History of* *the Navy of the* *United States of* *America*	Charles Goodyear vulcanises rubber
1840	Poe *Tales of* *Grotesque and* *Arabesque* Cooper *The* *Pathfinder*; *Mercedes of* *Castile*	*The Dial* ed. Fuller De Tocqueville *Democracy in* *America*, Vol. 2 Dana *Two Years* *Before the Mast*	William H. Harrison elected 9th President (Mar.–Apr. 1841)
1841	Longfellow *Ballads* Whitman *Franklin* *Evans* Cooper *The* *Deerslayer*	Emerson *Essays*	William Harrison dies John Tyler becomes 10th President (1841–5)
1842	Cooper *The* *Two Admirals*; *The Wing-and-* *Wing*		P. T. Barnum opens American Museum in New York City

1843	Cooper *Wyandotté* Whittier *Lays of My Home*	Prescott *History of the Conquest of Mexico*	Oregon Trail
1844	Cooper *Afloat and Ashore*; *Miles Wallingford*	Emerson *Essays, Second Series*	Texas annexed James K. Polk elected 11th President (1845–9)
1845	Poe *Tales*; *The Raven* Longfellow *The Belfry of Bruges* Cooper *Satanstoe*; *The Chainbearer*	Douglass *Narrative* Fuller *Woman in the Nineteenth Century*	Florida becomes 27th State Texas becomes 28th State US Naval Academy opens at Annapolis
1846	Melville *Typee* Hawthorne *Mosses from an Old Manse* Cooper *The Redskins*		Mexican War begins Acquisition of Oregon Donner Party Iowa becomes 29th State
1847	Emerson *Poems* Longfellow *Evangeline* Melville *Omoo* Cooper *The Crater*		Gold discovered in California American Medical Association founded
1848	Lowell *Biglow Papers* Cooper *Jack Tier*; *The Oak Openings* Bennett *Mike Fink* Poe *Eureka*	Marx and Engels *Communist Manifesto*	Wisconsin becomes 30th State Zachary Taylor elected 12th President (1849–50) Mexican War ends Mexico cedes California to US Revolutions in Europe
1849	Longfellow *Kavanagh* Cooper *The Sea Lions* Holmes *Poems* Whittier *Poems*	Parkman *Oregon Trail* Emerson *Addresses and Lectures* Thoreau 'Civil Disobedience'; *A Week on the Concord and Merrimack Rivers*	Mormons move into Utah
1850	Whittier *Songs of Labor* Hawthorne *The Scarlet Letter* Cooper *The Ways of the Hour* Poe *Works* Melville *White-Jacket*	Emerson *Representative Men* Susan Fenimore Cooper *Rural Hours*	Compromise of 1850 Fugitive Slave Act Zachary Taylor dies Millard Fillmore becomes 13th President (1850–53) California becomes 31st State

1851	Hawthorne *The House of the Seven Gables* Melville *Moby-Dick*	Parkman *The Conspiracy of Pontiac* *New York Times* founded	London Great Exhibition Isaac Singer patents sewing machine
1852	Stowe *Uncle Tom's Cabin* Hawthorne *The Blithedale Romance* Melville *Pierre*		Wells Fargo founded Franklin Pierce elected 14th President (1853–57)
1853	Hawthorne *Tanglewood Tales* Brown *Clotel*	Stowe *A Key to Uncle Tom's Cabin*	Gadsden Purchase from Mexico Commodore Perry arrives in Tokyo Bay
1854	Thoreau *Walden* Arthur *Ten Nights in a Barroom and What I Saw There*	Fitzhugh *Sociology for the South*	Kansas-Nebraska Act
1855	Whitman *Leaves of Grass* Longfellow *Hiawatha*	Barnum *Life*	
1856	Stowe *Dred* Melville *The Piazza Tales*	Emerson *English Traits*	James Buchanan elected 15th President (1857–61)
1857	Melville *The Confidence-Man*	*Atlantic Monthly* founded	Dred Scott decision John Frémont Expedition
1858	Longfellow *The Courtship of Miles Standish* Holmes *The Autocrat of the Breakfast Table*		Minnesota becomes 32nd State Central Park, NYC, opened First transatlantic telegraph cable
1859	Stowe *The Minister's Wooing*		Oregon becomes 33rd State John Brown's raid on Harper's Ferry
1860	Hawthorne *The Marble Faun* Holmes *The Professor at the Breakfast Table* Timrod *Poems*	Emerson *The Conduct of Life*	Abraham Lincoln elected 16th President (1861–5) South Carolina secedes from the Union Winchester repeating rifle
1861	Holmes *Elsie Venner*	Jacobs *Incidents in the Life of a Slave Girl*	Kansas becomes 34th State Civil War begins Jefferson Davis president of CSA First Battle of Bull Run Vassar College founded MIT founded

1862	Howe 'Battle Hymn of the Republic' Ward *His Book*		Second Battle of Bull Run Siege of Vicksburg
1863	Longfellow *Tales of a Wayside Inn*, Part 1 Bishop, 'When Johnny Comes Marching Home'	Hawthorne *Our Old Home* Alcott *Hospital Sketches* Lincoln 'Gettysburg Address' Thoreau *Excursions*	Emancipation Proclamation Battle of Gettysburg West Virginia becomes 35th State
1864	Whittier *In War Time* Brown *Clotelle*	Thoreau *The Maine Woods*	Sherman's march to the sea Nevada becomes 36th State
1865	Whitman *Drum-Taps* Whitman *Sequel to Drum-Taps*	Thoreau *Cape Cod*	Lee surrenders to Grant at Appomattox Court House Civil War ends 13th Amendment abolishes slavery Lincoln assassinated Andrew Johnson becomes 17th President (1865–9) Ku Klux Klan founded
1866	Whittier *Snow-Bound* Shaw *Josh Billings: Hiz Sayings* Longfellow *Flower-de-Luce* Melville *Battle-Pieces*		Reconstruction Civil Rights Act First oil well drilled in Texas First cattle drive from Texas to Montana
1867	Alger *Ragged Dick* Harte *Condensed Novels* Twain *The Celebrated Jumping Frog of Calaveras County*	Emerson *May-Day and Other Pieces*	Nebraska becomes 37th State Alaska purchased from Russia Alfred Nobel patents dynamite
1868	Alcott *Little Women* Shaw *Josh Billings on Ice*		Andrew Johnson impeached and acquitted Ulysses S. Grant elected 18th President (1869–77)
1869	Harte *Outcasts of Poker Flat* Stowe *Oldtown Folks*	Twain *Innocents Abroad*	First transcontinental railroad American Women's Suffrage Association founded First professional baseball team

1870		Emerson *Society and Solitude* Higginson *Army Life in a Black Regiment* Stowe *Lady Byron Vindicated*	Standard Oil Co. founded
1871	Whitman *Passage to India* Bryant *Poems* Eggleston *The Hoosier Schoolmaster*	Whitman *Democratic Vistas*	Great Chicago Fire Barnum's Circus founded
1872	Longfellow *Christus: A Mystery* Holmes *Poet at the Breakfast Table*	Twain *Roughing It*	Jehovah's Witnesses organised Yellowstone Park established
1873	Twain and Warner *The Gilded Age* Timrod *Poems* (new edn)	Gilpin *Mission of the North American People*	Remington typewriter Cable streetcar in San Francisco
1874	Cable 'Belles Demoiselles Plantation'	Custer *My Life on the Plains* Neal *Portland Illustrated*	Barbed wire invented
1876	Twain *Adventures of Tom Sawyer* James *Roderick Hudson* Melville *Clarel*	Emerson *Letters and Social Aims*	Colorado becomes 38th State Rutherford B. Hayes elected 19th President (1877–81) Battle of the Little Big Horn Alexander Graham Bell's telephone Philadelphia Centennial Exposition
1877	James *The American* Jewett *Deephaven* Bierce *The Dance of Death* Holmes *Poetical Works*		Reconstruction ends in the Southern states National railroad strike
1878	James *The Europeans* Bryant *The Flood of Years* Stowe *Poganuc People*	Charles Francis Adams *Railroads: Their Origins and Problems* Tyler *History of American Literature, 1607–1765* English Men of Letters series begins	Edison's phonograph Britain and Afghanistan at War

| 1879 | Cable *Old Creole Days* James *Daisy Miller* Tourgée *A Fool's Errand* | James *Hawthorne* Henry George *Progress and Poverty* | Edison's incandescent lamp Woolworth opens first 'five-cent' store Christian Science Church organised |
| 1880 | Longfellow *Ultima Thule* Cable *The Grandissimes* Henry Adams *Democracy* | Twain *A Tramp Abroad* | James Garfield elected 20th President (Mar.–Sept. 1881) Salvation Army organised |

General Bibliographies

General histories/handbooks of America and its literature

Bercovitch, S., ed. *The Cambridge History of American Literature* (6 vols to date, 1994–2003)

Boorstin, D. J. *The Americans: The Colonial Experience* (1958)

Boorstin, D. J. *The Americans: The National Experience* (1965)

Cook, C. and Waller, D. *The Longman Handbook of Modern American History, 1763–1996* (1998)

Cunliffe, M., ed. *American Literature to 1900* (1973)

Cunliffe, M. *The Literature of the United States* (4th edn, 1986)

Elliott, E., ed. *The Columbia Literary History of the United States* (1988)

Ford, B., ed. *The New Pelican Guide to English Literature, Volume 9: American Literature* (1988)

Garraty, J. A. and Carnes, M. C., eds *American National Biography* (24 vols, 1999)

Hart, J. D. and Leininger, P., eds *The Oxford Companion to American Literature* (6th edn, 1996)

Higginson, T. W. and MacDonald, W. *History of the United States from 986 to 1905* (1905)

Hughes, R. *American Visions: The Epic History of Art in America* (1997)

Johnson, T. H., ed. *The Oxford Companion to American History* (1966)

Ludwig, R. M. and Nault, C. A., Jr *Annals of American Literature, 1602–1983* (1986)

Salzman, J., ed. *The Cambridge Handbook of American Literature* (1986)

Scribner's American History and Culture (CD-ROM, 1998). Includes:

> Cayton, M. K., Gorn, E. J. and Williams, P. W., eds *Encyclopedia of American Social History* (1993)
>
> Graff, M. F., ed. *The Presidents: A Reference History* (2nd edn, 1996)
>
> *Dictionary of American Biography* Supplements Nine (1994) and Ten (1995)
>
> *Dictionary of American History* (7 vols, 1976)
>
> Ferrell, R. H. and Hoff, J., eds *Dictionary of American History Supplement* (2 vols, 1996)

Spiller, R. E., Thorp, W., Johnson, T. H. and Canby, H. S., eds *The Literary History of the United States* (3 vols, 1947)

Trent, W. P., Erskine, J., Sherman, S. P. and Van Doren, C., eds *A History of American Literature* (4 vols, 1918–21)

Tyler, M. C. *A History of American Literature, 1607–1765* (2 vols, 1879)

Walker, M. *The Literature of the United States of America* (2nd edn, 1988)

Ward, G. *The Writing of America* (2002)

Definitions of America and its literature

Bercovitch, S., ed. *Reconstructing American Literary History* (1986)

Bercovitch, S. *The Rites of Assent: Transformations in the Symbolic Construction of America* (1993)

Bercovitch, S. and Jehlen, M., eds *Ideology and Classic American Literature* (1986)

Chase, R. *The American Novel and its Tradition* (1957)

Chase, R. *The Democratic Vista* (1958)

Cologne-Brookes, G., Sammells, N. and Timms, D., eds *Writing and America* (1996)

Graff, G. *Professing Literature: An Institutional History* (1987)

Graff, G. and Warner, M. *The Origins of Literary Studies in America: A Documentary Anthology* (1989)

Green, M. *Re-appraisals: Some Commonsense Readings in American Literature* (1963)

Greenblatt, S. and Gunn, G., eds *Redrawing the Boundaries: The Transformation of English and American Literary Studies* (1992)

James, C. L. R. *American Civilization*, eds. Grimshaw, A. and Hart, K. (1993)

Jones, H. M. *The Theory of American Literature* (2nd edn, 1965)

Kammen, M. *People of Paradox: An Inquiry Concerning the Origins of American Civilization* (1972)

Kaplan, A. and Pease, D. E. *Cultures of United States Imperialism* (1993)

Limerick, P. N. *The Legacy of Conquest: The Unbroken Past of the American West* (1987)

Lipset, S. M. *The First New Nation: The United States in Comparative Perspective* (1979)

Lipset, S. M. *American Exceptionalism: A Double-Edged Sword* (1996)

Parrington, V. L. *Main Currents in American Thought* (3 vols, 1927, 1930)

Pease, D. E., ed. *Revisionary Interventions into the Americanist Canon* (1994)

Potter, D. M. *People of Plenty: Economic Abundance and the American Character* (1954)

Reising, R. *The Unusable Past: Theory and the Study of American Literature* (1986)

Ruland, R., ed. *The Native Muse: Theories of American Literature From Bradford to Whitman* (1972)

Shafer, B., ed. *Is America Different? A New Look at American Exceptionalism* (1991)

Spengemann, W. C. *A Mirror for Americanists: Reflections on the Idea of American Literature* (1989)

Spengemann, W. C. *A New World of Words: Redefining Early American Literature* (1994)

Spiller, R. E. *The Cycle of American Literature* (3rd edn, 1967)

Trilling, L. *The Liberal Imagination: Essays on Literature and Society* (1950)

Wiebe, R. H. *The Segmented Society: An Introduction to the Meaning of America* (1975)

Williams, W. C. *In the American Grain* (1925)

Thematic studies

Anderson, D. *A House Undivided: Domesticity and Community in American Literature* (1990)

Andrews, W. L. *To Tell a Free Story: The First Century of Afro-American Autobiography, 1760–1865* (1988)

Bauer, D. M. and Gould, P. *The Cambridge Companion to Nineteenth-Century American Women's Writing* (2001)

Brown, R. D. *Knowledge Is Power: The Diffusion of Information in Early America, 1700–1865* (1989)

Budd, L. J., *et al.*, eds *Toward a New Literary History: Essays in Honor of Arlin Turner* (1980)

Buell, L. *New England Literary Culture: From Revolution Through Renaissance* (1986)

Bush, C. *The Dream of Reason: American Consciousness and Cultural Achievement from Independence to the Civil War* (1977)

Davis, D. B. *Homicide in American Fiction, 1798–1860: A Study in Social Values* (1957)

Davis, D. B. *The Fear of Conspiracy: Images of Un-American Subversion from the Revolution to the Present* (1971)

Dekker, G. *The American Historical Romance* (1987)

Douglas, A. *The Feminization of American Culture* (1977)

Echeverria, D. *Mirage in the West: A History of the French Image of American Society to 1815* (1957)

Feidelson, F. *Symbolism and American Literature* (1953)

Ferguson, R. A. *Law and Letters in American Culture* (1984)

Fiedler, L. A. *Love and Death in the American Novel* (1960)

Fiedler, L. A. *The Return of the Vanishing American* (1968)

Fiedler, L. A. *An End to Innocence* (2nd edn, 1972)

Fisher, P. *Hard Facts: Setting and Form in the American Novel* (1985)

Frederickson, G. M. *The Black Image in the White Mind: The Debate on Afro-American Character and Destiny, 1817–1914* (1971)

Gates, H. L., Jr *The Signifying Monkey* (1988)

Gidley, M. and Lawson-Peebles, R., eds *Views of American Landscapes* (1989)

Greenfield, B. *Narrating Discovery: The Romantic Explorer in American Literature, 1790–1855* (1992)

Henderson III, H. B. *Versions of the Past: The Historical Imagination in American Fiction* (1974)

Jehlen, M. *American Incarnation: The Individual, the Nation, and the Continent* (1986)

Jones, H. M. *O Strange New World, American Culture: The Formative Years* (1964)

Jordan, W. *White over Black: American Attitudes toward the Negro, 1550–1812* (1968)

Kolodny, A. *The Lay of the Land: Metaphor as Experience and History in American Life and Letters* (1975)

Lawrence, D. H. *Studies in Classic American Literature* (1923; rpt. 1971)

Lease, B. *Anglo-American Encounters: England and the Rise of American Literature* (1981)

McWilliams, J. P., Jr *The American Epic: Transforming a Genre, 1770–1860* (1989)

Marx, L. *The Machine in the Garden: Technology and the Pastoral Ideal in America* (1964)

Miller, P. *The Life of the Mind in America: From the Revolution to the Civil War* (1965)

Mitchell, L. C. *Witnesses to a Vanishing America: The Nineteenth-Century Response* (1981)

Mumford, L. *The Golden Day: A Study of American Literature and Culture* (3rd edn, 1957)

Patterson, M. R. *Authority, Autonomy, and Representation in American Literature, 1776–1865* (1988)

Pearce, R. H. *The Continuity of American Poetry* (1961)

Pearce, R. H. *Savagism and Civilization: A Study of the Indian and the American Mind* (1988)

Poirier, R. *A World Elsewhere: The Place of Style in American Literature* (1966)

Rourke, C. *American Humor: A Study of the National Charact*er (1931)

Ruttenburg, N. *Democratic Personality: Popular Voice and the Trial of American Authorship* (1998)

Seelye, J. *Prophetic Waters: The River in Early American Life and Literature* (1977)

Seelye, J. *Beautiful Machine: Rivers and the Republican Plan, 1755–1825* (1991)

Slotkin, R. *Regeneration Through Violence: The Mythology of the American Frontier, 1600–1860* (1973)

Smith, H. N. *Virgin Land: The American West as Symbol and Myth* (1950)

Sollors, W. *Beyond Ethnicity: Consent and Descent in American Culture* (1986)

Spender, S. *Love–Hate Relations: English and American Sensibilities* (1974)

Sundquist, E. J. *To Wake the Nations: Race in the Making of American Literature* (1993)

Tanner, T. *The Reign of Wonder: Naivety and Reality in American Literature* (1965)

Tanner, T. *Scenes of Nature, Signs of Men* (1987)

Tanner, T. *The American Mystery: American Literature from Emerson to DeLillo* (2000)

Thomas, B. *Cross-Examinations of Law and Literature* (1987)

Tichi, C. *New World, New Earth: Environmental Reform in American Literature from the Puritans through Whitman* (1979)

Tompkins, J. *Sensational Designs: The Cultural Work of American Fiction 1790–1860* (1985)

Von Frank, A. J. *The sacred game: Provincialism and frontier consciousness in American literature, 1630–1860* (1985)

Ziff, L. *Writing in the New Nation: Prose, Print, and Politics in the Early United States* (1991)

Period studies

Chapter 2 A protoAmerican literature, 800 BC to 1611

Bodmer, B. P. *The Armature of Conquest: Spanish Accounts of the Discovery of America, 1492–1589*, trans. Hunt, L. L. (1992)

Boorstin, D. J. *The Discoverers* (1983)

Burgess, G. and Barron, W. R. J. eds *The Voyage of St Brendan: Themes and Variations* (2001)

Campbell, M. B. *The Witness and the Other World: Exotic European Travel Writing, 400–1600* (1988)

Cawley, R. R. *Unpathed Waters: Studies in the Influence of Voyages on Elizabethan Literature* (1940)

Cheyfitz, E. *The Poetics of Imperialism: Translation and Colonization from The Tempest to Tarzan* (1991)

Elliott, J. H. *The Old World and the New 1492–1650* (1970)

Fernández-Armesto, F. *Before Columbus: Exploration and Colonisation from the Mediterranean to the Atlantic, 1229–1492* (1987)

Franklin, W. *Discoverers, Explorers, Settlers: The Diligent Writers of Early America* (1979)

Friedman, J. B. *The Monstrous Races in Medieval Art and Thought* (1981)

Gillies, J. *Shakespeare and the Geography of Difference* (1994)

Greenblatt, S. *Marvelous Possessions: The Wonder of the New World* (1991)

Honour, H. *The New Golden Land: European Image of America from the Discoveries to the Present Time* (1975)

Jones, G. *The Norse Atlantic Saga* (1964)

Mackenthun, G. *Metaphors of Dispossession: American Beginnings and the Translation of Empire, 1492–1637* (1997)

Mason, P. *Deconstructing America: Representations of the Other* (1990)

O'Gorman, E. *The Invention of America* (1961)

Quinn, D. B. *North America from Earliest Discovery to First Settlements: The Norse Voyages to 1612* (1977)

Pagden, A. *European Encounters with the New World: From Renaissance to Romanticism* (1993)

Parks, G. B. *Richard Hakluyt and the English Voyages* (1928)

Rukeyser, M. *The Traces of Thomas Hariot* (1971)

Rowse, A. L. *The Expansion of Elizabethan England* (1955)

Rowse, A. L. *The Elizabethans and America* (1959)

Said, E. W. *Orientalism* (1978)

Scholes, R. *The Fabulators* (1967)

Todorov, T. *The Conquest of America: The Question of the Other*, trans. Howard, R. (1984)

Williamson, J. A. *The Cabot Voyages and Bristol Discovery Under Henry VII* (1962)

Chapter 3 From settlement to revolution, 1607–1783

Axtell, J. *After Columbus: Essays in the Ethnohistory of Colonial North America* (1988)

Bercovitch, S. *The Puritan Origins of the American Self* (1975)

Bercovitch, S. *The American Jeremiad* (1978)

Bercovitch, S., ed. *The American Puritan Imagination: Essays in Revaluation* (1974)

Boyer, P. and Nissenbaum, A. *Salem Possessed: The Social Origins of Witchcraft* (1974)

Breitwieser, M. R. *American Puritanism and the Defense of Mourning: Religion, Grief, and Ethnology in Mary White Rowlandson's Captivity Narrative* (1990)

Caldwell, P. *The Puritan Conversion Narrative: The Beginnings of American Expression* (1983)

Carroll, P. N. *Puritanism and the Wilderness: The Intellectual Significance of the New England Frontier 1629–1700* (1969)

Commager, H. S. and Giordanetti, E. *Was America a Mistake? An Eighteenth-Century Controversy* (1967)

Cronon, W. *Changes in the Land: Indians, Colonists, and the Ecology of New England* (1983)

Daly, R. *God's Altar: The World and the Flesh in Puritan Poetry* (1978)

Davis, R. B. *George Sandys: Poet-Adventurer* (1955)

Davis, R. B. *Intellectual Life in the Colonial South, 1585–1763* (3 vols, 1978)

Delbanco, A. *The Puritan Ordeal* (1989)

Demos, J. *Entertaining Satan: Witchcraft and Culture in Early New England* (1982)

Elliott, E. *Power and the Pulpit in Puritan New England* (1975)

Emerson, E. H. *Major Writers of Early American Literature* (1972)

Fender, S. *American Literature in Context, I: 1620–1830* (1983)

Fischer, D. H. *Albion's Seed: Four British Folkways in America* (1989)

Fliegelman, J. *Prodigals and Pilgrims: The American revolution against patriarchal authority, 1750–1800* (1982)

Fliegelman, J. *Declaring Independence: Jefferson, Natural Language, & the Culture of Performance* (1993)

Friedman, L. J. *Inventors of the Promised Land* (1975)

Fuller, M. C. *Voyages in Print: English travel to America, 1576–1624* (1995)

Gerbi, A. *The Dispute of the New World: The History of a Polemic, 1750–1900*, trans. Moyle, J. (1973)

Gilmore, M. T., ed. *Early American Literature: A Collection of Critical Essays* (1980)

Hall, D. D. *The Antinomian Controversy 1636–1638: A Documentary History* (2nd edn, 1990)

Haraszti, Z. *The Enigma of the Bay Psalm Book* (1956)

Heimert, A. and Delbanco, A., eds *The Puritans in America: A Narrative Anthology* (1985)

Karlsen, C. F. *The Devil in the Shape of a Woman: Witchcraft in Colonial New England* (1987)

Kibbey, A. *The Interpretation of Material Shapes in Puritanism: A Study of Rhetoric, Prejudice, and Violence* (1968)

Lang, A. S. *Prophetic Woman: Anne Hutchinson and the Problem of Dissent in the Literature of New England* (1987)

Lee, A. R. and Verhoeven, W. M., eds *Making America, Making American Literature: Franklin to Cooper* (1995)

McLeod, B. *The Geography of Empire in English Literature, 1580–1745* (1999)

Martin, T. *The Instructed Vision: Scottish Common Sense Philosophy and the Origins of American Fiction* (1961)

Miller, P. *Errand into the Wilderness* (1956)

Regis, P. *Describing Early America: Bartram, Jefferson, Crèvecoeur, and the Rhetoric of Natural History* (1992)

Scheick, W. J. *Design in Puritan American Literature* (1992)

Shea, D. *Spiritual Autobiography in Early America* (1968)

Shields, D. S. *Oracles of Empire: Poetry, Politics, and Commerce in British America, 1690–1750* (1990)

Vaughan, A. T. and Clark, E. W. *Puritans Among the Indians: Accounts of Captivity and Redemption 1676–1724* (1981)

Wright, L. B. *The Cultural Life of the American Colonies, 1607–1763* (1957)

Ziff, L. *Puritanism in America: New Culture in a New World* (1973)

Chapter 4 The new republic, 1776–1826

Davidson, C. N. *Revolution and the Word: The Rise of the Novel in America* (1986)

Downes, P. *Democracy, Revolution, and Monarchism in Early American Literature* (2002)

Elliott, E. *Revolutionary Writers: Literature and Authority in the New Republic* (1982)

Ellis, J. J. *After the Revolution: Profiles in Early American Culture* (1979)

Emerson, E. H. *American Literature, 1764–1789* (1977)

Fender, S. *American Literature in Context, I: 1620–1830* (1983)

Kerber, L. K. *Women of the Republic: Intellect and Ideology in Revolutionary America* (1980)

Lawson-Peebles, R. *Landscape and Written Expression in Revolutionary America: The World Turned Upside Down* (1988)

Norton, M. B. *Liberty's Daughters: The Revolutionary Experience of American Women, 1750–1800* (2nd edn, 1980)

Nye, R. B. *The Cultural Life of the New Nation, 1776–1830* (1960).

Petter, H. *The Early American Novel* (1971)

Ringe, D. A. *The Pictorial Mode: Space & Time in the Art of Bryant, Irving & Cooper* (1971)

Silverman, K. *A Cultural History of the American Revolution* (1976)

Tyler, M. C. *A Literary History of the American Revolution* (2 vols, 1898)

Warner, M. *The Letters of the Republic: Publication and the Public Sphere in Eighteenth-Century America* (1990)

Chapter 5 Growth and identity, 1812–1865

Aaron, D. *The Unwritten War: American Writers and the Civil War* (1973)

Baym, N. *Novels, Readers, and Reviewers: Responses to Fiction in Antebellum America* (1984)

Bell, M. D. *The Development of American Romance: The Sacrifice of Relation* (1980)

Bercovitch, S. and Jehlen, M., eds *Ideology and Classic American Literature* (1986)

Bewley, M. *The Complex Fate: Hawthorne, Henry James, and some other American Writers* (1952)

Bewley, M. *The Eccentric Design: Form in the Classic American Novel* (1958)

Brodhead, R. *Hawthorne, Melville, and the Novel* (1976)

Brodhead, R. *The School of Hawthorne* (1986)

Brooks, V. W. *The Flowering of New England, 1815–1865* (1936)

Brooks, V. W. *The World of Washington Irving* (1944)

Brown, H. R. *The Sentimental Novel in America, 1789–1860* (1940)

Buell, L. *Literary Transcendentalism: Style and Vision in the American Renaissance* (1973)

Cunliffe, M. *Chattel Slavery and Wage Slavery: the Anglo-American Context, 1830–1860* (1979)

Davis, C. T. and Gates, H. L. Jr. eds *The Slave's Narrative* (1985)

Fender, S. *Plotting the Golden West: American Literature and the Rhetoric of the California Trail* (1981)

Fussell, E. *Frontier: American Literature and the American West* (1965)

Gilmore, M. T. *American Romanticism and the Marketplace* (1985)

Harding, B. *American Literature in Context, II: 1830–1865* (1982)

Harrold, S. *American Abolitionists* (2001)

Irwin, J. T. *American Hieroglyphics: The Symbol of the Egyptian Hierglyphics in the American Renaissance* (1980)

James, C. L. R. *Mariners, Renegades, and Castaways: The Story of Herman Melville and the World We Live In* (1953)

Kaul, A. N. *The American Vision: Actual and Ideal Society in Nineteenth-Century Fiction* (1963)

Kelley, M. *Private Woman, Public Stage: Literary Domesticity in Nineteenth-Century America* (1984)

Kermode, F. *The Classic* (1975)

Levin, D. *History as Romantic Art: Bancroft, Prescott, Motley and Parkman* (1963)

Levin, H. *The Power of Blackness: Hawthorne, Poe, Melville* (1958)

Levine, R. S. *Conspiracy and Romance: Studies in Brockden Brown, Cooper, Hawthorne, and Melville* (1989)

Lewis, R. W. B. *The American Adam: Innocence, Tragedy and Tradition in the Nineteenth Century* (1955)

McWilliams, J. P., Jr *Hawthorne, Melville, and the American Character: A Looking Glass Business* (1984)

Matthiessen, F. O. *American Renaissance: Art and Expression in the Age of Emerson and Whitman* (1941)

Maxwell, D. E. S. *American Fiction: The Intellectual Background* (1963)

Meyers, M. *The Jacksonian Persuasion: Politics and Belief* (1957)

Michaels, W. B. and Pease, D., eds *The American Renaissance Reconsidered* (1985)

Miller, P. *The Raven and the Whale: The War of Words and Wits in the Era of Poe and Melville* (1956)

Noble, L. L. *The Life and Works of Thomas Cole*, ed. Vesell, E. S. (1964)

Pease, D. E. *Visionary Compacts: American Renaissance Writings in Cultural Context* (1987)

Porte, J. *The Romance in America: Studies in Cooper, Poe, Hawthorne, Melville, and James* (1969)

Porte, J. *In Respect of Egotism: Studies in American Romantic Writing* (1991)

Railton, S. *Authorship and Audience: Literary Performance in the American Renaissance* (1991)

Reynolds, D. S. *Beneath the American Renaissance: The Subversive Imagination in the Age of Emerson and Melville* (1988)

Reynolds, L. J. *European Revolutions and the American Literary Renaissance* (1988)

Schlesinger, A. M. *A Pilgrim's Progress: Orestes A. Brownson* (1966)

Sundquist, E. J. *Home As Found: Authority and Genealogy in Nineteenth-Century American Literature* (1979)

Sweet, T. *Traces of War: Poetry, Photography, and the Crisis of the Union* (1990)

Tallack, D. *The Nineteenth-Century American Short Story: Language, Form, and Ideology* (1993)

Taylor, W. R. *Cavalier & Yankee: The Old South and American National Character* (1961)

289

Trachtenberg, A. *Reading American Photographs* (1989)

Weisbuch, R. *Atlantic Double-Cross: American Literature and British Influence in the Age of Emerson* (1986)

Wills, G. *Lincoln at Gettysburg: The Words that Remade America* (1992)

Winters, Y. *In Defense of Reason* (1947)

Ziff, L. *Literary Democracy: The Declaration of Cultural Independence in America* (1981)

Chapter 6 Prospects for the Great Republic, 1865–1880

Bell, M. D. *The Problem of American Realism: Studies in the Cultural History of a Literary Idea* (1993)

Bridgman, R. *The Colloquial Style in America* (1966)

Brooks, V. W. *New England: Indian Summer* (1940)

Cash, W. J. *The Mind of the South* (1941)

Hook, A. *American Literature in Context, III: 1865–1900* (1983)

Lee, B. *American Fiction, 1865–1940* (1987)

Martin, J. *Harvests of Change: American Literature 1865–1914* (1967)

Morgan, H. W. *Unity and Culture: The United States 1877–1900* (1971)

Mumford, L. *The Brown Decades: A Study of the Arts in America 1865–1895* (3rd edn, 1971)

Pizer, D. *Realism and Naturalism in Nineteenth-Century American Literature* (1961)

Pizer, D., ed. *The Cambridge Companion to American Realism and Naturalism* (1995)

Trachtenberg, A. *The Incorporation of America: Culture and Society in the Gilded Age* (1982)

Warren, R. P. *The Legacy of the Civil War: Meditations on the Centennial* (1961)

Wilson, E. *Patriotic Gore: Studies in the Literature of the American Civil War* (1962)

Woodward, C. V. *The Burden of Southern History* (3rd edn, 1993)

Individual Authors

Each of the following entries is organised in up to three parts:

1 An outline of the author's biography and career as a writer.
2 Details of any existing definitive edition of the works, the scholarly Library of America edition and a selected list of letters.
3 A selected list of bibliographies, biographies, early reviews and recent or significant earlier criticism.

BEHN, Aphra (1640–89) may have been born Aphra Johnson in Canterbury, Kent, the daughter of a barber. This, like much of her life, is the subject of conjecture. Her mother was wet-nurse to Sir Thomas Culpepper, from a prominent Kentish family. As a child, Behn could have been educated in the Culpepper family, and would have learnt foreign languages from the refugee population in Kent. In the early 1660s the Johnsons seem to have moved to Surinam, Guiana, where Aphra had an affair with one William Scot. Behn returned to England in 1664, apparently pursued by Scot. In 1666 she married a German (or Dutchman) Johan Behn, said to be a 'London merchant', but just as likely to be a slave-trader. It was as a widow that same year that she was sent to spy for Charles II in Antwerp, where she was again associated with Scot. In 1668 she was threatened with debtors' prison. Shortly thereafter she turned to the pen. Between 1670 and 1689 she wrote occasional poetry and a number of plays, including her most popular, *The Rover* (1677), and *The Widow Ranter*, staged posthumously in 1689. She also published fiction: *Love Letters Between a Nobleman and His Sister* (1684) and *Oroonoko* (1688). She died on 16 April 1689, and is buried in the East Cloister of Westminster Abbey.

Todd, J., ed. *The Works of Aphra Behn* (7 vols, 1992–6).

Duffy, M. *The Passionate Shepherdess: Aphra Behn, 1640–89* (1977).
Goreau, A. *Reconstructing Aphra: A Social Biography of Aphra Behn* (1980).
Jones, J. 'New light on the background and early life of Aphra Behn', *Aphra Behn Studies*, ed. Todd, J. (1996).
Spengemann, W. J. *A Mirror for Americanists: Reflections on the Idea of American Literature* (1989), pp. 45–76.
Todd, J., ed. *Aphra Behn Studies* (1996).

BRACKENRIDGE, Hugh Henry (1748–1816), was born in Kintyre, a south-western headland of Scotland, the son of poor farmers who migrated to York County, Pennsylvania in 1753. He studied at the College of New Jersey (now Princeton University) from 1768 to 1774. At Princeton his friends included James Madison and Philip Freneau. While still an undergraduate he published, with Freneau, one of the earliest novels written in America, *Father Bombo's Pilgrimage to Mecca* (1770). A year later he co-wrote the Commencement Address with Freneau, and published it as *The Rising Glory of America* (1771). He served as a chaplain to George Washington's army from 1776 to 1778, and published two plays about incidents in the Revolution, *The Battle of Bunkers-Hill* (1776) and *The Death of General Montgomery* (1777). He also published *Six Political Discourses Founded on the Scriptures* (1778) and preached in Philadelphia *An Eulogium of the Brave Men who Have Fallen in the Contest with Great Britain* (1779). Brackenridge was not, however, destined to be a minister. He studied law for a year in

Annapolis, Maryland, then returned to Philadelphia, where in January 1779 he began the *United States Magazine* with Freneau. The magazine lasted twelve months. In 1780 he was admitted to the Bar, in 1781 began practice in Pittsburgh, and in 1801 moved to Carlisle, Pennsylvania. For the rest of his life he flourished as a literary lawyer. In 1786 he founded the *Pittsburgh Gazette*, a vehicle for his writing; and was appointed to the Pennsylvania Supreme Court in 1799. His publications reflected his frontier experience. He wrote poems in a Scots dialect indebted to Burns; in 1783 he edited two captivity narratives later reissued under the title *Indian Atrocities*; while his attempts to mediate during the Whiskey Rebellion led, in 1794, to *Incidents of the Insurrection in the Western Part of Pennsylvania*. Brackenridge is best remembered, though, for *Modern Chivalry*, begun in 1792 and regularly expanded and revised until 1815; and for *Law Miscellanies* (1814), a commentary on the relation of the US and the English Common Law that he considered calling the *Pennsylvania Blackstone*. He was married twice: in 1785 to a Miss Montgomery, and, in 1790, some while after her death, to Sabina Wolfe. He had one child with his first wife, Henry Marie Brackenridge, who became a lawyer and travel writer; and three with his second. He died on 25 June 1816.

Marder, D., ed. *A Hugh Henry Brackenridge Reader, 1770–1815* (1970).
Marder, D., ed. *Incidents of the Insurrection* (1972). Also includes some of his publications in periodicals.

Boyd, S. R., ed. *The Whiskey Rebellion: Past and Present Perspectives* (1985).
Marder, D. *Hugh Henry Brackenridge* (1967).
Newlin, C. M. *The Life and Writings of Hugh Henry Brackenridge* (1971).
Sapienza, M., ed. *Modern Chivalry in Early American Law* (1992).
Slaughter, T. P. *The Whiskey Rebellion: Frontier Epilogue to the American Revolution* (1986).

BRADFORD, William (1590–1657) was born in Austerfield, Yorkshire, and baptised on 19 March 1590. He joined a separatist group led by William Brewster (1567–1644) that moved in 1609 from England to Leyden, Holland, and then to New England in 1620, on the *Mayflower*. He was elected governor of Plymouth Colony in April 1621, and re-elected every year until 1656, except for 1633–4, 1636, 1638 and 1644. He may have been involved in writing *A Relation or Journall of the beginning and proceedings of the English Plantation setled at Plimoth . . .* (1622), known as *Mourt's Relation*, but is famous for *Of Plymouth Plantation*, which tells a story somewhat different from *Mourt's Relation*. It was begun in 1630, completed in 1651, but not published in full text until 1856. His first wife, Dorothy May, whom he had married in 1613, drowned in Cape Cod Harbour in 1620. She may have committed suicide. In 1623 he married Alice Southworth, with whom he had three children. He died on 9 May 1657 in Plymouth.

Ford, W. C., ed. *History of Plymouth Plantation, 1620–1647* (2 vols, 1912).
Morison, S. E., ed. *Of Plymouth Plantation, 1620–1647* (1952). A modernised edition.

Anderson, D. *William Bradford's Books: Of Plimmoth Plantation and the Printed Word* (2002).
Cave, A. A. *The Pequot War* (1996).
Smith, B. *Bradford of Plymouth* (1951).
Westbrook, P. D. *William Bradford* (1978).

BRADSTREET, Anne (1612?–72) was probably born at Northampton, the eldest daughter of Dorothy Yorke and Thomas Dudley. Dudley became steward to the Earl of Lincoln, and while two of his sons went to Emmanuel College, Cambridge, Anne was educated at home on the Lincoln estate in Sempringham. When she was sixteen she married

Simon Bradstreet, also of Emmanuel College. In 1630 she migrated to the Bay Colony in the *Arbella* with her parents and her husband. The migration, undertaken in the cause of Puritanism, also improved the status of her family. Dudley became deputy governor of Bay Colony, and then governor for four terms. Both Simon Bradstreet and a half-brother, Joseph Dudley, would become governors of the Colony. Her first known poem records a period of illness in 1632 and dates her age as nineteen. As well as much poetry, she wrote some prose 'Meditations' and a spiritual autobiography, 'Religious Experiences'. Probably without consent, her brother-in-law, John Woodbridge, took her work to London; it appeared there in 1650 as *The Tenth Muse Lately sprung up in America*, the first book of poetry published by an inhabitant of the colonies. The book was popular, and a second, expanded edition appeared in Boston as *Several Poems* in 1678, six years after her death. Bradstreet had eight children, two of whom transcribed work not in the two first editions. This material was published as *The Works of Anne Bradstreet, In Prose and Verse*, in 1867. She died on 16 September 1672 in North Andover, Massachusetts, where she had lived since 1645. The site of her grave is not known.

Hensley, J., ed. *The Works of Anne Bradstreet* (1967).

Berryman, J. *Homage to Mistress Bradstreet* (1956). A biographical poem.
Daly, R. *God's Altar: The World and the Flesh in Puritan Poetry* (1978).
Martin, W. *An American Triptych: Ann Bradstreet, Emily Dickinson, Adrienne Rich* (1984).
Rosenmeier, R. *Anne Bradstreet revisited* (1991).
Stanford, A. *Anne Bradstreet: The Worldly Puritan* (1975).
White, E. W. *Anne Bradstreet: The tenth muse* (1972).

BROWN, Charles Brockden (1771–1810), was born in Philadelphia, 17 January 1771, the fifth child of a prosperous, mercantile Quaker family. He studied at the Friends' Latin School in Philadelphia (1781–6) and was then apprenticed to a lawyer (1787–93). In 1793 he forsook the law to take up the uncertain occupation of writing, both in Philadelphia and New York City. He had already published a series of essays, 'The Rhapsodist', in the Philadelphia *Columbian Magazine* (1789). In New York in 1798 he began a period of runaway publishing: *Alcuin* (1798), a plea for women's rights, and four novels: *Wieland* (September 1798), *Ormond* (early 1799), *Arthur Mervyn* (Part 1, spring 1799), *Edgar Huntly* (summer 1799) and *Arthur Mervyn* (Part 2, summer 1800). A fifth novel, *The Memoirs of Stephen Calvert*, appeared in instalments in the magazine Brown also published at that time, *The Monthly Magazine and American Review*; it was never completed. Late in 1800 Brown returned to Philadelphia to enter the family mercantile business. It meant only a small abatement in his writing. Two epistolary novels, *Clara Howard* and *Jane Talbot*, were published in Philadelphia in 1801. From 1803 to 1807 he edited *The Literary Magazine and American Register*, which was succeeded by *The American Register; or General Repository of History, Politics and Science*. Both were vehicles for Brown's essays, and for an eighth novel, the *History of the Carrils*, left incomplete at his death. A ninth novel, the *Memoirs of Carwin*, intended as a sequel to *Wieland*, was also left unfinished and was included, firstly in William Dunlap's 1815 *The Life of Charles Brockden Brown*, and then – with *The Memoirs of Stephen Calvert* – in a collection published in 1822 in London. In 1803 he began political pamphleteering. *An Address to the Government on the Cession of Louisiana to the French* and *Monroe's Embassy* (both 1803), *The British Treaty* (1807) and *An Address on the Utility and Justice of Restrictions upon Foreign Commerce* (1809) pursue a mercantilist, imperial agenda. In 1804 he translated and edited Constantin Volney's *A View of the Soil and Climate of the United States of America*, and in 1805 wrote an introduction to John Blair Linn's poem, *Valerian*. Somehow, Brown found the time to marry Linn's sister, Elizabeth, in 1804, and have four children with her. He died in Philadelphia from tuberculosis on 22 February 1810.

Krause, S. J., ed. *Charles Brockden Brown, Three Gothic Novels: Wieland, Arthur Mervyn, Edgar Huntly* (Library of America, 1998).
Krause, S. J., *et al.*, eds. *The Novels and Related Works of Charles Brockden Brown* (6 vols, 1977–87).

Axelrod, A. D. *Charles Brockden Brown: An American Tale* (1983).
Clemit, P. *The Godwinian Novel: the Rational Fictions of Godwin, Brockden Brown, Mary Shelley* (1993).
Crain, C. *American Sympathy: Men, Friendship, and Literature in the New Nation* (2001).
Fleischmann, F. *A Right View of the Subject: Feminism in the Works of Charles Brockden Brown and John Neal* (1983).
Grabo, N. D. *The Coincidental Art of Charles Brockden Brown* (1981).
Ringe, D. *Charles Brockden Brown* (rev. edn, 1991).
Watts, S. *The Romance of Real Life: Charles Brockden Brown and the Origins of American Culture* (1994).

BYRD, William (1674–1744) was born in Westover, Virginia, on his father's plantation on the James River. He was educated in Essex, England, and studied commerce in Rotterdam and London. He was admitted to the English Bar in 1695 and, the following year, became the third colonist to be elected to the Royal Society (after John Winthrop and William Penn). 1696 also marked his return to Virginia, where he was elected to the colony's House of Burgesses. Byrd lived a transatlantic life for the next thirty years, acting in Virginia as a planter, politician, bureaucrat and amateur scientist; and in London as a representative of his colony, savant and man-about-town. He wrote the entry for Virginia in John Oldmixon's *The British Empire in America* (1708), the first attempt at a colonial history. In 1721 he published *A Discourse Concerning the Plague with Some Preservatives against it*, extolling the virtues of tobacco; and in 1725 *The Female Creed*, satirising the superstitions of women. Perhaps because of his misogyny, or perhaps because of his philandering, many of his courtships came to nothing. He was married twice: in 1706 to Lucy Parke, who died of smallpox ten years later, and in 1724 to Maria Taylor. From 1726 he lived in Virginia, with Maria, for the rest of his life. He rebuilt Westover, which still exists as a fine example of colonial architecture. In addition to planting, he was a prospector, Indian trader, slave trader – although he declared that he detested slavery – and unsuccessful land speculator. Much of his autobiographical and geographical writing was published posthumously. *A Description of the Dismal Swamp and a Proposal to Drain the Swamp* appeared in 1789. *The History of the Dividing Line betwixt Virginia and North Carolina*, probably written during a surveying trip in 1728, was not published until 1841, in a volume containing *A Progress to the Mines*, written in 1732, and *A Journey to the Land of Eden*, written in 1735. The satirical *Secret History of the Dividing Line* first appeared in 1929.

Tinling, M., ed. *The Correspondence of the Three William Byrds of Westover, Virginia, 1684–1776* (2 vols, 1977).
Wright, L. B., ed. *The Prose Works of William Byrd of Westover* (1966).

Davis, R. B. *Intellectual Life in the Colonial South, 1585–1763* (3 vols, 1978).
Lockridge, K. A. *On the Sources of Patriarchal Rage: The Commonplace Books of William Byrd and Thomas Jefferson and the Gendering of Power in the Eighteenth Century* (1992).
Marambaud, P. *William Byrd of Westover 1674–1744* (1971).
Smith, D. B. *Inside the Great House: Planter Family Life in Eighteenth-Century Chesapeake Society* (1980).

CLEMENS, Samuel Langhorne ('Mark Twain') (1835–1910) was born in Florida, a small Missouri town, on 30 November 1835, the son of an unsuccessful lawyer, slave-owner and land speculator. In 1839 the family moved to Hannibal, Missouri, where Clemens had a somewhat sporadic education. In 1848 he was apprenticed to a printer, then in 1851 worked as typesetter and journalist on his brother's newspaper, the *Hannibal Journal*, in which appeared his first published sketch. In 1853 Clemens left Hannibal, working first in St Louis as a printer and journalist, then in New York City, Philadelphia, Keokuk and Cincinnati. In 1857 he became an apprentice pilot on the Mississippi, receiving his licence in 1859 and working on steamboats until the outbreak of the Civil War. He served briefly with Confederate militia, then moved west as a prospector, speculator and freelance journalist. He was so unsuccessful that in September 1862 he turned to full-time journalism with the *Territorial Enterprise*, in the frontier town of Virginia City. It was with this paper, in 1863, that he first used the name 'Mark Twain'. His intemperate behaviour made Virginia City too hot for him, and he moved to San Francisco, where he again undertook newspaper reporting, and published 'Jim Smiley and His Jumping Frog' (1865), which he included in the collection, *The Celebrated Jumping Frog of Calaveras County, and Other Sketches* (1867). Clemens began lecturing; acted as a travelling correspondent in Hawaii (1866); and again in North Africa, Europe and the Middle East (1867). This last experience led to *The Innocents Abroad* (1869), an immediate success. In 1870 he married Olivia Langdon and took a part share in the *Buffalo Express*. In 1871 they moved to Hartford, Connecticut. A year later he undertook his first lecture tour of England. He published *Roughing It* (1872) and, with Charles Dudley Warner, *The Gilded Age* (1873). *The Adventures of Tom Sawyer* introduced Tom and Huck in 1876. Travels in Europe in 1878–9 resulted in *A Tramp Abroad* (1880). An interest in English and French history gave rise to *The Prince and the Pauper* (1882), *A Connecticut Yankee in King Arthur's Court* (1889) and *Personal Recollections of Joan of Arc* (1896). These were contrasted with fond memories of the West, which resulted in *Life on the Mississippi* (1883) and *The Adventures of Huckleberry Finn* (1884). In June 1891 the family left Hartford for Europe. While abroad he published *The American Claimant* (1892), *Tom Sawyer Abroad* and *The Tragedy of Pudd'nhead Wilson* (both 1894). In 1894 the failure of the too-intricate Paige typesetting machine led to bankruptcy. Clemens attempted to recoup his losses with a world lecture tour in 1895–6, settling in London and Vienna and not returning to the United States until 1900. Honours and financial security (at last) were accompanied by a pessimism barely concealed in *Tom Sawyer, Detective* (1896) and *Following the Equator* (1897); and clearly apparent in *The Man That Corrupted Hadleyburg and Other Stories* (1900), *What Is Man?* (1906), and *The Mysterious Stranger*, published posthumously in 1916. Twain died on 21 April 1910 at his home near Redding, Connecticut.

Anderson, F., *et al.*, eds *The Mark Twain Papers* (15 vols, 1969–).

Branch, E. M., *et al.*, eds *The Works of Mark Twain* (15 vols, 1967–).

Branch, E. M., *et al.*, eds *Mark Twain's Letters* (5 vols, 1988–).

Budd, L. J., ed. *Mark Twain: Collected Tales, Sketches, Speeches, & Essays* (2 vols, Library of America, 1992).

Cardwell, G., ed. *Mississippi Writings* (Library of America, 1982). Includes *The Adventures of Tom Sawyer*, *Life on the Mississippi*, *The Adventures of Huckleberry Finn* and *The Tragedy of Pudd'nhead Wilson*.

Cardwell, G., ed. *The Innocents and Roughing It* (Library of America, 1984).

Fishkin, S. F., ed. *The Oxford Mark Twain* (29 vols, 1997). Facsimiles of first editions.

Harris, S. K., ed. *Historical Romances* (Library of America, 1994). Includes *The Prince and the Pauper*, *A Connecticut Yankee in King Arthur's Court* and *Personal Recollections of Joan of Arc*.

Hill, H. L., ed. *The Gilded Age and Later Novels* (Library of America, 2002). Also includes *The American Claimant*, *Tom Sawyer Abroad*, *Tom Sawyer, Detective* and *No. 44, The Mysterious Stranger*.

Budd, L. J. *Our Mark Twain: The Making of His Public Personality* (1985).

Cardwell, G. *The Man Who Was Mark Twain: Images and Ideologies* (1991).

Cox, J. M. *Mark Twain: The Fate of Humor* (1966).

Emerson, E. *The Authentic Mark Twain: A Literary Biography of Samuel L. Clemens* (1984).

Fishkin, S. F. *Lighting Out for the Territory: Reflections on Mark Twain and American Culture* (1997).

Fishkin, S. F. *Was Huck Black? Mark Twain and African-American Voices* (1993).

Fishkin, S. F., ed. *A Historical Guide to Mark Twain* (2002).

Gillman, S. *Dark Twins: Imposture and Identity in Mark Twain's America* (1989).

Harris, S. K. *Mark Twain's Escape From Time: A Study of Patterns and Images* (1982).

Hutchinson, S., ed. *Mark Twain: Critical Assessments* (4 vols, 1993).

Kaplan, J. *Mr Clemens and Mark Twain* (1966).

LeMaster, J. R. and Wilson, J. D. *The Mark Twain Encyclopaedia* (1993).

Lynn, K. S. *Mark Twain and Southwestern Humor* (1959).

Messent, P. *Mark Twain* (1997).

Paine, A. B. *Mark Twain: A Biography* (3 vols, 1912). The first biography of Twain.

Rasmussen, R. K. *Mark Twain A to Z: The Essential Reference to His Life and Writings* (1995).

Robinson, F. G. *In Bad Faith: The Dynamics of Deception in Mark Twain's America* (1986).

Sewell, D. R. *Mark Twain's Languages: Discourse, Dialogue, and Linguistic Variety* (1987).

Smith, H. N. *Mark Twain: The Development of a Writer* (1962).

Smith, H. N., ed. *Mark Twain: A Collection of Critical Essays* (1963).

Sundquist, E., ed. *Mark Twain: A Collection of Critical Essays* (1994).

COLUMBUS, Christopher (1451?–1506) was born in Genoa, the son of a weaver. His date of birth can only be conjectured, and little is known about his young life. An early employment was with Genoese merchants in Lisbon, and it was from Lisbon that, he said, he travelled as far afield as Iceland and Elmina, on the Gold Coast. At least six years before his first voyage, Columbus sought patronage for an exploration westwards to the Orient. He eventually obtained a commission from Ferdinand and Isabella, the monarchs of Castile, and sailed westwards from the Canary Islands on 6 September 1492. He reached islands in the Bahamas – which, we do not know – on 12 October 1492. His journals describe subsequent landings at Cuba and Hispaniola, and a return to Lisbon on 4 March 1493. Ferdinand and Isabella claimed the lands for Castile, and rewarded Columbus with the titles of Viceroy of his 'discoveries', and Admiral of the Ocean Sea. His second voyage, with a much bigger fleet, began on 25 September 1493. He reached Dominica on 3 November by sailing south-west, establishing the route that would be most used in the age of sail. He spent much more time exploring the West Indies, leaving Hispaniola on 10 March 1496 and, pursuing a zigzag route eastwards, arrived in Cadiz on 8 June. He left the Canaries on his third voyage on 19 June 1498 and travelled first to the Cape Verde Islands, leaving them on 1 July and arriving off Trinidad on 31 July. During this voyage he at last landed on the South American mainland, at what is now Venezuela. He persisted in his view, however, that this was the Orient. He was increasingly at odds with the colony at Hispaniola, and this led to his return in October 1500 to Spain in chains. Exonerated by the Castilian court, he made a fourth and final voyage from the Canaries on 25 May 1502, travelling as far west as the Darien Peninsula. He arrived back in Spain on 7 November 1504. He soon began complaining of ill-health, and died in Valladolid on 20 May 1506. The so-called First Letter was the only primary document published in Columbus's lifetime. The Castilian court suppressed, and then lost, many of his documents. Substantial materials were only published in 1825, and Columbus's achievements finally established in 1828 for the English-speaking world by Washington Irving's *The Life and Voyages of Christopher Columbus*.

Jane, C., trans. *The Journal of Christopher Columbus* (1960).

Bushman, C. L. *America Discovers Columbus: How An Italian Explorer Became An American Hero* (1992).
Fernández-Armesto, F. *Columbus* (1991).
Morison, S. E. *Admiral of the Ocean Sea* (2 vols, 1942).
Phillips, W. D., Jr and Phillips, C. R. *The Worlds of Christopher Columbus* (1992).
Provost, F. *Columbus: An Annotated Guide to the Scholarship on His Life and Writings* (1991).
Sale, F. *The Conquest of Paradise: Christopher Columbus and the Columbian Legacy* (1990).

COOK or (less likely) COOKE, Ebenezer (1667?–1733?), was the son of a Maryland merchant and planter. Cook may have lived mainly in London until his father's death in 1711, when he returned to Maryland and sold the family plantation, Cook's Point. He practised law, and wrote occasional poetry for a press established in Annapolis, Maryland. He published *The Sot-Weed Factor* in London (1708), and both *Sotweed Redivivus* (1730) and *The Maryland Muse* (1731) in Annapolis.

Lemay, J. A. L. *Men of Letters in Colonial Maryland* (1972).

COOPER, James Fenimore (1789–1851) was born in Burlington, New Jersey, the son of a politician and land developer, William Cooper, and Elizabeth Fenimore. The next year the family moved to land that William had earlier named Cooperstown, at the edge of Lake Otsego, New York. Cooper entered Yale in 1803, and left without a degree in 1805 due to bad behaviour. He spent the years 1806 to 1810 at sea, in the merchant and US navies. William died in 1809, and just over one year later Cooper married Susan Augusta De Lancey; they had seven children. Although his father left a good estate, by 1820 Cooper was in the financial difficulties that prompted the start of his writing career. He wrote rapidly. He published *Precaution* (1820), followed by *The Spy* (1821), *Tales for Fifteen* and *The Pioneers* (both 1823), *The Pilot* (1824), *Lionel Lincoln* (1825) and *The Last of the Mohicans* (1826). He had lived with his growing family in New York since 1822. In 1826 he changed his name to James Fenimore Cooper, apparently to honour his mother, who had died in 1817. That same year he also moved to Europe, finishing *The Prairie* (1827) and writing *The Red Rover* (1828). Cooper lived in London for three months in 1828, where he completed *Notions of the Americans*. The whole family moved to Switzerland, then to Italy and Germany before returning to Paris in 1830. Cooper published *The Wept of Wish-Ton-Wish* (1829), *The Water-Witch* (1830), *The Bravo* (1831), *The Heidenmauer* (1832) and *The Headsman* (1833) before sailing for New York in 1833. *The Monikins* (1835), begun in Europe, did little to revive his declining American reputation; neither did conflicts over property rights with the villagers of Cooperstown, where he had returned to live in 1834. This experience, and the subsequent lawsuits, is reflected in four books published in 1838: *Chronicles of Cooperstown*, *The American Democrat*, and a pair of novels, *Homeward Bound* and *Home As Found*. During this period he also published five volumes collectively known as *Gleanings in Europe* (1836–8), based on his travel experiences, and the *History of the Navy of the United States of America* (1839). Declining royalties, and perhaps the continuing legal actions, now with newspaper editors, prompted even greater activity. In 1840 he published *The Pathfinder* and *Mercedes of Castile*; in 1841 *The Deerslayer*; in 1842 *The Two Admirals* and *The Wing-and-Wing*, based on naval exploits in the preceding century; in 1843 *Wyandotté*; and in 1844 two further seagoing adventures, *Afloat and Ashore* and its sequel, *Miles Wallingford*. In the mid-1840s he was also active in publishing naval history, and taking part in the controversy over the Somers mutiny. The Anti-Rent War provoked the Littlepage Trilogy: *Satanstoe* and *The Chainbearer* (both 1845) and *The Redskins* (1846). Five more novels expressed the sombre vision of his last years: *The Crater* (1847), *Jack Tier* and *The Oak Openings* (both 1848), *The Sea Lions* (1849) and *The Ways of the Hour* (1850). 'American and European Scenery Compared' was published posthumously in *The Home Book of the Picturesque* (1852). When Cooper died in Cooperstown, on 14 September 1851, he was writing a further history of the navy, and *The Towns of Manhattan*, an account of New York, most of which was lost in a fire at a printer's office. His daughter, Susan Fenimore Cooper (1813–94), was the first woman to publish an American environmentalist text, *Rural Hours* (1850). She also wrote valuable memoirs of her father, prefaces of fifteen of his novels for the 'Household Edition' of his works (1876–84), and a novel, *Elinor Wyllys* (1846), published under the pseudonym of 'Amabel Penfeather'.

Beard, J. F., ed. *The Letters and Journals of James Fenimore Cooper* (6 vols, 1960–8).
Beard, J. F., *et al.*, eds *The Writings of James Fenimore Cooper* (1980–).
House, K. S. and Philbrick, T., eds *Sea Tales: The Pilot, The Red Rover* (Library of America, 1991).
Nevius, B., ed. *The Leatherstocking Tales* (2 vols, Library of America, 1985).

Clark, R., ed. *James Fenimore Cooper: New Critical Essays* (1985).
Dekker, G. *James Fenimore Cooper the Novelist* (1967).
Dekker, G. and McWilliams, J. P., eds *Fenimore Cooper: The Critical Heritage* (1973).
Fields, W., ed. *James Fenimore Cooper: A Collection of Critical Essays* (1979).
Franklin, W. *The New World of James Fenimore Cooper* (1982).
Grossman, J. *James Fenimore Cooper* (1950).
House, K. S. *Cooper's Americans* (1965).
Johnson, R. and Patterson, D. *Susan Fenimore Cooper: New Essays on Rural Hours and Other Works* (2001).
McWilliams, J. P. *Political Justice in a Republic: James Fenimore Cooper's America* (1972).
Motley, W. *The American Abraham: James Fenimore Cooper and the Frontier Patriarch* (1987).
Peck, H. D. *A World By Itself: The Pastoral Moment in Cooper's Fiction* (1977).
Peck, H. D., ed. *New Essays on the Last of the Mohicans* (1992).
Philbrick, T. *James Fenimore Cooper and the Development of American Sea Fiction* (1961).
Railton, S. *Fenimore Cooper: A Study of His Life and Imagination* (1978).
Ringe, D. A. *James Fenimore Cooper* (1988).
Taylor, A. *William Cooper's Town: Power and Persuasion on the Frontier of the Early American Republic* (1995).
Verhoeven, W. M., ed. *James Fenimore Cooper: New Historical and Literary Contexts* (1993).
Wallace, J. D. *Early Cooper and His Audience* (1986).

CRÈVECOEUR, J. Hector St John de (1735–1813) was born in Caen, Normandy, the son of a large landowner, and baptised Michel-Guillaume-Jean de Crèvecoeur. He was educated in Caen and Salisbury, England, training as a surveyor and cartographer. The French army employed him in Canada during the French and Indian War as both a surveyor and soldier. He was wounded during the siege of Quebec in 1759 and resigned his commission, moving to New York, speaking English and changing his name to J. Hector St John. He worked as a surveyor and trader, travelling widely. In 1765 he became a naturalised New Yorker. In 1769 he married Mehitable Tippet and bought a farm in Orange County, NY, the inspiration for his *Letters from an American Farmer*. His peaceful life as a farmer was interrupted by the Revolution. He was fined and imprisoned by patriots because of his neutrality. Attempting in 1779 to return to France to establish his family's inheritance, he was imprisoned for three months by the British in New York City, and then shipwrecked off Ireland. He sold the manuscript of his

Letters in London before arriving in Normandy in August 1781. The *Letters* were published in 1782 and were an immediate success. Crèvecoeur published a larger two-volume French edition in 1784, expanded to three volumes in 1787. In 1783 he wrote a report on America for the French government, and was appointed consul to the new states of New York, New Jersey and Connecticut. He arrived in New York in November 1783, to find that his wife had died in 1781. In 1785 Crèvecoeur returned to Paris, where he became a close friend of Thomas Jefferson, then American minister. His work as consul in New York resumed in 1787, and he was elected to the American Philosophical Society in 1789. He returned finally to France in 1790, farming near Paris and travelling widely to visit two of his three children and their families (the third had migrated to New Jersey during the Reign of Terror). In 1801 he published in Paris *Voyage dans la haute Pensylvanie et dans l'état de New-York*, a three-volume account of his travels forty years earlier. It was not translated into English until 1964. He died in Sarcelles, near Paris, on 12 November 1813. Some essays and a play, 'Landscapes', were first published in 1925 as *Sketches of Eighteenth-Century America*.

Moore, D., ed. *More Letters from an American Farmer* (1995).
Stone, A., ed. *Letters from an American Farmer and Sketches of Eighteenth-Century America* (1981).

Allen, G. W. and Asselineau, R. *St. John de Crèvecoeur: The Life of an American Farmer* (1987).
Crèvecoeur, R. de *Saint John de Crèvecoeur: sa vie et ses ouvrages* (1883).
Mitchell, J. P. *St. Jean de Crèvecoeur* (1916).
Philbrick, T. *St. John de Crèvecoeur* (1970).
Rice, H. C. *Le cultivateur américain: Étude sur l'oevre de Saint John de Crèvecoeur* (1933).

DICKINSON, Emily (1830–86), was born at 'The Homestead', the house in Main Street, Amherst, Massachusetts, where she lived for all but fifteen years of her life. Her father, Edward, and her older brother, Austin, were leading figures in the life of Amherst and the college that had been founded there in 1821. Dickinson went to Amherst Academy and Mount Holyoke Female Seminary, ending her formal studies in 1848. In 1855 she visited her father in Washington, for he had been elected to the US House of Representatives; and in 1864–5 she visited Boston for eye treatment. Otherwise, Dickinson chose to live in Amherst and, after 1865, entirely within the bounds of the Homestead. If anything, the self-imposed confinement enhanced her vivid imagination. She read widely, and her letters reveal a limited number of intense friendships. Dickinson's earliest known poem dates from 1850. In 1862 she sent a sample of her poetry to Thomas Wentworth Higginson, a leading Boston radical and man of letters who, in an article in the *Atlantic Monthly*, had encouraged women to send him their work for publication. The relationship, almost entirely conducted by mail, produced no immediate result; only ten poems were published in her lifetime. Her younger sister, Lavinia ('Vinnie'), discovered a large number after Dickinson's death. Vinnie persuaded Mabel Loomis Todd, who had a love-affair with Austin Dickinson from 1882 until his death in 1895, to edit them. Todd published collections of the poems, co-edited with Higginson, in 1890 and 1891; a selection of Dickinson's letters in 1894; and a third collection of poems in 1896. Todd's publication of Dickinson's writing was suspended when she and Vinnie had a legal dispute over Austin's will. Austin's daughter, Martha Dickinson Bianchi, published a further selection of poems as *A Single Hound* (1914), followed by two memoirs in 1924 and 1932 and two further collections of poems in 1929 and 1935. Bianchi died in 1943, and the burden of publishing passed to Todd's daughter, Millicent Todd Bingham, who published yet more poems as *Bolts of Melody* (1945). 'Complete' scholarly editions of the poems, published in 1955 and 1998, have caused some controversy. Dickinson's apparently simple, cloistered life led critics into a minefield of complexity.

Franklin, R. W., ed. *The Poems of Emily Dickinson: Variorum Edition* (3 vols, 1998).
Johnson, T. H., ed. *The Complete Poems of Emily Dickinson* (1955).

Bingham, M. T. *Ancestors' Brocades: The Literary Discovery of Emily Dickinson* (1967).
Blake, C. R. and Wells, C. F. *The Recognition of Emily Dickinson: Selected Criticism Since 1890* (1968).
Cameron, S. *Lyric Time: Dickinson and the Limits of Genre* (1979).
Cameron, S. *Choosing Not Choosing: Dickinson's Fascicles* (1992).
Clarke, G., ed. *Emily Dickinson: Critical Assessments* (4 vols, 2003).
Erkkila, B. *The Wicked Sisters: Women Poets, Literary History, and Discord* (1992).
Howe, S. *My Emily Dickinson* (1989).
Howe, S. *The Birth-Mark: Unsettling the Wilderness in American Literary History* (1993).
Leyda, J. *The Years and Hours of Emily Dickinson* (1960).
Longsworth, P. *Austin and Mabel: the Amherst Affair and Love Letters of Austin Dickinson and Mabel Loomis Todd* (1999).
Loving, J. *Emily Dickinson: The Poet on the Second Story* (1988).
Martin, W. *An American Triptych: Ann Bradstreet, Emily Dickinson, Adrienne Rich* (1984).
Martin, W., ed. *The Cambridge Companion to Emily Dickinson* (2002).
Sewall, R. B. *The Life of Emily Dickinson* (1994).
Smith, M. N. *Rowing in Eden: Rereading Emily Dickinson* (1992).
St Armand, B. L. *Emily Dickinson and Her Culture: The Soul's Society* (1984).
Wolff, C. G. *Emily Dickinson* (1988).

DOUGLASS, Frederick (1818–95) was born on a large plantation near Tuckahoe, Maryland, the son of an unknown white father and Harriet Bailey, a slave who named him Frederick Augustus Washington Bailey. From the age of six until he was twenty he worked for a number of slave-masters, his unwillingness to submit to discipline ensuring that he frequently changed jobs. His last work as a slave was as a caulker in a Baltimore shipyard. He escaped from Baltimore in September 1838, travelling to New York City and marrying Anna Murray, a freedwoman whom he had met in Baltimore. They moved to New Bedford, Massachusetts, where he began work as a caulker and adopted the surname Douglass to evade recapture. Douglass had learnt to read and write secretly as a slave. He began reading Garrison's *The Liberator* in New Bedford, and in 1841 his eloquence impressed Garrison, who hired him as a lecturer. His lectures both made him prominent and increased the risk of recapture. In 1845 he published *Narrative of the Life of Frederick Douglass, An American Slave*. The book was a great success, but augmented the dangers from slave-hunters. He sailed to Britain in August 1845, undertaking celebrated lecture tours and receiving enough money to buy his freedom. He returned to the United States in 1847, moved to Rochester, New York, and began the *North Star*, and later *Frederick Douglass' Paper*, creating a rift with Garrison, because the journals campaigned on a platform of rights issues, and because Douglass espoused direct action. He assisted escaped slaves, in 1852 published *The Heroic Slave*, a short novel about a slave revolt, and in 1859 helped to plan John Brown's raid on Harper's Ferry, Virginia. He fled to Canada, and then England when the raid failed, but returned the following year. He campaigned for emancipation during the Civil War, but was disappointed by the failure of Reconstruction after it. Douglass moved to Washington, DC, where two projects, the *New National Era* and the Freedman's Savings Bank, both failed. Political appointments restored his finances. In 1882 Anna died, and two years later he married Helen Pitts, a white woman who had been his secretary. The mixed marriage displeased his relatives and abolitionist colleagues. Douglass continued regardless to campaign in an atmosphere of decreasing civil rights. When he died, on 20 February 1895, he was by far the most influential African-American, but his fight for Black liberty was far from being won.

Blassingame, J. W., ed. *The Frederick Douglass Papers: Speeches, Debates, and Interviews* (5 vols, 1979–92).
Foner, P. S., ed. *Life and Writings of Frederick Douglass* (5 vols., 1950–75).
Gates, H. L., ed. *Frederick Douglass: Autobiographies* (Library of America, 1994). Contains *Narrative of the Life of Frederick Douglass*, *My Bondage and My Freedom* and *Life and Times*.

Andrews, W. L., ed. *Critical Essays on Frederick Douglass* (1991).
Martin, W. E., Jr *The Mind of Frederick Douglass* (1984).
McFeely, W. S. *Frederick Douglass* (1991).
Quarles, B. *Frederick Douglass* (1948).
Sundquist, E. J., ed. *Frederick Douglass: New Literary and Historical Essays* (1990).

EDWARDS, Jonathan (1703–58), was born in East Windsor, Connecticut, the son and grandson of leading ministers. He entered Yale at age twelve, and graduated top of his class in 1720. In 1726 he shared the pulpit of Solomon Stoddard, his maternal grandfather, at Northampton, Massachusetts, succeeding him on Stoddard's death in 1729. Over twelve hundred of his sermons survive in manuscript. Edwards's first publication, *God Glorified in the Work of Redemption*, from a 1731 Harvard lecture, contained the belief in justification by faith which would remain a constant theme in his theology. His best-known sermon, 'Sinners in the Hands of an Angry God' (1741), is his most strenuous defence of his beliefs. His *Faithful Narrative of the Surprising Work of God* (1737) described the religious revival in Northampton that was part of the 'Great Awakening'. The awakening polarised congregations and, in *Some Thoughts Concerning The Present Revival of Religion* (1742), Edwards denounced extremism and proposed but did not name his wife, Sarah Pierpoint Edwards, whom he had married in 1727, as the model of 'meek' religious enthusiasm. The controversy continued, and Edwards tried to answer it with a *Treatise Concerning Religious Affections*, an examination of the psychology of religion often regarded as his most important work. Edwards's increasing belief in justification by faith alone led him to reject the 'Half-way Covenant'. This put him at odds with his congregation, who dismissed him in 1750. He moved to the Massachusetts frontier town of Stockbridge, where he preached to the Native Americans and published attacks on liberal theology, including the one known briefly as *Freedom of the Will* (1754). In 1758 Edwards accepted the presidency of the College of New Jersey (later Princeton). He had always been in frail health, and he died from a smallpox inoculation shortly after taking up the post. *The Nature of True Virtue* (1765) and *The History of the Work of Redemption* (1774), both published posthumously, contain the essence of his later thought.

Ramsay, P., *et al. The Works of Jonathan Edwards* (22 vols, 1957–2003).

Fiering, N. *Jonathan Edwards's Moral Thought and Its British Context* (1981).
Hatch, N. O. and Stout, H. S., eds *Jonathan Edwards and the American Experience* (1988).
Johnson, T. H. *The Printed Writings of Jonathan Edwards, 1703–1758: A Bibliography* (1940).
Lesser, M. X. *Jonathan Edwards: A Reference Guide* (1981).
Levin, D., ed. *Jonathan Edwards: A Profile* (1969).
Miller, P. *Jonathan Edwards* (1949).
Scheick, W. J. *Critical Essays on Jonathan Edwards* (1980).
Tracy, P. J. *Jonathan Edwards, Pastor: Religion and Society in Eighteenth-Century Northampton* (1980).

EMERSON, Ralph Waldo (1803–82), was born in Boston, the son of a Congregational minister. He attended Boston Latin School and Harvard University, where he began the journals he kept all his life. He graduated from Harvard in 1821, and then taught, leaving to visit Georgia and Florida to cure a pulmonary illness. He was ordained minister of Boston Second Church and married his first wife, Ellen Tucker, in 1829. He seemed destined for a calm clerical life, but Ellen died in 1831, and in 1832 he resigned his pastorate, feeling unable to give communion. In 1832–3 he toured Europe, meeting Carlyle, Coleridge and Wordsworth. On returning to Boston he began giving the lectures that became a major source of his essays, the most famous being 'The American Scholar' in 1837, and 'The Divinity School Address' in 1838. In 1835 he married Lydia Jackson (calling her 'Lidian') and settled in Concord, Massachusetts, developing a circle that included Hawthorne, Margaret Fuller and Thoreau. In 1840–4 he and other Transcendentalists issued *The Dial* as a vehicle for their ideas, edited first by Fuller and then by Emerson. He published *Nature* in 1836, but it was his first (1841) and second (1844) series of *Essays* that fully established his reputation. In 1847–8 he revisited France and England, giving on his return a series of lectures on England that then became *English Traits* (1856). A third visit to the Old World in 1873 included, for the first time, Egypt. He continued giving lectures until the mid-1870s, publishing them as collections: *Addresses and Lectures* (1849), *Representative Men* (1850), *The Conduct of Life* (1860), *Society and Solitude* (1870) and *Letters and Social Aims* (1876). An 1870 series of lectures at Harvard was published posthumously as the *Natural History of Intellect* (1893) by his editor, James Elliott Cabot. His poetry was collected in *Poems* (1847) and *May-Day and Other Pieces* (1867).

Bloom, H. and Kane, P., eds *Emerson: Collected Poems and Translations* (Library of America, 1994).
Gilman, W. H. *et al.*, eds *The Journals and Miscellaneous Notebooks of Ralph Waldo Emerson* (16 vols, 1960–82).
Porte, J., ed. *Emerson in His Journals* (1982).
Porte, J., ed. *Emerson: Essays and Lectures* (Library of America, 1983).
Rusk, R. L. and Tilton, E. M., eds *The Letters of Ralph Waldo Emerson* (9 vols, 1939–94).
Spiller, R. E. *et al.*, eds *The Collected Works of Ralph Waldo Emerson* (5 vols, 1971–).
Von Frank, A. J. *et al.*, eds *Complete Sermons of Ralph Waldo Emerson* (4 vols, 1989–92).

Allen, G. W. *Waldo Emerson: A Biography* (1981).
Buell, L. *Literary Transcendentalism: Style and Vision in the American Renaissance* (1973).
Buell, L., ed. *Ralph Waldo Emerson: A Collection of Critical Essays* (1993).
Burkholder, R. E. and Myerson, J. *Emerson: An Annotated Secondary Bibliography* (1985).
Burkholder, R. E. and Myerson, J. *Emerson: An Annotated Bibliography of Criticism, 1980–1991* (1994).
Cadava, E. *Emerson and the Climates of History* (1997).
Cavell, S. *Conditions Handsome and Unhandsome: The Constitution of Emersonian Perfectionism* (1990).
Chapman, J. J. *Emerson and Other Essays* (1898).
Ellison, J. *Emerson's Romantic Style* (1984).
Gougeon, L. *Virtue's Hero: Emerson, Antislavery, and Reform* (1990).
Harding, W. *Emerson's Library* (1967).
Konvitz, M. and Whicher, S., eds *Emerson: A Collection of Critical Essays* (1962).
Loving, J. *Emerson, Whitman, and the American Muse* (1982).
McAleer, J. *Ralph Waldo Emerson: Days of Encounter* (1984).
Myerson, J., ed. *A Historical Guide to Ralph Waldo Emerson* (2000).
Newfield, C. *The Emerson Effect: Individualism and Submission in America* (1996).
Paul, S. *Emerson's Angle of Vision: Man and Nature in the American Experience* (1952).
Poirier, R. *The Renewal of Literature: Emersonian Reflections* (1987).
Porte, J. *Representative Man: Ralph Waldo Emerson in His Time* (rev. edn, 1988).
Porte, J. and Morris, S., eds *The Cambridge Companion to Ralph Waldo Emerson* (1995).
Richardson, R. D., Jr. *Emerson: The Mind On Fire* (1995).

Robinson, D. *Emerson and The Conduct of Life* (1993).
Sealts, M. M. *Emerson on the Scholar* (1992).
Van Leer, D. *Emerson's Epistemology: The Argument of the Essays* (1986).
Whicher, S. *Freedom and Fate: An Inner Life of Ralph Waldo Emerson* (1953).

FRANKLIN, Benjamin (1706–90) was born in Boston, the fifteenth child of a tallow chandler and soap boiler. After a brief formal education, Franklin began working for his father in 1716, and from 1718 until 1723 was apprenticed to his brother James, a printer, contributing the 'Dogood Papers' (1722) to James's *New England Courant*, and on occasion managing the paper. The brothers argued, and Franklin moved to Philadelphia and worked, again, in a print shop. In 1724, with a promise of credit from William Keith, the governor of Pennsylvania, Franklin sailed to England to buy his own press. Keith defaulted on his promise, and Franklin worked for two London print shops, gaining some notoriety by publishing *A Dissertation on Liberty and Necessity, Pleasure and Pain* (1725). He returned to Philadelphia in 1726, and then began his own press, in 1729 buying the newspaper, the *Pennsylvania Gazette*, and contributing letters under such pseudonyms as Anthony Afterwit and Alice Addertongue. The popularity of Franklin and his press were further increased by the long-running *Poor Richard's Almanack* (1733–58), containing Franklinian apophthegmatic gems. Many of them were collected in 1758 as *Father Abraham's Speech* and, later, as *The Way to Wealth*, a title which Franklin may have enjoyed although it was not his own. In 1730 Franklin began living with Deborah Read. They had two children and cared for an illegitimate child that Franklin had already sired. Franklin was the ultimate polymath. In 1727 he founded the Junto, a Philadelphia debating society; in 1729 published *A Modest Enquiry into the Nature and Necessity of a Paper Currency*, an influential pamphlet; in 1731 founded the Library Company of Philadelphia, the first subscription library in the colonies; began the first German language newspaper in 1732; organised the Union Fire Company in 1735; invented the Franklin Stove in 1740–1; in the mid-1740s discovered the bipolar structure of electricity and published his findings as *Experiments and Observations on Electricity* (1751); in 1747 published *Plain Truth*, a proposal for a militia company; and was instrumental in founding the first hospital in the colonies, and the academy which became the University of Pennsylvania. In 1748 Franklin retired from printing, becoming a sleeping partner in his press. In 1753 he was appointed deputy postmaster-general for the colonies, and in 1757 travelled to London as agent for Pennsylvania. He worked in England for much of the time until 1775, meeting with likeminded sceptics. As relations soured between the colonies and the British government, his facility with satires and hoaxes, originally directed against colonial humbug, was now turned into propaganda with such pieces as 'Rules by Which a Great Empire May Be reduced to a Small One' and 'An Edict by the King of Prussia' (both 1773). In 1774 Franklin was dismissed as colonial deputy postmaster-general, and while he was at sea, returning to Philadelphia, the battles of Lexington and Concord began the Revolutionary War. Immediately on his return he was elected to the Continental Congress, was the oldest signatory to the Declaration of Independence, and in 1776 went to France as the leading and most active representative of the new nation. He returned to the United States in 1785, leaving behind a large band of French admirers, many of them female. His final five years were spent in reform politics and making gadgets. He died in Philadelphia on 17 April 1790. He wrote so much in so many different styles and under so many names that the full extent of his corpus may never be known.

Crane, V. W., ed. *Benjamin Franklin's Letters to the Press* (1950).
Labaree, L. W. and Willcox, W. B. *The Papers of Benjamin Franklin* (36 vols to date, 1960–).
Lemay, J. A. L., ed. *Benjamin Franklin: Writings* (Library of America, 1987).
Lemay, J. A. L. and Zall, P., eds *The Autobiography of Benjamin Franklin: A Genetic Text* (1981).

Aldridge, A. O. *Benjamin Franklin and Nature's God* (1967).
Brands, H. W. *The First American: The Life and Times of Benjamin Franklin* (2000).
Breitwieser, M. R. *Cotton Mather and Benjamin Franklin: The price of representative personality* (1984).
Buxbaum, M. *Benjamin Franklin: A Reference Guide* (2 vols, 1983, 1988).
Cohen, I. B. *Benjamin Franklin's Science* (1990).
Dull, J. *Franklin the Diplomat: The French Mission* (1982).
Hanna, W. S. *Benjamin Franklin and Pennsylvania Politics* (1964).
Lemay, J. A. L. *The Canon of Benjamin Franklin, 1722–1776: New Attributions and Reconsiderations* (1986).
Lemay, J. A. L. *Benjamin Franklin: Optimist or Pessimist?* (1990).
Middlekauff, R. *Benjamin Franklin and His Enemies* (1996).
Morgan, E. S. *Benjamin Franklin* (2002).
Randall, W. *A Little Revenge: Benjamin Franklin and His Son* (1984).
Sayre, R. F. *The Examined Self: Benjamin Franklin, Henry Adams, Henry James* (1964).
Seavey, O. *Becoming Benjamin Franklin: The Autobiography and the Life* (1988).
Van Doren, C. *Benjamin Franklin* (1938).
Wright, E. *Franklin of Philadelphia* (1986).

FRENEAU, Philip Morin (1752–1832), of Huguenot ancestry, was born in New York City on 2 January 1752. From 1768 to 1771 he studied at the College of New Jersey (Princeton University), where he was friendly with Hugh Henry Brackenridge and James Madison. While still an undergraduate he and Brackenridge published one of the earliest novels written in America, *Father Bombo's Pilgrimage to Mecca* (1770), and the next year they co-wrote the Commencement Address, publishing it as *The Rising Glory of America* (1771). He became a teacher, and then acted as secretary to a planter in Santa Cruz, West Indies. On return from Santa Cruz in 1778 he enlisted in the militia, and for a short while also became a privateer; he had supported the Revolution since 1775 with satirical poems. In 1780 he was captured and held for six weeks in the British prison-ship *Scorpion*. After recovering from his release, he worked on the *Freeman's Journal*, then from 1784 sailed trading vessels in the West Indies. In 1791 Freneau edited the New York *Daily Advertiser*, but shortly moved to Philadelphia to edit Jefferson's *National Gazette* (1791–3). Two further editorships were unsuccessful. After 1799 Freneau spent some time farming, and some time as master of a small freighter. He married Eleanor Forman in 1790; they had four children. He published the following collections during his lifetime: *The American Village* (1782), *Poems* (1786), *Miscellaneous Works* (1788), *Poems Written Between the Years 1768 and 1794* (1795), *Letters on Various Interesting and Important Subjects* (1799), *Poems Written and Published During the American Revolutionary War* (2 vols, 1809) and *A Collection of Poems on American Affairs* (2 vols, 1815). He died on 18 December 1832.

Leary, L., ed. *The Last Poems of Philip Freneau* (1945).
Pattee, F. L., ed. *The Poems of Philip Freneau, Poet of the American Revolution* (3 vols, 1902).

Axelrad, J. *Philip Freneau: Champion of Democracy* (1967).
Bowden, M. W. *Philip Freneau* (1976).
Leary, L. G. *That Rascal Freneau: A Study in Literary Failure* (1941).
Marsh, P. M. *The Works of Philip Freneau* (1968).
Vitzthum, R. C. *Land and Sea: The Lyric Poetry of Philip Freneau* (1978).

HAWTHORNE, Nathaniel (1804–64), was born in Salem, Massachusetts, on 4 July. His father, Nathaniel Hathorne (Hawthorne added the 'w' to his name in 1825), and his mother, Elizabeth Manning, both came from families who had settled in Massachusetts in the seventeenth century. In 1821 Hawthorne entered Bowdoin College, where he made long-term friends of his classmates Henry Wadsworth Longfellow and Franklin Pierce. He graduated in 1825, and devoted himself to writing. Initially he published anonymously: *Fanshawe* in 1828 and then short stories and sketches for newspapers, magazines and annuals. He published a number of books for children: *Peter Parley's Universal History* (1837), *Grandfather's Chair, Famous Old People* and *Liberty Tree* (all 1841), *Biographical Stories for Children* (1842), *True Stories from History and Biography* and *A Wonder-Book for Girls and Boys* (both 1851) and *Tanglewood Tales for Girls and Boys* (1853). He first came to critical attention in 1837 when Longfellow enthusiastically reviewed a collection of eighteen short works, *Twice-Told Tales*. In 1842 Hawthorne added twenty-one tales to make a two-volume version of *Twice-Told Tales*. That same year he married Sophia Peabody, sister of the educationalist Elizabeth Palmer Peabody. In 1846 he published a further collection, *Mosses from an Old Manse*, its title taken from the house in Concord where he first lived with his wife. In 1850 Hawthorne published his first novel, *The Scarlet Letter*, quickly followed by *The House of the Seven Gables* (1851), a final collection, *The Snow-Image* (1851), and a third novel, *The Blithedale Romance* (1852). Hawthorne held three political appointments. The first, as measurer of salt and coal at Boston Custom House, lasted from January 1839 to November 1840. The second, as surveyor of Salem Custom House, ran from April 1846 until June 1849. The third resulted from Hawthorne's campaign biography of his old classmate, the *Life of Franklin Pierce* (1852). Pierce was elected President in November 1852, and in July 1853 Hawthorne sailed with his family to Liverpool to take up a four-year appointment as US consul. The fond if delayed reminiscence, *Our Old Home* (1863), was the fruit of his time in England, while his fourth and final complete novel, *The Marble Faun* (1860) resulted from a two-year stay in Italy (1857–9). Hawthorne returned to Concord in 1860. He died in 1864, leaving a number of projects incomplete. They were published as *Septimus Felton* (1872), *The Dolliver Romance* (1876) and *Dr Grimshawe's Secret* (1883). *Note-books* from his experiences in the USA, England, France and Italy were edited by his family.

Bell, M., ed. *Nathaniel Hawthorne: Collected Novels* (Library of America, 1983).
Charvat, W., Pearce, R. H., Simpson, C. M., *et al.*, eds *The Centenary Edition of the Works of Nathaniel Hawthorne* (23 vols, 1962–97).
Pearce, R. H., ed. *Nathaniel Hawthorne: Tales and Sketches* (Library of America, 1996).

Baym, N. *The Shape of Hawthorne's Career* (1976).
Bell, M. D. *Hawthorne and the Historical Romance of New England* (1971).
Bercovitch, S. *The Office of 'The Scarlet Letter'* (1993).
Berlant, L. *The Anatomy of National Fantasy: Hawthorne, Utopia, and Everyday Life* (1991).
Colacurcio, M. *The Province of Piety: Moral History in Hawthorne's Early Tales* (1984).
Crews, F. *The Sins of the Fathers: Hawthorne's Psychological Themes* (1966).
Crowley, J. D., ed. *Hawthorne: The Critical Heritage* (1970).
Gale, R. L. *A Nathaniel Hawthorne Encyclopedia* (1995).
Harding, B., ed. *Nathaniel Hawthorne: Critical Assessments* (4 vols, 1998).
Herbert, T. W. *Dearest Beloved: The Hawthornes and the Making of the Middle-Class Family* (1993).
James, H. *Hawthorne* (1879).
Martin, T. *Nathaniel Hawthorne* (rev. edn, 1983).
McWilliams, J. P., Jr *Hawthorne, Melville, and the American Character: A Looking-Glass Business* (1984).
Mellow, J. R. *Nathaniel Hawthorne in His Times* (1980).
Miller, E. H. *Salem Is My Dwelling Place: A Life of Nathaniel Hawthorne* (1991).
Miller, J. H. *Hawthorne and History* (1991).
Millington, R. H. *Practicing Romance: Narrative Form and Cultural Engagement in Hawthorne's Fiction* (1992).

Mitchell, T. R. *Hawthorne's Fuller Mystery* (1998).
Newberry, F. *Hawthorne's Divided Loyalties: England and America in His Works* (1987).
Pfister, J. *The Production of Personal Life: Class, Gender, and the Psychological in Hawthorne's Fiction* (1991).
Reynolds, L. J., ed. *A Historical Guide to Nathaniel Hawthorne* (2001).
Swann, C. *Nathaniel Hawthorne: Tradition and Revolution* (1991).
Turner, A. *Hawthorne: A Biography* (1980).

IRVING, Washington (1783–1859), was born on 3 April 1783 in New York City, the youngest of eleven children of a Scottish merchant. He began studying law in 1799 and was called to the Bar in 1806, but practised little. In 1802 he published theatre reviews in his brother Peter's *Morning Chronicle*, using the name 'Jonathan Oldstyle'. He visited Europe in 1804, returning in 1806 to assist in the family business, and to write, with his brother William and James Kirke Paulding, the satirical periodical *Salmagundi* (1807–8). In 1809 he published, under the name 'Diedrich Knickerbocker', the burlesque *History of New York from the Beginning of the World to the end of the Dutch Dynasty*, revising it in 1812, 1819 and 1848. He edited the *Analectic Magazine* (1813–14), and in 1815 sailed to Liverpool, taking over the British branch of the family business. The firm was dissolved in 1818 and, encouraged by Sir Walter Scott and Francis Jeffrey, Irving began writing full time. The result was his most popular collection, *The Sketch Book of Geoffrey Crayon, Gent.* (1819–20), which had sequels in *Bracebridge Hall* (1822), and, resulting from his travels, *Tales of a Traveller* (1824, about Germany), *The Alhambra* (1832, about Spain) and the 3-volume *Crayon Miscellany* (1835), including *A Tour of the Prairies*, *Legends of the Conquest of Spain* and *Abbotsford and Newstead Abbey*. The extended stay in Spain (1826–9) as a diplomatic attaché was most fruitful, leading also to *The Life and Voyages of Christopher Columbus* (1828), which established the voyager's abiding fame, the *Chronicle of the Conquest of Granada* (1829) and *Voyages of the Companions of Columbus* (1831). After three years as secretary of the US Legation in London, Irving returned to New York, then visited the South and West. As well as *A Tour of the Prairies*, this resulted in *Astoria* (1836) and the *Adventures of Captain Bonneville* (1837). He went back to Spain as US ambassador (1842–5), returning in his home in Tarrytown-on-Hudson in 1846. This final period led to a full-length biography of his favourite author, *Oliver Goldsmith* (1849), *A Book of the Hudson* (1849), *Mahomet and His Successors* (1850), *Wolfert's Roost* (1855) and the *Life of George Washington* (1855–9). He died on 28 November 1859, soon after the publication of the fifth volume of this long-planned project. Despite a natural charm and amiability, he never married.

Myers, A. B., ed. *Washington Irving: Bracebridge Hall, Tales of a Traveller, The Alhambra* (Library of America, 1991).
Pochmann, H. A., Kleinfield, H. L. and Rust, R. D., eds., *The Complete Works of Washington Irving* (30 vols., 1969–89).
Tuttleton, J. W., ed., *Washington Irving: History, Tales and Sketches* (Library of America, 1983).

Antelyes, P. *Tales of Adventurous Enterprise: Washington Irving and the Poetics of Westward Expansion* (1990).
Boden, M. W. *Washington Irving* (1981).
Brooks, V. W. *The World of Washington Irving* (1944).
Hedges, W. L. *Washington Irving: An American Study 1802–1832* (1965).
Myers, A., ed. *A Century of Commentary on the Works of Washington Irving* (1976).
Roth, M. *Comedy and America: The Lost World of Washington Irving* (1976).
Rubin-Dorsky, J. *Adrift in the Old World: The Psychological Pilgrimage of Washington Irving* (1988).
Springer, H. *Washington Irving: A Reference Guide* (1976).

Wagenknecht, E. *Washington Irving: Moderation Displayed* (1962).
Williams, S. T. *The Life of Washington Irving* (1935).

JAMES, Henry, Jr (1843–1916), was born in New York City, into a wealthy and intellectual family. A brother, William James (1842–1910), was a distinguished psychologist and philosopher, and a sympathetic goad to Henry's writing. James began publishing both fiction and criticism in 1864, setting a precedent that he would follow all his life. His first extended fiction, *Watch and Ward*, was published in serial form in 1871. Over a period of six years he published *Hawthorne* (1879) and a series of novels which made him the most sophisticated observer of transatlantic cultural relations: *Roderick Hudson* (1875), *The American* (1876–7), *The Europeans* (1878), *Daisy Miller* (1879), *An International Episode* (also 1879), *Confidence* (1880) and *The Portrait of a Lady* (1880–1). Beginning with *Washington Square* (1881), James wrote several novels of social realism, and a number of unsuccessful plays. He returned to the transatlantic theme with even greater sophistication in *The Wings of the Dove* (1902), *The Ambassadors* (1903) and *The Golden Bowl* (1904). These, together with many of his earlier works, extensively rewritten, were published with his Prefaces as the New York Edition. All his professional life, James had extended his interest in human consciousness by writing ghost stories. 'The Turn of the Screw' (1898) and 'The Jolly Corner' (1908) are the most frightening. He also wrote biography, autobiography and travel books. From 1896 he lived at Rye, a small town in Sussex near the English Channel. He died in 1916, now a British citizen, but leaving an international legacy that impacted on critical theory as well as American and English literature.

Aziz, M., ed. *The Tales of Henry James, 1864–79* (3 vols, 1973).
Blackmur, R. P., introd. *The Art of the Novel: Critical Prefaces* (1962).
Edel, L., ed. *The Complete Tales* (12 vols, 1962–4).
Edel, L., ed. *Letters* (4 vols, 1974–84).
Edel, L. and Powers, L. A., eds, *The Complete Notebooks* (1987).
Horne, P. *Henry James: A Life in Letters* (1999).
Stafford, W. T., ed. *Henry James: Novels 1871–80: Watch and Ward, Roderick Hudson, The American, The Europeans, Confidence* (Library of America, 1997).
Strouse, J., ed. *Henry James: Complete Stories 1864–74* (Library of America, 1999).
The Novels and Tales of Henry James (The New York Edition, 26 vols, 1907–17).
Vance, W., ed. *Henry James: Complete Stories 1874–84* (Library of America, 1999).

Blair, S. *Henry James and the Writing of Race and Nation* (1996).
Bridgman, R. 'Henry James and Mark Twain', *The Colloquial Style in America* (1966).
Edel, L. *The Life of Henry James* (rev. version, 1977).
Edel, L. and Laurence, D. H., eds *A Bibliography of Henry James* (1999).
Freedman, J., ed. *The Cambridge Companion to Henry James* (1998).
Gard, R., ed. *Henry James: The Critical Heritage* (1968).
Kaplan, F. *Henry James: The Imagination of Genius* (1992).
Kelley, C. P. *The Early Development of Henry James* (1965).
Lewis, R. W. B. *The Jameses: A Family Narrative* (1991).
Long, R. E. *The Great Succession: Henry James and the Legacy of Hawthorne* (1979).
Matthiessen, F. O. *The James Family* (1947).
Poirier, R. *The Comic Sense of Henry James: A Study of the Early Novels* (1960).
Putt, S. G. *The Fiction of Henry James* (1968).
Rowe, J. C. *The Theoretical Dimensions of Henry James* (1984).
Tanner, T. *The Reign of Wonder: Naivety and Reality in American Literature* (1965).
Taylor, A. *Henry James and the Father Question* (2002).

JEFFERSON, Thomas (1743–1826) was born at Shadwell, the Virginian estate owned by his father, Peter Jefferson, a farmer and surveyor. He studied at the College of William and Mary (1760–2), and practised law (1767–74) until the growing conflict with Britain drew him fully into politics. He had been elected to the Virginia House of Burgesses in 1769, and remained a politician for much of the time until his term as third President ended. In 1769 he also began building 'Monticello' to his own design on a summit near Shadwell. He married Martha Wayles Skelton in 1772; they had six children, and she died in 1782. In 1774 he published *A Summary View of the Rights of British America*. He was a member of the Continental Congress (1775–6) and largely responsible for drafting the Declaration of Independence, although his colleagues altered its long indictment of George III. In 1779 he was elected Governor of Virginia, his term ending in 1781. While the British occupied Virginia in 1781, he wrote his only book, *Notes on the State of Virginia*, first published in Paris in 1784. By that time Jefferson had joined John Adams and Franklin in Paris, and in 1785 he replaced Franklin as US minister to France. He returned to the US in 1789 to become the first Secretary of State. In 1796 he became vice-president to John Adams, and in 1800 was elected President after a bitter battle with Adams. He was inaugurated in Washington, the new city that he had helped to plan. During his two terms Jefferson invited Paine to return to the US; was accused of keeping an 'African concubine', Sally Hemings (accusations supported by DNA testing in 1998); authorised the Louisiana Purchase and commissioned the Lewis and Clark Expedition; and maintained an uneasy neutrality during the Napoleonic Wars. Jefferson retired to Monticello in 1809. In 1814 he turned his attention to public education. He offered his library of 6,000 volumes to Congress, thereby founding the Library of Congress. The University of Virginia was built to his design and his curriculum. In 1812 he began corresponding once again with his old colleague and enemy, John Adams; their letters constitute a great debate about the nature of republican culture. They both died at home, Adams in Quincy, Massachusetts, Jefferson at Monticello, on 4 July 1826, the fiftieth anniversary of the Republic.

Boyd, J. L., *et al.*, eds *The Papers of Thomas Jefferson* (30 vols to date, 1950–).
Ford, P. L., ed. *The Writings of Thomas Jefferson* (10 vols, 1892–9).
Lipscomb, A. A. and Bergh, A. E., eds *The Writings of Thomas Jefferson* (20 vols, 1903).
Peterson, M. D., ed. *Writings* (Library of America, 1984).

Adams, W. H., ed. *Jefferson and the Arts: An Extended View* (1976).
Adams, W. H., ed. *The Eye of Thomas Jefferson* (1976).
Becker, C. *The Declaration of Independence: A Study in the History of Ideas* (1922).
Berman, E. D. *Jefferson Among the Arts: An Essay in Early American Esthetics* (1947).
Boorstin, D. J. *The Lost World of Thomas Jefferson* (1948).
Ellis, J. J. *American Sphinx: The Character of Thomas Jefferson* (1997).
Lehman, K. *Thomas Jefferson: American Humanist* (1947).
Lockridge, K. A. *On the Sources of Patriarchal Rage: The Commonplace Books of William Byrd and Thomas Jefferson and the Gendering of Power in the Eighteenth Century* (1992).
Malone, D. *Jefferson and His Time* (6 vols, 1948–81).
Miller, C. A. *Jefferson and Nature: An Interpretation* (1988).
Peterson, M. D. *The Jefferson Image in the American Mind* (1960).
Peterson, M. D. *Thomas Jefferson and the New Nation: A Biography* (1970).
Peterson, M. D., ed. *Thomas Jefferson: A Reference Biography* (1987).
Shuffelton, F. *Thomas Jefferson: A Comprehensive, Annotated Bibliography of Writings about Him* (2 vols, 1983, 1992).
Wills, G. *Inventing America: Jefferson's Declaration of Independence* (1978).

LONGFELLOW, Henry Wadsworth (1807–82) was born in Portland, later to become part of Maine. In 1825 he graduated from Bowdoin College in the same class as Nathaniel Hawthorne. He was offered a Chair in Modern Languages at Bowdoin provided he study in Europe. From 1826 to 1829 he visited France, Spain, Italy and Germany; and from 1829 to 1835 he taught at Bowdoin. He published *Outre-Mer: A Pilgrimage beyond the Sea* in two parts in 1833–4, and as a book in 1835. In 1834 he accepted the Smith Chair of French and Spanish at Harvard, again with the proviso of further study. His first wife, Mary Potter, whom he had married in 1831, died after a miscarriage while they were in Europe. Longfellow taught at Harvard from 1836 until 1854. In 1839 he published *Hyperion*, a prose romance, and *Voices of the Night*, his first collection of poems, including 'A Psalm of Life'. *Ballads and Other Poems*, published in 1841, included 'The Village Blacksmith' and 'The Wreck of the Hesperus'. In 1842 he contributed *Poems on Slavery* to the abolitionist movement. In 1843 he married Frances Appleton. Her wealthy father gave them as a wedding present Craigie House, the Cambridge mansion where Longfellow had first lodged in 1836. They lived happily there until Frances was killed in a fire in 1861. After Longfellow's death the house became a historic site. He published *The Spanish Student*, a poetic drama, in 1843; three anthologies, *The Waif* and *The Poets and Poetry of Europe* in 1845 and *The Estray* in 1846; *The Belfry of Bruges and Other Poems*, including 'The Bridge', in 1845; *Evangeline* in 1847; *Kavanagh*, his last novel, in 1849; *The Seaside and the Fireside* in 1850; and his two greatest triumphs, *The Song of Hiawatha* in 1855 and *The Courtship of Miles Standish* in 1858. *Tales of a Wayside Inn* was published in three parts; the first, including 'Paul Revere's Ride', appeared in 1863, the second in 1872 and the third in 1874. *Flower-de-Luce* (1866) included 'Killed at the Ford'. Between 1865 and 1867 he published a translation of Dante's *Divine Comedy* in three volumes; while in 1872 he brought together *The Golden Legend* (1851) with *The Divine Tragedy* (1868) and *The New England Tragedies* (1871) to form another triptych, *Christus: A Mystery* (1872), an enormous dramatic poem. His last publications were *The Masque of Pandora* (1875), an opera, and two collections: *Kéramos* (1878) and *Ultima Thule* (1880). *In the Harbor* (1882) and *Michael Angelo* (1882–3) were published posthumously. He died on 24 March 1882, at the height of his fame.

Hilen, A. *The Letters of Henry Wadsworth Longfellow* (6 vols, 1966–82).
McClatchy, J. D., ed. *Henry Wadsworth Longfellow: Poems and Other Writings* (Library of America, 2000).

Arvin, N. *Longfellow: His Life and Work* (1963).
Buell, L. *New England Literary Culture: From Revolution Through Renaissance* (1986).
Hilen, A. *Longfellow and Scandinavia* (1947).
Longfellow, S. *Life of Henry Wadsworth Longfellow* (3 vols, 1891).
Wagenknecht, E. *Longfellow: A Full-Length Portrait* (1955).
Wagenknecht, E. *Henry Wadsworth Longfellow: His Poetry and Prose* (1986).
Williams, C. B. *Henry Wadsworth Longfellow* (1964).

MATHER, Cotton (1663–1728), was born in Boston, Massachusetts, on 12 February 1663. He was the son of Increase Mather (1639–1723), to whom he devoted a biography, *Parentator* (1724). Increase Mather had, in 1670, published a biography of his own father, *The Life and Death of Richard Mather*. Richard Mather (1596–1669) had migrated to New England in 1635, and was one of the translators of the *Bay Psalm Book*. Cotton Mather's mother was Maria Cotton, the daughter of John Cotton (1584–1652), who had migrated from Boston, Lincolnshire to Boston, Massachusetts in 1633; who wrote the 'Preface' to the *Bay Psalm Book*; and whose widow had married Increase in 1656. Cotton Mather inherited a strong sense of his family, of its role in New England, and of the need to maintain and record 'the New England Way'. Among his many books and pamphlets, for instance, was a biography (1691) of John Eliot, another translator of the *Bay Psalm Book* and a missionary to the Native Americans. Mather wrote an autobiography, *Paterna*, unpublished but used by his son Samuel in *The Life of the Very Reverend and Learned Cotton Mather* (1729). Mather entered Harvard before he was twelve years old, receiving a Bachelor's degree in 1678 and a

Master's in 1681. He was ordained in his father's Boston church, Old North, in 1685; their popular, vigorous joint ministry lasted until Increase died. Threats to 'the New England Way' came from Anglicanism imported from Britain, and locally from witchcraft and from more liberal Congregationalism. Mather published defences of the rebellion against Sir Edmund Andros in 1689 and a eulogy in 1697 of the governor who replaced Andros, Sir William Phips. His best known text was *The Wonders of the Invisible World* (1692), an account of the Salem witch trials. Probably his greatest achievement, and certainly his longest, was *Magnalia Christi Americana* (*The Great Works of Christ in America*, 1702), a seven-part ecclesiastical history of New England. *The Christian Philosopher* (1721) shows that Mather saw no contradiction between science and religion. He wrote numbers of botanical and medical tracts, leading to his election to the Royal Society in 1713. He was also an early, if controversial, advocate of inoculation against smallpox. As a scientist, as well as in his *Bonifacius: An Essay to Do Good* (1710), Mather anticipated Franklin. Mather died on 13 February 1728.

Levin, D., ed. *Bonifacius: An Essay to Do Good* (1962).
Magnalia Christi Americana (complete, 3rd edn, 1853; rpt. 1979).
Murdock, K. B., ed. *Magnalia Christi Americana* (Books I and II, 1977).
Scheick, W. J., ed. *Two Mather Biographies: Life and Death and Parentator* (1989).
Silverman, K., ed. *Selected Letters of Cotton Mather* (1971).
Van Doren, M., ed. *The Life of Sir William Phips* (1929).

Breitwieser, M. R. *Cotton Mather and Benjamin Franklin: The price of representative personality* (1984).
Holmes, T. J. *Cotton Mather: A Bibliography of his Works* (3 vols, 1940).
Levin, D. *Cotton Mather: The Young Life of the Lord's Remembrancer, 1663–1703* (1978).
Middlekauff, R. *The Mathers: Three Generations of Puritan Intellectuals, 1596–1728* (1971).
Silverman, K. *The Life and Times of Cotton Mather* (1985).

MELVILLE, Herman (1819–91), was born in New York City, the son of Allan Melvill, a merchant, and his wife Maria, daughter of a revolutionary hero, General Peter Gansevoort. The loss of the family fortune meant that Melville had a makeshift education that, with the death of his father in 1832, had to be fitted in between jobs as a bank clerk, shop- and farm-worker, and schoolteacher. In 1839 Melville (as he now spelt his name) both had his first piece published, and began signing on as a seaman. He worked on and off as a seaman with the merchant and US navies until 1844. On his discharge he wrote the story that would be published in 1846 in London as *Narrative of a Four Months' Residence*, and in New York as *Typee*. The book caused a sensation. In 1847 Melville published *Omoo*, a sequel to *Typee*, which maintained its success, and gave him enough money to marry Elizabeth Shaw, the daughter of Lemuel Shaw, Chief Justice of the Massachusetts Supreme Court. A third novel, *Mardi*, followed in 1849. It was much less popular than its predecessors, but Melville still had enough steam up to write *Redburn* (1849), *White-Jacket* (1850) and *Moby-Dick* (1851); and to buy a farm in Pittsfield, Massachusetts, with money loaned by Lemuel Shaw. However, reviews of *Moby-Dick* were mixed, and he obtained poor terms for his next novel, *Pierre* (1852), which then caused a scandal with its hints at incest. Melville turned to short stories, publishing fourteen in periodicals, and collecting some of them as *The Piazza Tales* (1856). He also published *Israel Potter* as a serial, before it appeared in book form in 1855. By 1856 Melville was in financial difficulties again. He was rescued by Shaw, who was so worried about his son-in-law's health that he also financed a trip to Europe and the Middle East. *The Confidence-Man* was published while Melville toured Europe; it failed. Melville now turned to poetry, but could find no publisher. In 1863 he sold the farm to his brother Allan, his wife buying Allan's New York home with money inherited from her father, who had died in 1861. In 1864 Melville visited Civil War battlefields, writing poems that were published as *Battle-Pieces and Aspects of the War* in 1866. Late that year he was appointed an inspector of customs, a post he would hold until 1885. In 1876 he published *Clarel*, twenty years after visiting the Holy Land. His final books were published privately in editions of twenty-five copies: *John Marr and Other Sailors* in 1888 and *Timoleon and Other Ventures in Minor Verse* in 1891. When he died, in New York City on 28 September 1891, he left some poems entitled 'Weeds and Wildings Chiefly', unpublished, together with the sketch, 'Daniel Orme,' and *Billy Budd*.

Hayford, H., ed. *Herman Melville: Pierre, Israel Potter, The Confidence-Man, Tales, and Billy Budd* (Library of America, 1985).

Hayford, H., Parker, H. and Tanselle, G. T., eds *The Writings of Herman Melville* (15 vols, 1968–).

Tanselle, G. T., ed. *Herman Melville: Redburn, White-Jacket, Moby-Dick* (Library of America, 1983).

Tanselle, G. T., ed. *Herman Melville: Typee, Omoo, Mardi* (Library of America, 2000).

Arvin, N. *Herman Melville* (1950).

Bellis, P. *No Mysteries Out of Ourselves: Identity and Textual Form in the Novels of Herman Melville* (1990).

Brodhead, R., ed. *New Essays on Moby-Dick* (1986).

Chase, R. *Herman Melville, A Critical Study* (1949).

Dimock, W. *Empire for Liberty: Melville and the Poetics of Liberalism* (1989).

Franklin, H. B. *The Wake of the Gods: Melville's Mythology* (1963).

Gale, R. L. *A Herman Melville Encyclopedia* (1995).

Garner, S. *The Civil War World of Herman Melville* (1993).

Herbert, T. W. *Marquesan Encounters: Melville and the Meaning of Civilization* (1980).

Higgins, B. and Parker, H. *Herman Melville: The Contemporary Reviews* (1995).

James, C. L. R. *Mariners, Renegades, and Castaways: The Story of Herman Melville and the World We Live In* (1953).

Jehlen, M., ed. *Herman Melville: A Collection of Critical Essays* (1994).

Lee, A. R., ed. *Herman Melville: Critical Assessments* (4 vols, 2001).

Levine, R. S., ed. *The Cambridge Companion to Herman Melville* (1998).

Leyda, J., ed. *The Melville Log: A Documentary Life of Herman Melville, 1819–1891* (2 vols, 1969).

Martin, R. K. *Heroes, Captains, and Strangers: Male Friendship, Social Critique, and Literary Form in the Sea Novels of Herman Melville* (1986).

McWilliams, J. P., Jr *Hawthorne, Melville, and the American Character: A Looking-Glass Business* (1984).

Miller, E. H. *Herman Melville: A Biography* (1975).

Olson, C. *Call Me Ishmael: A Study of Melville* (1947).

Parker, H. *Reading Billy Budd* (1990).

Parker, H. *Herman Melville: A Biography* (2 vols, 1996, 2002).

Parker, H. and Hayford, H. *Moby-Dick as Doubloon: Essays and Extracts (1851–1970)* (1970).

Renker, E. *Strike Through the Mask: Herman Melville and the Scene of Writing* (1996).

Rogin, M. P. *Subversive Genealogy: The Politics and Art of Herman Melville* (1983).

Samson, J. *White Lies: Melville's Narrative of Facts* (1995).

Spanos, W. V. *The Errant Art of Moby-Dick: The Canon, the Cold War, and the Struggle for American Studies* (1995).

Spark, C. L. *Hunting Captain Ahab: Psychological Warfare and the Melville Revival* (2001).

Thomson, L. R. *Melville's Quarrel with God* (1952).

Yannella, D., ed. *New Essays on Billy Budd* (2002).

Young, P. *The Private Melville* (1993).

MORTON, Thomas (1580?–1647), describes himself in *New English Canaan* as a soldier's son and 'of Cliffords Inne gent', which suggests he was a lawyer. Otherwise, little is known of his life until he became involved in lawsuits over the property of a widow, Alice Miller, whom he married in 1621. In 1624 he sailed to New England and established a colony that, after he became leader, he named Ma-re Mount. He traded firearms and alcohol with the natives for furs. This led to his being deported to England in 1628. In 1629 he returned to Ma-re Mount, only to be deported again late in 1630. *New English Canaan* was first published in London, but seized by agents of the Massachusetts Bay Company. He then published it in Amsterdam in 1637. In 1643 Morton sailed to New England for the third and final time. He was arrested again, this time for publishing *New English Canaan*, and spent several months in jail in Boston. He was released in 1645 and moved to Maine, where he died in 1647.

See: Connors, D. F. *Thomas Morton* (1969).

NEAL, John (1793–1876) was born in Falmouth, now Portland, the largest city in Maine. The son of a Quaker teacher, he was educated at various local schools until the age of twelve. He then became a shop assistant, teacher and portraitist. From 1814 until 1816 he ran a dry-goods store in Baltimore with John Pierpont, the grandfather of J. P. Morgan. In 1816 he began studying law, financing himself by writing. Neal wrote furiously, and by 1823 he had a flourishing law practice. He contributed to the *Baltimore Telegraph* and a periodical, the *Portico*; and assisted Paul Allen in the *History of the American Revolution* (1819). He published a narrative poem, *The Battle of Niagara* (1818), a five-act blank verse tragedy, *Otho* (1819), and five novels. *Keep Cool* (1817) was followed in 1822 by *Logan*, about the Iroquois Chief admired by Jefferson. In 1823 he published *Seventy-Six*, obviously about the Revolution, *Errata, or the Works of Will. Adams*, and *Randolph*. This last novel contained an attack on the Baltimore politician William Pinkney. Pinkney's son challenged Neal to a duel. *Keep Cool* had partly been a tract against duelling. Neal followed its advice, kept cool, and sailed to Britain. He wrote a large number of articles on American life and letters, particularly for *Blackwood's Edinburgh Magazine*. Its owner published Neal's novel about New England and the Revolution, *Brother Jonathan*, taking its title from the stereotype of the shrewd Yankee. In 1827 Neal returned to Portland, practising law, fighting for women's rights and against racism, and writing, still furiously. He published four more novels: *Rachel Dyer* (1828, about the Salem witchcraft trials), *Authorship* (1830), *The Down-Easters* (1833) and *True Womanhood* (1859). He edited three journals: the *Yankee* in 1828, promoting the utilitarianism of his English friend Jeremy Bentham; the *New England Galaxy* in 1835; and *Brother Jonathan* in 1843. He also published *One Word More* (1854), a religious tract; popular novels about Indian adventures; his autobiography, *Wandering Recollections of a Somewhat Busy Life* (1869); a collection of children's sayings, *Great Mysteries and Little Plagues* (1870); and a guide to his home town, *Portland Illustrated* (1874). He died in Portland on 20 June 1876.

Pattee, F. L., ed. *American Writers: A Series of Papers Contributed to Blackwood's Magazine by John Neal* (1937).

Fleischmann, F. *A Right View of the Subject: Feminism in the Works of Charles Brockden Brown and John Neal* (1983).
Lease, B. *That Wild Fellow John Neal and the American Literary Revolution* (1972).
Orestano, F. 'The Old World and the New in the national landscapes of John Neal', in *Views of American Landscapes*, eds. Gidley, M. and Lawson-Peebles, R. (1989).
Orestano, F. *Dal Neoclassico al Classico: John Neal e la Coscienza Letteraria Americana* (1990).
Sears, D. A. *John Neal* (1978).

PAINE, Thomas (1737–1809) was born in Thetford, Norfolk, England, the son of a Quaker corsetmaker and his Anglican wife. He studied at Thetford Grammar School, and at the age of thirteen was apprenticed to his father. In 1756 he ran away, spending six months as a sailor before living in London and then working as a corsetmaker in Kent. He married Mary Lambert in 1759; she and a child died during confinement in 1760. He was an excise officer in Lincolnshire from 1762 to 1765 and in Lewes, Sussex, from 1768 to 1774. In the intervening period he was again a corsetmaker and teacher in London. He had married again, to Elizabeth Ollive, in 1771; they separated in 1774. In October that year he migrated to Philadelphia. A letter of introduction to Benjamin Franklin secured him the job as editor of the *Pennsylvania Magazine*. He was soon moving in republican circles. In January 1776 he published *Common Sense*; it was a great success. Once the United States had declared independence, Paine joined the militia. While serving with Washington in December 1776 he published *The American Crisis*. Twelve more essays with this title were published between 1777 and 1783. He obtained a number of US government appointments, some of which were controversial. In 1786 he published *Dissertations on Government*, supporting a central bank and attacking inflation, at the same time developing a design for a wrought-iron bridge. The next year he returned to Europe, seeking funds for the bridge project. In 1791 and 1792 he published the two parts of *The Rights of Man*, an answer to *Reflections on the Revolution in France* by Edmund Burke, whom he had met in England. He was tried in England for treason and sentenced to banishment, but had already fled to France. In 1792 the French Assembly made him a citizen and he was elected to the Convention, but when the moderate republicans lost power his citizenship was revoked and he was arrested. During eleven months in jail he wrote *The Age of Reason*. In 1797 he published *Agrarian Justice*, a pioneer land reform pamphlet. In 1802 he returned to the United States at the invitation of President Jefferson, but he achieved little more, and when he died on 8 June 1809 he had been forgotten.

Conway, M. D., ed. *The Writings of Thomas Paine* (6 vols, 1894; rpt. 1996).
Foner, E., ed. *Thomas Paine: Collected Writings* (Library of America, 1995).
Foner, P. S., ed. *The Life and Major Writings of Thomas Paine* (1945).

Aldridge, A. O. *Man of Reason* (1960).
Aldridge, A. O. *Thomas Paine's American Philosophy* (1984).
Ayer, A. J. *Thomas Paine* (1988).
Claeys, G. *Thomas Paine: Social and Political Thought* (1989).
Foner, E. *Tom Paine and Revolutionary America* (1976).
Fruchtman, J., Jr *Thomas Paine, Apostle of Freedom* (1994).
Keane, J. *Tom Paine: A Political Life* (1995).

POE, Edgar Allan (1809–49), was born in Boston, Massachusetts on 19 January 1809, the second son of itinerant actors. He was soon orphaned; his father deserted the family in New York, and then his mother died in Richmond, Virginia, in 1811. Poe became the ward of John and Frances Allan, a well-to-do, childless Richmond couple. He was never legally adopted, and was often completely at odds with the commercial attitudes of John Allan. Nevertheless, he sometimes added the name of his foster-father to his own. He accompanied the Allans to London, where he went to school from 1815 to 1820, and then continued his education in Richmond when they returned to Virginia. He attended the University of Virginia for one session, in 1826, but left after running up large debts. In 1827 he moved to Boston, published *Tamerlane and Other Poems*, and enlisted in the US Army under the name Edgar A. Perry, quickly rising to the rank of sergeant-major. Poe left the army in 1829 and lived with relatives of his natural father, the Poes and the Clemms, in Baltimore, while arranging the publication there of *Al Aaraaf, Tamerlane, and Minor Poems*. Allan assisted him to enter West Point as an officer-cadet in 1830, but they argued conclusively and Poe's cadetship ended in an expedient court martial. He moved to New York City, where he published *Poems by Edgar A. Poe* (1831), then returned to his aunt, Maria Clemm, in Baltimore, and published his first short story, 'Metzengerstein', in 1832. In 1836 he married Maria Clemm's daughter Virginia; they had earlier engaged in a private ceremony. From 1831 the three had formed a permanent, if peripatetic, household. From 1831, too, Poe held editorial jobs with magazines, publishing in them his poems, tales and savage reviews, interrupted by periods of hack-work and hunger. He worked for the *Southern Literary Messenger* in Richmond (1834–7); for *Burton's Gentleman's Magazine* (1839–40) and *Graham's Magazine* (1841–2), both in Philadelphia; and for the New York *Evening Mirror* (1844–5). Poe published *The Narrative of Arthur Gordon Pym* (New York City, 1837), *Tales of the Grotesque and Arabesque* (Philadelphia, 1840), a further collection of *Tales* and *The Raven and Other Poems* (both New York City, 1845). Poe had long wished to launch his own magazine, and in early 1845 he joined the *Broadway Journal*, taking a financial as well as an editorial interest. Then Poe's circumstances deteriorated. The magazine closed in January 1846. In January 1847 Virginia died of tuberculosis. Poe was frequently drunk and deranged, unsuccessfully courted three women in an attempt to stabilise his life, and in November 1848 attempted suicide. He died in Baltimore on 7 October 1849, returning to New York from an attempt in Richmond to start a journal and to remarry.

Mabbott, T. O., ed. *Collected Works of Edgar Allan Poe* (3 vols, 1969–78).
Ostrom, J. W., ed. *The Letters of Edgar Allan Poe* (rev. edn, 1966).
Pollin, B. R., ed. *Collected Writings of Edgar Allan Poe* (4 vols, 1981–6).
Quinn, P. F., ed. *Poetry and Tales* (Library of America, 1984).
Thompson, G. R., ed. *Essays and Reviews* (Library of America, 1984).

Buranelli, V. *Edgar Allan Poe* (2nd edn, 1977).
Carlson, E. W., ed. *The Recognition of Edgar Allan Poe: Selected Criticism Since 1829* (1967).
Clarke, G., ed. *Edgar Allan Poe: Critical Assessments* (4 vols, 1991).
Davidson, E. H. *Poe: A Critical Study* (1957).
Elmer, J. *Reading at the Social Limit: Affect, Mass Culture, and Edgar Allan Poe* (1995).
Hayes, K. J., ed. *The Cambridge Companion to Edgar Allan Poe* (2002).
Hoffman, D. *Poe Poe Poe Poe Poe Poe Poe* (1972).
Jacobs, R. *Poe: Journalist and Critic* (1969).
Kennedy, J. G. *Poe, Death, and the Life of Writing* (1987).
Meyers, J. *Edgar Allan Poe: His Life and Legacy* (1992).
Muller, J. P. and Richardson, W. J., eds *The Purloined Poe: Lacan, Derrida, and Psychoanalytic Reading* (1988).
Quinn, P. F. *The French Face of Edgar Poe* (1957).
Regan, R., ed. *Poe: A Collection of Critical Essays* (1967).
Rosenheim, S. *The Cryptographic Imagination: Secret Writing from Edgar Poe to the Internet* (1997).
Rosenheim, S. and Rachman, S., eds *The American Face of Edgar Allan Poe* (1995).
Silverman, K. *Edgar A. Poe: Mournful and Never-Ending Remembrance* (1992).
Silverman, K., ed. *New Essays on Poe's Major Tales* (1993).
Symons, J. *The Tell-Tale Heart: The Life and Works of Edgar Allan Poe* (1978).
Thomas D. and Jackson, D. K. *The Poe Log: A Documentary Life of Edgar Allan Poe, 1809–1849* (1987).
Thompson, G. R. *Poe's Fiction: Romantic Irony in the Gothic Tales* (1973).
Walker, I. M., ed. *Edgar Allan Poe: The Critical Heritage* (1986).

RALEGH, Sir Walter (1552?–1618) was born the son of a country gentleman in Hayes Barton, Devon, England. All his life he spoke with a broad Devon accent, pronouncing his name 'Rawley', the way he frequently wrote it. The preferred scholarly spelling has been 'Ralegh' for some time. Much of his early life can only be conjectured: he was probably educated in South Devon, and he was recorded in 1572 as a member of Oriel College, Oxford, which suggests that he may have been born about twenty years earlier. In 1569 he went to France as a volunteer in the Huguenot army, and may have stayed there for five years. In 1580 he fought in Ireland. The famous incident of the cloak and mud-puddle may have occurred the following year. He was a favourite of the Queen until she imprisoned both Ralegh and Elizabeth Throckmorton in 1592 for a suspected affair. After their release they married. Ralegh had been advocating English colonial settlement for some time before he sailed in 1585, arriving at Roanoke Island on the Carolina Outer Banks in June and settling six hundred colonists there. The settlement was evacuated a year later. A second expedition was sent to the land, which the Queen had now named the Virginia, in 1587. The entire group of settlers disappeared. In 1594 Ralegh sailed to Trinidad and then up the Orinoco in search of El Dorado. He published the account of his expedition, *The Discoverie of the Large, Rich and Bewtiful Empyre of Guiana*, in 1596. When James I succeeded Elizabeth in 1603, he imprisoned Ralegh on suspicion of plotting his removal. While in prison, Ralegh wrote his *History of the World*. He was released in 1616 in order to undertake a further expedition to the Orinoco. He sailed in June 1617, but the expedition was a disaster and, at the behest of the Spanish ambassador, James imprisoned him. He was beheaded on 19 October 1618. While Ralegh certainly smoked tobacco and had planted potatoes in his garden, stories that he was responsible for their introduction to England are probably exaggerated.

Latham, A. and Youings, J. *The Letters of Sir Walter Ralegh* (1999).
Ralegh *The Discoverie of the Large, Rich and Bewtiful Empyre of Guiana*, ed. and introd. Whitehead, N. L. (1997).

Armitage, C. M. *Sir Walter Ralegh: An Annotated Bibliography* (1987).
Greenblatt, S. J. *Sir Walter Ralegh: The Renaissance Man and His Roles* (1973).
May, S. W. *Sir Walter Ralegh* (1989).
Quinn, D. B. *Ralegh and the British Empire* (1947).
Quinn, D. B., ed. *The Roanoke Voyages, 1584–1590* (2 vols, 1955).
Youings, J., ed. *Ralegh in Exeter 1985* (1985).

ROWSON, Susannah (1762–1824), was born in Portsmouth, England, the daughter of a naval officer, William Haswell, whom she followed to Massachusetts in 1766. The family returned to England in 1778. They were destitute, and the young woman helped by writing songs for Vauxhall Gardens, a popular place of entertainment in London. In 1786 she published her first novel, *Victoria*, and married William Rowson. She soon became the breadwinner, and began writing in earnest. In 1788 she published *A Trip to Parnassus*, a poetic critique of the theatre, and *Poems on Various Subjects*. No copies of either text have been found. That year she also published *The Inquisitor*, a collection of views of London life seen by an 'Invisible Rambler'. In 1789 a second novel, *Mary, or the Test of Honour*, appeared, followed by *Charlotte* and *Mentoria* in 1791 and *Rebecca* in 1792. The Rowsons moved to the US in 1793. None of her work achieved great popularity in England, but the fate of *Charlotte* in the United States was quite different. It was first imported in 1792 then published in 1794 by Mathew Carey, who changed its title in 1797 to *Charlotte Temple*. For more than a century it remained the first best-seller in the United States. In 1793 the Rowsons had moved as actors to Philadelphia, where she published a play, *Slaves in Algiers* (1793) and an epistolary novel, *Trials of the Human Heart* (1795). In 1796 the Philadelphia theatre failed, and the Rowsons moved to another theatre in Boston, but in 1797 that theatre failed too. Rowson now opened Boston's first school for girls, but continued to publish. A novel, *Reuben and Rachel*, appeared in 1798; *Miscellaneous Poems* in 1804; and another novel, *Sarah, the exemplary wife* in 1813. She wrote several textbooks for young ladies in the years 1805–22. *Charlotte's Daughter*, a sequel to her most popular novel, appeared posthumously in 1828. Susannah Rowson died on 2 March 1824 in Boston.

Lawson-Peebles, R. 'International embarrassment: A transatlantic morphology of blushing, 1749–1812', in *Revolutionary Histories: Cultural Crossings, 1775–1815*, ed. Verhoeven, W. M. (2002).

Parker, P. *Susannah Rowson* (1986).

Vail, R. W. G. *Susanna Haswell Rowson, the author of Charlotte Temple. A bibliographical study* (1933).

SMITH, John (1580–1631) was born in Lincolnshire, the son of a tenant farmer. His autobiography, *The True Travels, Adventures, and Observations of Captaine John Smith* (1630), may not be entirely reliable. He may have received some elementary teaching from the father of Anne Hutchinson before being apprenticed to a merchant in King's Lynn. He then soldiered in Europe, visited Scotland, returned home, and travelled to the Mediterranean. He joined Austrian forces fighting Turkey and was promoted to captain. He was captured in Transylvania, but escaped, returning the England by means of Russia and Morocco. In 1606 he was chosen for the governing council of Virginia. He spent much of two years in Virginia exploring Chesapeake Bay, his work resulting in *A True Relation of . . . Virginia* (1608), the first account of the colony published from experience, *A Map of Virginia* (1612), and *The Generall Historie of Virginia, New-England, and the Summer Isles* (1624), which tells the Pocahontas story. Smith returned to England in 1609 and criticised the Virginia Company. Supported by West Country merchants, Smith explored New England in 1614 and 1615, publishing *A Description of New England*, a promotional tract, in 1616. It seems that during the second voyage he was captured by pirates and taken to France. Smith escaped and returned again to England; it is unlikely that he did any more travelling. He attacked Ralegh's search for gold in *New Englands Trials* (1620), promoting instead the careful mercantilism he had learnt in King's Lynn, a message repeated in his last pamphlet, *Advertisements for the unexperienced Planters of New-England, Or Anywhere* (1631). He also published two manuals of seamanship in 1626 and 1627, which suggests that had the Pilgrim Fathers accepted his offer of leadership, they would have set up their city on a hill further south. He died in London on 21 June 1631.

Barbour, P. L., ed. *The Complete Works of Captain John Smith, 1580–1631* (3 vols, 1986).

Barbour, P. L. *The Three Worlds of Captain John Smith* (1964).

Dolle, R. F. 'Captain John Smith's satire of Sir Walter Raleigh', in *Early American Literature and Culture: Essays Honoring Harrison T. Meserole*, ed. Derounian-Stodola, K. Z. (1992).

Emerson, E. *Captain John Smith* (1971).

Hulme, P. *Colonial Encounters: Europe and the Native Caribbean, 1492–1797* (1986).

Lemay, J. A. L. *The American Dream of Captain John Smith* (1991).

Tilton, R. S. *Pocahontas: The Evolution of an American Narrative* (1994).

Vaughan, A. T. *American Genesis: Captain John Smith and the Founding of Virginia* (1975).

SMITH, William (1727–1803), was born near Aberdeen, Scotland, the son of a small farmer. He graduated from King's College, Aberdeen in 1747 and began teaching in Abernethy, Scotland. In March 1751 he migrated to New York, where he taught and published *Indian Songs of Peace* (1752). *A General Idea of the College of Mirania* (1753) caught the attention of Benjamin Franklin, who assisted Smith to become first provost of the College of Philadelphia in 1756. He visited Britain in 1753 to take orders in the Anglican Church, and on his return became involved in Pennsylvania politics on the side of the proprietary Penn family. In 1755 he published *A Brief State of the Province of Pennsylvania*, and in 1756 *A Brief View of the Conduct of Pennsylvania*, attacking the

Quaker-dominated Assembly for failing to protect the Colony from Indian attack. The Quakers imprisoned him, together with William Moore (1699–1783), a Pennsylvania politician and judge. While in prison, Smith courted Moore's daughter Rebecca, marrying her in 1758. By 1762 Smith had been awarded three British honorary doctorates and had become a leading Anglican in America and an important administrator of cultural activity in Philadelphia. He reported to Lambeth Palace on the state of the Church in the colonies, and in 1765 published his popular *Historical Account of the Expedition against the Ohio Indians . . . under the command of Henry Bouquet*, describing new methods of Indian fighting and frontier settlement. He tried to steer a middle course during the revolution, answering Tom Paine's *Common Sense* with *Plain Truth* (1776). He was imprisoned briefly and lost his post as provost. He moved to Maryland, where he taught. In 1789 the charter of the College of Philadelphia was restored and Smith reappointed, staying in the post until the College became the University of Pennsylvania in 1791. Smith died in Philadelphia on 14 May 1803. Two volumes of his pamphlets and sermons were published shortly afterwards.

Smith, W. *Works* (2 vols, 1803).

Gegenheimer, A. F. *William Smith: Educator and Churchman* (1943).
Jones, T. F. *A Pair of Lawn Sleeves: A Biography of William Smith* (1972).
Lawson-Peebles, R. 'The problem of William Smith: An Aberdonian in Revolutionary America', in *Aberdeen and the Enlightenment*, eds. Carter, J. J. and Pittock, J. H. (1987).
Smith, H. W. *Life and Correspondence of the Rev. William Smith, D.D.* (2 vols, 1879–80).

STOWE, Harriet Beecher (1811–96) was born in Litchfield, Connecticut, the daughter of Lyman Beecher, a popular evangelical minister. She was a precocious child, quickly excelling in Litchfield Female Academy and then in Hartford Female Seminary, run by her elder sister, Catherine Beecher. She taught composition at the seminary from 1829 for three years. Catherine and Harriet moved with the family when in 1832 her father became president of Lane Theological Seminary, Cincinnati, Ohio. Harriet taught in Catherine's Western Female Academy, wrote a geography primer, temperance stories and sermons for periodicals, and New England sketches eventually collected in *The Mayflower* (1843). In 1836 she married a professor in the Lane Theological Seminary, Calvin Ellis Stowe, who encouraged her writing. The Stowes moved to Bowdoin College, Maine, in 1850, and in 1851 she began publishing *Uncle Tom's Cabin* serially in an anti-slavery journal, the *National Era*. The story's popularity was confirmed when it was published in book form in 1852. The resultant financial security prompted the Stowes to leave Bowdoin and settle in Hartford, Connecticut, where they became neighbours of Samuel Clemens. In 1853 Stowe published *A Key to Uncle Tom's Cabin*, answering criticisms that her tale was exaggerated. In 1853 she also undertook a tour of Britain, resulting in *Sunny Memories of Foreign Lands* (1854). In response to the Kansas-Nebraska Act (1854), she wrote her second, more combative anti-slavery novel, *Dred: A Tale of the Great Dismal Swamp* (1856). In 1859 she published *The Minister's Wooing*, her first novel of New England life. During a second European tour Queen Victoria had given an audience to Stowe. A third, spent partly in Italy, resulted in *Agnes of Sorrento* (1862). In that year she also published her second New England novel, *The Pearl of Orr's Island*. *Religious Poems* (1867) was followed by the biographical *Men of Our Times* (1868) and a third New England novel, *Oldtown Folks* (1869). In 1869 Stowe again visited England, meeting Lady Byron. *Lady Byron Vindicated* (1870) included revelations of incest and caused a scandal. Her reputation damaged by this venture into sexual politics, Stowe returned to New England themes: *Pink and White Tyranny* and *My Wife and I* (both 1871), *Sam Lawson's Oldtown Fireside Stories* (1872) and *We and Our Neighbors* (1875). Her last novel, *Poganuc People* (1878), was based on her childhood in Litchfield. She died in Hartford on 1 July 1896.

Sklar, K. K., ed. *Harriet Beecher Stowe: Three Novels* (Library of America, 1982). Includes *Uncle Tom's Cabin*, *The Minister's Wooing* and *Oldtown Folks*.

Ammons, E., ed. *Critical Essays on Harriet Beecher Stowe* (1980).
Ashton, J. W. *Harriet Beecher Stowe: A Reference Guide* (1977).
Boydston, J., *et al.*, eds *The Limits of Sisterhood: The Beecher Sisters on Women's Rights and Woman's Sphere* (1988).
Crozier, A. *The Novels of Harriet Beecher Stowe* (1969).
Caskey, M. *Chariot of Fire: Religion and the Beecher Family* (1978).
Gossett, T. *'Uncle Tom's Cabin' and American Culture* (1985).
Hedrick, J. D. *Harriet Beecher Stowe: A Life* (1994).
Hildreth, M. H. *Harriet Beecher Stowe: A Bibliography* (1976).
Lowance, M. I., Westbrook, E. E. and De Prospo, R., eds *The Stowe Debate: Rhetorical Strategies in Uncle Tom's Cabin* (1994).
Tompkins, J. *Sensational Designs: The Cultural Work of American Fiction 1790–1860* (1985).
Stowe, C. E., ed. *The Life of Harriet Beecher Stowe, Compiled from Her Letters and Journals* (1889).
Stowe, C. E. and Stowe, L. B. *Harriet Beecher Stowe: The Story of Her Life* (1911).
Sundquist, E. J. *New Essays on Uncle Tom's Cabin* (1986).

TAYLOR, Edward (1642?–1729) was born in Sketchley, Leicestershire, the son of a dissenting farmer. He was a schoolteacher until he was ejected for refusing to subscribe to the 1662 Act of Uniformity. He migrated to Massachusetts in 1668 and entered Harvard. After graduating in 1671 he was called to the frontier town of Westfield, in the Connecticut Valley, where he served as minister and doctor for the rest of his working life. His first poetry was a long verse-drama called 'God's Determinations Touching His Elect', completed around 1682. He then turned to 'Preparatory Meditations', a sequence of 217 poems written as preliminaries for administering the Sacrament. He also wrote occasional poems; a long interpretation of the Bible, 'Harmony of the Gospels'; and numbers of sermons on typology and in debate with Solomon Stoddard, a nearby and more liberal minister. Taylor was twice married and had fourteen children, five of whom died in infancy. He retired from the ministry in 1725, and died at Westfield on 24 June 1729. He carefully preserved his work, but published little of it. It passed to his grandson, Ezra Stiles (1727–95), who became president of Yale. Taylor's poetry was unearthed at Yale and a selection first published in 1937. Many of Taylor's manuscripts have been published since then.

Davis, T. M., Davis, V. L. with Parks, B. L., eds *Edward Taylor's Harmony of the Gospels* (4 vols, 1983).
Grabo, N. S., ed. *Edward Taylor's Christographia* (1962).
Stanford, D. E., ed. *The Poems of Edward Taylor* (1960).

Gatta, J. *Gracious Laughter: The Meditative Wit of Edward Taylor* (1989).
Grabo, N. S. *Edward Taylor* (rev. edn, 1988).
Hammond, J. A. *Edward Taylor: Fifty Years of Scholarship and Criticism* (1993).
Rowe, K. E. *Saint and Singer: Edward Taylor's Typology and the Poetics of Meditation* (1986).
Scheick, W. J. *The Will and the Word: The Poetry of Edward Taylor* (1974).

THOREAU, Henry David (1817–62), was born in Concord, Massachusetts. He entered Harvard in 1833, paying his way by teaching in Canton, Massachusetts, where he met and was deeply influenced by Orestes Brownson. Shortly after graduating from Harvard in 1837, Thoreau met Emerson, who encouraged him to write. Much of Thoreau's early poetry and essays were published in *The Dial*, which Thoreau helped Emerson edit in 1843. In 1838 Thoreau had opened a private school in Concord, with his elder brother John. They closed their school in 1841, and John died the following year. Thoreau wrote and, after much revision, published *A Week on the Concord and Merrimack Rivers* in 1849, as a record of their 1839 summer vacation building a boat, rowing and walking, and as a tribute to John. To have time to write, Thoreau lived with the Emerson family in 1841, then in 1843 tutored the family of Emerson's brother William in Staten Island. In New York City, Thoreau met the newspaper editor Horace Greeley, who became his literary agent. Metropolitan life did not suit Thoreau, however, and when Emerson bought land at Walden Pond, Thoreau built a cabin there and lived in it for more than two years. He gave lectures on his experience of the simple life, and they in turn were developed into *Walden, or Life in the Woods* (1854). In 1846 Thoreau was jailed for refusing to pay his poll tax. His 1848 lecture on this experience became 'Resistance to Civil Government' (1849). Thoreau lived the remainder of his life in Concord, engaging in such reform activities as abolitionism. Yet he also made excursions to such places as Cape Cod, the Maine Woods, Canada and – in an attempt to improve his health – Minnesota. Like his brother John, Thoreau had long suffered from tuberculosis, and he died of it in Concord on 6 May 1862. His essays and extracts from his journals were gathered into a number of posthumous publications: *Excursions* (1863), *The Maine Woods* (1864), *Cape Cod* (1865), *Letters to Various Persons* (edited by Emerson, 1865), *A Yankee in Canada* (1866), *Early Spring in Massachusetts* (1881), *Summer* (1884), *Winter* (1888) and *Autumn* (1892). Collected editions of his writings were published in 1894 and 1906; and have been in process since 1971.

Dean, B. P., ed. *Faith in a Seed: The Dispersion of Seeds and Other Late Natural History Writings* (1993).
Harding, W. and Bode, C. *The Correspondence of Henry David Thoreau* (1958).
Harding, W., Witherell, E. H., *et al.*, eds *The Writings of Henry David Thoreau* (11 vols, 1971–).
Sayre, R. F., ed. *Henry David Thoreau: A Week, Walden, The Maine Woods, Cape Cod* (Library of America, 1989).
Witherell, E. H., ed. *Henry David Thoreau: Collected Essays and Poems* (Library of America, 2001).

Borst, R. R. *A Thoreau Log: A Documentary Life of Henry David Thoreau 1817–1862* (1992).
Bridgman, R. *Dark Thoreau* (1982).
Buell, L. *The Environmental Imagination: Thoreau, Nature Writing, and the Formation of American Culture* (1995).
Cain, W. E., ed. *A Historical Guide to Henry David Thoreau* (2000).
Cameron, S. *Writing Nature: Henry Thoreau's Journal* (1989).
Cavell, S. *The Senses of Walden: An Expanded Edition* (1981).
Fink, S. *Prophet in the Marketplace: Thoreau's Development as a Professional Writer* (1992).
Garber, F. *Thoreau's Fable of Inscribing* (1991).
Harding, W. *The Days of Henry Thoreau* (rev. edn, 1982).
Harding, W. and Meyer, M. *The New Thoreau Handbook* (1980).
Hildebidle, J. *Thoreau: A Naturalist's Liberty* (1983).
Howarth, W. *The Book of Concord: Thoreau's Life as a Writer* (1982).
Krutch, J. W. *Henry David Thoreau* (1948).
Milder, R. *Reimagining Thoreau* (1995).
Myerson, J., ed. *The Cambridge Companion to Henry David Thoreau* (1995).
Neufeldt, L. N. *The Economist: Henry Thoreau and Enterprise* (1989).
Paul, S. *The Shores of America: Thoreau's Inward Exploration* (1958).
Paul, S., ed. Thoreau: *A Collection of Critical Essays* (1962).

Peck, H. D. *Thoreau's Morning Work: Memory and Perception in A Week on the Concord and Merrimack Rivers, the Journal, and Walden* (1990).
Richardson, R. D., Jr *Henry Thoreau: A Life of the Mind* (1986).
Sayre, R. F. *Thoreau and the American Indians* (1977).
Sayre, R. F., ed. *New Essays on Walden* (1992).
Walls, L. D. *Seeing New Worlds; Henry David Thoreau and Nineteenth-Century Natural Science* (1995).

TWAIN, Mark: See CLEMENS, Samuel Langhorne.

TOCQUEVILLE, Alexis de (1805–59) was born in Paris, the son of an aristocratic Norman family. He studied law and became an assistant magistrate. In 1831 de Tocqueville and his friend Gustave de Beaumont were commissioned by the French government to study the US prison system. They arrived in New York in May 1831, and travelled for nine months, returning to France in February 1832. They published their joint report, *On the Penitentiary System in the United States and Its Application in France*, in 1833. The visit also led to de Tocqueville's two-volume *Democracy in America* (1835, 1840), the most distinguished publication emerging from early nineteenth-century European tourism. The success of the first volume resulted in the award of the Légion d'Honneur and election to the Chamber of Deputies in 1839 and French Academy in 1841. After the Revolution of 1848, de Tocqueville and de Beaumont served on the committee that wrote the Constitution of the Second Republic. In 1849 de Tocqueville was elected vice-president of the Assembly and, for a short while, minister of foreign affairs. He was arrested and briefly imprisoned after the *coup d'état* of 1851 and creation of the Second Empire. De Tocqueville turned again to writing, publishing *The Old Régime and the Revolution* in 1856. This project, a historical sociology of the French Revolution, was not completed. De Tocqueville died in Cannes on 16 April 1859 from tuberculosis. In 1839 he married an Englishwoman, Mary Mottely; they had no children.

De Tocqueville, A. *Democracy in America*, trans. Lawrence, G., ed. Mayer, J. P. (1967). A recent translation.

Boesche, R. *The Strange Liberalism of Alexis de Tocqueville* (1987).
Drescher, S. *Dilemmas of Democracy: Tocqueville and Modernization* (1968).
Jardin, A. *Tocqueville: A Biography*, trans. Davis, L. and Hemenway, R. (1988).
Mayer, J. P. *Alexis de Tocqueville: A Biographical Study in Political Science* (1960).
Pierson, G. W. *Tocqueville and Beaumont in America* (1938).
Zetterbaum, M. *Tocqueville and the Problem of Democracy* (1967).

WHITMAN, Walt (1819–92), was born in Huntington, Long Island. He left school at the age of eleven to became an apprentice printer, and later a teacher. He moved to New York City in 1842 to work as a journalist and editor, publishing a number of short stories and poems of a conventional nature, and a temperance novel, *Franklin Evans; or the Inebriate* (1842). Jobs as an editor and journalist followed in Manhattan, Brooklyn and New Orleans until 1851. He then worked for some three years in Brooklyn as a builder while writing occasional newspaper articles and working on his verse. Whitman published the first edition of *Leaves of Grass* himself in July 1855, and followed it with a second edition fourteen months later. Further, amended and expanded, editions followed in 1860, 1866–7, 1871, 1876, 1881 and 1891–2. For ten years from 1863 he held posts in the US civil service in Washington, DC. In 1873, following a stroke, he moved to Camden, New Jersey, where he lived the remainder of his life, in modest circumstances and sometimes indifferent health, but enjoying growing international fame. Major collections of poems, issued as *Drum-Taps, Sequel to Drum-Taps* (both 1865) and *Passage to India* (1871), were later incorporated into *Leaves of Grass*.

Whitman's major prose works were *Democratic Vistas* (1871) and the autobiographical *Specimen Days and Collect* (1882). He died in the row house in Mickle Street, Camden, which he had bought in 1884.

Allen, G. W., Bradley, S., *et al.*, eds *The Collected Writings of Walt Whitman* (22 vols to date, 1961–)

Allen, G. W. *The Solitary Singer: A Critical Biography of Walt Whitman* (rev. edn, 1985).
Asselineau, R. *The Evolution of Walt Whitman* (2 vols, 1960, 1962).
Clarke, G., ed. *Walt Whitman: Critical Assessments* (4 vols, 1996).
Erkkila, B. *Whitman the Political Poet* (1989).
Erkkila, B. and Grossman, J., eds *Breaking Bounds: Whitman and American Cultural Studies* (1996).
Folsom, E. *Walt Whitman's Native Representations* (1994).
Greenspan, E., ed. *The Cambridge Companion to Walt Whitman* (1995).
Hindus, M., ed. *Walt Whitman: The Critical Heritage* (1971).
Kaplan, J. *Walt Whitman: A Life* (1980).
Loving, J. *Emerson, Whitman, and the American Muse* (1982).
Loving, J. *Walt Whitman: The Song of Himself* (1999).
Morris, R. *The Better Angel: Walt Whitman in the Civil War* (2000).
Murphy, F., ed. *Walt Whitman: A Critical Anthology* (1969).
Myerson, J. *Walt Whitman: A Descriptive Bibliography* (1993).
Price, K. M. *Whitman and Tradition: The Poet in His Century* (1990).
Reynolds, D. S. *Walt Whitman's America: A Cultural Biography* (1995).
Reynolds, D. S., ed. *A Historical Guide to Walt Whitman* (2000).
Thomas, M. W. *The Lunar Light of Whitman's Poetry* (1997).
Warren, J. P. *Walt Whitman's Language Experiment* (1987).
Zweig, P. *Walt Whitman: The Making of the Poet* (1984).

WHITTIER, John Greenleaf (1807–92) was born near Haverhill, Massachusetts, on the farm of his devout Quaker parents. Their poverty meant that he had only a limited formal education. In 1826 he published a poem, 'The Exile's Departure', in *The Newburyport Free Press*, edited by William Lloyd Garrison. It began a lifelong friendship between the two. Late in 1828 Garrison secured for Whittier the editorship of the Boston political weekly *American Manufacturer*. He subsequently edited, or was associated with, a number of journals, including the *New England Weekly Review*, the *National Era*, an anti-slavery journal, and the *Atlantic Monthly*. Many of his poems first appeared in such journals. In 1831 he published a collection of pieces, *Legends of New England* and a long narrative poem, *Moll Pitcher*. In 1833 he published an abolitionist pamphlet, *Justice and Expediency*, and later that year became a founder of the American Anti-Slavery Society. In 1835 he was elected to the Massachusetts Legislature, and the following year published in book form a second narrative poem, *Mogg Megone*. In 1838 he published *Poems*, a collection of anti-slavery verse expanded from an unauthorised edition issued the previous year. In 1843 he published a regional collection, *Lays of My Home*; *Ballads and Other Poems* in 1844; his final anti-slavery collection, *Voices of Freedom*, in 1846; and his only novel, *Margaret Smith's Journal*, in 1847. *Songs of Labor*, including 'Ichabod', appeared in 1850. The pattern of publishing every year or two continued until Whittier's death. The growing popularity of abolitionism established his reputation, which was enhanced by *In War Time and Other Poems*, including 'Barbara Frietchie', and particularly *Snow-Bound*, which was both a great critical and financial success. His seventieth birthday was the occasion for the dinner which caused Samuel Clemens so much embarrassment; his eightieth for more widespread and less controversial celebrations. Sickly throughout his life, he nevertheless outlived most of his generation, and was still highly popular when he died on 7 September 1892. He never married.

The Writings of John Greenleaf Whittier (7 vols, 1888–9).
Pickard, J. B., ed. *The Letters of John Greenleaf Whittier* (1975).

Frank, A. J. von *Whittier: A Comprehensive Annotated Bibliography* (1976).
Kribbs, J. K., ed. *Critical Essays on John Greenleaf Whittier* (1980).
Leary, L. *John Greenleaf Whittier* (1961).
Pickard, S. T. *Life and Letters of John Greenleaf Whittier* (1894).
Pollard, J. A. *John Greenleaf Whittier: Friend to Man* (1949).
Wagenknecht, E. *John Greenleaf Whittier: A Portrait in Paradox* (1967).
Warren, R. P. *John Greenleaf Whittier's Poetry: An Appraisal and Selection* (1971).

WIGGLESWORTH, Michael (1631–1705) was born, the son of a Puritan tradesman, on 18 October 1631 in Yorkshire. In 1638 the family emigrated to New England. Wigglesworth graduated from Harvard in 1651 and, due to self-doubt and recurrent illness, did not formally take orders until 1657. He preached and lived in Malden, Massachusetts from 1654. The following year he married Mary Reyner. She died in 1659. Wigglesworth, struggling with his health, spiritual and physical, as well as that of his congregation, began writing *The Day of Doom* in 1661. It was published the next year, and was an immediate and lasting success, going through several American and English editions within a century. In 1662, following a drought, Wigglesworth wrote 'God's Controversy with New-England'; it was not published until 1873. In 1670 he published *Meat Out of the Eater*, a series of poetic meditations reissued in 1717 and 1770. He married Martha Mudge in 1679. She died in 1690, and the following year he married Sybil Sparhawk or Sparrowhawk. Their son, Edward Wigglesworth (1693–1765) was a Congregational minister and the first Hollis Professor of Divinity at Harvard. Michael Wigglesworth died in Malden on 10 June 1705.

Bosco, R. A., ed. *The Poems of Michael Wigglesworth* (1989).
Morgan, E. S., ed. *The Diary of Michael Wigglesworth, 1653–1657: The Conscience of a Puritan* (1965).

Crowder, R. H. *No Featherbed to Heaven: A Biography of Michael Wigglesworth, 1631–1705* (1962).
Hammond, J. *Sinful Self, Saintly Self: The Puritan Experience of Poetry* (1993).

WILLIAMS, Roger (1603?–83) was born in London and educated at Cambridge. In 1629 he became a chaplain to a prominent Puritan family but, more radical than his employers, left for Massachusetts Bay, arriving in February 1631. Also too radical for the Bay theocracy, he moved quickly between Boston, Salem and Plymouth, finally becoming pastor at Salem in 1634. His 'levelling' views led to a sentence of banishment, but he escaped to Narragansett Bay before he could be deported to England. In 1636 he named his home Providence, having obtained land from the Narragansett tribe. It would become the capital of Rhode Island. In 1643 he returned to England, befriending Milton and Cromwell, receiving a patent for Providence Plantations, and publishing a number of works, including *A Key into the Language of America* (1643) and *The Bloudy Tenent of Persecution* (1644), a defence of freedom of conscience. Williams returned to Providence in 1644 and served as its leader, but on finding that he had been displaced, sailed again to England in 1651 to have his patent reconfirmed. While in England he published another contribution to the literature of religious freedom, *The Bloudy Tenent Yet More Bloudy* (1651). Back in Providence, he was again elected leader, but presided over a colony riven by political and religious argument. In the 1660s he found himself marginalised by Quaker settlers, whom he debated in *George Fox Digg'd Out of His Burrowes* (1676). Williams's house was burned during King Philip's War and he joined the militia, fighting the tribe he had befriended. He was buried with military honours in Providence early in 1683.

Lafantasie, G. W., *et al.*, eds *The Correspondence of Roger Williams* (2 vols, 1988).
Miller, P., ed. *The Complete Writings of Roger Williams* (7 vols, 1963).

Byrd, J. P. *Religious Liberty, Violent Persecution, and the Bible: The Challenge of Roger Williams* (2002).
Coyle, W. *Roger Williams: A Reference Guide* (1977).
Gaustad, E. S. *Liberty of Conscience: Roger Williams in America* (1991).
Gilpin, W. C. *The Millenarian Piety of Roger Williams* (1979).
Miller, P. *Roger Williams: His Contribution to the American Tradition* (1953).
Morgan, E. S. *Roger Williams: The Church and the State* (1967).
Spurgin, H. *Roger Williams and Puritan Radicalism in the English Separatist Tradition* (1989).

WINTHROP, John (1588–1649), was born at Edwardston, Suffolk on 12 January 1588, the son of a well-to-do lawyer. He attended Trinity College, Cambridge (1603–5), leaving to marry Mary Forth, in the first of four fortunate marriages. Winthrop became a Puritan in his youth. By 1627 he had become an important lawyer in London, but economic depression and religious conformism decided him to join the Massachusetts Bay Company. In 1630 he sailed on the *Arbella*, having written 'A Modell of Christian Charity'. He had already been elected governor, and he served, either as governor, assistant- or deputy-governor, until his death. His *Journal*, begun on 29 March 1630 and ended shortly before his death, records events both large and small in New England. It was first published in 1790, and in an expanded edition in 1825. With his wives Mary Forth (1605–15), Thomasine Clopton (1615–16), Margaret Tyndal (1618–47) and Martha Coytmore (1647–49) he had sixteen children, eight of whom survived to be adults. Winthrop died on 26 March 1649. His first child, John Winthrop Jr (1606–76), was governor of Connecticut and the first colonial to be elected Fellow of the Royal Society.

Dunn, R. S., Savage, J. and Yeandle, L., eds *The Journal of John Winthrop 1630–1649* (1996).
Ford, W. C., Mitchell, S. and Forbes, A. B., eds *Winthrop Papers, 1498–1649* (5 vols, 1929–47).
Hall, D. D., ed. *The Antinomian Controversy 1636–1638: A Documentary History* (2nd edn, 1990).

Battis, E. *Saints and Sectaries: Anne Hutchinson and the Antinomian Controversy in the Massachusetts Bay Colony* (1962).
Dunn, R. S. *Puritans and Yankees: The Winthrop Dynasty of New England, 1630–1717* (1962).
Hill, C. *The World Turned Upside Down: Radical Ideas During the English Revolution* (1972).
Kibbey, A. *The Interpretation of Material Shapes in Puritanism: A Study of Rhetoric, Prejudice, and Violence* (1986).
Morgan, E. S. *The Puritan Dilemma: The Story of John Winthrop* (1958).
Moseley, J. G. *John Winthrop's World* (1992).

Index

Longman Literature in English Series

General Editors:
David Carroll, formerly University of Lancaster
Chris Walsh, Chester College of Higher Education
Michael Wheeler, University of Southampton

Pre-Renaissance English Literature
English Literature before Chaucer *Michael Swanton*
English Literature in the Age of Chaucer *Dieter Mehl*
English Medieval Romance *W. R. J. Barron*

English Poetry
English Poetry of the Sixteenth Century *Gary Waller (Second Edition)*
English Poetry of the Seventeenth Century *George Parfitt (Second Edition)*
English Poetry of the Eighteennth Century 1700–1789 *David Fairer*
English Poetry of the Romantic Period, 1789–1830 *J. R. Watson (Second Edition)*
English Poetry of the Victorian Period, 1830–1890 *Bernard Richards*
English Poetry since 1940 *Neil Corcoran*

English Drama
English Drama before Shakespeare *Peter Happé*
English Drama: Shakespeare to the Restoration, 1590–1660 *Alexander Leggatt*
English Drama: Restoration and Eighteenth Century, 1660–1789 *Richard W. Bevis*
English Drama of the Early Modern Period, 1890–1940 *Jean Chothia*
English Drama since 1940 *David Rabey*

English Fiction
English Fiction of the Eighteenth Century, 1700–1789 *Clive T. Probyn*
English Fiction of the Romantic Period, 1789–1830 *Gary Kelly*
English Fiction of the Victorian Period, 1830–1890 *Michael Wheeler (Second Edition)*
English Fiction of the Early Modern Period, 1890–1940 *Douglas Hewitt*

English Prose
English Prose of the Seventeenth Century, 1590–1700 *Roger Pooley*
English Prose of the Nineteenth Century *Hilary Fraser with Daniel Brown*

Criticism and Literary Theory
Criticism and Literary Theory, 1890 to the Present *Chris Baldick*

The Intellectual and Cultural Context
The Seventeenth Century, 1603–1700 *Graham Parry*
The Eighteenth Century, 1700–1789 *James Sambrook (Second Edition)*
The Victorian Period, 1830–1890 *Robin Gilmour*

American Literature
American Poetry of the Twentieth Century *Richard Gray*
American Drama of the Twentieth Century *Gerald M. Berkowitz*
American Fiction, 1865–1940 *Brian Lee*
American Fiction since 1940 *Tony Hilfer*
Twentieth-Century America *Douglas Tallack*
American Literature before 1880 *Robert Lawson-Peebles*

Other Literatures
Irish Literature since 1800 *Norman Vance*
Scottish Literature since 1707 *Marshall Walker*
Indian Literature in English *William Walsh*
African Literatures in English: East and West *Gareth Griffiths*
Southern African Literatures *Michael Chapman*
Caribbean Literature in English *Louis James*
Canadian Literature in English *W. J. Keith*

Future Titles
English Poetry of the Early Modern Period, 1890–1940
The Romantic Period, 1789–1830